America's Transition:

Blueprints For The 1990s

Edited By
Mark Green &
Mark Pinsky

DEDICATION

To Sandy Chapin — and to the memory of Harry Chapin,
who helped found the Democracy Project in 1981 and who said,
"The radical ideas today become the popular policies tomorrow."

America's Transition: Blueprints For The 1990s
A publication of Democracy Project, Inc., 215 Park Avenue South,
Room 1814, New York, NY 10003, (212) 674-8989.

Library of Congress Catalog Card Number: 88-51693

ISBN 0-924168-00-5

Printed in the United States
First Edition

1 2 3 4 5 6 7 8 9 10

Book Design by Mark Pinsky
Cover Design by Tom Kleupful, Drentel, Doyle Partners

CONTENTS

JUSTICE POLICY

SOCIAL POLICY

INTRODUCTION:
Values For Democracy

Mark Green

I. THE POLITICAL PREDICATE

America is in transition, even if the executive branch is not.

Belying the comfortable metaphor of George Bush's "friendly takeover" of the Reagan Administration, great changes are occurring both in our country and world. Planetary warming hints at ecological disaster. Despite a falling dollar, our status as a debtor nation endures. Real wages have been nearly stagnant for 15 years, as our largest companies grow ever larger via acquisition rather than production. In the past 30 years, America has lost its nuclear monopoly and half its share of the world GNP. The Soviets are experimenting with pluralism, at the risk of unparalleled internal turmoil. Democracy and debt seem to be on a collision course in Latin America.

These developments offer both opportunity and peril for the 41st President and 101st Congress. But diverting America from responding well are the multiple crises Ronald Reagan has bequeathed us. This is an empirical rather than an ideological conclusion, for it's hard to ignore his accumulation of neglected needs.

The non-partisan Government Accounting Office, for example, issued 23 simultaneous reports (right after the election) urging dramatic federal action to address problems created or exacerbated by the Reagan Administration. In the spirit of his invocation that "facts are stubborn things," consider Reagan's good-bye "gifts," according to the GAO: it will cost $100 billion-plus to modernize the nation's nuclear weapons production plants; $50-$100 billion to rescue savings and loan associations; $20 billion to repair public housing; $5 billion for federal prisons. Then there's the $100 billion to clean up toxic waste dumps and yet another $100 billion to repair our crumbling infrastructure. The GAO never even got to the mountainous federal deficit and trade deficit or to the fact that the world's greatest democracy has the West's lowest incidence of voting and highest incidence of children in poverty.

We now see the difference between good acts and good acting and how popularity is not the same as problem-solving. For the rhetoric of patriotism, the rhetoric of get-off-our-backs and the rhetoric of morning-in-America did little to concretely improve the quality of our lives. In sum, for George Bush, George Mitchell and Jim Wright, our national leaders as we enter the 1990s, the era of avoidance is over.

Reagan's legacy includes not only unmet needs but also unanswered questions. Who now will pay these long overdue bills? How can we avoid their recurrence? Who among our elected officials has admitted these problems, much less answered them? Who has a new paradigm for our new world?

To date, the answer is not George Bush. His campaign resolutely refused to engage such "gloom and doom" topics, implying even that opponents were unpatriotic for raising them. Compare, as a result, the three major national elections last November: Canada's election turned on its historic free-trade agreement with the U.S.; Israel's turned on the issue of land-for-peace; and America's turned on whether Jehovah's Witnesses should have to pledge allegiance to the flag. Stressing flags and furloughs may have been a winning political formula, but it will now take a microscope to detect Bush's mandate for change.

Nor does his personal history offer much hope. In 25 years of public life, in prominent appointive and elective office, it's hard to associate him with any cause or idea. True, neither FDR nor JFK showed much evidence of being bold leaders before their presidential victories, and both rose to the occasion. We can only hope that Bush's career and campaign prove to be, as Mark Twain said of Wagner's music, "better than it sounds."

And for all their voluminous energy, conservative think tanks won't fare much better. They started out the 80s with a few ideas that were not particularly new or useful — taxes are evil, the Soviets are evil, government is the problem. Whatever their prominence then, due to a sympathetic conservative president, these groups have little relevance today to our trade debt, latchkey children, depletion of the ozone, untrained workers, or to an urban crisis in education, housing, health care and crime. A philosophy that disdains all public sector action yet forgives all private sector conduct cannot solve such problems, nor even seriously discuss them.

Together, George Bush and the conservative movement have much in common with Harry Truman and the liberals of the late 40s, who won an election they weren't supposed to because of an inept opposition and who, after the Roosevelt ascendancy, had largely run out of steam and ideas.

Hence, *America's Transition: Blueprints for the 1990s.*

In the spirit of the President-elect's generous remark of November 9th — "If [liberals] have got some good ideas as to how to move this country forward, I need them" — the 58 authors of these 38 chapters offer their best ideas to the next President and Congress.

The authors, each with deep experience either in government or on government, were asked to propose bold, practical, progressive alternatives for their respective agencies or subjects. All shared two primary assumptions.

First, America too often suffers through campaigns without content and victories without vision. (One Bush aide told George Will during the primaries, "Every time you take a position, you know you'll make someone angry"; and at the Democratic Platform hearings, one participant confided, "No one ever lost because of something he didn't say.") We've just gone through a second straight presidential election where the winner articulated no positive agenda. Timid politicians have historically allowed public-minded citizens to play a significant role in setting the national agenda. In the modern era, Martin Luther King and Ralph Nader are the most prominent examples.

Second, the public does want change — not radical change but real change. Extensive polling in 1988 by the bi-partisan Americans Talk Security and Public Agenda Foundation revealed large majorities who feared Japan economically more than the Soviets militarily and who would pay higher taxes if the funds were earmarked for health care, education and the environment. Any national leader reading these surveys should be reminded of the French statesman Alexandre Ledru-Rollin, who said of his countrymen, "Ah, well, I am their leader, I really ought to follow them."

While the Democracy Project is a non-partisan institute, we are not unaware that a self-professed conservative president may not easily embrace a self-professed progressive critique. Historically, however, remember that it was Richard Nixon who signed the legislation creating EPA and OSHA, who advocated generic welfare reform and, of course, who went to China. Similarly, Ronald Reagan's only significant achievements in his second term were the INF agreement and the elimination of most corporate tax loopholes, ideas associated more with liberals than conservatives. If liberal groups had predicted such results in, respectively, 1969 and 1981, they would have been laughed off the op-ed pages. As the Nixon and Reagan examples show, objective events and conditions can play a larger role than ideology in determining policy.

Indeed, remember Bush's campaign emphasis on a "kinder, gentler nation." However expedient and rhetorical, this formulation — especially his speeches arguing for child care, calling himself an "environmentalist," looking forward to being "the education president" and advocating ethics reform — do obligate him to pursue more compassionate solutions. Even "liberal" solutions.

And while the *presidential government* (again) is surely right-of-center, the *congressional government* (again) is more liberal. Constitutionally, it still takes two to tango. Because of November's dual mandate (the Republican presidential nominee got 54% of the popular vote; Democratic congressional candidates 58%),* America seems to be is evolving increasingly toward a kind of National Unity Government, as Israel has had, where nothing gets done unless the heads of both branches and parties agree on a bi-partisan basis.

Already, despite a popular Republican president, the last Democratic Congress initiated and enacted a far-ranging program, including welfare reform, trade legislation, plant closing notification, civil rights restoration, clean water, catastrophic health insurance — and even helped arrange a cease-fire in Nicaragua. Since George Bush can claim no obvious issues mandate and demonstrated not only no coattails but no coat (for the first time since 1960, the incoming President's party lost seats in the House and Senate), the 101st Congress may prove to be more than a match for the 41st President. And should a President Bush be unreceptive to progressive alternatives, the Democracy Project looks forward to reaching out to the newly assertive Congress and to becoming a vertebra in the spine of The Loyal Opposition.

America's Transition, then, like parallel volumes from the Heritage Foundation and Hoover Institution, does not seek to repeal the election result. Rather, we too would like to contribute our community's best vision for the post-Reagan era. Of course, disembodied policies without a sympathetic politician is as ineffectual as a politician without policies. But in the broader context of interested constituencies, movements and lobbyists, an agency-by-agency agenda can serve as a catalyst of change. It can also help avoid good policies being disparaged as "radical," which economist Lester Thurow defined merely as any idea less than three years old.

---

* While there were only three instances in American history pre-1956 when the party winning the White House lost control of Congress, it has happened six of nine times since then. And if the Republican Party looks secure in the executive branch, Democrats appear likely to increase their congressional dominance: during those five Republican presidential victories out of six elections from 1968 and 1988, Democrats *increased* their majority in the House; and if the historic pattern of the first off-year election holds true, Democrats in 1990 are likely to add to their 55 seat Senate majority, especially since many of the 17 incumbent Republicans who will be running first won in the cushy Republican years of 1984 and 1978.

II. FIVE VALUES

This volume contains over 500 concrete suggestions for the President, Cabinet officers, agency heads and Members of Congress. But more important than the bricks and mortar of a building is its foundation, on which all rests. Clearly Reagan and Bush have a very few understandable themes, involving less taxes and government, while Democrats seem to flit from one framework and slogan to another. Michael Dukakis tried to define himself as the sum of his position papers, but it still didn't add up to a coherent whole.

So what's the big idea?

The progressive philosophy believes in a mixed economy that combines a competitive marketplace with an accountable government policing abuses and providing those services which private enterprise can't or won't — from clean air to safe streets to food for the hungry. Ralph Nader's "overview" and all the regulatory chapters illuminate one businessman's observation to authors Leonard Silk and David Vogel: government without business is tyranny, and business without government is piracy.

Ayn Rand conservatives seem to believe that private greed can provide for all public needs. According to their philosophy, it's fine when people freely organize into private corporations, but illegitimate when citizens organize themselves into public legislatures to improve their condition. But sometimes, laissez *isn't* fair — price-fixing, pollution, poverty. That's where government comes in. That's why Abraham Lincoln progressives agree with the still resonant words of our 16th president: "The legitimate object of government is to do for the people what needs to be done, but which they cannot, by individual effort, do at all, or do well, by themselves."

In that tradition, *America's Transition* describes how a fair and frugal government can improve the quality of our lives. Threaded throughout these disparate chapters on different topics are five preeminent values that provide the foundation of all the individual proposals. Taken together, these values — **strong democracy, demand-side growth, children first, post-cold war peace** and **respect for law** — comprise a fresh approach as much at odds with prevailing conservative orthodoxy as Copernicus was from Ptolemy.

* **Strong Democracy.** For America to fulfill its revolutionary promise, our citizens need to adhere to the twin principles of patriotism — *participation* and *mutuality*.

A century ago, 80% of Americans voted (about the average of our current Western allies). In 1960, it was 63%; in 1988, 50%; and in the last non-presidential election, 38%. Americans who once crossed the oceans to fight for democracy now don't cross the street to exercise it.

How do we know when a democracy is dying? When a mine collapses, there's irrebutable evidence of failure. But a democracy? Surely one measure is the number of its residents who consider it worthwhile to choose the representatives who govern their lives. If too many don't vote, however, will officials know what is in the broadest national interest? Will some communities fail to be heard — while others are heard too loudly? If a 50% turnout is still a democracy, is 38%? 10%? What about when Americans with incomes under $5000 vote at half the rate as those over $50,000, giving the affluent one-and-a-half ballots each compared to the poor?

Two of the reasons for this steady decline of participation are registration requirements and special interest PACs.

Cumbersome voter registration laws were erected a century ago to discourage new black and immigrant voters. Yet while other laws with an invidious intent have been prohibited, such as literacy tests, registration laws endure. Isn't it foolish, for example, that 500 high school graduates each separately try to find their way to one Board of Elections to register rather than having one Board representative go to the school to register everyone in a day? Indeed, states with same-day and mail-registration (Minnesota, Wisconsin) regularly get turnouts 10%-20% higher than traditional registration states.

Also, the proliferation of PACs — half of all Members of Congress get half of all their funds from legislatively interested donors — discourages participation. Citizens may not bother voting when Members seem more interested in their contributors than their constituents. Office holders predictably don't go out of their way to bite the hand that funds them. The result: Congress tilts to organized interests rather than average citizens; good people are priced out of seeking public office; Congress suffers staleness as insulated incumbents serve near life-time tenures; and voters turn off — *e.g.*, while one in three voters thought their voice didn't count in 1966, according to a Harris Poll, now *two* out of three believe so.

"The solution to the problems of democracy," Governor Al Smith of New York once said, "is more democracy." Using the Smith Rx, the White House and Congress should enact Senator Alan Cranston's Universal Voter Registration Act, further reduce or eliminate PAC influence (as Philip Stern urges subsequently), provide for free TV time for general election congressional candidates and fix elections on non-work days, say, the second Saturday in November. Call it "Democracy Day." To enact this empowerment program only requires that Democrats in the Congress vote their beliefs and Republicans — long frustrated at their minority status because of how PACs entrench incumbents — vote their self-interest.

As for mutuality, a strong democracy needs to emphasize that citizens have not only rights but obligations. To sit on juries. Pay taxes. Obey laws you don't like. Assist those worse off. "You have got to have the same interest in public affairs as in private affairs," said President Teddy Roosevelt, "or you cannot keep this country what this country should be."

Especially in an era of tight budgets, mutuality also means meeting reasonable conditions if receiving a federal benefit. As Robert Kuttner and Stuart Eizenstat discuss, citizens and corporations who receive public benefits have responsibilities to the taxpayers who confer them — from students paying back loans to corporations not fleeing the community that provided inducements to invest there.

Ultimately, a strong democracy is a primary value because, without it, powerful interests can stymie the national interest and overwhelm all other values. Without PAC reform, for example, we should not be surprised that military contractors continue to dominate the defense budget process and that *one* Stealth Bomber costs more than providing pre-natal care for all pregnant women in poverty.

* **Demand-side Growth.** While "supply-side" conservatives want to give incentives to owners to produce, "demand-side" progressives want to spur economic growth by providing workers with an adequate income to signal producers where to invest. It's the difference, to steal a phrase, between trickle-*down* and trickle-*up* economics.

We are all familiar with the supply-side theory, pioneered by Andrew Carnegie in the 1920s and popularized by the Reagan Administration. In an update of Say's Law — that supply creates its own demand — Reaganites concluded that the best way to produce sustained growth was to concentrate on stimulating well-off investors to save, invest and produce more. This emphasis, however, conveniently led to a flood of corporate giveaways and upscale tax breaks.

The results? Savings and investment *fell* after enactment of Reagan's tax and budget program in 1981, and the distribution of wealth predictably worsened. The planned, massive distribution from labor to capital produced the greatest disparity between the wealthiest-fifth and poorest-fifth of American families in 40 years, as $9.50 in income was added at the top for every $1.00 lost at the bottom. While the average American workers earned $281 a week in 1983, he or she earned only $276 a week (in constant dollars) by 1988.

This policy failure, however, was accompanied by a political success. George Bush won the economic argument of 1988 by citing his Administration's 69 consecutive months of sustained growth and by attacking "the failed policies of the past" (a.k.a., Carter-Mondale). This is triply ironic. First, as author Robert McElvaine has documented, economic growth under Democratic Administrations over the past half century has been *six times* greater than under Republican Administrations. Second, the reason for continuous growth was a hyper-Keynesian deficit-spending (financed from abroad) that Reagan had denounced in 1980 as inflationary. And now, Reagan blames "big liberal spenders" for the deficits that created the borrowed prosperity he and his successor brag about! But for the intellectual dishonesty, you almost have to admire the audacity of their argument.

Compounding supply-side's failures, however, is its 1990s descendent — austerity. Precisely because of Reagan's legacy of debt, many in the business community urge slashing wages, consumer spending and federal entitlements in order to reduce the deficit and encourage capital formation. Which brings to mind Oscar Wilde's observation that, "Nothing succeeds like excess." Why further squeeze the middle class to further enrich an elite who previously simply pocketed, rather than invested, their tax cuts?

According to authors Robert Eisner, Nancy Barrett, Robert Kuttner, James Galbraith and Robert Reich, it's foolish to believe we can impoverish ourselves into prosperity. If the goal is to keep our wages "competitive," do we keep depressing them to the level of Korea, or Sri Lanka? The austerity school would so reduce individual and federal spending as to risk the kind of severe recession that would certainly depress the very savings and investments they seek.

The Economy section of *America's Transition* is based on a very contrary and very essential value — demand-side growth. If average Americans have an adequate wage, their spending will create markets that manufacturers will supply. Keynes once wrote about the Depression's lack of consumer demand, "The patient does not need rest, the patient needs exercise!" He understood that owners and managers won't build a factory unless there are consumers who want the product, regardless of how much idle capital is around. Say's Law should have died during the Depression, when there was supply without demand. Instead, "demand-side law" assumes that demand creates supply and that there's no fixed trade-off between spending and saving. More consumer and government spending can spur *more*, not less, jobs, output and savings. Any risk of added inflation would today appear modest due to world surpluses, low inflation and no recent experience with "demand-pull" inflation.

Demand-side growth is a happy alternative to *laissez-faire*/austerity and industrial planning. It believes that the engine of a strong economy is well-paid work, which then pulls along productivity, innovation and profits. This value leads naturally to a sequence of policies described both in this book and by Jeff Faux's Economic Policy Institute:

In *labor markets*, we need a "new social contract," in Kuttner's phrase, that can cheat the traditional "trade-off" between inflation and unemployment: labor gets secure, well-paid work and lifelong retraining while management gets a high-quality workforce and labor peace. This means a liveable minimum wage, more management-labor collaboration in the form of greater employee participation and stock ownership and government investment in retraining since the private sector habitually underinvests here. The U.S. could look to Sweden, which prefers to subsidize re-employment rather than unemployment: so while our labor market outlays go 80% for unemployment compensation and 20% for retraining, in Sweden the ratio is reversed.

In *fiscal policy,* say Eisner and Barrett, we should stop obsessing on our budget deficit as the only economic enemy. The deficit should be *gradually* reduced but not so precipitously as to trigger a recession.

In *monetary policy,* Galbraith urges a White House-Fed accord: lower interest rates followed by higher taxes, which can ease the deficit without reducing consumption and provoking a recession.

In terms of *third world debt,* Galbraith and Richard Feinberg urge that lending nations negotiate a writedown so that debtor nations can afford to be consumers of our exports. The chapter by Samuel Berger and Sidney Harman, as well as *The Cuomo Commission Report* of 1987, stress that we have to understand that debt and trade is not a zero-sum game — we prosper when others do.

* **Children First.** Until very recently public policy didn't consider children to be of significant concern. *Parents* raised children, not government. Indeed, when Congress began advancing child care for struggling working families in 1971, President Richard Nixon attacked and dismissed it as a version of big brother socialism. By 1988, Vice-president George Bush was campaigning for a child care tax credit because "child care is nothing short of a family necessity."

What happened between Nixon's indifference and Bush's concern was a confluence of demographic and economic trends that elevated the issue of children, especially children in poverty.

The simultaneous increase in single-parent families and decline in the real value of the minimum wage, for example, has produced a poverty rate among children (18%) that is the highest of any industrial democracy. The 70s and 80s also saw an unprecedented influx into the workforce of women with children...yet without safe, affordable, quality child care. There has been a large increase this decade in reported cases of child abuse, teenage pregnancy, school dropouts. Because of Reagan Administration cuts in pre-natal care and child immunization, there are more low birth-weight babies and the risk of infant death for minorities in America exceeds that of many Third World nations. Last, as American education scores and employees' skills have fallen in our world marketplace, many business groups began calling for increased spending on education.

This unusual alliance of the compassion lobby *and* the corporate lobby helped make the issue of children more prominent in the 1988 presidential campaign than the issue of, for example, *contra* aid.

Any governing agenda must think of children first for an obvious reason: as non-voters and non-consumers, they cannot always signal the powers-that-be about their special needs. Nor is the market-place a sufficient guardian. Consider this letter to the *Wall Street Journal* about the dangers of foot-long "toys" called lawn darts: parent David Snow referred to David Stockman's "half-baked theory of how free-market forces will address and correct product safety — that is, company x markets an ill-conceived product that kills and injures thousands. The company loses its shirt in tort actions. It removes the product from the market. Who needs the CPSC! I will convey this to my little girl the next time I go to her grave."

Taken altogether, Reagan Administration family policies have been pro-life, pre-birth; but once the fetus became an infant, the government ran away from home. It's an odd priority to think that large corporations need tax incentives to be productive but that you ruin a child if you give him or her a hot lunch.

Instead, chapters by Marian Wright Edelman, Robert Greenstein, Stuart Eizenstat and Norman Fruchter explain why the future of our children must be a prominent value in our society. A policy of "Children First" requires at least two indispensable approaches. First, laws should have a "children's impact statement," so that legislators can anticipate how proposed legislation might help or hurt the most vulnerable among us. Second, spending on children should be considered more an investment than an expenditure. Since every dollar spent on pre-natal care saves over $3 in avoided hospitalization of premature babies and since early education programs now will help equip the workforce of the next century, policy should be guided by the prudent ethic of pay-now-or-pay-later.

A Children First program would include universal pre-natal care, parental leave and child care in the workplace, drug treatment on demand, stronger product safety regulation, expanded Headstart, WIC, school nutrition and student loan programs, and a higher minimum wage and "earned income tax credit" so working families do not live in poverty. There can be no better pro-family policy or use of taxpayer funds than investing in the minds and bodies of children.

* **Post-Cold War Peace.** The first obligation of government is peace — the protection of its citizens from external aggression. No society can pursue growth, equity and excellence at home if it is not free from subjugation abroad.

America's post-war foreign policy has largely brought us peace, but at the cost of an immensely expensive arms race and the risk of nuclear incineration. Now, however, a once-a-generation development is underway that could diminish this cost and risk: the cold war — the central fact of the post-war era — is probably defunct.

Mikhail Gorbachev is clearly unlike predecessors who indolently allowed their country to decay from the lack of political and economic freedoms. Gorbachev's much-discussed drive for *glasnost* and *perestroika*, however, clearly aims to rescue his country from bureaucracy and stagnation.

But what should the U.S. response be? To date, American leaders have largely been spectators without a strategy. President Reagan deserves praise for finally appreciating the need to trade proposals rather than insults. But there's still no consensus answer to the following obvious question, posed by *The New York Times*: "If Mikhail Gorbachev succeeds in reforming the Soviet economy, will Moscow pose more or less of a threat to Western security?"

Isn't the answer less? A U.S.S.R. that evolves from a military economy to a civilian one, allows more pluralism and markets, increasingly (though slowly) frees refuseniks, renounces world struggle and advocates nuclear reductions is good for the U.S.. In an era of nuclear parity, where more nuclear weapons do not purchase more safety and where the reason we survived today is that the Soviets chose not to launch any of their 25,000 nuclear weapons, the only enduring way to peace is to reduce tensions through negotiations.

That means, as Stephen F. Cohen argues in his chapter, that we must meet Gorbachev halfway. How long can he make concessions without responses? For unless he can demonstrate real gains to *his* hard-liners — say, American arms reductions to match his or Western loans at market rates for domestic investment — Gorbachev may fail and be succeeded by a traditional cold warrior.

So while the value of peace required the "containment" of Stalin's U.S.S.R. at the height of the Cold War, today the same value requires a shift from mere containment to cooperation. Not because it may be in their interest but because it's in *our* national interest. The U.S. must continue to be skeptical and vigilant ("trust, but verify"), but also to show our own "new thinking" to seize an opportunity that could produce huge dividends in three areas:

1. *Nuclear Arms.* As described by Paul Warnke, *et. al.*, the new president should pursue the promising initiatives begun at the Reagan-Gorbachev summits. Unlike all prior weapons in history, nuclear weapons exist to deter and not be used; each side, consequently, must avoid destabilizing weapons — those capable of launching a first strike and "winning" a nuclear exchange — since their very existence may provoke a preemptive attack. Also, it's time to spend a bargaining chip called SDI to obtain a great compromise: both sides slash their ballistic weapons to below the number needed to trigger a "nuclear winter" and both keep any strategic defense systems in the lab. Last, the world will be safer with a comprehensive test ban treaty. If John Kennedy had persuaded his Pentagon to accept the

treaty he desired, rather than only the Limited Test Ban, today there would be no hydra-headed MIRVs and no undetectable nuclear-tipped cruise missiles.

2. *Conventional Arms.* In the early 1960s, the Pentagon budget was based on America's ability to fight two large wars and one small war at the same time. But Secretary of Defense Melvin Laird changed a 2-1/2 war strategy to a 1-1/2 war strategy after the Chinese threat effectively disappeared. The next Defense Secretary should similarly pursue possible savings if the Soviets join the Chinese as a former obsession.

The most obvious place to start would be Western Europe, where the U.S. spends 60% of its defense budget defending NATO. Because of the dramatic U.N. announcement about unilateral Soviet troop reductions, a President Bush can now match or top President Gorbachev in advancing a post-cold war peace. The U.S. should at least agree to a "defensive defense" strategy where both sides could repel an attack though not launch one. Or Bush could make a bold, historic counter-proposal that would establish him as a world leader for peace: a complete, mutual withdrawal of all superpower troops from Eastern and Western Europe. Given Gorbachev's stated goals of peace and rights, it will not be easy for him to refuse; and since our NATO allies fear a Soviet invasion (not a Polish one), how can they protest our withdrawal once the Soviet threat disappears?

Whatever does happen in Europe, our overall goal must be military *sufficiency*, not superiority, since the latter is both unobtainable and self-defeating. The chapter by Gordon Adams *et. al.* explains how to save some $40 billion annually yet maintain a sufficient defense.

3. *Regional Conflicts.* Especially after Vietnam and Afghanistan, both superpowers have expensively learned that there are limits to their power to dominate third world events and countries.

In the 1990s, let's test Gorbachev's assertion that there is no longer a military solution to any of the great political conflicts around the world. Already, several regional conflicts are being resolved — the Iran-Iraq war, Mozambique, perhaps Angola. If Soviet-American relations continue to warm, it should not be inconceivable to attempt understandings about such hot spots as Nicaragua, South Africa, the Middle East and Cuba. (One doubts, for example, that Gorbachev wants to send Castro several billion rubles a year in perpetuity — or that Castro wants to be so dependent forever.) Beyond discussing such difficult regional conflicts, the U.S. should aggressively challenge the U.S.S.R. — with whom we once cooperated to win a World War — to now cooperate in addressing such common problems as world hunger, nuclear proliferation, environmental hazards, terrorism and AIDS.

Unfortunately, an influential "war-is-inevitable" lobby (the phrase is Reagan's) considers negotiations with Soviets, much less concessions, a sign of weakness. Because its members prosper in proportion to the Soviet menace, these cold warriors begrudge the recent avalanche of Soviet concessions and retreats. But why impose the stereotypes of the 50s on the 80s? Why resent American success? Instead, the new President and Congress should encourage this mutual post-cold war peace, for an obvious reason: "Gorbachev needs to end the cold war to save his economy," writes Ronald Steel. "So do we."

* Respect for Law. Throughout our history, Americans — and their leaders — have displayed a special fidelity to law and ethics. If anything, our revolution militantly rejected arbitrary government and embraced the principle that no person is above the law — or, as Roman lawmakers put it, *Fiat justitia ruat caelum* ("Let justice be done, though the heavens fall.").

Recall how George Washington became the first victorious general in history to walk away from power when he completed his second presidential term. Recall how Senator Paul Douglas would return every gift sent him worth more than five dollars. And recall how Dwight Eisenhower vetoed a natural gas rate deregulation bill that he avidly supported because a natural gas lobbyist had tried to bribe a New Jersey senator before final passage.

It's a sharp drop from Paul Douglas to Edwin Meese, Michael Deaver, Lyn Nofziger, Robert McFarlane, Rita Lavelle, Paul Thayer — not to mention Oliver North and dozens of lesser-knowns who feathered their nests at taxpayer expense and who seemed to take literally their constitutional oath to "*execute* the laws faithfully." "For God's sake," said Elliot Richardson, the Republican four-time Cabinet secretary, "are we not entitled to hope that the next Administration will be a little less sleazy?"

Over in the regulatory agencies, contempt for law has been not only by commission by also by omission. At a recent hearing of the House subcommittee on consumer protection, Chairman James Florio (D-NJ) lost his patience after being told how the chairman of the Consumer Product Safety Commission persistently refused to recall obviously dangerous products. Said Florio, "Our dilemma is: When the law is the law and the regulators are not carrying it out, what do we do? Pass another law?"

Based on sheer numbers, the Reagan Administration has documentably been the least ethical and lawful in decades, with the sole exception of the Nixon crew. But why? Why did an Administration calling for a return to family values, religious ethics and a "strict construction" of the law wind up betraying these very standards? Two forces stand out — ideological fervor and personal profiteering.

This Administration's policies from the first have been framed in crusading terms. The Soviet Union was simply "the evil empire"; government was a symbol of "waste, fraud and abuse." In the face of such universals, congressional restrictions — otherwise known as laws — can appear to be technical, trivial, even avoidable. To zealots like North, the law is not an end but merely a means to an end.

Beyond ideology, Reagan's profiteering officials have often brought the habits of the marketplace into public life. Their conduct demonstrates that you can take appointees out of the private sector, but you can't always take the private sector out of appointees.

A new administration and Congress have the opportunity to again spotlight the value of law. First, a President Bush should nominate, and the Senate confirm, only people who will pledge allegiance to public service and ethics. People such as FDR's Frances Perkins and Truman's George Marshall and Kennedy's Stewart Udall and LBJ's John Gardner and Ford's Edward Levi and Carter's Cyrus Vance — all were more interested in making history than money.

Second, above all other positions, the Attorney General and each federal judge should be "a meet person, learned in the law" (Judiciary Act, 1789), and not merely a Daniel Manion who passes a reactionary saliva test. In the section on Justice, Stephen Gillers and Mark Gitenstein discuss how to choose such people.

Third, President Bush should sign the ethics bill his predecessor vetoed, a bill to discourage executive *and* congressional branch members from personally cashing in on their public office. And he should make clear that any appointee who failed to faithfully comply with a law's letter and spirit would be out on his ear the next day. Ronald Reagan never once publicly reproached his dozens of derelict appointees, enduring silently an Elliott Abrams who explained away lying to Congress by saying that no one had instructed him to tell the truth. Yet what makes America "a light unto the nations" is our respect for law and ethics. Without it, the necessary bond of trust between the governed and their governors may break.

III. A DECADE OF TRANSITION

73 and 100. These benchmarks artificially constrain the real transition for America. For there are only 73 days between election day and inauguration day within which to name the cabinet and sub-cabinet, prepare an inaugural address, draft a legislative program and revise the outgoing president's budget; and in-coming administrations invariably concur with Bob Haldeman's assessment that "your power is going to start eroding from January 20th on."

At the same time, all successors are invariably compared to FDR's famous First 100 Days, when the greatest domestic crisis of the century and an overwhelming Democratic Congress gave Roosevelt carte blanche to fight the Depression.

In 1989, however, the problems are both too long-term and undramatic to fit neatly into these accepted timeframes. Dropout rates of 50% in our center cities, annual $150 billion deficits and the depletion of the world's ozone layer took decades to accumulate; their solutions may take no less. Appreciate that some of the significant public policy reforms this half century, such as integrated schools, the federal securities laws and passive restraints in cars, all took a decade or two of great effort by committed advocates. Consequently, *America's Transition* assumes not a 73 day or a 100 day but a 10 year transition if America is to meet the challenge of change. As Justice Arthur T. Vanderbilt of the New Jersey Supreme Court once wrote, "Reform is not for the short-winded."

A longer perspective is especially appropriate for advocates from the progressive mainstream. Converting proposals into policies in President Bush's reign will not be easy. Even beyond getting his signature on legislation, there are a series of institutional hurdles in Washington. There's the special interest crowd and the war-is-inevitable crowd, which are both well-positioned to oppose challenges to their prerogatives. Also, global economic competition can frustrate the economic innovations of any particular nation; in a world with unregulated hundreds of billions in Yen and Eurodollars moving at computer speed between Exchanges and dollar-an-hour laborers toiling for third world competitors, national attempts to influence wage rates or industrial practices may falter.

Then there's the deficit hurdle, which is Reagan's way of vetoing activist government long after he's gone. How does a successor propose new programs when there aren't enough funds for old ones? The contributors to *America's Transition* attempt to address the deficit conundrum in three ways.

First, many proposals entail reforms without revenues, *e.g.*, creating a system of private Certified Toxic Auditors; limiting PAC influence; making the EPA a cabinet agency; strengthening GATT; choosing judges and justices more because of their integrity than their ideology. Many of the greatest democratic advances of the century — the Wagner Act, Voting Rights Act, Freedom of Information Act — did not require big expenditures or big centralized bureaucracies.

Second, other proposals can be funded with "earmarked revenues" or "mandated benefits." For example, a reasonable cap on deductible mortgage interest payments and a speculator's tax on windfalls from resales could generate revenues earmarked to low-interest loans for young, first-time homebuyers — which nicely raises the question of whether society should subsidize second homes for our parents or first homes for our children. Or federal law could require that companies over a certain size provide employees with, say, health insurance and child care, an approach that passes the costs onto entities which can most efficiently provide them.

Third, big-ticket items — the billions needed to provide drug counseling and treatment on demand or to extend Headstart and nutrition programs to all qualifying children — can only be funded by a re-ordering of federal priorities. A combination of described military savings, farm program savings, tax increases on the wealthiest (even a 38% top bracket for incomes over $100,000 is less than the 50%-70% rate of the 70s) and slightly increased economic growth could yield some $80 billion annually. If half went to deficit reduction and half to essential investments, the progressive agenda of this volume could be well launched in the 1990s. (Forty billion dollars, by the way, was precisely what President Reagan reallocated from domestic to defense spending to implement his political goals.)

In conclusion, *America's Transition* — and our earlier companion book, *Ideas That Work: 60 Solutions For America's 3rd Century* — demonstrates that the progressive community has a governing, pay-as-you-go agenda. But does it have the self-confidence to govern? Did it in 1980, 1984 and 1988 lose only elections, or heart as well? Certainly, its policies have taken a back seat in the 70s and 80s, for several reasons. The three greatest liberal leaders of the 60s were gunned down; Vietnam and Watergate impeached the credibility of government, which is often the instrument of liberal change; OPEC and Khomeini tainted the American President in 1979, who happened to be a Democrat; and Democrats didn't field their best line-up for president in 1988. Hence, five of six presidential defeats.

But no public philosophy worth its salt should default because of a defeat. Conservative Republicans certainly didn't in 1964. Suppose, for example, that Republican race-baiting in fact contributed to Dukakis's defeat. Would anyone seriously contend that Democrats surrender their historic commitment to civil rights? Should they trim their values because Dukakis inexplicably flopped in the second debate, failed to respond to the slander of liberalism, ran unpersuasive ads or was tactically outmaneuvered?

True, the Democrats' big loss back in 1984 "created the temptation to accept the victor's version of the truth," Governor Mario Cuomo said at the time. "[But] the principles to believe in are working, so I don't see any reason for abandoning them simply because the Republican candidate won the presidential election."

His words are still timely. The progressive mainstream has a message, even if it lacks a (presidential) messenger. Until our generation's tough idealist comes forward, we offer this program of hope to help the new President and Congress keep pace with the new America and World.

Economic Policy

OVERVIEW:
The Principles of a Progressive Economics

Robert B. Reich*

For the past eight years the United States has been governed as much by a public philosophy as by a particular president or party. That public philosophy — call it Reaganism — says in broad strokes: Get the government off our backs. Turn loose the power of the free market. Everyone can benefit from the wealth that trickles down — and if you don't it's your own damn fault.

This public philosophy has given context and meaning to a variety of specific policies that conservatives have been advocating all along — efforts to reduce income taxes, cut public spending, eviscerate government regulation of business and transfer public responsibilities to the private sector. Now these separate initiatives could be understood as part of a grand design: *viz.*, economic growth via Ayn Rand.

Animating this public philosophy is not just its coherence but also its self-serving caricature of the liberal, progressive philosophy: Economic growth is bad for flowers and other living things. Let big government spend more of others' money. Don't make more wealth, but redistribute what wealth we still have from producers to victims. Social justice is the preeminent value.

If the choice were between economic growth and social justice, growth wins every time. But that's not the choice. A new generation of progressives is now embracing a public philosophy that regards savings and investment, productivity, competitiveness and entrepreneurship as essential to social justice. Specifically, entrepreneurial progressives are now saying this: Genuine prosperity is possible only when the means of achieving it, as well as the fruits of it, are widely shared.

1. Savings and Investment. Progressives are in favor of increased savings and investment, but not the way conservatives define it. They view every cut in public spending as a net saving, and every private-sector expenditure as a new investment. Ronald Reagan's

---

* *Robert B. Reich teaches political economy at Harvard University's John F. Kennedy School of Government. His most recent books are* Tales of a New America *and* The Power of Public Ideas.

huge budget deficit is his secret plot to remain in the White House long after he officially retires. Conservatives would like nothing better than for his successors to obsess about reducing the budget deficit — and thus feel unable to spend new money or launch new programs.

Yes, America needs to increase its total savings to invest in our future productivity, without going even deeper into debt to foreigners. But progressives understand that many of the things we as a nation should spend money on are really *public* investments in our future capacity to produce wealth: education, training, day care, commercial research and development, roads, ports, bridges, sewage treatment facilities, airports.

The Reagan Administration pulled the plug on these public investments. It reduced primary and secondary school funding by about $800 million, and proposed far more drastic cuts. It cut college loans and grants to the tune of $3 billion. It cut back on training and retraining. Federal spending on commercial research and development is only 10 percent of what it was nine years ago. And we're investing only 1 percent of the nation's gross national product in infrastructure like roads and bridges, compared to 2.5 percent in the mid-1960s.

The effects of this underinvestment may be invisible until an eighteen-year-old wants a job but can't read or do simple mathematics, until America loses another major technology to the Japanese or until a bridge collapses or raw sewage washes up on our beaches. Yet in the long run such abdication steadily erodes our collective capacity to generate wealth. The next president and Congress must bring the budget deficit under control, but only within the context of the larger task of investing in our collective future.

2. **Productivity.** Progressives want to spur American productivity gains, which have stagnated at about 1 percent a year during this Administration, but not the way conservatives define the task. The conservative formula is to encourage American corporations to slim down — replacing skilled workers with automated machines, laying off long-term employees without incurring severance and pension costs, and substituting part-time workers. If fewer workers can produce the same amount as before, then — presto ! — each remaining worker is more productive.

But this form of productivity gain also can boost unemployment and reduce personal income overall. American farmers and auto workers are becoming ever more productive. Yet unless there's something more productive for ex-farmers and ex-auto workers to do, they won't necessarily share in the new-found prosperity. In the early 1980s, American manufacturers did become more productive, but at the cost of about 2.5 million workers who lost their jobs. A majority of these workers found new jobs that paid substantially less than the ones they left behind. Thus while productivity rose, average wages (adjusted for inflation) actually declined.

The new president must support measures to improve the productivity of every citizen in the nation — rather than the output of American corporations per employed worker. This goal requires a fundamentally different set of policies, designed to continuously upgrade the skills of American workers, to aid them in shifting to ever-more productive jobs and to bring unemployed and partially-employed Americans into the productive system.

3. Competitiveness. Progressives favor improving American competitiveness, but not the way conservatives want to. Conservatives understand the task as improving the nation's trade balance and the profitability of American corporations. This can most readily be achieved, they assert, by getting foreign nations to buy more from the United States, and American consumers to buy less from foreigners. And the easiest way to accomplish *this* is to cut or hold back Americans' real wages, and to allow (or encourage) the value of the dollar to decline relative to foreign currencies. These measures will improve the trade balance by making American goods relatively cheaper in global markets.

But this formula has a discomforting side effect: It will reduce the standard of living of most Americans. A competitive strategy dependent on reductions in real wages — through "give-backs" and other concessions of unionized workers, "two-tier" wage contracts that give new workers lower pay, a low minimum wage and subcontracts to non-unionized and part-time workers — will be successful ultimately when the take-home pay of Americans drops to that of workers in Brazil or South Korea. Allowing or encouraging the value of the dollar to drop will have much the same effect, because everything Americans then purchase from abroad will be that much more expensive. By the time a Japanese car sells in the United States for $30,000, America surely will be more competitive, but most Americans also will be much poorer.

Conservatives speak of the wondrous means by which free markets in goods and currency inevitably discover what each nation can do best. They blissfully ignore the dramatic successes of Japan, South Korea and other Pacific nations over the past decades in shifting their economies toward higher-valued products, and they turn a blind eye to the overwhelming dominance of sovereign governments in managing global trade. Progressives disdain this free-market blather, but also don't believe that the only alternative is to protect American jobs from foreign competition — which will make everything we purchase from abroad more expensive.

Washington should seek to improve American competitiveness in order to enhance the overall living standards of Americans. This objective can be achieved only by increasing the skills of all Americans, while shifting the nation's industrial base so as to make use of the higher skills. America needs to move out of mass production, large-batch production and primary commodities — all of which less-developed nations with lower-skilled work forces are coming to dominate. The nation should move toward more customized, flexible and technologically-sophisticated production, which depend to a greater extent on knowledge services like engineering and marketing. Such a transition is already occurring — as exemplified by everything from steel mini-mills to customized semiconductor chips — but the pace is too slow to maintain our standard of living free from debt to the rest of the world. In addition to continuous education and training, a more speedy transition depends on government policies designed to quickly transform basic research and invention (like superconductors) into new products and production techniques.

    4. Entrepreneurship. Finally, progressives celebrate entrepreneurship, but not the conservative variety. When conservatives speak of entrepreneurs, they envision maverick inventors, financiers and tough-guy chief executive officers whose autobiographies now grace the shelves of American bookstores. There's no secret to stimulating entrepreneurs like these. Just pay them princely sums, reduce their taxes and move government regulations out of the way.

    The progressive vision of entrepreneurship is fundamentally different, and more closely tied to motivating groups of people to do their best. In an advanced economy as complex as ours, innovation and growth have come to depend less on lone geniuses and charismatic chief executive officers than on creative teams with common commitments. The evidence is all around us — in small, highly-successful companies that have shared both the responsibilities and the benefits of success among all their employees; in communities that have turned around their economies through partnerships among firms, unions, universities and grass-roots citizens organizations and in previously-moribund American factories that have been revived through worker ownership.

    To foster a more collective vision of entrepreneurship, workers need to have a greater stake in corporate America. Big differences in remuneration and responsibility between those at the top of companies and those at the bottom reduce team spirit and divide enterprise into "us" and "them." The next president should emphasize policies designed to enhance worker participation and spread the benefits of productivity improvements: tax incentives for profit-sharing and gain-sharing, employee stock ownership and worker buyouts.

    "Savings and investment," "productivity," "competitiveness" and "entrepreneurship." For eight years Reagan conservatives have claimed these terms as their own. Their version has emphasized the importance of reducing overall labor costs, and of stimulating a relatively few individuals to great feats of entrepreneurial daring. This public philosophy promises immediate prosperity for a few, and asks us to trust that others will share in the prosperity eventually.

The progressive vision is sharply distinct. When progressives speak of achieving economic growth, we don't subordinate social justice as a value to be traded off against growth, or to be added on when growth is achieved. In this vision, a more egalitarian society is understood as a means of achieving prosperity, and intrinsic to it. Rather than aim to reduce labor costs, progressives focus on the importance of increasing labor's value.

Such a public philosophy implies four related precepts:

* First, government has a key responsibility for investing in our future capacity to produce wealth — in our citizens' education and training, and in our ability to live and work constructively together.

* Second, far greater numbers of Americans than now can become more productive members of society. As a large number of us do so, every one of us gains. Here, too, government has a major role.

* Third, the evolution of our system of production is a public as well as a private responsibility. Corporations can compete either by reducing labor costs or by investing in new skills and higher-valued production. The nation as a whole has a strong interest in encouraging the latter.

* Fourth, a more egalitarian workplace can generate greater wealth for all. Large disparities in power and remuneration undermine teamwork and thus inhibit productivity. Efforts to reduce such disparities and to democratize the workplace therefore can yield significant economic benefits.

The last Democratic Administration found the values of social justice and economic growth, ultimately, to be in bitter conflict. President Carter spoke eloquently about the problems of the poor, and undertook a number of initiatives designed to ameliorate them. But then, with inflation raging, he felt he had no choice but to appoint Paul Volcker as chairman of the Federal Reserve and to watch passively as Volcker choked off the money supply, plunged the economy into recession and thus imposed the heaviest casualties in the inflation fight upon America's poor and near-poor.

Ronald Reagan has demonstrated the reverse side of the same phenomenon: By appearing to aim for economic growth first and foremost, it has been possible for him to accomplish (or take credit for) a few key economic objectives, like tax reform and deregulation, and to be largely forgiven the huge budgetary mess he's created. The American public has been remarkably willing to allow Reagan to sacrifice social justice, as exemplified by the steadily-widening gap between the nation's rich and poor, without evidence that his economic policies have succeeded. Jimmy Carter's brief interregnum ended with double-digit inflation; Ronald Reagan's is ending with 12-digit indebtedness to the rest of the world.

By reestablishing the connection between prosperity and justice, the next president can offer a new vision of where America should be heading. He can then point with pride to a nation whose new prosperity is widely shared, precisely because the means of achieving it are widely shared.

FISCAL POLICY:
The Treasury Department

Nancy S. Barrett & Robert Eisner*

SUMMARY OF RECOMMENDATIONS

The economic program of the new administration and Congress must be dedicated to full employment and economic growth. Fiscal policy, with consistent support from the monetary authority, is key to that objective.

Measures of the Federal budget deficit are critically misleading. They do not separate capital from current expenditures and they do not adjust for inflation. Substituting current depreciation for Federal investment spending would reduce the measure of the deficit by some $70 billion. With even a modest 3 per cent rate of inflation, recognizing the "inflation tax," which reduces the real value of outstanding government debt, would show the *real* deficit to be another $60 billion less.

An initial target for the deficit might be one that prevents it from increasing the ratio of debt to GNP. This target can and should be adjusted on the basis of the movement of the economy, needs for public and private investment and monetary policy. In no case should the new administration set balancing the conventionally measured budget or even reducing its deficit as its "number one priority."

Focusing on the wrong things has given us the fiscal straight-jacket of Gramm-Rudman, arbitrary cuts in needed government services, foolish calls for general tax increases and frightening threats to cut Social Security for the elderly and the disabled. Americans struggling to make ends meet are told that they have been on a "consumption binge," that we can only be better off in the future by accepting austerity, by making ourselves worse off now. Some insist that we must slow down the economy with tighter fiscal and monetary policy to reduce the risk of future inflation, to cut the trade

* Nancy S. Barrett is Chair of the Department of Economics at American University. Robert Eisner is William R. Kenan Professor of Economics at Northwestern University and President of the American Economic Association. The authors are grateful for helpful comments from James K. Galbraith. The authors alone, however, and neither the universities nor the American Economic Association, are responsible for the views here expressed.

deficit or to correct our low savings rate. We call for a different strategy, one that entails a new commitment to more growth, to high employment and to increasing productivity.

Easier money and lower interest rates will increase investment, exports, income and employment. There should be neither regressive, distortionary "incentives for saving and investment" nor fiscal austerity programs intended to increase saving by reducing consumption. Raising taxes and cutting total government spending are likely, as they depress income and output, to reduce rather than raise national saving and investment, and all the more so if they entail cuts in public investment.

Social Security trust funds, however they are labelled, are effectively part of the Federal budget. Balancing the rest of the budget while we accumulate large Social Security surpluses drains the public of purchasing power and risks creating a recession. The Social Security surpluses should be used to finance investment in public infrastructure: in roads and bridges, in housing, in land, natural resources, health, research and, most important, in the education and training of our young. Real capital accumulation, and not paper accumulation of surpluses, is the only way to provide appropriately for the support of those retired and the prosperity of the Nation.

The new administration and Congress should:

* Show fiscal prudence and responsibility by insisting upon an easier monetary policy, changing the fiscal-monetary mix and reducing real interest rates without raising taxes or depriving the economy of necessary stimulus.

* Permit — and encourage foreign authorities to permit — dollar exchange rates to seek their market levels, thus stimulating exports and relieving our trade deficits.

I. THE CHALLENGE OF FULL EMPLOYMENT

Every percentage point of officially measured unemployment has been estimated to take at least two percentage points from the Nation's real gross national product. This lost output means fewer consumption goods when poverty remains a serious problem, fewer capital goods at a time of great concern over the need for more investment, a reduced tax base to fund government programs and services and fewer resources for meeting global needs.

Further reduction of unemployment will facilitate the movement of workers out of declining industries and regions. It will improve our ability to adjust to structural changes relating to trade and environmental needs. It will increase potential output, raise productivity and dampen political resistance to change.

High employment means not only greater output now but more saving and investment for the future. With more employment and output we can consume more — have our cake now — and also have and consume more later. In short, high employment, a worthy end in itself, is also a precondition for general economic progress.

The unemployment figures generally cited understate the number of people who experience joblessness. In addition to the totally unemployed usually counted, there are those partially unemployed and "discouraged workers," who have given up looking for work and fall out of the data. For the first quarter of 1988, when this "official" rate was 5.7 percent, the Bureau of Labor Statistics's full-time equivalent measure of total unemployment amounted to 10 million people, a full 8.8 percent of the adjusted labor force.

Major differences in policy prescriptions stem from differences in the estimates of how low unemployment can be allowed to get without the danger of kindling inflation. Despite the record of official unemployment rates averaging 3.5 percent in 1968 and 1969, with inflation little greater than now despite all the pressures of war spending, many in the last decade accepted the notion that we could not dare aim for unemployment rates below six or six and one-half per cent without risking "accelerating" inflation.

Clearly, there is a point to which we cannot lower unemployment by providing increased purchasing power and aggregate demand without bringing forth intolerable inflationary pressure. If we were to reach that point, restrictive fiscal and monetary policy would be in order. But now, with average unemployment already a full percentage point below the previously supposed minimum, and considerably lower in many states, there is no convincing evidence of inflationary pressure from overly tight labor markets. Analysts are beginning to suggest that perhaps we can get unemployment down to 5 per cent, even to the old "full-employment" target of 4 per cent, without more inflation.

There is here an important lesson for policy makers. The relation between unemployment and inflation is complicated and frequently murky. Confounding the conventional wisdom, unemployment and inflation have both been generally declining since the end of 1982. High and growing aggregate demand, such as may be brought on by stimulatory fiscal policy, generates more output and employment and reduces unemployment. But there never has been an excess-demand inflation in this country except in connection with war. Prudence is always in order but cutting demand is not the way to combat inflation brought on by supply-side factors such as the huge oil price hikes of the 1970s or the drought of 1988. Throwing the economy into recession and throwing American workers out of jobs is not the way to combat any inflation. We should certainly not allow outworn economic theories or dubious econometrical models to justify following that path now.

Inflation can and should be fought by insisting upon a full measure of competition, domestic and international. Inflationary Pentagon and other government buying practices, price supports, quotas, tariffs and other interventions contributing to inflation should be opposed.

The challenge for economic policy is to develop a strategy for achieving a low unemployment target and reducing the unemployment disparities that now exist across geographic regions and demographic groups. This is not a matter merely of helping the unfortunate. It is a way of increasing total output and hence the well-being of the Nation as a whole.

II. BUDGET DEFICITS (NOMINAL AND REAL) AND AGGREGATE DEMAND

In our economy, firms hire workers not because of orders from GOSPLAN and not because of noble sentiments from the Vatican. Rather, they do so if, and only if, they find it profitable. And they cannot find it profitable unless they can sell the goods and services that additional workers would produce. This means that to avoid recession and unemployment there must be adequate effective aggregate demand. That demand must be equal to the value of all that would be produced if everyone wanting to work had a job working as much as he or she wished. Unfortunately, as historical experience has repeatedly confirmed, we have no guarantee that the free market economy, notwithstanding all its other virtues, will always or even generally generate full employment demand on its own.

We have painfully learned that ignorant or foolish government policies can aggravate shortages of demand and consequent departures from full employment. Yet, without adequate demand — or purchasing power — our necessary efforts to improve labor markets and educate and train people for work are foredoomed. We may provide the supply of qualified labor, but they will not find jobs if there is not the demand for what they can produce.

Government fiscal policy — appropriately supported by the monetary authority — can make all the difference, for good as well as evil. The essential points are simple. By buying goods and services, whether missiles or milk, star wars or schools, government provides direct demand and supports output and employment. By "transfer payments" or the provision of income without return, as in Social Security or veterans' benefits or scholarships, government offers private citizens the means to demand goods and services, also supporting output and employment. And by increasing or decreasing taxes, government takes from or adds to the ability of the private sector to make purchases and sustain output and employment.

There is no escaping the fact that increased government spending, whether in itself useful or not, creates demand and thus stimulates the economy. Cuts in taxes, similarly, by boosting private spending power, also stimulate the economy. And reductions in spending and increases in taxes *both* slow the economy. A further critical insight is gained by recognizing that an excess of government spending over taxes — the very budget deficit so widely deplored — adds to the wealth that the public holds in the form of that government debt. And when people feel wealthier, for whatever reason, they spend more. Hence, budget deficits, by adding to the (paper) wealth of the private sector, bring increases in private spending — spending of all kinds, it turns out, for consumption of domestic output, for investment and for imports.

Because government fiscal policy affects the overall level of aggregate demand, the fact is that budget deficits can be too small as well as too large. If a shortage of aggregate demand prevents the attainment of full employment, a lesser deficit, let alone a balanced budget or a surplus, will make the situation worse. This then is not necessarily an argument for larger deficits, for there are possible countervailing forces. But it must be kept clearly in mind that, if we are truly committed to high employment, we must not violate that commitment in pursuit of the elusive god of the balanced budget.

This same reasoning shows that the notion that budget deficits are passing a tax burden to future generations is also misguided since, with a high-output, high-growth strategy, we can have more output both now and in the future. The only way in which current policy (including deficit spending) can adversely affect the future is if it results in lesser total national accumulation of capital, public and private, physical and human and intangible. An austerity program aimed at slowing the economy will *reduce* investment. It will thus bring sacrifice now that will only result in more sacrifice later.

Our faulty measures of the Federal budget deficit have sadly confused popular discourse and the formulation of sensible policy. We thought we had deficits, for example, during the Carter years. While they were much lower than the subsequent ones in the Reagan Administration, many mistakenly saw in those nominal deficits the cause of accelerating inflation. In fact, the inflation, brought on by oil and other supply shocks, entailed a substantial, implicit "inflation tax" on holders of the Federal debt and the money it backed, reducing the real value of the government debt. Since a deficit must reflect a net increase in the debt, and a surplus a reduction, the supposed deficits of the Carter years were in effect real surpluses. These surpluses reduced private wealth and, along with tight money, they brought on the mini-recession of 1980 which contributed significantly to the Reagan triumph.

The Reagan Administration initially pursued the tight fiscal and monetary policies they inherited, and did so with sufficient force and persistence to bring on that record recession of 1982. In a great political irony, however, for quite different purposes, they dramatically reversed the thrust of fiscal policy in the latter half of 1982 and thus brought on the recovery which has continued to this time.

Simply enough, the huge military buildup against the then "Evil Empire" and the huge cuts in taxes, along with a break in inflation due largely to the reversal of the oil price increases that drastically cut the inflation tax, gave us by the latter half of 1982 enormous real budget deficits. They constituted the greatest shift from real surplus to real deficit on record, and the economy responded. Any objective analysis must begin with the acknowledgement that the very large deficits were a major, probably critical, factor in the recovery, just as prior real surpluses contributed in a major way to the recession. And it was the continuing deficits, repeatedly adding to the public's wealth in the form of Treasury obligations, which have been a major factor in keeping the recovery going.

We now must face the fact that, if we are to reduce the deficit further — it already dropped very substantially in 1987, to $150 billion, from $220 billion the previous year — we have to be sure that such deficit reduction does not abort the recovery and throw us into a new recession with all the associated losses in output, employment and investment (not to mention, a higher deficit!). That dictates that additional cuts in the deficit should be part of a change in the fiscal-monetary mix that will insure aggregate demand sufficient to attain and maintain full employment.

Specifically, monetary policy — the supply of monetary reserves and credit by the Federal Reserve — must help to bring on substantial reductions in real interest rates. Lower interest rates will stimulate home buying and residential construction along with business investment in plant and equipment. Lower interest rates will also reduce foreign demand for the dollar and permit a further decline in our still excessive exchange rates, thus continuing and expanding our recent boom in exports. Output, employment and investment will rise and, with them, tax revenues from our higher incomes. Government expenditures for unemployment and low-income transfer payments will then also decline and reductions in the budget deficit will accumulate. Moreover, as interest payments on the debt are part of government outlays, each percentage point of interest that the Treasury saves will reduce the deficit directly by some $20 billion dollars. And these deficit reductions will take place in the one way that makes sense, the achievement of a prosperous economy.

This suggests the desirability of a "New Accord," in James Galbraith's phrase, between the incoming administration and the Federal Reserve. Easing of monetary policy will in itself reduce the deficit. Fiscal restraint to reduce the deficit further will be matched by sufficient monetary expansion to sustain continued economic growth.

In searching for a desirable fiscal-monetary mix we need a meaningful guide for overall budget policy. In a growing economy, a nominal budget balance could prove treacherous. It would imply a constant nominal debt and, with inflation, a permanently declining real value of government debt and hence of the private assets which that debt represents. This would be a continuing depressant to aggregate demand.

An initial target with far different implications would be one that makes sense to any individual or business — to keep debt in proportion to income. With a growth of nominal income or GNP of some 7 percent per year, that means that the Federal debt can grow at 7 percent per year. Thus, with a GNP of $4,500 billion and a total Federal debt of $2,400 billion at the end of the last fiscal year, if each grew by 7 percent, we would have debt of $2,568 billion and a GNP of $4,815 billion, still in the same 8 to 15 ratio. But this would mean an increase in the debt of $168 billion or, precisely, a deficit of $168 billion, pretty much in the range currently forecast for fiscal 1988. Thus "balance," in the sense of debt staying in a constant proportion to income or product, currently implies a conventionally measured "deficit" equal to some 3.7 percent of GNP, which may be contrasted with the fiscal 1983 recession deficit of 6.2 per cent.

All this is not to say that such a deficit is desirable, although it is as good a target to start with as any, and clearly better than Gramm-Rudman balance. Important further considerations, though, include the shape of the economy. Does it need more purchasing power to bring effective demand to the full employment level, or less if we are really convinced that the economy is overheated? This brings us back to considerations addressed earlier regarding the appropriate employment and output target. To stimulate the economy we might need a larger deficit, to slow it down a lesser one.

The gross Federal debt held by the public was 120 per cent of GNP at the end of 1946 and fell to 28 per cent by 1980, before rising back to 43 per cent in the last eight years. If we consider the relatively low 1980 ratio more appropriate — although it is not obvious why we should — we might note the implications of keeping it constant, rather than the current ratio. The total Federal debt, including holdings of the Federal Reserve, Social Security, retirement and other trust funds, is larger than the debt held by the public, and came to just about one third of GNP in 1980, as contrasted with its current 53 per cent. Maintenance of the 1980 debt-to-GNP ratio, with 7 per cent annual growth in GNP, would thus imply a deficit equal to about one-third of that 7 per cent, or some 2.3 per cent of GNP. Even this, then, would imply a fiscal 1989 deficit of about $115 billion. Holding the deficit at that level, some $50 billion below where it is now, would in fact bring the debt-GNP ratio back down to its 1980 figure in about a dozen years. The ratio would then decline further, with GNP growth, if the deficit were not raised back to 2.3 per cent of the considerably larger GNP at that time.

A second consideration would be the finances of state and local governments. Are the Federal deficits partially counterbalanced, as they usually are, by state and local surpluses? It is after all the thrust of all government spending and taxes which affects aggregate demand in the economy, and in view of sizeable intergovernmental transfer payments, there is a direct link between federal outlays (deficits) and state and local revenues (surpluses). Along with the calendar 1987 Federal deficit of $152 billion (on national income account), it may be noted, there was a combined state and local surplus of $44 billion.

III. NATIONAL SAVING AND CAPITAL FORMATION

A third, critical consideration for the long run economic health of the Nation is the relation of the budget to capital formation. Individuals need not hesitate in running huge "deficits" when they borrow to invest in new homes. Businesses routinely borrow, and hence run what would count as deficits in Federal accounting, when they build new plants or buy expensive equipment. Similarly, government borrowing and deficits may well be in order if they relate to government investment. It is rarely good policy, at any level, to try to pay out of current income for investment which will add to income in the future.

Government investment, as the Office of Management and Budget points out in its annual budget documents (*Special Analysis D*), involves not merely acquisition of brick and mortar (and missiles) but also investment in research and development and education and training, which add to the human and other intangible capital that have so much to do with future productivity. If the Federal government kept its accounts like any private business, it would put capital expenditures in a separate capital budget and include in the current account only capital depreciation. That would reduce our measure of this year's deficit by some $70 billion. More to the point, the separate capital budget could give us a better notion of the extent to which Government fiscal policy is making appropriate provision for our future well-being.

A final important consideration is the impact of the government budget on private capital formation. But here conventional arguments are suspect. It is usually pointed out that the identity between national saving and national investment implies that the more private saving is offset by government dis-saving, the less must be private investment. But this is true only in relation to a given level of income or output. However, since fiscal policy can affect the level of income, it is not the case that reducing the budget deficit will necessarily increase total saving and investment.

First, efforts to reduce the government deficit, whether by raising taxes or by reducing expenditures, can drive down income and output and thus reduce private saving. If the reduction in output, as is likely, discourages private investment, then income and saving, along with investment, are reduced all the more. The fallacy in the view that government deficits drive down private investment is the false premise that private saving is fixed, irrespective of the level of national income. Second, if the reduction in the deficit stems from reduced government investment, the total of investment, public and private, may well be lowered even further. A similar contraction is entailed in proposals for private saving incentives. Not only are these proposals generally regressive, but they restrict demand and thereby discourage investment.

The historical record is instructive. Over the period 1959 to 1984, at least, larger cyclically adjusted and inflation-adjusted deficits were generally followed by greater *increases* in private investment, while lesser deficits and surpluses were followed by lesser increases or actual *declines* in investment. Contrary to the usual concern that deficits "crowd out" investment, we have generally had "crowding in."

There have recently been suggestions in a number of quarters that the developing surpluses in the Social Security funds be used to increase national saving. It has been argued that the rest of the budget should be balanced so that the "unified budget" to which we usually pay attention would come into substantial surplus: 1.5 percent of GNP by 1993 and increasing amounts thereafter. Such a policy runs serious risks as it confuses *attempts* to save more, or government efforts to force more saving, with the actual achievement of saving.

Creating such an overall surplus in the government budget means creating an equal deficit in the private sector. Individuals and business will be paying into the government more than they are getting back and their wealth in the form of the government bonds that they hold will be declining. In such a situation there is every reason to believe that private spending will decline. This in turn will bring further declines in production and income. The private sector will be saving less, both because it is paying more in taxes than it is getting back from government and because of these additional reductions in private income. Again, the fallacy that less spending means more saving is based on the false premise of fixed output. Lower private spending reduces GNP and shrinks the income base from which saving flows.

Advocates of developing an overall surplus in the Federal budget suggest that by thus reducing the outstanding Federal debt and even using the Social Security funds to make private investments, we would reduce rates of interest and encourage capital formation. This can prove a dangerous illusion. Over and over it has been found that giving business funds through tax concessions or making the cost of funds less will do little or nothing for business investment unless the demand for output is strong and growing. Business generally does not find it profitable to invest in new plant and equipment if it cannot sell the production of its existing capital stock. Adequate liquidity and low interest rates are important, but these should be pursued directly by the monetary authority, that is, the Federal Reserve, not government trust funds.

A more sensible use of the Social Security surpluses would be to finance public investment expenditures. The current expenditure or consumption portion of the Federal budget may well be in surplus if we are running "deficits" (which private business accounting would not classify as deficits) in our capital accounts. Using Social Security surpluses to finance rebuilding of our roads and bridges, investing in our land and natural resources, maintaining and expanding our stock of housing and, most important, investing in our intangible capital of research, health and education is a better way to provide for the future. For in a very real sense, it is not the paper or accounting entries in Social Security funds which maintain those retired. It is rather the production of those working. And that depends overwhelmingly on the skills and abilities and total capital endowment that they will have in the future, the fruits of the investments we make now.

Of course, once full-employment (maximum) income is achieved, private saving can no longer be increased by further expansion of income. At full employment, increases in investment can only be achieved by reductions in consumption-type public expenditures or by increases in taxes which reduce private consumption, both of which mean a lower federal budget deficit. This brings us back to the proposition that reductions in the budget deficit, if they are not to be self-defeating, must be prudent and accompanied by a monetary policy easy enough to guarantee that full employment demand. It also brings us to the real issue of fiscal policy that addresses appropriately the question of priorities, for the government and for the Nation.

IV. OTHER TARGETS AND CONSTRAINTS

Productivity. Productivity growth is the key to sustained increases in real living standards and higher future output. The past two decades have witnessed a major slowdown in productivity growth, and an absolute decline in real wages. For many families, living standards have been maintained by a second earner (although millions of single-earner families have dropped below the poverty line). But as the movement of women into the labor force tops out, families will no longer be able to offset falling real wages in this way.

Productivity growth is also the key to controlling inflation and improving our international competitiveness. Thus, productivity needs to take center stage with full employment as a major policy target. The way to advance growth in productivity, and real wages, is investment in the broadest sense.

The key to promoting business investment is a prosperous, full-employment climate and low real interest rates. In such an environment, there would be little need to second guess business decisions, and no need for the wasteful, distortionary and inequitable investment tax credits and other investment "incentives" that have littered our tax code and that we have only begun to weed out in our recent tax overhaul.

Major investment needed to raise productivity and future output growth is in social capital — infrastructure, such as roads, bridges, public parks and human capital. There is a major role for government in support of basic research, but particularly in education and training. And productivity-enhancing investments in human beings will also serve to improve labor force mobility and employability.

The Trade Deficit. The vulnerability of the U.S. economy to sizeable impacts from the international economy is of fairly recent vintage, and the appropriate policy targets in this area are not well understood. It must be emphasized that there is no reason to make support of the dollar a policy objective. A great deal of our present difficulties stem from tight money policies which sometimes had the purpose and have always had the effect of making the dollar too expensive, thus causing unemployment in our trade-sensitive industries. The dollar should be allowed to fall to whatever market levels are consistent with low interest rates and a full-employment economy. Fixing or "protecting" the dollar gets us into a trap that can be as bad as fixing on a "natural" rate of unemployment or achieving some arbitrary budget deficit figure.

"Competitiveness" internationally is essentially a matter of exchange rates, as we are being reminded at the moment by our growing export boom. But productivity growth is key to our international competitiveness *with a rising standard of living*. A falling dollar makes our products more competitive abroad, but it also raises import prices, forcing us to pay more in exports for the goods we import. Raising our productivity growth can make up for this deterioration in our terms of trade.

Net foreign investment in the U.S. is the opposite side of the coin of our current account deficit. (The current account is essentially the trade balance together with the balance of international transfer payments, including interest.) The former *must* go with the latter. When we buy Toyotas and Mercedes, the Japanese and Germans accumulate dollars. They may invest them in bonds, stocks, motels, gambling casinos or manufacturing plants. Such investment is not necessarily bad. To the extent it creates jobs and productivity, increases in present and future output could more than offset the interest payments that flow abroad.

It is true that net foreign investment in the U.S. represents a claim on our assets and, as such, a subtraction from our potential national saving. But foreign investment will stop when, and only when, our current account deficit ends. And it will be reversed when, and only when, our current account deficit becomes a surplus, taking us back fundamentally to exchange rates. The increase in foreign investment in this country has been due to the overvalued dollar that created the trade imbalance. It will be reversed with a policy of lower interest rates and whatever further decline in the dollar proves necessary.

We have heard repeatedly that the United States has become "the world's greatest debtor nation." It is suggested that this is something of a national disgrace, if not a calamity.

For one thing, the phrase is misleading. The figures on which it is based do not refer to debt, per se, but rather to the difference between the value of American assets in other countries and foreigners' assets in the United States. Our assets are reported by the Department of Commerce to be worth some $400 billion less than foreigners' assets here. But there is a difficulty with the figures, well known to the statisticians that compile them but apparently unknown to those who publicize them. This relates to the fact that a major component, direct investment (as opposed to pure financial claims), is calculated at original cost. As U.S. direct investment abroad was to a considerable extent made some years ago, it has appreciated enormously in value.

Foreign investments here are on the average more recent, and hence have not appreciated as much. This difference is compounded by the very large decline in the value of the dollar since 1985, which increases the dollar value of this unmeasured appreciation of our foreign assets all the more. Thus 180 billion Francs of investment in France, worth $20 billion when there were 9 Francs to the dollar, are worth $30 billion now when 6 francs are enough to buy a dollar. Preliminary figures from estimates that one of us (Eisner, in collaboration with Paul J. Pieper) is preparing, suggest that the $400 billion of "net debt" that has been the object of considerable rhetoric is wiped out when direct investments abroad, along with Treasury gold holdings, are taken at current market value in dollars.

All this is not to say that continued current account deficits will not eventually get us to the point where our net investment position with the rest of the world is negative. But this should be taken in perspective. Even if we continued to run a current account deficit of $150 billion per year for the next five years (a highly unlikely event as our exports surge in response to a lower value of the dollar), foreigners would have accumulated $750 billion of claims on American assets. At a 4 percent real rate of interest (and we would hope it would be less) that would come to $30 billion of annual interest or investment income that we would be paying to foreigners. In a $6 trillion economy that would be just one-half of one percent of GNP. We do not mean to suggest that this is trivial, but it is hardly the stuff of national disaster. The sacrifice of one percentage point of employment as the consequence of an austerity policy to avoid it, we may recall, would cost some two percent of GNP.

Relations Among Policy Targets. Clearly, there are many synergies in our policy targets; achieving any one of them makes it easier for us to reach the others. Productivity performance will be enhanced in a full-employment, high-output economy, creating strong incentives for business investment without government involvement and distortions in the tax system. High productivity growth lowers the amount of inflation potential in a variety of ways, including reduced increases in import prices, declining pressure for compensating wage increases and lessened pressure for protectionist measures that raise prices directly. Reduction of the trade deficit is likely to entail some restoration of high-paying jobs in manufacturing. A growing economy will generate the tax revenues to support governmental programs, where needed, for human capital development that will both reduce structural unemployment and increase future productivity potential. As the next president focuses on the policy mix to achieve these goals, he should appreciate that their attainment can be thwarted by our fixations on budgetary balance, supporting the dollar and reacting to the *fear* of inflation.

V. THE POLICY MIX

The most important single tool for reaching full employment and maximum output is the provision of aggregate demand. The traditional macroeconomic policy instruments — government expenditures, taxes and changes in the money supply — affect the economy by stimulating (or restraining) aggregate demand. Increasing government spending, reducing taxes and expanding the money supply all have stimulative effects on GNP. Reducing government spending, raising taxes and restricting the money supply restrain GNP. Any of these policy instruments may be used to affect the *aggregate* of employment and output.

However, reliance on one or the other will have quite different effects on the *distribution* of output among consumption, investment and public programs, and on the international balance. The Reagan years were characterized by a mix of tax reductions, monetary restraint and increases in government (military) expenditures. On balance, this was stimulative, the impact of the tax reductions more than offsetting the restraining influence of high interest rates, and unemployment fell from almost 11 percent in December 1982 to below 6 percent in 1988.

This mix fueled increases in consumption, raised real interest rates and created a large Federal budget deficit. The high interest rates in themselves had a detrimental effect on investment but that effect was offset by the general stimulus to demand (and, perhaps, also by business tax reductions). High real interest rates also contributed to an overvalued dollar that drastically curbed exports. Thus, as the economy expanded, personal consumption and military outlays rose at the expense of exports and non-defense public goods while foreign claims on our assets increased. It is important to recognize that this imbalance was the outcome of the policy *mix* rather than of the overall degree of stimulus.

In fact, the areas most critics see as problematic — high interest rates, budget and trade deficits, low productivity growth — are all related to the policy mix, not the amount of stimulus. Few should fault a policy for creating additional output and bringing unemployment down from double-digit rates. However, a policy mix that creates high budget deficits with high real interest rates translates into sizeable trade deficits, and a corresponding growth in foreign investment in U.S. financial instruments, real estate and business enterprises. To say that the budget deficit has "caused" high interest rates and the trade deficit, or that the budget deficit is "being financed by foreign capital" misses the fundamental point that these are the simultaneous outcomes of a policy mix that combined major fiscal stimulus and relative monetary restraint.

But restraining aggregate demand is not the way to high employment and output, since austerity will only reduce output and make it more difficult to reconcile competing claims on the GNP "pie." Instead, a change toward more stimulative monetary policy and the less stimulative budget policy that the easing of credit would permit will create a more investment-oriented economy and reduce both the budget and trade deficits. Any further reduction in the Federal deficit should be part of a shift in the mix and not a general reduction in demand. Moreover, a shift in the policy mix will rectify the current imbalances, without resorting to the spending cuts implied in the Gramm-Rudman approach.

A policy emphasizing lower real interest rates would stimulate domestic investment and promote a decline in the dollar, thereby stimulating net exports, reducing the trade deficit and net foreign investment in the U.S. The budget deficit will then decline without higher tax rates because, as the economy grows, the tax base will expand. There will be little, if any, need for general tax increases, especially if military spending is held in check and cut down to size.

This fiscal dividend in the form of a larger tax base is substantial. The Congressional Budget Office estimated in 1988 that reducing unemployment by one percentage point will increase tax revenues by 1993 by $43 billion. More people at work also translates into smaller outlays on unemployment insurance, food stamps, AFDC and other transfer payments. CBO estimates that outlays on these items would be reduced by $24 billion, for an overall deficit reduction of $67 billion for each percentage point reduction in unemployment. In fact, in the past, periodic tax cuts have been required simply to offset the tendency of the budget to move into surplus and depress the economy as the tax base expanded with economic growth. As mentioned earlier, lower interest payments on government debt will also contribute to deficit reduction.

One side effect in this scenario will be the increase in import prices associated with a declining dollar. Since import prices are included in the Consumer Price Index and Producer Price Index, there is a danger that the impact of higher import prices on these closely watched indexes will suggest a need for monetary restraint. However, it is essential that international price adjustments be permitted to take place if the falling dollar is to correct our current trade imbalance. And it is equally essential that they not be mistaken for the harbingers of the continued inflation of an overheated economy.

Offsetting the effect on import prices, lower interest rates mean lower mortgage interest costs that make housing more affordable, and lower costs as well for automobiles and other consumer purchases. Lower interest rates also reduce business costs, and these benefits will be passed on to consumers in a competitive business environment. The stimulus to demand associated with lower interest rates will increase employment in housing and other construction, a source of relatively high-paying jobs.

VI. THE COMPOSITION OF OUTPUT

The shift in the policy mix — large increases in military spending and massive tax reductions combined with monetary restraint — had a dramatic impact on the composition of output. It is clear from Table 1 that despite the many structural changes that occurred during the 1970s — the OPEC oil price shocks, transition to flexible exchange rates, changes in domestic monetary regimes and increased openness of the economy to international trade — it was not until the advent of the Reagan Administration that the distribution of output among its major components was sharply affected.

TABLE 1
SHARES OF REAL GNP, PERCENT

	1973	1979	1983	1987
Personal Consumption Expend.	61.6	62.8	65.4	65.4
Gross Private Domestic Invest.	19.0	18.0	15.4	18.0
Business Fixed Investment	11.6	12.2	11.0	11.7
Government Expenditures for				
Goods and Services	20.6	19.1	19.8	20.2
Federal	8.4	7.4	8.4	8.8
Defense	6.2	5.1	6.3	6.9
Nondefense	2.2	2.3	2.1	1.9
State and Local	12.2	11.7	11.4	11.4
Net Exports	-1.1	+0.1	-0.6	-3.5
Exports	8.8	11.2	10.6	11.1
Imports	10.0	11.1	11.2	14.7
Federal Budget Surplus or Deficit,				
NIA, percent of GNP	+0.6	+0.4	-5.2	-3.4
Real Interest Rate				
(Corporate Aaa bond rate minus				
current % change in gross fixed				
investment implicit price deflator)	1.9	-0.1	12.2	7.5
Real Exch. Rate 2 Years Earlier	n.a.	93.1	100.8	132.0

Source: *Economic Report of the President, February 1988,* and *Economic Indicators,* April 1988.

Throughout the turbulent 1970s, consumption, investment, government spending and net exports commanded roughly the same shares of the GNP pie. In fact, conventional wisdom to the contrary, consumption *and* business investment increased somewhat and the Federal government captured a smaller share.

Following the Reagan Administration tax cuts in 1982, the consumption share of output rose significantly, from 62.8 percent in 1979 to 65.4 percent in 1987. With real GNP rising 19.6 percent over this period, that meant quite a surge in real consumption. Moreover, despite all the hoopla about reducing the role of government, the Federal share of the GNP pie grew from 7.4 percent in 1979 to a whopping 8.8 percent in 1987. This stemmed from a more than 35 percent increase in the defense share, from 5.1 percent to 6.9 percent, accompanied by a 21 percent decline, from 2.3 percent to 1.9 percent, in the Federal nondefense share of GNP.

The big, offsetting item to the increases in consumption and government shares was the decline in net exports, from +0.1 percent to -3.5 percent. The explanation for this is to be found right in the addenda at the bottom of Table 1. It is not directly the budget deficit, which was much higher as a ratio of GNP in 1983 when the decline in net exports was still modest. (Of course, recessions reduce imports, which is *not* the way to "cure" the trade deficit.) The explanation is in the exchange rate, tabulated as of two years earlier to allow for the well-known lag in trade adjustment. What happened, simply enough, was that the tight money and high interest rates of our policy mix raised the relative real costs of our goods to foreigners, as shown by the increase in the real, trade-weighted, average exchange rate from 93.1 to 132.0, by no less than 42 percent. It is a miracle that they bought them at all!

It appears that the high real interest rates shown on the table did far more damage to the trade deficit (net exports) than to the investment share. The share of gross private domestic investment was roughly the same in 1987 as it had been in 1979, while the share of business fixed investment dropped only slightly. Clearly neither the budget deficits nor even the entire policy mix brought crowding out of investment. What is true is that the recession of 1982-83, as do all recessions, knocked the bottom out of investment, reducing its share substantially, as shown in the table for 1983. Conversely, as study after study confirms, the greatest stimulus to investment is the growth in demand and output.

A new policy mix, that would entail lower real interest rates and exchange rates and a somewhat reduced budget deficit, would raise exports, cut imports and expand total output. This might bring a somewhat reduced *share* to consumption without reducing the absolute amount of real consumption. Private investment would be higher and, with a reduced share to the military, vital public investment could be raised significantly. The elimination of our trade deficit, with the consequent return to current account balance, would mean that foreigners would stop acquiring our assets at a rate greater than we are acquiring theirs.

VII. THE BUDGET AND TAX PROGRAMS FOR THE FUTURE

The austerity approach that currently guides the terms of reference for the economic policy debate is bound to the shibboleth of budget balance. The budget deficit is viewed the culprit in manifold ills of the economy, real or imagined. This perception could well tie the hands of an incoming administration wishing to undertake needed initiatives that entail increased spending.

Continued economic growth will increase the tax base and reduce the deficit, even with no change in policy. But since much of the public views the deficit as a symbol of fiscal mismanagement and government irresponsibility, the positive, prudent measures to keep the budget and deficit in line should be made clear. Restraint in military spending, easier money and lower interest rates and the gains from an expanding economy will bring tangible reductions in the deficit without general tax increases. Indeed, there have already been sizeable reductions in the deficit. In fiscal year 1987, the unified budget deficit stood at 3.4 percent of GNP, relative to 6.3 percent in fiscal 1982. On a current policy basis, the deficit is projected to be 2.6 percent of GNP in fiscal 1989. Further deficit reduction can and should come, as indicated above, as part of a change, coordinated with the Federal Reserve, in the fiscal-monetary mix. It must be emphasized that *the main threat to continued deficit reduction is a recession*, an outcome that is far more likely if austerity measures are pursued than under this chapter's policy scenario.

Taxes. We see little, if any, need for overall tax increases, especially if military spending is contained. Indeed, at some point in the next administration, tax *reductions* may be needed to offset the "fiscal drag" of the expanding tax base. In general, the goal should be to close tax loopholes and to keep marginal rates as low as possible while preserving the progressivity of the tax structure.

The Reagan Administration tax reform greatly reduced the progressivity of tax rates, and some of this might well be restored. For instance, the feature of the current tax law whereby the effective rate rises to 33 percent for incomes (for married persons filing joint returns) between $71,900 and $149,250 and then goes back down to 28 percent, might be corrected. One possibility then is to leave the top income rate at 33 percent (or even to go back to the 1987 rate of 38.5

percent) for incomes over $149,250 (or still higher figures in the future as a result of indexing). This would restore some progressivity and at least eliminate regressivity at very high incomes.

The regressive features of payroll taxes could be reduced by applying them to the full wage and salary base. This would allow for a rate reduction on all incomes, which would reduce labor costs to firms and contribute further to the overall progressivity of the federal tax system. Over half of all households pay more in payroll taxes than they do in income taxes, so that the regressive impact of payroll taxes offsets what little progressivity is left in the income tax system for these families.

Social Security. There is no excuse for reducing Social Security entitlements, although a case can be made for raising benefits but making them more fully taxable after some income cutoff, thus maintaining their average after-tax value. And it should be clearly understood that the growing surpluses in the trust funds are part of the budget; no accounting tricks can eliminate their impact on the economy. Just as trust fund receipts are part of the current revenues of the government, Social Security payroll tax payments are part of the overall tax burden. Building Social Security trust fund surpluses, though, has nothing to do with providing income security for the baby boomers when they retire well into the next century. What they get then will depend only on what the economy is then able to produce and on how society then decides how to divide its output. That means it will depend on the number of people working and on their human and physical capital.

Other budget issues. Undue attention to the deficit has diverted us from the more important issues of setting priorities and determining the appropriate size of government in the economy. One approach to implementing social investment priorities would be the development of a capital budget that would enable us to track public investments as opposed to outlays to meet current needs. A capital budget could also provide a reference point for an appropriate amount of non-cyclical deficit financing, since borrowing for social investment would not have the connotation of "fiscal irresponsibility" that would be associated with borrowing to meet current (consumption) expenditures.

A related innovation would be the implementation of GNP budgeting (as a supplement to the government budget), in which we would track the shares of output being devoted to various activities such as health, education, environmental renewal and the like. This would make the distinction between private and public provision of these goods and services less critical than the overall level at which they are being provided. Where the private sector is meeting a need, there would be less concern with government involvement; the government would become involved when there is a gap between societal needs and private sector outputs. Thus, a GNP budget would serve as a frame of reference for debating and establishing *national* priorities.

MONETARY POLICY:
The Federal Reserve

James K. Galbraith*

SUMMARY OF RECOMMENDATIONS

In its first month in office, the new administration should reach an accord with the Federal Reserve, through Chairman Alan Greenspan or his successor, to sharply restructure macroeconomic policy. Over its first year, a new administration should put in place the international and domestic conditions required for sustained growth and a managed transition of the U.S. price level, consistent with improving U.S. competitiveness and more balanced trade. The Federal Reserve's role must be to assist in this process: in negotiating over international monetary coordination, in settling the debt crisis and in ensuring the fundamental stability of the American banking system even as individual institutions adjust.

Specifically, the administration should:

* Raise personal and corporate income tax rates enough to generate about one percent of GNP in revenue, effective in January, 1991.

* Lower interest rates immediately. This will stimulate American businesses and homebuyers, generating genuine economic expansion. If Europe and Japan fail to match our interest cuts, we should allow the dollar to fall against their currencies.

* Act, with Japanese cooperation, to settle the Third World debt crisis. This should involve a managed writedown of foreign debts, accompanied by a plan to provide stable finance to developing countries.

* Strengthen the Federal Reserve's power to curb excessive financial speculation. To prevent panics in the financial community, the Fed should perform a supervisory function over arbitrage between stock and futures markets, as recommended by the Brady Commission.

* James K. Galbraith is an Associate Professor at the Lyndon B. Johnson School of Public Affairs at the University of Texas in Austin. He was formerly Executive Director of the congressional Joint Economic Committee. The author would like to thank Marlene Miller for her capable research assistance.

I. BACKGROUND

The Federal Reserve is an independent agency of the federal government, insulated from executive power and operating under a broad delegation from Congress. Its charter is the Federal Reserve Act of 1913, as amended (principally in 1933 and 1935), which vests authority over monetary policy in a Board of Governors of the Federal Reserve System and a Federal Open Market Committee.[1] Discount rate and regulatory powers are reserved to the Board, while open market operations are decided by the Committee. A Chairman of the Board of Governors, appointed by the President to a four-year term, generally exercises strong leadership over both bodies.

Since 1951[2] the Federal Reserve has enjoyed substantial discretionary powers over credit conditions, and so over the pace of economic growth. Its powers have been used in general support of steady expansion over the past two decades. However, on five major occasions the Federal Reserve has found it necessary to tighten credit in order to fight inflation: in 1967, 1970, 1974, 1979-80 and 1981-82. Recessions resulted from the last four of these occasions, with unemployment reaching nearly eleven percent at the trough of the most recent and serious recession in December, 1982.[3]

The weaker efforts of 1967, 1970 and 1979-80 failed to provide effective relief from inflation, and so set the stage for episodes of price, wage and/or credit controls, and later (when these failed or were abandoned) for the severe measures eventually taken. The deep recessions of 1974-5 and 1981-2 did have the intended effect, and were in fact followed by a period of sustained growth and industrial restructuring. Unfortunately, there is no evidence that permanent relief from inflation can be achieved by cyclical policies whether mild or severe. Each expansion, including the most recent, has eventually given rise to fears of renewed inflation.

II. RECENT POLICY

Federal Reserve policy since 1979 may be divided into three phases. A severely restrictive phase of slow money growth and high interest rates began with the appointment of Paul Volcker as Federal Reserve Chairman by President Carter in the summer of 1979; this tightness greatly deepened with the arrival of the Reagan Administration in 1981 and continued until the summer of 1982. There followed nine months of strongly expansionary policy (falling interest rates and rapid money growth), as the Federal Reserve sought to end the recession and to stave off serious difficulties in the financial system. From May 1983 to the present, a long phase of incomplete accommodation ('leaning against the wind') and high real interest rates has prevailed, with intermittent moves toward easier conditions in response to financial shocks (such as banking and savings and loan crises in 1984 and 1985 and the stock market break of October 1987). International forces have also become increasingly important, as the authorities sought first (in 1985) to correct the gross overvaluation of the dollar and then to hold the line at the new parities achieved by early 1987.

Given the reactive posture of monetary policy, fiscal forces have largely driven the economy since 1983, principally the enormous rise in the federal budget deficit from 1982 to 1984. Since 1985 the stimulus from the deficit has weakened. With the fall of the dollar, the decline of the deficit as a force for growth has been partly made up for by a recovery of exports to advanced country markets in 1987-88. This substitution, however, is incomplete. Overall, economic growth has slowed, while exchange rate realignment has sparked fears that inflationary pressures are returning.

On balance, the macroeconomic record of this decade has been good by comparative standards but weak by historical ones. After the serious 1982 recession, the U.S. has enjoyed growth, price stability and rising employment for five years. While this performance is comparable to Japan's and greatly superior to that of Europe, it is not as good as American experience in the nineteen-sixties, when unemployment rates were lower and growth even more robust. The price, too, has been a large and increasing load of debt, both domestic and foreign, the burden of which threatens to curtail precisely those forces by which growth and price stability have been achieved. Also, patterns of growth have been unbalanced, with an enormous inflow of manufactured imports on the one hand and stagnation of industrial exports on the other. From 1982 through 1986, the most advanced U.S. export industries were priced out of global markets for investment goods. In that time they have lost competitive ground to the Japanese and Germans, with doubts arising as to whether this ground can be recovered as more favorable macroeconomic conditions return.[4]

Problems arise from the policy mix particularly because the effects of fiscal policy fall first and hardest at home, while those of monetary policy tend to be felt rapidly around the world. Thus the tight-money policies of 1981-2 had unforeseen global effects, including bringing a rapid end to debt-financed growth in Latin America and elsewhere. The U.S. recovery of 1983-85 occurred as recession in the world economy continued; this and the high dollar produced stable prices in the U.S. but a monumental destabilization of the U.S. balance on trade and current account. Offsetting U.S. deficits were record current-account surpluses in Japan, Germany, Taiwan and other rapidly developing East Asian states, and in the debt-stricken countries of Latin America.

Especially important from the standpoint of the U.S. trading interests has been the financial strangulation of developing economies in Latin America, Africa and parts of Asia. The import levels of these countries have fallen by over 40 percent since 1980, and estimates of annual U.S. exports lost to this Great Depression of the Developing World range from $20 to $60 billion. There is no sign that the strategy of debt management since 1982, which has been carried out partly under Federal Reserve supervision, can succeed in restoring high rates of growth and reasonable progress in living standards to the developing countries.

Since 1985, the need for export-led growth has forced monetary policymakers to be increasingly sensitive to international conditions. Support for the dollar at the extraordinarily overvalued rates of 1981-85 ended with the Plaza Hotel accords of September 1985, following which the dollar fell sharply in comparison with the yen and D-mark, nearly to 1980 levels. As noted, some recovery of U.S. exports followed: about fifteen percent in real terms in 1987, with further progress reported in 1988.

However, the dollar remains well above levels that would restore current-account balance even today, for two reasons. First, the underlying competitive level of the dollar for U.S. industry has undoubtedly declined since 1980, reflecting the deep stagnation of advanced U.S. manufacturing industry in the first half of the decade. Second, the dollar has not yet depreciated significantly (if at all) in relation to currencies of major developing countries with whom we conduct a large share of our trade, especially of exports. For these reasons the current account deficit remains large, and downward pressure on the dollar continues.

III. PRESENT CONDITIONS

The Federal Reserve is (for the moment) properly wary of the risks of a new recession. Thus disturbances such as the stock market crash of October 1987 provoke prompt crisis management to assure stability of effective demand and undiminished liquidity of the financial system. Yet the Federal Reserve is equally averse to a rise in the inflation rate above the two-to-four percent rates of the past several years. Since most of the threat of rising inflation stems from rising prices of imports, this has led to a desire, so far as consistent with avoiding recession, to "hold the line" on the external value of the dollar.

So long as the developing country depression continues, the strategy of sustained growth led by exports at present exchange parities cannot succeed fully. A slowdown may be on the horizon already as the markets of Japan and Europe finish restocking American goods. At the same time, few domestic levers to support sustained growth in the American economy are available. Particularly as Gramm-Rudman-Hollings and other measures keep up pressure for reduction of the federal budget deficit, there is little political scope either for large increases in government spending or for new tax reductions to keep up the growth of domestic effective demand. The most favorable prospect is for a GNP growth rate of around 3 percent, with the threat of disruption from many possible sources. From the standpoint of policy, to achieve even this modest result will require effective attention to external conditions.

It now seems clear that inflation is returning, although how soon and how virulently remain open questions. Structural changes in U.S. employment have weakened the role and power of labor since 1980, while internationalization continually exposes more American workers to the pressure of foreign cost competition. Depression in the developing countries and in oil markets reduces the threat of rising costs in the supply of commodities and manufactured imports. On the other hand, the falling dollar has reduced competitive cost pressures on a wide range of manufactured imports from advanced countries and import-competing home goods. And, as the expansion ages and the unemployment rate continues to fall, there may come a point when conditions in U.S. labor markets begin to tighten. It would be prudent, therefore, to anticipate a continuing rise in inflation unless intervening events, such as a recession, prevent it.

IV. THE AUSTERITY OPTION

The current-account deficit, falling dollar, and fears of rising inflation have led to muffled calls from some quarters for a "quick fix," to be achieved by policy-induced slow growth or even recession in 1989 or 1990. An austerity policy is needed, in the view of its advocates, to "nip inflation in the bud." This view is shared by the remnant of monetarist economists in view of recent high rates of money growth, by those advocates of the "natural rate" hypothesis who view the present unemployment rate as too low and by certain figures in the business and financial communities (such as Peter Peterson, Albert Wojnilower and Charls Walker) who have been crusading for national value-added taxation. Federal Reserve Chairman Alan Greenspan may be sympathetic to these views, as he has said he regards an eventual recession to be inevitable, and has pointed to 1989 as the earliest date when one might occur. There is, also, a conventional view that new administrations are more likely to tolerate recession in their first years in office, when they do the least damage to eventual prospects for re-election.

Action to bring on a recession would be momentarily effective against inflation. Imports would fall more rapidly than exports, and the dollar would rise, reducing the current account deficit and suppressing the upward trend of costs and prices. A new round of industrial scrapping would clear out industrial deadwood among high-cost U.S. manufacturing firms, while sharply higher unemployment would depress the growth of wages. The U.S. economy would emerge more competitive on world markets, and a sustained round of resumed growth would be possible without serious fear, for another few years, of resumed inflation.

Yet this scenario also contains certain large problems and difficulties.

First, are the costs of recession itself, in unemployment, lost investment and scrapped capacity. Given the large rise in the share of services employment relative to manufacturing since 1980, the unemployment rate might not rise as much in a new industrial recession of comparable severity as it did in 1981-82. But the effects on remaining manufacturing employment would be very severe. Much of the subsequent recovery would simply consist of regaining lost ground, if indeed that could be done.

Second, the U.S. financial structure and the system of international payments would sustain heavy damage if a U.S. recession persisted for more than a few months. Latin America, particularly, would quickly suffer a sharp loss of foreign exchange reserves, precipitating a payments crisis and loss of solvency for the largest American banks. Similar effects would be felt in export-dependent areas of the U.S. economy where the financial structure is already weakened (such as the farm belt and Texas). It is conceivable that a such a crisis could get out of hand.

Third, the competitive advantage gained through recession would consist of a more equal wage structure between the U.S. and emerging manufacturing centers in Japan and the Third World. This is a poor result, insofar as it further removes the U.S. from its traditional source of trading strength in high-wage, advanced-technology manufacturing sectors. The U.S. presently relies on exports of computers, aircraft, industrial machinery, chemicals, energy equipment and other advanced goods. It will become a competitive exporter of passenger cars and other standardized manufactures when and only when American autoworkers are paid on a par with those of Yugoslavia, Spain and Korea. Sensible policy will seek to avoid such a result, which is manifestly in conflict with the policy objective of "good jobs at good wages."

For these reasons, a monetary strategy for the next administration must avoid the austerity option at all costs. Instead, the U.S. economy needs a redefined relationship between the Federal Reserve and the administration, with new goals and responsibilities for each.

V. A NEW ACCORD

The role of the Federal Reserve in the next administration must be part of a defined strategy for sustained expansion and managed adjustment of prices. The administration must, particularly, reach an early understanding with the Federal Reserve on the tasks of monetary policy given the goals and objectives of the President, his Cabinet and Congress. Such an accord could take the following lines.

First, the fact must be faced that an upward adjustment of the price level for commodities and assets in the United States, spurred by dollar depreciation and higher import costs, is not only inevitable[5] but essential. U.S. exports cannot flourish if they are not priced competitively, and to achieve competitive pricing means to pay more, comparatively speaking, for the goods we buy from the countries who buy ours. Higher dollar prices for developing country goods will also help restore real incomes and economic growth in those regions, raising worldwide growth rates and demand in investment sectors that rely on American suppliers. Higher relative prices for manufactured imports will help restore the competitiveness of some U.S. import-competing industries, and damp the explosive demand of U.S. consumers for East Asian manufactures. Asset price increases in the U.S. (particularly in real estate) may also be the only practical means to prevent a runaway crisis of financial institutions in certain parts of the country. All of these changes have been long delayed by the conduct of fiscal and monetary policy under Reagan and Volcker, at great cost to underlying U.S. manufacturing strength. They must now come, and quickly.

The task of policy must be to accept the needed transition and move beyond it to a new structure of acceptably stable prices as quickly as possible. The Federal Reserve, traditional ally of the creditors, must agree to remain neutral as the transition occurs. The new administration must take responsibility for institutional changes that compress the transition into a short time, and so prevent the return of chronic and destructive inflation.[6]

Within this framework, the priorities of the Federal Reserve must be, first, to sustain economic growth; second, to work under administration direction on international monetary coordination; third, to help organize an international settlement of the debt question; and fourth, to help curb the wasteful speculative practices that have so weakened corporate financial structures in this decade.

1. Economic Growth. To sustain economic growth, the Federal Reserve should move immediately toward a structure of lower interest rates as the new administration moves toward reduction of the budget deficit. It is vital that the timing of these offsetting moves be arranged so that monetary stimulus is in place before the effects of fiscal tightening are felt. There is all the difference in the world between an export-, housing- and automobile-led expansion tempered by higher taxes, on the one hand, and a consumption-led recession slowed by falling interest rates on the other.

A Federal Reserve commitment to sustained growth could also prove vital to the administration's success in getting Congress to accept the other half of the bargain: sharp and definitive federal deficit reduction. Ideally, such action should take the simple and flexible form of a rise in personal and corporate income tax rates sufficient to raise about one percent of GNP in new revenues.[7] This politically unpalatable course could be made far smoother if the Chairman of the Federal Reserve were to link it to an immediate reduction of interest rates, and to guarantee, so far as it is within the Federal Reserve's power to do so, to work to sustain growth and prevent fiscal restriction from leading to recession.

2. International Monetary Coordination. The Federal Reserve needs to help assert, as it has not done effectively in the past two years, U.S. economic and particularly monetary leadership among advanced nations. The enactment of effective legislation for deficit reduction, and specifically of a tax increase, is perhaps a prerequisite for success in this effort. But with that achieved, all pertinent branches of the U.S. government must work to assure that the American objective of high worldwide growth rates becomes accepted internationally, and specifically that it prevails over the hyper-conservative policy values of the present government in Germany.

3. The Debt Crisis. The Federal Reserve has played a leading role since 1982 in keeping the structure of financial relations between developing countries and their private commercial bankers intact. This was reasonable strategy so long as hope existed for the success of stabilization and adjustment programs and for a return to creditworthiness in private capital markets by affected debtor countries. No such hope exists any longer, and it is time for a change of strategy.

The compelling national interest of the United States now lies in writing down the debts as far and as quickly as possible, and in providing for ways and means to restart economic growth in Latin America and elsewhere on a sustainable basis. This is vital on three grounds: national and hemispheric security; democracy and human rights; and the importance of growing markets for the advanced-technology investment goods in which U.S. manufacturing industry specializes. To be effective, a debt writedown must be comprehensive and as nearly complete as resources permit, in order to free export earnings of the developing countries to be applied to new purchases of development-related investment goods.

To arrange a large-scale debt writedown will evidently require a large international effort, in which the leadership of the president of the United States must be paramount. Among other advanced nations, Japan most strongly shares the U.S. national interest in a rapidly developing world economy. Japan also enjoys both the disposable resources and the discretionary power in world financial matters (created by its gigantic current account surplus), while its relatively small contribution to the common defense has raised questions about how best to structure Japan's role and responsibilities in international relations. At the same time, European attentions are taken up by preparations for the forthcoming 1992 liberalization of trade within the European Community, and by the trade opening with the East.

A joint U.S.-Japan initiative to settle the debt crisis thus seems to be the most promising possibility.[8] Such an initiative might be based on negotiations between creditor and debtor governments over the appropriate valuation of past debts, followed by a re-purchase of those debts from the banks, financed by loans from the Japanese and other participating creditor nations, such as Taiwan. A successful operation of this kind could lead to new trading rules for the Pacific region as a whole, and to a financial structure capable of providing sound and sustainable finance to developing countries once the incubus of past debts has been removed.

Against the national interests served by a debt settlement lie only those of a few banking institutions[9] that have failed, over five years, to lay aside sufficient reserves, by withholding dividends and otherwise, to remain solvent in the event of a debt writedown. Their problems can be managed through aggressive use of the Federal Reserve's lending and regulatory powers, as well as those of other federal agencies; their reluctance to participate also can be allayed by regulatory action, such as directed writedowns and subordination of old debts to new. There is no basis for the fear that a managed writedown of the debts would necessarily entail an unmanageable crisis in the American financial structure.[10] The Federal Reserve must serve, however, as the nation's guardian and guarantor of overall financial stability as the reorganization of weak institutions within the financial sector proceeds.

4. Curbing Speculation. A structure of stable prices, alongside low and stable interest rates and expanding opportunities for profitable investment in advanced manufacturing in the United States, will all work to dampen the waves of purely speculative financial market activity that have so scarred the Reagan years.

The Federal Reserve has not been, in recent decades if ever, a strong influence against speculative activities by banks and other financial market players. It may be that the most promising policy measures to limit the flagrant abuses of the past few years lie in other domains: for example in turnover taxes, higher margin requirements, stronger disclosure requirements, antitrust enforcement, more effective enforcement of existing securities laws, and legal restrictions on greenmail, poison pills and other questionable practices. Nevertheless there are some steps in which the Federal Reserve necessarily would be involved.

Two of these concern arbitrage across different financial markets, particularly where the liquidity of the financial system as a whole may be affected. These are: intermarket arbitrage, most notably between stock and futures markets, and international arbitrage that takes advantage of the staggered opening and closing hours on financial markets across the globe.

The Reagan Administration's own commission on the stock market crash of October 1987 (the Brady Commission[11]) has produced a strong argument in favor of a consolidated supervisory role for the Federal Reserve over intermarket arbitrage. Such arbitrage, involving strategies of "portfolio insurance," enabled just a few players to spur enormous changes in the value of all stocks at critical times on October 19 and the surrounding days. In part, this occurred because of imperfect information: investors on the commodity markets were not aware that trading had not opened in certain stocks on the morning of the 19th, for want of bids. An intermarket supervisory mechanism could have acted to halt disruptive futures trading, and so provided a "circuit breaker" that might have forestalled the ensuing panic. As the Brady Commission urges, the Federal Reserve is well-suited for this role.

The issue of time-zone arbitrage is more complex, and would require further study to determine the extent of the developing risks and the appropriate nature of the response. To examine these questions is again an appropriate responsibility for the Federal Reserve.

VI. A POLITICIZED BOARD?

The Federal Reserve Board is by statute and tradition insulated from executive power. Its seven Governors serve in fixed fourteen-year terms, with one seat falling open every two years. The Chairman is appointed for a term of four years unrestricted by fixed dates. Thus Chairman Greenspan is scheduled to continue in office until four years after his appointment, or until mid-1991.

All of the incumbent Governors are appointees of President Reagan. All are Republicans, except for the most recent appointee. Of the Republicans, all but one have played active roles in the Republican Party at the local, state or Federal level, including service on Reagan-Bush campaign committees, contributions to candidates and party organizations, and service in the Reagan Administration.[12]

This pattern of appointments to the Federal Reserve Board is not unusual, as past administrations have also tended to name members of the president's own party.[13] But the extent to which time and circumstance have permitted the Reagan Administration to dominate the Board *is* unusual and may create genuine difficulties for any future Democratic administration. The question whether a new administration will face a politicized Federal Reserve Board must be raised.

The present Board, a mixture of businessmen and former business and bank economists, is neither better nor particularly worse than in the past. It is a new Board: at present, the senior member is Martha R. Seger, appointed in 1984. Lacking academic distinction, it seems strong in practical experience and in a concern with concrete business conditions of a kind sometimes absent from previous Boards. Moreover, it has been willing to exercise on occasion its independence of view, as when a majority appointed by Reagan (known at the time as the "Gang of Four") voted for a more relaxed policy in February of 1986, administering a telling defeat to Chairman Volcker. The lessons to be learned from that occasion are mixed. Among political observers the Board's action was viewed as having been taken in the Administration's political interest. But it was also clearly the right action, one that properly rejected an early move toward austerity. Whether the same Board, now expanded by several new appointments, would make a similar judgment in the changed political and economic circumstances of early 1989 is impossible to predict.

The internal politics of the Board changed abruptly in June of 1987. For a year or more before that time, the Board was broadly divided between an expansionist majority and an increasingly conservative Chairman.[14] When Paul Volcker resigned and was replaced by Alan Greenspan, the Board closed ranks behind its new Chairman. Gone was the strong impulse toward expansion and dollar depreciation. The result was a period of drift over the summer of 1987,[15] during which the Federal Reserve followed gradual moves toward tighter money and higher interest rates that were initiated by the German *Bundesbank*. This phase came to an abrupt end with the stock market crash in October of 1987. What has followed has been described earlier: a period of cautious maneuvering between the devil of a falling dollar and the deep sea of recession, in the hope that the channel is not completely blocked in the fogs just ahead.

VII. IMPLICATIONS FOR POLICYMAKING

All of the important policy initiatives described above are matters of the short run. The Federal Reserve must act quickly, effectively and in coordination with the new administration on all monetary and financial matters, from macroeconomic policy to the debt to regulatory questions. Without such cooperation the administration's initiatives will be doomed. The question is therefore how to secure cooperation, and quickly.

The president does retain certain instruments of unilateral power. Formal authority over exchange rate policy rests with the Treasury, not with the Federal Reserve. The Treasury also has the leadership role on matters relating to the debt. Banking regulators under the Comptroller of the Currency and the FDIC share responsibility with the Federal Reserve over matters of bank regulation affecting the debt. Yet none of these instruments is strong enough to overcome a Federal Reserve Board in determined opposition.

Much depends on the attitude of the Chairman. If honest agreement between the Chairman and the new administration can be reached, then it is likely that the Board and Federal Open Market Committee will be prepared to follow suit. To that end, the new president should promptly initiate discussions with Mr. Greenspan in order to ascertain his views. If in good faith agreement cannot be reached, then the president should be prepared to request Mr. Greenspan's resignation. Mr. Greenspan, for his part, should be prepared to offer to step aside. In the higher interests of both the Federal Reserve and the administration, both should strive to avoid a distracting public and perhaps legislative battle over the proper role of the Federal Reserve within the government of the United States.

VIII. ORGANIZATION AND FUNCTIONS

The Federal Reserve's structure features numerous anomalies, accidents of history and artifacts of past political compromise. Among these are the independence of the Board itself, the lack of coordination of the chairman's term with that of the president, the off-budget status of the agency, its penchant for secret operation and the role of the District Reserve Bank Presidents on the FOMC. Some of these bear changing on their merits, even though the case for urgency in doing so may be weak.

The Board's formal and practical independence is substantial and at times it is useful to the executive branch. The independent Board is both a powerful instrument and a convenient scapegoat, as in 1981-82 when the Reagan Administration sought a recession but hoped to avoid political responsibility for it. Yet there can be no principled defense of this arrangement. Clear lines of responsibility running from the president downward would clearly make for a more rational and better coordinated policy structure with a proper degree of accountability to the voters. Concerns about "politicization" — often voiced in connection with monetary policy but rarely on other matters — may be dismissed as specious in a democracy that is based on accountability to the voters.

How can better coordination and accountability be achieved? Theoretical possibilities range up to abolishing the Federal Reserve altogether (by, for example, making it a sub-agency of the Treasury). As a practical matter, though, much more modest steps could have strong effects. The chairman could be made, for example, a member of the president's cabinet, with a term of service like that of other cabinet officers. At the least, the chairman's term could and should be made coterminous with that of the president, so that an incoming president would not be saddled for three years or longer by his predecessor's appointee. Short even of the above, an administration could be given a formal seat on the Open Market Committee, so that its voice and views are regularly heard.

Budget independence and secrecy are two among many ways that the Federal Reserve has sought, with the help of its allies, to seal itself off from congressional oversight and public scrutiny. The arguments for this special treatment are unpersuasive. Congressional review of the agency's expenditures might strengthen the presently weak processes of oversight, which would be a good thing. Nevertheless, such review does not constitute a threat to the Federal Reserve's basic mission, any more than the fact that the agency is presently constituted under an act of Congress constitutes such a threat.

On the secrecy question, economists universally agree that the Federal Reserve could release complete records of its policy actions to the public at the time they are taken without any damage to the agency or its decisions; close observers in the markets have this information almost immediately in any event. More timely and public notice of FOMC decisions might even strengthen the effectiveness of the conduct of monetary policy.

The make-up of the Federal Open Market Committee is a final anomaly worthy of brief comment. The problem is that the five Presidents of district Federal Reserve Banks, who sit on the FOMC in rotation, are not qualified "officers of the United States" under the terms of the appointments clause of the Constitution, that is, appointed by the president with the advice and consent of the Senate. Instead, they draw their formal authority from the Boards of Directors of the district banks, which include certain private parties, notably local bankers. Thus the FOMC is formally a public-private body, a hybrid, which cannot legally under the Constitution set policy for the United States.[16] Remedies for this anomaly could consist either of vesting the FOMC's function in the Board, or of changing the method of appointment of district bank Presidents.

It may be that none of these structural and organizational issues merit the investment of significant political energy on the part of the new administration. Yet to advance one or more of them, such as the budget question, might prove a useful way to secure the Federal Reserve's agreement on the important questions of short-run macroeconomic and financial strategy. Myths aside, the Federal Reserve is a quintessentially political body, and a new administration should not shy from treating it as such. There may be no choice.

NOTES

[1] The FOMC consists of the seven Governors and five of twelve Presidents of the regional Federal Reserve Banks, who sit on a rotating basis.

[2] In March of 1951 the Federal Reserve's obligation to support bond prices at wartime levels was terminated. In 1953 all obligation to support bond prices ended, and the agency assumed its modern macroeconomic function.

[3] In most cases other forces, such as oil shocks, precipitated or reinforced contractionary pressures by the Federal Reserve. Yet in each case the Federal Reserve's deliberate actions were a decisive factor. See the recent account by William Greider, *Secrets of the Temple* (New York: Simon & Schuster, 1987), for detailed discussion.

[4] In the *New York Times* of May 5, 1988, Barry Bosworth is quoted as follows: "The United States had a real domination in capital goods, and the damage to it seems irreversible." For an opposing view see my book, *Balancing Acts: Technology, Finance and the American Future)*, forthcoming January 1989 (Basic Books).

[5] This assumes that no recession supervenes.

[6] Detailed discussion of these changes, which could involve such steps as synchronization of wage negotiations and new powers to help the President to influence inflation expectations, lie beyond the scope of this paper. See my article in *Challenge*, "Using the Presidency to Fight Inflation" (March-April 1985), and forthcoming book.

[7] This target is sufficient to bring the deficit of the consolidated government sector into balance in real terms at high employment, and is probably the most sensible choice of medium-term fiscal policy objective. See my paper, "The Strategy of Export-led Growth," *Challenge*, May 1988. Note that the effective date of such higher tax rates should be delayed, so as to allow the effects of monetary easing to be felt before those of the tax increases kick in.

[8] With the European Community perhaps taking special responsibility for African debts.

[9] Bank of America and Manufacturers Hanover would be insolvent if forced to write down their developing country exposure to secondary market values (about 48 cents on the dollar on average) that prevailed in February, 1988. Chase Manhattan and Chemical Bank would probably be insolvent at discounts of around 70 cents on the dollar. No other large American banks are in significant danger from this problem.

[10] It is quite possible, on the other hand, that an unmanaged writedown incident on an American recession could have such a catastrophic effect.

[11] *Report of the Presidential Task Force on Market Mechanisms*, Washington: GPO, January 1988.

[12] Documentation of the past political activities of Board members can be found in the record of their confirmation hearings.

[13] A significant exception was the renomination of Paul Volcker, a Democrat, by President Reagan in 1983.

[14] See Greider's account, *Secrets of the Temple*, pp. 698-706.

[15] Described in some quarters as the "interim chairmanship of Gerhard Stoltenberg."

[16] Numerous court challenges on this point have reached a dead end with the recent refusal of the Supreme Court to review adverse appeals court rulings. Indeed it now appears that no person or class of persons, public or private, has legal standing to challenge the constitutionality of the FOMC in court.

TRADE & COMMERCE:
Department of Commerce &
U.S. Trade Representative

Samuel Berger & Sidney Harman*

SUMMARY OF RECOMMENDATIONS

In ancient China, it is said, the bureaucrats separated the wheat from the chaff. They then carefully catalogued the chaff and discarded the wheat.

We approach the question of the next administration's policies toward trade and commerce not by cataloguing the chaff, but by identifying those values which should drive the policies.

America today faces a serious competitive problem in an increasingly global economy. Unless we deal with that basic reality in a forthright and urgent manner, we face an inevitable decline in our standard of living. The warning signs are there if we choose to see them.

* *In 1987, Americans bought $170 billion more from others than we sold to them.* Financing that trade deficit requires that we either sell off our assets or borrow from abroad. Interest payments to foreign bondholders of our federal deficit alone could exceed $75 billion by 1992 — the equivalent of a 2% drop in our standard of living. By comparison, the 1981-82 recession — the worst since the Great Depression — lowered Americans' standard of living by about 2.5%.

* *Consumers, here and abroad, are voting with their pocketbooks.* Last year, Americans spent nearly one dollar in four on goods produced elsewhere. To some degree that reflects the residual effects of the bloated dollar policies of 1981-85, which provided a discount for imports even as they taxed U.S. exports. But the resilience of the import share of the U.S. market three years after dramatic devaluation of the dollar indicates that more than price is involved in those consumer choices. The fact is that today there are few products or

---

* *Samuel Berger is an international trade attorney in Washington and former Deputy Director of the State Department Policy Planning Staff. Sidney Harman is chief executive officer of Harman International, a former Undersecretary of Commerce and co-author of* Starting With The People.

services which we alone produce; "Made in America" is not a sinecure in a competitive global economy.

* *America is not keeping pace with our major trading competitors in the investment and innovation which will create tomorrow's jobs and markets.* Our average annual investment in the 1980s has declined by more than a third from levels sustained from the 1950s through the 1970s. Japan spends 47% more than the U.S. — and Germany 32% more — on civilian research and development. One result: about half the new patents issued by the United States today go to foreign companies and individuals (compared with about 25% twenty years ago) while the number of new U.S. patents issued to Americans has declined by almost 40%.

The United States will enter the 21st Century a poorer nation unless we accept the reality of the global economy and develop a competitiveness strategy for America's success. This has two, interrelated dimensions: *internal* (those actions which must occur in the individual firm or industrial sector) and *external* (those policies which government can exercise with respect to other nations).

Thus, in reviewing trade and commerce, we start with the workplace. We stress manufacturing and seek to make the individual industry and firm the centerpiece of analysis rather than government devices designed to improve trade and commerce.

To help open the global marketplace to more, not less, trade, Washington in the 1990s should stop merely defensively protecting select industries and take the trade offensive:

* The new president and Congress should help strengthen GATT, rather than undermine it — and develop an overall strategy to replace the Reagan Administration's sector-by-sector ad hoc approach.

* Unilateral actions must be pursued as a conditional device to force the opening of markets abroad and not to close our markets to avoid competition.

* We need to create a new quasi-public "Export Corps" to train executives to seize opportunities in the global marketplace and to develop a state-of-the-art information system of economic trends and marketing information.

I. THE INTERNAL DIMENSION: QUALITY AND MANUFACTURING

While government has a vital role to play, there is little it can do to help American industry become more efficient and competitive unless American industry proceeds on the basis that what it does itself is crucial.

A vibrant manufacturing sector is critical to the nation's future. Ninety-five percent of research and development in the private sector is done at manufacturing firms. Wage scales in manufacturing are significantly higher than those in the information/service area. Together, these two elements make manufacturing vital. Further, the largest user of information and services would disappear if manufacturing were to continue to decline. If the United States is to regain its ascendancy in trade and commerce, it must make the individual firm and the workplace the plenum.

Unfortunately, American companies generally have not been in the forefront of advanced management thinking and correspondingly advanced manufacturing processes. The present and predictable global competitive struggle demands lean but value-driven management, emphasizing collegial, horizontal arrangements rather than mean, autocratic, command-down, vertical arrangements.

Happily, a new industrial mutant is emerging in this country that stresses the value-driven, collegial model. Consider, for example, the question of ownership in the new industrial mutant. It is traditionally — and correctly — defined in terms of equity. In private companies, that equity generally is held by a handful of managers. In public companies it generally is held by large institutions and independent investors, while management holds a very small percentage.

An additional definition of ownership in the newly emerging industrial firm is that "the company belongs to the people who inhabit it." This suggestion implies another kind of equity — call it emotional or psychic equity. The environment in which the work is done must encourage those who do it to feel that "this is my company — my contribution really matters." It is the antithesis of the perspective America inherited from Henry Ford and Frederick Taylor. That perspective holds that the company belongs to those who own the capital, and that workers are, in effect, dispensable and replaceable parts of its machinery.

In the new environment, traditional experts give way to multidisciplined generalists; the martinet yields to the facilitator. How many chief executive officers of our industrial companies would be reelected if those who voted were not the owners of the companies' securities, but rather those who worked in the companies' offices and plants? It is not a capricious question. Nor should one assume that if such an election were ever to occur, workers necessarily would vote for the most amusing personality or the union representative. The leadership of a company is critical to its people and, overwhelmingly, they know it. The Chief Executive Officer who has earned their respect and their trust is almost certain to be a successful and competitive leader. People want that for reasons of personal satisfaction and personal security.

THE MANUFACTURING CONTINUUM

During the past thirty years, many companies have chosen to separate the product spectrum into its parts: product design and development, product manufacturing and product marketing. Many have acted to retain the two poles of the spectrum (design and marketing), while "farming out" the product manufacturing. "Farming out" has sometimes taken the form of shopping for the lowest cost producer in the lowest cost labor market: "we design the product and we know how to merchandise it — anyone can stuff the boxes and load the boards." Others have settled for placing their trade name on products already designed and produced by other firms in other nations.

The abandonment of manufacturing, frequently labeled the "hollowing of the corporation," has had perverse effects on the fundamental competitiveness of firms over the long term, while permitting some to prosper in the short term. For firms and the nation, however, short-term profit can become long-term disaster. The reason is that product innovation and product quality are heavily dependent on the conjunction of design, manufacturing and marketing. It is a critical continuum. Progressive managers recognize that unless they directly and certainly control production of the product, they will become victims of their own expediency.

These three elements of the continuum actively inform and illuminate each other. True product quality arises from that intertwining and mutuality. True product differentiation can only arise when the firm "rolls its own." Nor does it make sense for firms to opt in and out of manufacturing as a function of currency exchange. It is, of course, true that when the dollar is weak, domestic manufacturing looks more attractive as pricing of our products abroad becomes more competitive and pricing of imports tends to rise. But gearing up for manufacturing and turning it off as a function of currency is a prescription for industrial malaria. The dollar was weak in 1971 after the dismantling of fixed foreign exchange rates. It was strong in 1975, weak in 1977, strong in 1980 and weak again in 1987. Given the lead time, set up and dismantling costs, a firm would be in deep trouble if it decided to manufacture only when the dollar turned weak, and to discontinue manufacturing when it turned strong. Sadly, numbers of companies are returning to manufacturing only on the basis of this currency crutch. It is, predictably, a doomed policy.

Consider quality. The primary advocates in this country, W. Edwards Demming and Philip Crosby, have been more respected in Japan than at home. Their definition of quality was "precise conformation to specifications." A more demanding definition has been followed by some firms: "performance and reliability at the highest level of customer need and acceptability."

Because quality is so much the consequence of a firm's (and its employees') state of mind, we propose a new definition: "performance and reliability *beyond* the highest level of customer need and acceptability."

When driven by such a definition, the processes and organizational character of a firm committed to the manufacturing continuum will undergo radical change. Instead of the traditional "push" approach to assembly line manufacturing, a new "pull" approach will develop. In the push approach, manufacturing engineers set standards, time and motion studies and the workers drive to meet the standards, "pushing" the product to the next operator on the line. It is a procedure which subordinates quality to quantity and, in the end, proves very costly because of high reject rates and scrap at the end of the line.

The pull approach in a company environment that promotes psychic ownership focuses on doing it right the first time. Workers may stop the line if necessary to assure that faults are corrected, so that each worker pulls the product from the previous operator. The same view carries from one assembly or production line to the next: "we do not permit the part or the product to move unless it is right."

With such perspective institutionalized in the firm, it is natural for management to move it to its vendors. "The company will no longer accept material or parts which are less than 100%, and we will help you to develop procedures which assure it." If vendors are delivering zero defect material, the company can arrange to have it arrive only as it is needed ("Just In Time") and can eliminate its own costly incoming inspection department and apparatus.

GLOBAL MARKETING

Because America's geography and economy seemed to promise limitless domestic markets, few firms have approached marketing abroad as a central priority. The approach has been, essentially, "we make what we see as right for the U.S.. If you want it, come and get it." That ethnocentric view has characterized products ranging from furniture to automobiles to shoes. Clearly, it will not work in foreign markets which have many choices, including their own developing industries. And clearly, the problem has been exacerbated by the fact that many U.S. companies have promoted the development of foreign firms by using them as product sources.

American firms can no longer afford such myopia. We need those foreign markets for reasons of national trade balance, and firms need them if they are to sustain adequate sales and employment. To sell in other markets, however, requires a serious commitment to the effort. An anthropological approach is better than a colonial one. Respect for the culture of the other market, reflected in products that respond to its needs (e.g., smaller, more gas-efficient automobiles in Europe) is essential. The employment of nationals in key posts is not only a sign of respect, but a wise way to assure a correct interpretation of the market needs. Emphasis on market share, coupled with determination to stay during tough as well as easy times, is equally essential. Americans continue to buy Japanese products today, despite higher prices, because they want them and because they trust them.

NEW TECHNOLOGY

Remarkable leaps have been made in the creation of new manufacturing machinery and related technology. Most of the advances have been achieved in Europe and Asia (notably Germany, Italy and Japan).

Too many American companies, however, have moved indiscriminately to incorporate this new technology in offices and plants by merely "throwing money at the problem." The usual result: disappointment and confusion.

The purpose of any new manufacturing technology should be to help improve productivity. To accomplish that goal, consultation with those who will operate the new machines is critical. In the first place, they know more about the work than virtually anyone else; the best and most self-confident manufacturing engineers invariably agree with this view. In the second place, they will surely do what they can to make the new equipment successful if they have recommended or approved it.

The best of the new manufacturing technology works hand-in-glove with the most progressive workplace environment. The new machines should not be seen as direct replacements for some number of humans. Rather, they tend to elevate the level of the work and introduce greater discretion for the office or factory worker. Consider that the new numerically controlled lathes can do a better, more precise and more efficient job than the old mechanical lathes in the hands of lathe-operator craftsmen. But the new lathes, if improperly attended, can also destroy very costly raw material. The lathe operator, in the right environment, becomes a lathe manager and almost certainly learns new skills (e.g., how to service the controlling computer).

The combination of new management attitude and new worker role can lead most directly to greater flexibility in the manufacturing process. It can sharply reduce set-up and changeover time and it can contribute directly to improved performance and reduced costs.

JOBS AND TRAINING

Even as the new technology can enhance internal productivity, it can lead to greater job security rather than be a threat to jobs — if it is appropriately employed and if the workers are participants in the decision.

In the introduction to this chapter, we argued that policy should be value-driven. Consider job training and retraining as a specific example. If national policy aims to train workers when they are made redundant by technological, trade or structural conditions, we are led to one set of policies. If policy proceeds on the basis that the dynamic of the workplace provides the best available environment in which to determine what skills should be developed, then programs which encourage up-skilling and parallel-skilling *in the workplace during the active work week* will be endorsed.

Unfortunately, policy still works the first way. The recently enacted trade bill incorporates a revision of traditional Trade Adjustment Assistance. The revision is called EDWAAA (Economic Dislocation and Worker Adjustment Assistance Act). Although the thinking in the proposed legislation extends the old approach so that provision for retraining is triggered by job loss for structural as well as trade reasons, the basic orientation is the same. Training and other aid will occur *after* the old job has been lost. All experience (and common sense) makes clear that this is the worst time and circumstances in which to attempt retraining. The employee is in the trauma of lost employment and an uncertain future — a difficult circumstance in which to learn anything. And the choice of what to teach or learn is made more risky by the fact that it is being done in the abstract.

Consequently, national policy should encourage continuous retraining in the workplace, which increases the likelihood that specific skills will be learned. Again start with the workplace as the plenum and more relevant policy can emerge.

II. THE EXTERNAL DIMENSION: TRADE POLICY

While we need to focus on how and what American firms produce, it also is true that American companies do not operate in an economic vacuum. There are cross-currents beyond the factory wall, the interaction of private and government decisions which determine the climate of global competition.

As noted above, other elements of government policy beyond the scope of this chapter play a far greater role in determining that climate than trade policy: fiscal, tax, monetary and exchange rate policies, even our approach to Third World development and debt. But a well-conceived and executed trade policy can contribute to global economic growth, as the U.S. experienced during the simpler times from the early 1950s to the late 1970s, when a reduction in average tariffs worldwide from levels approaching 40% to less than 5% helped contribute to unprecedented global growth averaging 3.3% per year.

The challenges faced by the next administration are far more daunting, both intellectually and politically. The boundaries between trade and investment, goods and services and trade and capital flows are eroding, undermining the continuing relevance of existing trade institutions. For example, the equivalent of $300 billion is traded from one currency to another *each day*, with profound consequences for trade in goods but with little international controls. More than two-thirds the cost of developing a new aircraft is spent on services — software, design and engineering — yet services, together with most agricultural and energy trade, are outside the scope of the GATT system.

The easy trade problems of reducing tariffs largely have been solved. The new challenges — non-tariff barriers, government subsidies, structural problems of overcapacity in steel and other sectors, trade distorting domestic agricultural policies, foreign investment, high technology, trade in domestically sensitive service industries — require a far greater measure of political leadership and imagination.

From the outset, the next administration and Congress must understand more clearly that the arena of corporate decision-making and private competition is global and that many other governments are far more active partners in that competition than ours.

IT STARTS WITH PRESIDENTIAL LEADERSHIP

America's resurgence as a premier economy must begin with an accelerating change in public culture and conceit — a new consciousness that quality and excellence are the cornerstone of continued prosperity, that America is part of a global economy and that we can only prosper in a world where others prosper as well.

At the same time, the American people must be convinced that our conception of shared well-being and commitment to open trade are shared by our trading partners. Americans must believe that their government will be as vigorous and clear-eyed in defending their interests against economic predation as it will be in protecting them from more traditional threats to our security.

This shift in public attitudes can only come with forceful presidential leadership. America's trade and competitive posture must become "presidential issues." This has not been the case with the Reagan Administration nor, for that matter, with any of its modern predecessors.

In our system of government, only the president can define the agenda, shape national priorities and crystallize emerging public attitudes. Just as President Reagan honored the private heroism of a Lenny Skutnik, the next American president can shine the spotlight of national and international attention on American enterprises that are showing the way toward renewed American competitiveness and leadership. Moreover, as President Carter demonstrated on energy, and President Reagan on SDI, elevating an issue to the presidential level changes the dynamic of decision-making internally, and the prospects for progress internationally.

By the same token, the new challenges we face in the international arena — agricultural subsidies and foreign investment, for example — go to the heart of domestic politics and national sovereignty. They cannot be solved by Trade Ministers, however talented and elevated. They require the active engagement of heads of state, to a degree unmatched in earlier negotiations.

FROM REACTION TO CREATION: CHANGING THE FOCUS OF U.S. TRADE POLICY

For most of the past two decades, U.S. trade policy was driven largely by the consequences of an unprecedented import expansion into the U.S. market. From 1980 to 1985, imports into the U.S. rose 41%, while U.S. exports fell by 3%. As a result, U.S. trade negotiators clocked the bulk of their hours, and the lion's share of their globe-trotting, negotiating various arrangements to protect import-sensitive American industries, from steel to autos to textiles.

This element of trade policy cannot be ignored. Temporary protection for American industries and workers seriously injured by surges in imports can be a legitimate response by government, one that is envisioned under Article XIX of the GATT. Americans will not continue to support efforts to liberalize the international trading system unless they are convinced that they have swift, affordable and effective remedies within that system. In appropriate circumstances, such as the case brought in the early 1980s by the Harley Davidson motorcycle company under section 201 of the Trade Act of 1974, interim relief from imports can provide the additional profitability and cash flow that will enable a U.S. industry to modernize or reposition itself so that it can compete with imports when relief is terminated.

The Omnibus Trade and Competitiveness Act of 1988, crafted by the Congress, strengthens that section 201 process by assuring that it focuses more sharply on what the domestic industry can and must do during the relief period to adjust to new competition. For example, it encourages an industry seeking relief to submit an adjustment plan and encourages the president to seek specific commitments from the domestic industry to reinvest its protection-induced extra profits to become more competitive. The new administration and Congress should insist upon such adjustment plans — and *condition* any import relief — on progress toward fulfilling specific commitments to reinvest, modernize or reposition the industry.

But if the '70s and '80s have been a period of trade defense, then the '90s must be a time of trade offense, as we shift the focus from trade protection to trade expansion, from import relief to market access and export promotion.

There are several reasons which compel such a shift of emphasis. Most obviously, the simple fact is that eliminating our current account deficit will require roughly a $200 billion annual increase in net exports. Our trade policy needs aggressively to reinforce the competitive opportunities now presented by currency realignments and growing American competitiveness, and support what will need to be an export-driven U.S. economy for the next several years. Moreover, it would be foolish to engage in indiscriminate market closing now, when American exports are on the rise and our trading partners, experiencing the discomfort of deteriorating trade balances themselves, may be all too willing to seize any pretext for reciprocal market closing. Finally, a focus on reciprocal market opening and access is essential to reinforce a renewed American commitment to quality and competitiveness, for Americans must know that purchasing decisions will be based on rationality, not nationality.

There are three instruments of trade policy for achieving the goals of promoting trade expansion and global growth: multilateral negotiations, bilateral negotiations and unilateral actions. Each has a role to play. They must be blended into a mutually reinforcing strategy by Washington throughout the 1990s:

1. Multilateral negotiations. Dominating trade policy is the ongoing round of GATT negotiations — negotiations with loftier ambitions and scantier domestic support than any since the GATT was launched in 1947. The new administration must decide the priority it will give these multilateral negotiations, for most other trade policy decisions will be affected by that judgment.

An increasingly popular view in Congress and among some trade commentators is that the GATT system is beyond repair and relevance — that, at best, it should be relegated to a secondary or residual role in our international trade strategy, while the focus of our attention should shift to "pluri-lateral" negotiations among like-minded nations or bilateral negotiations such as the U.S.-Canada Free Trade Agreement. Incoming officials will quickly need to decide what to do with the Uruguay Round — to pursue an ambitious agenda or cut our losses and take a minimalist approach.

A minimalist approach would be a serious mistake. The next president should raise, not lower, the stakes. First, an increasingly global economy needs stronger global institutions. We need to narrow, not widen, the gap between multinational corporate decisions and international trade discipline. More balkanization into regional groupings defies and retards the intensifying economic reality of globalization. Second, America's leadership inevitably suffers from the spectacle of wild swings in direction and policy from one administration to another. Since the United States government has invested its credibility in a far-ranging GATT agenda, we cannot now abandon that agenda without undermining American leadership. Finally, over the next decade we need to integrate the developing countries more fully into the international trading system, not perpetuate a system in which they neither assume the responsibilities nor gain the full benefits of closer cooperation. This is best achieved through global negotiations.

Certainly, our commitment to the GATT negotiations should neither be unconditional or exclusive. Other arenas and groupings among like-minded countries can provide the impetus for broader progress in the GATT, and the alternative if there is stalemate. On some issues, such as developing rules for international investment, codes which begin with the participation of a core group of countries but which invite others to join for reciprocal advantages can be a useful avenue for progress.

But at the outset, the 41st President and 101st Congress must move quickly to reaffirm America's leadership in pressing for a stronger and more embracing international trade regime. They must restate the case for such a course to the American people and reaffirm, in a global context, John Kennedy's wisdom that "a rising tide lifts all the boats." They must challenge Americans to see their future in terms of the national interest, not their narrow interest, because progress will not come without *mutual* concessions — reciprocal actions by the U.S. and our trading partners to reduce trade barriers. And, perhaps most importantly, they need to do what the Reagan Administration failed to do: develop a domestic constituency in support of a bolder approach to these negotiations.

Despite some progress, much of the hard work will fall to the next administration: creating a more open trading system for farm products even as we grapple in 1989 with our domestic farm programs in writing the 1990 farm bill; developing a framework of international discipline to deal with burgeoning trade in services, such as financial, telecommunications, engineering and data processing, now outside the GATT system; designing a strong and effective regime for protecting intellectual property rights against foreign infringement and pirating; and achieving a better international consensus on what practices represent legitimate government support for enhancing the competitiveness of its industries, and which are ultimately counterproductive for the international economy.

Perhaps most importantly, these negotiations must strengthen the machinery of international trade discipline if a multilateral trading system is to be preserved. It makes little sense to invest in the creation of new rules if the mechanisms for compliance are illusory. GATT as an institution must be strengthened. Today, the GATT Secretariat has a professional staff of less than 200 people. It must be enlarged. It must be given power to monitor compliance by member countries with their obligations. It should be given authority to initiate complaints. The paralysis of consensus decision-making must be eased. In effect, it must become a full-fledged global institution, like the World Bank and the IMF, an independent force to operate in the general interest.

The formula for progress in these negotiations was well stated by Council on Foreign Relations trade authors Michael Aho and Jonathan Aronson: it will require "the pressure of time limits, top level political intervention, the spotlight of public commitment and the fear of failure."

2. Bilateral negotiations. Multilateral negotiations to strengthen and expand the international trading system, which necessarily will extend over a protracted period, cannot replace country-to-country negotiations to resolve vexing issues of specific market access.

Here too, a more effective strategy must be developed by Washington in the 1990s. How do we approach the complex problem of market barriers and trade distorting practices among our major trading partners, particularly Japan, the European Community and the newly industrialized countries? The approach adopted by the Reagan Administration, particularly since 1985, has been essentially legalistic — sector-by-sector and barrier-by-barrier negotiations which have focused largely on procedural reforms that seek to eliminate discriminatory practices against foreign goods and services. Some American trade negotiators, like the Commerce Department's former Counsellor for Japan, Clyde Prestowitz, have argued that this approach, which can be met by delay and circumvention of agreements already achieved, is humiliating and ultimately unproductive for the United States. They urge more comprehensive, results-oriented bilateral negotiations which seek to establish specific goals, timetables and obligations.

However, it is unrealistic to expect, in the context of complex, asymmetrical economies and cultures, that governments can regulate trade flows or assure results. Moreover, from the perspective of both USTR resources and political realities, it is hard to image how comprehensive negotiations can proceed simultaneously both in GATT and in a series of super-bilateral negotiations, particularly if tough political concessions in one arena are subject to renegotiation in the other.

At the same time, the Reagan Administration too often has proceeded on an *ad hoc* basis, not focusing on those areas where the potential dividends for American goods and services are the greatest. We have defused our negotiating capital and credibility with items of marginal importance, such as aluminum baseball bats and access to Japan for American law firms. Our negotiating agenda too often has been driven by the "squeaky wheel," without regard to whether the market for squeaky wheels in the offending country justifies the effort.

The 1988 Trade Act provides a sensible middle course for the new administration. It requires the USTR to establish, at the outset, clear negotiating priorities: those practices, in those countries, which have the greatest restrictive impact on American exports. It concentrates our negotiating energies and capital on opening markets which hold the greatest opportunity for significant export growth by U.S. firms.

3. Unilateral actions. Particularly with American exports on the rise, retaliation against the trade-distorting practices of our trading partners is neither cost- nor risk-free. American manufacturers can be cut off from components and materials they need to be competitive in this market and others. And with current U.S. restrictions on steel, autos, textiles, machines tools and a host of other sectors, our market is not nearly as pristine and open as we like to believe. However, it is inescapably the case that access to the U.S. market provides the leverage sometimes needed to force our trading partners to make the difficult political decisions necessary to open their markets.

American negotiators must be armed with a credible threat, unequivocally backed by the president, that where internationally accepted standards are being violated, unilateral American actions will be taken when negotiations fail. There is a clear difference between closing our markets on a conditional basis as a device for opening markets, and closing our markets merely to avoid competition.

We also must face the reality that other governments are far more actively involved in support of their international industries — or at least are involved in a more purposeful way — than ours. To assure that American industries are not disadvantaged by that disparity, we need to devise competitive approaches to such programs as mixed export credits until negotiations can produce a satisfactory reduction of such practices by our trading partners.

U.S. EXPORT PROMOTION

Developing an export mentality fundamentally is a task for the private sector, as we disenthrall ourselves from the comfortable post-war notion that we can sustain our prosperity from a bountiful and isolated domestic market. However, there is much more that government can do to assist American companies to identify and seize their exporting opportunities.

Over the past twenty years, there have been at least six distinct national export campaigns launched by the federal government. They have had mixed success. In general, they have lacked presidential leadership, adequate resources and a pervasive sense of national urgency. It remains true that about one percent of American industries are responsible for 80% of American exports, that 250 American companies are responsible for 85% of all American exports and that there are some 20,000 American companies, principally small and medium size firms, which are capable of exporting but are not organized to do so.

These smaller firms see the risks as too great and lack adequate information about export opportunities. Yet the efforts of the federal government to assist these companies are divided and underfunded. For example, the United States government has 110 field offices of the SBA, 48 domestic offices of the Department of Commerce, 124 foreign offices of the Department of Commerce and 73 other countries where export promotion functions are served by the Department of State. Moreover, the American government generates and collects mountains of potentially useful data on international price trends, local and foreign competition, demand forecasts and foreign market opportunities, but lacks an effective delivery system to make this data available, in useful form, to American companies.

Among our major trading partners, Great Britain and France, for example, spend three times the amount of the United States on export promotion. Many have quasi-public entities which are responsible for identifying export opportunities. Most have a far more professional, high-level, career-oriented commercial service.

Consequently, the next administration should establish a quasi-public entity to consolidate, streamline and strengthen our export promotion efforts. It would work closely with the private sector, and with state and local governments which have increasingly moved into the vacuum. It would nurture, over time, a high-prestige commercial service — career professionals who would have the resources, the flexibility and the incentives to specialize in countries and sectors. It would recruit and train, from the top ranks of American college and graduate schools, an "Export Corps," providing a training ground for a new generation of more culturally adept and internationally minded business leaders. And it would seize the challenge issued by the House Subcommittee on Economic Stabilization — to "organize knowledge for action" — developing an effective, state-of-the-art, user-friendly delivery system for information on international economic trends and marketing opportunities.

ORGANIZING THE MACHINERY OF GOVERNMENT

To elevate trade and international economic considerations to a more central role in policy decisions and to speak with one clear voice to the world, some have proposed a unified Department of International Trade and Industry, along the lines of Japan's MITI. We believe such an effort would be a mistake. Such government reorganizations usually expend more in time, energy and political capital than they gain in shifting priorities or emphasis. It is not very productive for the next administration to spend its first few years negotiating with 19 Congressional committees and subcommittees over the contours of a new Trade Department. Moreover, collapsing the functions of the USTR and the Department of Commerce into one agency does not, in any meaningful way, advance the objective of integrating the various strands of American international policy into a more coherent whole. It simply replaces two Cabinet officers with one, who still faces across the table the Secretaries of State, Defense and Treasury.

Rather, we would urge a return to the original conception of the USTR as a high-level, White House-based, principal coordinator of trade policy and chief negotiator, with less emphasis on USTR's expanding role as administrator of trade policy. In this sense, the 1988 Trade Act may move us in the wrong direction, shifting greater administrative responsibilities to the USTR, which may diminish his or her ability to serve as the Chief Executive Officer, rather than Chief Operating Officer, of American trade policy.

As long as America has diverse security, foreign policy and economic interests in the world, there will be divergent priorities within the various departments of government. In the final analysis, what may be as important as determining the interagency coordinating mechanism for international economic policy is to assemble a team that appreciates the accelerating reality that America's economic competitiveness lies at the core of our security in the world.

THE FIRST 100 DAYS

We have described the general approach Washington should adopt to reestablish America's global economic leadership. The new administration faces an unusual array of early challenges as it fashions its trade policy and establishes its leadership. Here are several principal early tasks:

1. Getting Organized. To a greater degree than other areas of government where authority is more clearly defined, it is essential that the new administration act quickly to establish an interagency structure that facilitates the integration of domestic and international economic policies. The structure adopted assures that the United States government speaks to our trading partners with one clear voice, in the name of the president. This was not the case in the Reagan Administration. As negotiator Prestowitz has written: "The people with whom we negotiate...manipulate our system...because [it] is so disorganized that they can keep us in a state of continuous paralysis."

The new president should establish an Economic Security Council, chaired by the president and including the Secretaries of State, Defense, Treasury, Commerce, Labor, the Director of the Office of Management Budget, the Chairman of the Council of Economic Advisors and the U.S. Trade Representative. A USTR should be selected who, by stature and personal relationship, clearly speaks directly and personally for the president in international negotiations. And the USTR should be given principal responsibility for coordinating American trade policy and conducting trade negotiations.

2. National Trade Policy Agenda. The Trade Act of 1988 requires that the president submit to the Congress, no later than March 1 and each year thereafter, a report on the national trade policy agenda for the year. Building upon the bipartisan consensus formed around the 1988 Trade Act, this agenda can provide the vehicle for building a new partnership between the president and the Congress on the direction of American trade policy.

Congress cannot *conduct* trade policy anymore than it can conduct foreign policy. However, it is equally true that Congress intends to assert itself more actively than in the past in *shaping* American trade policy. Consequently, the new administration should move quickly to enlist the active participation of the Congressional trade leadership in the GATT negotiations. These negotiations are the last, best hope for preserving and strengthening the multilateral trading system. The new president, at an early date, should strongly and clearly affirm his commitment to ambitious goals for these negotiations. And our hand will be strengthened in those negotiations if other world leaders perceive the president and the Congress to be united in that commitment.

3. Super 301. A central provision of the 1988 Trade Act is the so-called "Super 301" procedure. This requires that the USTR, by April 30, 1989, identify those foreign unfair trade barriers, and those countries, which have the greatest restrictive impact on U.S. exports. USTR then will initiate negotiations with those priority countries for the elimination of these practices, with retaliation possible if no agreement is reached.

The key to successful pursuit of the Super 301 procedure lies in establishing clear priorities — identifying objectives which have support in the international community and American industries that will take full advantage of greater market access. An approach which is carefully targeted and unequivocally backed by the president from the outset can be successful. An approach which unrealistically seeks to respond to every complaining constituency is destined to fail.

4. Steel Quotas. On September 30, 1989, the regime of steel quotas that are in place with 20 countries is scheduled to expire. U.S. steel producers seek a continuation and expansion of the quotas for at least another five years.

Steel quotas, which have contributed to the recovery of the U.S. steel industry, also encourage U.S. steel-using manufacturers to expand operations abroad, rather than here at home. The new administration should fashion a steel policy which addresses the concerns of American steel producers — excess worldwide capacity and subsidization by some countries of their steel industry — without handcuffing the efforts of steel-using manufacturers across the country to become more competitive. This could include directly addressing such problems as pension reform and tax relief, while engaging in global negotiations to address overcapacity and subsidization, without continuing the costly import quotas that burden our manufacturing industries.

5. East-West Trade. With the West Europeans and Japanese moving quickly to provide new credits and technology to the Soviet Union, the new administration must fashion a coherent approach to East-West trade. The underlying question is one of foreign policy and national security: is it in America's interest to see the economic reforms and modernization efforts initiated by Secretary General Gorbachev succeed? We believe it is. While clearly we need to restrict western technology which could enhance Soviet military capabilities, the continued reluctance of the United States government to approach Soviet trade in a more cooperative manner simply means that Western European and Japanese companies will enjoy the benefits of such trade. We will lose our ability to lead the Western Alliance unless we fashion a balanced approach to trade with the Soviet Union.

6. European Integration. The European Community is moving steadily toward its objective of integrating its internal market by 1992, creating the largest market in the world. In general, this is a healthy development for the global economy to the extent that it will stimulate more rapid growth within Europe. There also are dangers for American firms, however, if the liberalization of trade within the European Community is accompanied by unjustifiable barriers to products and services from outside countries. The new administration must move quickly to make clear to the Europeans that it will watch the intricate integration process carefully, and that we will not sit by if such integration becomes a pretext for "Fortress Europe."

   7. Foreign Investment. There is a risk that "trade protectionism" of the 1980s will be replaced by "investment protectionism" of the 1990s. The question of foreign investment in the United States is a complex and difficult one, which needs to be stripped of its intensifying emotional content. What is a necessary national security industrial base in an era of global manufacturing? What are the net benefits or costs to the United States economy from foreign direct investment, *i.e.,* new factories and foreign-owned production in the United States? What further information do we need about foreign investment in the United States to make intelligent public policy judgments without subjecting American companies abroad to similarly burdensome requirements? Most importantly, how do we reduce our *need* for foreign capital to finance budget and trade deficits?

LABOR POLICY:
The Department of Labor

Robert Kuttner*

SUMMARY OF RECOMMENDATIONS

The next Secretary of Labor needs to accomplish such familiar elements of a deferred labor agenda as labor law reform and a higher minimum wage. But beyond that, the new administration and Congress should broker a new social contract between labor and management, in which workers get employment security and the prospect of steady upgrading and management gets a more highly skilled and flexible workforce.

This new social contract will require a novel concept of collective bargaining, a new concept of the corporation and of workers as stakeholders and new imaginative functions for government. But the payoff to the economy and to workers is immense. Specifically:

* Government, including the Departments of Commerce and Labor, should help create co-determination in corporate governance. Collaborative measures between labor and management should be encouraged, so long as they provide genuine shifts in power toward workers. The increase in productivity that such measures create will help America compete in the global economy.

* Pension funds should be immune from management raids, and should be a source of capital for new corporate forms. Private pensions should be collapsed into an earning-based second tier of Social Security.

* Unemployment compensation should give way to lifetime learning and retraining. This will increase the overall skills of the workforce, and ease periods of unemployment for both labor and management.

* Government should implement wage subsidies to ensure that every worker with a fulltime job earns enough to keep a family out of poverty.

---

* *Robert Kuttner is economics correspondent of* The New Republic, *a columnist for* Business Week *and author of, among other books,* The Life of the Party *and* The Economic Illusion.

* Government should systematically seek to convert low wage, dead-end jobs into para-professional jobs with career ladders.

I. INTRODUCTION

A progressive government ought to pursue policies that permit more creative social contracts between labor and management, and a more constructive role for trade unions. Such an approach would require a greater government role in promoting, financing and serving as guarantor of new models of labor-management collaboration. And it would mean a more substantial public responsibility for sharing the costs and benefits of necessary shifts in the skills of the work force in a competitive global economy.

In the 1980s, government became more hostile both to trade unions and to the idea that public policy needs to pay attention to labor markets, to the quality of the labor force or to the labor's constructive influence upon productivity. All three issues are linked, both as substance and as politics.

Politically, in virtually every industrial democracy, trade unions provide the most reliable key electoral constituency for political parties that believe in a mixed economy. There is a close correlation between the strength of organized labor and the ability of progressive administrations to govern successfully. In nations with weak or fractious labor movements, the Right is the usual majority party. In nations with strong, unified labor movements, the Center-Left party begins with a powerful ally. In the United States, a hostile national administration and a turbulent climate of industrial transition have combined to weaken trade unionism in this decade.

Substantively, labor's enthusiastic support for industrial transitions depends on some social guarantee that such transitions will benefit the workforce, rather than take place at labor's expense. A society grows more productive by substituting capital for labor, and by applying new technologies. When workers have reason to view those transitions as a source of increased living standards and improved opportunity, rather than as threats to their livelihood, positive sum gains result.

Therefore, a progressive labor agenda for the post-Reagan era in the U.S. ought to include three mutually reinforcing elements. First, government needs to help the labor movement reinvent itself — both as a valid policy goal per se, and to revive a political constituency for progressive politics and government. An authentic brand of co-determination can help accomplish that. Traditional "business unionism" probably cannot.

Second, government ought to radically reform the structure of pension funds, their governance, their influence on both capital markets and their role in worker ownership. The present system is perverse. Not only are most pensions beyond the control of workers, but the practice of tying pensions to individual firms allows pension assets to be raided in takeover attempts, often at the expense of workers. In capital markets, pension funds, which logically ought to be a source of stable, patient capital, instead are managed in the interest of short-term performance, which paradoxically fuels the very takeover game which harms workers. Many find themselves displaced by capital which represents their own deferred savings. Instead, pension fund capital could help underwrite restructurings that truly benefit and empower workers.

Third, government needs to devise an active labor market policy, which would provide opportunities for lifetime learning, retraining sabbaticals and job upgrading, as industrial transitions occur. Again, ideally trade unions can be at the center of such a retaining and upgrading strategy.

II. CO-DETERMINATION: A NEW SOCIAL CONTRACT?

All three of these issues are of course closely linked. Consider first the question of co-determination. The idea that more collaborative labor-management relations would be good for the U.S. economy has long been a tantalizing concept, floating just at the margins of serious economic debate.

Micro-economically, less adversarial labor-management relations could lead to gains in productivity and competitiveness. Macro-economically, it could encourage workers to accept benefits other than higher wages, such as job security or retraining opportunities, which would allow the economy to "cheat the Phillips curve" and enjoy tight labor markets with less inflationary pressure. The usual "trade-off" between inflation and unemployment is not an iron law of economics. Rather, it results primarily because we lack institutions of constructive social bargaining. In a *laissez-faire* economy, low unemployment gives workers the bargaining power to demand wage increases in excess of real productivity gains. Fearing inflation, the authorities then keep the money supply too tight and public spending too low.

But with a serious social compact, we could run a high growth, full-employment economy, without wage-driven inflation. Workers could be assured job opportunities and lifelong training and retraining; industry would be assured a high quality workforce and labor peace.

Government would invest in substantial upgrading of worker skills and restructuring of industry.

The broad and idealized appeal of this approach, however, tends to blind many advocates of quality-of-worklife strategies to the central question of power. The idea seems to be that all moves in this direction are to be encouraged, regardless of who is ultimately in charge and regardless of how much authority is genuinely handed over to workers. In a highly competitive economy, where firms are under ruthless cost-cutting pressure, benign bargains tend to be scrapped when the going gets rough and one side — management — retains all the power. Unions, consequently, have tended to resist the conventional version of an incomes policy, viewing such proposals as, in power terms, a one-way street.

The conservative or neo-liberal version of this approach includes the "Tax-based Incomes Policy" (TIP), which was in vogue in the late 1970s and which would give workers and firms tax incentives for restraining wages. A variation on the same theme is Professor Martin Weitzman's proposal for a "Share Economy," in which pay packages would be partly based on a share of the firm's total earnings rather than on a fixed wage.

Weitzman's model claims that if the marginal cost of labor is lower than the average cost, this novel compensation system would reduce unemployment. And perhaps it would. But the Share Economy strategy, like the TIP strategy, fails to change the governance of the firm. In fact, it gives workers another downside risk associated with entrepreneurship — the opportunity to take pay cuts during downturns — without offering workers the control that usually belongs to the entrepreneur. The progressive version of co-determination looks to enhance the institutional standing of workers and of trade unions, and not just to induce wage restraint for its own sake.

In principle, there is widespread support, among managers, trade unionists, public officials and economists, for a new, more collaborative system of labor-management relations. The core idea is that the old system is bad for productivity, for flexibility, for the competitiveness of the American economy, and that it no longer even effectively protects workers.

However when one presses the point, the idea embraces contradictory practical meanings. Many enthusiasts of labor-management collaboration innocently hope to attain productivity gains and to move beyond "adversarial" relationships without the need for substantial institutional change. To some in management, the goal is lower wage costs, more docile workers and weaker unions. To others, it means genuine sharing of responsibility and authority.

As we begin to think seriously about what a more collaborative system of industrial relations really implies, and how it would look institutionally, several paradoxes become evident:

First, the move toward more collaboration comes during a period of intensified competition, both globally and domestically. As a result, the same pressures that impel us to invent a more constructive system leave us with far less slack in the system to facilitate the necessary transitions. A firm faced with ruthless cost-cutting pressures is hard pressed to guarantee that workers who accept greater flexibility will not be laid off. A manager whose competitors are underpricing him cannot guarantee that a bargain exchanging flexibility for job security will necessarily stick.

Ironically, it would have been much easier to invent a system of more collaborative industrial relations back in the 1950s, when there was money in the system for wage and pension increases, and when unions had more industrial penetration and more power. But the system's very stability in the 1950s undermined any incentive for such change.

The old system, which lasted roughly from the late 1930s to the late 1970s, is often called "business unionism." It offered a kind of crude social contract in which government guaranteed workers' rights to bargain collectively for wages and working conditions, and in turn most large companies reluctantly tolerated unions. The unions refrained from challenging management prerogatives. Employees sought security in industry-wide master contracts and in an elaborate set of job classifications and work rules. The old industrial relations system was a kind of armed truce, balanced and undergirded by labor's ability to inflict damage, by industry's ability to live in a predictable competitive environment and by government's willingness to enforce the ground rules.

The ability of American trade unions to deliver benefits to their members and the ability of government to broker a generation of social peace was covertly dependent on American economic pre-eminence internationally, and on tacit toleration of oligopoly at home. We did not have ruthless price competition in the basic industries, and that created an umbrella where unions could bargain for master contracts and regular raises, and industry could pass the cost along to customers. But an interdependent global economy, based on an imperfect mix of open trade and national industrial strategies, leaves industry with far less of a cushion.

The postwar period of industrial stability is now history, and so is the old basis for labor power. The century old slogan, "Take wages out of competition," which has been the rock solid principle of traditional trade unionism, is a dead letter in many industries. On the contrary, wages are back in competition, not only between firms, but between different plants within the same firm, and even, under "two-tier" arrangements, between different generations of workers doing identical jobs in the same plant. Industry-wide master contracts, the basic instrument of postwar labor solidarity in the U.S., have all but vanished.

Thus all the major preconditions of the old social contract have dissolved. Global competition and deregulation have ended oligopoly; the strike no longer has the force that it once did; many companies are much more anti-union; and, if one more assault were required, the National Labor Relations Board (NLRB) is no longer impartial.

The power balance between labor and management has shifted — except in one dramatic respect. Management may have more power today to weaken unions, but at the same time management needs labor's cooperation more than ever. At one time in the history of mass production, it may have been possible to design machines to be idiot-proof, and to deploy human drones as one more interchangeable part. However, the very nature of the new technology demands smart, flexible, inventive human workers, who can respond creatively to situations not anticipated in manuals or programmed into assembly lines. It is not enough to have brilliant engineers and dumb workers, if in fact it ever was.

But while the new economy gropes toward a more collaborative labor-management culture, the traditional social organization of the corporation resists it. And this suggests a second paradox: the current weakness of organized labor makes it easier for management to resist sharing authority in a meaningful way. Many Quality of Work Life experiments seem to show great promise, but when a real crunch comes, management usually retains the real power. And next time, workers are far more wary of QWL. Employee Stock Ownership Plans are gaining popularity, but only a small fraction of them have produced real participatory management and power sharing as well as profit sharing. In short, given the impact of heightened competition on industrial relations, genuine collaboration is all the more imperative — and all the more difficult to accomplish.

A further paradox involves the mismatch between skills and jobs. As a whole, the U.S. needs a more highly skilled, better trained workforce. But too many of the available jobs still demand only minimal skills. Too many employers seem bent on reducing labor costs in the short run rather than creating high-wage, high skill jobs for the long run. Society has no mechanism for steadily upgrading the quality of work and of the work force. Among corporate personnel officers in the service sector, the most common complaint is that they can't find high school graduates competent to read instructions or to do basic arithmetic, or to show up on time, to take five-dollar-an-hour jobs — not that they have advanced training programs going begging.

It is a staple of the labor economics literature that firms generally underinvest in training — for the perfectly rational reason that a worker newly trained at company expense is entirely free to go to work for a competitor. This is a classic case of an "externality": the person called on to make the decision doesn't get the full benefit or suffer the full cost. So optimal social decisions are not always made by private actors. Society does have real shortages of workers in certain highly skilled craft occupations, such as machinists, but we have far too few mechanisms to train them. There is of course the obvious need for schools to do a better job equipping new workers with basic skills, but also the more subtle need for systematic upgrading of the workforce throughout one's productive life.

III. NEW ROLE FOR GOVERNMENT

In order to help labor and management break out of this trap, which serves neither, government must play a very different role. The old industrial relations system offered a very limited three way social contract, in which government was a player, but only as arbiter of collective bargaining under the Wagner Act framework, not as an active party helping labor and management to invent new ways of collaborating. Rather, government's function was to allow labor and management to bargain for shares of a growing pie, in an economy whose institutions were, in retrospect, remarkably stable.

Today, the economy is undergoing radical restructuring, as it must. But the benefits and costs are very unequally distributed; the few mechanisms available to ease the pain are minimal and defensive; and there are even fewer mechanisms or resources to convert the turbulence into broadly based opportunity. The principal engine of restructuring today is the hostile corporate takeover, which forces firms to engage in a degree of radical reorganization, either defensively or under new management, that the old stable system would never have accepted.

Economists can debate whether the outcome is beneficial in the long run — my own view is that the effect is mixed at best — but it is clear that neither workers nor society have a seat at that bargaining table, and that the financial climate in which a large number of companies are bent out of shape either executing or resisting takeovers makes long-term workplace collaboration all but impossible. The added financial and institutional turbulence of a takeover economy only intensifies the underlying industrial turbulence. As a result, innovative social contracts between labor and management that might be devised are usually stillborn.

This is most vividly illustrated in industries experiencing the most dramatic shake-ups. Consider, for example, airlines and steel. In the case of Eastern Airlines, the prospect of bankruptcy brought both labor and management to the very brink of a radically new form of social contract, in which management gave workers partial ownership and shared authority both on the shop floor and boardroom, and workers departed from the adversarial tradition, began thinking like profit-maximizing managers, and agreed to a more flexible form of compensation in which wages were reduced and part of their pay was based on gross earnings. In its first year, the new approach saved tens of millions of dollars, and Eastern was able to run in the black for the first time in years.

But the competitive pressures of de-regulation, the old habits of traditional management, the inability of Eastern's several unions to pursue a common strategy, the fact that labor still was only a minority owner and management's option to sell out to a new owner or to declare bankruptcy all snuffed out this new bargain before it had time to mature.

In the steel industry, the integrated mills are in the midst of a long-term restructuring, which will leave the United States with fewer mills, reduced production capacity, a fraction of the workers it once had, but a far more productive and dynamic industry in what remains. Along the way, a much more collaborative industrial relations culture is struggling to be born.

For example, at LTV Steel, labor and management agreed to an experimental arrangement at one plant in Cleveland, of the sort long advocated by industrial relations experts. The old book of job categories would be thrown out; workers would be paid according to one of three skill levels and made available to perform any of several jobs; most workers would be salaried; there would be job-security guarantees and new shop floor authority for the workforce.

Shortly after that agreement was struck, LTV went into bankruptcy — in part because the cost of pensioning off its workers exceeded the savings it achieved from closing excess capacity. The only institution we have for socializing some of this cost is the Pension Benefit Guarantee Corporation (PBGC), which has become a kind of backdoor Ministry of Industrial Restructuring in a society that does not believe government ought to be in that business at all. So instead of facilitating collaboration or spending public money to lubricate new bargains, taxpayer money goes only to mop up the cost of private failure and to ease a little of the pain inflicted on workers.

This suggests the first of the three policy proposals recommended in this chapter. In cases such as Eastern or LTV, where government plays the passive role of offering the protection of the bankruptcy law, or the bail-out of pension liabilities, or the temporary shelter of trade injury protection, the federal government needs to play a far more affirmative role in bringing about co-determination and restructuring arrangements, both as guarantor of the bargain and as supplier of technical assistance and sometimes of public capital.

Obviously, new mechanisms are necessary to increase the prospects that an Eastern Airlines or an LTV Steel might succeed as novel cases of collaborative industrial relations, rather than being remembered as two more entries on the list of failures. In the Eastern case, government played virtually no role. Labor and management negotiated a bargain against a background of very difficult market conditions, and there was no third party guarantor. When market conditions worsened again, management demanded another round of union belt tightening, superceding the earlier bargain; labor refused, and the company was sold. Labor was denied a chance to buy the company itself.

Suppose government had had a real seat at the table. Suppose, specifically, that government had contributed capital to the deal by buying some stock with full voting shares. And suppose government, as a part-owner, made it clear to management that its long-term interest was in seeing whether this novel, productivity-enhancing bargain between labor and management be given more time to prove itself, rather than subject to a fire sale when the going got rough. Eastern might then have been able to surmount a period of difficult market conditions; and the new social contract would have had a chance to prove itself. At minimum, management would have been denied the unilateral option of selling out to a third party.

Government — through the Departments of Labor and Commerce — should establish an Office of Economic Collaboration to facilitate such novel approaches, and should demand in return for any benefits that it confers that unilateral selloffs be prohibited while the new co-determined system matures.

Suppose, in the steel case, that instead of consummating restructurings through hostile takeovers, bankruptcy courts and PBGC bailouts, government took a more affirmative approach to the restructuring, and served as guarantor of some of these very promising bargains. Like the airlines case, that would also require a new agency, not just as a kind of neo-Reconstruction Finance Corporation to pump in capital, but also to help broker and enforce "positive-sum" labor-management bargains by taking a seat at the table.

Steel and airlines are of course the *most* difficult cases. In more normal cases, it would take less capital and less subsidy and less government intrusion to achieve some real gains. The takeover controversy also offers an opportunity. Recently we have observed dozens of firms — Goodyear, Boeing, Dayton Hudson, Gillette — running to state governments begging for protection against hostile takeovers on the ground that the new owner would be less loyal to the regional economy. Several states have now passed laws on the Indiana model granting that protection. It seems inconceivable that Congress will let this state-by-state approach continue; eventually we are going to get some national set of rules.

But in the meantime, many state governments are giving this protection away, in violation of the usual norms of capitalism, and in violation of their own self-interest. In these legislative crusades, trade unions are often reduced to the role of caboose on the train; they help established management lobby for the protective legislation, because the unions have little alternative and they often prefer the devil they know to the devil they don't know.

Before Massachusetts reflexively goes to bat for good old hometown Gillette, which after all has been very quick to locate production overseas when that seemed convenient and to weaken its unions when it had the opportunity, Massachusetts ought to inquire not just what the country can do for Gillette but what Gillette can do for the country. Government — and labor — ought to get something in return. A firm seeking shelter from the market discipline of a hostile takeover ought to be subject to some other forms of discipline and accountability. This might be the time for government to acquire some preferred stock, not just as a convenient device to block the raider, but to vote those shares (or delegate that voting power to employees) in order to infuse the company with a public purpose of working to generate local employment, at good wages and rapid productivity growth.

But isn't this a little bit socialistic — government selectively buying preferred stock, and voting shares? No more so than the Pension Benefit Guarantee Corporation, the Chrysler bailout, the Air Force subsidy of development of numerically-controlled machine tools and state laws preventing shareholders from maximizing their gain by tendering shares to corporate raiders. The difference is that our version of a mixed economy is far more likely than the current one to produce equitably shared, dynamic gains.

Traditional trade unionism and the traditional welfare state, comprised of pension funds, unemployment compensation and the like, was an effort to socialize some of the gain and some of the pain of pure capitalism, during a period when the American economy was enjoying both steady growth and institutional stability.

But today's global economy, with its intensified global competition and industrial transition, requires new forms of corporate governance. If a firm wants society to shelter it from the risk of hostile takeovers or give it subsidies, it must offer some alternative form of accountability to the usual sorts of market discipline. One could imagine an alternative corporate form. The corporation would not be vulnerable to hostile takeovers — but in return it would have authentic power sharing and worker co-determination at every level from the shop floor to the boardroom.

Plugging into a long, well-established legal and financial tradition which holds that shareholders are owners and owners are decision-makers, is probably far better strategically and philosophically than inventing a new regulatory overlay at odds with that of tradition. It makes more sense to devise a system in which workers and public officials receive stock in exchange for a special market preference, and vote their shares to demand a collaborative mode of management. Firms needn't seek federal assistance, but if they do they may then have to tolerate a federal voice at the firm representing taxpayer-investors, as any major institutional investor would expect. Alternatively, the Federal *quid pro quo* could be greater worker participation.

It may well be that government should begin this effort experimentally on a moderate scale, in a few companies at a time. Worker buyouts and public sector involvement should no longer be limited to the basket cases. Government should create a new framework where contributions of public capital translate into shares of ownership and influence, and that influence is used to produce positive sum gains for worker, firm and society. A firm that lives by the free market risks perishing in the free market.

IV. PENSION FUNDS

This raises the second issue — the role of pension fund capital. Pension funds are, of course, deferred wages. The present regulatory schema fails workers on several counts, even on the narrow test of providing income for their retirement. Workers who change jobs lose benefits. Pension savings are often available to be raided, based on the fiction that they are "overfunded." And a firm with a generous pool of pension assets often finds itself the target of either a hostile raid or a pre-emptive raid by its own management. ERISA — the Employee Retirement Income Security Act — creates a labyrinth of regulation, but it fails to give workers the most elementary protections against the raiding, or termination, of pension funds.

The next administration ought to bring about radical pension fund reform. Ideally, private pension funds should be collapsed into an earning-based second tier of social security. The present system of social security would continue, as a pay-as-you-go system. The second tier would be based on earnings histories and paid-in contributions, but funds would no longer be under control of corporate trustees, and the accrual of funds would follow the worker wherever he went. Only this degree of reform would permit full portability and full

protection against either raiding or termination and far tougher con-
flict-of-interest strictures to prohibit managers from using pension assets in corporate takeover contests. All firms should be required either to have pension plans that met a minimum standard, or to pay
into a pool for workers in small firms without such plans.

A fully funded, earnings-related pension system would also provide a large pool of capital under social control. Some of this capital
could be used to finance restructurings or worker buyouts. Even if the
present system of company-based pension plans were continued, further reform is needed both to curb abuses and to assure that when
pension fund capital, or ESOP capital, is used in restructurings, it results in authentic worker control or co-determination.

V. RETRAINING

The third element of labor market policy involves a necessary
socialization of the costs of labor market transitions — retraining and
re-employing those with inadequate or superceded skills. Often, as
the Eastern and LTV cases suggest, the invention of collaborative labor-management bargains during periods of rapid industrial restructuring founders on the very real problem that there is no place to put
the excess labor. Productivity gains literally mean more output for
less labor input; unless the industry happens to be a rapidly expanding one, it is all but impossible to negotiate collaborative bargains *in
one company.* Even forward looking bargains like the last round of
auto contracts cannot quite guarantee full job security for all workers,
because they cannot predict market conditions. And, of course, workers without strong unions have no such protection at all. The traditional system we have for separating employment security from job
security — namely unemployment insurance — costs society a lot of
money, but doesn't buy very much besides a short-term dole. Trade
adjustment assistance was essentially a more adequately paid version
of the unemployment compensation, for selected workers.

Therefore, it is necessary to drastically overhaul the system we
have for sharing the costs of labor market transitions, and in the
process use those outlays to continuously upgrade the skills of the entire workforce. When a worker is laid off because of a restructuring,
or a downturn in the business cycle, the choice ought not to be short-
term unemployment compensation versus a lower-paid job elsewhere.
If the worker is 58, perhaps an early retirement plan makes sense;
but if he is 38, he should be a candidate for a retraining sabbatical.

At present, we have small programs for helping to train disadvantaged young workers, and for re-employing workers displaced by
industrial transition. But about 80% of our total labor market outlays
go for unemployment compensation. Other industrial nations invest

much more heavily in subsidizing labor market transitions. Sweden's ratio of outlays is the reverse of ours: less than 20% of manpower outlays go to pay the cost of idleness and more than 80% go to subsidize retraining and re-employment.

The Swedish system continuously upgrades the workforce and allows workers to welcome rather than resist industrial restructurings that improve productivity in the long run. When the Swedish unemployment rate rises, the national labor market board can declare that funds are now available for workers to take paid sabbaticals, to learn new skills. This opens up jobs for other workers, reducing the overall unemployment rate and upgrading the productivity of the entire workforce at the same time. The labor market board can also use labor market subsidies as tools of regional or sectoral industrial policies.

For example, if a town has lost a major employer, say a shipbuilder, a local ad hoc tripartite committee of business leaders, labor representatives and local government can get funds to conduct a study and determine what kind of new industry might be suitable, given the local labor force. The local committee can then submit a proposal to the national labor market board, which in turn can offer a prospective employer subsidies to pay the cost of retraining and part of a few years' wages.

This system, in effect, uses a labor subsidy as a capital subsidy, and as a delicate tool of planning. Unlike the caricatures of economic planning, which invariably feature some heavy-handed bureaucratic czar attempting to "pick winners and losers," this approach is locally-based and relies on entrepreneurs to identify opportunities. It allows government and trade unions to play a constructive role, with the additional benefit of targeting development to localities with high unemployment, and continuously upgrading worker skills. It is far better than our characteristic system of enticing new development by means of bargaining away needed local tax base.

In the United States, during the past seven years, while the federal government has been enraptured with a primitive version of *laissez-faire*, it has fallen to the states to refine home-grown versions of business- government-labor collaboration. In California, for example, a portion of the unemployment insurance tax was split off to finance a separate agency called the Employment Training Panel. The Panel enters into contracts with employers to subsidize the cost of retraining or upgrading the skills of workers. The existence of this program makes it cost-effective for employers to upgrade jobs. The firm gains, and so does society. Unions are only marginally involved in most Panel contracts, but they could become far more directly involved as sponsors.

Typically, a local junior college is used to provide the training, which has the added benefit of augmenting the resources of this often-ignored part of our job training system. In some seasonal sectors of the economy, such as construction, traditional unemployment compensation makes sense. But as a system of helping people laid off from jobs to which they will never return, unemployment insurance is too limited.

Changing the emphasis of our labor market subsidies, from subsidizing unemployment to subsidizing re-employment, would accomplish several other goals that serve the broader objective of a more collaborative and competitive economy. First, an approach like the Swedish system of labor market boards or the California Employment Training Panel encourages firms to focus on their internal labor markets. By socializing part of the cost of training, it compensates for the tendency of managers to underinvest in upgrading the skills of their workers. It also can be part of a national strategy of constantly working to create good, high skill, well-paid jobs rather than cheap ones.

Most importantly for our goal of a new social contract between industry, government and labor, the existence of an active labor market policy makes it possible to negotiate new productivity-enhancing agreements, because it creates a temporary place to put excess labor. This not only has direct payoffs in terms of the productivity of the labor force as a whole, but it also facilitates more collaborative management by making it possible for labor to operate more flexibly. Retraining sabbaticals and re-employment subsidies are one more element of the bargain for government to bring to the table, and one more benefit that can substitute for wage inflation.

VI. LOW WAGE WORK AND JOB UPGRADING

A further important challenge for the next administration and Congress is the systematic upgrading of low-wage service sector work. Service sector work, on average, pays lower and more mal-distributed wages than the manufacturing work which it is replacing. Most of the new jobs will be service sector jobs, but roughly half of the jobs created during the 1980s pay an annual wage of less than $11,000. There are essentially two possible strategies for upgrading service sector work — wage subsidy and professionalization.

A number of academic experts, such a Professor Robert Lerman of Brandeis University and Professor David Ellwood of Harvard's Kennedy School have urged that the present welfare system be converted to a system of wage subsidy, using a revised version of the earned income tax credit (EITC). For example, if the head of a household earned $200 a week as a fast food cashier, the Labor Department would make up the difference between that wage and the poverty level for that worker's family. There would have to be experiment and refinement of this approach, to make certain that employers did not lower prevailing wages in order to have the government make up the difference. But this strategy represents a substantial improvement over "welfare" approaches because it rewards the holding of a job with a higher standard of living.

There is also a need for the Labor Department to initiate pilot programs aimed at the systematic upgrading of work in the human services, which is expected to be a major growth area. For example, home health care is both a more cost effective and dignified alternative to nursing home care for the elderly. Yet home health care services are available only sporadically, and are notoriously underfunded. As a consequence, the work is typically a "secondary labor market" job — low paid, without fringe benefits or career ladders and subject to predictably high turnover. The system treats home health care workers as comparable to housemaids.

A home health care worker, however, could just as logically be a para-professional, analogous to a visiting nurse. This would require greater training, higher pay and the creation of career paths. But for society, the greater expense would be well worth the cost if it kept more people out of nursing homes. There are dozens of other service occupations, where professionalization would be an avenue both to more productive provision of the service, and better-paid careers.

VII. FROM PARTICIPATION TO CO-DETERMINATION

A very good co-determination model was devised under Secretary Ray Marshall's leadership during the Carter Administration — the COSH Group. With a modest amount of public funding and Labor Department encouragement, in-plant Committees on Occupational Safety and Health began involving themselves intimately in plant safety. This gave workers and unions a new systematic capacity to protect the labor force, but it also led ineluctably to areas of "management prerogative" that were conventionally off-limits in the American system of labor relations. This role did not come easily to some unions. But at a time when labor is in a defensive mode, trade unions need to recoup by involving themselves far more directly in the process of corporate governance, and not just by devising such new services as credit cards.

It goes without saying that a more progressive government will need to pursue several traditional labor objectives, including labor law reform, increasing the minimum wage and protecting pension funds from raids. The structure of labor law, which in principle guarantees workers a fair vote on whether to join a union, has become hopelessly undermined by new management techniques of harassment and by a conservative National Labor Relations Board which seldom inflicts penalties for violations. But beyond restoring government to its traditional role of honest broker in collective bargaining, it is also essential that a sympathetic government create the political and economic space to help the labor movement involve workers much more intimately in corporate governance as well as production, and to invent a true social contract appropriate to the present economic era.

Labor-management collaboration during a period of heightened competition, technological change and corporate restructuring requires more than better labor laws or training in participatory management. It requires a new conception of the governance of the corporation, of the corporation as a social creature, of workers as stakeholders in the corporation and of government as guarantor of an effective social contract. It requires new institutions and new imagination. The payoff is immense: a more productive and competitive economy, a much better prospect of high growth macro-economics without inflation and a reinvigorated domestic trade union movement that provides a durable constituency for progressive government and politics.

The accumulated public debt and the other dismal legacies of Reaganomics are not sufficient excuse for an economics of austerity. America came out of World War II with a public debt more than 100% of the Gross National Product. Today, the debt is only about half of the GNP. Yet the War bought something for that debt. It produced an unprecedented collaboration between labor, industry and government. It built a generation of skilled workers and advanced technology, and a burst of consumer purchasing power, which fueled the postwar economic boom and paid off the debt.

Today the challenge is to duplicate that great national feat, but in peacetime. Two generations ago, depression followed crash, war followed depression and prosperity finally followed war. In learning from history, we need to change the sequence and skip over some of the stages.

Postwar prosperity was built on social partnerships, not on *laissez-faire*. The worst possible legacy of Reaganomics would be a legacy of cramped political imagination and austerity economics. The alternative is an economics of partnership.

RURAL ECONOMICS:
Department of Agriculture

William A. Galston & Susan E. Sechler*

SUMMARY OF RECOMMENDATIONS

In framing policies for the Department of Agriculture, the next administration will face three key challenges.

First, it must restrain the costs of the basic commodity programs while increasingly directing their benefits toward smaller and newer farmers. Second, it must develop new approaches to rural economic development as well as new instruments for implementing those approaches. And third, it will confront a new policy context: agriculture and rural America are far more exposed — and vulnerable — to the vagaries of the international economy than ever before. Whichever way one looks — toward commodity prices, food quality, exports, natural resources, rural manufacturing — the massive facts of rapid world economic shifts and increased global competition loom large.

And in this decade of huge budget deficits and the Gramm-Rudman squeeze, the cost of agricultural commodity programs has multiplied many times over. As U.S. producers find themselves more highly dependent on exports than ever before, our country could be lurching toward an agricultural trade war. At a time when new ideas are desperately needed for rural America, legislators, bureaucrats and interest groups with vested interests in the status quo have a near-stranglehold on the policy process.

Perhaps most troubling: while there is no serious alternative to USDA for implementing rural policies, the Department tilts strongly toward large and powerful agricultural producers at the expense of the smaller and more vulnerable. It also prefers agriculture at the expense of other rural economic sectors, producers at the expense of

---

* William A. Galston is Professor of Public Affairs at the University of Maryland and author of, among other books, A Tough Row to Hoe: The 1985 Farm Bill and Beyond. He was formerly the Director of Economic and Social Programs at the Roosevelt Center for American Policy Studies. Susan E. Sechler is Director of the Rural Economic Policy Program of the Aspen Institute. She formerly served as Deputy Director for Economics, Policy Analysis and Budget in the Department of Agriculture.

consumers and short-term economic imperatives at the expense of longer-term health, safety and environmental considerations.

Like most other sectors, therefore, the rural economy can benefit only from macroeconomic policies that attempt to stabilize prices, currency values, interest rates and debt at sensible levels. The full program outlined in this article would produce a net savings of at least $3 billion annually over the current baseline projections while promoting both growth and equity for rural America. Beyond macroeconomic stability, a number of sector-specific goals can be identified for agricultural and rural policy:

* *A phased reduction of acreage eligible for price/income supports to domestic production levels, with a tilt toward smaller producers.* This would reduce federal outlays, assist family-sized farms and increase the competitiveness of our commodities in world markets.

* *An effective cap on payments to producers.* By cracking down on widespread abuses of farm incorporation and reorganization designed to avoid the $50,000 limit on outlays to individual producers, the next administration could end the scandal of seven figure checks to sharp operators and save taxpayers nearly $1 billion each year.

* *Expanded markets for U.S. commodities.* Through a cease-fire in the international subsidies war, meaningful agricultural negotiations under GATT and a reorientation of agricultural research toward value-added products, the U.S. could increase both revenues and global market share.

* *An all-out attack on agricultural sources of groundwater pollution.* By expanding the demonstration program in low-input agriculture, assisting farmers in moving toward less intensive production methods and using the 1990 farm bill to reduce dependence on fertilizers and pesticides, USDA can make an important contribution toward a key environmental goal of the next decade — curbing groundwater pollution before it becomes an economic and social crisis.

* *Create new federal leadership for rural development.* The next president should appoint a board to oversee new rural research, collect and disseminate information and explore the effects of regulatory and other national decisions on rural interests. By jump-starting coordination, this approach could help break through the institutional restraints that thwart innovative rural development.

* *A strengthened commitment to consumer needs.* By organizing food safety and nutrition programs under one administration umbrella, holstering inspection, labeling and education programs, developing effective policy responses to nutrition research and participating in efforts to rid our food supply of harmful pollutants and chemicals, USDA could take the lead in addressing rising public concerns about the safety and nutritional content of the food we consume.

I. STRUCTURE AND FUNCTION

Founded during the Lincoln Administration in 1862, the United States Department of Agriculture (USDA) is the oldest department of the federal government not tied to one of the traditional portfolios (foreign affairs, the exchequer, justice, defense and public lands). Its annual operating budget of about $67 billion and its payroll of more than 112,000 persons are exceeded only by the Departments of Defense, Health and Human Services and the Treasury. USDA has offices or committees in nearly every county.

USDA has undergone numerous reorganizations during its long life, typically at least once per administration. The current structure under the Secretary and Deputy includes two under-secretaries and seven assistant secretaries, nearly all with jurisdiction over a group of agencies organized by function.

Many of USDA's activities are important but obscure. Here is a list of some of the major agencies and programs:

Reporting to the Under-Secretary for International Affairs and Commodity Programs: the Agricultural Stabilization and Conservation Service (ASCS) administers most of the farm price and income programs; with more than 150 representatives in American embassies around the world and a corps of analysts at home, the Foreign Agricultural Service (FAS) seeks to monitor world market conditions and expand outlets for U.S. farm products. FAS also administers the export subsidy programs.

Reporting to the Assistant Secretary for Marketing and Inspection Services: the Agricultural Marketing Service (AMS) directs or monitors a range of activities in the areas of marketing, product inspection and grading and operations of facilities. It also buys bulk food for donation to institutions and the needy; the Animal and Plant Health Inspection Service (APHIS) is responsible for the control and eradication of pest and disease problems in agriculture; the Agricultural Cooperative Service (ACS) provides information about, and technical assistance to, farmer cooperatives; the Food Safety and Inspection Service (FSIS) inspects meat and poultry for wholesomeness and truthful labeling.

Reporting to the Under Secretary for Small Community and Rural Development: the Farmers Home Administration (FmHA) offers loans and grants to farmers for land acquisition, operations and emergencies, to rural communities for public facilities and to rural communities and individuals for subsidized housing; the Rural Electrification Administration (REA) helped extend electric power to rural areas (during the New Deal) and continues to supply electric and telephone cooperatives with subsidized credit; in cooperation with thousands of private insurance agents, the Federal Crop Insurance Corporation (FCIC) directs the operations of the crop insurance programs.

Reporting to the Assistant Secretary for Food and Consumer Services: the Food and Nutrition Service (FNS) administers the school lunch program, the food stamp program and the Women's, Infants' and Children's (WIC) food-voucher program and other nutrition programs; the Office of the Consumer Advisor.

Reporting to the Assistant Secretary for Science and Education Administration: the Agricultural Research Service (ARS) conducts federal research in 150 laboratories located around the country and abroad; the Cooperative State Research Service (CSRS) coordinates and provides funding for research conducted primarily in agricultural experiment stations located at land grant universities; the Extension Service (ES) coordinates and provides funding for education programs conducted primarily through state Extension Services based at land-grant universities.

Reporting to the Assistant Secretary for Economics: the Economic Research Service (ERS) is the Department's social science research and analysis agency; the National Agricultural Statistical Service (NASS) collects data from farmers and agribusiness on the performance of the agricultural sector; the World Agricultural Outlook Board (WAOB) coordinates and estimates data relating to world crop and market conditions.

Reporting to the Assistant Secretary for Governmental and Public Affairs: a series of small offices to handle congressional, state, interest group and press relations.

In addition to the Deputy and assistant secretaries, the General Counsel, Inspector General, Office of Budget and Policy Analysis and two major agencies report directly to the Secretary: the U.S. Forest Service (USFS) is responsible for the management of nearly 200 million acres of national forest and wilderness lands; the Soil Conservation Service (SCS) administers conservation, water-quality and environmental-improvement programs.

All in all, the Department operates 250 separate programs. The largest are those pertaining to farm programs and exports, rural development and farm credit, conservation and consumer nutrition and safety. The nutrition programs are dealt with elsewhere in this volume, and the details of the housing programs, research and education and food inspection, although important, could not be treated adequately within the confines of this brief chapter.

II. THE POLITICS OF AGRICULTURE

During the two past decades, a number of shifts have occurred in the relative balance of power among interest groups that seek to influence the agricultural and rural policy process. The clout of the general farm organizations has waned and the influence of groups representing individual commodities has increased significantly. In part, this shift was inevitable: each commodity group can achieve a high degree of internal unity behind a narrowly focused legislative agenda, such as increasing the price support for corn or retaining import quotas for sugar. But, more importantly, the basic structure of agricultural policy-making has been conducive to this shift.

Although there are virtually hundreds of statutes relating to food and agriculture, the major legislative vehicle is the quadrennial farm bill, which is organized into titles dealing with the different commodities. In addition, the House Agriculture Committee is divided into subcommittees that mirror, and provide convenient points of access for, the producer commodity groups. Attempts to assert sector-wide leadership — or to stimulate an umbrella policy that overrides commodity-specific concerns in favor of the most good for the most people in the economy as a whole — have rapidly fallen victim to the commodity-specific demands of the would-be leader's home state or district as an election nears.

Other shifts have reflected broader political trends. For example, during the late 1970s, groups representing consumers and smaller producers gained a hearing at the highest reaches of USDA. Consumer interests were promoted through high level appointments and the impact of programs and trends on the structure of U.S. agriculture was examined carefully. During the 1980s, by contrast, the policy process has been dominated by the larger producers and by post-production agribusiness.

Another change has been the rising impact of environmental groups on agricultural policy. As public awareness of such hazards as soil erosion and groundwater pollution has increased, environmental organizations have been able to bring about some changes in relevant agricultural policies. In the 1985 farm bill, for example, a new "Conservation Reserve" was established to take highly erosive land out of production, farmers' eligibility for federal subsidies was made increasingly conditional on their adoption of sound conservation practices, and new programs were authorized to promote "low-input" agricultural techniques that would minimize the use of fertilizers and pesticides.

The politics of agricultural policy are played out at the state and local level as well. Many of USDA's functions are administered by individuals and committees in the states and counties. Each state, for example, has its own ASCS director, and county ASCS committees play key roles in overseeing programs dispensing to their neighbors billions of dollars annually. Each state also has its own FmHA director, and county FmHA supervisors wield substantial authority. The Extension Service has 21,000 employees. The Soil Conservation Service has 3,000 field offices, one in virtually every county.

Three other broad political points are also worth noting.

First, in the formulation of agricultural and rural policy, Congress is at least as important as the executive branch. The geographical concentration of agriculturally dependent counties — and the fact that *every* senator has a "farm problem" — ensures a continuing cadre of senators, representatives and senior staff members who will give those interests top priority. This cadre is strategically placed in the key committees and subcommittees. Executive branch proposals that have not been adequately coordinated with this cadre are apt to be regarded as "dead on arrival."

Second, congressional attitudes towards agricultural and rural issues do not divide neatly along party lines. For example, in spite of the public perception of Democrats as the party of the "little guy," some of the strongest support for agricultural programs that pay out huge sums to wealthy individuals comes from Democrats representing large rice and cotton producers. Conversely, midwestern Republicans who generally stand four-square for "fiscal integrity" tend to draw the line when significant cuts are threatened in agricultural programs. In general, there is bipartisan congressional support for key (and expensive) elements of the agricultural status quo.

Third is the important but often overlooked question of public support for the programs administered by the Department. For example, while the consuming public is increasingly concerned about broader questions of food safety, including pesticide and other chemical residues, the Department tends to limit its concern for food safety to its responsibility for meat and poultry. Why? Because there are only a few consumer groups to pressure the Department (far fewer than commodity and industry groups), USDA staff tend to underestimate the magnitude of consumer concern.

And, finally, despite the fact that 77 percent of the value of farm production is concentrated in the top 14 percent of producers, whose net worth is ten times the average for families in the United States, polls indicate that farmers and farm programs remain enormously popular with most Americans. Whether this generalized support will survive times of fiscal tough choices is hard to predict.

III. THE REAGAN RECORD

In the eyes of traditional farm interests, USDA has emerged from the Reagan years better off than many federal agencies. No administration has the flexibility to change dramatically the basic programs without legislative authorization, and unlike some other agencies that do not have strong congressional support, many parts of USDA remain functioning bureaucracies with reasonable morale and continuity of personnel.

UNITED STATES DEPARTMENT OF AGRICULTURE
Program Level
(Dollars in Millions)

	1981	*1987*	*Plus/minus*
Commodity Credit Corporation	12,672.0	30,795.0	+143%
Export Programs	3,773.4	4,301.9	+14%
Farm Loans	8,293.0	3,091.0	-62%
Community Loans	1,662.0	679.0	-59%
Housing Loans	3,493.0	2,039.0	-41%
REA Loans	6,391.0	1,210.0	-81%
Food Assistance Programs	16,186.0	19,466.0	+20%
Research and Extension	943.0	1,251.0	+32%
Soil Conservation Service	589.0	643.0	+9%
Others	2,955.0	3,544.0	+20%
GRAND TOTAL:	56,957.4	67,019.9	+18%

At the same time, because the most powerful and consistent congressional interventions have promoted the interests of larger farmers, the balance of programs and priorities has shifted significantly since the 1970s. Expenditures for price/income support programs and for trade promotion have soared from an average of $4.0 billion during the Carter Administration to an average of $17.3 billion during the first six years of the Reagan Administration. And, while increased poverty has required that total expenditures for the food and nutrition programs grow, the FNS staff has been cut by more than 30 percent and requirements for participation have been tightened.

The Commodity Programs. Since the Depression of the 1930s, federal commodity programs have sought to maintain farm income through a combination of price guarantees, direct income supplements and supply management.

The effectiveness and expense of these programs is largely determined by events in the broader economy, such as the rate of inflation, interest and exchange rates and the vagaries of the weather. At the outset of the 1980s, for example, commodity program levels and approaches were based on the premise of continued rapid inflation. Although agricultural prices and land values had already begun to slip, the 1981 farm bill built that assumption into its structure of government-guaranteed minimum prices for specific commodities. However, inflationary predictions proved to be unjustified. World market prices for basic commodities collapsed, while government programs held guaranteed prices far above market levels. In response, government costs soared while exports fell.

For the 1981 farm bill, the new administration proposed to end income payments for farmers, set the price-supporting loan rates at 75 percent of current market prices, eliminate all the tools of supply management (cropland set-asides and diversions), withhold price support for sugar, greatly reduce support for dairy products and virtually eliminate the peanut program. By proposing such drastic program changes, the Administration squandered any opportunity that might have existed for more modest but meaningful reform, and Congress wrote the farm bill along traditional lines.

Early in 1985, in the midst of the worst rural shakeout since the Great Depression, the Reagan Administration once again proposed fundamental policy alterations that would have reduced farm income substantially, at least in the short-term. Congress rejected this approach as a non-starter, seized control of the policy process and passed a two-track policy: while price supports were to be reduced to enhance the international competitiveness of our commodities, farm income was to be shielded from the consequences of lower market prices through increased direct subsidies ("deficiency payments") to individual producers. By maintaining farm income, it was hoped, the agricultural credit system could be stabilized and an all-out rural banking crisis averted.

This strategy scored some successes, but at great cost. In 1980, farm price/income stabilization programs totalled $2.8 billion. By 1986, the cost of these programs had increased nearly ten-fold, to $25.8 billion. No other major budget item — not defense, not even interest on the national debt — rose so rapidly during this period. While commodity prices have stabilized, the continuing wide gap between market prices and government benchmark ("target") prices ensures large outlays for years to come, unless price guarantees are reduced or the overall structure of the programs altered. (The summer 1988 drought has changed this equation temporarily, but seems unlikely to alter the long-term relationships.)

Exports. Of all the markets in the agricultural economy, exports have been the most unstable in the boom-bust cycle of the past decade. Agricultural exports rose from $6.7 billion in 1970 to over $43.8 billion in 1981, and our annual agricultural trade surplus reached $26.6 billion. At the peak, four of every ten planted acres were producing for export. Then, for the reasons discussed in the previous section, the bottom fell out. Between 1981 and 1986, our annual agricultural exports fell by 40 percent, and our trade surplus declined by 80 percent, to less than $6 billion.

By reducing guaranteed prices toward world-market levels and by increasing efforts to promote exports, the 1985 farm bill stabilized this free-fall by 1987 and even helped increase exports modestly. Congressional pressure forced the Administration to take further action, first to subsidize wheat sales to the Soviet Union, then to broaden export subsidies for a wide range of commodities. Still, this limited recovery has lifted our exports to an annual rate of only $33.5 billion, 23 percent below the 1981 peak.

But U.S. export policies, stemming from domestic economic and political problems, have led to escalating trade frictions with other nations, which have comparable difficulties. The European Community's Common Agricultural Policy restricts imports of U.S. commodities, stimulates over-production and then discharges the surplus onto world markets through massive export subsidies. Japan employs quotas and other barriers to fix the level of U.S. commodity imports at far lower levels than might otherwise prevail, although agreements reached in the summer of 1988 seem likely (if actually implemented by the Japanese government) to improve moderately U.S. beef and citrus exports. The Reagan Administration has worked hard to move agricultural trade to center-stage in the current phase of GATT negotiations (the "Uruguay round"), but has failed to achieve significant international movement toward its proposed ten-year phase-out of all national agricultural subsidies and the creation of a global free market in commodities.

Conservation. It is hardly surprising that awareness of the agriculture-conservation link has grown during the past decade. The increasing use of herbicides and pesticides since World War II has raised fears about diminished food safety and increased groundwater pollution. The agricultural production boom of the 1970s brought vast stretches of land — much of it marginal at best — under cultivation and heightened the risk of long-term soil erosion.

On the whole, the 1980s have witnessed some advances in agricultural conservation policy. Recognition of basic problems — in particular, soil erosion and water pollution — has increased. Because of congressional intervention, funding for USDA's traditional conservation programs, administered by the Soil Conservation Service, has been spared deep cuts. Perhaps most importantly, conservation forces succeeded in their efforts to include a significant Conservation Reserve in the 1985 farm bill, to obtain funding for the Reserve and to ward off annual legislative sneak attacks that would have crippled its operations. Since its inception, the Conservation Reserve has attracted more than 25 million acres of highly erosive land. The ultimate objective is a total of 40-45 million acres. On the minus side, although a number of states have adopted new initiatives to limit the adverse effects of agricultural production on water quality, there has been very limited work at the USDA.

Rural Development. The traditional identification of "rural America" with "agriculture" has become less and less appropriate over the past two decades. With the growth of rural manufacturing starting in the 1960s, and of rural tourism and retirement in the 1970s, agriculture now constitutes only about one-fifth of the rural economy. In spite of a brief economic upsurge, rural America once again suffers from a shortage of job opportunities and persistent poverty at rates well above the national average. Also, it continues to struggle with distinctive problems of housing, schooling and infrastructure. Nevertheless, the tilt of federal policy toward agriculture at the expense of rural economic development has, if anything, intensified.

In the face of simultaneous declines in three sectors vital to the rural economy — agriculture, natural resources and basic manufacturing — the Reagan Administration has mounted an all-out assault on federal rural development programs. Nearly all have been reduced substantially: since 1980, real expenditures have decreased by 65 percent, or $17 billion, compared to a decline in all nondefense discretionary spending of 20 percent.

While rural programs comprise only a small percentage of domestic spending, nearly 60 percent of the "savings" in the President's 1989 budget were slated to come from nine rural programs. In addition to significant cuts at the Department, major items affected by these budget cuts include the Small Cities component of the Housing and Urban Development's Community Development Block Grant (CDBG) program, the Environmental Protection Agency's wastewater-treatment grant program, the public-works grant program administered by the Economic Development Administration, and both direct and guaranteed loans for individual businesses made by the Small Business Administration.

While there have been signs of renewed congressional interest in rural development over the past year, the subject has in general lacked new ideas, an institutional focus for sustained effort and well placed support.

One reason for this is the confused role the USDA plays in the rural development policy dialogue. Rural development authority with the Department is dispersed to at least three agencies, none of which has development as its primary mission.

The largest rural development program authority is located in the Farmers Home Administration, the original and fundamental role of which is to be the lender of last resort for farmers. It has acquired more recently the lead responsibility for rural housing assistance. This mixture of housing, development and farm loans creates a difficult environment for rural development. The training of local FmHA personnel is agriculturally oriented, with no requirement for formal backgrounds in economics or development. The agency's community outreach is also oriented to production agriculture. At the national level, its importance as an agricultural banker, with outstanding loans of approximately $65 billion, overshadows its role as a development agency. As a bank, FmHA has one of the most popular and politically successful constituencies — farmers. The intended beneficiaries of development programs — poor people and communities — are far less popular. Thus, FmHA lacks either the incentive or the expertise to create and vigorously administer innovative rural development programs.

Consumer Concerns. While consumers have become increasingly concerned about food and nutrition, USDA has not developed a consistent or clear role for these concerns. Sharing responsibility with the Food and Drug Administration and with the Environmental Protection Agency for monitoring the food supply, USDA has for the most part narrowed its role to inspecting meat, poultry and grains. During the 1970s, the Department began to take more aggressive positions on nutritional issues through such innovations as the Dietary Guidelines. In recent years, however, the Department has retreated in deference to more traditional producer perspectives.

IV. GOALS FOR THE NEW ADMINISTRATION

Unlike the boom of the late 1970s or the bust of the mid-1980s, the situation in rural America facing the next president and Congress is ambiguous.

On the favorable side, the seven-year shakeout of farmers is slowing. Those who remain have become more flexible and have adopted more effective techniques for production and financial planning. Many surviving farmers have used high payments under the 1985 farm bill to pay off debt, which is now down $50 billion (about 25 percent) from its 1983 peak. Costs of agricultural production — in particular, land, fertilizer and energy — are considerably lower than they were five years ago. After plunging by about one-third nationwide, the price of land has stabilized at levels close to its real productive value. As a result, the rate of rural bank failures has begun to decline. Meanwhile, lower commodity prices, a cheaper dollar and more energetic export promotion have combined to lift exports out of their slump.

On the negative side, the modest underlying improvement in the agricultural sector and its top producers has come at the expense of a vastly increased dependence on the public treasury, generating a clash both with the fiscal realities of the Gramm-Rudman-Hollings era and with other rural priorities. The exodus of population from rural areas has resumed, and there has been a resurgence of rural poverty to nearly 18 percent of the rural population (although only a small percentage of the poor are actually farmers). Intellectually and programmatically, rural development is a near void. Multilateral agricultural trade negotiations are at an impasse, and an all-out trade war in this area is a distinct possibility. Finally, rural America is now highly dependent on the performance of the national and international economy, but it is largely isolated from national and international economic policy making.

V. STRATEGIES FOR '89-90

An omnibus farm bill is not due to be considered until 1990, a year after the new president takes office. This fact is both a challenge and an opportunity for 1989: a challenge to pursue strategies short of a new farm bill, and an opportunity to prepare — intellectually and politically — for what is sure to be a wrenching, year-long battle to redirect the course of agricultural policy.

1989

1. **Appointments are critical.** The next administration will face its first test *before* the inauguration. If real changes are to be made, appointments at both the national and state levels must not foreclose a fair hearing for new approaches. The USDA Secretary and senior deputies must be individuals who are not captives of the traditional interest groups, yet who understand rural economic problems and development opportunities and who are prepared to consider seriously the plight of the smaller, less powerful groups and communities in rural America.

USDA's congressional liaison and intergovernmental relations offices, traditionally dumping grounds for those to whom minor favors are owed, must be staffed with competent and loyal workers who can ensure that proposed policy changes receive a fair hearing. Outside Washington, the state directors of FmHA play a vital role in implementing policy. Although senators and other state political figures traditionally play the leading role in designating these directors, the next administration and Congress must carefully review nominees to ensure that they will not sabotage efforts to return FmHA to its historic mission.

2. Work toward an effective payment cap. In theory, direct government payments are limited to $50,000 per person annually. In practice, the legal definition of a "person" makes widespread evasion of this limit possible and even easy. Persons are defined, not just as individuals but also as members of joint operations or as entities such as limited partnerships, corporations, associations, trusts or estates that are actively engaged in farming. Creative uses of incorporation and reorganization can thus result in payments far in excess of $50,000 accruing to individuals. In a 1987 study, the General Accounting Office carried out a survey of farm practices and estimated that annual payments resulting from legal evasions of the $50,000 cap were nearing $1 billion.

In March 1987, USDA proposed a series of steps, in the form of recommended amendments to the 1985 farm bill, to restrict these abuses. These steps were revised and incorporated into H.R. 3042, a bill introduced by Representatives Charles Schumer (D-NY) and Silvio Conte (R-MA) later that year and praised for its potential effectiveness in an October 1987 GAO report.

On grounds of both fiscal prudence and basic equity, these efforts should be resumed early in the next administration. With median family income under $30,000, it is difficult to understand why average Americans should be subsidizing six-figure payments to individual producers, many of whom are far above average in wealth. Institution of an effective payment cap would send a message that would receive widespread support and also save an estimated $1 billion annually.

3. Existing credit programs should be administered aggressively — and where necessary reoriented — to help smaller and beginning farmers. Under the Farm Credit Act Amendments of 1987, the Secretary of Agriculture was made a member of an "Assistance Board" charged with selling up to $750 million of farmland now in the Farm Credit System inventory to qualifying, family-sized farms. The next Secretary should directly oversee the implementation of this project to ensure that the intention of Congress is honored.

The 1987 amendments also targeted the sale of FmHA inventory property toward family-sized operations, a provision the next Secretary should promote by ensuring FmHA's use of seller-financed installment sales.

The recent trend to replace FmHA direct loans with loan guarantees should be reversed. Loan guarantees, which are twice as large on average as direct loans and command higher interest rates, undermine the public purposes of this program by serving the interests of fewer, larger and better-off borrowers at the expense of smaller and beginning farmers.

4. Help develop effective measures to counter groundwater pollution. While the Water Quality Act of 1987 clearly makes EPA the lead agency in addressing groundwater pollution, USDA must play an important supporting role. Key steps include:

* expanding the recently established demonstration program in low-input agriculture;

* enhancing assistance available to farmers who want to move toward less intensive production methods; and

* exploring ways of encouraging deintensification of production, along with reduced dependence on fertilizers and pesticides, in the 1990 farm bill.

5. Begin to create new federal leadership for rural development. At present, rural development efforts have no effective focus, for three principal reasons. First, the agency — FmHA — that oversees many of the remaining rural development programs is dominated by its agricultural loan activities, and the priorities within this long-established agency are unlikely to change any time soon. Second, the constituencies in favor of, or benefitting from, rural development are relatively weak, and their interests are seldom articulated effectively at the national level. Finally, rural development is bound to be largely a state and local responsibility, and federal services can only work if they can be efficiently delivered to the states and localities. No such delivery mechanism now exists, and the odds are long against any quick transformation of existing FmHA or Extension Service infrastructures.

A fresh start is essential. The next president should appoint a presidential board to oversee the competitive allocation of a research-and-demonstration fund for new rural-development initiatives, to disseminate the results of these activities and to collect and distribute more widely the important research already taking place in the states. In addition, the new board should initiate policy discussion aimed at analyzing, understanding and potentially altering the effect of regulatory and other national decisions directed at industries that have an impact on rural areas. One example of this would be the telecommunications industry, in which regulation has the potential of effecting economic growth in distant areas.

After a few years perhaps, the activities of this board might be transferred to a revitalized rural development office within USDA. But, for now, rural development needs a jump-start, and that can only occur if it is liberated from its current institutional fetters with support at the highest levels.

In addition, we suggest the following steps.

* The Business and Industry Loan Guarantee program, now funded at an annual level of roughly $100 million, should be terminated. This program now funds only a limited number of large-scale business development projects, and the most direct beneficiaries are commercial lenders, few of whom qualify as needy or deserving.

* The Rural Development Loan Fund, now supported by only $14 million annually, should be expanded significantly. The RDLF extends below-market-rate loans to local community development groups for re-lending or direct equity investments in rural businesses in economically depressed areas.

* Existing community facility programs (primarily water and wastewater treatment) should be targeted more directly on the neediest communities that still lack basic services.

6. Encourage a strong consumer presence in decision process and programs. The office of the Assistant Secretary for Consumer Affairs should be reorganized to include supervision of the Meat and Poultry Inspection Service. Remarkably enough, despite the growing popularity of fish in the American diet, there is currently no inspection of fish. Inspection services should be expanded to include fish and other seafood.

The growing recognition — summarized in the recent Surgeon General's report — of health problems stemming from Americans' high fat diet deserves an effective response from USDA. This would include consumer education, coupled with persuasion and incentives designed to move producers toward lower-fat products with commercial appeal.

USDA must cooperate with — and when possible take the lead in — efforts to ensure that all foods are as free as possible from harmful pollutants and chemicals. (At present, foods such as fish and chicken to which Americans tend to turn for a lower-fat diet pose greater than average risks.) USDA should be open to the mounting body of scientific evidence identifying certain plant and animal growth hormones as human health hazards.

7. Comprehensive efforts should be undertaken to expand markets for U.S. commodities. The export dependence of U.S. agriculture is a long-term fact of life that cannot be wished away. So a key challenge facing Washington is to ensure that foreign markets are growing and as wide open as possible to the most extensive range of U.S. raw commodities and processed product. While this will have to be a multiyear if not permanent effort, some important steps can be taken early in the next administration. One of those steps — debt relief for developing nations — is discussed in another chapter. Suffice it to say that no sector of the U.S. economy was hit harder than agriculture by the debt crisis, which forced developing countries to halt and reverse the expansion of their agricultural imports, and no sector would benefit more from U.S. debt policies more sensitive to the interests of producers.

8. Push for open markets. After strenuous efforts, the Reagan Administration succeeded in placing agricultural trade on the agenda for the current round of GATT negotiations. Since then, international talks have stagnated or even regressed. The Administration advanced an ambitious program for eliminating agricultural subsidies entirely over the next decade, creating the perfect free market of classical economists' dreams. As many experts predicted, however, our trading partners were not willing even to consider such a proposal, let alone adopt it.

The next administration will accordingly face a situation in which GATT negotiations are underway without either an agreed agenda for agricultural trade talks or a realistic U.S. bargaining position. An early challenge will be to formulate the outlines of such a position and sell it to other important producer — and consumer — nations as a workable framework for these complex negotiations.

This approach must have two overarching components — an interim agreement to prevent current skirmishes from developing into an all-out agricultural trade war, and a long-term settlement that promotes a more open system of international competition.

In our view, the heart of the interim agreement must be a "ceasefire in place" — that is, a mutual agreement to freeze all export subsidies at current levels: not only the quantity receiving subsidies but also the rate of subsidy per unit. And, it should extend to all features of national agricultural programs that have the purpose or effect of subsidizing exports.

As for the long-term, since the no-subsidy stance is politically unacceptable, the most feasible approach might be to distinguish between features of domestic agricultural programs that transfer income to farmers and those that distort international markets. The former should remain outside the bounds of the GATT negotiations, while the latter should be addressed and minimized. The essential elements of this approach are as follows:

* It is unreasonable to expect that all countries will adopt the same domestic policies or move to free-market systems for agriculture.

* Existing policies should be altered to ensure that all increases in agricultural output above current levels receive a market return.

* All subsidies on products entering international markets should be phased out.

* Policies that substantially reduce consumption should also be phased out.

In the U.S. context, these policies would mean, at a minimum, the gradual termination of direct export subsidies and the phased withdrawal of price/income subsidies on that fraction of domestic production entering world markets. Maintenance of the current price/income support structure for domestically consumed production would, however, be permissible under this approach.

Additional products. In recent decades, most agricultural research has been directed toward increasing agricultural productivity in basic commodities. This strategy has led to the relative neglect of what has become the fastest growing sector of the international market: value-added products. In the next administration, USDA should use the leverage provided by the federal contribution to the Cooperative State Research Service to increase the volume of value-added research carried out at the land-grant colleges.

1990

The central task of agricultural policy in 1990 will be the drafting of new omnibus farm legislation. The key goals of the bill should be the following:

* In this era of collision between fiscal stringency and unmet social needs, outlays must be kept to a minimum. However, it is important to remember that, when the Reagan Administration attempted to cut off farm benefits precipitously, it lost control of the process. It will be critical, therefore, to propose a longer-term phase down.

* The bill should seek to redress the severe current inequities between commodity subsidies on the one hand, and rural-development assistance on the other.

* The bill should build on the experience and progress of the 1980s in the area of conservation and make significant headway toward reducing water pollution.

* The agricultural provisions of the bill must be consistent with the administration's negotiating strategy in the international trade arena.

A farm bill that promotes those goals might contain the following features:

1. Commodity programs

* Loan rates should be restructured to interfere minimally, if at all, with world market rates. (A multiyear moving average of world prices might work well as a rate-setting mechanism.)

* The program acreage base eligible for income supports should undergo a phased reduction, by commodity, toward domestic production levels. For example, if 40 percent of all U.S. wheat is produced for export, then eligible program acreage should be reduced over time to 60 percent of its current level.

* Program acreage reductions should be tilted to assist smaller producers on some sort of sliding scale. While many variants are possible, the basic idea is that producers with larger than average acreage in a particular commodity would incur a larger percentage reduction than would producers with smaller than average acreage.

* The effective payment limits of $50,000 per person discussed in the previous section should be incorporated into the bill.

* Commodity programs that flatly violate fairness and common sense should be reexamined from the ground up. For example, the sugar support program uses import quotas to maintain domestic prices at levels three to four times higher than world market prices, yielding windfalls to a few large producers. Besides bilking U.S. consumers, this program has highly negative effects on the economies of small, sugar-dependent nations throughout the Western hemisphere and interferes with our capacity to conduct effective regional diplomacy.

2. Rural Development

As required, the development initiatives discussed in the previous section should be incorporated in the 1990 farm bill. In particular, information developed in the study of a state block grant rural development program should be carefully reviewed.

Small businesses constitute an important potential growth sector for the rural economy. Evidence suggests that a serious obstacle to small business development is the reluctance of traditional rural banks, many of whom barely survived the mid-1980s, to extend small business loans, especially in the newer and more speculative parts of the economy. An effective way of breaking the logjam would be to create a secondary market in small business loans, along with lines of federally sponsored secondary markets in other sectors. Individual lenders would be able to sell, say, 90 percent of the face amount of each new small business loan to a new secondary market facility. The retained ten percent would provide an incentive not to make large numbers of excessively risky loans. Suitable loan limits and other regulations would be required to ensure that the secondary market remained targeted toward true small businesses.

3. Conservation

The Conservation Reserve should be reexamined to ensure that it is promoting its objectives as efficiently as possible. Some studies suggest, for example, that it is not oriented sharply enough toward its ostensible target — highly erosive lands that should never have been brought into production. Also, the USDA cap on bids for acreage entered into the Reserve has, in fact, become a target price for bidders, eliminating most incentives to offer land below the price cap and actually raising program costs.

VI. CONCLUSION

If the incoming administration tries to reform everything in agriculture — or in agricultural programs — all at once, the fresh start will become a foolish start. The department needs to be reoriented toward a better balance between producers and consumers, between large and small producers, between concentration and communities, between agriculture and the rest of the rural economy. This chapter has proposed a moderate, balanced and carefully phased set of policy initiatives that would, over time, enhance economic growth, foster social equity and reduce current burdens on the federal treasury and the American taxpayer. We believe that if they were adopted, rural Americans — indeed, all Americans — would benefit significantly.

The authors wish to thank the following individuals who generously offered ideas and advice as we struggled to draft this article: Kenneth Cook, Norman DeWeaver, David Freshwater, Ellen Haas, Dale Hathaway, Brian King, William Motes, John Pender, J.B. Penn, Robert Rapoza, Brandon Roberts, Gene Severens, Marty Strange.

Military &
Foreign Policy

OVERVIEW:
Foreign & Military Policy

Theodore C. Sorensen[*]

The next president of the United States, as the following chapters confirm, will be faced on January 20, 1989 with unprecedented opportunities. The winds of political change, driven in large measure by the pressures of domestic economic stagnation, are continuing to blow through the Soviet Union. Bipartisan support for verifiable arms reductions agreements, as demonstrated by the Senate roll call vote on the INF Treaty, has reached a new peak in the United States. The failure of Marxist economies in Eastern Europe, Africa, Latin America and Asia has diminished the appeal of Third World revolutionaries urging upon their impoverished compatriots a similar route. The banner of human rights — originally and rightfully an American banner, if we would only consistently uphold it — is being raised in defiance to more and more totalitarian regimes of every ideological shade and stripe. And the United Nations, no longer a feckless, futile forum of the weak, is once again a potentially important player in the resolution of regional conflicts.

But the 41st president will also face unparalleled problems: some postponed or mishandled, including Central America and Mexico, and some newly global in scope but unyielding to quick solution, such as trade, debt, narcotics, pollution and terrorism.

The chapters that follow set forth a variety of prescriptions for these and other problems. Some of these prescriptions are more specific than others. Some are more realistic than others. Some — on arms control linkage and budget priorities — are inconsistent with others. All are worthy of the new president's consideration.

But whatever his ultimate decision on such proposals, he should also bear in mind the pitfalls and perils that await him in the national security field. For this field contains land mines and quicksand, requiring caution as well as skill and wisdom, as well as courage. In actions on any of the proposals in the chapters that fol-

[*] *Theodore C. Sorensen is a partner in the New York law firm of Paul, Weiss, Rifkind, Wharton & Garrison and former Special Counsel to the President, 1961-64. He is the author of* Kennedy *and* Decision-Making In The White House.

low, our new president should beware the temptations that have lured many of his predecessors into error or worse. They are many.

1. First is the temptation to keep on campaigning — to continue responding to popular demands of the moment instead of the long-term public interest, oversimplifying complex issues for the sake of a ten-second "sound bite" on the evening television news, raising more questions than answers, delivering more rhetoric than responsible actions. There will be pressure from his party and friends to play politics with foreign policy, to restaff the Departments and agencies involved in national security affairs — and our embassies around the world — with his own ideologues and political donors. The campaign habit is hard to break. It has been the president-elect's *raison d'etre* for over a year. It brought him success. It is easier than governing, than making decisions and accepting responsibility.

But campaigning will not suffice. Hard choices in national security affairs must be made, not postponed. The president's foreign policy pronouncements, unlike campaign promises, have real consequences. His words, now reaching multiple audiences, allies and adversaries as well as American voters, must be weighed with greater care. The frustrating processes of consultation are now more important than news media deadlines and headlines. Campaign oratory to the contrary notwithstanding, there is no "Republican" or "Democratic" answer to drug trafficking, terrorism, Lebanon, Third World debt or a host of other problems — only the answer or approach most consistent with our national interests. The best politics in the White House is to pursue the best available — not necessarily the most publicly appealing — policies.

2. A second and related temptation is to make change for the sake of change. There is much to be said for a new broom sweeping clean, throwing the rascals out and throwing their policies out with them. Show them who's boss. We have been through the Truman Doctrine, the Nixon Doctrine, the Carter Doctrine, the Reagan Doctrine — now it's time for the new president's doctrine.

Not necessarily. In foreign affairs, continuity is the soul of strength. Our allies — and even the Soviets and their allies — are disheartened by continued zigzags in American foreign policy. It suggests unsteadiness and unreliability, dangerous attributes in an adversary and disabling attributes in a leader.

Morever, in the last year of the Reagan Administration, the ideologues of the Far Right have been largely gone from leadership positions in the White House, National Security Council, Central Intelligence Agency and Departments of State and Defense. With certain exceptions (such as Central America), policy has been increasingly made by pragmatists. Belatedly the advantages of negotiation over confrontation with the Soviet Union have been real-

ized. Not every expensive weapon system or budget item sought by
the military in fiscal 1988 was approved. Not every pro-American
oppressor was embraced. Many changes are still required, in policies
and priorities as well as personnel. But there is much on which to
build.

3. A third overlapping temptation for the president-elect in
organizing and staffing a new administration is to bring all national
security decision-making into the White House. The State Department, he will observe, is filled with people linked to the policies
and approach of his predecessor. Its bureaucracy seems impenetrable,
immobile, unimaginative, unresponsive. The glamour and glory of
foreign policy — the summit meetings, the state visits, the address to
the United Nations, the reviewing of troops and other great "photo
opportunities" — are presidential prerogatives, and more importantly, the Constitution makes him our chief diplomat and commander-in-chief. The nuclear age has reinforced the gravity of those sole
and unique responsibilities. Virtually every recent president has discovered that he can act in foreign affairs with greater speed and
fewer leaks by entrusting an increasingly large National Security
Council staff and relegating the Department of State to a secondary
role.

But, as two of the following chapters make clear, that approach
will not work. Of course, the president must lead; he must coordinate;
he must proclaim policy; he must look to his own staff members as
sources of advice, innovation and initiative as well as channels of information from the Departments. But an active, responsible, involved
Department of State and foreign service remain indispensable to both
the formulation and the implementation of a coherent and effective
foreign policy. Those career officers who served the nation by loyally
and professionally serving President Reagan can serve his successor
with equal loyalty; and to ignore their advice or diminish their role
would be a tragic waste of talent.

Stirring and reshuffling the Department of State in each new
president's term can be healthy. The Secretary of State must be the
chief executive's "main man," not the bureaucracy's front man. He can
lead and mold and mobilize the Department as an effective instrument for the president, but only if he — and not the National Security Advisor, Secretary of Defense, Director of Central Intelligence or
anyone else — is clearly seen by both American and foreign diplo-
mats as the president's principal advisor, spokesman and emissary in
the world of foreign affairs.

4. Fourth, the new president will be tempted to rush into one or
more new foreign policy initiatives — to push promptly for some
dramatic breakthrough, some bold action, proving his mettle, putting
the world on notice. After all, it is a heady experience to win the

presidency of the most powerful nation on earth, to move into the Oval Office, to be saluted by generals and respected by experts and cheered by the multitudes. Every new occupant of the Oval Office senses that he has a magic touch, that he can do no wrong. He knows that his "honeymoon" with the Congress, press and public may be short-lived, that the time to act is now.

It was in that context that John Kennedy fell into the Bay of Pigs, Lyndon Johnson fell into the Tonkin Gulf and Jimmy Carter fell into a sweeping revision of our arms control offer that only startled and antagonized the Soviets. Those are but a few of the many examples of the folly of early over-eagerness. Clearly, the president's first half year in office is not a time for inaction. If he has made full and effective use of the transition to plan and prepare, if he has received helpful and expert advice in policy from this volume and elsewhere, he can "hit the ground running." But he must choose his priorities with care and he must look before he leaps — look hard at the problems and personnel he has inherited and at the realistic prospects for success or failure of any bold new initiatives urged upon him.

The transition months, both before and after his Inauguration, form a period in which he must get to know the strengths and limitations of his new advisors and how best to utilize their skills, evaluate their advice and weigh one against another. It is a period when they too must feel their way cautiously, examining the intractability of the persistent world problems handed to them and the practicality of solutions brought to the new team by careerists presumably unable to sell those proposals to the previous team. It is a period when both the president and his new team should consult with their counterparts in friendly countries, drawing upon their wisdom and experience before sailing off into uncharted waters.

5. This last piece of advice brings to mind another temptation that looms large in the eyes of all new presidents — the temptation to go it alone in foreign affairs, unhindered by the restraints of allies, the resistance of neighbors. Bold leadership requires bold action. Consultation with other countries is painfully slow, risking costly and possibly fatal leaks and delays. Consent is frequently begrudging or denied, for other countries have their own interests, their own politics, their own economic objectives and historical relationships. Collective innovation is an oxymoron. Because the United States is more powerful than others, it has more responsibility, an obligation to lead and to act; and because it is more powerful than others, it is criticized and resented, yet asked to carry more than its fair share of the Free World's burdens. A president who wishes to make his mark may find it watered down to invisibility through rounds of consultation.

Not every American initiative requires clearance with our allies, much less their participation or even cooperation. But there are few global problems that we can resolve alone. The world is large, its problems stubbornly resist solution and our resources are limited. We have no monopoly on diplomatic, military, paramilitary or intelligence skills. Others have contacts, specialties and relationships that we lack. In the eyes of world law and world opinion — and both matter more in the long run that we have sometimes realized — a unilateral action by the United States is often far less defensible than a genuine multilateral action taken by this country together with its allies.

In Latin America, for example, the traditional antipathy to intervention by this country among political leaders across the spectrum inevitably undermines whatever side or cause such American intervention is intended to support. Truly regional efforts by the Latin Americans themselves, even when encouraged and assisted by the United States, may be less satisfying to presidents yearning to demonstrate machismo but more likely to produce results.

6. A sixth and similar temptation attractive to most Twentieth Century presidents is the possibility of bypassing Congress, often simultaneously shutting out the American press and public as well. No meaningful foreign policy is possible with 535 Secretaries of State on Capitol Hill. In the national security area, the Framers intended presidents to innovate and Congress to deliberate. In diplomatic and military matters, secrecy, dispatch and flexibility are often unavoidable necessities, and neither the role nor the structure of the legislative branch is suited for these purposes. The president, charged with primary responsibility for preserving and advancing our national security and Constitutionally empowered to do what he determines to be necessary, must be able to act when action is required, without waiting for congressional debate or authorization — just as John F. Kennedy acted alone during the Cuban missile crisis.

But times have changed since Kennedy. The Congress has reasserted its role; the consequences of the "imperial" American presidency — in Vietnam, Laos, Iran, Central American and elsewhere — remain fresh in our minds; and a more probing and skeptical press has made lasting secrecy on controversial executive actions virtually impossible. The truth will out; and a Congress scorned is a Congress prone to impose even heavier restrictions on executive action. Overlapping committee jurisdictions, multiple demands for executive branch testimony, the possibility — particularly in the Senate — of a small handful of ideologues endlessly delaying majority approval of necessary action all add to every president's frustration with our system of shared, divided and balanced powers. But that is our system; and Congress is not to be denied.

7. Last on the list is the temptation that encompasses all the others — the temptation to meddle, or to cause the United States to meddle, in international matters that are effectively beyond the reach of the president and the country as a whole. Foreign policy looks deceptively attractive. Merely by making pronouncements he can "make" foreign policy, with no need for appropriations and legislation. He is the commander-in-chief of "his" own Armed Forces. Those are all "his" helicopters and military attaches. Domestic economic policy, by comparison, seems as complicated and intractable as a great ocean liner, difficult to speed up, turn around or repair. It involves or offends more special interest groups than foreign policy, more campaign contributors, more Capitol Hill lobbyists. Meetings on fiscal, monetary, agricultural, urban and similar problems can be boring; meetings on crises and challenges in far off places are often fascinating.

But in truth the demarcation line between foreign and domestic problems is no longer clear. Many of our most pressing problems in international affairs are economic, largely dependent on our efforts to improve productivity, trade, education, job training and deficit reductions. Domestic issues — including inflation, crime and the environment — are in turn dependent on our international efforts on trade, narcotics, pollution and other fronts. Money spent on weapons is not available for health care. Debt relief for foreign governments without some relief for American farmers is unthinkable. Adventuring abroad without strong economic, industrial and political bases at home is dangerous.

There are no longer any easy answers to international problems. There are no longer American answers to every international problem. Nuclear war and the nuclear arms race are not "winnable" in any meaningful sense for either the United States or the Soviet Union. Superior armaments are no longer enough to maintain a position of unchallengeable leadership and strength in world affairs. The world has changed, and the next president will need to exercise restraint as well as leadership, to avoid the traps and pitfalls described above through patience and prudence as well as wisdom. But that is why he was elected — not because these problems were easy.

Nevertheless, the opportunities remain: the opportunity to enhance the security of this nation and the rights of humans everywhere, the opportunity to end the arms race and redeploy vast resources to fulfilling our own needs for infrastructure and institutions, the opportunity to leave the White House in four or eight years with the ultimate satisfaction of having helped to make this country — indeed, this planet — a safer, more hopeful place for all mankind.

SOVIET RELATIONS:
The President's Historic Opportunity

Stephen F. Cohen*

SUMMARY OF RECOMMENDATIONS

The next American president will have both a historic opportunity and an obligation to end the decades-long U.S.-Soviet cold war. The opportunity awaits him in Moscow — in the anti-cold war thinking and foreign policy reforms adopted by Mikhail Gorbachev since he was chosen Soviet leader in 1985. The obligation is dictated by the fact that the cold war, with the arms race as its most characteristic expression, has become the greatest threat to America's national interests. The president will have to translate his anti-cold war commitment quickly into bold U.S. actions and proposals. The following steps are especially important:

* In his inaugural address, the president should assure Gorbachev that the United States is now ready for open-minded negotiations on every disputed issue. To implement that process vigorously and consistently, he should appoint to all relevant foreign policy positions only people deeply committed to the anti-cold war effort.

* In the same speech, the president should accept Gorbachev's standing offer of an immediate U.S.-Soviet moratorium on the testing of all nuclear weapons and devices. The moratorium will arrest the nuclear arms race and give up the snails-pace process of arms limitation talks to catch up with the torrid pace of weapons technology.

* No less important, the president must not rush into a buildup (or "modernization") of conventional weapons, which account for almost 80 percent of U.S. defense expenditures. Instead, he should explore fully Gorbachev's extraordinary offer to reduce conventional forces in Europe in "asymmetrical" ways that will eliminate perceived Soviet superiorities.

* The president must also seek to diminish conflicts that fuel the arms race. As the largest suppliers of weapons to the Third World

---

* *Stephen F. Cohen is Professor of Politics and Director of the Russian Studies Program at Princeton University. His books include* Bukharin and the Bolshevik Revolution; Rethinking the Soviet Experience *and* Sovieticus: American Perceptions and Soviet Realities.

countries, the United States and the Soviet Union should agree to replace all military aid with economic assistance. And as a symbol of post-cold war cooperation, he could propose the creation of an American-Soviet Youth Corps to send doctors, teachers, agronomists and engineers to those countries, instead of weapons and soldiers.

* In the same spirit, the president ought to propose a special U.S.-Soviet task force, composed of visionary thinkers from both countries, to design other forms of cooperation in, for example, halting nuclear proliferation, combatting terrorism, protecting the earth's environment and exploring outer space.

* Mindful of the Soviet Union's abiding concern about its 4500 mile border with China, the president should renounce any intention of a Washington-Beijing alliance against Moscow, and announce that his administration will not supply any kind of weapons to Beijing.

I. THE OPPORTUNITY

The next American president will have both a historic opportunity and an obligation to end the decades-long cold war between the United States and the Soviet Union. The opportunity already awaits him in Moscow — in the anti-cold war thinking and foreign policy reforms adopted by Mikhail Gorbachev since he was chosen Soviet leader in 1985. If the president lacks the vision and courage to seize the opportunity, he will be neglecting the best and largest interests of the United States.

That is because the cold war, with the U.S.-Soviet arms race as its most characteristic expression, has become the greatest threat to America's national interests in two profound ways. Above all, it threatens our national survival. As Carl Sagan has aptly said, since 1945, "the United States and the Soviet Union have booby-trapped the planet with almost 60,000 nuclear weapons," far more than enough to destroy every city on earth and "probably enough to destroy the global civilization." The United States exists today only because no one in Moscow, and no accident anywhere, has sprung the trap. Nor is there an infallible system, computerized or otherwise, to protect us against such a mishap. That is the lesson of Korean Air Lines Flight 007, Challenger, Chernobyl and Iran Air Flight 655, disasters resulting from human and "high-tech" fallibility and auguring much worse.

The cold war also is sapping America's economic health, which is as important for real national security as are weapons. In present-day dollars, according to Sagan's calculations, the United States has spent roughly $10 trillion on the cold war during the last four decades. Imagine all the economic, educational, medical, cultural and scientific sacrifices that has meant. Today, as U.S. defense spending approaches $300 billion a year, most of it directed against a perceived Soviet threat, the problem has become starkly evident in the decline of many of our non-military industries, the largest budget and trade deficits in our history and the number of our fellow citizens who live in poverty.

Nor is the cold war over, contrary to euphoric reports in the media, inspired by four Reagan-Gorbachev summit meetings since 1985. The nuclear and conventional arms race goes on, its fast-paced technology speeding far ahead of the political half-measures taken to constrain it. The ratified INF Treaty, which promises to remove and destroy American and Soviet intermediate range missiles in Europe, is important as a first symbolic act of nuclear abolitionism. But the two sides have given themselves three full years to abolish missiles capable of carrying, at most, only four percent of their stockpiled nuclear warheads. Discussions now focus on a so-called START agreement that would eliminate 30 to 50 percent of the strategic arsenals. By the time it is negotiated, ratified, verified and fully implemented, technological geniuses on both sides are likely to have invented new nuclear weapons that formally comply with the treaty but are even more deadly than those to be abolished. Meanwhile, both sides contemplate a "modernization" of conventional weapons, and a full range of underlying cold-war conflicts — ideological, political and regional — continue to rage around the world.

In reality, three years of mostly inconclusive negotiations and media atmospherics could not possibly end an historical phenomenon of the magnitude of the cold war, whose ideological origins date back 70 years to the Bolshevik revolution; whose modern-day embodiment in the arms race has been underway since 1945; and whose dynamics are sustained on both sides by a powerful array of institutions, elites and popular attitudes formed over those decades. Despite episodes of detente going back to the 1930s, and even a U.S.-Soviet military alliance during World War II, virtually all of us — American and Soviet citizens alike — are children of the twentieth century's cold war. Not surprisingly, many officials and citizens have come to accept it as the only possible relationship, even as a virtuous one.

To go beyond this mountainous legacy of cold war to a valley of safer U.S.-Soviet relations therefore will require a long march and bold leadership on both sides. Events since 1985 tell us that the journey is now possible if the next American president meets Gorbachev halfway. President Reagan, to his lasting credit, went farther in that direction than most people thought possible. But it has not been nearly enough, and not only because the cold war goes dangerously, needlessly on. Even the modest progress in arms control achieved since 1985 has been due largely to a long series of concessions by Gorbachev. No national leader can safely persist in such one-sided compromises to a foreign adversary, least of all Gorbachev, who is deeply embattled in a struggle with powerful opposition to his far-reaching domestic reforms, or *perestroika*, and to his conciliatory policies toward the West.

It is time for comparable U.S. initiatives and compromises. After all, it was the Soviet leadership, not democratic America, that responded to the growing perils of cold war with "new thinking," boldness and flexibility. To do no less is the real challenge, and historic opportunity, that awaits the next president.

II. OBSTACLES AND OPPOSITION

And yet, a great many influential Americans in both political parties are sternly warning the next commander-in-chief against any such policy. Some of them are theological cold warriors for whom there can never be an alternative U.S.-Soviet relationship, no matter how great the necessity or possibility. But the majority of these influential advisors belong to the self-described "bipartisan center" — a large company that includes many of yesterday's officials and policy intellectuals whose worn conceptions obscure today's historic changes and opportunities. They speak of policy toward Gorbachev's Soviet Union in abstract jargon and empty cliches about "toughness" and "negotiating from strength," as though everyone else advocates dealing from weakness. In effect, by insisting that U.S. policy never deviate from "bipartisanship" and its "center," they reflexively oppose the new anti-cold war thinking and measures that America so urgently needs.

While there are significant differences between our wild-eyed cold warriors and statesman-like centrists, they are united by their opposition to a fundamentally new course in U.S.-Soviet relations. Their recommendations vary, from a policy of escalated cold war and arms race to one of indifference or business-as-usual toward Gorbachev's leadership. Given the influence they exercise in policy circles, their essential arguments need to be examined.

A shrinking but still vocal group of "experts" even maintains that Gorbachev's reforms in Soviet foreign policy are not really changes but a "propaganda trick," or that they remain merely words, not deeds. The facts tell us otherwise. The revisionist ideas Gorbachev calls "the new thinking" in foreign policy have been circulating for many years at lower levels of Soviet officialdom. In 1985, along with many of their longtime proponents, they came to power with Gorbachev. Though not uncontested in the Soviet national security elite, those ideas reflect new perspectives on the world order and international relations. In practice, they comprise an anti-cold war orientation toward the West that is the only foreign policy compatible with Gorbachev's equally historic political and economic reforms at home. That is why, for almost four years, and at risk to his own position as leader, Gorbachev has been arguing strongly against Soviet cold-war dogmas about national security and East-West relations, some of which date back not only to the Brezhnev era but to Stalin and even Lenin.

Despite protests even among his Politburo colleagues, Gorbachev has insisted, for example, that "the nuclear threat" and other "common human concerns" must take precedence over traditional Marxist-Leninist concepts; that national security for the Soviet Union can derive only from "mutual security" for the United States; that such security for both countries can be achieved only through political negotiations and military build-downs, not build-ups; that, accordingly, "reasonable sufficiency" should replace superiority and possibly even parity as a guideline for defense spending in Soviet strategic and conventional doctrine; and that conflicts in the Third World and elsewhere must be avoided or resolved so as not to jeopardize this necessary process of demilitarizing East-West relations. Most fundamentally, perhaps, he has rejected the original Soviet dogma that cold war is inevitable because of the nature of the American capitalist system. (Our cold warriors insist, of course, that it is inevitable because of the nature of the Soviet communist system.)

And in fact, Gorbachev's words have already been translated into some important deeds. People associated with "the new thinking" have replaced officials of the Brezhnev "stagnation era" throughout the foreign policy establishment, from the Central Committee Secretariat to the Foreign Ministry. Meanwhile, new thinking has been expressed in actual foreign policy, from Gorbachev's concessions to U.S. negotiating positions on nuclear weapons and his offer to eliminate perceived Soviet advantages in European conventional forces to his withdrawal of Soviet troops from Afghanistan. Considering that great power policy-making is almost always deeply conservative and exceedingly slow to change, what more evidence do we need that fundamental shifts are underway in the Soviet leadership's thinking and behavior?

Even worse, many American analysts who do acknowledge the authenticity of Gorbachev's reform efforts in domestic and foreign policy nonetheless still oppose a fresh U.S. response. The cold warriors among them see in Gorbachev's reforms and concessions only signs of Soviet weakness to be exploited by an unrelenting hardline policy of military buildup and political ultimatums — a chance at last to "win" the cold war, whatever that might mean. Such proposals are illusory and fraught with danger. No Russian government, however encumbered with problems, will capitulate to the United States. As Andrei Sakharov has argued, "All historical experience indicates the opposite." The result of such a U.S. policy would be a deeper, more perilous cold war, including an uncontrollable nuclear weapons race both on earth and in space. In the process, it would gravely, probably mortally, wound Gorbachev's leadership, depriving his reform programs of the economic resources and political coalitions they need to survive at home.

This prospect raises a question rarely asked by Americans: What is the political alternative in the Soviet Union if Gorbachev fails? In the short term, a post-Gorbachev leadership is likely to attempt a more moderate kind of reform — less radical economic changes without the Gorbachevian "excesses" (as they are derisively called by his opponents) of radical anti-Stalinism, *glasnost* and *demokratizatsiya*. Given the country's enormous economic and social problems, such a leadership would almost certainly fail. The logical contender would then be the Party's counter-reformist, neo-Stalinist wing, which already is clamoring for a revival of despotic state power, including pogrom-like repressions; for a reimposition of social order; for an end to Gorbachev's "Americanization" of Soviet life; for an end to liberalization in East Europe; and for a cold-war (even iron-curtain) face to the West. Any American who really cares about human rights and international security in the nuclear age should be deeply concerned about this possibility. Apparently, our cold warriors do not care.

The "bipartisan center," on the other hand, probably does care but seems to want to do more or less nothing in response to the historic opportunity represented by Gorbachev. These influential advisors propose a kind of aloof, wait-and-see policy, as though the United States plays no role at all in the cold war or the arms race — as though Gorbachev should or could end them alone, without an active American partner. As President Reagan once remarked, "It takes two to tango."

Recoiling from any new anti-cold war approaches, centrists offer various rationalizations. U.S. policy, they warn, must be based on America's national interest, not on Gorbachev. Furthermore, Gorbachev is an aberrant or eccentric Soviet leader who is likely to fail or be overthrown, and the United States has no real influence over the political struggle raging in the Soviet Union. And if his economic and political reforms were to succeed, might not the Soviet Union emerge as a more formidable and thus more dangerous adversary to the United States? These are serious questions that deserve an answer.

It is certainly true that U.S. policy must be based on American national interests, but it is also true that Gorbachev's domestic and foreign policies are in America's interests. Indeed, they correspond to much of what we have long demanded and hoped for from the Soviet government. Unlike any imaginable alternative, Gorbachev's policies hold out the possibility of a Soviet nation engrossed for decades in almost Herculean internal reforms; the possibility of a considerably better economic and political life for the great majority of Soviet citizens, from factory workers and peasants to intellectuals, from Baltic peoples and Ukrainians to Russian Jews; and, above all, the possibility of an end to the apocalyptic dangers and corrosive military expenditures of the 40-year arms race. If nothing else, is not the possibility of billions of dollars freed to restructure our own economic life and help our own people in America's national interests?

It is also true that Gorbachev's domestic reforms face enormous political opposition and structural obstacles, and that eventually he may be deposed. But it is not true that he is an eccentric or isolated leader without broad support. He did not come to power in 1985 accidentally or alone, as many American commentators seem to think, but at the head of a resurgent reform movement that had existed inside the Communist Party since the early 1960's. During its more than three years in power, Gorbachev's *"perestroika* party," as some of its adherents term it, has found many supporters among officials and citizens in all walks of life, as well as many opponents. No one can predict the outcome of this fateful struggle, but it is nonsense to say that Gorbachev and his reforms are already doomed.

And though the struggle is essentially an internal Soviet one, it is both untrue and irresponsible to deny that the United States will play an important role in its outcome, for better or worse. Gorbachev has wagered much of his personal authority on the hope that eventually the United States will meet him halfway in new thinking and bilateral compromises. If it does not, his position as leader in both foreign and domestic policy will be greatly weakened. More generally, if we rudely rebuff or simply remain aloof from his calls to reduce cold war tensions and end the arms race, Gorbachev will never be able to persuade recalcitrant Soviet elites to reallocate large resources from the military to the civilian economy, or to undertake the risks inherent in his program to decentralize and liberalize the political system. We may not hold Gorbachev's fate in our hands, and yet it is hardly independent of what we do.

But do we want him to succeed? Should we fear a reformed Soviet system as a greater threat to the United States? Such a perspective offends common sense and America's professed ideals. Gorbachev's advisors frankly admit that their large-scale reforms will take "several decades." During that long historical period, America also will have a chance to become stronger by turning inward to its own economic problems and neglected citizens. Moreover, where is the potential danger if Gorbachev's reforms transfer huge quantities of rubles and scarce technology from the Soviet military-industrial complex to consumer goods, services and welfare; give citizens more freedom, a larger role in decision-making and more access to the West; and persuade this and subsequent generations of Soviet officials to seek their legitimate destiny in reform at home rather than in expanded power abroad? Let us heed Sakharov, who struggled and suffered for the changes finally underway: "The West and the entire world also have an interest in the success of reforms in the U.S.S.R."

To argue otherwise is to betray what our own government has professed ever since the beginning of the militarized cold war with Stalin's Soviet Union: that America awaits and would welcome a different Soviet Union, one with a more open society and political process, with more private enterprise and human rights, with less repression and fewer barriers to Western influence — because such a Soviet Union would be a more acceptable and less dangerous member of the world community. That prospect now stands before us, beckoning us to meet it halfway. If the United States rejects it, if we in effect ally ourselves not with the forces of Soviet reform but of counter-reform, we will be sending a profound, probably irreversible message to future Soviet generations and leaders — and to ourselves. We will be saying that no matter how great the opportunity for an alternative, America prefers the cold war and the nuclear arms race forever.

III. GENERAL PRINCIPLES AND TEN PROPOSALS

That historic decision will be made, through action or inaction, by the next American president. If he has the wisdom and resolve to join Gorbachev in an all-out effort to end the cold war, he will no doubt be traduced by our cold-war lobbies and gravely reproached by the "bipartisan center." But he has nothing to fear politically from the American people. Recent opinion polls show that the public is weary of cold war tensions and military buildups, fearful of nuclear weapons, open-minded about Gorbachev's overtures and deeply alarmed by America's economic and social problems.

From the beginning of his administration, the president need only speak candidly to the people. He must say that Gorbachev's proposals represent a long-awaited possibility, though not yet a certainty, of ending the cold war, and that he is determined, for the sake of America's best interests, to begin his presidency by testing Gorbachev's sincerity rather than new weapons. He should emphasize that the long journey to a post-cold war relationship is certain to include temporary setbacks and disappointments, and that the realistic destination is not likely to be a U.S.-Soviet friendship or alliance.

Very different historical experiences, dissimilar political systems and real conflicts have made our two nations natural rivals for the foreseeable future.

The president must explain that the joint quest, based on a U.S.-Soviet partnership in survival, is for a relationship in which cooperation and tolerance displace the most dangerous conflicts, and in which the residual rivalry can be expressed primarily in non-military ways. If the United States and the Soviet Union must compete, let us do so not in an arms race that threatens everyone and benefits no one, but in a compassion race to improve the lives of our respective peoples and those of less developed countries. Let us compete to demonstrate in real accomplishments rather than in ideological assertions which is the more caring system, American democratic capitalism or the Soviet socialism with a human face, of which Gorbachev speaks. And let that competition go on indefinitely.

For this to happen requires a new American thinking about the Soviet Union and about real national security in a changing world in order to overcome decades of our own cold-war dogmas and reflexes. Only the president from his "bully pulpit" can provide this kind of leadership. He alone has the authority and the nation's constant attention. And he more than anyone else can shift the politically acceptable mainstream of media discourse, which has featured a dialogue between cold warriors and chilly warriors during the Reagan years, to a national discussion about how to achieve a new U.S. Soviet relationship.

As the leader of this discussion, the 41st president should introduce two important principles. First, while Americans dislike many aspects of its behavior, the Soviet Union is a legitimate great power with rightful interests in world affairs. Recognizing this principle of political parity, the United States is prepared to join the Soviet Union in an expanded process of negotiations to end the cold war through mutual concessions that safeguard the reasonable interests of both countries. (The president might add that it no longer matters which nation bears greatest responsibility for the history of the cold war, only that both sides agree it must stop.) Clinging to a specious analogy, cold warriors will cry, "Appeasement!" but the president will reply that there is no one-way street to mutual security or to the end of the cold war.

Second, the president must take the leading role in demilitarizing American thinking about the Soviet Union by fully rehabilitating the principles and practice of political diplomacy and accord. All of our underlying conflicts with the Soviet Union are political ones. This does not mean that the United States should disarm unilaterally or be militarily weak. It does mean that we must stop seeking solutions to political conflicts by inventing new weapons systems, as both sides have done for so many years. The goal is to replace that overwhelmingly military relationship with a diplomatic one. It also means that no arms control agreements will ever be stable without larger political accords to protect them against the underlying conflicts, as we learned with SALT II and the ABM Treaty and as will be true of INF, START and any other treaties to come.

If the next president wants to provide such anti-cold war leadership, he will have to translate it very quickly into bold U.S. actions and proposals. The pace of the arms race, growing conflicts around the world, and Gorbachev's embattled position at home leave no time for the prolonged ritual of muscle-flexing by a new incumbent. Ten steps are particularly important:

1. The president should, preferably in his inaugural address, assure Gorbachev that the United States is now ready for open-minded and good-faith negotiations on every disputed U.S.-Soviet issue, without exception. To initiate this expanded process of negotiations as quickly as possible, he should send one or two of his closest personal associates to Moscow to convey his own preferred agenda of discussions and to learn Gorbachev's.

2. In his inaugural speech, the president also should accept Gorbachev's longstanding offer of an immediate U.S.-Soviet moratorium on the testing of all nuclear weapons and devices, including space-based anti-missile systems. Such a moratorium, which can be reliably verified, is crucial. It will stop the ongoing nuclear arms race, because weapons that cannot be tested will not be deployed, and thus are unlikely to be funded. It will thereby give the snails-pace process of arms limitations talks much-needed time to catch up with the torrid pace of weapons technology. And it will be a dramatic indication of U.S.-Soviet determination to end the nuclear arms race forever.

3. No less important, the president must not compensate by rushing into a buildup (or "modernization," as it is euphemistically called) of conventional weapons. These armaments and the requisite troops account for almost 80 percent of U.S. defense spending. If they continue to grow, no substantial budgetary funds will ever be liberated for non-military purposes, and another dimension of the cold war will go on, perhaps even intensify. Instead, the president should explore fully Gorbachev's extraordinary offer to reduce Soviet and U.S. conventional forces in Europe in "asymmetrical" ways that will eliminate the perceived Soviet superiority in various categories. Having always wished for fewer Soviet troops in Central and Eastern Europe, how can we not prefer this alternative to yet another costly buildup?

4. What may be the Soviet Union's changing role in both Eastern and Western Europe also requires a far-sighted response by the presi-

dent. The Brezhnev doctrine, formulated to justify the Soviet invasion of Czechoslovakia in 1968, seems to have been officially repudiated under Gorbachev. According to a recently declared "Gorbachev doctrine," as a Soviet newspaper has termed it, Moscow now acknowledges that every ruling Communist party in Eastern Europe is "fully autonomous in its actions" and thus no longer subject to the threat of Soviet military intervention. If so, the president should respond positively to this development by fully normalizing U.S. political and economic relations with all of those governments. He also should encourage growing political and economic relations between our Western European allies and Moscow. Since the Soviet Union is in significant respects a European nation, such relations ought to be viewed as part of a healthy normalization of European politics, not as a threat to U.S. interests. If the Atlantic Alliance is really based on the shared democratic values of its members, why the constant alarm that Moscow may somehow deceive or "decouple" America's NATO allies?

5. Aware that even the most determined measures to end the arms race will fail without equal efforts to diminish U.S.-Soviet political conflicts everywhere, the president should propose substantive and symbolic acts of cooperation in the Third World, the scene of so many present and potential superpower collisions. Above all, as the largest suppliers of arms to those regions, which serve only to increase the murderous nature of indigenous civil wars, the United States and the Soviet Union must agree to replace military aid with economic assistance. They must also negotiate a code of mutual restraint banning direct or covert use of superpower forces, proxies and even military "advisors" in those regional conflicts. In addition, as a potent symbol of a post-cold war era of cooperation, the president could propose the creation of an American-Soviet Youth Corps that will send to Third World countries not weapons and soldiers but young doctors, teachers, agronomists and engineers, who together can heal, teach, cultivate and build. When they return home, these young people may become future leaders of a post-cold war world.

6. In the same spirit, the president should propose the formation of a special U.S.-Soviet task force, composed of visionary thinkers from both countries, to design other forms of cooperation; for example, strengthening the United Nations' peace-keeping capabilities, halting nuclear proliferation, devising anti-terrorism measures, fighting world-wide diseases and hunger, seeking safe sources of energy, protecting the earth's environment, exploring outer space and resolving regional conflicts already underway. The task force will not replace foreign policy bureaucracies in either country, but it must be far more creative than they have proved to be over the years.

7. One exceedingly dangerous regional conflict requires the president's urgent attention. Acknowledging that both superpowers have vested interests in the Middle East and that no lasting peace settlement there is possible without the support of both, he must ask the Soviet Union to rejoin multilateral negotiations, from which it has been excluded since 1978. In return, the president will expect the Soviet Union to restore full diplomatic relations with Israel, which it broke off in 1967, and to persuade Syria and the PLO to recognize irrevocably Israel's right to a secure existence.

8. In addition, the president should respond positively to some promising improvements under Gorbachev affecting Soviet Jews who wish to emigrate and those who do not. The Jackson-Vanik and Stevenson amendments, passed by Congress in 1974, severely limited U.S.-Soviet trade by linking it to Jewish emigration from the Soviet Union. In light of recent developments, the president should promise to seek ways to expand the economic relationship between the two countries.

9. It is also important for the president to acknowledge publicly that the Soviet Union, like the United States, is understandably alarmed by perceived threats in neighboring countries. In particular, perhaps as much as 15 to 18 percent of Soviet defense spending, and a quarter of the country's troops, are directed against China, with whom it shares a 4500-mile border. With this in mind, the president should renounce any intention of a Washington-Beijing alliance against Moscow, the so-called "China card," and announce that his administration will not supply any kind of weapons to China. The United States seeks a flourishing political and economic relationship with Beijing, not a military one. Indeed, the president could add that he applauds the growing signs of a detente in Sino-Soviet relations.

10. Finally, so that all these initiatives can be pursued vigorously and consistently, without the internecine conflicts that characterized previous U.S. administrations, the president should appoint to all the relevant foreign policy positions only people deeply committed to his anti-cold war effort.

IV. IF NOT NOW, WHEN?

Some people will say that such proposals to end the cold war reflect a naivete about Soviet intentions and about harsh political constraints on American presidential leadership. But almost four years of Gorbachev's policies give us ample reason to believe that he will respond with still more initiatives and concessions of his own. As for presidential leadership, perhaps we have forgotten what it ought to be — not political recipes cunningly prepared to appeal to the greatest number of bipartisan tastes, but an understanding of the nation's real interests and the courage to pursue them. Nor should we forget that the remarkably bold Gorbachev emerged out of the far harsher and more constrictive political world of the Soviet Communist Party apparatus. Are we to believe that American democracy cannot produce a comparable leader to meet him halfway?

When Gorbachev's radical proposals to solve his country's problems were opposed by his own centrists, he replied defiantly: "If not now, when? If not us, who?" Given a historic opportunity to end the cold war, we can rightfully ask: If not now, when? If not the next president, who?

NUCLEAR DEFENSE:
The Seven Vital Principals

Paul C. Warnke
Philip G. Schrag
David A. Koplow*

SUMMARY OF RECOMMENDATIONS

In developing nuclear defense policy, the next president should keep in mind the enduring principles of sound deterrence. The most important principle is that strategic nuclear forces can deter a nuclear attack, but they cannot be used to win a nuclear war. A second critical principle is that some weapons deployments can actually increase the likelihood of nuclear war by inducing the Soviet Union, in a serious crisis, to launch a pre-emptive nuclear strike against those weapons.

The Reagan record on nuclear defense is mixed. The Intermediate Nuclear Forces Treaty contributes positively to nuclear stability by recognizing that intermediate range nuclear missiles are not really useful for the purpose of fighting a war and by eliminating some weapons that might invite pre-emptive attack. But because of his focus on a purported 50% cut in strategic weapons and his preoccupation with strategic defense, President Reagan squandered an opportunity to negotiate deep cuts in missiles with multiple, independently-targetable warheads (MIRVs) — weapons that pose the greatest threat of sudden, pre-emptive nuclear strike. The President also edged the world closer to the brink by deploying MX missiles in vulnerable silos, planning to deploy Trident II missiles in a version that could pose a first-strike threat to Soviet silos, and abandoning the effort to negotiate a ban on underground nuclear weapon tests.

---

* Paul C. Warnke is a lawyer in Washington, D.C. He was formerly Director of the Arms Control and Disarmament Agency (ACDA) and Chief Arms Negotiator under President Carter, and served in the Defense Department under President Johnson. Philip G. Schrag is a Professor of Law at Georgetown University and former Deputy Counsel of the ACDA. He is the author of Listening for the Bomb: A Study of Arms Control Verification Policy (forthcoming). David A. Koplow is Professor of Law at the Georgetown University Law Center and a former Special Assistant to the Director of ACDA.

The 41st president — working closely with the 101st Congress — should try through renewed negotiations to move the deterrent systems of both countries away from MIRVed missiles:

* He should build on the START negotiations conducted by the Reagan Administration, but should place greater emphasis on the restriction of MIRVed ICBMs.

* In exchange for the elimination of a significant number of MIRVed Soviet missiles, he should be willing not to deploy the most destabilizing version of the Trident II missile.

* He should, however, leave room in a negotiated agreement for the United States to build new single-warhead missiles for deployment both on land and at sea.

* To slow the qualitative arms race and to discourage the proliferation of nuclear weapons to other countries, he should work toward a ban on all nuclear weapons tests. This effort might begin with a verifiable agreement between the U.S. and the Soviet Union to ban all testing above a very low yield threshold.

The Reagan era has been a period of lost opportunity and poor strategy in nuclear defense policy. Not only have precious national resources been squandered "building up to build down," and not only have opportunities been missed to curb the nuclear arms race, but this Administration's policies and practices in the past eight years have actually increased the risk of nuclear confrontation and war.

I. BACKGROUND

THE CURRENT STOCKPILE

The United States has traditionally diversified its nuclear forces among a variety of delivery systems. The "triad" of nuclear arms includes: intercontinental ballistic missiles (ICBMs), capable of flying from silos in the U.S. to targets in the U.S.S.R. within about 30 minutes; submarine-launched ballistic missiles, carried quietly aboard submarines capable of hiding for sustained periods in deep ocean waters; and intercontinental bombers, armed with nuclear bombs or air-launched missiles. Describing this armada as a "triad" actually understates its diversity, because each "leg" of the forces contains a number of different types of missiles, submarines or aircraft, each with its own characteristics and basing patterns. The multiplicity of platforms greatly complicates the task of any potential aggressor who might attempt to attack and disable all U.S. strategic forces simultaneously.

The U.S.S.R. sustains a considerably less diverse triad. For example, while the U.S. keeps only about 18% of its 12,000 strategic nuclear warheads on fixed (and therefore relatively vulnerable)

ICBMs, the U.S.S.R. continues to mount a majority of its 11,000 strategic warheads on this least survivable type of platform.

Each nation has frequently modernized its strategic nuclear forces, adding new generations of arms at irregular intervals. The U.S. is now replacing portions of all three legs of the triad. The Minuteman ICBMs are being supplemented by fifty large MX missiles and may be further augmented by the Midgetman missile still on the drawing board. The fleet of Poseidon submarines and their Trident I missiles is being phased out in favor of larger Trident submarines and more accurate Trident II missiles. And the aging force of B-52 bombers is being equipped with long-range cruise missiles and supplemented by B-1 and "Stealth" bombers.

ARMS CONTROL AGREEMENTS

The arms control efforts of every president since Dwight D. Eisenhower have produced several important agreements. To some degree, these efforts have channeled and slowed the pace of the nuclear arms race, although they have not yet fundamentally changed the dangers we face.

The 1972 SALT I agreements included a "freeze" on the two sides' numbers of missile launchers, as well as a mutual agreement not to build territorial defenses against ballistic missiles. These agreements were followed by the 1979 SALT II Treaty, which would have capped the strategic arsenals on both sides at agreed levels and required Soviet reductions. In 1980, Ronald Reagan campaigned on the accusation that the treaty was "fatally flawed," but even his Administration for almost six years tacitly agreed with the Soviets to abide by the obligations of this unratified treaty pending the negotiation of another agreement. In the fall of 1986, however, the U.S. deliberately exceeded one of the deployment limits established by the treaty.

The START negotiations (the Reagan Administration's renaming of SALT) included some dramatic — and perhaps ill-advised — proposals, such as the idea, blurted out at the Reykjavik summit, of promptly eliminating all strategic ballistic missiles. But the talks have failed so far to produce concrete results, largely because of the Reagan Administration's fixation with the "Strategic Defense Initiative" (SDI). The Soviets have been unwilling to cut a substantial deal regarding strategic offenses until they know the shape of future "Star Wars" defense forces. President Reagan, in return, has clung to three successive SDI illusions: first as a perfect defense, then as a tool to improve deterrence, and finally as an "insurance policy" — but it has resisted using SDI as a bargaining chip, even when substantial Soviet concessions could have been obtained in return. Indeed, at the Moscow summit, President Reagan reiterated his vision of SDI as an impenetrable shield, something nearly all physicists reject as technically impossible for the foreseeable future.

Regarding shorter-range nuclear weaponry, the Treaty on Intermediate-range Nuclear Forces (INF) was signed in December, 1987, and instruments of ratification were exchanged at the Moscow summit. The INF Treaty is a modest but useful accomplishment, banning medium-range ground-based missiles and incorporating a panoply of unprecedented verification measures. The treaty calls for the scrapping of hundreds of nuclear missiles by both sides, though the arms to be dismantled will constitute only a very small fraction of the superpowers' nuclear arsenals.

Other important arms control agreements limit the parties' conduct of nuclear explosions. The Limited Test Ban Treaty of 1963 confined the tests to underground chambers, and the Threshold Test Ban Treaty of 1974 restricted the size of these underground explosions to the equivalent of 150 kilotons of TNT. Both sides appear to have observed the 150 kiloton treaty, but it has never been brought into force; although two previous Republican administrations had deemed its verification provisions adequate, President Reagan has opposed ratification, pending Soviet acceptance of additional monitoring provisions.

THE STRUCTURE OF THE AMERICAN DEFENSE POLICY APPARATUS

Several government agencies participate in the process of formulating U.S. defense policy. The Departments of State and Defense, of course, have the largest roles. Actually, in most inter-agency groups, the Pentagon sends two semi-independent representatives: one from the Joint Chiefs of Staff, or its subunits, and the other from the civilian side of the Department, the Office of the Secretary of Defense.

Another major player is the U.S. Arms Control and Disarmament Agency (ACDA). A small, independent organization created in 1961, ACDA is independent of the State Department although its Director acts under the direction of the Secretary of State. ACDA has statutory responsibilities for organizing and leading American arms control efforts. Under President Carter, ACDA usually played a key role in the arms control process, generating new ideas and advocating them within the bureaucracy. In the Reagan years, however, ACDA has been relegated to a lesser status, and the agency's prominence, effectiveness and autonomy have been drastically reduced.

In addition, the National Security Council staff plays a key role in arms control deliberations, sometimes serving as a neutral "coordinator" of the efforts of the primary agencies, and sometimes more directly influencing policy. As the occasion warrants, other agencies, too, are involved. Because the Department of Energy, for example, controls the design and testing of nuclear weapons through its contracts with Livermore and Los Alamos National Laboratories, it helps to make nuclear test ban negotiating policy. Similarly, the National Aeronautics and Space Administration has been involved in deliberations about weapons in space.

II. PRINCIPLES FOR NUCLEAR DEFENSE POLICY

Seven principles can help shape and inform U.S. defense policy over a relatively long period of time. Although none of them is revolutionary, it is useful, in periods of presidential transition, to step back from the pressures of the moment and contemplate certain enduring, long term standards.

First Principle. *Realistically, the sole function of our strategic nuclear arsenal is to deter nuclear attack.* Understandably, some strategic thinkers assume that the U.S. strategic nuclear arsenal can achieve a variety of missions: to deter conventional attacks on the U.S. or its allies; to coerce the U.S.S.R. or other antagonists to adopt polices more to our liking; or to fight and "win" a nuclear war. In fact, however, strategic nuclear forces are simply not that useful: they are much too powerful — and they carry too great a danger of triggering a suicidal global nuclear war — to constitute a credible threat in response to low-level provocations.

This is not to say that nuclear weapons are unimportant. Indeed, their central mission — deterrence of nuclear attack by the U.S.S.R. or others — remains of utmost salience. But it does mean that the U.S. defense policy cannot rely on strategic nuclear forces as the solution to most military problems.

The intellectual battle over strategic theory — that is, over whether nuclear weapons can be used for purposes other than the deterrence of nuclear war — has never been settled. As a result, every American administration and every Congress has had to revisit this issue each time a new strategic weapon is designed and proposed by the military services. The results have been incoherent; we have some strategic weapons that are particularly suited to deterrence and others that could be regarded as best suited for fighting a nuclear war.

Second Principle. *The quality of a deterrent force should be measured by two factors: the credibility of the threat that it can and will be used to retaliate after a nuclear attack, and the degree to which it does not invite or provoke a preemptive nuclear attack.* One important attribute of a nuclear deterrent is obvious: every potential attacker must fear that launching a nuclear attack would result in devastating retaliation, so that any hope of "winning" a nuclear war is quickly abandoned. But the second important attribute is more subtle. A badly designed deterrent force can actually make nuclear war more likely by presenting the other side with incentives to launch a nuclear war preemptively. A good deterrent, therefore, does not encourage an attack on itself.

When there is no international crisis, this second feature of a deterrent force is less important. Neither the civilian nor the military leaders of either superpower would seriously contemplate launching a surprise, unprovoked nuclear attack on the other superpower. But in a very serious political and military crisis, if war seems likely to break out within days, leaders may well ask themselves and their staffs whether their nation could be better off if it launches a preemptive nuclear attack on the other side. So long as the answer is negative, diplomacy may resolve the crisis. This situation is termed "crisis stability."

If, however, the answer for either side is positive, the world is in danger. And if the answer for both sides is positive, and both sides realize it, the leaders might well run for their buttons.

Certain aspects of a nuclear weapon system, therefore, could make preemption seem desirable. To understand these perverse features, imagine that you were in charge of either superpower's military forces. First, you would analyze your own vulnerability. If your adversary's weapon delivery system were so accurate and powerful that it could destroy most of your nuclear weapons before you could launch them, you might feel compelled to put your weapons on a "launch on warning" hair trigger. You might even feel a necessity to try to destroy the adversary's weapons preemptively, before they could be launched against you.

In addition, you would analyze your adversary's potential vulnerability. If your adversary's very threatening system were "vulnerable" to attack — that is, if there were a good chance that you could destroy the major portion of it by shooting at it before it is launched — then you would feel an even stronger incentive to try to attack it early in a crisis. In this way, both features — vulnerability on either side — lead to greater instability and greater danger of uncontrolled escalation in a crisis.

As a result, both the United States and the Soviet Union should ideally have strategic nuclear forces that are relatively unthreatening to the other side's nuclear arsenal, while still promising devastating retaliation against the other side's military facilities and economic infrastructure. The nuclear forces should also be perceived as able to survive a preemptive attack in sufficient quantities to be able to "ride out" the aggression and still retaliate with massive, unacceptable damage to the attacker.

While it may seem obvious that U.S. forces should be configured with these characteristics in mind, it may be less obvious — or at least less than obvious to the Reagan Administration — that it is also in the U.S. interest that the Soviet Union have forces that are survivable and that do not threaten the survivability of our forces. That is, if unrestricted American technological growth, coupled with the failure of arms control, left the Soviet Union relatively more vulnerable to a hypothetical preemptive attack, the reaction of the Soviet leadership would likely be starkly adverse to U.S. interests. The U.S.S.R. would be very unlikely to "capitulate" to the apparent U.S. edge (no more than we would, if the situation were reversed) but would respond, instead, by redoubling its military efforts, developing new arms and creeping ever closer to a policy of preemption or launch on warning.

From all of this, there emerges a certain tension between the best strategy for *deterring* a nuclear war and the best strategy for *winning* one. The weapons and policies that would be most useful for the purpose of avoiding a nuclear attack in the first place (e.g., weapons that are accurate enough to hit military bases but not to destroy missile silos) are not the same as the weapons and policies that would be most useful for implementing a nuclear war-winning strategy (e.g., weapons that could preemptively attack the other side's silos and communications nodes).

There can not be a gross disjunction between these two goals, of course. In order to provide any kind of a credible deterrent, a weapon must be potentially useful in combat, too. Conversely, any nuclear weapon that has a true combat significance also provides at least some contribution to the deterrence function as well. But the goals do diverge at some point: counterforce weaponry (strategic weapons that can destroy the other country's strategic retaliatory forces) are very valuable in the "warfighting" mode, but they may be worse than useless for deterrence since their deployment may incite the other side's fears that a potentially disabling first strike is possible or planned.

In short, making war more "thinkable" — such as by devising weapons and policies that would contribute to the United States' ability to conduct a limited, protracted nuclear war — may also make nuclear war more likely. National security depends, at base, on nuclear deterrence, and the strategic nuclear weapons in the U.S. arsenal will have utterly failed in their central mission if they are ever used at all.

Third Principle. *Technological advance is vital to American security, but some innovations take the world closer to the brink of war.* American technology has been able to make frequent changes in our weaponry. Within the past several years, new generations of nuclear weapons have been devised; stealth technology has advanced; newer, quieter submarines have been discovered; and progress has been made in research on ballistic missile defense.

Unfortunately, while many of these technological advances confer a short-run advantage to the innovating country, in the longer term they can be disadvantageous to both superpowers. Several inventions, such as advances in missile guidance technology, have reduced crisis stability by making preemptive nuclear attack seem more advantageous.

Perhaps the best publicized example of opening this type of technological Pandora's box is the U.S. experience with MIRVs, multiple, independently-targetable re-entry vehicles. In the late 1960s, when American innovation first developed the methodology for placing more than one warhead on a missile, MIRVs seemed to many people to be an opportunity to deter the Soviets from building an anti-ballistic missile system. With MIRVs, the United States could proliferate offensive weapons more easily than the Soviets could build systems to shoot them down.

Within a few years, however, the Soviet Union mimicked the American developments, and began to MIRV its own, much larger, force of ICBMs. American defense analysts soon realized that the multiple warheads on heavy Soviet missiles had become the single most important threat to the viability of the U.S. force of land-based missiles. Some nuclear theorists even came to believe that the Soviets might think that they could use a relatively small number of their biggest MIRVed missiles to destroy the entire U.S. ICBM force, while leaving all of their other missiles in reserve to deter American retaliation for their first strike. The attempt to "out-invent" the U.S.S.R. ultimately backfired, leaving us less secure than we were before we hit upon the MIRV idea.

Nor is MIRV an isolated example. The Reagan Administration's initiation of a new arms race in strategic defenses, prompted by the illusion of an effective Star Wars technology, may provide another disastrous application of the principle as the Soviets, sooner or later, follow our lead into the world of exotic defenses.

Technological innovation can be a wonderful asset to a carefully-considered defense policy. But mindless, unguided technological growth, driving to invent — and to deploy — anything that can be invented, is more likely to disrupt security than to enhance it. Judicious management of the technological possibilities, including negotiated restraint where appropriate, is therefore the better course.

Fourth Principle. *Limited resources available for defense will always require hard choices among competing programs.* National survival will always have first call on America's resources. But even with this priority, some demands will go unmet. The public fisc cannot hope to finance all the competing proposals for nuclear arms. Careful choice is therefore required, keeping in mind the first principle, which is that sound nuclear programs are those that enhance the deterrence of a nuclear attack.

The Reagan Administration's approach to defense budgeting, instead, has been simply to throw money at the Pentagon, refusing to make the hard, but necessary, choices. It has spent, and misspent, billions to provide too little in real military muscle. By pouring money into Star Wars, and attempting to buy new arms for each leg of the triad simultaneously, the Administration has stretched the defense dollars too thin. It has failed to pursue any sustainable sense of priorities.

Fifth Principle. *Relations with the Soviet Union must be expected to reflect a mixture of competition and cooperation.* International life is unavoidably dominated by the complex, sometimes unpredictable relationship between the U.S. and the U.S.S.R., a relationship with life-or-death consequences.

We have, at the same time, much that divides us and much that drives us together. Our two nations differ fundamentally in their cultural and social history, in their economic and political organization, in their aspirations and plans for the planet, and in their relations with their allies and neighbors. There is a great deal to dislike about the Soviet Union, a great deal to fear and a great deal to try to change.

At the same time, the two superpowers also have an immense shared interest in survival. For more than forty years, this shared interest has kept our disagreements from erupting into war. The fundamental test for U.S. policy, therefore, is to manage the complexity of the U.S.-U.S.S.R. connection: competing effectively where we must, but cooperating usefully where we can.

Sixth Principle. *Defense procurements and arms control agreements are related, necessary components of overall national security policy.* It is sometimes imagined that there is inherently a permanent, irreconcilable antagonism between defense procurement and arms control, as if the Defense Department and the Arms Control and Disarmament Agency were little more than warring barons competing for influence. While a certain amount of clash is inevitable, and indeed desirable, in formulating national policy, it is also important to remember that the ultimate objective — an objective shared by all participants — is the promotion of U.S. national security.

The centrality of deterrence makes obvious the need for procuring at least certain types of nuclear weapons. But arms control also has some unique properties. Only negotiated agreements can actually reduce the threat facing the United States and it allies — there are no other ways to cut down the number or change the types of nuclear missiles currently pointed at us. The arms control process is also a singular tool for enhancing mutual understanding and for building the personal and institutional connections that can make use of force less likely.

Seventh Principle. *The arms control process must be sustained and strengthened.* It is very difficult to negotiate and implement an important arms control agreement. Strong forces, in both the U.S. and the U.S.S.R., will continue to oppose restraints on military deployment.

The United States government must therefore nurture the institutions and the processes of arms control. The next president should appoint skilled, stable leadership for the agencies and the delegations charged with negotiating agreements. They should conduct the negotiations in a confidential, orderly fashion, trying to keep them as free as possible from the glare of publicity and public posturing. The United States must be able to manage its domestic political process so that negotiated treaties can be ratified and brought into force promptly. For after the failure to ratify SALT II, the reputation of the U.S. as a reliable negotiating partner in the arms control arena has been compromised, and it needs to be restored. The overwhelming Senate approval of the INF Treaty has helped do so.

Attention to the negotiating process also means that the United States must make its negotiating proposals realistic and consistent. Consider, for example, verification. The INF Treaty has greatly expanded the range of possible inspection options. Nevertheless, the President should make verification proposals that are really needed, not simply "nice to have." The appropriate standard of verification, as described by Secretary Shultz, is one of "effective" verification, ensuring that any treaty breaches would be detected in time for the U.S. to mount an appropriate response before the strategic balance could be materially affected. Insistence upon far more stringent detection capability — demanding that an arms control treaty must incorporate a "perfect" capability to detect instantly any violation, however inconsequential — is too often simply an opponent's tactic for resisting any agreement at all.

Finally, enhancement of the arms control process also means exorcising the ghost of "linkage," the doctrine that would hold progress in arms control hostage to progress in other, unrelated areas of U.S.-Soviet relations. Linkage has often been a potent tool of arms control opponents, providing cover for a host of other, less respectable motives for criticism of a treaty. But strategic nuclear arms control is simply too important to U.S. national security interests to be sidetracked by the ups and downs in U.S.-Soviet relations.

We will always have differences with the Soviet Union, and some of these differences will be profound. But it is self-defeating to link these other matters to arms control: it does not aid in the resolution of either the arms control problems or the other matters for the entire set of U.S.-Soviet concerns to be tied into a single, intractable package. Arms control, after all, is not a reward for acceptable Soviet behavior; it is a policy we pursue in our nation's own interest.

III. RECENT DEVELOPMENTS

CHANGES IN CRISIS STABILITY SINCE 1970

With these principles in mind, we can evaluate the strategic forces of the United States and the Soviet Union and their efforts to achieve effective arms control agreements.

Over the past twenty years, by deploying strategic nuclear forces whose purposes can be perceived as winning a nuclear war rather than merely deterring one, the United States and the Soviet Union have departed from the first principle. In doing so, they made the world a considerably more dangerous place than it was in 1969, for example, when President Nixon assumed office. Some of this change resulted from an aspect of the third principle, the inevitable, but not necessarily benign, march of technology. For example, the United States' Minuteman missiles became more accurate — and therefore more threatening to the Soviet Union's fixed land-based missiles — in the late 1970s and early 1980s simply because engineers designed improved guidance systems for them. Although many members of Congress were aware of the evolution of these missiles into more effective counterforce weapons, the change occurred so gradually that there was no significant public debate of the kind that normally accompanies the deployment of an obviously "new" system such as the MX missile.

The most destabilizing development of the last twenty years, however, was not the gradual improvement in missile accuracy but both sides' deployment of missiles with MIRVs. As a result of this deployment in the mid-1970s, either side could begin to consider scenarios such as one side using only a small fraction of its strategic forces to destroy a major portion of the other side's land-based ICBMs in a preemptive attack, while retaining a large number of residual missiles to deter a retaliatory strike by the opponent's remaining forces. Furthermore, while the deployment of MIRVs on submarine-launched missiles was bad enough (because each missile could target several land-based ICBMs), their deployment on silo-based ICBMs was folly itself, as measured by the second principle. It turned each side's most potent counterforce weapons into what the other side's military might perceive to be sitting ducks for a preemptive strike.

Similarly, the United States' replacement of a large number of Polaris and Poseidon nuclear missile submarines by a smaller number of newer Trident submarines has had a mixed effect on the prospects for avoiding nuclear war in a serious political crisis. Because they are quieter and can remain at sea for longer periods of time, the Trident submarines are even less vulnerable to attack and therefore less likely to invite one. But to the extent that the Soviets ever become able in the future to detect and track the movements of some of our submarines, we would be much better off having a larger number of smaller submarines, because then the Soviets would have less chance of finding nearly all of them at the same time.

Of course, not all changes in nuclear technology are destabilizing. These three negative developments (improved missile accuracy, MIRVs and bigger submarines) contrast with other nuclear force changes which have improved deterrence by strengthening retaliatory forces without threatening or tempting preemption. For example, the development of mobile ICBMs could significantly help deterrence, since they could be moved around periodically to hide them from a preemptive surprise attack, while still filling a retaliatory role.

Mobile ICBMs do have two features that tend to impair stability. First, any new mobile system, like any new missile system, is likely to include the latest technical advances in guidance systems. So a new, more accurate, mobile system built by either side may be seen as contributing to a first-strike capability against the other side's strategic forces. This negative feature, however, could be countered in part by the mobility of the forces against which these more accurate missiles would be aimed and in part by moving toward single warhead systems rather than MIRVs, so that the use of such missiles to destroy ICBMs would deplete the attacker's forces on more than a one-for-one basis.

Second, the argument is made that mobile missiles present serious verification problems. But verification of compliance with numerical deployment limitations requires knowing only the numbers, and not the locations of, the other side's missiles. The Soviet Union's willingness (in the INF Treaty) to agree to cooperative verification measures (such as inspections of missiles as they leave a factory) can make it possible to know how many mobile missiles the Soviet Union has deployed, even if we are not certain of their exact locations at any given time.

Improvements in manned bombers, too, are a stabilizing trend. To the extent that new bombers are able to ride out the effects of a distant nuclear explosion, and to attack Soviet targets with bombs or with long-range air-launched cruise missiles without being shot down, they offer improved retaliatory capability. But since even the fastest bombers and cruise missiles imaginable would take hours to reach Soviet borders, they cannot be perceived as threatening a pre-emptive strike; they would get there long after the other side's ICBMs had been launched, and could therefore only be used in a re-taliatory capacity. The worst that can be said about either the B-1 or the Stealth bomber programs is that they are very expensive and may not be the best investments of increasingly scarce defense dollars; yet unlike MIRVed missiles, they do not make it more likely that a serious crisis will end in nuclear war.

THE REAGAN RECORD

The Reagan Administration's record in terms of making nuclear war less likely is a mixed one. The INF Treaty, eliminating inter-mediate range missiles in Europe, is a positive development, which contributes to nuclear stability in three ways. First, it reinforces the first principle, for it apparently accepts the premise that the only genuine purpose for nuclear forces (except perhaps for very short range battlefield weapons) is the deterrence of nuclear attack. U.S. Pershing and ground-launched cruise missiles in Europe could not have been used against the Soviet Union, even after a Soviet conventional force attack, without making an all-out nuclear exchange virtually inevitable. The agreement of the U.S. and its allies to dismantle the INF weapons acknowledges this reality.

The INF Treaty also bows to the second principle. The presence of Pershing missiles in Germany, which cut Moscow's nuclear attack warning time from 35 minutes to about 8 minutes, could only have made Soviet leaders more jumpy in a period of crisis. The Pershings were therefore obvious targets for a launch-on-warning mentality or a preemptive attack that could easily have begun an escalating nuclear war.

Finally, the verification provisions of the treaty are entirely consistent with the sixth and seventh principles. These ground-breaking measures will pave the way for cooperative verification measures that could make it possible to reach future arms control agreements that will have considerably greater significance.

Aside from the INF Treaty, on the other hand, the Reagan Ad-ministration's stewardship over nuclear arms control policy has been a failure. It was, of course, a refreshing moment when the President, after scuttling the SALT II Treaty and railing for six years against the "evil empire," became, at the Reykjavik summit, an ardent ad-vocate of far-reaching nuclear arms control. But the particular strategic arms treaty that his Administration has worked to achieve — a Strategic Arms Reduction Treaty (START) to cut each side's strategic nuclear weapons by 50% — does not make its central focus the need for greater strategic stability.

President Reagan had, after all, the good fortune to be dealing with General Secretary Mikhail Gorbachev, a Soviet leader willing to embrace new ideas in arms control, such as the sweeping verification provisions of the INF Treaty. Applying the second principle, we can see that the items of nuclear hardware most likely to prompt the Soviets to launch a preemptive attack are their vulnerable, but potent, fixed, land-based MIRVed ICBMs. The President's principal objective should have been to obtain the Soviet Union's agreement to eliminate them, or at least to reduce their numbers to a very low level. To destroy the Soviet MIRVed ICBM force, he should have been willing to agree to eliminate the United States' MIRVed Minuteman and MX missiles. Similarly, he should have focussed on eliminating MIRVed missiles in the Soviet submarine-launched forces as well, even at the price of converting U.S. submarine-launched forces to single-warhead missiles.

Cutting strategic nuclear forces by 50% is good public relations; it's an easily understandable and instantly popular idea, with a nice round number at its heart. Making nuclear war less likely will, however, require greater attention to the qualitative mix of weapons in each side's arsenal, as opposed to simply reducing the numbers of such weapons.

Unfortunately, the Reagan Administration's emphasis on "deep cuts" in the numbers of deployed weapons not only misses the point about reducing the likelihood of nuclear war but may also leave United States forces with less than an optimal mix of strategic weapons — perhaps even making us worse off than we are today. This perverse effect could occur a) if a START agreement incorporated, as the U.S. has proposed, provisions reducing each side's strategic nuclear arsenal to no more than 1600 delivery vehicles, carrying no more than 6000 warheads, of which no more than 4900 warheads could be on ballistic missiles and b) if the treaty did not at the same time include requirements, or at least compelling incentives, to move away from MIRVs and back to single-warhead systems.

Under these circumstances, both the Soviet Union and the United States would probably be driven to sustain a strategic nuclear force structure that is far too concentrated and therefore far too vulnerable. On the U.S. side, for example, we would probably proceed with the full complement of 20 planned Trident submarines, each with 24 missiles carrying 8 MIRVs — accounting for 3840 of our quota. The 50 planned MX missiles would use another 500 warheads, so 4340 (almost 90%) of our allowed 4900 ballistic missile warheads would be carried on only 70 platforms. And the Soviets would have 4900 ballistic missile warheads available to aim at these 70 targets.

The wiser course, instead, would be to use the arms control agreement as an opportunity to promote a restructuring of both superpowers' strategic nuclear forces. Even if this means sacrificing some of our (and of the Soviets') newest, most powerful, most technologically sophisticated missile systems, we should seek to move to a situation in which the stability — not just smaller numbers — of forces is paramount. This means shaping the START agreement, and shaping our unilateral defense acquisition policies, to favor smaller, more numerous submarines and single-warhead, mobile ICBMs.

Although President Reagan's most important arms control initiative did not reflect the best policy that the United States could have chosen, reducing strategic weapons by 50% and capping the superpowers' strategic arsenals at much lower than present levels is considerably better than continuing an unrestricted arms race. Unfortunately, President Reagan not only failed to ask for the best possible deal, but, as of this writing, he has failed to get any deal at all. The Moscow summit in May, 1988 produced no significant agreements and wasted a major opportunity for progress.

The failure of that summit was virtually inevitable, for three reasons. First, the Reagan Administration had agreed in principle at the Reykjavik and Washington summits to the 50% cuts and the various sublimits of a START agreement without first determining the mix of weapons it would want within the allowed constraints. After these summits, the armed services began to bargain among themselves with respect to which weapons would be retained, and the Administration was unable to make the necessary resource allocation choices before the Moscow meeting.

Second, the Soviets sought a mutual ban on long range nuclear-armed sea-launched cruise missiles. Since conventionally armed cruise missiles and nuclear-armed cruise missiles are indistinguishable at a distance, a ban of this sort would require the United States and the Soviet Union to board each other's ships, at least periodically, to verify that no nuclear-armed missiles were on board. The U.S. Navy strongly opposed allowing Soviet sailors to inspect American ships, and the Administration supported the Navy. As a result, although the U.S. is usually trying to persuade the reluctant Soviets to agree to more inspection, in this case the United States was unwilling to take seriously a Soviet offer for cooperation that could have helped to eliminate the arms race in sea-launched cruise missiles.

Third, the President became so committed to the Strategic Defense Initiative (Star Wars) that he was unable to compromise on this issue with the Soviets, who insisted on compliance with the ABM Treaty's restrictions on testing and deployment of anti-ballistic missile technology, as initially interpreted by both sides.

Additionally, five other aspects of President Reagan's nuclear defense policy are clearly steps in the wrong direction. These five policy initiatives are 1) the deployment of MX missiles in vulnerable basing modes, 2) the planned deployment of Trident II missiles in a first strike configuration, 3) the high level of funding accorded to the Strategic Defense Initiative, 4) the abandonment of the attempt to negotiate a ban on all nuclear weapon tests and 5) the Administration's neglect of intelligence systems that are needed to monitor Soviet compliance with arms control agreements.

Early in his first term, President Reagan proposed to deploy 100 MX missiles in old Minuteman silos, even though fixed ICBM silos were becoming increasingly vulnerable to preemptive attack as Soviet missiles became more accurate. Congress then limited the deployment to 50 missiles, while the search for a more survivable basing mode drags on.

Putting any MXs into vulnerable silos is doubly foolish. Because the MX is an extremely accurate weapon, with ten MIRVs per missile, the Soviets could think that the United States planned to use it preemptively against Soviet silos if war should seem likely. Still worse, deploying such threatening missiles in easily targetable silos sends Soviet military planners the message that if war seems inevitable, it would be rational to begin it by trying to knock out the MX missiles before they could be launched.

In May, 1988, the Administration announced a new plan to put MX missiles on specially built railroad cars that would normally remain on military bases but would fan out onto the nation's commercial rail system in time of crisis. This plan is no improvement. While on the bases, the missiles would be vulnerable to a sudden, surprise nuclear attack, and beginning to move them out of those bases during a crisis could tempt the Soviets to launch such an attack before they could be effectively dispersed.

Similarly, the Reagan Administration decided to replace the existing Trident I missile in Trident submarines with the more advanced Trident II missile, beginning in late 1989. The Trident II missile could in principle contribute to stability because it is capable of much greater ranges than the Trident I. With this missile, the Trident submarines will be able to use even larger ocean areas for concealment, and the United States' deterrent will be less vulnerable to surprise attack, even if the Soviets' very poor ability to keep track of the locations of Trident submarines were eventually to improve.

But the Administration was not content to deploy Trident missiles so configured as to make it harder for the Soviets to attack American missile-launching submarines. It developed two different versions of this new missile. One version will contain twelve Mark-4 warheads, each with 100 kt. of explosive. Mounted on Trident II missiles, these warheads will have a 50% chance of being able to land within 900 feet of a target such as a missile silo, and will, as a result, have about a 50% chance of destroying a silo hardened against 3000 pound per square inch overpressures. The other version will use eight 475 kt. Mark-5 warheads; these more powerful warheads will have more than an 80% chance of destroying the same targets.

From the perspective of a Soviet general, Reagan's decision to deploy the Trident II missile with Mark-5 warheads makes no sense as a retaliatory threat. Why? Because most military and industrial targets are not highly hardened against nuclear blast effects, and are therefore vulnerable to the Mark-4 version of the Trident II missile. The government's decision to deploy the Mark-5 version of the Trident can only be seen as intended to shoot at hardened military targets such as missile silos. But it is useless against silos whose missiles have already been launched in a first strike, and this version of the Trident II could only, therefore, play a role in *initiating* a nuclear exchange. For a Soviet general, then, the conclusion is obvious: once the most powerful version of the Trident II missile is deployed, if there is a political crisis, Soviet missiles must be launched before they can be attacked by these highly accurate SLBM weapons.

The third and best known of President Reagan's mistakes in nuclear policy was his insistence on devoting substantial sums of money — he proposed five billion dollars for FY 1989 — to develop defenses against Soviet ballistic missiles. In principle, an instantly deployed and perfectly operating Star Wars system could improve deterrence by making ballistic missiles obsolete. As a result, populations would be perfectly protected; second-strike nuclear delivery systems (such as manned bombers) would become invulnerable to preemptive attack and could be used only for retaliation; and the world would return to the relatively safer deterrent system that prevailed in the 1950s.

But there are several problems with a Strategic Defense Initiative. To begin with, given the problems of locating and shooting down thousands of Soviet missiles and decoys in a period of just a few minutes, most physicists who have studied the anti-missile problem think that Star Wars could never be made to work; in addition, the Soviets can devise inexpensive countermeasures (e.g., by multiplying the number of missile decoys) that could readily negate the SDI system. Second, the cost of deploying Star Wars would be staggering; many estimates exceed a thousand billion dollars, dwarfing all other budgetary demands.

Most plans for Star Wars systems depend on satellites in fixed earth orbits to shoot down or at least locate Soviet ballistic missiles. But it is obviously easier to shoot down a satellite than for the satellite to shoot down or direct fire to a large number of warheads accompanied by decoys and chaff. The Reagan Administration's only answer to this challenge was that, somehow, the satellites would be able to defend themselves.

But even if some kind of anti-ballistic missile system could be built, and at an acceptable price, no known or foreseeable technology will make it perfect or instantly deployable, and therein lie the dangers of preemptive war. Suppose the United States were about to deploy a system that could effectively neutralize Soviet missiles. Would the Soviet military stand idly by, knowing that the Soviet Union's missile force was about to become useless while the American missile force would still function as planned? Or imagine that the United States deployed a Star Wars system that could destroy 95% of whatever Soviet warheads remained usable after an initial American volley. During a crisis, would Soviet military planners feel confident that the United States would refrain from attacking preemptively, or would they worry that U.S. leaders would regard as "acceptable" the damage that could be done by the Soviet warheads that would survive the initial U.S. attack and then penetrate the Star Wars defenses?

Doubts such as these caused the United States to work very hard, in the late 1960s and early 1970s, to persuade the Soviets to abandon the idea of strategic missile defense, and to sign the 1972 Anti-Ballistic Missile Treaty, which enshrines the concept of nuclear deterrence by requiring each country's cities to be forever defenseless. Ironically, it is now the Soviets who are trying to teach us the theory of deterrence that we persuaded them to accept when they signed that treaty. And our own government is undercutting the treaty by claiming, in a legal "reinterpretation", that it permits tests of exotic SDI systems. Fortunately, Congress has so far prohibited such tests.

The Reagan Administration's fourth major arms control error came in its 1982 decision to take an enormous leap backwards by terminating the nearly successful negotiations for a comprehensive ban on nuclear weapon tests. Technological "improvements" in nuclear weapon designs make the world a less stable place by changing the nature of the deterrent system every generation. A test ban would significantly add to stability by freezing existing warhead and bomb designs, since neither the Soviet nor the United States government would add an untested design to its weapon stockpile.

If we and the Soviets had negotiated a nuclear test ban in 1950, after the Soviets developed the atomic bomb, there would have been no hydrogen bomb. If we had negotiated such a ban in 1955, there would have been no ballistic missiles; in 1965, no MIRVs; in 1970, no cruise missiles. A test ban negotiated now would prevent a race to develop various versions of strategic defenses which depend on nuclear detonations as well as other future types of nuclear weapons whose properties can only be guessed at.

In addition, many countries which are capable of building their own nuclear weapons within the next twenty years regard the failure of the United States and the Soviet Union to stop nuclear weapons tests as evidence that the superpowers are not serious about ending the nuclear arms race, and they use this failure as a justification for their own nuclear weapons research. This is why the effort to halt such tests was at the center of President Carter's nonproliferation policy.

Unfortunately, the Reagan Administration valued the development of new types of nuclear weapons more highly than ending this aspect of nuclear weapons competition. It refused to continue comprehensive test ban negotiations, even after the Soviets demonstrated, in an agreement with the Natural Resources Defense Council, that they were willing to accept seismic monitoring stations on their territory. The President refused to accept General Secretary Gorbachev's invitation for an immediate mutual moratorium on testing, even after the Soviet Union unilaterally stopped testing for eighteen months. The State Department even issued a statement to the effect that a test ban could not be negotiated so long as nuclear deterrence was an element of national security — presumably forever.

Finally, it is worth noting the Administration's failure to attend diligently to the needs of treaty verification. This omission is perhaps surprising — for the Reagan Administration has been vociferous in launching allegations of Soviet treaty violations. But the past eight years have seen a deterioration in U.S. satellite monitoring capability; our ability to inspect the Soviet Union by remote sensors has lagged. This degradation is partly a transitory phenomenon, due to the general upheavals in the U.S. space program, but it is also largely due to the predictable operation of the fourth principle, regarding limited funding capacity. As more and more monies are diverted to insatiable projects like SDI, less is available for less glamorous but more important demands such as satellite reconnaissance.

IV. GOALS FOR THE NEXT ADMINISTRATION

Against this background, the goals of the next administration with respect to nuclear policy are clear. It should not expect to make major departures from the system of nuclear deterrence that has prevailed since the late 1940s. But within that system, certain policy changes should be implemented which emphasize that the purpose of strategic nuclear weapons is to prevent a nuclear war, not to try to win one.

The new administration should refocus strategic arms control negotiations to concentrate on unstable types of nuclear weapons rather than absolute numbers of nuclear weapons. Every effort should be made to move the deterrent systems of both countries away from MIRVed missiles, particularly the increasingly vulnerable ones such as those in fixed silos, and toward single-warhead missiles and slower but less vulnerable weapons such as bombers. For example, a principal goal of the United States should be to eliminate as many MIRVed land-based Soviet ICBMs as possible, including the entire force of SS-18s, the weapon in the Soviet arsenal that is most threatening to American strategic forces. Of course the Soviet Union will not give up these forces without significant American reductions in similar systems. So the new administration should be prepared to agree to dismantle the 50 MX missiles that are currently operational or in the process of being deployed. They are the most threatening and destabilizing of U.S. ICBMs, and they are too exposed to possible Soviet attack. Furthermore, dismantling them would allow the U.S. to deploy up to 500 warheads on other, more stable, systems and still remain within the limits and sublimits of any strategic arms control agreement.

Similarly, in future negotiations, in exchange for elimination of a significant number of MIRVed Soviet missiles, the United States should be willing not to deploy the silo-killing Mark-5 version of the Trident II missile, the version with the 475 kiloton warhead. The United States should also be willing to agree, in exchange for an appropriate Soviet concession, that it will not test or deploy a system of defense against strategic missiles. SDI has proved to be a potent bargaining chip, but it should be played before it loses its value — as it will when it proves infeasible to develop at an acceptable cost, or, indeed, at any cost.

In strategic negotiations, the United States should create room for itself to develop and deploy two new types of missiles, a mobile, single-warhead land-based missile such as the proposed Midgetman, and an equivalent single-warhead submarine launched missile. It should, however, seek agreement that neither side will ever again build a new type of MIRVed strategic missile.

Any prospect of complete nuclear disarmament is a long way off. When nuclear arms are reduced to very low numbers of weapons (e.g., 200 per side), the value of hidden caches and the threat from possible small nuclear forces of other countries would be much greater than they are today; to get below that level, we would need a level of constant, intrusive world-wide inspection that can barely be imagined at this point.

Meanwhile, we and the Soviets should try to work ourselves back to a more stable and less provocative deterrent. To pave the way, arms control agreements should encourage each side gradually to convert their missile forces on both sea and land to single-warhead systems, and to make the land-based systems less vulnerable by making them mobile.

A ban on underground nuclear testing should also be a major goal for the new administration; given General Secretary Gorbachev's demonstrated willingness to break new ground in permitting monitoring and onsite inspections on Soviet territory and his interest in halting nuclear weapon tests, major new restraints on nuclear testing are easily within grasp.

Whether the ban should extend to *all* nuclear tests or only to those that can be detected and identified with a reasonable number of seismic monitoring stations in both countries is a matter about which people can reasonably differ. Even a ban on tests above five kilotons would make a major difference in slowing the pace of new developments in the nuclear arms race. Given the much greater non-proliferation value of a complete, world-wide ban on testing, and the relative insignificance of the tests that could be conducted with very low yields, the United States and Soviet governments might well prefer to seek a truly comprehensive test ban.

Of lesser significance, the United States and the Soviet Union should confirm to each other that the only purpose of strategic weapons is deterrence, by declaring that neither will be the first to use strategic nuclear weapons against the territory of the other country or its major allies. Such a statement should not extend to a commitment to refrain from using battlefield nuclear weapons in Europe; such weapons have some plausible value in halting a major conventional attack. By contrast, there is no plausible basis for being the first side to use strategic nuclear weapons against a superpower or its close allies; such use would inevitably lead to mutual destruction. In theory, using strategic weapons to attack a few targets in the Soviet Union might persuade the Soviets to halt a tank attack on Germany, but in practice the Soviets would probably retaliate for strikes at their homeland by using nuclear weapons on European or American targets, and escalation to general nuclear war would be almost inevitable.

Finally, pursuant to the seventh principle, the new administration should improve the government's policy-making machinery to enhance the development of a rational nuclear defense policy. First, the president must personally ensure that his administration is not torn apart by feuding between the National Security Advisor and the Secretary of State that seems to have become endemic, as seen by the public battles between Kissinger and Rogers, Brzezinski and Vance, Allen and Haig and Poindexter and Shultz. Unless the president has a clear idea of why he wants some other arrangement, the Secretary of State should be the principal architect of foreign policy, and the Advisor's role should be to help the president to review the various options available to him, rather than to run a rival State Department out of the White House basement.

Second, the Director of the Arms Control and Disarmament Agency, virtually powerless during the Reagan years, should be restored as the principal person proposing and executing the President's arms control policies. Given the Agency's tiny size (about 200 people, including clerks and secretaries), this will be possible only if the Director has the complete confidence of the Secretary of State. Therefore, the president should allow his Secretary of State to decide who the Director of the Arms Control and Disarmament Agency will be, and the Secretary should choose a person in whom he or she has total confidence and to whom the Secretary can delegate considerable authority. In addition, to the extent that the Director is not personally also the ambassador who heads the U.S. teams at various negotiations, all such ambassadors should report to the Director rather than to the State Department. This practice, which prevailed during the Carter Administration but was later abandoned, is necessary to prevent circumvention of the Director and a chaotic form of policy-making.

Finally, a point that should be obvious nevertheless needs to be made. Arms control delegations, and the staff groups that develop their instructions, should be composed only of people who support the President's policy. Dr. Herbert York, who served as President Carter's ambassador to the nuclear test ban talks in 1979, reports that the groups supposedly supporting him were filled "with people more than half of whom were generally opposed to having a successful result," who were able to "take every small issue and raise it to a cabinet-level issue so that it took several months to decide anything."

We have a government of checks and balances, in which each major branch and indeed each major official has some impact on overall policy. But the next president would be making a mistake if he were to imagine that he can simply preside over a bureaucracy in which hundreds of people with intensely different views about nuclear defense policy fight never-ending battles among themselves. The president and his senior advisors must make some basic policies, and they must make it clear that those in the government who do not agree with those policies are welcome to transfer to agencies and projects where they will find their work more compatible with their views. Some important changes are needed in nuclear defense and arms control policies, and when the president has set his course, it should not be impeded by subordinates who take it upon themselves to save the country from the people's choice.

CONVENTIONAL DEFENSE:
The Defense Department

Gordon Adams
Stephen Alexis Cain
Natalie J. Goldring*

SUMMARY OF RECOMMENDATIONS

During the Reagan Administration, defense budgets have exceeded all previous peacetime levels. Inadequate management of defense spending, most recently exemplified by the Pentagon procurement scandal, has left a burdensome legacy. Spending growth has occurred without sound long-term planning, strong central direction of the Pentagon bureaucracy or the guidance of a coherent national security strategy. So the next president and Congress must establish restraints on current and future defense budgets to encourage the military services to eliminate waste and cancel unneeded programs.

The legacy of the defense budgets of the 1980s will inevitably shape the options available to the new administration. Substantial amounts of defense spending are already obligated in contracts. Further impetus for spending growth will arise from the cost of the weapons bought during the buildup, and from political and bureaucratic pressures to produce the next generation of weapons.

It is now possible to achieve greater national security at lower cost, especially in light of improved U.S.-Soviet relations and negotiations to reduce both nuclear and conventional defense forces. The following proposals are a beginning.

* Because the Pentagon will have to live with budgets that do not grow beyond the rate of inflation, it should prepare five year defense plans based on a range of assumptions about its budget, including zero real growth and reductions of two to three percent after inflation each year.

* The continuing development and production of the full range of currently planned strategic nuclear weapons should be reconsidered,

*Dr. Gordon Adams is Director of the Defense Budget Project in Washington, D.C. and author of The Iron Triangle: The Politics of Defense Contracting. Stephen Alexis Cain and Natalie J. Goldring are, respectively, the senior budget analyst and European analyst at the project.

and work on SDI should be limited to long-term research. These actions could yield substantial savings with little security risk. Strategic force plans should be reevaluated within the framework of a START agreement.

* The new president should examine proposals for new conventional forces skeptically, particularly those which involve acquiring weapons for deep strikes against Warsaw Pact forces. At the same time, the administration should pursue a verifiable European conventional arms reduction agreement. Such an agreement could decrease the concentration of those conventional forces along the NATO/Warsaw Pact central front that are most clearly designed for offensive use.

* The Defense Department should set priorities among the new weapons scheduled to enter production during the next administration. Some should be deferred until development and testing are completed, and others could be cancelled outright.

* Finally, the next administration needs to strengthen management at the Pentagon. It should fully implement the "Goldwater-Nichols" legislation, which increases the power of the Secretary of Defense, the Joint Chiefs of Staff and the theatre commanders relative to the individual services. It should also seek to reform the weapons acquisition process, requiring more competition and independent cost analysis and reducing concurrency between development and production. The next administration should also consider forming a new civilian acquisition agency to handle weapons purchases.

I. THE REAGAN LEGACY

The Reagan Administration's broad agenda of national security commitments cannot be reconciled with the limits on defense resources imposed by the federal deficit. Moreover, the next administration will have to deal with the increasingly visible problem of waste and fraud in defense acquisition, as well as errors and failures in military performance.

Given the growing mismatch between commitments and resources, it will be essential to reexamine the relationship between U.S. defense goals, missions and military forces and the funds available to them.

The Reagan Administration broadened the definition of the threats to American national security and of the military missions U.S. forces would need to fulfill. As Secretary of Defense Caspar Weinberger stated in 1982, "We might decide to stretch our capabilities, to engage the enemy in many places or to concentrate our forces and military assets in a few of the most critical arenas.... [T]he decision on how large our overall defense effort ought to be must be based on much broader and more fundamental judgments than some arbitrary and facile assumption about the number of `wars,' or fronts, that we must be prepared for."

The Defense Department's internal *Defense Guidance* defined this expanded national security mission more explicitly. American security, the *Guidance* argued, was best ensured by having the ability to fight and prevail in a protracted nuclear war, to bring war directly home to Soviet ports, to open a front against the Soviets in Asia, to carry out major combat activities in the Middle East, to maintain control over the high seas and to intervene rapidly with a significant level of military force in combat situations in the Third World.[1]

These goals provided the justification for significantly larger defense budget requests than those of preceding years. However, these goals were less useful as guidance for budget and force planning since they could be used to support almost any military procurements. According to an analysis by the Joint Chiefs of Staff, in order to carry out the Weinberger strategy, U.S. armed forces would have to grow from 16 to 23 Army divisions, from 13 to 24 aircraft carriers, from 24 to 44 air wings and from 304 to 1,308 airlift aircraft. The defense budget would have to be $750 billion higher than projected in the plan for FY 1984 through FY 1988.

Defense budgets and actual defense spending rose rapidly in the 1980s, though the force structure actually grew little despite the demands of the new strategy. The Pentagon budget doubled from $144 billion in FY 1980 to $295 billion in FY 1985, an average annual growth rate of 9.3 percent after inflation. By 1985, growth in defense spending began to conflict with attempts to control the federal deficit. Largely as a result of the Gramm-Rudman-Hollings deficit reduction legislation, passed in October 1985, defense budgets have been reduced 10 percent from FY 1985 to FY 1989.

By undertaking a rapid buildup without careful planning, the Reagan Administration has left a mixed legacy for its successor. This legacy includes an extensive modernization of military equipment, growing difficulties in controlling high levels of defense spending, a "bow wave" of new weapons systems emerging in the early 1990s, a danger of decline in the readiness and sustainability of existing conventional forces, uncertainty about the ability of these forces to perform their missions and uncertainty about the ability of the DOD to manage its budget and acquisition processes properly.

1. Defense Modernization. The centerpiece of the Reagan military buildup has been the modernization of U.S. strategic and conventional forces. Arriving in office in 1981 with a firm commitment to increase defense spending, the Defense Department allocated significant new funding to the acquisition of military hardware, primarily for programs projected by the Carter Administration. (The only major hardware programs initiated by the Reagan Administration in FY 1982 were the B-1B bomber and two new nuclear aircraft carriers.) As a result, Defense Department procurement budgets rose 113 percent after inflation between FY 1980 and FY 1985.

This growth in procurement helped fill out conventional forces with equipment first produced in the late 1970s or early 1980s. Approximately one-third of U.S. main battle tanks are now M-1 Abrams, 13 percent of armored fighting vehicles are M-2 Bradleys, 19 percent of attack helicopters are AH-64 Apaches, 13 percent of utility helicopters are UH-60 Black Hawks and 13 percent of navy combat aircraft are F/A-18s Hornets. Virtually none of these weapons had been fielded when President Reagan took office.

Most of these upgrades, however, cost significantly more than the force modernization programs of the Ford and Carter years. Comparing the first seven years of the Reagan administration to the previous seven, the Reagan Administration bought only five percent more fixed wing combat aircraft while paying 56 percent more for them, after adjusting for inflation, 73 percent more helicopters while paying 292 percent more and nine percent more tanks while paying 104 percent more. It is not clear that the increased capabilities of the new weapons justify their significantly higher cost.

2. Difficulty in Controlling Defense Spending. The rapid modernization program will also reduce the next administration's ability to control defense spending and to set its own budget priorities. The share of defense funding devoted to "investment" (procurement, research and development and military construction) increased from 38 percent in FY 1980 to 45 percent in FY 1988. This commitment to rapid defense "modernization" has created intense pressure for high defense spending in the 1990s.

When appropriations for defense investment grow rapidly, actual spending tends to lag behind budget authority, creating a backlog of appropriated but unspent funds. This backlog results because Congress "fully funds" weapons programs in a single appropriation, but the weapons take several years to build with payments made to the contractors in increments. Thus, while overall DOD budget authority grew 40 percent after inflation from FY 1980 to FY 1988, the backlog of unexpended funds grew 100 percent after inflation, to an estimated $266 billion. More than 80 percent of this backlog has been obligated to contracts and will almost certainly be spent in the coming years, barring the politically and legally difficult act of breaking defense contracts. As a result, although defense budgets began to fall in FY 1986, actual defense spending did not begin to decline in real dollars until FY 1988.

Because of these obligated defense funds, the share of defense spending that is "relatively uncontrollable" (due to prior-year contracts) rose from 20 percent in FY 1976 and 27 percent in FY 1980 to an estimated 40 percent by FY 1987, according to Office of Management and Budget (OMB) data. This "stern wave" of spending — e.g., when spending commitments already made push up levels of defense spending "from behind" — will limit Washington's ability to control overall defense spending.

3. Commitments to New Weapons: The "Bow Wave". The Reagan Administration's modernization program may well continue into the 1990s, as a new wave of programs emerges from the rapidly-expanding R&D budgets of the 1980s. Several new weapons are soon scheduled to enter production, including the C-17 cargo plane, SSN-21 submarine, LHX helicopter, the V-22 Osprey aircraft, a new Army tactical combat missile and new Air Force and Navy attack/fighter aircraft. A number of new strategic weapons programs are on the way as well. If all of these new weapons are produced, demand for defense procurement funding in the 1990s will increase competition for budget resources. Either defense budgets will have to rise, or funding to maintain readiness will need to be cut.

4. Military Readiness. The readiness of U.S. military forces may begin to suffer as a result of DOD's focus on military hardware. One early result of the Reagan defense budgets was an improvement in the salaries, morale and quality of defense personnel. In 1980, for example, just over half of Army recruits had high school degrees, as did over 70 percent of Navy and Marine Corps recruits and just over 80 percent of Air Force recruits.[2] By FY 1987, over 90 percent of new enlistees to all four services had high school degrees.[3] Military pay rose 39 percent during the same period.

Furthermore, the budget which funds the training of military personnel and the maintenance of military equipment (operations and maintenance — O&M) grew 29 percent after inflation between FY 1980 and FY 1989. However, statistical measures of training and maintenance do not show the same kind of improvement as pay and measures of prior education, and O&M funding started decreasing in FY 1985. Troops are spending less time in training and education programs today than in 1980. Flying hours for pilots of Army and Air Force tactical aircraft increased in the early 1980s, but have not improved in recent years, while Navy and Marine Corps flying hours have not changed throughout the decade. Data on "depot maintenance" backlogs, which reflect the amount of unrepaired military equipment, also show little improvement.

"Sustainability," or the ability to undertake combat for prolonged periods of time, has also not improved as much as one would have expected in light of the increase in resources. The services have moved closer to the targets they set for filling stocks of spare parts, support equipment and ammunition, crucial ingredients for sustaining combat. But they are now likely to fall short of their goals, since funding for these items has been cut back sharply recently.

Given the emphasis placed on military hardware, it will become increasingly difficult to provide adequate funding for readiness and sustainability in the future, a dilemma which will have to be resolved by the next administration and Congress.

5. Military performance. It is clear that the funding growth of the past seven years has significantly improved U.S. combat capability. U.S. military forces were not often used in combat during the Reagan Administration. The exceptions were the limited military operations in Lebanon and Libya and the invasion of Grenada. The policy justifications of all three actions can be questioned, and the Lebanon and Grenada operations exposed serious performance problems. The Lebanon operation was a failure, and while the invasion of Grenada could be considered militarily successful, there too the U.S. military had problems planning and organizing an operation in a combat environment.[4] In Lebanon, the use of the battleship *New Jersey* to fire artillery rounds into the hillsides was ineffective. Moreover, the Marines operating near Beirut were not only deployed in an extremely vulnerable location, but were also not provided adequate intelligence on military threats and the local political situation.

The Grenada operation was an apparent military success. Again, there were serious intelligence failures. In addition, poor coordination of communications between the military services made it difficult to use naval artillery to support Army units on the shore. A key problem was the incompatibility of communications equipment among the Army, Navy and Marines. In addition, despite relatively light ground fire and limited local resistance, the military lost nine helicopters (two in a collision) and took a week to carry out what had been planned as a two-to-three day effort.

According to a Senate Armed Services Committee staff report on the operations of DOD, the Joint Chiefs and the services, the problems in Grenada suggest "deficiencies in the planning and preparation for employment of U.S. military forces in times of crisis."[5] The report also concluded that the services often resist the authority of the Office of the Secretary of Defense on major issues and compete with or duplicate each other on minor ones.

6. Organization and Management. The management capabilities of the Defense Department and the military services during the Reagan Administration have created considerable concern. Attention has focused on DOD's system for managing the acquisition of weapons from the private sector. Debate and investigations in 1983 and 1984 examined the manner in which the Defense Department acquired spare parts; reviews in 1986 and 1987 focused on contractor abuse of federal procurement regulations. The integrity of the entire defense acquisition system was called into question by the procurement scandal of 1988, which focused on possible bribery, fraud and contractor collusion involving, principally, Navy contracts.

A great deal of Congressional and executive branch energy has been invested in the 1980s in attempting to reform DOD management. Among other actions, Congress has mandated the creation of a DOD Inspector General's Office, set the terms for increased competition in defense procurement, required contractor warranties on defense hardware and strengthened restrictions on the movement of DOD personnel to contracting companies with which they dealt while in public office or uniform.

In a 1985 report, the Senate Armed Services Committee attributed a significant part of the management problem to the weakness of the Secretary of Defense and the Joint Chiefs of Staff vis-a-vis the individual services. Furthermore, the JCS was found to be performing poorly as an advisor to the Secretary of Defense and the President. The Committee also found that defense missions were poorly integrated into the planning and budgeting process, and Congress was taken to task for "micromanagement" of defense budgets and acquisitions.[6] While these difficulties are long-standing, they were exacerbated by Secretary Weinberger's policy of decentralizing authority.

7. Constraints on Future Budgets. Perhaps the most significant defense legacy of the Reagan Administration is the federal deficit. In response to its rapid growth, the Gramm-Rudman-Hollings Act of 1985 set deficit reduction targets and required that defense and domestic spending share equally in any spending cuts carried out under that Act. This critical legislation turned the federal budget into a "zero sum game" among taxes, domestic spending and defense.

In response to deficit reduction pressures, Congress froze the FY 1986 defense budget at approximately the FY 1985 level. Subsequent automatic Gramm-Rudman-Hollings cuts in March 1986 reduced defense budget authority four percent (after inflation) below the FY 1985 level. Secretary Weinberger sought significant budget increases in FY 1987 and FY 1988 to make up for these cuts, but Congress reduced defense funding below inflation in both of those years. The White House/Congressional "budget summit" of November 1987 led to an agreement that defense funding for FY 1989 would be $299.5 billion, a slight decrease below FY 1988 in real terms and ten percent below the FY 1985 level in constant dollars.

While defense budgets remain substantially higher than in any peacetime year prior to the Reagan Administration, the end to budget growth makes it vital to reevaluate DOD budget assumptions, plans and programs. Although the FY 1989 budget submission by Secretary Carlucci appeared to make some concessions in this direction, it contained an optimistic forecast that defense budgets would rise two percent after inflation each year between FY 1990 and FY 1993. Further reductions will be needed by the next administration.

II. THE CHANGING GLOBAL CONTEXT FOR U.S. SECURITY POLICY

The Reagan defense program and budgets were based on the assumption that the Soviet threat was relentlessly expanding and that U.S. defenses were dangerously weak after a decade of neglect. The threat and the neglect were both described in sweeping terms, and revitalization of the U.S. military was considered essential for national security and foreign policy.

There have unmistakably been important changes in the international situation since 1980. In particular, the rise of Mikhail Gorbachev has made a dramatic difference in the internal and external policies of the Soviet Union. In the foreign policy arena, General Secretary Gorbachev moved quickly to conclude an agreement with the United States eliminating intermediate-range nuclear forces. The reductions brought about through this treaty, while militarily insignificant, are politically important. They may be a precedent for significant reductions of strategic forces and for unequal reductions in conventional military forces in Western Europe.

The opportunities posed by Soviet policy changes can already be observed in Soviet and Eastern European proposals for the Conventional Stability Talks (CST) in Vienna. However, the United States continues to define Soviet intentions in Europe as threatening and Warsaw Pact conventional forces as significantly superior to those of NATO. Nuclear arms control, it is often argued, makes it necessary for the United States and its European allies to expand their spending on conventional forces, so that NATO can still deter the Warsaw Pact. From this perspective, it has been common for U.S. spokespersons to call for "beefing up" conventional forces in Europe and to "bash" the NATO allies for what is described as their failure to carry a fair share of NATO's conventional military burden.

The realities of the conventional military balance in Europe and of the allied contribution to NATO's forces are significantly more complex and not nearly as unfavorable as this viewpoint suggests. NATO member countries maintain active duty military forces numbering well over five million people, along with large military reserves. NATO anti-armor forces, fighter aircraft and surface naval forces surpass those of the Warsaw Pact. The alliance also has significant advantages in logistics and support, and it substantially outspends the Pact on defense overall. In addition, our NATO allies make a major contribution to the alliance's military capabilities.[7]

This section focuses on policy options for forces in the European theatre, which consume approximately 60 percent of the U.S. defense budget.[8] Changes in Soviet policy and lower tensions in Central Europe present a new opportunity for progress in conventional arms reductions in this arena. Properly negotiated, such reductions could decrease the military confrontation in Europe while enhancing stability. Although such agreements are complex and would take years to implement, substantial political and budgetary rewards could follow for both alliances.

New possibilities for change may be arising in the area of superpower competition in the Third World as well. The agreement on Soviet withdrawal from Afghanistan is a sign that the Soviets may be rethinking the usefulness of military intervention in the Third World. Consequently, there is a possibility for future U.S.-Soviet cooperation in resolving regional disputes, or at least in reducing superpower involvement in them. U.S. and Soviet efforts to defuse the Iran-Iraq war also indicate such a trend. Further evidence of changes in Soviet thinking came in "The Requirements for Stable Co-Existence in U.S.-Soviet Relations," a recent report by a U.S.-Soviet group which included high ranking Soviet Communist Party officials together with former U.S. government officials. The group's statement recommended that the superpowers refrain from intervening militarily in local conflicts, either directly or through proxies. Adoption of such a policy by the U.S. and the Soviet Union could reduce the possibility of larger wars developing out of Third World conflicts.

Even though these new opportunities have become evident, there are signs that U.S. security policy may be focusing on increasing forces for intervention in the Third World, which have already been built up substantially during the 1980s. The Reagan Administration and its Commission on Integrated Long-Term Strategy have stressed the importance of devoting more U.S. military resources to forces designed for Third World conflict, and to aid for the participants in these conflicts, both governments and rebel groups.[9] Thus, in a time of shrinking budgets and expanding diplomatic opportunities, the Pentagon is seeking to continue to expand its missions, goals and forces for the Third World.

The next administration faces a new set of budgetary dilemmas and opportunities. The major dilemma stems from the growing gap between defense resources and commitments to global military capabilities, missions and goals. The new administration will be forced, as a result, to rethink national security policy. The opportunities grow out of the changes taking place around the globe, which make arms reductions and new forms of international cooperation possible.

III. THE OPPORTUNITIES FOR CHANGE

1. Strategic Forces. The new administration will face important decisions involving strategic weapons programs (see "Nuclear Defense" chapter). A significant number of the weapons programs in the procurement "bow wave" of the late 1980s and early 1990s are strategic nuclear weapons: the Air Force's Stealth bomber, Midgetman missile, advanced air-launched cruise missile, short range attack missile (SRAM II) and rail-garrison basing for the MX missile, the Navy's Trident II missile and the first phase of the Strategic Defense Initiative.

While conventional forces account for a much larger share of DOD resources than do strategic programs, the latter nonetheless absorb substantial amounts of funding — approximately $45 to 55 billion per year in the late 1980s. Strategic weapons funding has already received high priority in the budgets of the 1980s, and it is likely to grow even further if new strategic systems enter production and are eventually deployed. Given funding constraints, this growth may crowd out funds for conventional forces. However, if the new administration emphasized conventional programs, it could obtain substantial savings by cancelling some of the new strategic weapons and decreasing funding for the Strategic Defense Initiative. Decisions in this area need to be made early in the new term; the Reagan Administration has already given substantial budgetary and political momentum to these programs.

While the current arms control negotiations would seem to offer an opportunity to reduce strategic weapons spending, DOD currently plans to continue all of its strategic modernization programs, with the possible exception of the Midgetman missile, in the framework of a strategic arms reduction agreement. The United States could comply with the treaty by dismantling older weapons, while building the new systems as planned, saving little money.[10]

By contrast, arms control could produce substantial budgetary savings if it resulted in the cancellation of some new strategic programs, leaving both the United States and the Soviet Union with strategic forces consisting primarily of weapons already paid for and a mix of old and new forces. For instance the United States could forego production of the Trident II D-5 missile, the rail-mobile MX missile and the Stealth bomber, if we could thereby gain reciprocal restrictions on Soviet programs. The United States could also upgrade the force by deploying Advanced Cruise Missiles on the B-1B bomber and by building a silo-based version of the Midgetman missile. Another option would be to proceed with the D-5, Advanced Cruise and rail-mobile MX missiles, while saving money by foregoing the Midgetman missile and B-2 bomber. Such a treaty could save the United States as much as $10 to $15 billion per year in funding for strategic offensive weapons during the 1990s.[11] In addition, by restricting the SDI budget to some $2 billion per year, enough to sustain vigorous research but not enough for deployment, the Defense Department could save between $3 and 6 billion annually from current plans during the next president's term.

2. Policy Options for European Security. Military analysts generally agree that the U.S. should work with its allies to provide an effective deterrent to and defense against an attack by the Warsaw Pact. There is substantial disagreement, however, over how best to accomplish this objective. Even before the INF Treaty was signed, some analysts and military leaders suggested that action was necessary to redress a perceived Soviet/Warsaw Pact advantage in conventional forces. They emphasized procuring new weapons systems, especially those employing advanced technologies. Other analysts argue that European security can best be ensured through continuing the arms control process, focusing on conventional arms reductions. Others have proposed reconfiguring NATO and Warsaw Pact military forces in a more defensive mode as a way to decrease the likelihood of war in Europe.

* New Technologies and Follow-on Forces Attack. Analysts who support the continued modernization of NATO's nuclear and conventional forces argue that upgrades are necessary to replace nuclear forces eliminated by the INF treaty and to provide a conventional deterrent to Warsaw Pact attack. The Reagan Administration opposes reductions in the remaining tactical nuclear forces in Europe, arguing that these weapons — and even new ones — are essential to deter a conventional Warsaw Pact assault.[12]

In addition, DOD plans to acquire new conventional weapons systems designed to carry out deep strikes behind the Warsaw Pact front lines as part of the new NATO strategy of "follow-on forces attack." These include new intelligence and communications systems to assist in processing combat information and in targeting distant enemy forces rapidly, and longer-range conventional missiles to target Warsaw Pact troops, armor and supplies well behind the front lines.[13]

These programs are likely to be costly,[14] exacerbating the budget problem. The services seem to be proceeding with these acquisitions virtually without reference to the forthcoming conventional arms control talks. In light of the budgetary and arms control implications of these technologies, the new administration should review, in concert with our allies, the wisdom of proceeding with them. By terminating or deferring weapons designed for follow-on forces attack, the next administration could save approximately $1 billion per year;

savings would be significantly higher in later years when these weapons are scheduled to reach full-scale production.

    * *Reductions in Conventional Arms.* Conventional arms control is a second security option for the European theatre. In the past, the Soviets were apparently unwilling to accept intrusive verification measures or to acknowledge asymmetries in military forces, making arms reduction difficult. However, the INF Treaty carries out unequal reductions in nuclear forces, and the Soviets have stated their interest in conventional arms control, including asymmetrical reductions when necessary. The INF treaty also provides precedents for significantly more intrusive new verification procedures.

    Successful reductions in U.S. and European active duty military forces, in tandem with the Warsaw Pact, could increase military stability and save budgetary resources on both sides.[15] Through such negotiations, NATO and the Warsaw Pact could reduce their equipment and manpower levels, with each alliance retaining the capability to deter an attack by the other.

    Even if conventional reductions were achieved, however, they would most likely take time to negotiate and implement, since the issues involved are quite complicated. Potential roadblocks include reaching a common understanding on the existing balance of forces, establishing effective verification and enforcement procedures, and ensuring that an agreement would restrict offensive potential without decreasing defensive capabilities.

    It is also important to preserve relationships within the NATO alliance while pursuing such negotiations. For example, retaining some U.S. forces in Europe could reassure the West Germans that the U.S. is committed to their defense and discourage them from expanding their own conventional forces.

    * *Defensive Deployments and Changes in Doctrine.* A number of European defense analysts and increasing numbers of Americans are exploring the prospects for restructuring conventional forces in Europe. Such strategies are often described as "defensive defense," "nonprovocative defense" and "alternative defense." While the details of these proposals differ, they all would redesign forces so that they are no longer suitable for an attack on an adversary.

    Without committing fully to defensive defense as an overall doctrine, it may be possible for NATO and the Warsaw Pact to take some steps that would reduce the offensive capabilities of each side's forces without eliminating their deterrent value. The likelihood of reaching a defensive defense posture could be increased by negotiating restrictions on offense-oriented deployments such as forward based tanks, bridging equipment, destabilizing "deep strike" weapons and long-range attack aircraft. At the same time, NATO capabilities to withstand tank charges could be reinforced with barriers and mines that could be put in place quickly.

* Summary. Each of these European conventional force options needs to be considered in relation to the others. The Department of Defense is proceeding with a major effort to modernize its tactical nuclear and conventional forces, without examining the impact of this effort on conventional arms control negotiations. Analysts, particularly in Europe, are assessing alternative defense options, yet this work receives little attention in the United States and does not have a significant effect on arms control negotiations.

The next administration must consider whether upgrades of short-range nuclear weapons and enhancement of deep strike capabilities provide the most cost-effective and safest means of enhancing deterrence in Europe. This review should also explore the desirability of defensively-oriented options and their effect on stability in Europe.[16] Both of these options should be evaluated in the context of conventional arms reduction talks. Fiscal pressures on NATO and the Warsaw Pact could combine with diplomatic opportunity to allow both alliances to reduce military spending while increasing security.

3. New Starts versus Existing Programs. On a more immediate level, the new administration will need to decide whether to produce all of the new conventional weapons systems currently in the development stage. By moving rapidly towards production of the next generation of weapons, the Reagan Administration has created substantial pressure for its successor to produce them. It may be wise, in spite of this pressure, to cancel or postpone production of some of these weapons. The funds saved could help maintain efficient rates of production for systems currently in production.

If new starts proceed as planned, current production programs will bear the brunt of budget reductions. For example, the Air Force and the Navy are each planning to produce new, advanced tactical aircraft in the 1990s, while slowing down or even cancelling production of current fighter and attack aircraft programs (F-15, F-16, F-14, F-18, A-6, AV-8B) in order to free funds for new ones. It would be less costly to defer acquisition of the new aircraft, while buying those already in production at efficient rates. The Navy faces a similar choice with respect to new nuclear attack submarines, and the Army with respect to the next generation of helicopters.

Most current production programs began in the late 1970s and early 1980s, and therefore employ highly advanced technologies. The costs and technological capabilities of these programs are well defined. New production programs, on the other hand, involve technological hazards and unpredictable costs, potentially squeezing already limited future budgets and providing the services with fewer weapons and less certain capabilities. Given DOD's historical tendency to underestimate the costs of its new weapons, the new generation of weapons represents a substantial risk.

Moreover, in most cases, the new generation of hardware will be significantly more expensive than the old, continuing the trend of trading quantity of weapons for technological sophistication or "quality". Given budget constraints and the bow wave problem, the next administration should carefully review plans for new weapons starts and focus resources on improvements that can be made to existing generations of equipment, improving capability at much lower costs. Incremental gains may be more useful militarily than completely new technologies, and significantly less expensive. A prudent restructuring of the conventional weapons modernization program, emphasizing systems currently in production while deferring new starts, could save as much as $30 to 40 billion from Pentagon plans annually in the early 1990s.

William W. Kaufmann has described a strong conventional defense program for FY 1990 through FY 1994 which would save $192 billion from the program projected in the Pentagon's most recent five-year plan. Savings would come through replacing equipment at slower rates, while holding several new weapons in development, deferring production of systems such as the Army Tactical Missile System, the LHX helicopter, the SSN-21 submarine and the V-22 tilt-rotor aircraft. Kaufmann's proposal would also eliminate plans to expand the Navy any further, cutting it back to 570 ships while phasing out the three oldest aircraft carriers.[17]

4. Readiness and Sustainability versus Hardware. The new administration will also need to decide whether to give budgetary priority to investments in weapons or on the readiness and sustainability of military forces. Increases in defense spending during the 1980s have improved military readiness less than one might have expected because of the priority given to purchasing new military hardware. The risk of continuing this emphasis is that readiness and sustainability will deteriorate.

Since weapons are not delivered until one to four years after they are funded (even longer in the case of ships), weapons purchased with the high procurement appropriations of the mid to late 1980s will be fielded during the new administration. These new weapons will increase the demand for readiness and sustainability funding since, in most cases, they will be more expensive to operate and support than their predecessors.

The curve of funding for readiness and sustainability may already be falling behind these expanding needs. Beginning the next round of weapons modernization so soon after the last major set of modernizations would put readiness and sustainability funding further in jeopardy. Even if cuts in overall defense spending are necessary, the 41st President and 101st Congress should protect funding in such areas as depot maintenance, education and training, sailing and flying hours, all of which directly affect the readiness of the armed forces. In addition, more attention needs to be devoted to the adequacy of munitions levels for all of the services, and to shortfalls that may exist in funding for spare parts and support equipment for existing hardware.

5. Effective Management. A major part of the defense problem over the past decade results from the Defense Department's internal organization and its management of the acquisition process. Reorganizing DOD, reducing "waste, fraud and abuse," and prosecuting lawbreakers will not, in and of themselves, bring defense commitments in line with resources or control defense spending. DOD reorganization is an important ingredient in this process, however, since it could create more effective channels for communicating strategy and military needs to budget planners and budget limitations to strategic planners. Reform of the acquisition process can also play a role in reducing defense costs in the long term, thus helping meet military requirements within constrained budgets.

Before it initiates new proposals, the next administration should take a close look at the DOD reorganization legislated in the "Goldwater-Nichols" Act of 1987. The most important changes intended by this law are strengthening the role of the Joint Chiefs of Staff, designating their Chairman as the chief military advisor to the President and giving the Commanders of the Unified and Specified Commands increased responsibility for linking theatre defense needs to the DOD planning and budgeting process.[18]

These changes begin to address the twin "Achilles heels" of DOD planning and budgeting: the excessive autonomy of the military services and the lack of a clear relationship between military strategies, forces and missions and defense budgeting.[19] If DOD planning and budgets are defined less in terms of the separate interests of the military services, they are likely to be more effective. The heads of the military commands have an overview of the requirements for a given theatre (e.g., Europe or Southwest Asia), or military function (e.g., transportation). Their direct involvement in budget planning will help link budgets and missions more closely while setting constraints on the "sovereignty" of the services. As with many such reforms, however, these are just a beginning; the proof of their effectiveness lies in their implementation.

More "jointness" among the services and the strengthening of the central role of the Secretary of Defense could reduce inter-service logrolling and rivalry. In the longer run, the next administration should explore the relationships among military missions, seeking to eliminate redundancy and rivalry. As a first step, consideration should be given to redefining the Army's role in providing close air support to ground troops, a mission currently assigned to (and performed with reluctance by) the Air Force.

The other crucial DOD management issue concerns the acquisition process. A number of "reforms" have been legislated in this area over the past seven years, with at best unclear effects.[20] Perhaps the most significant change was the creation of an acquisition executive in the Defense Department. When the procurement scandal hit, the second such executive, Robert Costello, had already begun to weaken some of the reforms previously implemented: for example, the progress payment rate (payments for work done made monthly to contractors) will be raised from 75 percent to 80 percent in FY 1989; and fixed price contracts will be used less often for research and development.[21]

Congressional legislation cannot, by itself, produce effective Defense Department management. DOD also has had difficulty in restructuring its own acquisition process. As a result, it is essential to have a White House committed to reforming the acquisition process, setting budgetary limits as a management tool and fully supporting a Secretary of Defense and staff who understand the acquisition and budgeting processes. Without these conditions, reforms may occur, but little is likely to change.

Within the framework of such a commitment, some basic changes might contribute to more effective DOD acquisition:

* Greater competition in contracting needs to be encouraged, and DOD needs to report accurately and in detail on the extent to which such competition actually takes place.

* The use of detailed, independent DOD cost analyses of proposed weapons programs to compare with cost data reported by contractors could provide a measurement tool for keeping contractor costs proposals under better control.

* The investigative work and reporting of the Defense Department's Inspector General's office should be increased as one means of monitoring DOD acquisition practices and the implementation of acquisition policy reform.

* Serious efforts are need to reduce concurrency between the development and testing of major weapons programs and their actual production (concurrency is the practice of initiating production of a weapons program while development and testing program are still under way). Pressures to move rapidly to the production state while a system is still being developed and tested have raised production costs while making it more costly to cancel weapons systems (since substantial amounts of money are expended on production before testing is completed and a cancellation decision can be made). The DIVAD air defense gun was cancelled after $1.8 billion had been spent and more than 50 guns produced. Even though all 100 B-1B bombers

have been produced, upgrades to ensure that they will be effective penetrating bombers through the 1990s could cost an additional $8 billion. Problems of this kind may occur with the B-2 (Stealth) bomber and the Army's Tactical Missile System, both of which are being acquired with high levels of concurrency.

* The next administration should consider removing the military services from the process of negotiating, signing and supervising contracts for research, development and procurement of weapons and supplies. Instead, a civilian corps could be charged with managing and the acquisition process. This change would mirror acquisition management process in a number of allied countries, which appear to have significantly fewer management problems.[22]

IV. STRATEGIES FOR THE NEW ADMINISTRATION

The legacy left by the defense policies of the 1980s has created an urgent need for immediate action. Yet there are substantial obstacles to implementing many of the changes proposed in this chapter. The new administration will be able to control only a limited portion of defense spending, and it will have to deal with budgets already in place or proposed by the departing administration. There will also be opposition in the bureaucracy and the Congress to cuts in defense spending or cancellation of new systems.

Important policy details and choices concerning most weapons programs, however, inevitably involve the services. Thus, it must be made clear from the beginning that services choices are also constrained by resource limits and that priorities must be set. The new President and Secretary of Defense should make realistic projections of total defense funding over the next five years and instruct the services to adjust their plans to these levels. Given the current level of the defense budget and the need to reduce the federal budget deficit, the most that the services should expect is for their budgets to keep pace with inflation. DOD should develop program options based on zero real growth as well as on annual reductions of two to three percent after inflation, contingencies which are likely and which, with good management planning, should pose no threat to national security. Even after annual real reductions of three percent, defense funding in FY 1994 would be 19 percent higher after inflation than the FY 1980 level.

In addition to setting a long-range plan, it will be important to reflect defense priorities and policies in actual budgets as soon as possible. The president's first budgets will be crucial policy statements, affecting policies and programs which might be difficult to reverse later. Shortly after taking office, the new administration should be prepared to review the priorities set in the FY 1989 budget (which will be in progress when the 41st president takes office) and submit revisions to the FY 1990 budget (which the outgoing administration will have already submitted to Congress). Because of the proportion of these budgets committed to ongoing programs, major cuts will be difficult. Yet, actions early in the president's term can translate into significant savings later on.

One of the first tasks for the new administration will be to carry out the policy review described in this chapter. Only with a realistic assessment of missions, forces and capabilities can we construct a coherent, affordable plan for our defense. Any attempt to solve national security problems simply by increasing spending is doomed to failure.

NOTES

1 Quoted in detail in Richard Halloran, *To Arm a Nation: Rebuilding America's Endangered Defenses* (1986), Chapters 7 and 9.

2 Caspar W. Weinberger, *Annual Report to the Congress for Fiscal Year 1986* (February 1985), p.110.

3 Frank C. Carlucci, *Annual Report to the Congress for Fiscal Year 1989* (February 1988), p.152.

4 Material for this section is drawn largely from Richard Gabriel, *Military Incompetence: Why the American Military Doesn't Win* (1985); Richard Halloran, *To Arm a Nation*; James Coates and Michael Kilian, *Heavy Losses: The Dangerous Decline of American Defense* (1985); U.S. Congress, Senate, Committee on Armed Services, *Defense Organization: The Need for Change*, Staff Report (October 16, 1985), pp.363-70.

5 SASC Report, p.15.

6 SASC Staff Report, pp.81-82.

7 See Gordon Adams and Eric Munz, *Fair Shares: Bearing the Burden of the NATO Alliance* (Defense Budget Project, 1988). On the complexities of the conventional force balance in Europe, see Joshua M. Epstein, *The 1988 Defense Budget* (The Brookings Institution, 1987), pp.36-45; John H. Mearsheimer, "Numbers, Strategy and the European Balance," *International Security*, 12, No.4, pp.174-185; and Barry R. Posen, "Is NATO Decisively Outnumbered?," *International Security*, 12, No.4, pp.186-202; Senator Carl Levin, *Beyond the Bean Count: Real-*

istically Assessing the Conventional Military Balance in Europe (January 20, 1988). For an alternative view of the balance, see James Thomson and Nanette Gantz, "Conventional Arms Control Revisited: Objectives in the New Phase," RAND-N2697-AF (December 1987).

[8] This figure includes the costs of U.S. conventional forces in Europe or committed to redeployment in Europe, as defined in the NATO Defense Planning Questionnaire. It does not include U.S. strategic nuclear forces or a substantial part of the U.S. Navy. See DOD, *United States Expenditures in Support of NATO* (April 1985), unclassified introduction, p.2.

[9] Fred C. Ikle, *et al.*, *Discriminate Deterrence: Report of the Commission on Integrated Long-Term Strategy* (U.S. Government Printing Office, January 1988), pp.13-22.

[10] Congressional Budget Office, *Modernizing U.S. Strategic Offensive Forces* (CBO, November 1987), pp.40-45; Robert S. Norris, William M. Arkin and Thomas B. Cochran, *Nuclear Weapons Databook Working Paper: Start and Strategic Modernization* (Natural Resources Defense Council, December 1, 1987), pp.14-16.

[11] Stephen Alexis Cain, *The START Agreement: Strategic Options and Budgetary Impact* (Defense Budget Project, July 1988).

[12] Carlucci, *Annual Report to the Congress, Fiscal Year 1989*, pp. 242-243.

[13] See Office of Technology Assessment, *New Technology for NATO: Implementing Follow-On Forces Attack* OTA-ISC-309 (June 1987).

[14] For detailed cost data see *ibid.*, pp. 32-33.

[15] See Jonathan Dean, *Watershed in Europe: Dismantling the East-West Military Confrontation* (1986).

[16] Dean, *Watershed in Europe*, pp. 61-75.

[17] Testimony before the Defense Policy Panel of the House Budget Committee, June 21, 1988.

[18] See *PL 99-433*, "Goldwater-Nichols Department of Defense Reorganization Act of 1986," which provides that the Chairman of the Joint Chiefs of Staff shall be the "principal military advisor to to

the President, the National Security Council and the Secretary of Defense."

[19] See SASC study, *op.cit.*, pp. 4-5 and Stubbing, *op.cit.*, pp. 109-159.

[20] One year after its report the presidential "Packard Commission" expressed disappointment at the slow process of implementing its proposed reforms, which had been accepted by the Secretary of Defense. See John H. Cushman, Jr., "Pentagon Seen Changing Little in Arms Buying," *The New York Times*, July 15, 1987, pp. A1, B28.

[21] There is also growing defense industry opposition to the previously legislated acquisition reforms. See Rowan Scarborough, "Study: Profit Policies Imperil Weapons Firms," *Defense News, 9*, No. 18, p. 15.

[22] See General Accounting Office, *Weapons Acquisition: Processes of Selected Foreign Governments*, NSIAD-86-51FS, (February 1986); GAO, *Defense Organization: Advantages and Disadvantages of a Centralized Civilian Acquisition Agency*, NSIAD-87-36, (November 1986); and Andrew C. Mayer, "Military Procurement Procedures of Foreign Governments: Centralization of the Procurement Function," Report No.84-229 F, (Congressional Research Service, December 11, 1984).

HUMAN RIGHTS:
State Department

Holly Burkhalter & Aryeh Neier[*]

SUMMARY OF RECOMMENDATIONS

The new administration can do much to make human rights a key aspect of U.S. foreign policy. After years of the Reagan Administration's highly politicized human rights rhetoric, vast quantities of military assistance to governments which abuse their own people and virtual contempt for U.S. human rights laws, the American people are ready for a change in the 1990s.

The new president should insist that the State Department and our embassies abroad report accurately and thoroughly on human rights issues in every country. Ambassadors should be instructed to meet with and support human rights monitors abroad, and the U.S. should publicly condemn gross abuses of human rights by friend or foe.

The administration and Congress should make a thorough evaluation of U.S. foreign aid, and put our allies on notice that political imprisonment and killings, torture and disappearances by the authorities will result in a reduction or cessation of goverment-to-government assistance.

In keeping with new U.S. trade law, Washington should undertake a review of the labor rights practices of our trading partners and take steps to limit or suspend trade benefits to those countries which accrue an unfair trade advantage through suppression of unions or other violations of worker rights.

The new president should pay up our dues to interntional human rights organizations such as the Inter-American Commission on Human Rights, and work with our allies to pressure abusive governments to improve their human rights performances.

The following are key suggestions contained in this chapter regarding a vigorous human rights policy in the next administration:

* The new president should appoint a Secretary of State and advisors in the Defense Department, the NSC, the Treasury De-

[*] *Holly Burkhalter and Aryeh Neier are, respectively, Washington Representative and Vice-Chairman of Human Rights Watch, a New York-based human rights organizaiton including Americas Watch, Helsinki Watch, Asia Watch and Africa Watch.*

partment and the U.S. Trade Representative's office who share his commitment to human rights.

    * U.S. representatives at the State Department and in our embassies abroad should seek ways of supporting and protecting human rights monitors.

    * The U.S. should seek the cooperation of our allies in isolating abusive governments and in denying them international assistance, including multilateral development bank loans.

I. INTRODUCTION

    Despite the Reagan Administration's declared intention to repudiate the human rights legacy of the Carter presidency, the executive branch has been unable to avoid the issue thanks to constant scrutiny of its policies by the Congress, the press and the human rights community. Credit is also due to certain bureaucratic procedures put in place during the Carter years that were retained and even improved. For example, the first country-specific human rights reports required by law were skimpy and politicized under Presidents Ford and Carter but grew better with each passing year. The improvement continued throughout the Reagan Administration as political officers in embassies abroad became more familiar with the task and the State Department's Human Rights Bureau succeeded in persuading the Department's regional bureaus to speak more frankly about most governments.

    Despite the institutionalization of certain human rights activities, however, the Reagan Administration has failed to promote human rights on many occasions, and has frequently pursued policies which themselves caused great suffering. The explanation for these failures has generally included one or more of the following factors:

    * The Administration ignored human rights problems in some countries because it feared jeopardizing cordial relations with allies. An example was the executive branch's reticence about publicly condemning gross abuses of human rights in Tibet by the Chinese.

    * The Administration deprecated reports of human rights abuses because it feared that public criticism of an ally might weaken the offending government either within the country or internationally. This is a partial explanation for the executive branch's consistent policy of putting a good face on the deplorable human rights situation in El Salvador. Elliott Abrams, the Administration's first Assistant Secretary of State for Human Rights and Humanitarian Affairs and later the Assistant Secretary for Inter-American Affairs, emerged as a particular champion of El Salvador's deplorable human rights record.

* The U.S. itself was directly responsible for gross abuses of human rights by supplying considerable military and economic aid to forces which committed human rights violations and which could not exist, much less prevail, without outside assistance. The *contra* war against Nicaragua is the obvious example.

* The U.S. soft-pedaled criticism or failed to disengage from abusive regimes in the hopes that continued supportive relations would mitigate the repressive policies. The Administration's policy of "constructive engagement" towards South Africa is a case in point.

* The Administration ignored human rights violations or even lauded abusive governments through apparent ignorance, as in the case of Secretary of State George Shultz's January 1987 trip to Liberia, when he praised the Doe Government for nonexistent "progress" on human rights and described Liberia's grossly fraudulent election as "quite open."

* The Administration provided aid and maintained close relations with military institutions in countries with weak civilian governments, thereby bolstering the very elements which continued to engage in gross abuses of human rights. This policy, which was frequently justified on the grounds that U.S. relations with military forces had a "humanizing" effect on them, might be seen in U.S. relations with Guatemala following the election of President Vinicio Cerezo.

* The Administration refused to speak frankly about human rights abuses in an effort to encourage certain countries to distance themselves from the U.S.S.R. One example is the U.S. silence on human rights abuses in Yugoslavia.

* The United States equated protection of human rights with the mere holding of an election, meanwhile failing to denounce the destruction of civilian institutions. The Administration's policy towards Haiti in 1987 and 1988 demonstrates this approach.

* The Reagan Administration denied or explained away human rights abuses against certain victims, or even invited attacks upon them, because of their alleged political views. In the case of El Salvador, the Administration justified attacks on civilians living in conflict zones by the armed forces on the grounds that the victims were guerrilla sympathizers.

* The Reagan Administration used its reports and public statements as a platform to denounce human rights organizations and advocates with whom it disagreed, thus minimizing reports of abuses and jeopardizing the safety of monitors working in dangerous situations. For example, it attacked the principal human rights organizations in Honduras and the Philippines.

* The Reagan Administration supported and nourished some despicable violators because they were deemed necessary to the success

of particular foreign policy objectives. Thus the CIA employed Argentine military figures responsible for the "dirty war" to train the Nicaraguan *contras* in Honduras, and, in turn, the U.S. refrained from criticizing the military for its terrible abuse in Argentina. And the U.S. maintained cordial relations with Panamanian military strongman Manuel Noriega until 1988 because of his perceived support for the *contras*.

* The Administration sacrificed opportunities to ameliorate abuses in a misplaced effort to penalize its adversaries. In Cuba, for example, the Reagan Administration abruptly ended the processing of exit visas for Cuban citizens, including several thousand former political prisoners, as a reprisal for Fidel Castro's refusal to take back the large numbers of criminals who came to the U.S. in the Mariel exodus. For several years, the U.S. refused to restore regular immigration procedures in order to "pressure" Cuba on the issue and heighten tensions within Cuba by closing off the "safety valve" that immigration provided.

Against this backdrop of contempt for human rights, a new administration could become an advocate for rights, not an apologist of abuses. Before turning to specific recommendations, however, it should be emphasized that the indispensable element of a successful U.S. human rights policy around the world is the commitment of the president, his cabinet and his advisors to consider the protection of human rights as an important factor in all foreign policy decisions affecting either friendly or adversary governments. At the same time, an administration should not try to pretend that human rights are being defended when policies have a demonstrably negative impact on human lives.

II. THE STATE DEPARTMENT

Most opportunities for the executive branch to influence human rights are in the domain of diplomacy. The administration possesses a wide variety of diplomatic tools to advance human rights in various countries, including public or private criticism of abuses; regular diplomatic intervention on individual cases or on persistent abusive practices; meetings with dissidents and human rights monitors; objective and detailed human rights reporting in the annual State Department Country Reports and in cable traffic to and from our embassies; on-site investigations of flagrant abuses by embassy personnel; attendance at symbolic occasions such as funerals or political trials and vigorous support for international human rights efforts such as resolutions and special investigative rapporteurs at the United Nations and the Organization of American States.

Diplomacy works both ways, however. There are also a host of diplomatic signals we should avoid sending because they minimize pressure on violators and squander U.S. opportunities to encourage improvement. For example, administration spokespeople in Washington or in embassies abroad should not engage in public apologies, excuses or justification of gross abuses by our allies. If the administration seeks to correct the public record when it believes that reports of human rights abuses are in error, it should never use the occasion to discredit human rights monitors abroad who are frequently at risk, and it should never excuse abuses because of the alleged political affiliation of the victims. Human rights reporting, be it in the public State Department Country Reports, statements to the press, or responses to Congress should be neutral and objective and not distort the facts to advance other interests. Obviously, the administration must pursue a variety of interests *vis a vis* foreign governments. But in so doing it should neither overstate the extent of human rights violations in adversary countries nor minimize violations in allied countries.

Specifically, the State Department Human Rights Bureau can play an important role in helping guide human rights diplomacy for the entire administration. Because of the lack of support for a consistent human rights policy by top officials in the Reagan Administration, a consensus appears to have developed within the foreign service that a stint at the Human Rights Bureau is not career-enhancing. Nonetheless, the Human Rights Bureau has had some committed and capable staff during the Reagan Administration, who have struggled to have human rights concerns taken into account by regional bureaus. And the actual procedures for communication between the various bureaus are in place and do not require tinkering: inter-agency groups, including representatives of the Human Rights Bureau, meet to discuss questions of aid and trade, and the Bureau appears to receive relevant cable traffic. Still, explicit expressions of support by the President and Secretary of State for the Human Rights Bureau would enhance morale there and promote the Bureau's mandate within the bureaucracy.

Beyond an enhanced esprit at the Bureau, there are some mechanical ways to improve its operations. For example, the new administration should take particular pains to see that human rights information is included in the briefing material for top U.S. officials when they meet heads of state in the U.S. or when they visit foreign capitals. Some of the worst blunders of the Reagan years involved such visits and public appearances. The Assistant Secretary of State should not only be sure that his or her staff checks off on the briefing material and talking points which are prepared, but should insist upon briefing top officials personally so that critical human rights concerns will be raised and inappropriate signals avoided.

The key to effective advocacy within the State Department is for the Bureau to be headed by a real human rights advocate, who views it as his or her job to force the bureaucracy to consider the human rights consequences of policy decisions. If the Bureau is overruled, it is too much to expect the Assistant Secretary of State for Human Rights to break publicly with the State Department or the White House, except in the most extreme circumstances. At the same time, however, the Human Rights Bureau should not ever be put in the position of publicly excusing abuses or championing repressive governments. If the administration implements policies which have an adverse affect on human rights, the Human Rights Bureau should not be called upon to defend those policies or minimize the human rights consequences of them.

While a vigorous Human Rights Bureau would do much to enhance the new administration's human rights policy, it would be a mistake to compartmentalize the issue within the Bureau. A senior deputy within each regional bureau, as well as the political and legal bureaus, should be made responsible for vetting policy decisions for their human rights consequences, and for coordinating policy with the Human Rights Bureau. The National Security Council and the White House press and protocol offices should also be made sensitive to human rights considerations, and placed in regular contact with human rights watchdogs in the Human Rights and regional Bureaus. Human rights considerations must also be made an explicit factor in policies and programs under the Defense Department, the U.S. Trade Representative and the Commerce Department as well.

III. U.S. EMBASSIES

Appointing ambassadors who share the new administration's human rights concerns is, obviously, one of the most important aspects of human rights policy. But a fine ambassador alone is not sufficient to outweigh mixed signals from the Pentagon, the Trade Representative or the White House. For example, the Reagan Administration's ambassador to Chile for the past several years has been Harry Barnes — a seasoned diplomat and an excellent human rights advocate. His efforts in Chile were significantly undercut, however, by United Nations Ambassador Vernon Walters, who led efforts to dilute or scuttle international human rights initiatives on Chile, and maintained warm relations with Chilean military figures. The moral is, ambassadors who are committed to human rights function best with strong support from Washington.

Embassies should require not just the human rights officer (who is frequently a junior staff person) to monitor human rights, but *all* embassy personnel to be alert to human rights developments and to assist in monitoring and reporting. In countries where there are severe human rights problems, a senior officer should oversee human rights activities for the embassy, with the frequent involvement of the ambassador. U.S. embassies abroad cannot substitute for local human rights groups, and overworked ambassadors and staff cannot be expected to investigate every reported human rights violation. Nonetheless, adequate financial and personnel resources should be made available to embassies in countries with particularly poor human rights records so that reports of egregious abuses can be investigated.

In some embassies, "clientism" means that the embassy neither wants to nor can objectively monitor and report on human rights. Examples abound in both the Reagan and Carter Administrations: the failure of embassies to report squarely on human rights in Guatemala in the 1980s and Iran in the 1970s are well known. In such cases, which will be brought to light by the contrast between the reports emanating from human rights groups and those of the embassies, the Secretary of State should be willing to send in a high level representative such as a senior deputy from the Human Rights Bureau to undertake a study, or to make diplomatic representations.

Occasionally, the human rights situation becomes so serious that special monitoring teams should be put together for individual studies. Consider the Reagan Administration's decision to employ an independent investigator to examine the causes of refugee dislocation in Mozambique in March 1988. The investigator, a refugee specialist, interviewed Mozambican refugees and compiled a lengthy report detailing horrendous abuses by the RENAMO guerrillas, which was then publicized widely by the State Department.

IV. INTERNATIONAL ORGANIZATIONS

The United States should support strongly international human rights initiatives. The new administration should press the Senate to ratify the human rights covenants. The U.S. should pay up its contributions to the United Nations and the Organization of American States, and should consider enhanced contributions to their human rights instruments, such as the UN's Working Group on Disappearances and the Inter-American Commission on Human Rights of the OAS. The United States' representatives to these bodies should encourage specific and detailed reporting and condemnation of abusive governments, either friend or foe. During the Carter Administration, the U.S. representative to the Inter-American Commission on Human

Rights pushed strongly for the OAS to cite specific countries, and to adopt resolutions urging violators to carry out the Commission's recommendations. While the Commission continued to issue substantive human rights reports in later years, the Reagan Administration discouraged the naming of names by the OAS, which then abandoned the practice.

Certain international humanitarian organizations, notably the United Nations High Commissioner for Refugees and the International Committee of the Red Cross, play an extremely important role in protecting human rights and mitigating suffering. Contributions to these organizations — with no strings attached — should be increased. Moreover, the United States should use its diplomatic influence to encourage governments with poor human rights records to permit confidential visits and humanitarian activities by the International Committee of the Red Cross. ICRC presence is particularly important in situations of international or non-international armed conflict.

V. BILATERAL ASSISTANCE

U.S. law prohibits economic and military assistance to governments engaged in a pattern of "gross violations of internationally recognized human rights." These prohibitions were enacted in the mid-1970's by an activist, post-Watergate Congress sickened by the Vietnam War and a spate of brutal military takeovers in Latin America. In the same period, Congress ended a twenty-year program of aid and training to foreign police forces. These laws (and the best instincts of the Carter State Department) limited U.S. aid to Latin American dictators, though there is little evidence that they inhibited U.S. aid to human rights abusers in Asia and the Middle East. By the early 1980's, however, human rights laws fell almost entirely into disuse, with the Reagan Administration requesting and the Congress granting aid to repressive regimes around the world.

The new administration should assess how the military and economic aid we are providing to governments around the world affects human rights and the stability of civilian governments. Obviously, the question must be raised whether aid recipients face the kind of internal or external threat which poses a security risk to the U.S., and whether U.S. aid is justified on these grounds notwithstanding gross violations of human rights. It will likely be found, for example, that Turkey's strategic significance justifies the large amount of military aid it receives, and that military aid is required for the Aquino Government in the Philippines because of the significant threat to that government posed by the NPA guerrillas. In those cases, aid should be accompanied by public expressions of concern about abuses. The U.S. should also use aid as a lever to encourage such governments to purge torturers and killers from the armed forces and police, and to enact disciplinary procedures to prevent recurrences of abuse.

Leaving aside security considerations, many in Congress and the executive branch see military and police aid as a tool for reforming military forces which commit human rights violations — particularly in countries headed by civilian presidents, as in Guatemala and El Salvador. In fact, however, we do not believe that the case can be made that aid to foreign military forces limits human rights abuses or enhances civilian rule. A generation of U.S.-trained officers led bloody military coups in Argentina, Chile, Guatemala, Uruguay and Brazil. And U.S. training and aid to police forces under the auspices of AID's Office of Public Safety strengthened repressive foreign police forces around the world and, in some cases, expanded their capability for political repression considerably, as in the case of Brazil, Vietnam, Guatemala, Uganda and others. Police and military involvement in torture, political killings, disappearances and political imprisonment is not generally a function of poor training or lack of resources.

Political will — including a demonstrated commitment to investigation and punishment of violators within the police and military — is required to end gross abuses of human rights. No amount of technical training and aid absent that commitment will humanize or professionalize police forces. The case of Argentina is perhaps the most striking example of what can be achieved through such leadership: when President Alfonsin took office, he ended the practice of political imprisonment, torture and disappearances virtually overnight, and did so without foreign aid or training.

Some scholars have proposed that U.S. aid and training should be aimed at subordinating elite and powerful military establishments to civilian rule. The National Democratic Institute has proposed that *civilian* leaders from Latin America be provided with training in military issues so as to break the military's monopoly on the information needed to make national decisions on security, and that military and civilian leaders should be integrated in "confidence building" programs. And human rights advocates in Congress have proposed that the U.S. limit its direct dealing on military questions to the civilian head of state. Ideally, we should provide any aid directly to him and force the country's military to negotiate with their own president and legislature, rather than the U.S. ambassador or Congress.

While there is room for creative new approaches to the aid question, U.S. funds alone can't endow weak civilian governments with the authority to bring powerful and repressive military forces to heel. In general, U.S. assistance to military and police forces which are engaged in political abuses tends to nourish them — both symbolically and materially — and often at the expense of the civilian government.

While U.S. military aid and training is not sufficient to end human rights abuses, neither can it be said that the mere suspension of aid to repressive regimes inevitably mitigates their abuses. For example, the United States prohibited military aid to Guatemala on human rights grounds from 1977 to 1985, yet that country's military carried out the bloodiest repression in the hemisphere's history, killing scores of thousands of civilians. Similarly, an embargo on military aid to Chile since 1976 did not appear to restrain General Pinochet's reign of terror. In such cases, human rights policy should reflect an ancient maxim of medical practice: *Primum non nocere* (first do no harm). At the very least, the United States should disassociate itself from the violators, deprive them of aid and encourage our allies to do the same, and lead a campaign to ostracize them internationally.

The issue of aiding foreign governments in combatting their own drug problem will likely be an important foreign aid policy question confronting the new president and Congress. The U.S. is already heavily involved in supplying anti-narcotics assistance through a variety of means, including the Drug Enforcement Administration and the Defense Department. U.S. troops have even been involved directly, as in the case of Bolivia. Though the issue is clearly one of great importance to U.S. interests, Washington should scrutinize anti-drug programs carefully for their human rights consequences.

The following rules should apply: 1) U.S. support for a "war" on drugs should not enhance military power at the expense of civil authority. Extraordinary measures, such as the militarization of certain geographic zones and suspension of constitutional guarantees, should be discouraged. 2) Practices such as extrajudicial executions, torture and long-term imprisonment without trial are unacceptable and should not be employed against alleged drug traffickers. If such measures characterize foreign countries' anti-drug efforts, U.S. aid should be withdrawn. 3) "Drug wars" should not be used as a cover to achieve other ends, such as suppression of ethnic groups or political dissidents, and U.S. aid should be strictly limited to anti-narcotics efforts. For example, there is abundant evidence that the Burmese Government used U.S. anti-narcotics assistance to wage war against fractious ethnic tribes. 4) The human and environmental impact of U.S.-supplied defoliants should be carefully studied. There is evidence that massive use of anti-drug chemicals in Thailand and Burma has had a destructive impact on the lives and resources of some of the world's poorest and most defenseless people.

In the past several years, both the Congress and the Administration have displayed increasing interest in providing economic assistance to "civilian" institutions in various countries. The National Endowment for Democracy received some $18 million in fiscal year 1988, including $1 million for election monitoring activity in Chile, $600,000 for civilian institutions in South Africa and $1 million for Poland's Solidarity. While the notion of supporting civil society is attractive, the new administration could enhance this goal by adopting a multilateral approach and working with our democratic allies in supporting programs. Multilateral programs to support free independent press institutions, human rights groups, labor unions and political groups would be harder to be stigmatized by foreign governments. And the approach would provide some insulation from U.S. efforts at control or manipulation of recipient groups, and encourage more pluralism in the civil sector receiving the funds.

VI. MULTILATERAL ASSISTANCE

U.S. human rights law requires that American representatives to the multilateral development banks (World Bank, Inter-American Development Bank, Asia Development Bank and African Development Bank) must oppose loans to countries whose governments are engaged in a pattern of gross violations of internationally recognized human rights. The Reagan Administration has all but ignored the requirements of the law, and has opposed (through abstention, not by a "no" vote) only a handful of loans. An important issue at the banks is not just the United States' own vote, but the efforts it makes at the banks with other countries' representatives to "channel assistance toward countries other than" those which violate human rights.

The new administration should, of course, obey the law and vote against loans to governments with particularly poor human rights records. What about the question of influencing other countries' votes? While it would be desirable to have the support of our allies so that loans could actually be denied to gross violators, extensive U.S. politicization of the international lending agencies is not necessarily desirable. The sword cuts both ways: during the Reagan Administration, Nicaragua lost millions of dollars in multilateral development aid because of U.S. arm-twisting in the international financial institutions. In general, the U.S. representatives to the banks should mobilize their political resources against large structural adjustment loans to abusive governments. Structural adjustment loans — which account for as much as 20% of multilateral lending today — are particularly important in shoring up governments; they are also critical in persuading private banks to increase lending.

In addition to developing a workable human rights policy at the banks, the president and Congress should take a close look at the human consequences of the multilateral loans themselves. Critics in the development and environmental communities have reported on the damaging consequences to the environment and to tribal communities from numerous projects financed by the World Bank. Enormously expensive dams and internal migration projects in Brazil and Indonesia, for example, have uprooted tens of thousands of poor rural dwellers, ruined precious rain forests and disrupted fragile tribal cultures.

The Treasury Department's representatives to the development banks should work with other agencies of government as well as with environmental and development groups to come up with a strategy for evaluating the human impact of bank loans and ways of influencing the projects before the money is voted.

VII. HUMAN RIGHTS CONDITIONS ON TRADE

The issue of the loss of thousands of industrial jobs to third world countries, where wages are low and working conditions poor, has been raised throughout the 1988 campaign. And the 1988 Trade Act identifies worker rights abuses as "an unfair trade practice," permitting trade adjustments in reprisal.

Certain labor rights standards are already law, such as the 1985 provision of the Trade Act which conditions trade benefits under the Generalized System of Preferences upon governments' taking steps to assure the protection of fundamental worker rights (including freedom of association, freedom from forced labor, a minimum working age for children and humane conditions of labor). The statute also requires a yearly review process of petitions filed by private groups, and a report by the State Department on the status of labor rights in beneficiary countries.

The Administration's performance in implementing the law has been weak. While Chile, Rumania, Nicaragua and Paraguay lost their trade benefits on worker rights grounds, other more significant trading partners with poor labor rights records, including South Korea, got a clean bill of health. In one case, the U.S. Trade Representative, who is responsible for hearing petitions and bringing the abuses to the attention of beneficiary governments, refused even to review a petition on labor rights in El Salvador because the State Department opposed some of the unions which were particularly victimized.

A fresh approach should take a number of steps to enhance U.S. leverage on worker rights, as the new trade law requires. First, the U.S. Trade Representative should accept for review *all* petitions by human rights groups and labor unions, make a good faith effort to investigate them, and bring U.S. concerns to the attention of offending governments in the course of trade negotiations. Second, the State Department, in conjunction with the Labor Department, should upgrade the quality of its labor reporting (currently included in the State Department Country Reports on Human Rights). Labor attaches in our embassies abroad should meet with trade unionists from across the political spectrum, and make a particular effort to gather information on worker associations subjected to government repression. Third, the U.S. Trade Representative should publish the result of its annual review process, including the labor rights petitions which were filed, the office's evaluation of the allegations, a description of the representation made to the relevant government and a description of the government's response. Last, when governments fail to take steps to improve labor rights, trade benefits under the GSP should be revoked, as the law requires.

In addition to bilateral initiatives on labor rights and trade, the new administration should push for a working party at the General Agreement on Trade and Tariffs (GATT), and seek a multilateral agreement among GATT members which links respect for worker rights to trade relations. The U.S. offered a proposal for a labor rights working party at the GATT this year. This effort should be maintained and expanded in 1989, which should make particular efforts to obtain the support of our allies for the initiative.

There is one case where stronger trade sanctions are in order. That case is South Africa, with its pass law system; its extreme repression of labor union activity; political disenfranchisement of the black majority and consistent gross violations of internationally recognized human rights. The new administration should work with the U.S. Congress — not against it, as has the Reagan Administration — in finding ways to isolate South Africa economically, politically and diplomatically.

VIII. U.S. INTERVENTION

All the recommendations above stop short of calling for unilateral military intervention or U.S. efforts to overthrow foreign governments on human rights grounds. Though exceptions might be warranted when crimes against humanity are committed on the scale of Nazi Germany or Cambodia under the Khmer Rouge, the rule should be that military invasion, either directly or by proxy, should not be undertaken to promote human rights. For one thing, military intervention will likely worsen the human rights situation. For another, the actual reasons for the invasion are likely to be rooted in political and geopolitical considerations. The use, or abuse, of a human rights rationale to justify military intervention can only degrade the human rights cause.

Reagan's eight year effort to overthrow the Nicaraguan Government has been a bloody study in unilateral intervention. The creation and maintenance of an abusive and unpopular guerrilla force; direct physical attacks on the country, including mining its harbors; and a harsh trade embargo which has helped to beggar the economy have had devastating human consequences for Nicaragua.

Thanks to the Central American negotiations, led by Costa Rica's President Oscar Arias, U.S. intervention may at last be curtailed. At the time of this writing, a tenuous cease fire is in place and U.S. military aid to the *contras* has been suspended. Yet despite the terrors which intervention imposed on Nicaragua, the Democrats do not appear to a have a clear policy about its application elsewhere. Liberal Democrats in Congress clamored for intervention in Panama to remove the loathsome General Noriega, enthusiastically endorsed trade sanctions against Panama and cheered as the Administration reneged on its payments for the use of the canal. In a different case, many in Congress and the human rights community called for U.S. military intervention to disarm the Haitian army and paramilitary bands responsible for the massacre of Haitian voters in November 1987.

Human rights intervention should be aimed not at overthrowing governments or destroying their economies but at promoting human rights improvements, or, failing that, disengaging the United States from the abuses. In the case of Panama, U.S. policy should have been to withdraw support from General Noriega and promote reforms in the powerful Panamanian Defense Forces, rather than merely vilify the general and curry favor with his army in the hopes of provoking a military coup. In Panama, as in other countries, both the cause of human rights and U.S. strategic interests would have been better served by a consistent policy of support for democratic institutions, criticism of abuses by the authorities and pressure (in cooperation with our allies) for systemic reform.

THIRD WORLD DEBT AND DEVELOPMENT:
World Bank & International Monetary Fund

Richard E. Feinberg*

SUMMARY OF RECOMMENDATIONS

Traditionally, industrial countries provided capital to spur Third World growth. But since 1982, Third World nations have been obliged to transfer financial resources on a massive scale to industrial nations. This economically perverse and morally offensive transfer of resources from the poor South to the rich North is commonly referred to as the Third World debt crisis.

This crisis matters deeply to the United States. It threatens the solvency of money-center banks, is altering the structure of the U.S. financial system and has come to dominate the policies of the U.S.-created World Bank and International Monetary Fund (IMF). It has altered international trade flows and added to the U.S. trade deficit by forcing developing nations to trim their imports. It has become the central issue in U.S. relations with our hemispheric neighbors and with Sub-Saharan Africa. Financial pressures have unseated governments in developing nations and threaten fledgling democracies in Latin America.

Developing countries have been struggling to adjust their economies to these and other shocks caused by the international economy. Many governments in Latin America and Africa are seeking to make their public sectors more efficient, their industries more competitive and their social programs more equitable. Such reforms should generally benefit the LDCs (less developed countries) as well as the United States, since they promise to build heathier economies more integrated into global markets.

But the success of these reform efforts is jeopardized by the capital shortage caused by the reverse resource transfer. The paradox of

---

* *Richard E. Feinberg is Vice-President of the Overseas Development Council and formerly served in the Treasury and State Departments, as well as on the staff of the House Banking Committee.*

policy reform without capital investment is the central contradiction in the international debt strategy. A new debt strategy should better balance U.S. interests by sustaining the solvency of the U.S. banking system while stimulating growth in the debtor nations. Seeking to provide adequate capital for both creditors and debtors, a new initiative could be based on these five criteria:

* The net resource transfer should be consistent with growth targets. The World Bank and IMF should set country targets for new lending and debt restructuring that leave enough capital in the LDCs to permit adequate investment and growth.

* Countries should be treated on a genuinely case-by-case basis. Some nations have strong enough export performance to be able to fully meet interest obligations and reach growth targets. Other nations will require an alleviation of debt service.

* Debtor nations should pursue economic reforms that foster efficiency and equity. IMF and World Bank programs should explicitly address the distribution of the domestic benefits and costs of adjustment programs.

* Roughly equivalent contributions should be expected of all creditors. Each creditor can choose for itself whether it wishes to provide new monies or receive less debt service.

* All parties to the debt crisis should participate in designing the new policy framework. The U.S. government should convene a meeting of leading banks, major creditor and debtor nations and the IMF and World Bank to design a new debt strategy.

Such an international agreement, backed by friendly democratic states in the North and South, could be presented not merely as a banking or foreign aid issue but as a strategic initiative aimed at two major national security issues: the strengthening of economic development and political democracy in Latin America and Africa, and the reduction of the U.S. trade deficit through the growth of Third World export markets.

I. HISTORY OF THIRD WORLD DEBT

During the 1970s and early 1980s, developing countries borrowed heavily to finance balance of payments deficits caused by a volatile external environment — high oil prices, falling terms of trade and surging interest rates. Debt was also incurred to compensate for domestic policy errors such as chronic fiscal deficits, overvalued exchange rates and capital flight.

In the 1970s, commercial banks were flush with recycled petrodollars and other loanable funds and actively competed for Third World clients. Sluggish loan demand in the industrial world stimulated banks to turn to the rapidly expanding and credit-hungry developing countries. Fierce competition for market shares tempted inherently cautious banks to be aggressive; individual loan officers were rewarded more for the quantity than the quality of their international portfolios. U.S. bank exposure to non-oil exporting developing countries jumped from an estimated $34 billion in 1975 to $103 billion by 1982.

When commercial bank economists calculated that their less developed country clients would be able to service their mounting debts, they used a series of economic assumptions which seemed reasonable at the time but which history proved to be overly optimistic. Few analysts working in the banks or elsewhere foresaw the OPEC-induced energy price hikes or the nature and depth of the global recession of the early 1980s. These unanticipated twists of fate caught many LDCs in a double bind: real interest rates sharply increased, and with them the interest payments due on floating-rate debts at a moment when downward movements in most commodity prices had cut into LDC foreign exchange earnings. Alarmed at the sudden deterioration in creditworthiness of many LDCs, bankers closed their lending windows, effectively driving nations to the brink of default. The cumulative result was the famous telephone call from Jesus Silva Herzog, the Mexican Minister of Finance, to the U.S. Treasury Department on August 12, 1982, announcing that the Mexican treasury was dry and without means to meet debt obligations.

To avert a financial panic, the U.S. government, the IMF and the commercial banks successfully collaborated to mount a rescue strategy based on three elements: the debtors should tighten their belts in order to live within the new financial constraints; the creditors should reschedule principal payments while continuing to receive interest payments; and official and private lenders should provide some new financing to cover a portion of interest payments to debtors implementing approved stabilization programs.

In the debt renegotiations that followed, creditors have extended more generous rescheduling terms — longer maturity and grace periods, lower spreads over their cost of funds, and smaller upfront fees. In addition, commercial banks generally maintained normal trade and deposit facilities. Nevertheless, heavy interest payments continued, and relations between debtors and creditors grew more tense.

II. THE BAKER PLAN

In response to these rising tensions, the international debt strategy was modified in October, 1985, by then Treasury Secretary James Baker. Baker placed a new rhetorical emphasis on the political requirement to move beyond austerity to renewed growth and urged the commercial banks to extend modest amounts of new loans to support economic reform. Baker also abandoned his lukewarm posture toward the World Bank and urged it to play a central role in the future global adjustment process.

By 1987, however, it became evident that the "Baker Plan" was stalled. First, LDC growth had not resumed. In 1986-87, Sub-Saharan Africa remained stagnant. For Latin America, growth in 1987 was 2.3 percent, one point lower than the already sluggish rates of the previous three years. The average inflation rate (weighted by population) had risen to a shocking 180 percent by the end of 1987. And second, creditors became increasingly unwilling to extend new loans. U.S. banks have continued to *reduce* their exposure in Latin America, and official lenders have failed to fill the gap. Reflecting a general loss of confidence, the value of Latin American debt in secondary markets plummeted.

The triple whammy of domestic economic stagnation, anemic export revenues and mounting debt obligations overwhelmed Baker's debt strategy, which failed to improve the creditworthiness of the debtors. According to the World Bank, the ratio of LDC debt to GNP rose from 26 percent in 1982 to 38 percent in 1987, while the ratio of annual debt service to export earnings remained at the 1982 crisis level of 21 percent, and much higher for many countries. The notable exception to these distressing trends are the rapidly industrializing East Asian nations, particularly the "four tigers" — South Korea, Taiwan, Singapore, and Hong Kong — where phenomenal export growth has permitted the successful management of debt obligations.

The "bottom line" in North-South economic relations is the net transfer of financial resources — new loans minus amortization and interest payments. In the five years before 1982, LDCs received *positive* net resource transfers of $147 billion in medium and long-term lending. From 1983-87, net transfers abruptly and massively turned a *negative* $85 billion. For heavily indebted Latin America, the net negative transfer was especially severe, totalling an estimated $147 billion from 1982-87. Latin American countries annually transferred 4-6 percent of their GNP, and 20-40 percent of their domestic savings. For Latin America the net transfer fell somewhat in 1986-87, reflecting the decline in market interest rates and the concessions granted by commercial banks, but the two-year outflow of nearly $40 billion remained burdensome.

III. COMMERCIAL BANK ADJUSTMENT

While most LDCs continue to flounder, commercial banks have significantly strengthened their positions. By limiting new lending to debt-stricken nations, the banks have lowered the ratio of their

LDC exposure to their total assets and to their expanding capital base. More recently, banks have set aside substantial provisions against possible losses on Third World debt. So while banks remain vulnerable, they are less hostage to Third World debt than they were in 1982.

This improvement in their balance sheets gives the banks greater flexibility in dealing with their LDC debts. While the banks remain opposed to granting large-scale relief, more recently they have been willing to absorb partial losses through various financial mechanisms:

* **Debt-equity swaps.** Commercial banks may sell debt at a discount to an investor who wishes to exchange the debt for local currency to help finance an investment. Debt-equity swaps have been particularly common in Chile and Mexico, although their use is circumscribed by LDC concern to limit monetary expansion resulting from such conversions and to regulate investment policy. Non-governmental organizations are seeking to use swap mechanisms to gain resources for their objectives; for example, environmentalists could use the local currency for land management.

* **Buybacks.** When their debt is selling on secondary markets at a very deep discount, LDCs may want to buy back their debt in order to cancel it. The banks can use buybacks to receive a quick cash infusion and clean their books of evidently bad debts. In 1988, Bolivia used bilateral aid flows to buy back about $400 million in commercial bank debt at 11 cents on the dollar.

* **Debt securitization.** Banks may want to trade loans at a discount in exchange for a negotiable security, particularly if that new security or bond is to be treated preferentially to other debts, is backed by collateral or is guaranteed by an international agency. In early 1988 commercial banks exchanged $3.7 billion in loans at 70 cents on the dollar, in return for $2.6 billion in 20-year Mexican government bonds partially guaranteed by Mexican-owned U.S. government bonds held in escrow by the U.S. Federal Reserve Board.

Mexico had initially hoped to reduce by $5-10 billion the $78 billion it owed to international banks. The deal fell short of expectations because of fundamental conflicts over price and debt, while Mexico wanted to gain substantial leverage from any use of its cash reserves for debt management. The creditors also wanted the new securities to be safe: the U.S. government bond secured the principal, but the banks were unable to persuade the U.S. government or the World Bank to guarantee interest payments, whose present discounted value on the 20-year Mexican notes much exceeds the principal amount.

This struggle over the size of the discount and the sharing of the remaining risk will be at the center of future debt negotiations. Because aspects of the conflict are zero-sum, future bargaining is likely to be tough. However, there are possible outcomes which may minimize total losses and even produce some gains for all parties: public policy by the next administration is essential to help fashion such politically palatable outcomes.

IV. REFORM IN DEVELOPING NATIONS

Developing countries have been struggling to adjust their economies to the repeated shocks caused by the international economy. Most immediately, they have had to adjust to fluctuating costs of borrowed capital and gyrating prices for their commodity exports. More fundamentally, developing countries are seeking to keep abreast of global technological changes which threaten the competitiveness of their factories and farms. To assure adequate capital and technological modernity, LDC governments are striving to reorganize their political economies.

Throughout the Third World, governments are working to restructure their public sectors in order to gain financial solvency. Budget deficits are being slashed, often by raising taxes, cutting capital expenditures and reducing subsidies to state-owned enterprises. Some governments are trimming functions better left to the private or nongovernmental sectors. To husband scarce public resources, governments are targeting essential public programs to benefit carefully defined social groups.

At the same time, public-private sector relations are being revamped in many nations. In post-colonial Africa, the private sector was often associated with colonialism and foreign ethnic groups, while a strong marxist influence in Latin America pictured the private sector as essentially exploitative and foreign-dominated. These sentiments still exist, but are losing force with the passage of time, the waning of orthodox marxism, the strengthening of indigenous capitalism and the rising influence of pragmatic technocrats. While few intellectuals advocate unfettered markets and most reject Chilean-style liberalization as entailing extreme social costs, the efficiency of price mechanisms is being widely recognized. Increasingly the private sector is seen as a dynamic engine of growth, and governments are viewing private business as a partner rather than as a threat. The East Asian success stories are being studied for lessons in cooperation between government and business.

To increase exports, many governments have devalued their currencies and offered other incentives to the export sector. While the exact formula varies across cultures, most LDC governments pursue some variant of industrial policy in which export promotion plays a major role. Governments often seek to lure foreign investors — with their access to technology, capital and markets — into targeted export industries.

Mexico, for example, is undertaking a series of structural adjustments aimed at making the public sector more efficient and at increasing export earnings. In an effort to reduce the budget deficit and concentrate limited state resources, many non-strategic state-owned firms have been privatized. To make industry more competitive, the peso has been sharply devalued, and external tariffs have been dramatically slashed, to a maximum rate of 30 percent.

Argentina is moving more slowly, but in a similar direction. Most Argentine economists and a growing number of businessmen and politicians recognize the need for fiscal discipline and policy reform. The government is gradually liberalizing foreign trade, reforming the financial system, and privatizing a few state-owned firms. In order to close a chronic fiscal deficit, the government is struggling to raise taxes while holding down public-sector wages and consumer subsidies.

In 1986, the countries of Sub-Saharan Africa submitted to a United Nations Special Session the "Program of Action for African Economic Recovery and Development," which amounted to a frank admission of past mistakes and promises of major policy reform. The Africans regretted the overprotection of industry, the neglect of small-farmer agriculture, and the unplanned extension of state responsibilities beyond managerial capacities. In the judgement of the World Bank, "about half of the countries in Sub-Saharan Africa are already committed to serious reform." Common reforms include raising prices to farmers in the export sector, depreciating the currency to compensate for domestic inflation, and narrowing fiscal deficits.

For the most part, such reforms should benefit the LDCs as well as the United States. They promise to build healthier economies more integrated into global markets. If introduced with care, they can also enhance local equity; for example, more carefully targeted social programs may better serve the truly poor, while higher prices to producers can benefit small farmers.

Nevertheless, the success of these many reform efforts is jeopardized by capital shortage. In Latin America, investment rates have fallen from 23 percent of GDP in the 1970s to 15 percent in 1986. In many Sub-Saharan African countries, gross investment has become too low to maintain the existing capital stock, no less to generate new projects. However smoothly functioning price mechanisms may be, it matters little if there is no capital to seek the highest returns. However competitive the exchange rate, exports will stagnate if there is no capital to invest in the traded-goods sector. However earnest a government may be in its efforts to provide a favorable climate to business, the private sector cannot respond if it lacks investable funds.

The paradox of policy reform without capital investment is the result of the central contradiction in the international debt strategy: the requirement that the LDCs fully service their debts and therefore suffer a massive capital drain at the same time as they are attempting to build a new productive structure. While a few LDCs may be able to generate enough exports and savings to accomplish both objectives simultaneously, most LDCs have faltered under the strain.

V. NEW PRIORITIES: REDEFINING U.S. INTERESTS

The debt crisis has been costly to important U.S. interests:

* American farmers and manufacturers have suffered. As a result of the contraction in Third World markets, U.S. exports fell from $88 billion in 1980 to $77 billion in 1985. If U.S. exports had grown in the first half of this decade at the same rate as in the 1970s, they would have reached about $150 billion. Moreover, the actual and potential employment loss (if exports had grown as they did in the 1970s) amounted to 1.7 million American jobs.

* Economic exhaustion is threatening centrist, civilian governments in Argentina, Brazil, Peru and the Philippines. Friendly nations, such as Jamaica, Costa Rica and Mexico are struggling with severe social dislocations. The association of structural change with inflation and unemployment is creating a backlash which is reviving unhealthy nationalism and fueling political polarization.

* The debt crisis is a chronic sore point in U.S. diplomatic relations with the Third World. Rather than being seen as a source of economic assistance, the U.S. is being cast as a callous commercial power coercing poor nations to transfer hard-earned savings to the world's wealthy banking centers. Seizing this opportunity, the Soviet Union and Cuba have mounted a propaganda offensive in Latin America.

When the debt crisis first struck, the primary threat was considered to be the vulnerability of the major money-center banks, which had more than 180 percent of their capital tied up in loans to Latin America alone. U.S. policy understandably gave priority to safeguarding the banks' solvency, and thus to assuring the continuation of debt service. The adverse effects on other U.S. interests were either not perceived at the time or were considered secondary. Moreover, the money-center banks quickly organized and exerted a powerful, concerted influence over creditor-government policies. U.S. exporters, which were more diffuse and whose interests were less centrally engaged, did not respond in as well-organized or vigorous a way.

Debtor governments have gained some marginal concessions in debt negotiations, but they have remain divided and been unable to challenge the strategy espoused by the better organized commercial banks. Despite repeated efforts, debtor governments have been unable to form a united front equivalent to the *de facto* creditor cartel. Each debtor nation sits in isolation across the negotiating table from the chosen representatives of the combined banking world.

The stability of its financial system remains a paramount U.S. national interest. Collapse of the money-center banks would have dire consequences for the entire economy. Fortunately, by building capital and lessening the weight of their LDC exposure, the banks are now able to deal more flexibly with Third World debt. It is now possible to craft debt policies which better balance competing U.S. interests by paying more attention to LDC growth and democracy.

The commercial banks have continued to record profits on most of their Third World debts, but most financial analysts — whether working for the banks or independent investors — believe that substantial losses will have to be taken before the debt crisis passes. Consequently, money-center banks' equity values are depressed, in some cases to below their book value, and banks' exposure in major Latin American debtors is valued in secondary markets at around 50 cents on the dollar. In preparation for the day of reckoning, banks have set aside reserves equal to 25-30 percent of Third World assets.

VI. A NEW INITIATIVE: CAPITAL FOR GROWTH

A new debt strategy should better balance U.S. interests by sustaining the solvency of the banking system while stimulating growth in the debtor nations. Seeking to provide capital adequacy for both creditors and debtors, a new initiative could be based on these five criteria:

1. The net resource transfer should be consistent with growth targets. The World Bank and IMF should set country targets for new lending and debt restructuring that leave enough capital in the LDCs to permit adequate investment and growth.

2. Countries should be treated on a genuinely case-by-case basis. Reagan Administration strategy has insisted that all LDCs service all debts. Some nations, such as South Korea and Colombia, have strong enough export performance and the actual or prospective access to private capital markets to be able to meet interest obligations and reach growth targets. Other nations will require an alleviation of debt service; for some nations, the relief can be temporary, while for others more permanent "bankruptcy" arrangements will be necessary.

3. Debtor nations should pursue economic reforms that foster efficiency and equity. While these objectives may sometimes conflict at the margin, in most LDCs there are abundant opportunities to improve the allocation of resources while alleviating poverty. In particular, IMF and World Bank conditionality should explicitly address the distribution of the domestic benefits and costs of adjustment programs and should provide interested governments with ideas on how to protect the more vulnerable groups. Furthermore, more rational and open trading regimes, and less hostile treatment of foreign investment, would generally serve the interests of both the LDCs and the United States.

4. Roughly equivalent contributions should be expected of all creditors. Each creditor can choose for itself whether it wishes to provide new monies or receive less debt service, negotiating with each debtor the exact choice of financial instruments. A formula such as the present discounted value of each creditor's contribution could be used to measure rough equivalence. The industrial countries should provide the World Bank, the IMF and the major regional development banks with sufficient resources and the clear mandate to sustain positive transfers to debt-ridden nations undertaking reform programs at least until they resume growth. Whereas it is unreasonable to expect commercial banks to become a source of net capital in the foreseeable future, they should reduce their receipt of net financial resources.

To allow for such equitable arrangements among creditors, the restructuring of public and private sector debts, which occur in separate forums, should be more closely coordinated.

5. All parties to the debt crisis should participate in designing the new policy framework. The U.S. government should convene a meeting of leading banks, major creditor and debtor nations and the IMF and World Bank, to design a new debt strategy. This wider representation is likely to produce an outcome consistent with a more balanced weighing of U.S. financial, commercial and foreign policy interests.

Such a consultative process would help heal the rift in U.S. relations with developing countries, and particularly with heavily-indebted Latin America. At home, an international agreement backed by friendly democratic states could be presented not merely as a banking or foreign aid issue, but as a strategic initiative — as essential for the economic viability and therefore endurance of Latin American democracies and vital for maintaining warm hemispheric relations. Such a U.S.-Latin American development initiative would further serve U.S. national economic security interests by stimulating U.S. exports, thereby reducing the U.S. trade deficit.

Multilateral participation is not without its risks. The debtors might press for exorbitant demands or indulge in polemics. However, if the United States convened the meeting, carefully selecting the time, place and participants, it should be able to guide the agenda.

Invitations could be reserved for Third World finance ministries and central banks — those bureaucracies that have behaved so responsibly to date and that would have every incentive to demonstrate that closer working relations with Washington can bring real rewards.

To facilitate procedures and maximize focus, the first meeting might be limited to the major Latin American debtors. Separate meetings could be convened to address the special problems of the second and third tier of debtors in Sub-Saharan Africa and parts of Latin America and Asia — those whose debts are relatively small from a systemic point of view and manageable with some special alterations, and those whose economic situation is so desperate that only highly concessional solutions seem valid. Bilateral debts — including export credits, concessional assistance and military aid — weigh more heavily for many poorer debtors. The Paris Club routinely reschedules high percentages of both principal and interest, but several European nations have agreed to outright cancellation. Arguing that Congress would immediately deduct the amount of any cancelled loans from new aid, the Reagan Administration has abstained from official debt forgiveness.

Overall, this net transfer reduction strategy would overcome the tensions between debt service and investment needs, between external obligations and domestic reform. It would further U.S. diplomatic and trading interests without jeopardizing the stability of the banking system. Indeed, the financial system would be strengthened in the long run.

VII. FINANCIAL ENGINEERING

This new debt strategy also provides the mechanisms for overcoming the conflicts regarding the pricing and securing of new financial instruments. Calculations of capital adequacy — of debtor nations and financial intermediaries — would help establish the depth of discounts. More cooperative relations among industrial-country governments, the multilateral agencies and the commercial banks would facilitate the sharing of the remaining risk. Where banks accept sizable discounts, or are willing to reduce interest payments, official agencies could partially guarantee debt service, for example, by insuring remaining interest obligations on a multi-year, rolling basis.

Once the basic framework has been established at the political level, financial engineers could go to work to fashion instruments that best meet the needs of all parties. New capital flows could be stimulated through creative collateralization or partial guarantee schemes. Methods for debt reduction mentioned above are debt-equity swaps, buybacks and debt securitization. Additional concepts include the conversion of debt or debt service into local currency, performance and commodity-indexed bonds tied to the debtor's economic performance or to an index of commodity export prices, partial interest capitalization and the partial write-off of existing loans. Creditor-country governments will have to work with banking regulators, accountants and tax authorities to remove unwarranted obstacles to the use of such instruments.

Since the capital markets have already anticipated substantial losses, cleaning up the banks' books could actually lift the banks' standing. A more rational debt strategy would also enhance the value of the banks' remaining exposure by increasing the capacity and willingness of the debtor nations to meet their payments obligations. With their leaner, clearer portfolios, the commercial banks would be better positioned to compete in the rapidly evolving world of integrated capital markets.

Calculations of the impact of debt relief on bank capital suggest that even in the event of significant write-offs, only a very few of the major U.S. banks might not be able to meet the capital requirements that the Federal Reserve has established for 1992. The few vulnerable banks might be able to restructure their operations to meet the capital ratio targets, or be absorbed by other players in the shifting world of global finance. Moreover, it might be possible to grant relief not through principal reduction but through interest-rate reduction or capitalization, thereby avoiding a direct "hit" to banks' capital bases.

VIII. BUDGET REQUIREMENTS

The proposed debt strategy has two budgetary costs. First, it requires authorizations for official agencies who must provide new growth capital to the Third World. They need additional funds to maintain positive net transfers, to be able to catalyze private flows and to have influence with developing countries in the design of economic reform strategies. Fortunately, the impact on the U.S. budget of major capital injections into the World Bank and IMF is surprisingly small. The World Bank is seeking a $75 billion general capital increase, but since only 3 percent must be paid in cash (the remainder being covered by guarantees), the U.S. direct contribution is only $420 million over six years. Since U.S. contributions to the IMF can be withdrawn upon request, they are counted as U.S. reserves and so are not a budgetary outlay.

The second potential budgetary cost results from any losses incurred by the commercial banks that are shared with the Internal Revenue Service. Estimating the revenue losses, however, is extremely difficult. In the past, banks have paid little to no U.S.

taxes on Third World business, but laws governing the taxation of foreign source income are changing and new IRS and other regulatory rulings are expected. Whatever the tax loss, however, it would at least partially be offset by the increase in tax payments coming from U.S. exporting firms and their workers that experience the benefits of more rapid growth in debtor nations. Moreover, under current policy the banks are certain to sustain losses — in perhaps even greater amounts and without the offsetting benefits.

IX. POLITICAL-BUREAUCRATIC STRATEGIES

Only the White House can provide the balance of interests and the decisive leadership required to deal successfully with Third World debt. To competently tackle the growing list of momentous international economic issues, the White House needs a greatly enhanced capacity for economic policymaking. Placing this new capacity within the National Security Council would make sense in terms of collating economic and foreign policy interests, but would only work if the NSC adviser or his/her senior deputy were genuinely interested in economics and understood the linkages.

The State Department's presence in the making of international economic policy has declined markedly. While the Treasury Department ought to remain the lead agency in international economic affairs, State needs to rebuild its capacity and clout to assure that foreign policy interests are taken into account, in order to balance Treasury's concentration on financial interests.

A new debt strategy would affect the operations of numerous regulatory bodies. The new administration should establish a Cabinet-level committee to coordinate the policies of the Federal Reserve Board, the Comptroller of the Currency, the Securities and Exchange Commission and the IRS, as well as the U.S. creditor agencies (Eximbank, the Agency for International Development and the Departments of Defense and Agriculture). In addition, the Financial Accountants Advisory Board (FASB) must be consulted and persuaded. Only a full-court press that involves all of these institutions will produce a coherent, consistent strategy.

And only a new president can provide the initial direction and credibility to undertake such an immense task. With his direction and a Cabinet-level committee, the governmental authorities in the creditor nations, commercial banks, international financial institutions and the debtor nations can then work together to severe this financial gordian knot.

NOTES

1 The World Bank, *World Development Report* (1988), Table 1.4, p.31.

2 *Ibid.*, p.30.

3 United Nations Economic Commission for Latin America and the Caribbean, *Economic Survey for Latin America and the Caribbean, 1987: Advance Summary*, April 1988, p.45, Table 16. U.N. ECLAC defines the net resource transfer to include short as well as long-term loans, direct investment and official transfers less net interest and profits.

4 World Bank, *op cit.*, p.28.

5 Inter-American Development Bank, *Economic and Social Progress in Latin America: 1987 Report*, p.24, Table III-1.

6 John W. Sewell and Stuart K. Tucker, and contributors, *Agenda 1988: Growth, Exports and Jobs in a Changing World Economy*, 10-11 (1988).

7 For a fuller set of recommendations for the World Bank, see Richard E. Feinberg and contributors, *Between Two Worlds: The World Bank's Next Decade* (1986).

8 For a fuller treatment see Overseas Development Council, *The Role of Banking Regulation in Third World Debt Strategies*, May 1988.

9 Unpublished, author's calculations.

INTELLIGENCE:
National Security Council &
Central Intelligence
Administration

Jeffrey Richelson*

SUMMARY OF RECOMMENDATIONS

The new president and Congress need to initiate major reforms with regard to both the NSC and the intelligence community.

With respect to the NSC, the new administration should:

* Clearly define and limit the functions of the NSC staff, even before legislation is passed. NSC staff should be barred from operational activity.

* Establish a workable NSC committee system in a short period of time, rather than emulate the year-long process of the Reagan Administration.

* Establish a component of the NSC charged with monitoring policy implementation.

The Director of Central Intelligence will have numerous tasks ahead of him. A crucial task will be to convince the president that his support is required both to back the DCI in his inevitable struggles with the Secretary of Defense and other intelligence agency heads and to help attain legislative action in the required areas. Beyond that the DCI should:

* Draft an Executive Order that enables the DCI to establish control over the entire intelligence community.

* Implement changes in intelligence priorities and secrecy restrictions.

* Develop intelligence charters in cooperation with the congressional oversight committees.

* Develop a coherent plan for matching priorities, collection systems and analytic capabilities within a reasonable time period.

---

* Jeffrey Richelson is a consultant to the National Security Archives and the author of several books, including The U.S. Intelligence Community and American Espionage and the Soviet Target.

* Substantially narrow the gap between collection capabilities and analytic capabilities.
* Regard covert actions as an exceptional tool to be used only in special circumstances, given the long-term failures of CIA covert actions in Guatemala, Iran and Chile.

I. HISTORY

The present structure of the U.S. intelligence community has evolved from a combination of legislative action and executive branch initiatives. The fundamental legislation, which established both the National Security Council and Central Intelligence Agency, is the National Security Act of 1947. The Act established the NSC to:

* Assess and appraise the objectives, commitments and risks of the United States in relation to our actual and potential military power for the purpose of making recommendations to the president about national security; and
* Consider policies on matters of common interest to the departments and agencies of the Government concerned with the national security, and to make recommendations to the president.[1]

Thus, the NSC was to coordinate the formulation of national security policy and offer policy recommendations. In order to carry out this function, it was to have a staff, headed by a civilian executive secretary appointed by the president.

The CIA was assigned five functions. It was to advise the NSC on the national security intelligence activities of Government departments, make recommendations to the NSC on the coordination of those intelligence activities, correlate and evaluate intelligence relating to national security and disseminate that information, provide "services of common concern" for the intelligence community and "perform such other functions and duties related to intelligence affecting the national security as the National Security Council may from time to time direct."[2]

The CIA was thus conceived of as an agency that would a) take the intelligence products of other agencies and produce a final product for the NSC, b) manage organizations such as the Foreign Broadcast Information Service (which monitors foreign radio broadcasts) and distribute its data throughout the intelligence community and c) conduct espionage operations. The provision in the National Security Act authorizing the CIA to perform "such other functions" was intended, according to a now declassified internal CIA memo, to permit the CIA to conduct conventional spying operations, not covert action.[3]

Both the NSC and CIA have evolved in ways not envisioned by their founders. The prominent role that has come to be played by most national security advisers was not foreseen — indeed the terms "Assistant to the President for National Security Affairs" and "National Security Adviser" were not coined until the Eisenhower and Johnson Administrations respectively. Nor has the intermittent use of the NSC staff to monitor policy implementation (primarily under Eisenhower and Nixon/Ford) followed from the original intent of the National Security Act. Finally, while both Henry Kissinger and Zbigniew Brzezinski conducted sensitive diplomatic missions, the operational use of the NSC as exemplified by Oliver North was solely a Reagan Administration innovation.[4]

While the CIA never attained the degree of control over the intelligence production process that was envisioned by its founders, it has attained a primary position in the intelligence community. It has been the major source of national intelligence production, particularly of the National Intelligence Estimates. Its Directorate of Operations is responsible for clandestine human source collection and covert action operations. Its Directorate of Science and Technology has played a pivotal role in the development of technical collection systems such as the U-2, SR-71, KH-11 and Rhyolite that have provided much of the hard data the United States collects on the Soviet Union and other denied areas of the world.

Other components of the intelligence community have been established by classified presidential directives or departmental/service regulations. Of major importance are the National Reconnaissance Office (NRO) and National Security Agency (NSA), both of which are housed in the Department of Defense. NRO is responsible for management of satellite reconnaissance operations while NSA is charged with intercepting foreign communications and non-communications signals (e.g. missile telemetry, radar signals).

Within the military services are fifteen different intelligence units. Some provide manpower to run oversees listening posts under the direction of NSA. Others are involved in intelligence analysis, human source collection, counterintelligence and monitoring nuclear detonations. Of particular importance are the service scientific and technical intelligence centers which study the capabilities and vulnerabilities of foreign weapons systems.

II. THE REAGAN YEARS

There are several notable aspects of NSC operations during the Reagan Administration. One is the high turnover rate of National Security Advisers: in eight years there have been five occupants of the position, compared to one during the Carter period and two during the Nixon-Ford years. Second, the NSC committee system grew to a bewildering array of committees. While previous administrations operated with a very limited number of Cabinet and sub-cabinet level committees (seven under Nixon and two under Carter) to deal with policy issues, an original three Reagan Senior Interagency Groups (for foreign policy, defense and intelligence) expanded to 25 by mid-1987, with 55 subordinate Interagency Groups.[5] Finally, as noted above, while both Kissinger and Brzezinski undertook sensitive and sometimes clandestine diplomatic missions while occupying the national security adviser's post, the extensive covert/paramilitary support operations of Oliver North were unprecedented.

Without full access to the secret history of U.S. intelligence activity during the Reagan Administration, it is not possible to draw up a completely accurate balance sheet. Successes — in terms of analysis, collection or intelligence technology — may still be hidden. It is possible, however, to identify some of the notable events that have occurred since 1981.

As a result of prodding by Senate Intelligence Committee Chairman David Durenberger, Director of Central Intelligence William J. Casey oversaw the production of a 40-page National Intelligence Strategy outlining the priorities and objectives of the intelligence community for the 1985-1995 period. The extent to which the document truly guides the activities of the intelligence community in a coherent fashion remains to be seen. However, the preparation of the document was an important first step in establishing a single statement of intelligence priorities and objectives to guide the entire intelligence community over a prolonged period of time.

There has been a substantial increase in the production of National Intelligence Estimates. CIA analysts have been instrumental in improving intelligence methodologies and thus reducing uncertainty concerning various aspects of Soviet strategic capabilities and behavior — in particular Soviet missile accuracy, nuclear test yields and the economic burden of military spending on the Soviet economy. On the other hand, there have been accusations, by the House Permanent Select Committee on Intelligence, National Intelligence Officer John Horton and others, that the content of estimates on Central America, Mexico and Soviet involvement in terrorism were influenced by political pressure.[6]

Several former intelligence officers were identified as sources of information to hostile intelligence services, resulting in varying degrees of damage to U.S. intelligence operations. Edward L. Howard provided the KGB with information that allowed it to identify several CIA sources within the Soviet Union. A former NSA employee provided information to the KGB about U.S. targeting of Soviet communications links and a secret project to tap a Soviet communications cable in the Sea of Okhostsk. The Howard case in particular reflected poorly on the CIA's judgement in handling an individual who received highly sensitive information and had shown signs of instability.[7]

The CIA was also embarrassed when KGB defector Vitaly Yurchenko left his CIA escort in a Georgetown restaurant to redefect to the Soviet Union. Although part of the reason for Yurchenko's discontent was beyond the control of the CIA, it is generally agreed that the CIA's handling of Yurchenko left much to be desired. At least as embarrassing was the revelation that a high percentage of the CIA's Cuban assets were actually serving as double-agents for the Cuban counterintelligence department.[8]

As a result of such setbacks, DCI William Webster has revamped the CIA's counterintelligence operation. Webster established a post of Associate Deputy Director of Operations for Counterintelligence, which considerably raised the status of the CIA's counterintelligence chief. Additionally, under the new framework, the new Associate Deputy Director can draw not only on the counterintelligence personnel from the Directorate of Operations but also on analysts from the Directorate of Intelligence and personnel from the Office of Security.

The CIA did apparently develop good sources within Eastern Europe. A high priority of William Casey was expansion of the CIA's human assets in Eastern Europe and the Soviet Union. By the end of Casey's tenure the agency had approximately 25 reporting sources from Eastern Europe. Among those, before he defected, was a long-time CIA informant who served on the Polish general staff and provided the CIA with advanced information on General Jaruzelksi's martial law plans.[9]

Perhaps the most damaging loss suffered by the intelligence community during the 1981-1988 period was the product of a decision made in the Ford Administration and reaffirmed in the Carter Administration: to make the space shuttle the delivery vehicle for all military satellites. The loss of the space shuttle as a satellite delivery vehicle, along with the fourteen month grounding of the Titan 34D booster, prevented the launch of any reconnaissance satellites. The result was that between August 1985 and October 1987 the U.S. was left with only a single aging KH-11 photo reconnaissance satellite to perform a mission usually performed by a two-satellite constellation. In addition, launches of new generations of imaging (i.e. photo reconnaissance and radar imaging) and signals intelligence satellites, designed for shuttle launch, have been delayed.

Also, the Reagan Administration has restored paramilitary covert action to a place as a prime instrument of foreign policy. U.S. aid to both the Contras and Afghan rebels has been significant, and in the latter case has undoubtedly affected the course of the war through the provision of Stinger missiles.

III. BUDGET

The budget for the entire intelligence community and its components is classified. Most recent estimates place the present budget at between 20 and 25 billion dollars. The bulk of the funds go to personnel expenses and the expenses involved in the research and development and operation of technical collection systems.

The budgets for individual components would appear to be approximately $1.5 billion for the CIA, $4 billion for NSA, $3-4 billion for NRO and up to $6 billion for the military components of NSA (with a total of 38,000 personnel and 60 overseas locations). The vast majority of the remainder of the budget is accounted for by the DOD and military service intelligence organizations.

Because of the classified nature of even aggregate budget figures, much less individual programs, it is difficult to suggest the precise budget figures required to accomplish a proposed set of intelligence activities. However, given the cost of surveillance systems required for general U.S. intelligence requirements and monitoring compliance with the INF and a future START treaty — ranging from several hundred million dollars for signals intelligence satellites to up to $2 billion for radar imaging satellites (satellites which produce photographic-like images through the use of radar rather than conventional camera systems) — it is hard to imagine a budget less than one in the $20-$25 billion range. Any savings that might be achieved by the eventual termination of the more costly covert action programs (such as aid to the Afghan rebels) or reduction in the several layers of military service intelligence bureaucracy would be more than overridden by the additional costs for the new surveillance systems.

IV. THE NEXT AGENDA

The next administration will need to address a variety of issues — procedural and substantive — with regard to the NSC and intelligence community. Some issues are virtually as old as the NSC and post-war intelligence community. Others have arisen or become more salient due to recent domestic and international events.

PROCEDURAL REFORMS

Each administration has established an NSC committee system and method of operation to suit the management style of the incumbent president. The next president needs to select a national security adviser who is perceived as an extension of the president's involvement in national security affairs and has direct access to and a personal rapport with him.

The next administration will need to develop a streamlined and workable committee system, avoiding the proliferation of committees that hampered the proper and effective functioning of the NSC during the Reagan Administration. Also, a segment of the NSC staff should be given the specific function of overseeing the implementation of policy by monitoring and reporting on the relevant actions of the State Department, Defense Department and intelligence community.

At the same time the NSC staff should be very explicitly barred from bureaucratic operations or covert intelligence activities. Such involvement prevents objective monitoring of implementation as well as possibly introducing bias in staff recommendations to those formulating policy.[10]

DIRECTOR OF CENTRAL INTELLIGENCE

The primary procedural issue with respect to the intelligence community is the role of DCI. Less significant, but still important, is the issue of defense intelligence organization.

From its very creation, the role of DCI has been a subject of controversy, being seen as a threat to the power and independence of the other intelligence agencies. In addition, the desire of the Secretary of Defense and military chiefs to be able to direct "their" intelligence assets has often placed the DCI up against their formidable opposition in exerting control over the intelligence community.

The first major extension of the DCI's power came with the advent of the Carter Administration. President Carter's DCI, Stansfield Turner, sought day-to-day control as well as budgetary control over the National Reconnaissance Office and National Security Agency. Turner argued that economic and other nonmilitary intelligence may be more important to the president and national decisionmakers than tactical military intelligence. Turner was opposed by Secretary of Defense Harold Brown, who argued that without control of NSA and NRO the military would not be able to properly advise the president on military matters.[11] Turner attained only a portion of his goals. When President Carter signed Presidential Directive 17, he assigned Turner responsibility for approving the budgets (but not daily control) of the NRO and NSA.

The underlying issues that made the powers of the DCI a subject of contention at the beginning and end of the Carter Administration still prevail. Satellite and other forms of technical collection can provide valuable information to both senior-level decisionmakers and strategic intelligence consumers (e.g. the President, Secretary of State, CIA) and tactical intelligence consumers (e.g. the military services and military commanders overseas) and thus create competing demands. This problem, known in the community as the "national-tactical interface," is likely to become even more acute. As the U.S. has deployed real-time collections systems (systems which can collect the data and transmit it back to Washington or another location virtually instantaneously) such as the KH-11 and a variety of real-time SIGINT systems, tactical users, such as theater commanders, can see a great value in the constant flow of intelligence data concerning the movements of opposing forces. The establishment of a variety of programs and installations to provide and receive such data reflects this value. As real-time capabilities expand and programs grow, strategic and tactical users will be in greater competition, which will manifest itself both in the selection of intelligence targets and in the nature of new technical collection systems.

A related issue of importance is the ability of the DCI to establish collection and analysis priorities. Within the national intelligence category there are many choices to be made as a variety of different types of intelligence fall in that category — military, political, economic, scientific and even sociological. The choice of collection and analysis priorities can have a significant impact on how senior decisionmakers will deal with a variety of situations.

Contrary to Harold Brown's complaint, we need to, if anything, enhance the power of the DCI to include day-to-day control over NRO and NSA and greater control of collection and analysis priorities.

One suggestion that has often been made is to separate the head of the intelligence community from the day-to-day control of the CIA. Thus, the proposed National Intelligence Act of 1980 and pending legislation have called for the establishment of a Director of National Intelligence. Its advocates argue that such a separation would place the head of intelligence community closer to the president (both physically and personally), allow the Director of National Intelligence to focus on the major intelligence issues and induce the heads of intelligence agencies other than the CIA to view the DNI as an impartial arbiter of intelligence decisions.

However, such a separation would probably be a setback for centralized direction of the intelligence community. The result would be a Director of National Intelligence with far less actual power than the present DCI since any DNI would have few resources compared to CIA, DIA, NSA and NRO. A resourceless DNI's attempt to direct their activities would be a losing battle. It was acknowledged in the 1975 Murphy Commission report that:

...to function as the President's intelligence adviser, it is essential that the DCI have immediate access to and control over the CIA facilities necessary to assemble, evaluate and reach conclusions about intelligence in all functional fields including political, economic, military and scientific subjects.[12]

The president's intelligence director also needs to have significant control over the development of technical collection systems and the other aspects of CIA activities (counterintelligence, HUMINT, covert action). In addition, separation of the DCI from the CIA will also retard the flow of information through the intelligence community, adding the Director of the CIA to the head of NSA and the Director of Naval Intelligence as guardians of "their" information.

Within the Defense Department and military services there is also need for reform. At the very least, the powers of DIA need to be strengthened to allow it to better direct and evaluate the intelligence production of the military service intelligence units. The more drastic solution of abolishing those service intelligence units is unlikely to be either politically feasible or managerially efficient.

PRIORITIES

One of the most important policy issues confronting the new administration is the question of priorities. Despite the vast resources devoted to intelligence collection, the United States cannot begin to collect complete information on all aspects of world affairs relevant to U.S. foreign and defense activities. Decisions on priorities can be of immense importance in determining future policy. Failure to collect in-depth information on a subject can mean an inadequate understanding of a particular problem or area of the world or an inability to deal with crises or combat situations when they arise.

A significant portion of U.S. intelligence collection and analytic activities has been devoted to the collection of intelligence relevant primarily to war-fighting. Included is much of the massive data base of potential nuclear targets from which actual war plans are developed. Some military experts, such as Edgar Uslamer, argue that gathering such information is an essential element of deterrence and that identifying and tracking "relocatable targets" (i.e. mobile ICBMs and mobile command posts) must be an extremely high priority for U.S. intelligence.[13]

Others, including the author, would argue that war with the Soviet Union is extraordinarily unlikely — precisely because the probable costs of such a conflict are too large to risk. Rather, the first priority of U.S. intelligence collection and analysis should be to permit the United States to conduct policies that help reduce conflict, promote further reform in the Soviet Union and Eastern Europe, encourage the further development of democratic and prosperous societies and determine the impact of a variety of international problems on the United States.

Specifically, the collection and analysis activities of the intelligence community should seek, with respect to the Soviet Union and

Eastern Europe, to determine the internal opposition to Gorbachev, implications of economic and other events for the stability of Gorbachev's rule, the ethnic situation in the Soviet republics, the impact of the "yellowing" (i.e., the increasing proportion of Asians) of the Soviet armed forces on military and foreign policy (as opposed to simply how to exploit the yellowing in wartime) and developments in Hungary, Czechoslovakia, Poland and East Germany. Outside the Soviet Bloc, collection and analysis should seek to provide understanding of the internal situations in a variety of non-European nations (including Brazil, Mexico, the Philippines, Argentina, Indonesia and others). It is also important for the intelligence community to focus on the likely impact of international economic events on the United States and to assess the threat from such problems as international narcotic trafficking, terrorism and nuclear proliferation.

Along with establishing such priorities it will be necessary to increase funding to allow the CIA and other intelligence agencies to hire a sufficient number of qualified analysts who can cover developing political, sociological and economic events throughout the world, whether it be ethnic problems in the Soviet Union, trends in the Arab world or the international debt crisis. Many CIA analysts have neither visited the country they are responsible for nor speak the native language. At other times understaffing has hurt intelligence community performance. Thus, the CIA had only one analyst assigned to Iran during the last days of the Shah's rule while NSA had only one individual assigned to Cuba during the Soviet brigade crisis.

A second issue of great importance facing the incoming administration is what technical collection resources will be deployed. No significant resources should be devoted to developing reconnaissance LIGHTSATs — that is, producing a large number of relatively cheap, limited capability satellites as means of insuring a continuing capability in the event of war. Diverting resources into LIGHSATs would inevitably sacrifice the advanced capabilities needed for supporting national security decision-making and treaty monitoring, a trade-off that would diminish U.S. national security.

Rather, it is important to produce a sufficient number of advanced space collection systems, both imagery and SIGINT, to ensure that adequate backup spacecraft are available in the case of unexpected launch failures. Further, one lesson of the Challenger disaster is that the deployment of intelligence (and other critical satellites) *cannot* be assigned exclusively to manned systems. Future intelligence spacecraft should be designed so as to be launchable on both shuttle and expendable launch vehicles.

A third policy issue, and one of the most contentious issues in the area of intelligence activities, is the use of covert action — which can range from monetary aid to a politician or political party to paramilitary operations to overthrow a government. Both Gerald Ford and Ronald Reagan have proclaimed the right of the United States to conduct a variety of covert actions.

Is this legitimate conduct for a democracy? Since U.S. covert actions in the late 1940s in Italy and France helped establish relatively stable democratic societies free of communist control, one school of thought believes that such future interventions should not be automatically ruled out. Others would argue that unless the possible election outcome will result in a direct physical threat to U.S. territory or installations, the United States should let democracy take its course.

While one can create many theoretical scenarios in which U.S. covert action is appropriate, the reality is less encouraging. The history of U.S. covert action is replete with examples of operations which have produced disastrous results for the people of the targeted country. Subsequent to the U.S. inspired overthrow of the Guatemalan government of Jacobo Arbenz in 1954, Guatemala has been subjected to over thirty years of brutal right-wing dictators, complete with death squads. Similarly, the installation of the Shah brought both the repression of the Shah and the madness of the Khomeini regime. In Chile, U.S. covert action certainly contributed to the replacement of the democratically elected regime of Salvador Allende with the brutality of Augusto Pinochet. More recently, U.S. support of the Contras has meant aiding a group labeled by the Council on Hemispheric Affairs as one of the "worst human rights violators" in Central America.

Nor have U.S. long-term interests necessarily been enhanced. Certainly, the long-term outcome in Iran has cost the United States that nation as an ally and created a foe that assaults U.S. vessels and undertakes terrorist attacks. Even the U.S. support of the Afghan resistance may have some long-term negative effects. Among the resistance groups, the four most powerful are those that want to establish an "Islamic state."

The new administration, counseled by the relevant congressional leaders, should consider covert action an exceptional tool to be undertaken only in special circumstances. It should not be used to interfere in the electoral process of foreign countries. It should not be used to place propaganda or disinformation in foreign media channels. Nor should it be used to support groups who have little attachment to democratic values and individual liberties.

Covert action is a tool to be considered in undermining a terrorist group or leader of a nation that engages in terrorist attacks. It might also be considered in situations where groups which share democratic values are under attack from a dictatorial/authoritarian regime.

However, even if the above criteria are satisfied, its use must be considered with skepticism. Past experience indicates that covert manipulation is much easier on paper than in practice.

It is also necessary for Washington to review the present secrecy attached to many U.S. intelligence operations. True, the United States intelligence community is the most open intelligence community in the world. However, the openness is a relative one since absolute secrecy concerning intelligence operations has been so uncritically accepted in many countries.

Clearly, intelligence operations require secrecy in a variety of respects. Secrecy is mandatory when revelation of a piece of information would allow a target of intelligence collection to take countermeasures to deny the U.S. information or conduct effective deception operations. This would include the identities of human sources, aspects of tradecraft that would allow hostile security services to identify and track human sources, foreign security shortcomings that permit intelligence penetrations (e.g. the failure to encipher messages on an important communications link), the ability to decipher foreign communications and some advanced capabilities of technical collection systems.

Unfortunately, rather than restricting secrecy to areas where it is imperative, the intelligence community has, either by design or inadvertence, sought to protect legitimate secrets with a buffer of trivial "secrets." Consequently, information that would permit the public to better understand U.S. intelligence operations as well as the validity of government claims about foreign nations is hidden from public view.

Information that should be made public includes the basic NSC Intelligence Directives which regulate the activities of the intelligence community and the names, basic functions and costs of space reconnaissance and other technical collection systems. Such information would allow an intelligent public debate over the question of intelligence priorities.

A former head of the National Intelligence Council, Richard Lehman, wrote that in 1947 those who established the CIA:

accepted the tradition of total secrecy characteristic of other national [intelligence] systems, notably the British, as appropriate for an American system...

In hindsight, this appears to have been a mistake, because it prevented the education of the public and all but a few Congressmen in the realities of intelligence, and because it protected intelligence itself from the oversight that could have required a greater sensitivity to public interests.[14]

V. STRATEGIES

Pursuit of the initiatives suggested above must involve a combination of legislative initiative as well as Presidential, NSC and intelligence community initiative. In some cases new laws are appropriate, in others executive branch directives and regulations. In yet other instances it is necessary to rely on the initiative of those holding office.

Legislatively, amendments to the National Security Act can precisely define the functions of the National Security Council staff — specifying its role in supporting policy makers and overseeing implementation, while at the same time barring an operational role. In particular, an amendment should bar NSC staff members from conducting intelligence activities of any kind.

At present only the Central Intelligence Agency is chartered by an act of Congress. It is time to develop charters for other agencies of the intelligence community that would define the extent of each agency's functions and responsibilities. It is also important to establish by law the powers of the DCI, rather than depending on executive orders or presidential directives which lapse at the end of each administration and may be more easily ignored than legislation.

Legislation can be employed to relax some of the present unnecessary secrecy restrictions. The chartering process can bring organizations such as the National Reconnaissance Office and the Army's Intelligence Support Activity into the open. In other areas, only action within the executive branch would be feasible.

Finally, attainment of other goals must depend on the president and those in management positions at the NSC and intelligence community level. Creation of a workable NSC committee system, geared to the management style of the president and national security adviser, cannot be established by *a priori* principles. Only the president and those within the intelligence bureaucracy can establish new intelligence priorities and ensure adequate funding for collection and analysis activities.

NOTES

[1] U.S. Congress, House Permanent Select Committee on Intelligence, *Compilation of Intelligence Laws and Related Laws and Executive Orders of Interest to the National Intelligence Community* (1983), p.7.

[2] *Ibid.*, p.7.

3 Lawrence Houston, "Memorandum for the Director, Subject: CIA Authority to Perform Propaganda and Commando Type Functions," September 25, 1947.

4 Zbigniew Brzezinski, "The NSC's Midlife Crisis," *Foreign Policy*, Winter 1987-88, pp.80-99.

5 National Security Decision Directive 276, "The National Security Council Interagency Process," June 9, 1987.

6 U.S. Congress, House Permanent Select Committee on Intelligence, *U.S. Intelligence Performance on Central America: Achievements and Selected Instances of Concern* (1982), p.7. John Horton, "Why I Quit the CIA," *Washington Post*, January 2, 1985, p.A15.

7 David Wise, *The Spy Who Got Away* (1987).

8 *Ibid.*; Michael Wines and Ronald J. Ostrow, "U.S. Duped by Cuban Agents, Defector Says," *Los Angeles Times*, August 12, 1987, pp.1,14.

9 Bob Woodward, *Veil: The Secret Wars of the CIA* (1987), p.306; Bob Woodward and Michael Dobbs, "CIA Had Secret Agent on Polish General Staff," *Washington Post*, June 4, 1986, pp.A1,A31.

10 Brzezinski, "The NSC's Midlife Crisis."

11 Joseph Fromm, "Inside Story of the Battle to Control Spying," *U.S. News and World Report*, August 8, 1988, p.27.

12 Commission on Organization of the Government for the Conduct of Foreign Policy, *Report* (1975), p.98.

13 Edgar Uslamer, "Moving Targets," *Air Force Magazine*, May 1987, pp.23-25.

14 Richard Lehman, "Memorandum for [deleted]," July 9, 1975.

Regulatory Policy

OVERVIEW:
The Health and Safety of America

Ralph Nader*

In no other area of government does the president's philosophy of power emerge more clearly than that of government regulation of business. Under Ronald Reagan the catchword was deregulation. This meant a reduction in enforcement of existing standards, a near cessation in issuing new standards, a revocation of some major rules and a marked diminution of industry studies, data collection and their public distribution. In addition to this regulatory freeze were repeated legislative attempts to weaken the statutory foundations for regulatory agencies and departments, almost none of which passed Congress.

While these moves were couched in the rhetoric of "getting government off your back" or letting the free market work its will, the results were more in the direction of leaving the people defenseless against corporate misbehavior. The list of exposures, absent the restraint of law, reads like a description of daily human interactions. Because safety and fairness regulation was aggressively abandoned, there was less safe food, autos, drinking water, household products, workplaces, energy and drugs and more fraudulent impositions in the financial marketplace of banking, insurance and securities.

Some of the economic deregulation continuing from the Carter years (transportation, telecommunications) seemed on the whole beneficial but not without a resurgence of abuses — due to weak antitrust and safety enforcement — that may bring calls for re-regulation. Broadcast and cable deregulation is also leading to greater concentration of media ownership, avoidance of "public interest, necessity and convenience" tests for broadcasting and sharply higher prices for cable.

During the Carter and Reagan years, an elaborate network of anti-regulatory think tanks, led by the American Enterprise Institute and the Heritage Foundation, produced torrents of reports purporting to demonstrate the failure of all kinds of regulation and the superiority of unrestrained markets (with the notable exceptions of federal programs designed to subsidize some businesses directly or through tax expenditures). The anti-regulatory catechisms reached

---

* *Ralph Nader, the well-known consumer advocate, has started dozens of ongoing organizations advocating consumer and environmental interests.*

such a fever pitch that the nation's declining innovation, productivity and "competitiveness" were even attributed to the stifling hand of regulation. Using a cost-benefit formula invariably tailored to the corporate conclusion, Reagan's Office of Management and Budget even found itself calling the automatic passive restraint standard not cost-effective. This view was challenged by Professor William Nordhaus of Yale who concluded that simply in dollar terms, apart from the reduction of human tragedies, the air bag was massively cost-effective.

OMB and a rigged "cost-benefit analysis" may play an unusually large role in the next administration for one reason: George Bush was chairman of the President's Task Force on Regulatory Relief from 1981 on, and regularly held press conferences to announce revocation of rules which were designed to save life, prevent disease and assure the economic rights of consumers. Can he transcend facile dismissals of regulatory approaches and restrict statutory missions in consumer, environmental and workplace arenas?

The performance of regulatory agencies described by the succeeding chapters in this section expose shortcomings in meeting these statutory goals. These failures of the Reagan-Bush Administration reflect the vulnerability of laws to uncontrolled bureaucratic discretion and political manipulation that the drafters of these laws either did not anticipate or did not desire to prevent.

After the first wave of regulatory agencies — commencing in 1887 with the Interstate Commerce Act — was subjected to academic appraisal through the 1950s, the progressive view was that the regulatees were controlling the regulators. Studies documented how the railroads, trucking companies and airlines twisted the Interstate Commerce Commission and the Civil Aeronautics Board to be their legal price-fixers and promoters of their anti-competitive interests, rather than defenders of consumers and competition. Congressional hearings and other reports showed how industry lobbyists — routinely nourished by the revolving door of former regulatory appointees — shaped the agenda and output of these agencies. When cracks appeared in agency charters that unfairly facilitated the lobbyists' successes, the latter's influence on Capitol Hill blocked any corrective amendments. (The correlation of PACs and votes is illuminated by Philip Stern's concluding chapter.) Consequently, the learning curve of experience was not allowed to improve the consumer protection work of the regulators who labored under a framework largely frozen in an early 20th century format.

For decades, the supposed beneficiaries of these agencies — consumers — were neither encouraged, informed nor empowered to participate in formal proceedings. Barriers of secrecy, lack of standing to petition or sue the agency, judicial deference to agency decisions no matter how insupportable, unavailability of experts and the prohibitive cost to participate combined to shut out consumers. The result: a cushy agency culture that embraced the purported regulatees.

During the Carter Administration, some of these barriers were diminished in various regulatory agencies and departments. Outreach programs designed to involve consumers were initiated by the U.S. Department of Agriculture, the National Highway Traffic Safety Administration, the Federal Trade Commission and the Civil Aeronautics Board. Modest intervenor assistance funds were available, for example, at the FTC for impecunious petitioners who were deemed able to present unrepresented viewpoints at a rule-making proceeding. An elderly group received such funds to prepare and make a presentation regarding hearing-aids. The procedural doors seemed to be opening to average people who lacked their own trade association. The image of the regulatory process as a closed tunnel between the regulators and the regulated began to recede.

But substantively, the inflation of 1979 due to rising energy prices gave commerce and industry an opportunity to stall or stop health, safety and other regulatory initiatives. By the time Reagan took office in 1981, the deregulatory bandwagon was underway as conservative polemicists made government into an all-purpose scapegoat for industry's ailments. Secretary of Transportation Drew Lewis told an auto-dealers' convention in early 1981, for example, that as far as he was concerned there would be no auto safety standards issued in the first term. This comment reflected the vast discretion to decline program implementation and do so with subsequent administrative impunity. The (alleged) regulatory officials felt very secure in comprehensively doing nothing and the Office of Management and Budget seconded this inactivity, pressuring for a weakening of the *status quo* in ways of dubious legality.

Notwithstanding the nominal "independence" of major regulatory agencies from the political control experienced by Cabinet Departments, in reality their consumer beacon is similarly directed by the White House, the OMB and the Congress, in that order. The courts can modestly push regulators by revoking standards that are "arbitrary and capricious," as the Supreme Court unanimously did in 1983 to the Department of Transportation's recision of the passive restraint standard #208 (*e.g.*, air bags). The courts can order agencies in some situations to act or to disclose data that could lead to a rule-making procedure. But judicial reviews, due to institutional constraints and the paucity of consumer litigants with staying power, is a most general boundary for feckless and irresponsible behavior.

White House leadership and citizen participation rights (*e.g.*, freedom of information, citizen petitions, fairer agency procedures, broader citizen standing to sue) can create a climate for reducing widespread abuses of corporate power. By providing regulatory limits and useful reports for the media and citizenry, regulatory officials can enhance a "productivity of justice" which spells less economic waste and fewer human casualties.

Federal regulatory actions, however, are not the only approach. Let me highlight some of the multiple roads to common objectives.

First, the leverage of federal, state and local procurement dollars are hardly used to stimulate innovation, safety excellence and environmental care. Together, these procurement dollars exceed fifteen percent of the nation's gross national product. Governments buy many of the same products and services that consumers purchase — automobiles, drugs, detergents, light bulbs, energy, telecommunications and more. Bright spots in the use of government procurement have included models of energy-efficient buildings and the purchase by the General Service Administration of 5,000 air-bag-equipped cars in 1985 that brought Ford Motor Company, and later the rest of the auto companies, back into the air bag business. Procurement could quickly expand the market for recycled products and photovoltaic solar units. In an era of budget deficits, the use of procurement in this direction should prove to be popular and economical to taxpayers and consumers alike. GSA Administrator Gerald Carmen, a staunch Reaganite and cool toward regulation, had just such an enthusiastic response to the air bag procurement proposal when I placed it on his desk in 1982.

Second, if government can use billions of tax dollars to subsidize profit-making business every year, it can certainly justify legislated programs designed to empower citizens and facilitate their banding together in non-profit advocacy and self-help groups. The Illinois state government now permits inserts in its mass mailings which invite people to join the Illinois Citizen Utility Board, a non-profit consumer group created by state law and empowered to participate in utility regulatory proceedings with a right to judicial review. Parallel groups could develop if the Postal Service, the Social Security Administration, banks, insurance companies and other regulated sellers were required to use their delivery system or billing envelopes to carry an invitation to their customers. Such inserts could help them in informing their own community intelligence, not just to participate in legal forums but also to privately bargain with large sellers.

Some of these arrangements are under way. Illinois, Wisconsin and San Diego have citizen utility boards generated by laws requiring carriage of solicitations in utility monopoly billing envelopes at no cost to the company. A Supreme Court decision in 1986 limited this right, but the now Chief Justice Rehnquist dissented, leaving open a possibility of revision in a later case. Private consumer group bargaining is well established between large associations of elderly (the AARP) and group health insurance sellers. Public Citizen has established *Buyer's Up,* which is a non-profit group representing some 12,000 households, negotiating discount home heating oil contracts with Washington, D.C.-area fuel dealers. Group buying is a major priority for the consumer movement of the future.

Third, state action can move to fill in the vacuum created by federal abdicators. Worker right-to-know laws regarding toxics in the workplace started at the state level. Other examples include laws protecting non-smokers from cigarette smoke in public places, as well as the recent successful California initiative raising tobacco taxes for use in preventive medicine and health coverage for the indigent. In fact, state safeguards regarding banking services, radioactive waste transport and nuclear power plants, to name a few instances, have led the Reagan Administration to move for federal pre-emption — a strange turnaround for self-styled states' righters.

Fourth, the government can use its public assets, such as the leased public lands, and its numerous and varied business subsidy programs to condition the kind of behavior that is already part of national policy — whether it is curbing soil erosion, controlling water and air pollution or directing research and development funds in similar directions. The Chrysler loan guarantee could have included certain R & D missions furthering auto safety, emissions controls and fuel efficiency, among other options. Federal export financing can restrain destructive activities affecting the rain forests in the tropics. After all, implementing a workfare program in return for federal aid to dependent corporations should resonate among genuine conservatives.

The central concept is *quid pro quo* — if government is writing the checks, directly or indirectly through special tax preferences, then it has the right to set certain performance standards. Bailing out banks, for instance, can be conditioned in part on the banks periodically permitting inserts in their bank statements that invite depositors to join together in a financial consumers association. The opportunities on this pathway are many and consequential.

Lastly, an imaginative competition policy that enforces the antitrust laws can unlock many of the wasteful consequences which have emerged from a) the merger and acquisition binge of the last decade and b) certain joint ventures and other restraints of trade so wholly ignored by the FTC and the Justice Department.

Problem-solving, which deploys our society's humane value systems on behalf of our economy and environment, is inherently suspicious of monistic ideologies that constrict the mind and its imaginations — especially the mind of the president. Problem-solving must meet an empirical test, not a rhetorical abstraction. The actual benefits of regulation — as detailed in *Freedom From Harm*, published in 1986 by Public Citizen and The Democracy Project — must not be obscured. They light the way for a society seeking workable approaches that permit the rule of law to tame the reign of power. The history of regulation is sufficiently rich in lessons to both caution and guide us and the next president in this direction.

ENVIRONMENT:
Environmental Protection Agency

William Drayton*

SUMMARY OF RECOMMENDATIONS

In the 1970s the second great wave of public health legislation in U.S. history promised to protect Americans from the tens of thousands of man-made substances pouring into their environment.

Providing these promised protections at last is one of the two most urgent environmental priorities of the 1990s. Success will require rebuilding deeply damaged institutions, restoring the voluntary compliance with environmental laws lost in the 1980s and imaginatively seeking out better ways of getting the job done at each step of the process:

* *Research*. Strategically managed research on indoor pollution, waste disposal alternatives and reliable monitoring for toxics would save both thousands of lives and billions of dollars. What's needed is boldly focused researchers backed by a budget investment roughly twice the current shrunken 1/2 of 1 percent of governmental expenditures on the environment (0.0006 percent of society's overall clean-up budget).

* *Screening*. Tens of thousands of chemicals in commerce and pesticides in the food chain will remain untested regardless of the laws until economic, reliable short tests for the full array of health risks (not just cancer) are devised. The administration should create a national challenge competition to fill this critical missing link.

* *Standards*. The need to slow and prepare for the greenhouse effect and to break this decade's Clean Air Act and acid rain logjam are already high on the new Congress's agenda. Once it frees research, makes broad chemical screening possible and installs effective monitoring systems for toxics, the pace of standard setting and follow-on field compliance work should accelerate.

---

* *William Drayton, a former Assistant Administrator of EPA, is a MacArthur Fellow, Chair of the organization Environmental Safety, and President of Ashoka: Innovators for the Public. Jim Gomes helped develop this paper.*

* *Compliance*. Restoring voluntary compliance will require regaining the confidence of millions of decision-makers roughly simultaneously. Presidential leadership and credible field follow-through are all necessary. The Administration should make certified environmental auditors central to the new process — a skilled force equal to the vast, complex task of testing and certifying the safety of hundreds of thousands of sources of pollution — since government can no longer do the job alone. Such environmental auditors would also provide a third force that would serve as a buffer between government and business and a powerful political insurance against future periods of anti-environment reaction.

* *Resources*. EPA cannot do twice 1981's workload with the same purchasing power it had in 1975 (before any of the statutes to control toxics were passed). It and the states need both new approaches and an increase of over $800 million in the operating budget.

The last several years have confirmed the long-standing warnings of environmentalists that mankind's multiplying impacts on the planet are altering the atmosphere, oceans and climate dangerously. Suddenly we are becoming aware that we've punched alarming holes in the earth's protective ozone layer; that in twenty years a fifth of all current species of life will be extinct; that we've increased the level of carbon dioxide in the world's atmosphere 25 percent since 1900 and consequently are beginning to experience what will increasingly become dangerously disruptive rising temperatures and sea levels and that the complex chain of consequent effects threatens the climate, the habitability of some regions and much of the quality of life.[1]

So the new administration's second major environmental challenge is to provide global leadership to limit the damage. It should propose (1) a global protection research program; (2) new or strengthened policy institutions and (3) a package of specific steps to limit the greenhouse effect, such as disincentives for carbon dioxide emitting fuels, incentives for solar and other benign alternatives and protection for the world's forests. A new, more stringent treaty is needed to preserve the earth's protective ozone layer.

Cabinet status for EPA would help accomplish both goals.

I. THIS DECADE'S LEGACY

In 1981 two historic currents collided: the second great wave of public health law in U.S. history and the Reagan Administration. For the environment and the public's safety, the effects of this encounter have unfolded over the ensuing eight years with the fatefulness of a classical Greek tragedy.

At the beginning of the 1970s, America set out to control the few relatively easily observed pollutants then recognized as problems, e.g. biological oxygen demand in water and sulphur in the air. By the end of the 1970s, successful environmental regulation had reduced many of these pollutants significantly. For example, clean water regulation had cut biological oxygen demand by 71 percent, phosphates by 74 percent and heavy metals by 78 percent.

However, within a few years of EPA's birth, science was demonstrating that hundreds of other substances that had been let loose were dangerous (even though often all but invisible). The public demanded action. Large bipartisan majorities in Congress and Presidents of both parties joined to launch the second public health revolution in American history. Just as an earlier generation insisted on the "sanitary revolution" once it understood that cholera and other epidemics were the result of uncontrolled biological contaminants in the environment, in the 1970s America promised itself to control the new threat from man-made contaminants.

From 1976-1980, the country enacted a dozen major new or fundamentally amended statutes promising to protect the public. Tens of thousands of suspect substances were to be screened for safety and regulated when necessary. Drinking water, food, the air, where we work and live, the products and materials we use and our land were to be made safe again.

Moreover, our rivers and streams were to become "fishable and swimmable" again. Instead of smog obscuring national park vistas — even in the Rockies and the Sierras — visibility was to be restored so that we could see the beauty of this country again.

According to the government's own data, adding these new responsibilities to EPA's ongoing tasks doubled its workload over the first several years of the 1980s. The 1980s was the decade when we had to deliver on these promises. But in January 1981, the Reagan Administration came to office with a different agenda — to remove the regulatory restraints it perceived to be limiting personal freedom and economic growth, most especially those developed by EPA.

Recognizing that it probably couldn't repeal the environmental laws and that trying to do so would entail large political costs, the Administration set out instead to neuter them by denying them the institutional capacity to get the job done. First, it sought, through a carefully planned series of 10-15 percent "modest" reductions over two years, to cut EPA's (inflation-adjusted) purchasing power by 60 percent. An organization cut in half obviously could not do twice the work.

Its personnel policies were even more radical. EPA's work is enormously technical and depends on complex patterns of specialization and interaction learned over years of institution-building (three quarters of the Agency's senior civil servants at the start of the Reagan Administration were scientists and engineers). The Administration was only stopped at the last moment from implementing a coordinated series of "reorganizations," mass firings, and other personnel initiatives that, using its own figures, would have meant that by June of 1982 only 300 of the 5400 headquarters and research staffers working eighteen months before would still be at their desks. The rest would have quit, been fired or been involuntarily bumped elsewhere and (usually) demoted. By the fall of 1981, the Agency was already losing staff at the rate of 2.7 percent *per month*.

Aeschylus never described so sure a calamity as the uncomprehending meeting of this historic wave of preventative public health legislation with a new Administration committed to "regulatory relief". The deep damage caused by this fateful collision defines and limits the prospects for the next ten years. The worst came quickly. Between 1981 and 1983:

* The typical EPA protective program lost twenty to forty percent of its purchasing power — far less than the Administration planned but still devastating in the face of the programs' multiplying workloads. University and other independent researchers suddenly lost two-thirds of their EPA support.

* Business confidence that competitors were being made to comply with environmental law was compromised, and with it the voluntary compliance that is essential to effective regulation. By late 1983 the General Accounting Office reported 78 percent *non*compliance with one of the highest priority requirements of the hazardous waste law and 82 percent *non*compliance (much of it continuous and gross) with the Clean Water Act. Instead of climbing steeply as the dozen new statutes requiring protection against toxics took effect, business investment in pollution abatement *fell* 38 percent. This loss of voluntary compliance multiplied the Agency's and the states' workload many times. (Going from 98 to 96 percent compliance doubles the number of firms requiring enforcement action. Imagine what 80 percent *non*compliance means.)

* One government study after another showed the Agency unable to undertake more than token portions of the key tasks assigned it. For example, of the 66,000 existing chemicals in commerce EPA is supposed to review for safety, it has (incompletely) screened less than one percent in the last decade.

*A series of scandals had damaged the Agency's reputation for professionalism — essential for a quasi-judicial organization. The staff that stuck it out were embarrassed to tell people where they worked.

* The average Presidential level position in the Agency saw almost two dozen appointees resign or be forced out under a cloud over

these years. The Administrator, Anne Gorsuch Burford, was forced to resign; her chief confidant had to withdraw before confirmation and left Washington facing the risk of indictment and disbarment; the Assistant Administrator responsible for the Superfund program went to jail; etc.

After the scandals, cuts and consequent public alarm, new moderate leadership under first William Ruckleshaus and then Lee Thomas restored professional standards and calm. Their restoration of professionalism and decency towards the staff preserved enough of an excellent institution that eventual rebuilding remains possible.

However, stalemate settled over the budget: From 1983 to the present the Agency's inflation-adjusted resources have remained roughly constant. However, not cutting the budget further still left EPA in an impossible situation. Only one small program, Drinking Water, has more than half the resources it needs to deal with its workload. (It has 58 percent.) *The Administration's proposed budget for the 1989 fiscal year would give EPA the same real purchasing power it had in 1975* — before the enactment of any of the dozen statutes requiring it to protect the public from toxics as well as the few, relatively simple pollutants it was charged with controlling in 1975. The imbalance between workload and resources worsened in the 1980s as Congress added new stricter standards and procedures and required EPA to regulate hundreds of thousands of new firms. For example, the number of pollutants the clean water program must control has increased more than twenty fold. The number of sources of pollution it must regulate, not including millions of sources of "non-point" pollution (e.g., agricultural runoff), has almost tripled. Nonetheless, the program's real purchasing power has been cut 43 percent.

The states cannot fill this breach. Their workload has grown faster than EPA's because more of it entails direct field work, because they too must implement all the new toxics statutes and because they suffer most directly from the loss of voluntary compliance. Nonetheless, between the 1981 (pre-Reagan) budget and the Administration's proposed 1989 budget, EPA's financial support for the states, adjusted for inflation, has been cut back 24 percent.

The Administration asked for $1,566 million for the 1989 fiscal year (in 1988 inflation-adjusted dollars). Analysis prepared by Environmental Safety, which relies overwhelmingly on government's own workload data, suggests the real need is $2,926 million (in 1988 dollars). This assumes no fundamental changes in either the current statutes or in EPA's modus operandi. (See chart on following page.)

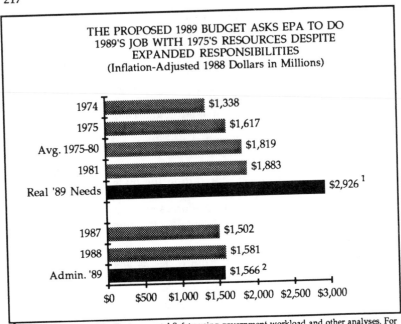

THE PROPOSED 1989 BUDGET ASKS EPA TO DO
1989'S JOB WITH 1975'S RESOURCES DESPITE
EXPANDED RESPONSIBILITIES
(Inflation-Adjusted 1988 Dollars in Millions)

1974 — $1,338
1975 — $1,617
Avg. 1975-80 — $1,819
1981 — $1,883
Real '89 Needs — $2,926 [1]

1987 — $1,502
1988 — $1,581
Admin. '89 — $1,566 [2]

$0 $500 $1,000 $1,500 $2,000 $2,500 $3,000

[1] Real needs estimated by Environmental Safety using government workload and other analyses. For further informatin, contact Environmental Safety.

[2] This figure includes $60 million in one-time compensation to pesticides firms for withdrawing two dangerous products. This hides a 3.7% further cut to EPA's muscle.

Not only has EPA been unable to implement the safeguards enacted in the last decade, but it has been severely handicapped and often entirely unable to address emerging problems. A few examples:

* Because pollution released inside a building can't disperse easily, concentrations inside are typically far higher than outside. People (especially the frail and vulnerable) spend much of their lives indoors. Yet the Reagan Administration has year after year sought to eliminate entirely even research regarding indoor pollution lest it trigger a massive new field of regulation. Indoor pollution of all sorts should be an urgent priority of the next administration.

* Action to control acid rain has been deferred for eight years.

* Knowing the levels of particular pollutants accurately in the air, water, and groundwater is fundamental for research, policy, standard-setting and compliance. EPA built national monitoring networks for the traditional pollutants it went after in 1970 but has not done so for the newer toxic pollutants. There is an urgent need to invest in developing effective monitoring tools to handle these new

pollutants. One consequence of this failure is that citizens can't learn what exposure levels they or their communities are experiencing.

* For at least fifteen years evidence has been mounting that the synergistic and cumulative impact of pollutants is significantly different from and more serious than the sum of the impacts of the individual substances. Yet the field's approach at each level (research, legislation, standards, field implementation) deals with one pollutant in one medium almost in isolation.

EPA should be a prime source of new ideas and experimentation in everything it does — from research to the design of individual consent decrees. That was its tradition, a tradition that has been losing ground to a sense of siege, of lost trust and respect, of the likely response to risk-taking being censure, not respect. This field cannot afford EPA becoming a bureaucracy.

II. A NEW ADMINISTRATION

A new administration and Congress will have to move quickly and very strongly if it is to escape the destructive logic of the last eight years. It must go about the long hard job of getting people to respect their biological and planetary limits.

BY INAUGURATION DAY

By Inauguration Day the new administration will have taken several fundamental decisions that will largely determine its ability to restore effective environmental protection. In each case inertia or inaction will lead to seriously harmful results.

First, the new government-to-be must replace the outgoing Administration's budget proposal with its own or live with the past's priorities for most of its first two years. This is a problem affecting all agencies, but the risks for EPA — for all the reasons expressed in the prior section — are especially great.

Those OMB staff who carried out the cutting are unlikely to propose significant change. Usually EPA gets its senior Presidential appointees late, long after State and Defense. Consequently, there may be no appointees of the new administration at the Agency until well after the budget has gone to Congress. Even if there are, they may not be familiar with EPA's complex budget and management needs.

If the Agency's budget needs are consequently not adequately addressed, it will be very difficult for the new administration to turn the Agency around. Even with quick, significant budget relief beginning in October 1989, it will be well into the new term before the Agency can begin to rebuild. It is urgent that the transition staff devote a good deal of its time to ensuring that the president-elect, his

White House staff and eventually his EPA appointees focus quickly on an honest, non-incremental set of budget options.

Second, the president-elect must think through how he wants to manage his line agencies. Does he want to lead through his line appointees? Or will he rely chiefly on large White House and OMB staffs, who in turn will try to keep the Departments in check through a series of controls? Given the painful history, this is an especially sensitive choice for EPA and several of the other regulatory agencies.

Almost all recent Presidents have started off saying they planned to follow the first model but have in fact fallen 70-90 percent into the second path. This pattern is largely set in the months right after the election. The president needs immediate help on his budget, and OMB is ready and anxious to show how essential it is. He needs other immediate staffing help, and the senior political and personal advisors who ran his campaign are the obvious, tried people to whom he will turn. Their skills, stature and role make them gravitate to White House jobs.

By contrast, most of the president's Cabinet appointees are not yet in place, let alone in effective control; and their deputies and assistants have not yet gone to, let alone emerged from, the by then clogged FBI clearance process.

Such a structure is an invitation for these staffs to cut the president off from his government. Their very drive to serve the president can be a snare if it lulls him not to make the considerable effort needed to lead his line Administration. Moreover, energetic staffers, especially if put in the bureaucratically ill-defined and insecure environment that has characterized many White Houses, are very likely to respond by competing with the departments for access, responsibility and power.

The problem of Executive Office/line department relationships is probably more troubled in the regulatory field and for EPA specifically than it is in most other parts of the government. The Agency perceives itself, properly, as a quasi-judicial agency responsible for setting difficult regulatory balances defined by statutory criteria. Strong interventions by (often junior) Executive Office staffers responding to requests from and appearing to rely heavily on information and interpretations provided by regulated parties often have seemed improper, especially during Administrations intent on rolling back regulation. In 1976 these interventions became an issue in the Presidential campaign, and President Ford's appointees at EPA unilaterally withdrew from OMB's "Quality of Life Review" after the election. It has again become a sharp issue over the last several years, with Congress holding repeated hearings and refusing to approve related Reagan Administration legislation.

A new administration needs a new approach if it is not to sink into this historical pattern of distrust, now etched in the behavior of the several bureaucracies and constituencies involved. If it shifts overall much more to Presidential leadership that works through the government's line appointees, making such a break will flow naturally. Even if the new President opts generally to work heavily through staff, he would be wise to insist on a redefinition of the particularly troubled Executive Office/EPA relationship.

This redesign should accomplish two key objectives. First, it should return true responsibility for balanced regulatory decision-making to the EPA Administrator. Letting the White House escape the role of semi-official court of last resort will allow it to shed a politically dangerous operating responsibility as well as put the burden for sensible decisions clearly with the one person and institution designed for the job. Second, the President should find an effective way to lead the Administrator and his or her other regulators. He should give them a few clear objectives and guidelines, challenge them to perform and hold them accountable. The common pattern of the President never seeing his regulators once appointed and leaving them to the small scale agendas of junior OMB staffers is an invitation to drift and disappointment.[2]

THE PRESIDENT'S AGENDA

The president-elect will probably have the opportunity to lead the country and world to a very few historic decisions. How well he understands the historic moment and how effectively he can focus his government's and his public's energies on these opportunities more than anything else will define his contribution.

Protecting the public from toxics or the planet from us are among the ideas he may want to consider. However, even assuming he does not set such a priority, it is most important that he and his senior environmental managers from the start of the administration lead the environment out of its distant ghetto to become a central, creative contributor to the development of whatever core goals the president does set.

Environmental considerations are becoming an essential ingredient in broader decision-making. How can one intelligently consider economic or energy strategy without considering the environment? A few strategic shifts in the structure of the economy could do more for environmental conservation and public health than years of work to add after-the-fact abatement controls. And now that the urgency of preserving the global atmosphere, oceans, forests, species and climate is becoming clear, the environment has also become both one of the most pressing opportunities for international collaboration and a newly important issue for foreign policy.

Creating millions of good new jobs will be a central objective of the new president. How might his environmental managers help him accomplish that goal? First, they should offer strategy options, e.g., the shifting of relative factor prices in the economy in favor of labor at the expense of natural resources. If the very heavy (almost 30 percent) taxes on hiring people (social security, unemployment, etc.) were phased down and equal revenues raised by new taxes on, or reduced tax breaks for, natural resources (land, energy, etc.), the country would benefit both from more jobs and greater natural resource conservation.

As the president's work flows from basic strategy towards design and implementation, his environmental team should continue to contribute. What are the environmental implications of the possible approaches under consideration? What alternative approaches should the administration consider? Just how might they work? As important, how can the environment help on the ground — be it by helping the U.S. pollution industry become a significant exporter or by helping build popular support for pro-jobs, pro-environment tax changes? The failure of the environment to deliver effective political support for the early Carter conservation-oriented energy policy is one of the major reasons his Administration later swung to synfuels.

As the world has become steadily more interdependent, our recent Presidents' historic opportunities and interests have become increasingly international. A global economy, for example, urgently needs global policies and institutions. Any President setting out to help in building them will learn, as the World Bank has, that ignoring environmental constraints leads to very painful consequences.

Helping build order in the world more generally could well be one of the new President's central commitments. As part of that pursuit, he would probably also want to lead this country towards respectfully collaborative, not unilateral, forms of leadership. If he does he should learn from Jean Monnet. Monnet laid the foundations for the gradual coming together of Europe over the last forty years by starting after the war with specific, immediately feasible collaborations. The president should look for precisely the same sort of politically and otherwise practicable likely early successes.

Dealing with the planet's pressing environmental problems is as important and promising an opportunity as he is likely to find. The environment is an issue with virtually universal popular and leadership support around the world, east and west, south as well as north.[3] It's a technical subject whose professionals collaborate easily across cultural, ideological and other barriers. Even during the most difficult years of Soviet-U.S. tension, the environmental link was productive and warm.

As the developing majority that lives in the world's southern continents has come to understand that economic progress — survival for many of the poor who depend most directly on the environmental commons — must rest on strong environmental safeguards, the popular environmental movement there has multiplied. Ten years ago Indonesia had almost no environmental groups; now it has over five hundred, not to mention some pesticide policies stronger than the U.S. Consequently, today the environment is one of the relatively few areas where a strong, skillfully handled, collaborative U.S. lead could find quick, widespread support in the southern hemisphere. It is also an opportunity to reach out to the rising post-independence generations our policies and institutions have so long and harmfully ignored.

Here, as in domestic policy, environmental managers in the 1990s should contribute to the development of policies important to the environment but not narrowly environmental. The world's destructive debt crisis is an obvious example. Investing/lending chiefly to large-scale, capital intensive, commonly politically managed projects was as much an environmental as a developmental and banking failure. Yet, despite the fact that the biggest and commonly most vital part of these economies consists of small farmers or new urban immigrant slum dwellers, we have been unable to find ways of getting economic credit and associated supports to these people. If we could break this logjam by adapting several successful models that exist, we would accomplish a number of critical goals all at once. We'd be offering many of these people economic hope and a stake in society. We'd be opening what is needed for a reversal of the currently perverse south-north capital flows — good, productive, mutually beneficial investment opportunities in the south. And we'd be making a number of quite essential environmental objectives plausible.

For example, if we want reforestation to occur on any scale, hundreds of millions of small farmers struggling on marginal lands are the key.[4] The economics should be favorable: by fencing a now barren, eroding hillside (to protect it from animals) and planting trees, a farmer will get some fodder in the first year, rich yields of fodder thereafter and, after several years, a growing income from the trees. Yet how can a farmer who is struggling to feed his family afford the necessary investment when credit costs 20 percent for 12 hours? America is the world's leader in finance and farming and it has enormous environmental sophistication. Why couldn't the Administration provide the leadership that would allow these U.S. talents to help the world solve so fundamental an economic and environmental problem?

These few simple examples suggest the importance of drawing the environment into the administration's center. Making EPA a

Cabinet Department would usefully symbolize the change. True, the nation's environmental constituencies and institutions have been under a long, destructive siege hardly conducive to bold strategic thinking. And the government's agencies are now especially ill-prepared, substantively and organizationally. On the other hand, there is nothing like an historic opportunity to reinvigorate institutions and movements.[5]

CONTROLLING ENVIRONMENTAL TOXICS

For almost a decade America has had statutes and regulations on the books promising to make our air, water, food and land safe and spelling out how the job should be done. Policy improvements are needed, but what's missing is implementation.

We've cut research; we've only screened a few chemicals and then for only a few of the possible risks; standard-setting lags proportionately; and voluntary compliance has crumbled dangerously because businessmen no longer believe that government is ensuring that everyone, especially competitors, will obey the law. Let's look at how to make each of these components work.

First, an across-the-board pre-condition. To safeguard the entire population against thousands of chemicals coming from millions of sources who must be induced to change their behavior is a task that one cannot imagine undertaking without a substantial team of highly trained and motivated professionals. The initial prerequisite for success is to rebuild the country's environmental team. These men and women must be given the necessary responsibility, freedom, resources and respect. They must have a non-bureaucratic, decentralized, yet integrated organizational framework in which to work. Scapegoating must stop. If society wants these safeguards, it must invest in the institutions and people essential to their implementation.

1. Research. The environmental field was called into being and is constantly being redefined by science. So it's hard to overstate the importance of a) reversing the budget cutting and related institutional damage; and b) installing strong research management capable of generating creativity in the laboratories.[6]

The deep budget cuts and intellectual timidity of recent years have been enormously wasteful. Not providing guarantees and other incentives for fundamental research in hazardous waste abatement techniques when it is clear the industry doesn't have sufficient market certainty to do so otherwise locks the country into ineffective remedies and billions in avoidably expensive investments. Not defining and updating what disposal techniques do and don't make sense for each major waste stream leaves ill-trained local junior engineers substituting their "best engineering judgement." And it forces legislatures to act blindfolded without being able to weigh the alternatives.

Not researching indoor pollution leaves some of the highest, most widespread and most easily corrected risky exposures unaddressed. Not researching how to prevent pollution through increased re-use, recycling and materials substitution leaves us dependent on expensive, often unreliable end-of-pipe treatment and disposal. It would be easy to list a hundred other similarly profligate failures to research.

No private company could survive, especially one operating in a new scientific field like the environment, with the government's current lack of research investment and weak strategic sense. Environmental research is now roughly 1/2 of 1 percent of government environmental expenditures — or some 0.0006 percent of society's overall clean-up expenditures.

2. Screening. One of these research omissions leaves the government able to screen only a tiny portion of the suspect substances it should by law be evaluating — and then only for a small portion of the potential risks.

There are over 66,000 chemicals now in use, and several thousand new substances are created each year. The Toxic Substances Control Act, the pesticides law, the Safe Drinking Water law and other statutes require the government to screen all these substances (and more) for possible risk and to impose safeguards where necessary. These laws can only be effective to the degree that such screening is possible.

A few statistics tell the story. Over the 1980s the government has been unable to complete action on 99 percent of these chemicals. In 1984 the National Academy of Sciences reported that we do not have adequate information to conduct health hazard assessments on over 90 percent of these chemicals and pesticides.

Moreover, when the government says it has screened a substance, the screen is almost always incomplete. It can spot acute, immediately visible effects. It has a quick, economic and reasonably reliable screen for cancer. However, from that point on it must rely heavily on animal tests, i.e., epidemiology by analogue — an analogue that is imperfect and that largely precludes observing many types of effect. How can one, for example, reliably spot and measure other than acute psychological change in a rat?

Until science can produce a set of economic, simple, quick tests for a full range of health risks, not just cancer, the environmental statues that depend on chemical screening will remain in very large degree empty promises.

EPA should launch a national five year competitive research program to develop such a battery of short tests. The Agency should go to 20-25 top quality research teams wherever they are around the country; explain the country's critical need; give each team two to five of the one hundred high volume, most suspect chemicals in use; and ask them (a) to do as comprehensive a risk analysis of each chemical as they can and, in the process, (b) to develop practical, easily used short tests for whatever health effects they can.[7] Their results on the first part of this charge will set the now largely idle standard setting and field implementation portions of these statutes very usefully to work. And engaging and motivating top investigators competitively to attack the critical lack of effective short tests in a thoroughly practical setting just might open the way to making the chemical screening statutes effective.

3. Standards. Despite these failures, we have learned enough to have created an extensive set of basic safeguards against unduly risky exposure to a great many suspect new substances our species has introduced into the environment. These safeguards are the law. Most have been the law for years.

There is, of course, a great deal more to do. How will the country keep automobile emissions from beginning to increase again in a few years, the current consensus projection? How can we help the Food and Drug Administration for the first time truly insure that food imports meet U.S. pesticides contamination standards? How can we best cut the emissions responsible for global warming and other atmospheric changes? The need to manage human behavior environmentally will always be creating new regulatory needs.

4. Compliance. In the 1970s almost everyone complied voluntarily with most of these laws.[8] Of 14,000 registered sources of air pollution in Connecticut during five years in the middle of the decade, for example, only 300 required administrative orders. And, of these, only 20-30 became enforcement problems. Regulation cannot succeed without this sort of voluntary compliance.

As noted, environmental regulation forfeited much of business's voluntary compliance in the 1980s. Restoring voluntary compliance is essential for the new administration. The best research and the best standards at the end of the day mean little unless they change behavior.

To succeed the next administration will have to regain both the attention and the confidence of hundreds of thousands of decisionmakers roughly simultaneously. After all, the collapse took place — even in the face of the very substantial pressures exerted by the expanding new rules of liability — largely because businesses correctly concluded that they could no longer assume that the government would ensure that their competitors were shouldering equal costs. Success will probably require a combination of a visible presidential intervention; a change in the regulatory process that simultaneously forces itself on everyone's attention; and a visibly adequate field capacity to be credible with a skeptical audience.

We probably cannot return to earlier arrangements. While the mistakes of the last decade have greatly hastened the drop-off in compliance, eventually something similar would probably have happened in any case. A thoughtful designer of institutions faced with the scale of 1988's task would not choose the same regulatory model adopted in 1970 to deal with the far simpler problems brought into focus by Earth Day.

There is only one other area where regulation must cover almost all of society — tax, securities and financial regulation. It has worked effectively for fifty years — without generating the chronic pattern of political backlash that has been so profoundly harmful to the environmental movement. Its success is certainly not because it is less intrusive or imposes smaller costs.

Environmental regulation needs to learn from its more successful financial cousin. Probably the most important single lesson is the value of creating a profession working at the interface between government and those subject to regulation. The environmental field could similarly develop certified public environmental auditors who would, rather like CPAs: (a) evaluate the procedures and safeguards of firms handling hazardous materials and certify in their annual reports whether or not they are doing so in a generally accepted safe manner; and (b) collect, lab test, certify and report ambient and work place conditions. They would be engaged and paid by business, held legally liable to the public and supervised by government.

A new profession of environmental auditors would do the vast volume of routine inspecting and evaluating the government is not now doing and never will be able to do. Even more valuable, they would develop and constantly evolve methodologies that fit the infinitely varied circumstances of particular industries, companies, processes, ambient conditions and laws. (They will need these tools to do their job and will have the specialized, current knowledge to develop them.) They would occupy the middle ground, and they would have the strongest possible interest in defending it. They would also act as much needed interpreters between government and business.

Government is already moving in this direction. California has established a registry of state-certified environmental auditors, to the applause of small business, which is unable to afford the in-house auditors the larger firms have hired or to evaluate the competency of available consultants in this new, highly technical field. A number of other states have started to require auditors for special purposes ranging from radon inspections to certifications that a property is environmentally safe at transfer. Most large companies that deal with dangerous substances have set up their own environmental auditors, and their work has created the sophisticated techniques that make the broad application of the idea now possible. The growing use of the idea in such diverse circumstances is a reflection both of its now proven utility and also of a growing awareness that the old approaches are no longer able to do the job.

Expanding the use of environmental auditors is one example of how the environmental field will have to experiment with new tools to enable it realistically and practically to get the massive job of the 1990s done. A few other examples will give a sense of the range of approaches needed.

EPA runs two of the country's largest capital public works programs. The wastewater treatment construction grants program needs to encourage innovation, ranging from novel treatment approaches to the introduction of assembly line modular treatment units that will be both cheaper and far more reliable than the traditional plant custom-designed for each small town. The Superfund must create new incentives that will induce, not inhibit, quick private clean-ups. Both need stronger means of ensuring contractor performance and project financial integrity.

The program charged with controlling automotive and truck emissions has traditionally focussed its attention on pre-manufacture prototypes and the subsequent manufacturing stage. As more states and cities are running mature periodic inspection and maintenance programs, they are building a model-specific data base regarding actual performance. This information opens the door to regulation based on performance, not prototypes.

As the Safe Drinking Water program finally begins to produce standards covering toxics, 40,000 public drinking water systems must start testing for these substances and reporting to their customers, a potentially powerful requirement that has barely been touched to date. Much more could be done by enhanced collaboration across agency lines, e.g., by providing financial and career incentives for inspectors of one agency to spot problems of concern to another. The opportunities are as endless as the need. The next several years must see a great deal of hard-headed but bold management experimentation.

5. Support. The recognition that the country must find new approaches extends well beyond issues of program design. The environmental field's most fundamental failure has been political.

EPA and its environmental public health work has been under terrible attack most of the last two decades. The damage done during the Reagan Administration chronicled above has not been unique. For example, Governors Grasso of Connecticut and Rhodes of Ohio and Mayor Beame of New York all led similar if less determined reactions. The almost universal support for environmental protection reflected in the polls is not organized. The "environmental" constituency has traditionally been overwhelmingly focused on conservation and recreation issues, and the health organizations view EPA distantly and with some ambivalence.[9]

Building a solid, sustainable, organized political base for environmental regulation is one of the new administration's most critical tasks. Without such a foundation we will never make our environment reasonably safe, let alone escape the terribly destructive policy swings of the last years.

There are three broad elements the next administration should pursue to build such a foundation:

* It should try to build the sort of professional intermediation that the introduction of certified public environmental auditors promises. One suspects that future reactions will be much less severe if such a profession has a chance to become a heat shield between the parties and as its members become established in city after city across the country.

* It should actively reach out to build new constituency alliances. The growing number of victims' groups is a very promising prospect. As the problems have gotten worse, and as the law has in all fields increasingly protects and compensates victims, people who have suffered personal and property damage have increasingly organized to press their common interests. There may also be new opportunities in the public health field as historic scars heal and as EPA's public health work begins to fit better with those of other agencies.

* EPA must build up such a solid reputation for quasi-judicial probity and professional competency that it formally becomes "good government" to give it respectful autonomy. The Internal Revenue Service and Securities and Exchange Commission won such standing.

PROTECTING THE PLANET

In July 1988 a senior member of the National Aeronautics and Space Administration, testifying to the Congress, summarized what has been emerging as a consensus among scientists: "Present global temperatures are the highest in the period of instrumental records.... The rate of global warming in the past two decades is higher than at any earlier time in the record. The four warmest years in the past century all have occurred in the 1980s. The global temperature in 1988 up to June 1 is substantially warmer than the like period in any previous year in the record." He concluded that this evidence provides "99 percent confidence" that what we're seeing is no normal chance fluctuation.

This greenhouse effect (caused by the buildup of carbon dioxide and other industrial gasses in the atmosphere) could well cause climate changes over the next two generations larger than the changes experienced throughout human civilization. The temperature increase could be as great as that accompanying the last glacial to interglacial transition. Such extremely rapid change would predictably cause important ecological and physical systems to fall out of equilibrium — which both makes prediction hazardous and threatens even larger losses than extrapolation might suggest. For example, forest ecosystems may not survive in the face of such rapid warming. Another example: rising oceans would wipe out most existing coastal wetlands, while man's defense of his coastal property would prevent the formation of compensating new marshes.

The impacts on human society could also be large. Continental interiors would probably bake. Favorable farming conditions might shift from the rich soil of the U.S. midwest to glacier-scraped regions of Canada. Much of Bangladesh would be covered by the ocean. What if the Gulf Stream, which defines Europe's weather, shifted? A thousand other projections and questions of profound consequence cascade down on us as a result of these giant forces we have accidentally let loose.

The greenhouse is only one of the things we are doing to our planet. We have been destroying its protective outer ozone layer. We have increased the acidity of rain and snow. Here we use the greenhouse as an exemplar of the broader problem.

Human society must learn to understand and manage its impacts on the planet, and to do so preventatively rather than after-the-mistake. This is environmental protection's next and most critical job. Providing the needed leadership must be one of the administration's two core, historic environmental responsibilities.

With so much at stake on the one hand, and with so much that is unknown and uncertain on the other, what specific steps should we take now?

1. **Launching a Defense.** First, it is mad not to invest seriously in the research necessary for us to understand how the planet's critical systems (atmosphere, oceans, climate) work and how human activity is affecting or might affect them. In 1987, EPA had only $1 million invested in studying atmospheric effects.

Second, this is an issue that requires global action. In 1985 more than two thirds of the world's carbon dioxide emissions did not come from the U.S., Europe and Japan. The highest rates of growth are in the developing countries of Asia and South America. It is not entirely accidental that the U.N. Environment Programme (UNEP) is located in Nairobi. We cannot protect ourselves, let alone the planet, with a U.S. program only. On this issue effective leadership must be global leadership.

The world needs to sit down together to develop a joint understanding and agreed strategies. The new administration could help launch such a collaborative effort. It could, perhaps jointly with others, propose a shared world research program. If this idea gets bogged down, the U.S. could immediately sharply expand its own research effort and encourage the scientists and governments of whatever other nations are willing to participate as active partners.

At the same time, the new president and Congress could seek to encourage the creation of stronger world environmental policy institutions ranging from informal policy forum (successful in developing the current consensus on controlling chlorofluorocarbons) to a strengthened UNEP. The July 1989 meeting of the UNEP Council could be a useful target date.

Most of the important advances in environmental history, after a pioneering period of citizen initiatives, have been launched with investments in research and associated policy staff. Such investments are neither too controversial or terribly expensive. But, by defining the problem and what could be done about it, and by working to build support, these seeming modest initial organizations usually become powerful engines of change.

2. Limiting the Damage. Beyond these obvious first steps lie rich fields of possible actions, first to delay or stop greenhouse warming (and other affects) and/or second to deal with the consequences of changes we either can't or won't avoid.[10]

How might one stop or, more likely, seek to retard the greenhouse effect? Some of the most important possible policies include: (a) encouraging conservation of carbon dioxide emitting fuels; (b) stimulating the introduction of solar and other benign energy sources; (c) charging users of carbon-emitting fuels an environmental penalty to encourage fuel conservation and switching with the revenue perhaps going, for example, to lower the high (payroll) taxes on employment or to encourage conservation and solar; (4) stopping deforestation and stimulating widespread tree farming; and (5) banning or limiting production of harmful gasses.

3. Adjusting to the Unavoidable. Preparing for and adjusting to the consequences of climate change requires a further array of policies and investments. If the farm belt is to become hot and dry, agricultural research had better begin developing crops and techniques that fit. If we want to allow new wetlands to develop along a receding coastline, then we'll have to look closely at Maine's new law that requires shoreline property owners to move any improvements they have made out of the way of natural change taking place along the coast. We'll have to start now designing long-lived capital investments to deal with likely changes — as Charleston, South Carolina, for example, is doing as they design a new sewer system to survive a rising ocean. These are only a few early, already obvious examples.

We can no longer take "nature" for granted. Our species' impact on the planet's fundamental life-supporting systems is too great.

NOTES

[1] In preparing this paper Jim Gomes, Sherry Hiemstra and the author talked with over 70 leaders from every environmental perspective and were enormously struck by the fact that three quarters gave priority to dealing with the new global issues. Four, certainly eight years earlier this clearly was not the case.

[2] The U.S. Regulatory Council, created in the late 1970s, was one organizational experiment that served this purpose. Never loved by OMB, it was dubbed "pro-regulation" and disbanded as quickly as possible in the first months of the Reagan Administration.

[3] See the Lou Harris Poll prepared in 1988 for the United Nations Environment Programme.

[4] In India, except for the limited public works department programs along road and railroad strips, government programs have generally failed. Most successful tree-planting has been done by rich farmers who can afford (and protect) it.

[5] The following sections try to give a sense of the nature and direction of the path ahead. Brief sketches of a few specific actions that seem important should help define the path more specifically. But space precludes this being a blueprint. It does not touch on major areas like conservation and recreation. However, the environmental community has worked together intensively for months to prepare a detailed study that truly deserves its title: *Blueprints for the Environment: Environmental Policies, Budgets and Administrators for a New Administration.*

[6] For a discussion of how environmental science might be better managed and given far greater sense of strategic purpose, see the author's chapter in *Science and Technology Advice*, edited by William T. Golden, Pergamon Press, 1988.

[7] The costs of this special program could properly be assessed against the affected industries under the Toxic Substances Control Act and Superfund laws.

[8] A few programs, especially pesticides control, have histories of chronic non-compliance that predates the 1980s.

[9] Most state health departments lost functions and resources when the new state environmental agencies were created.

WORKPLACE SAFETY & HEALTH:
Occupational Safety and Health Administration & Mine Safety and Health Administration

Margaret Seminario*

SUMMARY OF RECOMMENDATIONS

Our nation's workplace safety and health program is in serious peril. After eight years of neglect, the Occupational Safety and Health Administration (OSHA) has neither the will nor the resources to do its job. Major health and safety problems have not been addressed. Partly as a result, more than 10,000 workers are killed each year and one million seriously injured. Tens of thousands more die prematurely from long-term occupational diseases.

With a sympathetic 41st president and 101st Congress, major improvements can be made in health and safety protections for workers. New initiatives should be launched to educate managers and workers about hazards and to expand the participation of workers in workplace safety and health activities. Quality inspections, tough enforcement and correction of hazardous conditions should be top program goals.

Key recommendations to achieve these goals are:

* Appoint an Assistant Secretary who is committed to a strong OSHA and willing to work with labor and management to improve the program. OSHA faces an enormous task. It will take strong leadership and the input of unions and employers to make the program work.

* Set standards for priority safety and health hazards and speed up the standard setting process. Major safety and health hazards are unregulated and it now takes three to eight years to complete a regu-

---

* *Margaret Seminario directs the occupational safety and health activities of the AFL-CIO, where she has worked since 1977. She is a member of the National Advisory Committee on Occupational Safety and Health and the Federal Advisory Council on Occupational Safety and Health.*

lation. Standard setting needs to be improved to prevent unnecessary disease and injury.

* Develop new approaches to targeting inspections to dangerous worksites. With responsibility for 4.5 million workplaces and limited resources, OSHA must improve its targeting so the most hazardous worksites are inspected on a regular basis.

* Mandate at all worksites safety and health committees, which can inspect worksites and even shut down hazardous jobs and require training and education for front line supervisors. OSHA regulations and inspections will never cover all hazards or worksites. OSHA must stimulate expanded worksite safety and health activities, including safety committees and training, to address workplace hazards.

These new initiatives and program improvements will require a modest 10 percent increase in OSHA's budget and staff levels for each of the next four to five years.

I. OSHA HISTORY

The Occupational Safety and Health Act of 1970 set up a federal program of regulation and inspection to address worksite safety and health hazards. The law created the Occupational Safety and Health Administration (OSHA), assigning employers the responsibility to provide a safe workplace and granting workers and their representatives rights of participation and access to information.

The law covers all private sector workplaces except for those hazards and situations which are subject to regulations of another federal agency (e.g., radiation in nuclear facilities and pesticide exposures for farmworkers). Eighty million workers and 5.9 million workplaces are subject to the Act's requirements. State and local public employees are covered in those states which operate a state OSHA plan. A 1980 Executive Order extended OSHA regulations and inspections to federal civilian workers.

The primary functions of the agency are standard setting and enforcement. Ten regional offices and 85 field offices employing 1,800 people are responsible for enforcement and inspection activities. The remainder of the agency's staff, an additional 400 people, are headquartered at the national office in Washington, D.C.

OSHA has had a rocky history, suffering greatly during political transitions. In its early years, OSHA was opposed by the business community, particularly small business, as well as the Nixon Administration. With an inexperienced, unqualified staff and inadequate resources to do the job, it became an easy target by those who opposed the federal government's role here from the start. As a result, from

1971 to 1974, little progress was made in establishing a meaningful national safety and health program.

In 1975, OSHA began to make some progress with the appointment of Dr. Morton Corn, a respected safety and health professional, as assistant secretary. Efforts were launched to improve and expand the staff through in-house training and the hiring of qualified safety and health professionals. Important occupational health problems, like lead, noise, coke oven emissions and cotton dust were targeted and regulatory action on these hazards was initiated.

With the Carter Administration and the appointment of Dr. Eula Bingham, a toxicologist, OSHA continued to gain strength and credibility. Final standards were set on lead, cotton dust, arsenic, acrylonitrile, DBCP and benzene, and a policy for regulating cancer-causing substances promulgated. And the agency stepped up its enforcement activities against employers who violated the law.

For the first time, OSHA also directed significant resources towards involving workers in safety and health activities in the workplace. A major worker educational program, the New Directions Program, greatly expanded worker safety and health training through grants to unions, universities and employer groups. A promulgated regulation guaranteed workers and their representatives the right of access to worker exposure and medical records. And a worker right-to-know standard on chemical hazard information was proposed. All these measures attempted to involve workers more in their own worksite safety and health.

The significant achievements of the Carter Administration did not come without opposition. Indeed, the more serious the initiative, the greater the opposition. Legal challenges by the business community seeking to overturn standards became routine. Legislatively, there were yearly attempts to limit OSHA's authority through appropriations riders and, in 1980, a major reform bill was introduced which would have limited the agency's inspection powers. For the most part, however, these efforts were unsuccessful, and by 1980, after a decade of struggle, the agency had finally established its legitimate role in the regulatory arena.

Progress at OSHA came to an abrupt halt with the inauguration of President Reagan in 1981. Committed to a program of deregulation, the Reagan Administration immediately set out to roll back regulations and weaken enforcement activities of the agency. The President's Task Force on Regulatory Relief targeted major existing OSHA standards for review; and Executive Order 12291 gave the President's Office of Management and Budget broad authority to review and approve all major proposed and final rules prior to their publication.

At the agency itself, Thorne Auchter, a construction executive with no safety and health experience, though active in the 1980 Reagan campaign, was appointed Assistant Secretary for OSHA. The Reagan deregulatory platform, not the Occupational Safety and Health Act, became the blueprint for agency activity.

The Administration halted all work on new OSHA standards. A right-to-know standard on chemical hazards proposed by the Carter Administration was withdrawn, and rulemaking actions were halted on the carcinogens hexavalent chromium and nickel.

Instead, all efforts focused on weakening or revoking existing standards, particularly those targeted by the Task Force on Regulatory Relief: lead, cotton dust, noise, cancer policy and methods of compliance. The agency even took the unprecedented action of requesting the Supreme Court to suspend its ongoing review and rulings on the cotton dust and lead standards so that the standards could be revised — i.e., weakened. In both cases, the Supreme Court ignored the request and went on to uphold the existing standards.

Despite the Reagan Administration's best efforts, most OSHA standards were not weakened. Union litigation and pressure, congressional intervention and adverse public opinion derailed or tempered many of the planned actions. Over the eight years of the Reagan Administration, OSHA was forced to abandon its deregulatory agenda and even to issue new standards on Hazard Communication, ethylene oxide, asbestos, benzene, formaldehyde, field sanitation for farm workers and hazardous waste worker protections.

In June 1988, under the direction of Assistant Secretary John Pendergrass, the agency proposed to update permissible exposure limits for 428 toxic substances originally set in 1971 when the OSH Act went into effect. However, ignoring the contrary recommendations of its own National Institute of Occupational Safety and Health (NIOSH), the agency proposed to accomplish this goal by adopting industry accepted standards recommended by a private group, the American Conference of Governmental Industrial Hygienists.

OSHA's recent record on safety hazards has been equally dismal. Serious hazards like failure to lock out dangerous equipment during servicing or to provide protection to workers who enter toxic or oxygen deficient environments still are unregulated and claim hundreds of lives a year. Worse has been interference by the Office of Management and Budget, whose role has been greatly enhanced during the Reagan Administration. Under Executive Orders on Federal Regulation (E.O. 12291) and Regulatory Planning (E.O. 12498), OMB has attempted to influence OSHA's regulatory agenda and to weaken or block safety and health standards. For example, OMB, in 1984, cut out a short-term exposure limit from a court-ordered standard on ethylene oxide, thereby permitting high peak exposures to this cancer-causing chemical used to sterilize hospital equipment. A short-term exposure limit was only set after a second court order by the U.S. Court of Appeals for the District of Columbia.

In recent years, OMB has extended its intervention through the Paperwork Reduction Act. Through a broad interpretation of "paperwork," OMB has disapproved the requirements for cancer labeling in the formaldehyde standard and material safety data sheets in the construction industry under the Hazard Communication Standard.

So after eight years, the net result of the Reagan program is a few diluted standards, a handful of standards issued and a backlog of serious hazards in need of regulation. And OSHA enforcement activities were seriously weakened. Unlike standard setting, changes in enforcement policy do not require rulemaking and can be accomplished simply by administrative directive, or inaction.

In 1981, Thorne Auchter issued directives which greatly reduced the scope of OSHA inspection activities and limited the severity of citations and penalties. The agency instituted a series of policies exempting the majority of employers from routine safety inspections. For example, OSHA safety inspections were limited to the manufacturing, construction and maritime sectors. All other sectors (e.g., service, communication, transportation) were exempt from safety inspections except for investigations of complaints or fatalities and catastrophes. In the manufacturing sector, industries were exempt from routine safety inspections if the industry had a lost workday injury rate below the national average. Firms still subject to inspections could escape inspection if their injury logs showed a lower than average injury rate. Under this policy, 86 percent of all manufacturing employers were exempt from routine safety inspections.

For firms still subject to inspection, changes in policy reduced the level of seriousness of citations and proposed penalties.

Midway through the Reagan Administration, a number of well publicized catastrophes revealed the weakness of the agency's policies. Union Carbide's West Virginia plant, the sister facility to Carbide's Bhopal, India plant, was considered a "safe" plant and exempt from routine safety inspections. And in 1983, an immigrant worker, Stephan Golab, died of cyanide poisoning at the Chicago Film Recovery Plant. A few weeks prior to his death, OSHA had visited the plant, but failed to conduct an inspection because workplace records showed a low injury rate. The local district attorney prosecuted the company officials under state criminal law and won a murder conviction from an Illinois Court.

As a result of such situations, some changes were made in OSHA's exemption policy during the term of Labor Secretary William Brock. Citations and penalties were increased in particularly egregious cases. Consequently, Union Carbide was fined $1.3 million for failing to prevent toxic substance exposures and to keep accurate injury records at its Institute, West Virginia plant. In the past 2-1/2 years, there have been about 30 such major enforcement actions, the majority for recordkeeping violations against major employers such as Chrysler, Ford, Monsanto, IBP, John Morrel, Scott Paper and International Paper. Many of these cases have been settled by OSHA or the Solicitor of Labor's office, generally without any input by affected labor unions and without adequate requirements for abatement of practices and hazards.

Findings of major recordkeeping violations underscored the weakness in OSHA's exemption policy which relied upon employer injury records. In March 1988, responding to congressional pressure, OSHA dropped its records exemption policy and now requires at least a walk through of all facilities regardless of the employers' injury record.

II. OSHA/MSHA BUDGET AND RESOURCES

The resources available to OSHA to meet its responsibilities have always been small, particularly when compared to the task facing the agency. In FY 1987, OSHA had a budget of $228 million and 2,131 authorized positions. In FY 1988, the budget increased to $235 million and 2,352 positions as a result of the California State OSHA plan being returned to federal jurisdiction. Currently there are 65 million workers and 4.5 million firms covered by federal OSHA. (OSHA State Plans cover 1.4 million additional firms.)

Of the total FY 1988 budget, $109.9 million is earmarked for federal enforcement, which now covers 30 states (including the State of California). State program enforcement is budgeted for $40.5 million and standard setting activity for $6.5 million. With this budget the agency conducts approximately 60,000 inspections and issues three to four safety and health standards each year.

The limitations in the OSHA budget are particularly clear when compared to the funding and staffing levels of its sister agency, the Mine Safety and Health Administration (MSHA). MSHA is responsible for conducting mandatory inspections in coal mines and metal and non-metal mines.

To carry out its responsibilities to inspect 11,000 mines employing 320,000 workers in FY 1987, MSHA had a budget of $156.5 million and a staff of about 2,750. This level of resources translates into $489 spent for every worker covered. By comparison, the OSHA budget amounts to $3.60 for workers subject to that Act.

Like many other agencies, OSHA has been significantly affected by budget cuts during the Reagan Administration. Staffing levels, including the number of inspectors, have been cut by about 25 percent. In 1980, OSHA had about 1,125 inspectors in the field. As of September 1987, prior to the return of the California State Plan to federal jurisdiction, the agency had about 850 inspectors on staff.

There have been similar budget cuts in other OSHA programs, including standards development and education. The standards budget has been reduced from $7.4 million to $6.5 million, and the budget for worker education was slashed from $17 million to about $2 million.

Because of OSHA's limited resources, many serious safety and health hazards are not being addressed by regulations or enforcement activities. For example, there are major hazards in health care settings, including exposure to the AIDS and Hepatitis B viruses. Millions of workers are employed in this industry, yet only a small number of inspections are conducted each year in hospitals and other health care facilities and standards on infectious diseases have yet to be issued.

Similarly, ergonomic problems related to poor job design, which cause injury to the muscles, bones and nerves, are a serious problem for millions of workers. OSHA employs only one professional ergonomist.

To address the serious safety and health problems facing American workers, OSHA needs an increase in budget and staff. Providing a basic level of inspection coverage to high hazard workplaces and responding to complaints and fatalities would require a federal enforcement staff of approximately 1,800-2,000, an increase of 600 to 800 professional positions, an additional 60-80 laboratory positions and 120-160 clerical support positions. The cost of this increase (including salaries, benefits, non-personnel costs, equipment and travel) would be approximately $54-72 million.

The health standards office, with only about 30 professionals, is also understaffed. Five to ten additional professionals at a cost of $300,000 to $500,000 would greatly increase the capability of this office. Given the 80 percent cut in training and education programs and the importance of involving workers in their own workplace safety, an increase of $10 million in training and education programs should be sought. Funding and staff are also needed to develop programs on ergonomics and job design, and to establish an office of construction safety and health at the national office.

Any increases in OSHA's budget and staff should be phased in over time. The agency lacks the capability and pool of qualified individuals to expand immediately to the desired levels.

A phased-in expansion program with a 10 percent real annual increase in agency budget and staff (beyond increases for inflation and wage increases) for the next four to five years would lead to a program with adequate resources to monitor serious hazards and workplaces.

III. NEW PRIORITIES AND INITIATIVES

The next administration has the opportunity to launch new initiatives and achieve major gains in worker safety and health protections:

Standard Setting. OSHA's track record in standard setting is underwhelming. In its 17 years of existence, the agency has set only 19 health standards and 26 safety standards. Standards are usually established in response to a petition or a law suit, and generally cover only a single hazard and take 3-6 years to complete.

To improve standard setting, the agency needs to set clear priorities for standards while seeking the input of labor, management, NIOSH and the states. If OSHA has a clear regulatory agenda and acts on these standards, petitions and law suits for new standards will be less likely.

Standards should be set for toxic chemicals to which large number of workers are exposed, such as cadmium, chromium, nickel and methylene chloride. Exposures to the blood-borne diseases AIDS and Hepatitis B in health care settings must be regulated. Safety standards on lock out of dangerous equipment and unsafe trenches should be issued immediately.

OSHA should also move to develop generic standards like the Hazard Communication Standard which require employers to develop programs in key areas. Generic standards should be developed for exposure monitoring of toxic substances, medical surveillance and training.

The standard setting process also needs to be speeded up. The health standards directorate and safety standards directorate, now separate, should be combined and overseen by a new high-level career management person, who would be responsible for keeping standards activity on track. In addition, the Office of Regulatory Analysis, now in the Policy Office, should be brought into the Standards Directorate to better coordinate activity on standards development.

Enforcement. Recent major enforcement actions by OSHA have demonstrated that strong enforcement of the Act is still possible and desirable. However, there are fundamental problems with the agency's targeting system and procedures that must be changed to assure effective and consistent enforcement of the law.

As discussed, OSHA's current targeting system does not effectively direct inspections to the most hazardous operations in the most dangerous worksites. Instead, OSHA needs more information about hazards and conditions in particular workplaces before inspections are conducted. Past compliance histories are one source of information not currently utilized. Bureau of Labor Statistics data from the Annual Survey and Supplementary Data Systems may be another source, particularly if changes are made in these systems to collect more detailed data and remove some of the confidentiality restrictions which now exist. Certain hazardous operations (e.g., use of high hazard chemicals) could also be identified by requiring permits for these operations and/or direct reporting to OSHA.

During the past eight years, there has been little incentive for area directors and inspectors to conduct *thorough* inspections and to take *major* enforcement actions. In fact, during the early Reagan years, the inspection staff was disciplined or penalized for strong enforcement. For example, in 1982, after conducting several inspections of the Adolph Coors facilities, OSHA's Regional Director in Denver, Colorado, Curtis Foster, was relieved of his duties based on charges of improper hiring practices of inspectors in 1980. Foster fought these charges in the courts and in 1986 was ordered reinstated on the job.

Currently, performance evaluation criteria for enforcement personnel stress the number of inspections, yet there is no incentive or directive to conduct in-depth inspections of significant hazards. OSHA needs a clear policy of strong enforcement against serious hazards. Performance evaluation criteria and program directives need to be changed to create an incentive for conducting not only enough inspections but also enough *quality* inspections of serious hazards.

Construction Hazards. OSHA needs to improve its capabilities and programs for the construction industry. Construction is among the most dangerous industries, where serious hazards result in a very high injury and fatality rate. OSHA has devoted the majority of inspection resources to construction, which accounts for over 60 percent of all inspections. These inspections have been limited in their effectiveness. Still, construction inspections cover only about 320,000 workers each year, compared with 1.6 million workers in manufacturing, and result in relatively few serious citations. Better targeting programs and increased training for inspectors would improve this situation.

The agency should also increase its now nearly non-existent construction expertise at the national office. An Office of Construction Safety and Health should be established to develop and oversee regulation and enforcement in this dangerous industry.

Workplace Safety and Health Committees. The focus of the OSHA program is the promulgation of standards and enforcement of these regulations. Few attempts have been made, however, to expand safety and health programs to individual worksites, as is commonplace in many European countries and Canadian provinces. There, the development of worksite safety and health activities, through safety and health committees, is a major part of the national programs.

OSHA regulations on Hazard Communication and Access to Medical and Exposure Records now give workers and their representatives the right-to-know about chemical hazards on the job. OSHA should take the next step and give workers and their representatives the right to *participate* in worksite safety and health activities by promulgating regulations which mandate labor-management safety and health committees. These committees should have the right to inspect the job site, conduct accident investigations and shut down hazardous jobs.

Training and Education. Training of workers and first line supervisors is a critical element in job site safety and health. Though the agency has expanded training requirements on chemicals through the Hazard Communication Standard, agency resources devoted to training efforts have been significantly cut.

The New Directions Training and Education Grants Program should be expanded to support increased training and education activities by unions and employers. OSHA should also develop training materials and curriculum that can be used by workers and supervisor training. These materials would assist employers, particularly small businesses, to comply with standards and help ensure that workers receive adequate training.

Ergonomics. Ergonomic problems related to poor job design are widespread throughout American industry. For example, repetitive trauma disorders, such as carpal tunnel syndrome, have been documented in assembly line workers, meat packing, VDT operators and other occupations.

OSHA should develop a comprehensive program to address ergonomic problems through research, evaluations, standards, enforcement and training and education. Staff must be hired at the national office to develop regulations and training materials and at the regional offices to encourage enforcement actions on ergonomic problems.

IV. STRATEGIES

The appointment of an effective Assistant Secretary for OSHA will be key to the success of the next administration's safety and health program. The Assistant Secretary should be experienced in the safety and health field, a strong leader who is respected by both labor and management and who will seek input from these parties in developing programs and policies.

The next Assistant Secretary will have to rebuild the agency both in terms of staffing and moral. Many OSHA employees have understandably lost their sense of mission. New staff must be hired to fill vacancies and to expand the agency's programs. Both the current career staff and new personnel must be fully involved in the development and implementation of new programs so they have a stake in their success. Limiting involvement to only political appointees, which was a problem at OSHA during the Carter Administration, will not lead to long-term change.

Major improvements in OSHA's regulatory and enforcement programs can be accomplished within the context of the current legislation. Yet the Occupational Safety and Health Act of 1970 is 18 years old, and, save for a few appropriations riders, has never been amended or updated. Several legislative changes are needed to advance worksite health and safety activities, streamline OSHA standard setting and enhance OSHA's enforcement and abatement authorities.

Workplace safety and health programs, which include safety and health committees, expanded worker participation and enhanced training should be mandated by law as in other countries. Such programs will improve the capability of employers and workers to address safety and health problems. Legislating these measures would underscore their importance and preclude protracted litigation. Several states are considering such initiatives as a follow-up to worker right-to-know legislation. Federal action would achieve these gains for all workers.

OSHA standard setting is often a lengthy process; OMB requirements and intervention, the departmental review process and building a record that will withstand court review are reasons for some of the delay. Much of the delay, however, can be attributed to agency indecision and inaction. Statutory changes should be made which set forth reasonable time periods for standard setting and require agency justification to Congress if deadlines are not met. Such a provision wouldn't guarantee deliberate speed, but hopefully would expedite the promulgation of standards.

There is general agreement that OSHA needs to set generic standards which mandate programs or cover multiple hazards. This could be accomplished either by regulation under existing law, if the new OSHA assistant secretary were sufficiently motivated, or by new legislation mandating medical surveillance, environmental monitoring and training programs.

The major shortcomings in the enforcement provisions of the current OSHA law are its abatement provisions. If an employer contests a citation, there is no requirement to abate even the most serious hazards until the contest is resolved. This omission contrasts with the Mine Safety and Health Act, under which serious and life threatening hazards *must* be abated pending the outcome of the challenge. OSHA inspectors also do not have the authority to shut down dangerous life threatening operations without a court order. Again, their MSHA counterparts have this right.   Amendments should be enacted which give OSHA the same authority to require abatement of serious and life threatening hazards as exists under MSHA.

The penalty structure and criminal provisions of the OSH Act are also out of date and weak compared to other more recent safety and environmental laws. The maximum penalties are $1,000 per serious violation and $10,000 for willful violations. Criminal sanctions are permitted only for fatality cases involving a violation, falsification of records or reports or when advance notice of an inspection is given. The penalty structure should be updated and maximum penalties set at $25,000 per serious violation and $100,000 per willful violation to bring them in line with other similar statutes. Criminal provisions should be extended to cover all willful violations which result in disease or injury, whether or not there's a fatality.

For the next administration to improve the OSHA standard setting process, the role of the Office of Management and Budget must be reduced. Consequently, the next administration should rescind Executive Orders 12291 and 12498. To the extent that a centralized review by OMB is viewed desirable, a new process could be established by executive order which clearly limits OMB's role and reinforces the authority of regulatory agencies to set standards under their respective statutes. Any OMB review should be conducted as part of the public rulemaking process and all communications between the agency and OMB should be made part of the rulemaking record. (For more on OMB's proper role regarding paperwork and rulemaking, see the chapter on OMB.) OSHA's programs, particularly in the standard setting area, could be strengthened through increased coordination with other health and safety agencies, including the National Institute for Occupational Safety and Health (NIOSH), and the Office of Toxic Substances (OTS) at EPA. NIOSH and OTS have statutory responsibilities to recommend and refer standards to OSHA. These agencies have risk assessment and exposure assessment capabilities that could be of great use in the standard setting process. NIOSH and OTS are generally not involved in the development of standards, however, and participate only in later stages of rulemaking.

The Assistant Secretary for OSHA should establish a formal relationship with NIOSH and OTS/EPA heads to coordinate the activities of the three agencies on an ongoing basis.

OSHA should also attempt to increase coordination with the states. In recent years, for example, states have passed right-to-know laws and asbestos abatement laws; and they are undertaking criminal prosecution of safety and health violations under state laws. Going further, OSHA should consider developing programs, initially on a pilot basis, where state and local activities could complement the federal OSHA's work. Agreements could be made for states active on the right-to-know programs to enforce OSHA's Hazard Communication Standard. Similarly, OSHA could establish a system for referral of egregious cases to state and local prosecutors for possible criminal prosecution.

V. MINE SAFETY AND HEALTH ADMINISTRATION

The nation's 400,000 miners work in what continues to be the country's most dangerous occupation. Each year 130 men and women die on the job and more than 20,000 more are seriously injured.

The Mine Safety and Health Administration (MSHA) is charged with the responsibility of protecting the miners in the coal industry and metal and non-metal mines under the Federal Mine Safety and Health Act of 1977. Without question the mine safety law is the most stringent statute in the federal system of safety and health laws. Unlike OSHA, the mine safety law requires periodic mandatory inspections and extensive training for miners. MSHA inspectors have the authority to shut down dangerous jobs and order immediate correction of hazards.

During the past eight years, however, safety and health conditions in the mines have deteriorated, as the significant increase in non-fatal accident rates indicates. Both the serious and nonserious rates have steadily increased during this period; in the last two years these rates have increased dramatically.

This deterioration has occurred in large measure as a result of a conscious policy of nonenforcement by the Reagan Administration. The number of enforcement actions has been reduced, the size and number of fines for violation of the Act have been dramatically reduced. For example, roughly half of all fines are now a single penalty of $20 and the amount of penalties collected has dropped from $19 million in 1980 to $10 million in 1986. In addition, education and training activities and standards development have been curtailed.

Budget and Resources. Since 1980, there has been a decrease in MSHA's staff and budget in real dollar terms. In FY 1980, the agency had a staff of about 3,700 and a budget of $143.6 million; that year, 132,044 inspections were conducted. By FY 1987, MSHA had a budget of $156.5 million and staff of 2,900 to implement the mine safety law. With these resources the agency conducted a total of 108,140 inspections, or some 20% less.

Both Reagan budget cuts and a decrease in the number of active mines are responsible for the decline. Since the Mine Safety and Health Act requires a specified minimum number of mandatory inspections, a basic level of coverage in the mining industry has been maintained.

MSHA should be able to carry out its health and safety mandate with its current resources. The agency should also be able to encourage innovation in the elimination of accidents through better design.

One program area which could use modest increases is education and training. The MSHA law requires 40 hours minimum training for new miners. Education centers set up to conduct this training were closed in 1982, severely compromising the quality of training for many miners. These centers should be restored. An additional appropriation of $4 million will be required for this purpose.

RECOMMENDATIONS FOR NEW INITIATIVES AND PRIORITIES:

* **Accident Prevention.** There exists information and data on the causes of fatal and serious nonfatal accidents. But this information has been under-utilized causing needless "carbon copy accidents." Such information and accident analysis should be used to develop regulations which correct known dangers and to direct the education and training programs toward accident prevention.

* **Designing Out of Accidents.** Safety experts agree that the permanent elimination of accidents can be achieved only through the design of systems and machinery which eliminate or reduce the potential for accidents. For example, the introduction of the long wall miner system eliminates the risk of roof falls, the single largest cause of accidents in the conventional mining system. Much more needs to be done to develop innovative techniques to eliminate known accident causes.

* **Regulations.** Many of the regulations governing mining conditions are outdated and do not reflect the information gained from the study and analysis of past mining accidents. There is insufficient use made of accident data permitting the unnecessary repetition of accidents where cause and prevention are well known. Regulations should be adopted which address specific problems and conditions of modern mining.

* **Management.** The de-emphasis on enforcement has resulted in an increase in the non-fatal accident rate from 5.46 accidents per 100 miners in 1983 to 8.32 accidents per 100 miners in the first quarter of 1988. Those operators who violate the Act's provisions must be subject to strong enforcement actions and the assessment of stiff fines and penalties.

CONSUMER PROTECTION:
The Federal Trade Commission

Eddie Correia & William I. Rothbard[*]

SUMMARY OF RECOMMENDATIONS

The Federal Trade Commission is a small agency with an enormously broad mandate. With a FY 1988 budget of only $66.2 million, it is charged with policing "unfair and deceptive" business practices throughout the American economy. It is responsible for approximately half of all antitrust enforcement at the federal level; it is the only consumer protection agency with a broad national mandate to stop fraud and it is charged with enforcing a series of important rules regarding used cars, funeral homes, consumer credit and other business activities in every community in the nation.

This tiny agency has the potential to make a major contribution to fairness in the American marketplace. Unfortunately, the Reagan Administration concentrated its efforts on reducing its already small staff, attempting to limit its authority and redirecting enforcement priorities to insignificant cases.

The first priorities for a reinvigorated Commission are these:

* *Appointing new leadership.* Two vacancies on the Commission are likely to be available for appointments by the next president. These appointments are crucial for establishing a working majority. The appointment of a capable and committed chairman is, of course, the single most important action to insure a successful FTC. Next in importance, but also key, are the Directors of the Bureaus of Competition and Consumer Protection.

* *Increasing the budget and staff.* The agency has been allowed to shrink drastically during the Reagan years. Its budget should be increased by 25% over two years, primarily to restore enforcement staff and allow hiring committed young attorneys.

---

[*] *Eddie Correia is Chief Counsel and Staff Director of the Senate Antitrust, Monopolies and Business Rights Subcommittee and formerly was an advisor to the chairman of the FTC. William I. Rothbard is Of Counsel to the Los Angeles firm of Irell & Manella; he formerly served as counsel to the Senate Antitrust Subcommittee and as an advisor to the chairman of the FTC.*

* *Setting new priorities.* New priorities must be established quickly, particularly in the consumer protection area. Current rule-making initiatives which are not promising should be terminated. A limited number of major new initiatives should be carefully chosen and receive early attention, including, for example, increasing nutritional and health-related information available to consumers, focusing enforcement on national companies rather than small local firms and investigating cases of product design defects known to the manufacturer but not disclosed to consumers.

* *Proposing new legislation.* It is unlikely the FTC will have been reauthorized by the end of the 100th Congress. The new leadership should work with the Commerce Committees of both houses to obtain a reauthorization bill, which should include new statutory authority to allow the states to assist in enforcement of trade regulation rules and fraud cases, to investigate problems in the insurance industry and to obtain more effective redress for consumers.

I. THE FTC'S HISTORY

Understanding the FTC, where it is today and where it should go, requires a review of the Commission's controversial and schizophrenic history. Although difficult to believe today, the creation of the FTC was one of the major achievements of President Woodrow Wilson. President Harry Truman, writing fifty years later, even ranked Wilson as one of the great Presidents because of his role in establishing it.

CREATION OF THE FTC: HIGH EXPECTATIONS

The Federal Trade Commission was created in 1914 at the height of the Progressive Movement. The Sherman Antitrust Act of 1890 was widely viewed to have failed to prevent monopolies which eliminated competition and raised prices. President Wilson and his allies persuaded Congress to establish a new agency with wide-ranging powers to stop unfair, anticompetitive business practices. A key concern was to avoid authorizing the new agency to stop only a specified "laundry list" of bad practices. Thus, the legislative mandate was intentionally kept broad, and the FTC was given the authority to prohibit "unfair methods of competition." In addition to its authority to conduct administrative proceedings and issue injunctions against practices it found unfair, the Commission was authorized to collect information about business conduct and industry performance, to conduct wide-ranging studies of the economy and to recommend legislation to Congress.

The FTC was created to function independently from the Executive Branch and from any single political party or administration. Thus, the FTC Act called for the staggered appointment of five commissioners, who could be removed only for misconduct. No more than three commissioners could be from a single political party and the schedule of appointments made it likely no President could name more than three commissioners during a single four-year term.

The Congress and the Wilson Administration thought they were creating a powerful, independent agency with ample authority to ensure a fair, competitive marketplace. Two decades after its creation, the sculptures added to the Commission's headquarters on Pennsylvania Avenue — muscular public servants controlling the wild horse of unrestrained capitalism — still reflected the optimism of its founders.

"THE LITTLE OLD LADY OF PENNSYLVANIA AVENUE"

Through most of its 75 year history, the FTC has fallen far short of the high expectations of its creators. It has spent much of its early history attacking outlandish advertising claims by tiny firms for baldness creams, phony investment schemes, miracle cures and the like. While these claims no doubt harmed consumers, the Commission could make only a tiny dent in the fraudulent practices of hundreds of thousands of scattered small commercial enterprises.

From its inception, the Commission assumed that its legal authority to ban "unfair methods of competition" included the authority to attack fraud and deception as well as antitrust violations. In 1934, the Supreme Court unexpectedly held that proof of an "unfair method of competition" required showing that a competitor was injured. Thus, injury to consumers alone did not violate the Federal Trade Commission Act. Congress responded by amending the statute in 1938 to prohibit "unfair or deceptive practices" in addition to "unfair methods of competition." The definition of "unfair" practices has been a source of controversy surrounding some of the FTC's actions.

During the Depression, the Commission sponsored trade conferences, actually meetings of competitors, to devise rules of conduct. Although some of this activity could be viewed as facilitating helpful standardization practices and codes of ethics, it also amounted to Commission-sponsored collusion by competitors. The Depression also led to the passage of the Robinson-Patman Act, the antitrust law which prohibits giving an unfair price advantage to large companies. Much of the Commission's antitrust efforts up until the 1960s were devoted to enforcement of this Act, at the expense of failing to enforce other antitrust rules.

In enforcing the prohibition against "unfair and deceptive" practices, the Commission continued to focus on fraud by small, fly-by-night companies. It had no authority to impose stringent penalties or to seek redress for injured consumers. Instead, its only remedy was a simple order to "cease and desist," which required a lengthy administrative proceeding. Its efforts were like the cleaning crew after a sporting event; much energy was expended, but the next night the grounds were just as littered. The Commission failed to make any permanent impact on the clutter of unfair and deceptive practices in the American marketplace.

By the 1960s it was painfully obvious that the FTC, mired in trivial cases which required years of exhaustive administrative proceedings but which produced few meaningful results, had been a spectacular failure. It was a bureaucratic backwater which attracted few top-ranked graduates. It became known as the "Little Old Lady of Pennsylvania Avenue."

A NEW LEASE ON LIFE

In 1969, a report by Ralph Nader and other consumer activists was severely critical of the Commission's performance. Prompted by the Nader report, President Nixon asked the American Bar Association to undertake its own study. The ABA's conclusions were much the same — the Commission was a failure.

These reports gave the Commission a new lease on life. It began to set priorities for allocating its limited resources, rather than simply rely on complaints from the "mailbag." During the next decade the Commission launched dozens of major initiatives, including challenges to many basic practices of the automobile, oil and food industries.

The Commission also made a number of major policy changes in its consumer protection efforts. These included the adoption of a requirement that advertisers have "prior substantiation" of advertising claims. This policy caused something of a revolution in advertising practices and eventually won the support of the advertising industry. The "advertising substantiation" rule increased the truthfulness of advertising as well as the effectiveness of Commission enforcement. Rather than having to expend substantial resources proving a claim was false, the FTC could simply ask an advertiser to furnish its documentation and review its sufficiency.

In the mid-1970s, Congress gave the FTC substantial new legal authority to promulgate "trade regulation rules" — administrative regulations which applied to an entire industry. In addition, the Commission was authorized to seek monetary civil penalties against companies violating clearly established standards, monetary redress for consumers and preliminary injunctions in antitrust and consumer protection cases.

In 1977, President Carter appointed an aggressive consumer-oriented senior congressional aide, Michael Pertschuk, to be Chairman of the Commission. The FTC, armed with new legal tools and shed of its do-nothing image, seemed to be on the verge of the golden era of its history.

THE CARTER ADMINISTRATION AND THE CONGRESSIONAL REACTION

The Carter Administration took office with many of the major projects initiated during the Nixon and Ford Administrations about to be implemented. These included major monopolization cases against the oil and breakfast cereals industries, and an extensive investigation of possible monopolistic practices by the automobile industry. The Commission had also launched a series of rulemaking proceedings aimed at imposing tough new rules of conduct on several industries, including funeral homes, credit agencies, used cars, health spas and others.

The major new initiative of Chairman Pertschuk was a proceeding to develop a rule regulating children's advertising. Although the Commission set out a number of options for a final regulation, it was widely assumed that a final rule would ban much of the advertising intended primarily for very young children, e.g., on Saturday morning cartoon programs. In addition to rulemaking proceedings, the Commission continued to challenge marketing practices of major companies on a case-by-case basis. These efforts included bringing suit against major automobile manufacturers for failing to disclose known design defects in new cars.

It is possible to justify each of the new and aggressive initiatives launched by the FTC in the early and late 1970s. In most cases, it is even possible to trace their origins to concerns raised by key members of Congress. (For example, conservative members of Congress, including Senator Strom Thurmond, urged the FTC to look into the issue of children's advertising.) However, the FTC's policies during this period provoked a major and well-orchestrated political counter-attack by business groups. The Commission had taken on so many industries that it was comparatively easy to assemble an extremely broad lobbying coalition, whose purpose was to convince Congress to limit the FTC's authority.

Ironically, many of the initiatives begun during the earlier Republican administrations became branded as the product of a Democratic FTC out of control. To a large extent the Carter Commission had the responsibility of implementing these initiatives and of doing so when the political climate had shifted toward "deregulation."

An ominous sign of the FTC's vulnerability was an editorial by the *Washington Post* branding the Commission as the "National

Nanny." The attack on the FTC climaxed in 1979 with the passage of the FTC's reauthorization bill. That legislation limited the FTC's authority to pursue many of its major initiatives, including those involving funeral homes, insurance, trademarks, children's advertising and agricultural cooperatives.

The FTC during the Carter administration accomplished a great deal, but the political backlash weakened it and encouraged business lobbyists to seek congressional restrictions on its statutory authority. The FTC has still not recovered totally despite a much more pro-business orientation during the Reagan Administration.

II. THE REAGAN ADMINISTRATION'S FTC

Criticizing the FTC for "over-regulating" fit nicely into the Reagan campaign's theme of getting government off the back of business. In fact, President Reagan's choice as Chairman of the FTC, James C. Miller, also had headed the Office of Management and Budget's Task Force on Regulatory Relief. Thus, he was one of the officials most identified with the administration's deregulatory philosophy.

The Reagan Administration's FTC agenda had at least four goals: shrink the budget and reduce staff, including elimination of the Commission's ten regional offices; change enforcement priorities to focus on "hard core fraud" and only the most egregious antitrust violations; terminate most of the major ongoing rule-making proceedings which survived the legislative restrictions; and submit legislative proposals to restrict permanently the FTC's authority.

ANTITRUST

Along with the Justice Department, Chairman Miller's FTC attempted to revise radically the antitrust enforcement goals of the Commission consistent with the "Chicago school" approach advocated by Robert Bork and other conservatives. In general, this approach has several key premises: "vertical restraints," i.e., agreements between companies at different levels of the production and distribution chain, never present antitrust problems and warrant no enforcement effort; only horizontal mergers of companies with extremely large market shares can threaten competition and, then, only under special circumstances; "predatory pricing" and price discrimination by dominant companies virtually never harm competition and warrant little or no enforcement attention; and government is as much or more a culprit in limiting competition as private business.

These policy assumptions led the Miller FTC to make these changes in antitrust enforcement policy:

1. Resale price maintenance. The FTC refused to enforce the antitrust prohibition against "resale price maintenance" — manufacturers dictating prices to retailers. It did not bring any cases to enforce this antitrust doctrine, which was originally announced by the Supreme Court in 1911. In contrast, the Carter FTC had brought several of these cases, including one involving Levi Strauss jeans which resulted in an estimated savings to consumers of $75 million per year.

The "Chicago School" argues that manufacturers only agree with retailers to charge particular prices when these agreements promote point of sale services and product quality. Consequently, it is argued, fixing resale prices is actually beneficial to consumers because it reflects the decision of the manufacturer to obtain the most efficient mix of price and services for his product.

In fact, there are less harmful ways of ensuring that dealers adhere to manufacturer service and quality requirements. The antitrust laws allow manufacturers to require dealers to comply with non-price restrictions such as providing warranty service. Dictating prices to retailers, on the other hand, harms competition by preventing high volume retailers from competing on prices. A new administration should restore enforcement of this antitrust principle, which promotes greater choice and more vigorous price competition for consumers.

2. Merger Enforcement. The FTC under Chairman Miller followed a policy — extreme at first and moderated later — of challenging only very egregious mergers between competitors. Early in the administration, the FTC and the Justice Department issued new merger enforcement guidelines, describing which mergers would be viewed as harmful by the agencies. In general, these statements of policy were a useful and sound guide. However, both the FTC and the Justice Department sometimes ignored their own guidelines and limited antitrust actions only to mergers which substantially exceeded the guidelines' thresholds.

Some past antitrust enforcement efforts, particularly in the 1960s and early 1970s, had gone too far in challenging mergers which were competitively neutral and, in some cases, arguably procompetitive. The courts and the antitrust agencies also were somewhat slow to recognize the importance of foreign competition in preventing competitive harm from a merger of domestic firms in some cases. By the late 1970s, the FTC had come to rely increasingly on sound economic analysis of affected markets.

Reliance on economic analysis is unobjectionable. But during the last seven years, Commission economists constructed elaborate and unrealistic theories to explain how mergers between competitors with large market shares could not harm competition. The Commission accepted untenable assumptions about the definitions of markets as well as the likelihood new entry would offset any increase in prices resulting from higher concentration. The result: a substantial reduction in enforcement levels.

The Reagan Administration' s more passive role in antitrust enforcement can be seen in the following chart which shows the number and size of mergers over the last several years and the number of

MERGER ENFORCEMENT
BY THE REAGAN ADMINISTRATION

National Merger Activity

	Total Mergers	Total Value ($Millions)	Mergers Over $100 Million	Mergers Over $1 Billion
79	1529	34.2	65	3
80	1565	33.0	58	3
84	3158	126.0	191	19
86	4323	204.4	388	34
88	3701	167.5	299	—

The twenty-three largest mergers in U.S. history have occurred since 1981, including the five largest — Chevron-Gulf ($13.2 billion); Texaco-Getty ($10.1 billion); DuPont-Conoco ($8 billion); British Petroleum-Standard Oil ($7.6 billion); and U.S. Steel-Marathon Oil ($6.6 billion).
Source: *Mergers and Acquisitions*

Department of Justice

	Mergers Reported Under H-S-R*	Investigations Under H-S-R	Total Merger Cases Filed
79	861	51 (5.9%)	11
80	784	38 (4.8%)	10
84	1340	37(2.8%)	5
86	1949	40 (2.1%)	6
87	2533	—	6

* Hart-Scott-Rodino Act, which requires advance notification of certain mergers.

Federal Trade Commission

	Mergers Reported Under H-S-R	Investigations Under H-S-R	Enforcement Actions
79	861	79 (9.2%)	13
80	784	35 (4.5%)	13
84	1340	36 (2.7%)	8
86	1949	43 (2.2%)	6
87	2533	26 (1.0%)	9

Antitrust Personnel

	FTC	Dept. of Justice
79	568	872
80	575	883
84	398	619
87	307	549

actions by the FTC and the Department of Justice. The chart shows that as the number of large mergers increased, the number of investigations dropped.

Merger enforcement should focus on mergers between competitors, "horizontal mergers." However, some mergers between firms at different levels of the production and distribution process ("vertical mergers"), and some between firms in different industries ("conglomerate mergers") can present competitive problems under special circumstances. Nevertheless, the FTC failed to bring a single vertical or conglomerate merger case in seven years.

3. Monopolization. Monopolization cases involve dominant firms driving smaller firms from the market, or in some cases preventing their entry. Many monopolization cases involve predatory pricing, deliberately setting prices below costs in order to drive other firms from the market. The Commission essentially abandoned enforcement efforts in this area.

It is well recognized that enforcement decisions in this area should be made carefully so as not to discourage aggressive competition. As a general principle, enforcement is not appropriate unless the evidence is clear that a dominant firm intentionally engaged in below cost pricing in order to drive out smaller competitors. An example of such a case was one initiated by the Commission in 1974 against the Borden company. The final order was upheld by the court of appeals in 1982. However, the Commission under Chairman Miller weakened the order on its own initiative in order to establish a new policy regarding predatory pricing. The standards for unlawful conduct set out in the Commission order are extremely stringent and almost impossible to prove or enforce.

4. Robinson-Patman Act. These cases involve discriminatory pricing by manufacturers, typically sales to a large customer at a lower price than to a smaller firm. While this practice can harm competition, as with predation cases, the Reagan FTC philosophically opposed enforcement. Again, the FTC should not abandon enforcement of a statute that is the law of the land. Enforcement decisions should be made carefully to insure they promote competition and consumer welfare as well as the fair opportunity for small businesses to compete.

5. Health Care. The Reagan FTC did continue to enforce antitrust laws against anticompetitive activities in the health care industry, as well as other industries involving professional groups. To its credit, the Administration also strongly opposed legislation which would eliminate FTC jurisdiction over professionals, including physicians and lawyers. Enforcement actions have focused on collusive activity among professionals as well as mergers of hospital chains.

The Commission has established a creditable record in this area, and the program should be continued by a future administration.

CONSUMER PROTECTION

The FTC of the 1970s was aggressive in carrying out its responsibility to protect consumers. It targeted major corporate offenders, aggressively exercised new industrywide rulemaking powers and undertook a special obligation to protect society's most vulnerable consumers — children, senior citizens, minorities and the poor — from commercial exploitation. The Commission's enlarged presence encouraged more truthful advertising and increased deterrence of other unfair and deceptive practices.

While the FTC of the late 1970s was criticized for some aggressive initiatives, its basic enforcement mandate was not questioned until the arrival of the Reagan Administration. The Miller Commission pursued the Administration's general philosophy of deregulation by attempting to undermine many fundamental consumer protection policies as well as their statutory foundations.

1. Redefining "Deception." The meaning of "deceptive practices" for purposes of FTC enforcement had become well established in court and Commission opinions. Nevertheless, the Reagan Administration made a major effort to persuade Congress to enact a statutory definition, which would narrow the established one and prevent bringing certain categories of cases. For example, Chairman Miller proposed prohibiting deceptive advertising only if it deceived and substantially injured so-called "reasonable consumers." When he could not persuade Congress to enact this definition into law, the Commission issued a Deception Policy Statement establishing it as Commission policy. Since this definition protected only "reasonable consumers," it meant the 19th Century system of *caveat emptor* applied to everyone else. It also encouraged a return to the old FTC emphasis on case-by-case enforcement against fringe firms engaged in hard-core criminal fraud.

The Commission required its staff to engage in frequently unnecessary and sometimes futile information-gathering exercises before acting. In one case, for example, the Miller team withheld permission from the staff to obtain an order against the manufacturer of a defective, life-threatening seaman's survival suit while the staff considered whether a private wrongful death action would be a sufficient remedy. In another, it refused to challenge a deceptive children's ad because of evidence that a minority of viewing children were not deceived. This logic, the natural result of Chairman Miller's new deception policy, turned FTC law on its head. Evidence that a substantial number of consumers were deceived traditionally was enough to warrant enforcement action, especially in cases involving vulnerable groups such as children. Under the Reagan FTC, the same evidence led to no action.

2. Revised Enforcement Priorities. The Reagan FTC's emphasis on challenging only deceptive practices which met stringent fraud standards produced a dramatic decline in advertising enforcement. Ironically, it also resulted in a return to enforcement against small, local companies, the pattern of the Commission's early history. While the Nixon-Ford-Carter FTC focused its enforcement resources on major nationwide advertising campaigns by Fortune 500 firms, the Reagan FTC devoted its even scarcer resources to minor campaigns affecting relatively few consumers. In one illustrative year, the Commission brought a mere fifteen advertising cases, with only one involving a big-name ad campaign. In contrast, the advertising industry's self-regulation unit handled 110 cases (most involving the top 100 advertisers), and found 64 big campaigns to be deceptive.

3. The Ad Substantiation Rule. The Reagan FTC also attempted to undermine the Commission's rule requiring *prior* substantiation of advertising claims — the foundation of the Commission's advertising enforcement program. While this requirement was both popular with advertisers and had improved the credibility of commercial advertising, Chairman Miller viewed it as a prime example of government over-regulation. His attack on the rule produced such an uproar within the advertising industry, however, that he was quickly forced to abandon it.

The Commission continued to express reservations about the principle of prior substantiation and succeeded in significantly weakening ad substantiation standards in Commission orders.

4. Undisclosed Product Defects. In the late 1970s, the Commission implemented a policy of requiring automobile manufacturers to disclose known design defects to consumers. In several cases, the Commission negotiated redress orders, including, in effect, warranty adjustments. The Reagan FTC essentially abandoned this program, bringing virtually no significant product defects cases. Costly undisclosed defects remain a major consumer problem and deserve far greater enforcement priority than they received during the Reagan Administration.

5. Health Issues. Deception in health, food and drug advertising also enjoyed relaxed enforcement during the Reagan Administration. Since the publication of the landmark Surgeon General's report on cigarette smoking in 1964, the FTC had played a central role in requiring cigarette manufacturers to warn consumers of the health effects of their product. The FTC promulgated the first warning rule, conducted major law enforcement investigations of deceptive cigarette advertising practices and devised the current system of rotational warnings passed by Congress in 1984.

Moving away from this commitment, the Reagan FTC ignored trends of increased smoking by minors and failed to investigate seriously potentially unfair and deceptive cigarette advertising which might promote smoking by minors. Despite the influence of cigarette advertising on the decision to smoke, no significant investigation of cigarette marketing to children and teenagers has been undertaken by this Administration. (The Commission has challenged "low tar" claims and other tobacco advertising not directed to children.)

As a result of this lack of concern, the tobacco industry has felt free to be more blatant in its appeals to young potential smokers, including using relatively youthful-looking persons in its advertising, running ads in youth-oriented publications, and sponsoring and publicizing its products at high-profile sporting events. Youth-directed cigarette advertising poses major consumer protection concerns and should be thoroughly examined in 1989.

The Commission also relaxed enforcement against deceptive advertising for food and drugs, traditionally an area of substantial enforcement activity. While the Nixon-Ford-Carter FTC had brought a series of major cases against analgesics advertising and began an over-the-counter drug rulemaking proceeding, the Reagan FTC all but abandoned this area. And it terminated a rulemaking proceeding which would have required certain nutritional information to be furnished to consumers.

6. Trade Regulation Rules. The Reagan FTC also challenged many of the industrywide rulemaking proceedings under the Magnuson-Moss Act, which had been begun by previous Republican and Democratic administrations. These rulemaking efforts were intended to improve the effectiveness and fairness of law enforcement by setting out clear standards applicable to an entire industry. The Miller team established new evidentiary standards that were almost impossible to meet and then applied them to block rules that were in the final stages of development. So they prevented or delayed the promulgation of most of the pending rules, including ones applicable to sales of hearing aids and requirements for disclosure of nutritional information. Two important rules involving the funeral and consumer credit industries were approved over the objections of the Miller leadership and are in effect today. And the "used car rule" was also approved, but in a substantially weaker form than originally proposed.

While Magnuson-Moss rulemaking has proven to be far more complex, controversial and time-consuming than originally anticipated, if used appropriately it can still be an efficient and equitable enforcement tool. Yet it was used by the Reagan FTC as little more than an ideological whipping boy, a symbol of the evil of over-regulation.

7. Vulnerable Groups. Finally, the Reagan FTC has failed to continue the tradition of special concern and protection for the most vulnerable consumers. No group of consumers is more vulnerable than young children, yet the Miller Commission responded to the negative political fallout of the ill-fated "Kid-Vid" proceeding not by continuing to police unfair and deceptive children's advertising, but by doing nothing. Since 1981, practically every complaint against allegedly unlawful children's advertising has been denied. This is not surprising, given Chairman Miller's belief that it was not "legitimate" for the Commission to police unfair and deceptive children's advertising and decide whether children should be allowed to watch certain advertisements.

8. Injunctive and Consumer Redress Actions. The Reagan Commission did carry forward an enforcement priority of its predecessor FTC — the use of the agency's authority under section 13(b) of the FTC Act to seek injunctive and monetary relief for defrauded consumers. Section 13(b) actions have been an increasingly effective and popular element of the Commission's anti-fraud program. They can provide a fast and effective means of stopping harmful business practices and obtaining redress for injured consumers.

While the Commission deserves credit for its successes in this program, a number of improvements can be made. There is often undue delay and internal review of relatively simple cases. In addition, the Commission has too often brought suit against companies which have breached the Commission's "hard core fraud" standard, but which have almost no assets to satisfy a judgment. In some cases, the Commission has announced large monetary judgments with great fanfare when marginally solvent defendants could not possibly satisfy them.

INTERVENTION

In addition to its law enforcement responsibilities, a secondary but still significant function of the FTC has been the preparation of economic and industry studies. These analyses can enhance understanding of markets and economic regulation, and thus are an important adjunct to the Commission's overall goal of promoting competition and consumer protection. They also have the potential to influence public policymaking and business practices in particular industries. FTC proposals based on these studies have led, for example, to such landmark federal legislation as cigarette warnings and consumer credit protection, and to greater awareness and sophistication in the purchase of life insurance and generic drugs.

The Commission also has provided its analysis of competitive problems to other economic regulatory agencies, such as the International Trade Commission and Interstate Commerce Commission. These "interventions" have contributed to the development of sound regulatory policy to the extent that they are based on the Commission's own expertise in antitrust enforcement and analysis.

Commission interventions in the Reagan era took on much greater importance and commanded an unprecedented allocation of staff resources. Where these interventions remained rooted in the Commission's own expertise, such as in trade matters before the ITC and ICC, they continued to be useful. For the first time, however, many strayed far afield from the Commission's own institutional experience, and seemed driven more by the Administration's zeal for deregulation than by a desire to share objective economic insights. The Commission's lack of expertise and experience in the communications industry, for example, did not prevent it from filing comments with the Federal Communications Commission on such issues as broadcasting licensing, program syndication rights and communications satellites.

By converting Commission interventions into a tool of the Administration's ideological war on regulation, the Reagan FTC devalued an important program. To be useful and credible in the future, this program should be restored to its traditional function of providing information and analysis to other agencies on issues within the Commission's realm of institutional knowledge and experience.

III. BUDGET ISSUES

The FTC has suffered a steady and drastic decline in resources during the Reagan Administration. The table below shows the decline in the agency appropriation in current and constant dollars since 1978 (in millions).

	FY78	80	84	88
Actual	62.1	71.5	64.2	66.2
Constant	85.8	76.5	61	53.7
(1982 dollars)				

The result of the steady budgetary decline has been a dramatic reduction in the size of the FTC staff. Never a large agency, the FTC has shrunk from over 1700 employees in 1979 to 1011 as of October 1, 1987. By the end of 1988, the agency will have fewer than one thousand personnel, a decline of more than 40% in less than a decade.

FTC employees are concentrated in Washington, with approximately 190 people in the ten regional offices around the country. This small group is responsible for enforcing dozens of statutes and regulations applying to hundreds of thousands of businesses. The agency has historically allocated about half its resources to antitrust enforcement and half to consumer protection activities. Antitrust enforcement authority is shared with the Antitrust Division, which had 549 employees as of February 5, 1987. However, no other federal agency has authority to enforce the general consumer provisions of the Federal Trade Commission Act. Thus, fewer than 500 people, including administrative support personnel, are in theory responsible for enforcing the federal consumer protection laws.

The decline in FTC resources has clearly contributed to a reduction in significant enforcement activity. For example, the FTC is responsible for investigating proposed mergers which present possible competitive problems under the Hart-Scott-Rodino Act. The number of mergers reported to the FTC has continued to increase as staff resources have decreased. In 1980, there were 784 mergers reported to the FTC, at a time when the FTC had the equivalent of 575 workyears allocated to antitrust enforcement. In 1987, there were 2533 reported mergers but only 307 workyears allocated to antitrust. Thus, the ratio of staff to reported mergers declined by over 80%.

A new administration should request an increase in the FTC's appropriation for fiscal years 1990 and 1991 to restore at least half of the staff lost over the last decade. This would require a total increase of about 30% over two years, or funding of additional $10 million over projected levels in FY 90 and an additional $10 million increase in FY 91.

IV. NEW INITIATIVES

ANTITRUST

1. **Merger Enforcement.** Economic analysis should play an important role in antitrust enforcement generally, as Reagan appointees have said. The focus of merger enforcement, and, in fact, all antitrust policy, should be to promote competition, increase efficiency and benefit consumers. The Administration erred, however, in making unrealistic assumptions about market self-corrections in deciding which mergers to challenge. The problem was not that the Administration advocated reliance on economic analysis, but that its economic analysis was biased toward allowing harmful mergers.

It also correctly emphasized taking greater account of foreign competition and the development of world markets. In general, this perspective is correct. The courts have long recognized that foreign competition should be considered in analyzing the potential harmful effects of mergers. The issue, however, is not whether international competition plays some role in determining whether a merger is likely to reduce competition. The harder question is how much weight should be given to foreign competition in light of constraints on foreign production and formal or informal import barriers. For example, a merger of the largest producers of domestic crude oil could still present antitrust problems in light of the potential for oil-exporting countries to reduce exports.

As noted, the Administration essentially abandoned merger enforcement against conglomerate mergers. Because such mergers can present competitive problems under special circumstances, it is unwise to adopt a flat policy against challenging them. Enforcement against conglomerate mergers should generally be limited to cases where the decision of a firm to enter a new market by an acquisition is a substitute for a pro-competitive entry through investment in new capacity. Conglomerate merger enforcement based on a general concern about aggregations of political and economic power inherently raises policy issues going well beyond antitrust and is, therefore, better left to Congress.

In general, the merger guidelines developed by the Justice Department, with some input by the FTC, are a useful analytical tool as well as a guide to the government's enforcement criteria. The guidelines provide that a challenge to a merger would occur except in "extraordinary cases" if market concentration exceeds a "Herfindahl-Hirchman Index" (or "HHI") level of 1800 and the change in the index resulting from the merger exceeded 100. (The index is derived by adding the squares of each firm's market share; for example, an HHI index of 1800 is roughly equivalent to a market with four firms having 20% of the market and two firms having 10%.)

The empirical evidence for predicting harmful effects of particular mergers is extremely limited. Consequently, the guidelines developed by the Department are a reasonable attempt to state general principles which should be considered in bringing an enforcement action. Moreover, the market share thresholds, while they are clearly arbitrary to some extent, are also reasonable. Even though the numerical guidelines can provide a good guide to enforcement decisions, there can be wide swings in application, depending on how the agencies evaluate the relatively "subjective" elements of the analysis, including the identification of the proper product and geographic markets, the likelihood of new entry and the potential for collusion. For example, hearings before the Senate Antitrust Subcommittee showed that the Justice Department failed to challenge a merger which increased the HHI index by 585 in a market with an HHI concentration level of 3,025. It also failed to challenge another merger which increased the HHI by 864 in a market with a concentration index of 5,128.

While professing to follow the guidelines, the FTC took a very narrow view of what mergers it would challenge. The annual rate of FTC merger challenges declined by over 40% from the FY 79-81 period to the FY 82-87 period. This decline is particularly striking when compared to the steady increase in the number of mergers reported under the premerger notification program during this period. (The rate of premerger notifications increased almost 200% between the FY79-81 period and FY 87.)

2. Other Antitrust Enforcement Issues. The Reagan administration has adopted the position of conservative antitrust scholars, who oppose enforcing the antitrust laws against "vertical" agreements, i.e., those between different levels of the distribution chain, such as manufacturers and retailers. It has taken this position despite the long-standing Supreme Court doctrine that agreements between manufacturers and retailers to set retailers' prices are flatly unlawful. (Unfortunately, in its 1988 *Business Electronics Corp. v. Sharp Electronics Corp.* opinion, the Supreme Court substantially narrowed the scope of this principle. Congress is now considering legislation to reverse the holding of that case.)

The Chicago School argues that resale price-fixing does not warrant antitrust concern because manufacturers will never attempt to establish resale prices unless it leads to a more efficient allocation of resources by promoting retailer services. Manufacturers encourage retailers to offer services, it is argued, in order to prevent high-volume discount retailers from taking a "free ride" on the services offered by high price retailers.

The "free rider" phenomenon is elegant in theory but insignificant in practice. Most persons who shop at discount clothing or appliance outlets do not take advantage of free services offered by high price retailers. They simply take advantage of this alternative distribution system, which offers less luxurious showrooms, fewer sales clerks and lower prices. Moreover, the antitrust laws allow manufacturers to require their retailers to provide certain services, thus providing a less restrictive way of accomplishing the desired goal. In short, by refusing to enforce the prohibition against resale price-fixing, the Reagan Administration has taken a position harmful to vigorous price competition and to consumers who buy at discount outlets.

A new FTC should implement these steps to improve antitrust enforcement:

1) allocate more resources to antitrust enforcement and to investigating a larger percentage of proposed mergers which present possible competitive problems;

2) articulate clearer criteria for challenging mergers to avoid erratic swings in enforcement policy;

3) be more aggressive in challenging horizontal mergers through more realistic assumptions about the definition of relevant markets and the likelihood that entry of new firms will eliminate the anticompetitive potential of these mergers;

4) work more cooperatively with the State Attorneys General, for example, by sharing information about proposed mergers with them, a step that will probably require legislation;

5) restore enforcement of the per se rule against resale price maintenance; and

6) explore the possibility of obtaining consumer redress in antitrust cases. Because of the *Illinois Brick* opinion that indirect purchasers have no standing to sue price-fixers even if they suffer injury, consumers who pay higher prices cannot now sue for monetary redress. The Commission should seek new statutory authority to end the anomaly that the ultimate victim of antitrust violations can't sue.

CONSUMER PROTECTION

The Commission's consumer protection mission has suffered severe but not irreversible damage under Reagan-Miller. The job of the new administration is to restore the congressional vision of the FTC as an agency dedicated to economic justice for the consumer.

To accomplish this job, a new Commission must be willing to use the full range of its statutory authority to attack widespread patterns of deception and unfairness. It should utilize Magnuson-Moss rulemaking in appropriate cases. The Commission should consult with Congress to the extent possible to lay the groundwork for potentially controversial actions. As history has shown, the FTC, no matter how well-intentioned, cannot effectively and legitimately carry out its statutory mandate without the support of Congress and its authorizing and appropriations committees.

1. Enforcement Priorities. The new administration must reorder the enforcement priorities of the Commission so that it becomes first and foremost a law enforcement agency, rather than primarily a government-wide advocate for deregulation. It must redirect most of its energies to significant cases against national companies, leaving most small, hard-core fraud cases to local and state consumer protection authorities. It must also rededicate itself to protecting society's most powerless consumers: children, the elderly and the poor.

The new administration should reinvigorate several key consumer protection programs downgraded by the past Commission. These include the advertising substantiation and national advertising enforcement programs; the food, drug and cigarette advertising programs; the product defect program; and investigations into commercial exploitation of children, older consumers, the poor and non-English speaking minorities.

Youth-oriented advertising of cigarettes — a product responsible for the annual death of 350,000 Americans — has escalated during the 1980s and represents a public health as great as that associated with illicit drug abuse. Congress and government at all levels are now aggressively moving to restrict the use of cigarettes. Given the strong consensus that now exists in Congress for public action to limit the harmful effects of cigarette use, the next FTC should work with Congress to develop effective approaches to eliminating deceptive and unfair advertising of cigarettes, especially advertising aimed at minors who begin smoking without adequate appreciation of the risk.

New consumer issues also have emerged as a result of recent cultural and demographic trends. The immigration wave, especially from Latin America and the Far East, has created a new class of vulnerable consumers — many poor, uneducated and non-English speaking — unaccustomed to the American marketplace and easy prey for unscrupulous business practices. Older Americans, as the fastest growing segment of the population, are finding themselves the object of intensified marketing efforts at the very time that advancing age makes them more vulnerable to commercial exploitation. In addition, America's new emphasis on health and physical fitness has created unprecedented demand for health-oriented products and services, together with unprecedented opportunity for consumer abuse in this area. The next Commission should assign a high priority to studying such emerging consumer issues, and to developing an effective enforcement response.

2. Rulemaking. With regard to industry rulemakings, the new administration will inherit final or proposed rules that were not aggressively enforced or were simply allowed to languish during the Reagan period. Those few rules that became final, notably the Funeral, Credit and Used Car Rules, should be reviewed to see if they are being enforced effectively or are in need of possible modification. Enforcement of these rules presents special difficulties since they apply to thousands of business throughout the country while the Commission's enforcement staff has continued to decline. The Commission should work with state and local consumer protection officials, especially the State Attorneys General, to find effective ways to assure compliance with these rules.

Any other remaining rules that were begun long ago and yet not promulgated by the Miller FTC should be reexamined to determine if they are still needed or if some alternative enforcement approach would better suit today's market conditions.

3. Legislation. Certain legislative initiatives would greatly strengthen the Commission's ability to protect consumers. First, the new Commission should work with Congress to secure prompt reauthorizing legislation. An FTC reauthorization — which the Commission has not had since 1980 — will put the Commission on a solid footing for the first time in years and give its enforcement efforts a new legitimacy.

Second, the FTC's authority to obtain monetary redress for defrauded consumers under section 13(b) of the FTC Act is not well-defined. Because of continuing legal hurdles in securing redress, Congress should reexamine section 13(b) and, if necessary, pass legislation strengthening the FTC's authority to obtain effective and expeditious redress for injured consumers.

Third, congressional modification of the insurance industry's exemption from the federal antitrust laws would have the beneficial effect of restoring the FTC's jurisdiction over unfair methods of competition and unfair and deceptive practices in the promotion and sale of insurance. To its credit, the Reagan FTC has called for repeal of this exemption.

Congress also should repeal current statutory limitations on the Commission's ability to conduct studies of the insurance industry. Insurance consumers, such as elderly Medigap users, are victims of false advertising, misleading product information and high-pressure sales tactics that would be violations of Section 5 of the FTC Act in any other industry. As the chief consumer protection agency in the land, the FTC should have the authority to investigate an industry which takes in almost $400 billion each year in premiums.

Finally, legislation authorizing state attorneys general to enforce the FTC Act's ban on deceptive practices affecting more than one state would provide valuable back-up support to the FTC's consumer protection mission. Even a rejuvenated FTC will be constrained by budget deficits and severely limited resources from accomplishing all of its enforcement objectives. It can be assisted immeasurably by the state attorneys general, who have endorsed federal legislation giving them the legal authority to enforce the Section 5 ban on deceptive practices on a multistate basis. Such legislation has been introduced in the last two Congresses and should be a high priority for consumer legislation in 1989.

The FTC already has most of the statutory authority it needs to protect consumers. But no matter how much authority it has, in the end, as the Reagan-Miller Commission has shown, it will only be as good as its leadership, its people and its strength of commitment to economic justice. Enactment of this legislative program, however, will help the Commission to do its job better, assuming it has the will to do the job at all.

PRODUCT SAFETY:
Consumer Product Safety Commission

Robert S. Adler & R. David Pittle*

SUMMARY OF RECOMMENDATIONS

Established in 1972, the U.S. Consumer Product Safety Commission (CPSC) is the federal agency with the mission of reducing unreasonable risks of injury associated with consumer products. Its jurisdiction covers most household products except for items such as food and drugs regulated by other federal agencies. To address unreasonable risks of injury, the CPSC is empowered to issue and enforce safety standards, ban products, obtain product recalls and conduct consumer information programs.

Hailed as a "model" agency when it was first established, the CPSC almost immediately failed to meet the unreasonably high expectations that its founders held for it. This led to a severe disenchantment among agency supporters and critics culminating in the Carter Administration contemplating the abolition of the agency. From an ebb in 1978, the agency gradually regained much of its lost luster under the skillful leadership of Chairwoman Susan King, who succeeded in redefining the agency's mission and goals in a way that led to realistic expectations about agency performance.

The agency's rejuvenation came to an abrupt halt with the arrival of the Reagan Administration. Openly hostile to the existence of the CPSC, the Administration first sought to eliminate the Commission, but finding Congress unalterably opposed to that, the Administration then imposed enormous funding and staff cuts on the agency — the largest suffered by any of the federal regulatory agencies. In addition, the Administration appointed a series of "reluctant regulators" to the agency, leading to half-hearted and ineffective enforcement of the agency's authority.

---

* Robert S. Adler is Associate Professor of Legal Studies at the University of North Carolina School of Business Administration and former counsel to the House Energy and Commerce Committee. R. David Pittle is Technical Director of Consumers Union; he served from 1973 to 1982 as a commissioner of the CPSC.

Although popular with the American public by virtue of its product safety mission, the agency needs new leadership, greater resources and improved morale if it is to function properly. A new administration and Congress should:

* Decide whether the agency should remain as an independent, collegial body or should be transformed into a single administrator agency. Restore a meaningful measure of agency resources lost under the Reagan Administration.

* Although the current Reagan appointees cannot be removed until their terms expire, the president should either reorganize the agency or appoint additional Commissioners to move the agency in a more progressive direction.

* Abolish the "gag rules" in current law that prevent the CPSC — alone among federal health and safety agencies — from releasing in a timely manner information about potentially defective products.

* Streamline CPSC rulemaking procedures so that its ability to write safety standards in the event that industry voluntary efforts prove unsuccessful becomes credible. End the self-imposed policy restrictions on product recalls of the Reagan appointees that hamper effective protection of the public.

I. HISTORY

FROM "MODEL AGENCY" TO BASKET CASE

Congress passed the Consumer Product Safety Act (CPSA) in 1972, establishing the CPSC as a five member independent regulatory agency with a mandate to: (i) protect the public against unreasonable risks of injury associated with consumer products, (ii) assist consumers in evaluating the comparative safety of consumer products, (iii) develop uniform safety standards and minimize conflicting state and local regulations and (iv) promote research and investigation into the causes and prevention of product-related deaths, illness and injuries. Among other things, the agency has the following regulatory powers arising from its enforcement of five acts:

* set safety standards for consumer products
* ban products
* issue administrative "recall" orders to compel repair, replacement or refunds for products that present substantial hazards
* seek court orders to require the recall of imminently hazardous products

In addition to providing these powers, Congress required businesses under CPSC jurisdiction to report to the agency whenever they obtain information indicating that their products contain defects which "could create" substantial product hazards. These so-called

"15(b) reports" rapidly assumed, and continue to play, a major role in the agency's regulatory activities — especially as the agency's resources to find hazards have dwindled.

Congress enacted the CPSA during the so-called "consumer decade," the period from the mid-60's to the mid-70's when it established or statutorily strengthened a multitude of agencies. Expectations about the ability of expanded federal regulatory authority to improve consumers' lives ran high during this period. Nowhere were expectations higher than with the Consumer Product Safety Commission.

The need for such an agency grew out of the report of a study commission established in 1968 by President Lyndon Johnson. Called the National Commission on Product Safety (NCPS), this group estimated that consumer products injured 20 million Americans every year. Of these, 110,000 sustained permanent disabilities and 30,000 died at an annual cost (in 1970 dollars) of $5.5 billion. By any standard of measurement, the NCPS concluded, the exposure of consumers to unreasonable product hazards was "excessive." Accordingly, the NCPS recommended establishing a product safety agency.

In rapid response, Congress enacted the Consumer Product Safety Act, which for the first time established federal administrative jurisdiction over large numbers of consumer products. The CPSC's jurisdictional sweep is extremely broad. Estimates of the number of products under its purview range from 10,000 to 15,000. The number of businesses producing and distributing these products is well over a million. One way to visualize the agency's authority is to think of the types of products found in a large shopping mall. With the exception of the pharmacy and grocery stores (and even some items there), virtually everything in the mall falls within CPSC jurisdiction.

Congress and others involved in establishing the CPSC wanted a "model" agency. This meant that the CPSC must have strong regulatory authority, adequate funding, broad public participation (especially from consumers) in decisionmaking, widespread openness and substantial independence from White House influence. With these features, it would quickly establish a vast federal system of consumer product safety standards through open, democratic, efficient procedures.

The CPSC tried hard to be a model agency. It adopted an openness policy that required virtually all meetings between Commission employees and outside parties to be open to the public. It stretched the Freedom of Information Act to include virtually all Commission documents, including memoranda discussing legal weaknesses of agency rulemaking options from its general counsel's staff. It actively solicited rule-making petitions from members of the public and developed a policy that imposed virtually no formal requirements on petitions. And the Commission provided funding to consumers and consumer groups to participate in its rulemaking endeavors.

Conventional wisdom in the early 1970's held that the CPSC was the most powerful regulatory agency ever created. At the confirmation hearings of the first set of Commissioners in 1973, Senator Marlow Cook remarked that so great was the CPSC's authority that an honest person wouldn't want it and a dishonest one shouldn't have it.

Yet, by the time the Carter Administration settled in, conventional wisdom had taken a 180-degree turn. The new image of the CPSC was of an awkward, incompetent body that gave good intentions a bad name. The agency's founders had expected the CPSC to promulgate 15-20 safety standards per year. To the contrary, under the Consumer Product Safety Act, it had promulgated only three standards in five years — and one of them was a trivial standard for swimming pool slides (which earned the agency a "Golden Fleece" award from Senator William Proxmire). Moreover, the agency's attempts at openness had drawn criticism even from consumer groups who, angered that the release of legal memoranda might enable industry successfully to challenge agency rules, had accused the agency of confusing "openness with nakedness."

The rise and fall of the agency's reputation arose more from unreasonable expectations than from agency incompetence. Contrary to the views of critics, it was hardly the most powerful regulatory agency in Washington. Although it possessed the power to ban products and set safety standards, so did most other health and safety agencies. And, unlike some other agencies, the CPSC's rulemaking authority was heavily weighted with procedural requirements that made it virtually impossible to set standards at other than a snail's pace. Finally, and perhaps most important, the CPSC remained a tiny agency throughout its years — with funding and staff equal to roughly half that of the Federal Trade Commission, the next smallest regulatory agency.

From the low days at the beginning of the Carter Administration to the arrival of the Reagan Administration, the agency actually regained much of its lost luster. It did so not by churning out greater numbers of safety standards — to the contrary, under Chairman Susan King, the agency promulgated only 8 regulations in 3-1/2 years, fewer than under either of her Republican predecessors — but by successfully redefining the agency's role. The redefinition involved convincing the agency's critics in the Congress, White House and the press that (i) successful regulation depended more on the quality of regulations than quantity, (ii) some alternatives to mandatory standards — such as product recalls — presented results equal, if not superior, to standards, and (iii) within its limited resources, the agency actually operated fairly effectively and efficiently.

During the Carter years, the CPSC started to shift its focus away from mandatory standards. The agency began to push industry groups to upgrade voluntary standards rather than writing mandatory standards itself. Although these efforts produced a number of false starts and slow progress, in many cases they resulted in reasonably high quality and widely followed standards. In the more successful cases, such as a voluntary standard addressing the flammability of upholstered furniture, the key seemed to be that highly motivated industry officials mobilized product manufacturers to develop voluntary standards in the face of almost certain mandatory action by the CPSC.

THE REAGAN SABOTAGE

Shortly after President Reagan took office, his Director of OMB, David Stockman, denounced the CPSC (and FTC) in vivid terms: "They've created this whole facade of consumer protection in order to seize power in our society. I think part of the mission of this administration is to unmask and discredit that false ideology." Shortly thereafter, the Administration sought to abolish the CPSC. Congress flatly refused.

Although unsuccessful in its efforts to kill the Commission, the Administration was able to slash the agency's budget and staff 25 percent in 1981, far and away the largest reductions among all federal health and safety agencies. Thereafter, although the Administration sought large cuts in funding, Congress refused to cooperate, although there were substantial staff reductions. Eventually, Congress threatened to impose statutory personnel floors, leading the Administration to moderate its attacks and settle for small, but persistent, staff cuts each year.

Although Congress protected the CPSC from annihilation by the Reagan Administration, its Members, unsettled by the loss of many liberal, pro-CPSC Senators in 1980, perceived a national mood for deregulation. In response, Congress passed a set of amendments in 1981 that trimmed the agency's authority substantially. Among other things, Congress:

* tightened restrictions on the ability of the Commission to release information from which the identity of a consumer product manufacturer could be identified (the CPSC is the only health and safety agency with restrictions on the release of such information),

* imposed a virtual ban on the release of "15(b) reports" from manufacturers containing information about possible product hazards (other health and safety agencies such as National Highway Traffic Safety Administration (NHTSA) and Food and Drug Administration

(FDA) with analogous reporting requirements may freely release such reports),

* added numerous additional substantive and procedural requirements that must be met before the agency could promulgate safety standards or impose product bans,

* established an advisory panel on chronic hazards that must be convened and consulted before the agency could begin rulemaking with respect to products presenting a risk of cancer, birth defects or gene mutations.

The Reagan Administration also appointed a group of "reluctant regulators" as Commissioners of the agency. With one or two exceptions, all of the Reagan appointees have opposed both mandatory regulation and strong agency initiatives to push industry to develop voluntary standards. Instead, they have favored more passive measures. Despite occasional statements from the Reagan appointees insisting on a contrary intent, the agency, in practice, has unfailingly abandoned the development of mandatory standards upon the assurance, however unreliable, of an industry group that it would develop a voluntary standard. Even when the evidence demonstrated that satisfactory progress was not being made towards the development of an adequate voluntary standard, the Reagan-appointed Commissioners wouldn't bestir themselves. For example, when an industry group refused to permit CPSC staff to attend its voluntary standards meetings, the Commission simply acquiesced.

One measure of the Commission's relaxed approach to product safety was developed by the Consumer Federation of America (CFA), the Nation's largest consumer advocacy group. CFA compared the number of agenda items considered by the Commissioners during the period from 1978 to 1986. In 1978, the Commission considered 255 agenda items; in 1979, it considered 237; in 1985, it considered 95; and in 1986, it considered only 80. CFA concluded that "the only explanation for the decrease in agenda items in our view is the Commission's decreased vigor in addressing safety hazards."

By far the strongest proponent of the Reagan deregulatory philosophy is the Commission's current chairman, Terrence Scanlon. Consumer groups, Members of Congress from both parties and other critics perceive Scanlon as hostile to the agency's mission and intent on crippling its effectiveness. He acts as though the 1981 amendments require the agency to defer development of mandatory standards in order to permit industry groups to *begin developing* voluntary standards, a clear misreading of the law. In fact, the only restriction on the agency is that it cannot promulgate a mandatory standard if it determines that an industry group has *adopted* and *implemented* an adequate voluntary standard.

Scanlon's approach to the agency's recall authority causes even greater worries. Notwithstanding the agency's clear authority to do so, Scanlon has widely proclaimed his view that the CPSC should almost never seek the recall of defective products if the recall would involve more than one manufacturer at a time. Scanlon's reasoning is truly ironic. He insists that industry-wide recalls constitute "backdoor rulemaking." Yet, he strongly opposes government standards setting.

Moreover, he has insisted that the Commission engage in formal cost-benefit analyses prior to instituting recalls even though the law does not require them and they tend to bias decisions against recalls. Done well, recalls operate quickly and informally once product hazards are recognized. In most cases, meaningful data on costs, injuries or death cannot be readily obtained even though it is clear that the public is at risk from a dangerous product. To insist that the CPSC halt its efforts to recall a product — especially where the manufacturer is cooperating fully — in order to permit a CPSC economist to plot costs and benefits makes little sense except to one reluctant to see a recall system work effectively.

Undoubtedly the most controversial product hazard faced by the Commission during Scanlon's term has been All-Terrain Vehicles, commonly referred to as ATVs. ATVs are three and four wheeled motorized off-road recreational vehicles with balloon tires marketed for climbing sand dunes and scrambling through the woods. According to CPSC staff, as sales of these vehicles rose, so did injuries and deaths. From 1982 through March, 1988, at least 1037 people died using ATVs. Over 365,000 required hospital emergency room treatment from 1982 through April, 1988. Many members of Congress and consumer groups contended that these injuries and deaths stemmed from the inherently unstable design of ATVs.

Faced with this situation, Scanlon's fellow Commissioners, with Scanlon vigorously dissenting, voted to request the Justice Department to file an action seeking a court order declaring ATVs to be an "imminent hazard" under section 12 of the Consumer Product Safety Act. As part of the court order, they sought extensive notice, hazard warnings and consumer training with respect to ATVs. In addition, they asked for an order directing ATV manufacturers to offer refunds for all three-wheeled ATVs and adult-sized ATVs being used by consumers under 16 years of age. At the end of a long process of negotiation with the manufacturers, the Commission settled the case with weakened provisions for notice and training, along with a moratorium on the sale of *new* three-wheeled ATVs, but without a recall of *existing* vehicles.

At the same time, the House Appropriations Committee placed a provision in the current appropriations bill that bars payment of salaries for more than three Commissioners, in effect forcing the agency to operate as a three member body. Although a smaller Commission may make sense given the agency's limited resources, section 4(d) of the CPSA requires a quorum of three in order for the agency to conduct business. This permits any Commissioner effectively to prevent matters from being voted on if the Commissioner boycotts a meeting. The CFA believes that Chairman Scanlon, in 1986, resorted to a "no-show" strategy as a means of postponing a vote on several matters on which he was likely to be outvoted. Indeed, cancellations of Commission voting sessions in 1986 jumped by 87 percent over the previous year.

In response to the turmoil and decline of the Commission, Members of Congress increasingly have called for Scanlon's resignation. In addition, Congress has taken steps to involve itself more directly in the agency's affairs. Recent legislation introduced by the committees with direct jurisdiction to re-authorize the CPSC has included provisions directing the agency to take specific action with respect to a variety of products, e.g., All-Terrain Vehicles, sleepwear flammability, lawn darts, swimming pool slides, indoor air pollutants, toys with small part hazards and cigarette lighters. Said James Florio, Chairman of the House Consumer Protection Subcommittee, "... if someone is going to criticize [product-specific legislation] as micro managing, well, so be it. But it is unacceptable that we have this situation in this country dealing with product safety, and I am convinced that there is a consensus growing in the Congress that there is a need for action to get the Commission back doing what it is supposed to be doing."

II. PRODUCT LIABILITY VS. PRODUCT SAFETY

One of the early arguments advanced by the Reagan Administration in support of abolishing the CPSC was that the market promoted product safety through the private product liability system. (Somewhat inconsistently, the Administration then proposed legislation that would have restricted the rights of consumers to bring liability claims.) Is this contention valid?

The National Commission on Product Safety, the original group that recommended establishing a product safety agency, studied the common law tort system's effect on product safety and concluded that it was inadequate. "Despite its humanitarian adaptations to meet the challenge of product-caused injuries, the common law puts no reliable restraint upon product hazards."

Why not? We suggest several reasons. First, product liability litigation is a *post*-injury mechanism. It is not triggered until someone is injured, usually severely. In many cases, it will not serve a *preven-*

tive function until many persons have filed or successfully conducted lawsuits. Thus, there may be an inexcusable delay between the time a dangerous product enters the marketplace and the time when it is either removed or rendered less dangerous. Second, in certain instances, manufacturers may find it unnecessary or less costly to pay damages to victims of hazardous products than to produce safer products. (This is especially true for carcinogens where a long latency period renders causation difficult to prove in court.) Third, the impact of product liability litigation on industry is haphazard. Companies find it difficult to predict whether or how many successful lawsuits will be brought against them. Accordingly, they may well gamble by producing products that, although cheaper to produce, pose unacceptable risks of injury.

Fourth, litigants in lawsuits generally cannot muster the resources available to a government agency, even one as small as the CPSC, to conduct in-depth studies of product-related injuries and determine appropriate fixes for them. Fifth, the parties to a lawsuit are concerned with the particular factual nuances of their case and not with the more general aspects of risk associated with the product at issue. Again, this makes it difficult to generalize about the safety of a product simply by examining the results of one lawsuit. And last, there is no systematic follow-up from a lawsuit to determine whether the defect that caused an injury or death has been corrected.

In short, product liability lawsuits play a major role in *compensating* victims of defective products. In terms of *preventing* future injuries, their role, although at times powerful, is too unfocused and sporadic to be satisfactory to adequately protect consumers from product hazards.

III. BUDGET REQUIREMENTS

The CPSC is a regulatory speck compared to other federal health and safety agencies. For example, the Commission's budget ($32 million) is roughly one percent of the Environmental Protection Agency's ($2.4 billion) and less than eight percent of the Food and Drug Administration's ($420 million).

Once the Reagan Administration tried and failed to abolish the CPSC, it shifted to a strategy of starving the agency. In 1981, the Commission's worst budget year, the Administration sought, and obtained, a 25 percent cut in the agency's budget and staff. OMB Director Stockman candidly admitted that the cuts were "not designed solely to reduce the size of the federal budget ...." Rather, he said, they "form an integral part of the Administration's efforts to redirect regulatory policy." In other words, less funding meant less activity.

How much has it been cut? The CPSC's budget request for FY 1989 is $32.9 million and 532 full-time staff. This represents a 58.6 percent drop in constant dollars from its budget of $30.9 million in FY 1974. In its early years, the CPSC maintained 14 area offices throughout the country. Area offices conduct critical inspections to determine whether agency rules are being complied with, to investigate product-related injuries to determine whether products present unreasonable risks of injury and to provide safety information to consumers and industry. Because of cuts in funding and staff in 1981, the CPSC closed nine offices and, as of FY 1988, planned to shutter two more, leaving it with a grand total of three area offices for the entire United States.

In its emaciated state, the CPSC has moved from a preventive to a reactive status. As former Commissioner, Stuart Statler, put it, the agency operates more as the "ambulance at the bottom of the cliff instead of the fence atop it."

Because the CPSC is so small, policies regarding its budget are as much symbolic as financial. Just as abolishing the CPSC would have had no appreciable effect on the nation's deficit, doubling the agency's budget would similarly go unnoticed. However, budget decisions about the CPSC do play a major role in sending a message about the president's views regarding consumer protection, product safety and regulation. This is so because the CPSC is a highly visible agency. According to a 1982 Lou Harris poll, "Consumerism in the Eighties," the CPSC outranked Ralph Nader, the U.S. Congress and all other federal agencies in popularity among the American public. Attacking the CPSC was the Administration's way of signalling its dislike for product safety regulation.

Still, simply "throwing dollars" at the CPSC absent other major changes (discussed later) would be an exercise in futility. In fact, some of the most needed reforms at the agency either would save money or require no additional funding. Some agency functions, however, need more resources. In particular, the CPSC has cut in half its National Electronic Injury Surveillance System (NEISS), a network of hospital emergency rooms that regularly report on product-related injuries, to the point that it takes the agency roughly twice as long to collect necessary information on product-specific injuries as it did when NEISS was fully funded. Delays in gathering this information result in unnecessary deaths and injuries.

Similarly, the agency's field staff has been slashed so much that the agency cannot truly be considered to maintain a national presence. Injuries and deaths cannot be adequately investigated, companies cannot be inspected, state and local liaison with state and local governments cannot be sustained and the public cannot be informed without some restoration of the agency's original field operations.

As a measure of how a greater investment in the CPSC could return a dividend of fewer deaths and injuries, here is a partial listing obtained from agency insiders of pressing problems unaddressed or addressed inadequately by the agency: cigarette lighter fires, unstable bunk beds, potential carcinogens such as DEHP and nitrosamines in children's products, unstable and inadequate home playground equipment, acute and chronic hazards posed by formaldehyde in consumer products, unstable and inadequately designed off-the-road children's bicycles, permanent paralysis resulting from diving board accidents, deaths to children crushed by automatic garage door openers, acute and chronic hazards from indoor air pollutants, exploding gas barbecue grills, kerosene heater "flare-up" fires and circuit breakers that don't break circuits.

We suggest that a future budget of $40 million, or an increase of roughly $7 million over the current budget, is necessary and realistic. This would help restore the agency's injury data gathering capabilities as well as its enforcement strength. Should the new president seek an increase for the CPSC, he should make clear that an increase in no way signifies that the new administration intends for the agency to become a "regulate first, talk later" body. To the contrary, the agency should continue the tradition begun under Susan King, CPSC Chairman during the Carter Administration, (and carried to abusive extremes under Chairman Scanlon) of working cooperatively with industry groups to promote voluntary standards and product recalls.

IV. NEW PRIORITIES AND INITIATIVES

AGENCY ORGANIZATION AND STRUCTURE
1. **Decide Whether the CPSC Should Remain As a Collegial, Independent Agency or Be Transformed Into a Single Administrator Agency.** In recent years, some observers have suggested that the CPSC be transformed from its status as an independent collegial agency to that of a single administrator agency. Some, but not all, have further suggested that the agency be folded into a larger department, such as Health and Human Services. The arguments advanced in favor of the change are that a single administrator would operate more efficiently and expeditiously than a multi-headed body.

Those who favor retention of the CPSC's current status argue that better, more thoughtful decisions get made by collegial bodies. Commission policy setting often involves complex judgments about and occasional trade-offs among scientific data, engineering analyses, injury information and economic calculations. According to their argument, a collegial body with diverse viewpoints can make such complex judgments better than a single individual.

We make no specific recommendation about agency structure except to caution the new administration not to conclude that the agency's problems will be solved either by changing or retaining its collegial form. Far more critical to its success will be the quality of the people appointed to office, the commitment they bring to promoting product safety, the policy direction given them by the White House and the resources provided to them to carry out their mission. Furthermore, we would urge the new president not to expend his limited political capital in a fight to change the agency's structure if that would forestall other, more significant changes.

One "middle-ground" approach would be to preserve the current three-member status of the agency. Perhaps the best approach to this would be to appoint two new Commissioners immediately (this would require cooperation from the House Appropriations Committee in removing the restriction on paying more than three commissioners). Then, upon the expiration of Scanlon's and Graham's terms, the president should not appoint replacements. This would allow the administration the ability to assume immediate control of the CPSC, but allow it to revert to a three member size and thus not lock the tiny agency into a five member status indefinitely. Such an approach would likely be more acceptable to the House Appropriations Committee than simply enlarging the agency from its current size.

2. Reorganize and Strengthen CPSC Compliance Activities. Because of numerous personnel shifts and unnecessary procedures (e.g., cost-benefit analyses for recalls) imposed by Chairman Scanlon, the CPSC's compliance activities need to be thoroughly reviewed with an eye towards re-establishing an effective, aggressive system. One piece of good news in this respect is that many of the high quality CPSC staff have remained at the agency during the Reagan years. However, because of hostile leadership, they have been discouraged from enforcing the law and they are not organized very effectively.

3. Establish an Inter-Agency Liaison Group. One of the most effective innovations under the Carter Administration was the establishment of a liaison group among the federal health and safety agencies, including CPSC, FDA, OSHA and EPA. Under this arrangement, staff representatives regularly met to exchange information about products common to the jurisdiction of all agencies, e.g., formaldehyde, vinyl chloride and asbestos; to develop uniform procedures, such as reporting requirements; to exchange information relevant to compliance activities; and to discuss other common problems. The liaison group was widely regarded as a major success. Yet, the Reagan Administration immediately abolished this organization and replaced it with a far less effective and more politically controlled group. A new administration should re-establish a strong liaison among the federal regulatory agencies.

PROGRAMMATIC CHANGES

1. Emphasize the Administration's Commitment to the CPSC Without Creating Unreasonable Expectations. Although actions with respect to product safety count more than words, the new White House should use its bully pulpit to set some new directions for the CPSC. First, a new president should make clear his strong support for the life-saving mission of the CPSC. Second, he should indicate that he does not judge regulatory effectiveness by the number of safety standards issued or any other quantitative measure of regulatory actions taken. Rather, the key is for the CPSC to work effectively with all affected parties — manufacturers, distributors, retailers, importers, consumer groups and others — to protect members of the public from unreasonable risks of injury. Third, he should stress that industry must be prepared to cooperate with the CPSC if the nation's safety goals are to be achieved. This means that safety information must be shared with the agency and that good faith efforts to upgrade unreasonably dangerous products must be undertaken. If not, the CPSC must be prepared to take mandatory action.

These themes may sound platitudinous, but they are essential. Just as President Reagan's speeches proclaiming that government was the problem, not the solution, provided a framework for numerous specific policies, so too will the new president's remarks about product safety and the CPSC.

2. Abolish Unnecessary Restrictions on the Release of Essential Product Safety Information. Even those most opposed to government intervention in the marketplace usually will concede that it is appropriate for government to provide information to assist consumers in their decisionmaking about products. Unfortunately, the CPSC, unlike any other federal health and safety agency, operates under cumbersome, time-consuming and expensive restrictions when it comes to the release of safety information. These restrictions are found in section 6(b) of the CPSA.

Under section 6(b), before the agency releases information from which the identity of a manufacturer could be ascertained, it must first notify the manufacturer of the contemplated release of information, permit the manufacturer to comment on the information to be released, then take "reasonable steps" to assure (i) that the information is accurate, (ii) that disclosure is fair in the circumstances and (iii) that disclosure is reasonably related to accomplishing the purposes of the CPSA.

As interpreted and implemented by the CPSC, these "reasonable steps" require investigations, evaluations, product analyses, consumer complaint confirmation and other steps. Manufacturers not satisfied with the agency's actions have the right to be notified of an impending information release and the right to sue to enjoin its release.

Not unsurprisingly, a number of manufacturers have threatened lawsuits, leading the agency to engage in extensive negotiations in order to satisfy the manufacturers. Given the CPSC's limited resources, the agency understandably has been eager to avoid litigation over 6(b) matters. Consequently, manufacturers have found it relatively easy to intimidate the agency into withholding information about serious product hazards.

To repeat: the CPSC is the *only* federal health and safety agency with restrictions like these on the release of information. An FOIA requester at NHTSA, OSHA, FDA, EPA or the FTC would have immediate access to most product hazard information. Only the CPSC has its hands tied.

As originally interpreted by the CPSC, 6(b) applied only to instances in which the Commission itself *initiated* the disclosure of such information, such as safety bulletins, CPSC reports or press releases. Where outside parties requested information pursuant to the Freedom of Information Act (FOIA), the agency reasoned that it made little sense to follow 6(b) procedures since FOIA requesters would understand that the CPSC did not place its imprimatur on the information. Unfortunately, in 1980, after seven years and 50,000 FOIA requests handled by the agency under this interpretation, the U.S. Supreme Court ruled in *Consumer Product Safety Commission v. GTE Sylvania, Inc.* (447 U.S. 102 (1980)), as a matter of statutory interpretation, that the CPSA did not permit a distinction between CPSC-initiated disclosures and FOIA requests. Accordingly, the court required the agency to process *all* information releases under 6(b) procedures.

The Supreme Court's ruling proved to be a disaster both for consumers and the Commission. Prior to the decision, 85 percent of all requests for information under the Freedom of Information Act were answered within the 10 working days required under the FOIA. The remaining 15 percent were answered within 30 working days. Subsequent to the court's ruling, however, the number of FOIA requests answered within 10 days fell to 60 percent (these did not involve 6(b) issues) while the remaining requests that required 6(b) processing often took months, and even years, to process. In addition, information costs at the agency exploded. As of 1985, the agency spent roughly 13 staff years and $520,000 annually in direct costs to process information under 6(b) requirements.

Manufacturers and the Reagan Administration have defeated repeated congressional attempts to change 6(b). They have insisted that the CPSC review all information identifying manufacturers lest it turn out to be inaccurate and cause harm. Despite the years of contrary CPSC practice prior to the Supreme Court ruling, no instance of such harm has ever been documented. Moreover, even if such an occurrence were to happen, one must question whether it is an appropriate trade-off to keep the public uninformed about possible product hazards out of fear that a manufacturer on rare occasion might suffer from the release of inaccurate information.

3. Abolish Restrictions on the Release of "15(b)" Reports About Possible Substantial Product Hazards. Under section 15(b) of the Consumer Product Safety Act, businesses that obtain information about potentially hazardous defects in their products are required to notify the CPSC. This requirement is similar to ones enforced by the NHTSA with respect to motor vehicles and the FDA with respect to medical devices. Members of the public have access to reports of potential hazards at NHTSA and FDA as soon as they are filed.

Until 1981, the public also had access to "15(b)" reports at the CPSC. However, as part of the general CPSC bashing in that year, the Chamber of Commerce convinced Congress that, except for relatively narrow circumstances (e.g., if the agency brought an imminent hazard lawsuit in court), the public should be denied access to these reports. The Chamber's argument was that confidentiality would encourage manufacturers to file 15(b) reports. Unfortunately, this proved incorrect. To the contrary, the number of 15(b) reports, which had peaked at roughly 200 in FY 1979, dropped dramatically after the law was changed. In FY 1982, only 96 reports were submitted to the agency. (In recent years, the number of reports has crept upward from the low of 1981, but never has matched the high of 1979.) Clearly, confidentiality had no positive impact whatsoever.

On the other hand, the public has been denied access to important information about possible product hazards. Once again, manufacturers have gained unfair leverage in negotiating recalls with the agency.

A new administration should seek to repeal the confidentiality of "15(b)" reports. Again, consumer protection would be enhanced through traditional market mechanisms without costing the taxpayers a penny.

4. Stimulate Greater Reporting of Potential Product Hazards Under Section 15(b). It seems inconceivable with CPSC jurisdiction over 10,000-15,000 different products distributed by over one million businesses that only 100 to 200 instances arise nationwide that would lead a company to report a *possible* product hazard. When one considers that FDA receives roughly 18,000 such reports from a much smaller universe of manufacturers or that consumers file roughly 60,000 to 70,000 product liability lawsuits annually, one unavoidably concludes from the handful of 15(b) reports that this section is being widely ignored.

Indeed, the severest hazards involved in CPSC recalls have been uncovered by agency staff from information sources other than 15(b) reports. Clearly, something must be done to enhance this program.

One essential improvement is to increase agency communication with industry about the requirements of section 15(b). Of greater importance, however, is the need for additional resources, especially investigators, to uncover unreported and unrecalled hazardous products.

Another improvement would be to clarify more precisely which situations must be reported under the CPSA. Recently, the Commission took a major step backwards when, in response to industry complaints, it withdrew from the *Code of Federal Regulations* a series of written examples that the agency considered reportable under section 15(b). To clarify the scope of reportable events, a new administration should encourage Congress either to provide authority for the CPSC to write substantive rules regarding 15(b) or to amend the CPSA to include specific examples of reportable events. One useful step is a bill currently pending before Congress that would require 15(b) reports: (i) where a product has malfunctioned and the product would be likely to cause or contribute to death or serious injury if the malfunction were to recur, (ii) where a product is the subject of a liability claim or lawsuit involving an injury or death, (iii) where a product fails to comply with an applicable Federal or voluntary industry safety standard, (iv) where a product may contain a defect or (v) where a product otherwise may present a substantial risk of injury.

The critical point about this legislation is its emphasis on *potential*, as opposed to thoroughly documented, hazards. The CPSC must be apprised of risks at an early stage before injuries or deaths have begun to accumulate. Once the agency knows about the possibility of harm, it can assess in cooperation with the manufacturer whether or when remedial action is appropriate.

5. Streamline Agency Rulemaking Procedures. The Administrative Procedure Act (APA), 5 U.S.C. sections 551-559, provides the basic framework for federal agency rulemaking. In its most basic form, the APA requires an agency that contemplates rulemaking to provide notice to the public of the proposed rule, take comments on its proposed rule and promulgate a final rule if satisfied that no serious objections have been raised. Those aggrieved by an agency rule are free to challenge it in court if they feel it was not promulgated in accordance with the agency's legislative mandate or was not justified on the basis of available evidence.

Rulemaking at the CPSC must follow this basic model, but also must conform to a host of *additional* requirements not contained in the APA — in particular, many added in the 1981 amendments. These amendments impose "paralysis by analysis" on the agency. Under the CPSA as amended, the Commission must issue a formal Advance Notice of Proposed Rulemaking before it can promulgate a rule and evaluate comments about whether it should even begin rulemaking. Should the agency conclude after making numerous required statutory findings that rulemaking is appropriate, it must then conduct a preliminary regulatory analysis including a comprehensive cost-benefit analysis. If, after this, the CPSC still concludes that action is warranted, it must then propose its rule together with its regulatory analysis and take comments from the public. If, after reviewing the comments, the agency continues to believe that a regulation is warranted, it must publish a comprehensive final notice including elaborate findings about alternative courses of action considered, costs and benefits, its reasons for choosing to promulgate a regulation and specific findings that no adequate voluntary standards exist to deal with the problem.

The number and complexity of findings guarantees that the agency will rarely, if ever, undertake mandatory standards. Were there no formal requirements, the agency undoubtedly would engage in much of the same analysis called for in the law. The difference is that detailed legal requirements are a trap for the unwary. A failure on the Commission's part to follow the precise technical requirements of the law, however inadvertent or irrelevant to the requirements of a final regulation, would possibly be grounds for the invalidation of the regulation in court. Knowing this, industry lawyers are quick to raise endless objections based on these requirements every step of the way realizing that the agency will be forced to document in excruciating detail its compliance with the law.

If the new administration wants regulation be a credible threat in the CPSC's dealings with industry, it should support streamlining the rulemaking process. Due process in abundance for industry can be maintained even with streamlined procedures.

At a minimum, the requirement for an Advance Notice of Proposed Rulemaking should be made discretionary and some of the more irrelevant and burdensome requirements called for in the regulatory impact analyses should be abolished. Further, with respect to rules that simply require labels or specific instructions for products, all requirements not mandated by the Administrative Procedure Act should be abolished. Warnings and labels rarely have the economic costs associated with them that performance standards or bans do. Accordingly, the agency should be freer to consider and use this type of rule.

6. **Clarify the Role That Voluntary Standards Should Play in CPSC Activities.** As previously noted, the current group of Commissioners does not merely defer to voluntary standards; it grovels before

them. The Commission regularly halts agency action on the "hope" that industry groups will develop plans to write voluntary standards. It does so even where little, if any, evidence exists to demonstrate the likelihood of effective voluntary action. To paraphrase Will Rogers, the Commissioners have never met a voluntary standard they didn't like.

A new administration must restore proper balance to the Commission's relationship with the voluntary standards community. This need not result in large numbers of mandatory standards. Such a new balance would make clear industry's obligation to cooperate with the agency fully in its voluntary standards activities and affirm that the agency must insist on meaningful and credible progress from industry. This step requires no particular legislation. Rather, the agency must simply tighten its procedures for monitoring voluntary standards, establish deadlines for action, and move firmly to take mandatory action should it become clear that adequate voluntary action will not occur.

7. **Expand the Agency's Injury Data Capabilities.** An indispensable requirement for promoting effective product safety is to know which products injure, kill and sicken consumers. In this respect, one of the most useful activities undertaken by the CPSC is the acquisition and dissemination of injury data. Industry, consumers and the agency alike benefit from this information. Often, merely knowing that a problem exists virtually ensures its solution. Many manufacturers may not have an accurate notion of a product's potential for harm because they receive injury reports only for the products they personally make. They and other manufacturers refuse to share them out of fear of product liability lawsuits. Because the CPSC can gather this data nationwide, only it can often illuminate a risk that no one manufacturer could appreciate. Once aware of the situation, most manufacturers will attempt to fix it.

Unfortunately, as budget cuts have deepened, the CPSC increasingly has cut back on injury data collection. Cuts in information gathering have proven to be irresistible because the agency spends so much money in this area. To maintain its NEISS system in 60 hospitals — a number already too small — the agency spends hundreds of thousands of dollars annually. Yet, these expenditures must be made in order to provide the information necessary for the agency to determine which products present the greatest risks. For example, the NEISS system was instrumental in surfacing the hazards of ATVs.

A new administration must meet two immediate needs with respect to the CPSC's injury data systems. First, it must provide sufficient resources to enable them to function properly. Second, it must encourage the agency to expand data sources known to be useful that have historically been underutilized at the agency. For example, the CPSC receives thousands of consumer complaints every year. In a number of cases, these complaints have triggered investigations resulting in nationwide product recalls. Yet, while NHTSA has stated that consumer complaints to its hotline are its main data source for defect investigations, the CPSC does not use consumer complaints anywhere as effectively. In part, this is because the agency does not have the resources to receive or evaluate large numbers of consumer complaints. In part, it results from its inability to share this information in a timely fashion with the public — unlike NHTSA — because of section 6(b) restrictions.

FOOD & DRUGS:
The Food & Drug Administration

William B. Schultz[*]

SUMMARY OF RECOMMENDATIONS

The Food and Drug Administration has the broadest jurisdiction of any federal regulatory agency, being responsible for the safety of foods, drugs, cosmetics and medical devices. Although generally insulated from political pressures, there has been a major shift in the focus of the agency during the last eight years, as politics have frequently overridden science and in some cases the clear requirements of the law. The Reagan Administration accomplished this result by requiring the Department of Health and Human Services and the Office of Management and Budget to review important policy decisions of the FDA and by appointing commissioners who set a new tone for the agency.

As a result, the FDA allocated more resources to the approval of new drugs, long a priority of the drug industry, but it has allocated fewer resources to enforcement of food sanitation and the removal of unsafe and ineffective products from the market. During the 1990s, this orientation should be refocused by implementing the following recommendations:

* *Elimination of HHS and OMB Review.* The Commissioner of the Food and Drug Administration should have full authority to issue regulations pertaining to products within the FDA's jurisdiction, and HHS and OMB should not be permitted to overturn the Commissioner's decisions.

* *Enforcement of the Laws.* The Food, Drug and Cosmetic Act should be amended to give the FDA the authority to impose administrative penalties and to issue subpoenas; and the FDA's budget should be increased to give it sufficient resources to perform adequate fish inspections and the other tasks that are central to its mission.

* *Expediting Important Regulations.* To break its perennial logjam, the FDA should adopt a program to expedite the issuance of key regulations; this would include designating these regulations for fast-

---

[*] *William B. Schultz is a staff attorney at Public Citizen Litigation Group and an adjunct professor at the Georgetown University Law Center.*

track treatment; the simultaneous (rather than sequential) review of the regulations by the relevant divisions; and the adoption of internal timetables to which the agency would strictly adhere.

 * *Addressing the AIDS Crisis.* The next Congress and administration should insure that the agency is devoting adequate resources to evaluating the tests on AIDS drugs and vaccines; the Commissioner should reverse the policy of allowing foreign drug companies to market unapproved products through the mail to individuals in this country; and the Commissioner should take a leadership role in educating the public about the merits of the drug approval process.

I. INTRODUCTION AND OVERVIEW

The Food and Drug Administration is our oldest consumer protection agency. It also has the broadest jurisdiction, being responsible for regulating products that account for 25 cents of every dollar spent by American consumers. In addition to human drugs, the FDA is responsible for regulating medical and radiologic devices, vaccines, serums, blood, cosmetics and animal drugs. The agency also has jurisdiction over all food products, except for meat and poultry, which are regulated by the Department of Agriculture, and pesticides, over which it shares jurisdiction with the Environmental Protection Agency. It lacks jurisdiction over alcohol and tobacco. The FDA carries out its mission with only 7,300 employees and a budget of approximately $500 million.[1]

Congress adopted the first food and drug law in 1906. Perhaps because the agency is so old, it has never had the status of an independent regulatory agency such as the Federal Trade Commission or even a separate executive branch agency such as the Environmental Protection Agency. Instead, it has been a division of another agency since its creation, initially the Department of Agriculture, subsequently the Federal Security Administration, and in modern times the Department of Health, Education and Welfare ("HEW"), which was restructured as the Department of Health and Human Services ("HHS") in the late 1970s. The FDA is directed by a single commissioner who will be subject to Senate confirmation for the first time next year.

The agency is divided into sections that have been constantly renamed and reorganized during the past eight years. Currently, the principal divisions are the Center for Food Safety and Applied Nutrition, the Center for Drug Evaluation and Research, the Center for Biologics Evaluation and Research (which regulates vaccines and allergy treatments and diagnostic products), the Center for Devices and Radiological Health, the Center for Veterinary Medicine and the

National Center for Toxicological Research (the agency's research arm).

In addition, the FDA has an office of Chief Counsel, and various associate commissioners who are responsible for consumer affairs, regulatory affairs, public relations and legislative affairs. Historically, its Chief Counsel has played an active role in setting FDA policy, although this has been less the case during the current Administration. The quality of work done in that office has been among the best in the government.

The FDA regulates products in two basic ways. For the vast majority of products, the statute and regulations promulgated by the agency set a standard that products must meet. Examples are the requirement that food not be "adulterated" and that over-the-counter drugs be "generally recognized by experts" as being "safe and effective."[2] Products that are subject to this type of standard may be marketed without any prior review by the agency. However, products in violation of the standard are subject to injunction, seizure, as well as the criminal penalties provided for in the statute.[3]

On the other hand, beginning in 1938, Congress has enacted a series of statutes requiring that products within the jurisdiction of the FDA also be subject to *pre-market* review. This is essentially a licensing scheme, under which the product may not be sold until it is first approved by the agency. In 1938, Congress imposed the requirement that "new drugs" be "safe" and in 1962 it added the requirement that they be proven "effective" as well. Both effectiveness and safety must be proven by "substantial evidence," which the statute defines as "well-controlled clinical investigations."[4]

Congress also enacted laws requiring pre-market approval of food additives in 1958, and color additives in 1960.[5] Animal drugs were added to the list in 1962.[6] Each of these three laws contains a "Delaney Clause," prohibiting the FDA from approving these products unless the applicant has demonstrated that the substance does not cause cancer in humans and laboratory animals.[7]

Finally, in 1976 Congress adopted comprehensive legislation covering medical devices, although very few medical devices have actually been subjected to the pre-market approval requirements.[8]

The Federal Food, Drug and Cosmetic Act delegates all authority to the Secretary of the Department of Health and Human Services; prior to the Reagan Administration, the Secretary of HHS had delegated that authority to the Commissioner of the Food and Drug Administration.[9] As a result, before 1980, the agency had acted with extraordinary independence, at least in modern times. Because it was viewed as an agency charged with grappling with scientific issues, its decisions were rarely politically reviewed, much less overturned, by the Secretary of HEW or HHS.

This approach began to change in the Carter administration, though what started as an exception became the rule during the Reagan Administration. As one of his first official acts, incoming Secretary Richard Schweiker issued a regulation withdrawing the delegation for "highly significant public issues."[10] Today, the Secretary of the Department of HHS reviews virtually every regulation issued by the Food and Drug Administration.

Another important change made by the Reagan Administration is the expanded role of the Office of Management and Budget ("OMB"). As a result of Executive Order No. 12291 and Executive Order No. 12498, all significant regulations and plans for future regulatory initiatives must be reviewed by the OMB, in addition to HHS. On a number of occasions, this process has allowed special interest industry groups to undermine important health and safety regulations. On other occasions, it has substantially delayed the implementation of regulations by the FDA.

II. SIGNIFICANT POLICY RECOMMENDATIONS

When the Reagan Administration took office, it emphasized voluntary industry compliance instead of regulation and it signalled that enforcement of the law was no longer a priority. As a result, FDA enforcement actions declined by about 50% during the first four years and the agency's personnel shifted their philosophy of regulation.[11]

During the second half of the Reagan Administration, the Commissioner has set the wrong tone in other ways. For example, when six color additives turned out to cause cancer in animals, the FDA, taking directions from HHS, reinterpreted the Delaney clause rather than remove the dyes from the market, as required by law. The agency's decision was reversed by a unanimous panel on the U.S. Court of Appeals for the District of Columbia Circuit, in an opinion written by Judge Stephen Williams, a judge appointed by President Reagan.[12]

The most important new issue to face the agency during the Reagan Administration is AIDS. In response to criticism that the FDA has kept AIDS drugs from reaching patients, the Commissioner should have taken a leadership role in explaining the strength of our current approval process to the American public. In recent years, the agency has adopted regulations designed to expedite the approval process for AIDS drugs if they become available and to make such drugs available while they are being tested if they show promise. On the other hand, our laws do protect consumers against the fraudulent sale of products for which there is no evidence of effectiveness.

Rather than defend our current drug approval system, however, Commissioner Frank Young recently initiated a program whereby AIDS patients may purchase drugs directly from foreign drug manufacturers, even though those drugs are not approved by the FDA, and thus ordinarily would be seized if imported. In doing so, he has sent exactly the wrong message to AIDS victims, both undermining the confidence in our drug approval system and giving them false hope about these therapies.

The new administration should send a different kind of message. While voluntary compliance with the laws should be encouraged, it is no substitute for a vigorous enforcement program where laws have been broken. And while industry deserves timely decisions on applications to market new drugs and other products, the agency should place more emphasis on its consumer protection responsibilities, including its responsibility to withdraw products from the market that are unsafe or ineffective.

STRUCTURAL AND GENERIC RECOMMENDATIONS

1. The FDA Should Be Given Authority to Decide Matters Within Its Jurisdiction. OMB and HHS review of FDA decisions has severely undermined the agency's ability to carry out its mandate of protecting the public. For example, the FDA's decision to require a label on aspirin products to warn about Reye's syndrome, a rare but sometimes fatal disease that can occur when children with flu or chicken pot take aspirin, was overruled by OMB; its decision to ban six carcinogenic color additives was reversed by the Secretary; and HHS also overturned its decision not to regulate the interstate shipment of unpasteurized milk, which can contain salmonella and other forms of bacteria that can lead to illness.

In each of these cases, the FDA's decision was made after lengthy deliberations by the scientists and lawyers at the agency, only to be overturned when the affected industry successfully lobbied the political appointees at HHS and/or OMB. After litigation and Congressional oversight hearings, the FDA belatedly required the label on aspirin, banned five of the color additives, and regulated the interstate shipment of unpasteurized milk. But the delay caused by HHS and OMB review probably resulted in at least hundreds of needless deaths.

There is another, more subtle effect of HHS and OMB review. Today, FDA officials often choose not to issue important regulations because they know that OMB will not give its approval, or will seriously undercut the impact of the regulations by delaying its review. For example, recently the agency had to consider the question of regulating urethane, a carcinogen that has been found in many al-

coholic beverages. At the end of 1985, Canada had set limits on urethane in wine and liquor.

The FDA and industry began testing alcohol products for urethane
levels and identified at least 100 that have levels exceeding the
Canadian limits. The FDA seriously considered regulation, but, according to an article published in *Food Chemical News*, the Commissioner decided not to regulate urethane because he concluded that a
regulation might have difficulty obtaining clearance from OMB. Instead, he entered into voluntary agreements with the wine and liquor
industry under which the manufacturers would not meet the Canadian limits until 1995. The agreements are not enforceable by the
FDA.

In other instances, HHS and OMB review have caused long delays in issuing regulations. For example, the agency has taken 10
years or more to issue regulations covering particular categories of
over-the-counter drugs, and a significant part of this delay is at-
tributable to HHS and OMB review. And when the agency finally
completed its rules designed to speed up its review of new drug
applications, long a priority of the drug industry, it took the FDA
two years to finalize the regulation, largely because of the time required for HHS and OMB review. Thus, HHS and OMB review affect
the agency's ability to regulate in two fundamental ways: it has delayed regulation for an agency that is already extraordinarily slow,
and it has added a political element to decisionmaking which ought
to have an especially strong scientific base.

HHS and OMB review, however, is a double-edged sword.
Knowledgeable industry officials acknowledge that the public's loss
of confidence in the FDA has spurred activity in the states which
they regard as far less desirable than uniform federal regulation.[13]

For all these reasons, the FDA's authority to decide matters
within its jurisdiction should be restored by redelegating authority to
FDA and by revoking Executive Orders Nos. 12291 and 12498. HHS
and OMB would be permitted to comment on any proposed regulations, but the final decisionmaking authority would be given to the
Commissioner of the FDA. The president, of course, would always
have the power to replace any Commissioner who was not carrying
out the policies of his administration.

**2. The FDA Should Adopt Procedures for Expediting Important
Decisions.** For many years, the FDA has been the subject of intense
scrutiny and criticism by the drug industry, which has claimed that
there is a "drug lag" in the United States caused by the FDA. In response, the FDA created a fast track for the very small number of
new drug applications that are submitted every year for breakthrough drugs. When the new drug applications are in good order, it
is capable of reviewing these drugs relatively quickly. Although the

review of these drugs takes an average of two years (in part due to inadequacies in the new drug applications), FDA took only 107 days to review and approve the application for AZT, the only AIDS drug that has been licensed in this country.

Compared to its record in removing ineffective or unsafe products, the agency's record in approving new drugs looks fast. Thus the FDA has taken more than 25 years to review the effectiveness of prescription drugs that were on the market when Congress adopted the 1962 efficacy amendments; it took a similar period of time to decide the safety of color additives, many of which turned out to be carcinogens. One pre-1960 carcinogenic color additive (FD&C Red No. 3) is still on the market, pending further study, *28 years* after Congress directed the agency to decide whether all color additives were safe within the meaning of the Act.

The FDA's record in reviewing over-the-counter ("OTC") drugs is even worse. Directed in 1962 by Congress to decide the safety and effectiveness of over-the-counter drugs, the agency waited until 1972 to even establish the OTC Drug Review. By the early 1980s, its scientific panels had determined that two-thirds of all OTC drug ingredients are unsafe or ineffective for their claimed uses (most were deemed ineffective). Nevertheless, today the FDA has issued final regulations covering only about 20% of those ingredients.

The FDA's record in addressing serious health risks of single products has also been poor. Among numerous examples, tampons and toxic shock syndrome ("TSS") is typical. In the late 1970s, the link between TSS and Rely Tampons was discovered, and by 1981 the FDA had determined that women could reduce their risk of TSS by using less absorbent tampons. In 1982, it issued a regulation requiring tampon manufacturers to disclose this fact, but did not require any standardized absorbency labeling. So one manufacturer's "super" may actually be less absorbent than another manufacturer's "regular" tampon. Consequently, in 1984 the agency determined that a labeling regulation would be necessary. It was important for the FDA to act quickly since TSS can kill — at least 1600 women have contracted TSS since 1981, and 36 have died. Nevertheless, the FDA took four years to issue a proposed regulation, and has still not disclosed when it will issue the final requirement that manufacturers comply with standardized labeling.

Very often the FDA takes four to six years or even more to issue important regulations. It took eight years to issue the quality control regulations that were required by the Medical Device Act of 1976, and it still has not issued the regulations that Congress required be issued within one year in the 1984 Generic Drug Law. This delay is not explained by any statutory requirement, since the Administrative

Procedure Act only requires that the public be given a brief period of time to comment.[14]

This problem should be given high priority during the next administration. One approach would be to appoint a team within the Commissioner's office who would be assigned the job of expediting a small number of critically important regulations. This team would be given the authority to require relevant agency officials to set deadlines and help resolve differences within the divisions that can often delay the promulgation of regulations.

The team should also have the authority to require that divisions review regulations simultaneously. Currently, regulations are often reviewed sequentially; for example, the Chief Counsel's office might not begin its review until the OTC Drug Division had completed its work, which must in turn await a statistical review. To the extent possible, all divisions should review important regulations at the same time.

Such an approach was used for the regulations regarding investigational new drug applications that the agency issued in 1987. The agency was under a tight deadline because it had promised Vice President Bush's Regulatory Task Force that it would issue a final regulation within 60 days of the time it issued its proposal. Although the regulations were controversial, generating more than 200 comments and a Congressional hearing, the agency expeditiously issued a 40-50 page document 62 days after soliciting comment.

3. The FDA Should Aggressively Enforce the Food and Drug Laws. Upon taking office in January 1981, the Reagan Administration began talking more about "voluntary compliance" and less about enforcement of the laws. This theme was passed on to the Commissioner of the FDA who conveyed it to FDA employees. As a result, during the first four years of the Reagan Administration, enforcement actions at the FDA declined by about 50%. Anecdotal evidence suggests that the new policy has had an adverse impact on warehouse cleanliness, and on the quality of foods, drugs and cosmetics.

This policy jeopardizes the health of consumers and deprives them of the protections to which they are entitled under the Food, Drug and Cosmetic Act. It is also unfair to businesses that comply with the law, since their competitors are allowed illegally to cut corners and costs. The next administration — and Congress via oversight hearings — should emphasize civil and criminal enforcement actions to force compliance with the food and drug laws.

There are also a number of statutory amendments that would assist the FDA in its enforcement efforts. Although the Food, Drug and Cosmetic Act provides for criminal penalties, it should be amended to give both the courts and the Commissioner the authority to assess civil fines. The Act also should be amended to give the agency subpoena power required in connection with administrative proceedings. Finally, the statute needs to be amended to provide for administrative detention of adulterated and misbranded foods, mandatory food coding to facilitate food recalls, and additional authority to give the FDA access to records regarding adulterated foods and other products.

4. The New Administration Should Increase the FDA's Budget. During the Reagan Administration, FDA personnel have been cut from 8,000 to a little more than 7,000 employees. Given the scope and importance of the agency's mandate, this is simply insufficient to do the job. The imbalance between the personnel allocated to the FDA and to other agencies is demonstrated by the comparison between the 10,000 inspectors that the Department of Agriculture employs to inspect meat and poultry and the 700 inspectors that the FDA employs for all inspections. As a result, the FDA can allocate only a small percentage of these inspectors to perform fish inspections, even though adulterated fish are the source of a number of very serious health risks.

While budget increases will not be popular with the next president or Congress, the increases here would be relatively modest and would be justified because the FDA's mission is central to our public health.

DRUGS AND BIOLOGICS

1. The FDA Should Continue to Give High Priority to AIDS Drugs and Vaccines, But Acknowledge the Need to Protect Victims From Fraudulent Therapies. During the coming decade, the FDA's most visible activity will be the licensing and promotion of products designed to treat AIDS.

In order to consider what role the FDA should play in the AIDS crisis, it is necessary to understand the limits of the FDA's function. The FDA is not responsible for basic drug research. Therefore, it is not at fault if a promising therapy is being inadequately tested, or is not being tested at all. Instead the FDA's role is to approve testing procedures and evaluate test results.[15]

There have been two themes to the FDA's response to the AIDS crisis. First, the agency has made AIDS its highest priority and has allocated considerable resources to reviewing and approving AIDS therapies. In 1987, for example, the FDA carved out an exception to its regulations, designed to make lifesaving drugs available to more people while they are being tested for safety and effectiveness. Other modifications in its regulations explicitly allow the agency to curtail clinical research where early results are sufficient to justify a finding of substantial evidence of effectiveness. Even before the FDA adopted these regulations, it had appropriately invoked this procedure for AZT, the only drug that the agency has approved for the treatment of AIDS.

Second, the Commissioner has unfortunately tried to blunt criticism of the FDA by making it easier for AIDS victims to obtain drugs not even tested in this country, where there is no evidence of safety or effectiveness. In June 1988, over the objection of senior staff at the agency, the Commissioner announced to a group of AIDS victims that the agency would permit individuals to import unapproved AIDS drugs through the mail, for their own use.

This policy panders to the fears of desperately ill people who are extremely susceptible to medical fraud. It also could cause AIDS patients to forego more promising therapies in favor of unproven products that would not otherwise be available in this country. Finally, it threatens to undermine the public's confidence in the drug approval process, since it suggests that even the Commissioner believes that the system fails to make important drugs available to people when they need them.

During the foreseeable future, the FDA will be judged by how it responds to the AIDS crisis. The easy part is allocating adequate resources to evaluate drug and vaccine protocols as quickly as possible; the hard part is balancing the desires of individual AIDS victims for drugs, regardless of whether there is evidence that they work, against society's judgment that manufacturers should be prohibited from selling unproven drugs, even to terminally ill patients.

Another societal interest which raises even more difficult ethical issues concerns the benefits of drug research. Until recently, participation in drug research was the primary method by which individuals with untreatable diseases could gain access to unapproved and possibly beneficial drugs. This research was then used to separate effective treatments from those that are ineffective, to the benefit of future patients. As unproven AIDS drugs become available from foreign countries and elsewhere, it has become harder to convince patients to participate in clinical research. As a result, future patients will suffer, while it is doubtful that patients who currently have AIDS will benefit.

The FDA needs a coherent AIDS policy, one that includes input from a cross-section of interests on this issue, including AIDS patients, researchers and others. The Commissioner should either appoint such a task force or solicit comments on this issue, and then announce a unified plan.

2. The FDA Should Continue to Support Generic Drugs, and Adopt a Mandatory Patient Package Insert Program. Two significant consumer goals over the past 15 years have been reducing the marketing restrictions on generic drugs and requiring mandatory patient package inserts ("PPIs"). The Reagan Administration showed initial hostility to both programs. Early in the Administration, Secretary Schweiker delayed the FDA's "paper NDA" policy, which was designed to remove certain barriers to the approval of generic drugs that were copies of drugs first marketed after 1962. Subsequently, that policy was reinstated, and in 1984 Congress enacted the Drug Price Competition and Patent Term Restoration Act, which allowed manufacturers of generic drugs to file abbreviated new drug applications ("ANDAs") once the patent on the pioneer product has expired. Rather than conducting expensive clinical studies, a sponsor is required to demonstrate that its product is "therapeutically equivalent" to the pioneer product. As a result, generic drugs are much more widely available today than they were even five years ago.

The PPI program did not fare as well. After approximately five years of study, the FDA in 1980 implemented a pilot program that would have required PPIs for 10 widely-used prescription drugs, which accounted for one-seventh of the prescriptions sold in the United States. These inserts would have provided consumers with information about the approved uses of the drugs (many prescription drugs are prescribed for unapproved uses), their indications, side effects and what substances not to take with the product. This information is routinely provided with OTC drugs, but, with a few exceptions such as the birth control pill, is not given to prescription drug consumers.

One of the Reagan FDA's first acts was to revoke the PPI program, with the result that consumers do not gain access to this vital information. Restoring the program should be made a high priority of the next administration and Congress.

3. Is the Program for Approving New Prescription Drugs Jeopardizing Public Health? As mentioned above, one of the highest priorities of Reagan's FDA has been to speed up the drug approval process. This is a valid goal so long as the public health is not jeopardized and resources not diverted from more important projects.

During the past ten years, the agency has approved a number of drugs, none of which had significant advantages over existing treatments but which were eventually removed from the market because they turned out to cause serious conditions, including death. Examples are Selacryn, Zomax, Oraflex, three drugs for blood pressure, pain relief and arthritis that caused liver and kidney damage (Oraflex and Selacryn), and allergic reactions leading to shock (Zomax), all occasionally leading to serious injury and death. At the present time, there is no evidence of a direct connection between the agency's program to speed up the drug approval process and these drug tragedies. However, the agency's practice of approving disproportionate numbers of new drug applications in December of each year suggests that it may be trading protection of the public health for speed in drug approvals.

The next government should take a close look at this issue to insure that the health of the American public is not being sacrificed for speedier drug approvals.

4. Other Issues:

* *Pre-1938 Prescription Drugs.* The Food, Drug and Cosmetic Act exempts drugs first marketed prior to 1938 from the licensing requirements of the statute. However, the agency may require the manufacturer to submit evidence of safety and effectiveness if the labeling of the product has been changed since 1938.

Although the FDA has systematically reviewed the safety and effectiveness of all prescription drugs first marketed after 1938, it has never adopted a program for *pre*-1938 drugs. These drugs should be identified, evaluated to determine whether they continue to qualify for the grandfather exception to the statute, and then evaluated to determine whether they comply with the applicable requirements of law.

* *Over-the-Counter Drugs.* A 1978 internal management study was severely critical of the structure, pace and priorities of the OTC drug review, and a 1982 Report of the General Accounting Office reached similar conclusions. Nevertheless, in 1986, the Commissioner cut the personnel allocated the OTC Review from 38 to 21.5 full-time equivalent employees.

The Over-the-Counter Drug Review will continue to be an embarrassment to the agency until it issues final regulations identifying the requirements that OTC manufacturers must meet in order to comply with the Food, Drug and Cosmetic Act. Although the Commissioner has stated that the FDA will complete the OTC Review by 1993, in the past the agency has never complied with similar commitments.[16] The next administration should adopt an internal plan to meet this commitment. It should also expedite the publication of final regulations for categories of drugs where the agency has already issues proposed rules and received comments from interested parties.

Finally, there is currently very little effective regulation of OTC drug advertising claims, which is the responsibility of the Federal Trade Commission. As a result, drug companies make numerous misleading claims. Serious consideration shall be given to transferring the jurisdiction for regulating OTC drug advertising to the FDA, which has successfully and tightly regulated prescription drug advertising, and to giving the FDA adequate resources to enforce the prohibitions against false and misleading OTC drug claims.

* *The Prescribing of Prescription Drugs for Unapproved Uses.* The FDA regulates drugs, but has little legal authority over doctors. Although the Food, Drug and Cosmetic Act prohibits drug companies

from advertising or otherwise promoting their products for unapproved uses, nothing in the law prohibits a doctor from prescribing a drug to patients for indications that have never been approved by the agency. Instead, doctors are regulated by state licensing boards and possible malpractice lawsuits.

Two recent controversies raise questions about the wisdom of this wholesale exemption. The first is Accutane, a powerful drug that is effective in treating acne but that also causes birth defects in one in four children born to women who have used it during pregnancy. For this reason, the FDA has approved the drug only for severe recalcitrant cystic acne, but not for milder forms of acne. Although only about 70,000 women in this country have the severe form of acne, according to the drug's manufacturer, approximately 560,000 women have been prescribed the drug since 1982. As a result, according to the FDA's own estimates, there have been about 600 birth defects and countless numbers of unnecessary abortions.

The second example involves prescribing steroids to athletes. Although steroids are approved for a number of medical conditions, use of mega-doses for physical conditioning entails unjustifiable risks and has not been approved by the FDA. Nevertheless, as the highly publicized case of Olympic athlete Ben Johnson shows, widespread misprescribing of steroid products is a serious problem.

Legal experts are divided on whether the FDA has the authority to limit the prescribing authority of doctors. In the case of Accutane, the agency should prohibit dermatologists from prescribing Accutane to patients with less severe forms of acne than those approved by the FDA, with penalties imposed on physicians who violate the regulations; in the case of steroids, perhaps there should be a specific prohibition on prescribing these drugs to healthy athletes, with penalties attached.

The next government should determine once and for all whether the FDA has the authority to limit the prescribing of drugs to particular specialties and to prohibit prescribing for unapproved uses. If the Commissioner determines that he does not have this authority, then the agency should ask Congress to adopt legislation.

* *Direct Advertising to Consumers of Prescription Drugs.* Traditionally, prescription drug advertising has been directed only to doctors. FDA regulations have made it impractical to advertise prescription drugs to consumers; consequently, such advertising has generally been limited to advertising about price and the general reputation of a particular drug manufacturer.

In recent years, there has been increased interest in direct advertising of prescription drugs to consumers on the part of a few drug manufacturers, the advertising industry and certain elements of the media. In general, the medical profession, the pharmaceutical industry and consumer groups have opposed such advertising.

The failure of the Federal Trade Commission and the FDA to regulate over-the-counter drug claims effectively suggests that the FDA would not be capable of ensuring that prescription drug advertising is truthful and not misleading. While such advertising might have the marginal benefit of "educating" consumers about prescription drugs, such gains are more than outweighed by the injury caused by misleading advertising in the absence of an adequate enforcement capability by the agency.

* *Medical Devices.* Medical devices, regulated under the Medical Device Act of 1976, include products such as tongue depressors, which require little regulation, and pacemakers and heart valves, which should be carefully regulated by the federal government. One serious omission in the current law is the absence of a requirement for hospital reporting of injuries caused by medical devices. Instead, the law relies on manufacturers to report adverse experiences, even though a number of such events occur in hospitals but are not reported to manufacturers. Legislation to correct this omission was almost enacted during the last Congress and should be made a high priority.

Another serious problem is the excessive use of the 510(k) loophole under which new medical devices that are "substantially equivalent" to devices already on the market may escape the pre-market review required by the statute.[17] This loophole has almost swallowed up the Act, as every year the FDA permits hundreds and possibly thousands of 510(k) devices to escape the more stringent requirements of the Act. Again legislation should set a date after which a more thorough pre-market review would be substituted for the substantial equivalence determination.

* *Foods.* For most of the Reagan Administration, the Center for Food Safety was directed by Dr. Sanford Miller, who had been appointed during the Carter Administration. While the Center did not propose major programs advocated by consumer groups, it has been surprisingly successful in insulating many of *its* decisions from the politics of the Reagan Administration. The Center has been overruled, however, on a number of important and highly publicized decisions. Two examples are the Center's decision to ban six color additives and its decision to regulate the interstate shipment of unpasteurized milk. In each case, the FDA and Center were overturned by HHS but were vindicated when public interest organizations challenged the HHS decision in Court.

Two other significant failings of the current Administration are its proposal to allow food manufacturers to make health claims for foods and its failure to require that important nutritional information be disclosed on foods. The health claims issue arose when Kelloggs began advertising that its bran cereal helped protect against cancer. In the past, the agency had treated such claims as drug claims which would be permitted only if the sponsor demonstrated effectiveness under the standards of the drug provisions of the Food, Drug and Cosmetic Act. Kelloggs did not even attempt to make such a showing.

The FDA, however, has proposed a rule which would permit a wide variety of health claims to be made on foods with no effective regulation by the agency. Congressman Ted Weiss's Subcommittee on Intergovernmental Relations and Human Resources has concluded that the agency's proposal is illegal.[18] In addition, as is true with direct advertising of prescription drugs, the agency does not have the resources to monitor the fraudulent claims that are certain to be made. Therefore, the FDA should abandon its health claims proposal, and reimpose its longstanding requirement that manufacturers who make such claims must meet the standards of the drug provisions of the Act.

The FDA has also done a poor job in insuring that adequate nutritional information is provided on foods. For example, even though it has acknowledged the evidence that too much salt can lead to high blood pressure and heart disease, the FDA has relied on voluntary labeling to provide this information to consumers, a program which like many other voluntary industry efforts has largely failed.

In the next government, the whole issue of nutritional labeling should be reevaluated. Currently, only manufacturers who make some nutritional claims are required to place nutritional information on the product's label, the form and content of which is prescribed by the FDA. The agency should carefully consider what information should ideally be required on a nutritional label and require it for all foods, where practical.[19]

The FDA is also responsible for regulating "unavoidable" contaminants such as mercury in fish and aflatoxin. Some of these contaminants have serious health risks. For example, aflatoxin, which is found in some corn and peanuts, is one of the most potent carcinogens ever discovered. Although classified as unavoidable, often the levels of contaminants can be lowered by good harvesting, storing and manufacturing practices. The FDA has never issued regulations to cover these substances, but instead has relied on unenforceable "action levels," which are standards that it establishes without any public input. As a result, each time it brings a court action to enjoin the sale of a food contaminated with one of these substances, it must reprove its case. The next FDA should identify the most serious unavoidable contaminants and then issue regulations setting allowable tolerance levels.

* *Cosmetics.* As far as regulation is concerned, cosmetics are also a somewhat forgotten product. The Food, Drug and Cosmetic Act prohibits the sale of "adulterated" cosmetics and regulates color additives in cosmetic products.[20] However, although cosmetics are often ingested (particularly lipsticks), absorbed into the skin, and can irritate the eye, the FDA apparently has no statutory authority to require pre-market testing and does little to insure that they are safe or that their use entails no unreasonable risk.

Cosmetic manufacturers often make generally unsubstantiated claims, an example being claims that cosmetics will eliminate wrinkles and regenerate skin. With little regulation, competition in the marketplace emphasizes the claims rather than the quality of the products being produced. This entire area needs to be evaluated and a coherent program should be implemented to regulate cosmetics.

NOTES

[1] The FDA's overall staff was reduced by more than 10% during the Reagan years.

[2] 21 *U.S.C.* 321(p)(1), 342, 355.

[3] 21 *U.S.C.* 331-334.

[4] 21 *U.S.C.* 355(d); *United States v. Rutherford,* 442 U.S. 544 (1979).

[5] 21 *U.S.C.* 348, 376.

[6] 21 *U.S.C.* 360b.

[7] 21 *U.S.C.* 348(c)(3)(A), 360b(d)(1)(H), 376(b)(5)(B).

[8] 21 *U.S.C.* 360, *et seq.*

[9] However, Congress provided that only the Secretary of HHS could invoke the provision of the Act that authorized the agency to withdraw its approval of a new drug without providing an opportunity for a hearing in the case of an "imminent hazard." 21 *U.S.C.* 355(e)(5). This provision has been used only once, in the case of the diabetic drug Phenformin.

[10] 21 *C.F.R.* 5.11(a)(2)(1985).

[11] Public Citizen Health Research Group, *Decreased Law Enforcement at the Food and Drug Administration and the Occupational Safety and Health Administration FY 1981-1984* (1984).

[12] *Public Citizen v. Young,* 831 F.2d 1108 (D.C. Cir. 1987).

[13] The most visible example is Proposition 65 in California, a popularly adopted initiative that requires warning labels identifying carcinogens on all products.

[14] 5 *U.S.C.* 553.

[15] Approximately 250 drugs and vaccines are currently being tested for treatment of AIDS.

[16] The commitment was made in defense to a lawsuit brought by public interest organizations charging that the FDA has unreasonably delayed the OTC Drug Review, in violation of the Administrative Procedure Act. *Cutler v. Hayes,* 818 F.2d 879 (D.C. Cir. 1987) (currently on remand to the U.S. District Court for the District of Columbia).

[17] *See* 21 *U.S.C.* 360(k).

[18] Subcommittee on Intergovernmental Relations and Human Resources, *Disease-Specific Claims on Health Labels: An Unhealthy Idea,* H.R. Rep. No. 100-561 (1988).

[19] Legislative authority should be requested if the FDA determines that it lacks the authority to require a uniform nutritional label.

[20] 21 *U.S.C.* 361, 376.

AUTO SAFETY:
National Highway Traffic Safety Administration

Joan Claybrook*

SUMMARY OF RECOMMENDATIONS

Motor vehicle crashes are the leading cause of severe injury and death for Americans under the age of 44 in the United States, yet many such casualties can be mitigated or prevented with available vehicle technologies and effective state laws. In fact, the federal highway safety program, begun in 1966, has since that date saved over 150,000 lives and prevented millions of injuries.

Despite the opportunity to save thousands of additional lives annually, the Reagan Administration has chosen to ignore years of valuable research and instead serve as a conduit for industry objections to vital safety standards. It revoked life-saving motor vehicle standards, discontinued critical research programs, undermined valuable public information programs, often failed to enforce the safety recall requirements in the law, cut the funding for the federal regulatory and grant-in-aid safety and fuel economy programs by 50 percent (inflation-adjusted) and cut staff by 25 percent.

There are a number of actions the new administration and Congress can initiate within months of taking office that could result in saving an additional 7,000 lives and thousands of disabling injuries each year. These are:

* Issuance of effective motor vehicle crashworthiness standards for side impact and pedestrian protection.

* Improved brake and rollover safety standards for light trucks, large trucks and motorcycles.

* Enactment of state laws to achieve nationwide motorcycle helmet use, safety belt use, slower speeds and administrative license suspension for drunk drivers.

* Enforcement to assure that millions of vehicles with safety defects are recalled.

* Distribution of factual consumer information to help make the marketplace work.

---

* Joan Claybrook is president of Public Citizen and former Administrator of the National Highway Traffic Safety Administration.

In addition, the federal fuel economy standards, which by law are 27.5 mpg unless amended, should be gradually increased to conserve oil, reduce U.S. vulnerability in a future oil crisis, counteract the greenhouse effect and control inflation, with the additional benefit of preserving U.S. worker jobs.

I. INTRODUCTION

In 1987, 46,390 Americans were killed in highway crashes and 1.8 million suffered disabling injuries. In other words, that means 127 deaths a day, the equivalent of one major airline crash a day, every day of the year, a situation this nation would never tolerate from the airline industry.

The overall economic loss to society from auto crashes is at least $75 billion a year, about $700 per American family. This does not include the human costs of pain and suffering, or dependency from disability born by individuals, their families or friends. Motor vehicle crashes are the fourth leading cause of death, but the costs of these injuries are second only to those of cancer because the age at which they occur is much lower than for other leading causes of death and severe injury. Fully 32 percent of those killed on the highway are age 15 to 24, although this age group represents only 16 percent of the total population.

The National Highway Traffic Safety Administration (NHTSA) — located in the U.S. Department of Transportation — is the federal agency created in 1966 to reduce this carnage. Because of its potential to save lives and prevent injuries, it is one of the most important public health agencies in America.

For over half a century before 1966, while the death and injury toll mounted each year, the popular myth that highway crash injuries were both unpredictable and unavoidable was promoted by auto manufacturers and generally accepted as fact. But this terminology disguised the remedial nature of the problem. While the occurrence of a particular crash may be unpredictable, the type of human harm that occurs in crashes can be anticipated, and the total number of people killed and injured each year is predictable — by type of vehicle, by age, by type of crash, by sex — and, therefore, susceptible to reduction through preventive measures.

The Congress in 1966 gave the NHTSA a number of tools to reduce death and injury on the highway. For the first time the government was given authority to set safety standards for motor vehicles, not just for crash prevention (such as improved tires, brakes and lighting), but also for crashworthiness, or crash injury reduction (such as interior padding, safety belts and collapsible steering columns). Congress also authorized NHTSA to provide grants-in-aid to states to carry out highway safety programs dealing with such problems as drunk driving, pedestrian safety and enforcement of traffic laws. In addition, the agency was told to conduct research to support its actions, to develop experimental safety cars, to supply the public with information to enhance safety in the marketplace and to require the recall of defective cars.

From its conception, this agency has been controversial. The legislation was enacted in record time after it was revealed that General Motors had investigated Ralph Nader, the author of a searing critique of the auto industry who was urging enactment of the safety legislation. In response to the first proposed motor vehicle safety standards in December 1966, Henry Ford II threatened to close down the auto industry. The industry also tried unsuccessfully to stop NHTSA from publicly disclosing information about defective cars. In 1967 General Motors alleged that shoulder belts could harm car occupants, resulting in a three month delay of the standard. In 1970 Henry Ford ran full page ads in major papers condemning air bags, and in 1971 visited President Nixon with Lee Iacocca asking that the newly issued standard be revoked and a new fuel tank integrity standard not be issued.

In 1974 Congress revoked Ford's better idea: interlocking safety belts which required the belt to be buckled before the car would start. At Ford's suggestion and under White House pressure, NHTSA had adopted the interlock as a substitute for air bags, but neither the public nor Congress liked the result. As the most potent life-saving standard ever adopted, the air bag (and subsequently also automatic safety belts) standard became the major source of friction between safety advocates and the insurance industry on one side and the auto industry on the other.

It remains that today, even though the Reagan Administration reissued the standard after the Supreme Court by a vote of 9 to 0 overruled Reagan's 1981 revocation of the standard. Manufacturers now are installing air bags or automatic belts in 40 percent of all new cars this year. Mercedes started installing air bags as standard equipment in the driver side of its vehicles in 1985 and Ford Motor Company estimates it will install driver side air bags in one-half of its domestic production in 1990 models. But many auto dealers, after years of conditioning to oppose air bags, make little effort to inform customers about this technological vaccine, and some manufacturers, most notably General Motors, remain unenthusiastic about their capability to save lives.

In view of the modest cost for the reduction in casualties achieved, the next administration should evaluate them in a non-partisan fashion from the perspective of how air bags advance the public health rather than just measure the heat they generate in Detroit.

II. NHTSA SUCCESSES

The life saving achievements from the NHTSA programs are remarkable, particularly considering the organized industry opposition as well as government opposition during the Reagan years. Since 1966, more than 150,000 lives have been saved and millions of injuries mitigated as a result of the federal motor vehicle safety standards or the programs fostered by NHTSA grants-in-aid to the states. The major life saving programs, according to NHTSA data, analyses and estimates are:

* Over 100,000 lives have been saved by the federal motor vehicle safety standards, including collapsible steering columns, side impact strength, laminated windshields, interior padding and shoulder/lap belts.

* Between 32,000 and 65,000 lives and about $14 billion in fuel costs have been saved by the 55 mph national speed limit that was fully in effect from 1974-1986. In 1987, the Reagan Administration supported increasing it to 65 mph on rural interstate highways, causing nearly a 20% increase in deaths on these highways during the first few months after the state laws were changed.

* About 6,300 lives are now saved each year by state laws enacted and administered with the encouragement or leadership of NHTSA: child restraint use laws now in every state (290 lives); age 21 year old drinking age laws now adopted by every state (1,000); tougher state drinking and driving laws in some states (1,600); motorcycle helmet use laws in 23 states (350); and safety belt use laws in 32 states and D.C. covering about 85 percent of the population (3,100).

* About 133 million malfunctioning motor vehicles and millions of faulty parts have been recalled by manufacturers under the safety defect recall requirements of the 1966 law, saving thousands of lives.

Since 1981, the annual number of deaths has dropped by 3,000 (from 49,301 deaths), primarily because of demographic changes in the 15-24 year old high risk population (about a 9.5 percent reduction) and the enactment of child restraint, age 21 for drinking and belt usage laws. In 1988 and future years, the higher 65 mph speed limit will increase deaths and injuries. On the other hand, large-scale installation of air bags will reduce them.

In addition to saving lives, NHTSA administers the federal fuel economy program which saves consumers money and preserves the environment. Between 1975, when the Energy Conservation Act became law, and 1985, the average fuel efficiency of new U.S.-made cars doubled. Thus, each year the average owner of a 1985 model car saves about $100 on fuel costs (depending on the price of gasoline). By the year 2000, according to NHTSA, the cumulative fuel savings for cars and light trucks will be about 595 billion gallons compared to 1976 levels if the 1987 fleet savings are continued.

In addition to these savings, as many as 7,000 additional fatalities and thousands of disabling injuries annually could be prevented or mitigated. These savings could be achieved with vehicle design modifications that are both technologically and economically feasible, and by extending to all states laws governing rules of the road — such as motorcycle helmet use, safety belt use, speed limit and drunk driving laws. At least a thousand more lives could be saved per year if these state laws were enacted in every state and enforced. Few other government health programs can document similar achievements.

III. CRITIQUE OF REAGAN ADMINISTRATION ACTIONS

During the Reagan Administration, the auto safety and fuel economy programs have been attacked as costing manufacturers too much money and not being cost-effective. So life-saving standards were revoked, and others in proposal form have been indefinitely postponed or ignored. Still others have been delayed for years by the Secretary of Transportation or the White House Office of Management and Budget, while some have been reinstated after court challenges. Only one significant new safety standard, for high-mounted rear stop lamps, has been issued during this entire Administration, and it was proposed during the Carter years.

The initial Reagan Administration attack on the auto safety program was announced on April 6, 1981 in a document entitled "Actions to Help the U.S. Auto Industry." It listed 24 standards to be revoked, delayed or reviewed. Most were in fact later cancelled. The disdain shown by the Reagan Administration for the sanctity of life and the need for energy savings has been challenged by members of Congress, by the National Transportation Safety Board, the courts, the press, the Government Accounting Office and public interest groups. Here are their major critiques:

* **1981 Revocation of Key Lifesaving and Cost Saving Standards.** Automatic occupant restraints (air bags or automatic belts) are by far the most important life-saving vehicle safety standard ever issued, estimated to save 6,000 to 9,000 lives and 150,000 serious injuries per year when in all cars. This standard, due to have taken effect in September 1981, was targeted for immediate revocation by the Bush Task Force on Regulatory Relief. The standard was reissued in 1984 (to be fully in effect for drivers in 1990 models) following a 1983

Supreme Court decision initiated by insurance company/consumer lawsuits that overruled Reagan's 1981 revocation. Passenger-side air bags were subsequently delayed until 1993 models. A detailed cost-benefit analysis prepared for the insurance industry found the cost to the Nation was $2.4 billion for every year the standard was delayed (Reagan/Bush delayed it six years for drivers and ten years for passengers at a cost of over $17.5 billion).

   * **Failure to Issue Safety Standard Proposals.** When the Administration came into office, important proposed standards were pending, but little action was taken, and eight years later they have not been issued in final form. The primary ones are: side impact protection (1,000 lives could be saved annually); pedestrian protection (hundreds could be saved annually); and large truck vehicle underride guard.

   Also, a number of standards could and should have been issued, but the Administration failed to do so. These include: application of key car safety standards to vans and light trucks (automatic restraints, occupant containment, head restraints, roof crush, side impact protection); standards to mitigate excessive instability and rollover in vans and light trucks and to improve braking capability; large truck antilock braking, cab interior safety crashworthiness, improved occupant restraints and fuel system integrity; and shoulder harnesses in vehicle rear seating positions.

   * **Cutbacks in Key Consumer Information Programs.** Another area targeted by the Administration shortly after taking office was consumer information. Consequently, braking capability disclosure requirements by new car make and model were eliminated. The tire quality grading system, requiring disclosure of tire performance characteristics for treadware, traction and heat resistance was suspended in 1982 (and reinstated in 1985 following Public Citizen's lawsuit); *The Car Book*, listing performance characteristics such as vehicle crashworthiness, defect recalls, insurance discount or surcharge and frequency of repair by make and model was removed from publication in 1981. A proposal to label new cars with crash safety and insurance information was ignored. Key consumer information pamphlets were discontinued and removed from circulation. And requirements that tire dealers register with manufacturers the names of tire purchasers to assure notification if their tires are recalled was removed from the law at the request of the Reagan/Bush Administration and tire dealers.

   * **Failure To Effectively Enforce the Law.** The Reagan Administration not only revoked safety standards but was also lax about enforcing existing law, particularly requirements for recall of safety-related defects:

* Few formal investigations (one to three) are opened each year and they are not expeditiously resolved. Of the seven now pending, four are two to five years old.

* Not one "initial determination" of a defect or any recall order has been issued since 1983.

* Instead, NHTSA makes "informal" requests asking companies to voluntarily recall, most of which are refused (of 18 requests in 1986, only 2 resulted in recalls).

* The backlog of informal and formal investigations of vehicles suspected of containing safety related defects now totals about 48 million vehicles.

* At the end of 1986, the vehicles whose cases were still "in progress" had resulted in nearly 20,000 crashes, 7,000 injuries and 500 deaths.

Because of the embarrassing record of refusals to recall by auto companies, NHTSA has attempted to avoid disclosing to the public the particular cases in which it requests a manufacturer to institute a recall. Fortunately, the House transportation appropriations subcommittee recognized the importance of this issue and has periodically required such disclosure.

* **Destruction of Cost-Effective Fuel Economy Program.** In addition to cutting back safety standards, the Reagan Administration has cut back the fuel economy program.

Industry reporting requirements were severely reduced and the $8 million dollar fuel economy research program was eliminated in 1982, making evaluation of industry petitions and rulemaking far more difficult and more dependent on unevaluated industry claims. The standards for cars for 1986-1988 were reduced to 26 mpg — well below the 1985 statutory 27.5 mpg; the standards for light trucks and vans were set at 20.5 mpg (for two wheel drive vehicles), below what most companies numbers show they can achieve. Nor are fuel economy standards issued in a timely fashion. For example, reduced standards (between 26.5 mpg and 27.5 mpg) were proposed in August 1988 for 1989 models just coming off the production lines, making improvements infeasible. As predicted, the lower number was adopted.

The Reagan Administration also allied with the large auto companies to adjust EPA measurements to permit the companies to avoid paying fuel economy penalties. Smaller companies have paid $16 million in penalties.

The Reagan Administration has recommended elimination of the entire fuel economy program despite the obvious implications for a future energy crisis and the greenhouse effect. Along with U.S. auto companies, it claims that fuel economy standards threaten American jobs (i.e., U.S. companies will be forced to manufacture their large cars abroad). In fact, lower fuel economy standards are the culprit, allowing U.S. companies to import rather than manufacture 500,000 small cars in the U.S. in 1988 because they don't need to average them in their U.S. fleet to meet the existing standards.

* **Encouragement of a Needless, Dangerous Horsepower Race.** One of the least justified actions by the Administration has been encouragement of higher driving speeds. Despite overwhelming evidence of its payoff, the 55 mph speed limit was raised by Congress in April 1987 to 65 mph on rural interstate highways with the strong endorsement of the Reagan Administration. It resulted in a 20% increase in deaths on these rural interstates and has influenced the speeds traveled on all higher speed highways.

In addition, the safety standard requiring 85 mph maximum speedometer notation was revoked, paving the way for a new muscle car race, although it is common knowledge that the population most influenced in their driving habits by high-speed ads and cars with 140 mph speedometers are young males, who are already killed more than twice as frequently on the highway than any other population segment.

* **Failure to Encourage Reenactment Of Motorcycle Helmet Use Laws.** Curiously, while the Administration pressed for enactment of mandatory seat belt use laws, it refused to endorse mandatory helmet use laws — yet helmets are the most effective single source of protection for motorcycle riders.

Although less than 4% of all registered vehicles are motorcycles, they account for 9% of all vehicle-related fatalities (4000 fatalities in 1987). Nevertheless, motorcycle safety was not listed by NHTSA as one of its program priorities until March 1988. Although helmet use laws were not promoted by the Reagan Administration, since 1981 three states have enacted helmet use laws: Louisiana, Nebraska and Oregon (where the referendum got 69% vote).

IV. PRIORITIES IN THE UNFINISHED AGENDA

MOTOR VEHICLE CRASHWORTHINESS STANDARDS

Based on many years of research findings, we know that additional motor vehicle crash protection standards can annually save about seven thousand lives and avoid thousands of serious injuries; they are cost effective and could be quickly issued. The key areas are:

* Steering assemblies account for 25% of the total harm to occupants in all crashes, and 55% of the harm to drivers in frontal collisions. While air bags will partly mitigate this problem, the technology exists for more forgiving steering assemblies — self-aligning, self-centering and padded.

* Other interior component improvements could readily be adopted to better manage crash energy in frontal crashes just by extensions of existing technology. They include designing instrument panels to eliminate hard or dangerous portions and improving windshields with glass/plastic designs to absorb more energy and further mitigate ejection. A very simple addition, just one inch of padding on the front pillar and roof headers, will reduce head injuries by up to 50% at 20 mph impact speed (3,000 fatal head injuries occur each year from contact with these unforgiving areas). As many as 500 lives could be saved annually at a very modest cost.

* Side impact crashes cause 8,000 deaths per year and 25,000 serious injuries. Three hundred to 1,000 Americans could be saved every year if the long-delayed side impact standard is adopted (depending on its requirements) to reduce thoracic/abdominal injuries, head injuries from contacts with the front-pillar and side door ejection. This standard is needed because voluntary progress by industry has been minimal despite long-documented research findings.

* Rollover crashes kill 8,200 people per year, about 22% of all passenger vehicle deaths. Although three-fourths of them are in small cars, pickup trucks or vans, and the rollover fatality rate for these vehicles is six times that for large cars, this Administration claims that even a "decision" to develop a stability safety standard cannot be made for two years. A petition by Senator Tim Wirth to NHTSA for an initial requirement based on a vehicle's geometrically determined "stability factor" (related to track width and center of gravity height) was rejected in 1988, although Consumers Union's more general petition was accepted. In addition to a new safety standard for vehicle stability, existing roof-crush requirements for cars should be significantly upgraded and applied also to light trucks and vans.

* Rear seat shoulder harnesses should be required in all passenger vehicles because of clear evidence that lap belts (now the only requirement) sometimes cause severe injury and death in a crash when not worn low around the hips. At 32% usage of rear shoulder belts, 50 lives and 1,000 serious injuries would be prevented with shoulder harness/lap belt combinations compared with lap belts alone. The cost is estimated at about $14 for components and fuel costs over the life of the vehicle compared to $200 to $300 reported by consumers for retrofit in current model cars.

REDUCING PEDESTRIAN INJURIES

Pedestrian fatalities number about 7,500 annually and about 150,000 injuries. Indeed, pedestrians have a much higher probability of being injured than do occupants. Pedestrians are consistently involved in 2% of highway crashes but account for 16-18% of fatalities.

Research shows that many hundreds of fatalities and thousands of serious pedestrian injuries could be prevented, particularly in crashes of 20 mph and below (60% of pedestrian deaths occur on urban streets or residential roads and pre-impact braking occurs in 70% of the crashes). Long delayed standards to making striking vehicles more forgiving should be adopted to soften the front ends of cars, reduce hood stiffness, lower underhood components, eliminate frontal protrusions and lower the impact surface below the bumper. Some existing production models already incorporate many of these technologies. The cost is small, particularly if these features are design requirements for new models.

IMPROVING VAN AND TRUCK SAFETY

Over 7,800 people were killed in light trucks, vans and sport (Jeep/Samurai) utility type vehicles in 1987, accounting for about 20% of all motor vehicle occupant fatalities. Deaths in these vehicles increased 23% from 1983 to 1987. The death rate from rollover crashes in sport-utility vehicles is more than double that of passenger cars, and sport-utility vehicles are one of the fastest growing segments of the automotive market. These multipurpose vehicles are not now required to meet some of the most important passenger car safety standards, particularly automatic restraints, head restraints, roof-crush and side impact protection. If such standards were issued for these crash-prone vehicles, at least 2,000-3,000 lives per year could be saved.

Large trucks are involved in crashes that kill 4,750 and injure about 150,000 people annually. Most of these fatalities and injuries are not truck occupants but are occupants of other vehicles or pedestrians and bicyclists. Nevertheless, truck drivers sustained over 9 percent of all work-related fatalities (in 1984) and yet comprised only 1.8 percent of the employed work force in that year. One of every three tractor trailers can be expected to crash every year, a rate far higher than for passenger cars. Deficient braking systems could be a contributing factor in as many as one-third of these crashes.

The most important improvement to reduce death and injury from large truck crashes is improved handling and stability, including use of anti-lock braking systems; anti-lock brakes have been used for years on aircraft and more recently on luxury automobiles. Although a new anti-lock standard was proposed in 1979, the Reagan Administration will commit only to more studies, but no regulatory action.

Other truck standards are needed to protect truck occupants when crashes occur. 62% of truck occupant fatalities occur in rollover crashes, with 38% of them ejected. Other standards that should be issued are: cab interior protection, including more comfortable retracting belt systems with shoulder belts to prevent injury and ejection;

improved locks and hinges; roof crush limits (none now exist and little padding is installed); and more forgiving steering assemblies with power steering.

MOTORCYCLE HELMET USE LAWS AND ANTI-LOCK BRAKES

We know that helmet use in states with helmet use laws is almost 100% and that wearing helmets is the most important single action to prevent death and injury of motorcyclists. While total motorcycle deaths dropped in 1987 by a remarkable 13%, many more lives of this high risk group of young males could be saved with greater helmet use. Unhelmeted riders are three times more likely to incur a fatal head injury than an unhelmeted driver. Louisiana, the first state to repeal and then readopt a full helmet law, found a 30% reduction in fatalities in that year (1982), even though cycle registrations increased by 6%. Three states in 1988 have already passed helmet use laws without any support from the Reagan/Bush Administration, paving the way for the rich opportunity to encourage the other 29 states to do so. Anti-lock brakes should be required for motorcycles to improve stability and panic stopping for these vulnerable vehicle users.

CONTROLLING SPEEDS ON HIGHWAYS

We know that speed kills and that nearly half (20,000 in 1987) of all fatalities occur on roads with speeds posted above 54 mph. Driving speeds and deaths on these highways have increased since Congress authorized 65 mph speeds on rural interstate highways, yet vehicle manufacturers increasingly are building and advertising high powered cars in a new horsepower race. This race was facilitated by the elimination in 1981 of the standard setting 85 mph maximum notation on speedometers. Speedometers once again show 120 to 140 mph. The standard should be reinstituted along with cooperative efforts by federal and state governments and safety constituencies to limit deadly speeds on highways. Also, radar detectors, outlawed in some states, should be outlawed nationwide.

INCREASING SAFETY BELT USE

Safety belt used laws are now in place in 32 states and D.C. covering about 85% of the population. Usage rates in these states are about 50% (although it varies from 65% in North Carolina to 22% in Utah). Average usage in non-belt use states is about 30%. In 1987 belt use laws saved 3,100 lives and 37,000 moderate to critical injuries. About 700 additional lives could be saved with 50% belt use nationwide. With 85% usage, 10,000 lives total would have been saved in 1987. Belt use laws should be enacted nationwide and efforts should be made to increase usage with improved enforcement.

REDUCING ALCOHOL-INVOLVED CRASHES

Alcohol involvement remains a major factor in highway crashes. About 50% of all traffic fatalities, or 23,900, were alcohol related in 1986, an increase of 7% over 1985. One half of these fatalities are age 30 or below. The new state 21-year-old drinking laws initiated by the Congress, however, have made significant progress in saving lives in the 18-20 age group. Nevertheless, in 1987, 64% of the drivers under age 25 killed in single-vehicle weekend crashes were intoxicated, and 19% of teenagers age 15 to 19 involved in fatal crashes were drunk. Particularly vulnerable populations, such as pedestrians and motorcyclists, show heavy involvement of alcohol among fatalities. Although the results are likely to be more elusive than in other government efforts, a number of programs should be pursued to reduce alcohol involvement in highway injuries:

* Persuade all states, perhaps with incentive grants, to adopt administrative license suspension laws allowing licenses to be suspended on the spot, with subsequent administrative hearings (24 states have already adopted them).

* Impose stronger penalties, including stiffer fines and suspension of driver licenses, for youths under age 21 found to be drinking.

* Encourage judges to require installation of ignition interlock breathalizer systems for violators convicted of drunk driving (particularly repeat offenders) to prevent their car from starting if their breath contained alcohol; the cost of retrofitting cars would be $200 to $300.

* Press for enactment of tougher state dram shop laws placing liability on tavern owners for serving alcohol to people who are drunk or drinking heavily (many of these were eliminated or softened during the past few years under pressure from the food and restaurant owners during the insurance liability crisis).

* Increase the tax on alcohol and dedicate it to vastly increased alcohol rehabilitation services (this kind of support is often prohibitively expensive for alcoholics); a small increase would produce sufficient funds but would be strongly opposed by the alcohol industry.

CONSUMER INFORMATION

An informed consumer makes the marketplace work. Publication of factual, comparative information should once again become a priority, with issuance of the long-delayed proposed rule to require safety data on new car stickers. With air bags now being increasingly offered for sale, it is imperative that the government educate consumers on their performance and replacement after a crash (covered by insurance) both at point of sale and as reference material.

Vehicle crash testing should be expanded to cover side impact and rollover tests and light trucks and vans. Consumer alerts should once again be published on serious safety defects and tire quality. Grading comparative information should be widely circulated rather than ignored. *The Car Book*, which combines make and model data, should be circulated broadly.

ENFORCING THE LAW ON SAFETY DEFECTS

Failure to enforce the law breeds contempt for it among violators as well as the public. For this reason, and most importantly to reduce death and injury, NHTSA should vigorously pursue cases in response to consumer complaints and take enforcement action after asking the manufacturer to recall, rather than letting cases languish or simply closing them. NHTSA should also move quickly on all pending cases or inquiries to avoid the current situation in which 6.5 million suspected defective vehicles are beyond the 8 year statute of limitations.

IMPROVING FUEL ECONOMY

To conserve oil and counteract the greenhouse effect, fuel economy standards should be gradually increased above 27.5 mpg. But if this program is instead diminished or aborted, as the Reagan Administration has urged, hundreds of thousands of auto manufacturing jobs will be lost as U.S. companies import all their small cars from abroad. When the price of gasoline was high, the Administration argued that the marketplace obviated the need for federal standards; now that the price is lower, it argues the program is anachronistic. The purpose of the law is to achieve improved fuel economy regardless of the market.

We know that average fuel economy for existing automobiles can be improved above the statutory 27.5 mpg, the minimum number set by Congress for 1985 and later models (double the 1976 average mpg). Congress authorized the agency after 1985 to increase the standard or to set it as low as 26 mpg, whichever constituted "maximum feasible fuel economy." NHTSA set it at 26 mpg for 1986-88, and proposes 26.5 to 27.5 for 1988-90, although Ford, General Motors and Chrysler have exceeded 26 mpg by .4 mpg to more than 1.6 mpg since 1986. This has allowed Ford and General Motors particularly to build up credits and avoid paying penalties for failing to meet the standard in the past, and to import over 500,000 smaller fuel efficient cars (with a loss of about 175,000 U.S. jobs) because they did not have to produce them with U.S. parts to meet the higher 27.5 mpg standard. (The companies can average the fuel economy of cars which have 75% domestic content; U.S. manufacturer ("captive") imports are counted separately under the law.) In addition, in 1977 NHTSA easily modified a large

6 passenger Chevrolet to meet 27.5 mpg. Most cars are far smaller than this.

FUEL ECONOMY VS. SAFETY

Some critics argue that improved fuel economy will *reduce* motor vehicle safety. This can be the case for some types of highway crashes, but is not a necessary result.

First, 39% of all traffic occupant fatalities occur in single vehicle crashes (a single vehicle crash is usually front or front angle into a fixed object, not unlike two identical vehicles crashing into each other). As NHTSA's crash test program shows, many of newer small fuel efficient cars are *more crashworthy* than larger cars in single vehicle type crashes.

Second, 15% of all fatalities are pedestrians and bicyclists, and another 5% are motorcyclists in multivehicle crashes. For these individuals, heavy gas guzzlers pose a greater danger than lighter cars.

Third, to protect pedestrians, motorcyclists and occupants of other vehicles, all vehicles should be made less aggressive and more forgiving, resulting in greater protection for the more vulnerable elements on the highway.

Fourth, improving fuel economy means reducing weight, not necessarily reducing size. Large size cars can meet higher fuel efficiency standards with advanced technology and lightweight materials, as was demonstrated by the NHTSA with its large size and compact-size Research Safety Cars in the late 1970s. Its 2500 pound vehicle met 32 mpg average fuel economy and crashed without injury to occupants in single vehicle frontal crashes into a barrier at 50 mph and in side crashes at 40 mph — far above safety performance levels of current model cars, large and small.

Fifth, while automotive fuel efficiency has doubled since 1975, the fatality rate has dropped from 3.45 to 2.4 per 100 million miles of travel, and there are many safety improvements yet to be made in current model cars that could save thousands of lives per year (air bags, side impact protection and repeal of 65 mph speed limit).

FIVE MPH BUMPER STANDARDS

The five mph bumper standard, effective on 1980 models after lengthy rulemaking, should be reinstated. DOT's 1979 study found it was cost effective, saving consumers about $400 million annually. It was reduced by the Reagan Administration for 1983 models to 2.5 mph with promises of cost savings, reduced weight and a consumer information standard revealing the bumper performance of each new car sold. In fact, no price reductions were ever announced, weight savings do not begin to balance even a fraction of the cost of increased crash damage costs (the Insurance Institute for Highway Safety found damage ranging from $419 to $2,030 in 5 mph crash tests of 22 mid-size cars in 1987) and no consumer information requirement has ever been issued by NHTSA despite numerous promises since 1983. Thus, consumers don't even know if a car has a fully effective 5 mph bumper or not, and cannot make cost-effective car purchase decisions.

REINSTATING CRITICAL RESOURCES

The NHTSA has been budgetarily starved by the Reagan Administration as well as undermined by its leadership, who probably would not have used additional funding constructively. But with leaders supportive of the agency's mission, funding levels restored to inflation-adjusted levels of 1975 would increase agency capability. This would mean an additional $150 million and 233 additional staff.

These are small numbers for an entity with a major life-saving and energy conservation mission, as well as proven accomplishments. Compared to funding for National Institutes of Health programs, the Department of Defense, the Federal Highway Administration or the $75 billion in economic losses from highway crashes each year, these amounts are footnotes, but would have life-saving and cost-saving significance nationally when applied to NHTSA.

TELECOMMUNICATIONS:
Federal Communications Commission

Nolan A. Bowie
Angela J. Campbell
Andrew Jay Schwartzman*

SUMMARY OF RECOMMENDATIONS

Telecommunications policy addresses decisions concerning electronic transmission of information and intelligence, including voice, video and data. Although ever-greater technological innovations have increasingly blurred the distinctions between formats, the discussion which follows uses the traditional terms "mass media" and "telephone." The Federal Communications Commission (FCC), an independent government agency, is the primary telecommunications regulatory and policymaking body. The Commerce Department's National Telecommunications and Information Administration (NTIA) advises the executive branch on policy.

Telecommunications policy decisions are different in at least two respects from other important issues confronting the new president, such as arms control, health care, drugs and housing. First, the long-term consequences of telecommunications issues are neither immediately apparent nor easily explained, unlike the plague of drugs, for example. And second, the choices, wise or unwise, will have no significant near-term budgetary impact. There is economic elbow room to do the right thing.

Decisions which will be made in the next few years will largely determine whether future control of the distribution of information will be concentrated in a few hands or, as is technologically feasible, democratized far beyond current capabilities. For example:

---

* Nolan A. Bowie is Assistant Professor of Communications at Temple University. He was formerly Executive Director of the Citizens Communications Center. Angela J. Campbell is Director of the Citizens Communication Center and Assistant Professor of Law at Georgetown University Law Center. Andrew Jay Schwartzman is Executive Director of the Media Access Project. He was formerly staff counsel for the United Church of Christ Office of Communications.

  * Will every American ultimately have affordable access to a fiber optic cable that delivers programs, data, news and information?
  * Will the jobless be shut off from electronic employment listings of the future, which may replace newspaper ads?
  * Will cable TV operators be allowed to continue to operate as monopolists, owning the cable and also controlling program content?
  * Will direct-to-home satellite broadcasters have the right to refuse to sell time to one party's candidate for president?
  * Will we adopt the already developed Japanese "high definition" TV technology, which would be available only to those able to afford a special new set, or will we await an American-developed "compatible" system?
  * Will the increasing concentration of mass media ownership resulting from deregulation continue unabated?

  Over the long term, we must adapt these new technologies to the democratic process. All Americans deserve affordable access to information which reflects the diversity of our culture. Censorship by the government, or by excessively concentrated powers within the private sector, must be foreclosed. And personal privacy must be preserved.

  In the meantime, telephone service must be kept affordable and universally available. Protections can be designed to permit telephone companies seeking to enter competition with the cable industry to do so without abusing their massive monopoly power. The FCC's broadcasting Fairness Doctrine should be reinstituted. And a new president and FCC must pursue policies that increase ownership and employment of minorities and women in the mass media; slow the increasingly dangerous concentration of control of the mass media in fewer and fewer hands; and create a more flexible, adequately funded public broadcasting service.

I. RECENT DEVELOPMENTS

  Dramatic advances in telephone and broadcasting/cable technology have become commercially practical in the last decade. Cellular telephone, paging and other technologies are becoming readily available to many consumers. Just as public libraries democratized information access in the last century, we can soon provide audio and video "information services" giving universal access to consumer, health and job data. A vastly increased array of entertainment and news programming, much more fully representative of all elements of our culture, can be produced for distribution in a life-like high definition format via satellite or by fiber optic mechanisms. Individual viewers could view such material at a time of their choice.

However, while the regulatory agenda is increasingly concerned with determining the nature of telecommunications policy for the 21st century, the implementation has not promoted democratic values. Meaningful enforcement of major aspects of the Communications Act of 1934 has been largely abandoned over the last eight years. The Reagan Administration, with important assistance from the courts, has substituted marketplace forces for economic regulation at a key juncture. Telephone service has become much more expensive for low-volume consumers, as many fruits of new competition have been directed to business. Radio and TV have been substantially deregulated, further reducing accountability to historically underserved segments of the community. And President Reagan's veto has allowed repeal of the all-important Fairness Doctrine, at least temporarily.

Telephone Policy. The most significant development affecting telephone policy during the Reagan Administration was the 1981 settlement of the government's antitrust suit against AT&T. The consent decree required AT&T to divest its local telephone companies, thereby allowing consumers to choose AT&T or another long-distance company to handle long-distance calls from their home or business phones. U.S. District Court Judge Harold H. Greene, who administers AT&T's consent decree, continues to have a major impact on telephone policy.[1] The Reagan Administration and Congress have largely deferred many important telephone issues to Judge Greene. The Court has generally done a good job of administering the decree, but it is dangerous to allow a single person to retain indefinitely so much influence over telephone policy.

Other than 1984 amendments with respect to cable television, the Communications Act, with amendments, operates fundamentally as it has since 1934. The Reagan FCC has employed the inherent flexibility in the statute to implement its deregulatory policies.

The Reagan Administration philosophy has been to deregulate telephone service in the belief that competition, privatization and the unregulated marketplace would promote consumer welfare. But the quality and degree of competition that have resulted from these policies are limited and suspect. Benefits for business are mixed; benefits for individuals are few. The Administration claims there is now healthy competition in long distance service, but AT&T still dominates, holding about 80% of the domestic market. Of the other 561 competitors, MCI commands around 10%, and US Sprint 6%. AT&T also controls most international long distance calls.

The Administration proudly reports that about 93% of households have telephone service. While this is one of the world's highest rates, it falls 7% short of the declared goal of "universal service." The concept of universal service should mean the full and complete participation of the citizenry, regardless of the ability or willingness to pay.[2] Households without telephone service are disproportionately minorities; these "information poor" represent but one sign of a growing regional, racial and class "information gap."[3]

Belief in the "magic of the marketplace" has been official faith at the FCC since 1981. But in mid-1988, the Administration began to show a new flexibility in order to protect its constituencies. For example, responding to the Reagan social agenda, the FCC slapped stiff fines on "dial-a-porn." Similarly, telephone companies have been favored with a proposal for new "price cap" regulation which would be substituted for historic profit limitations. This would allow prices to go higher than would otherwise be the case.

Another recent initiative is NTIA's proposal to change telephone rules that would allow telephone companies to compete with cable in providing "broadband" services of the future. This proposal does deserve serious consideration by the new administration, but only if telephone companies are required to offer such service on a common carrier basis. In this fashion, the telephone company will not control the content of the programming or information services it would provide; rather, access to the system by program and service providers should be on a nondiscriminatory basis. Furthermore, the service should be available to all consumers at reasonable prices.[4] As a prerequisite to fundamental fairness, cable must also be allowed to compete in providing the kind of voice and data services which have traditionally been provided by telephone companies.

Mass Media. There is now a pitched debate within the broadcasting industry over whether opposition to the Fairness Doctrine should be dropped, and only the President's veto blocked legislation to reenact it.[5] Congress is poised to act in other areas as well. There is increasing public pressure to reimpose rate regulation, minimal service criteria and franchise obligations on cable TV systems. And the broadcasting and electronics industry, which in the past had fought against federal standard-setting, have begun a clamor for such assistance in the development of "high definition" television for the next decade.

Technology and deregulation have combined during the 1980s to alter the present and future structure of the mass media. Much of the emphasis has been on creating services available only to those who can afford them, such as pay cable. Moreover, many traditional restraints on media ownership have been relaxed or eliminated, leading to increased concentration at the expense of local ownership. Entry of minorities and women into ownership ranks has slowed down considerably.

Dissatisfaction has not been limited to consumers. More and more elements of the business and academic communities have begun to rethink their reliance purely on marketplace forces. Cable promised to bring scores of innovative services, with increased local orientation, to every household. It has evolved into something less; the numerous new channels are for the most part nationally distributed, and offer derivative, rather than innovative, service at prices which, thanks to deregulation, have soared.

II. BUDGET REQUIREMENTS

The FCC and NTIA are small agencies which expend most of their resources on personnel. Increased application fees have made the regulatory process somewhat more self-financing. Congress has in recent years given the FCC slightly more than it has requested, with fiscal 1989 appropriations totaling about $100 million.

The Reagan Administration has unsuccessfully attempted the ultimate deregulation of the airwaves by proposing in the last several budgets that some, and later all frequencies should be auctioned. This has been regarded by most telecommunications experts — and interested members of Congress — as being akin to selling off the Grand Canyon or the Mississippi River, and has been treated accordingly.

The incumbent Administration has also used the budget weapon to attack two important areas of telecommunications policy, public broadcasting and the NTIA's telecommunications facilities program. However, Congress has continued to support these programs at higher levels. Senator Ernest Hollings, who chairs the Commerce Committee as well as the appropriations subcommittee with telecommunications jurisdiction, has pressed for adoption of a "spectrum fee" for users of FCC regulated airwaves to finance public broadcasting. This proposal has broad implications for licensees, who might claim greater freedom from regulation or reallocation of the frequencies in exchange for these fees. Most progressive students of the Commission believe that the obligation to serve should not be made a negotiable matter.

The distribution, as well as the amount, of money for public broadcasting is likely to be a matter of continuing dispute. During the 100th Congress, the Senate proposed a radical reorientation, directing program funds to stations and substantially reducing the role of the Corporation for Public Broadcasting (CPB). Adjusting telecommunications policy to meet the new realities will not require significant new budgetary commitments. Of the recommendations contained below, only the suggestion for a National Endowment for Public Telecommunications might require even modest additional funding.

III. NEW PRIORITIES AND INITIATIVES

As we enter the so-called information age, new communications technologies can provide the necessary infrastructure to solve a variety of regulatory, social, political and economic problems. But this potential may not be realized without the formulation of sound public policy.

TELEPHONE AND INFORMATION POLICY

Information policy has an increasingly profound impact on free speech, privacy, productivity, jobs, trade and military security. The next president should begin the effort to define the values and interests that should be promoted in telecommunication and information policy. In addition, he should begin to define the long-range goals of public policy in these areas.

He should look to the Constitution and, particularly, the Bill of Rights. The Founders had an information policy: they used government as a tool to provide for the free flow of information. The Constitution authorized the Postal Service and post roads, and mandated a copyright and patent protection. The First Amendment insured that government would promote, and not restrict, the discussion of issues and ideas. The Fourth Amendment provides the broader basis of the right to a reasonable expectation of privacy, prohibiting the Government from unreasonable searches and seizures of personal information.

The president should follow the Congressional scheme, as embodied in the remarkably supple and effective Communications Act of 1934. It places priority on service to the public interest in decision-making, prohibiting the FCC from censoring information content, with the limited exception of obscenity and indecency. Title I, Section 1 of the Act emphasizes universal access to information and knowledge, stating the purpose of establishing the FCC as being

> to make available,...to all the people of the United States a rapid, efficient, Nation-wide, and world-wide wire and radio communication service with adequate facilities at reasonable charges, for the purpose of the national defense, for the purpose of promoting safety of life and property...,and for the purpose of securing a more effective execution of this policy by centralizing authority....

The president must promote the First and Fourth Amendment goals of maximizing the free flow of information to all the people of the United States — to provide policy initiatives that maximize the diversity of information content and source and thereby promote competition among information providers; to avoid censorship of information except to protect society against certain widely perceived threats to its stability (e.g., national security and obscene information); to protect the rights of creators or intellectual property (copyright and patents); and to maximize citizens' personal privacy rights. The challenge is to make "appropriate communication and information technology" as universal and easy to use as the telephone and television, while at the same time protecting and promoting privacy rights.

In meeting this constitutional and technological challenge, the president should not abdicate responsibility to the marketplace alone. The values at stake are too precious.

Left to its own devices, the private sector will not establish the infrastructure necessary to democratize communications and information dissemination. Because of its focus on short-term profitability in competitive markets, deregulation inhibits long-range development and planning. The function formerly (*i.e.*, pre-deregulation) served by Bell Labs must be replaced. In short, government should intervene to establish standards, to avoid the export of more jobs and to promote basic research. Among the central issues facing Washington are when and how to replace the existing copper-based telephone/cable TV plant with state-of-the-art fiber optic integrated telecommunications infrastructure.

The Integrated Services Digital Network concept, referred to under the acronym "ISDN," must be the object of immediate attention. How, when and by whom ISDN will be developed is one of the great issues of the coming decade. "ISDN" refers to a single network of fiber optic cable and switches into the home and office which will replace traditional telephone and cable connections. All voice, data, facsimile, telemetry, signaling (or dialing) and video can be delivered over this system.

Government will have to help select standards, which should insure common carrier regulation to separate control of content from control of the means of transmission. The structure should be interactive, using a broadband design capable of managing voice, data and video. This will encourage information providers to compete for audiences by providing large numbers of channels made available on a nondiscriminatory basis to programmers, data base providers and other users. This diversity offers the potential for realizing the First Amendment mandate of free and open expression, equally available to all.

With new technological capacities, the traditionally narrow focus of telephone regulators must be broadened, for they must now address a question of global sweep: How far can the gap between the cultural elite and poor people be expanded without causing irreversible negative social consequences?

The traditional availability of low-cost universal telephone service has been a democratizing force. As cable serves more and different functions, the goal of universality becomes ever more important to self-governance. Just as technology and living patterns transformed auto ownership from a luxury into a necessity, so too are new information technologies and changing public information needs blurring the distinction between services which are "basic" and those which we now regard as "enhanced." The minimum standard service must be defined to reflect such changing needs in an emerging information society.[6] Excessive delay in this exercise could so expand the gap between the information-rich and the information-poor as to threaten the most basic of the societal covenants.

The new administration should begin to confront another coming reality. Certain types of telephone service have traditionally contained both explicit and implicit subsidies in their rate structures.[7] Yet, even as information access becomes ever more critical for subsistence, these subsidies are being removed. Given the importance to society of information in electronic formats, Washington must find new ways to insure universal service to appropriate technologies and essential information. The special needs of the homeless, the poor and the physically challenged must be met in this area. For now, the new administration should expand existing programs designed to reach persons who cannot afford telephone service and take steps to increase access to telephone service by persons with disabilities that limit their uses of the telephone.

One particularly bold strategy could be adopted to capture the public's imagination and dramatize the importance of changing information technologies. The planned construction of a new government telephone system could be restructured to make its excess capacity available as a "lifeline" system of last resort for the information-poor. At $25-40 billion, this project, called FTS-2000, has thus far been mired in scandal and confusion. This gigantic fiber optic system with ISDN capability is presently conceived as being dedicated to government uses while "bypassing" entirely the private sector's network. By insuring that the system has broadband capability to transmit video as well as voice and data, the administration can help shape the future of private systems as well.

Revelation of the FBI's "Library Awareness Program" underscores the ever-present threat of unreasonable government surveillance.[8] Current personal privacy protections are insufficient for the technologies of the present, and will be even less so in the near future. The new president and Congress should establish a permanent federal privacy protection commission and initiate legislation defining the balance between expected privacy and legitimate police and national security functions in the new information age. The basic scheme of the Privacy Act of 1974 has been a useful start towards protecting citizens from governmental abuse of stored personal data, but the law is already obsolete and must be vastly modified to meet future needs, such as predisclosure notification to the individual.

The Reagan Administration's fundamentally flawed interpretation and implementation of the 22 year-old Freedom of Information Act (FOIA) can be partially reversed by administrative actions, such as liberalizing recently adopted fee waiver policies. More broadly, however, the FOIA has not kept pace with advancing information technology, particularly as it relates to computerized federal information and data bases. Only some of this revision is possible through executive order, such as requiring that information currently being released under FOIA in paper formats also be processed into useful electronic formats.

MASS MEDIA

The most fundamental mass media policy priority of the new administration should be to promote the availability of the broadest possible diversity of viewpoints in the marketplace of ideas. This can be achieved through promoting diversity of ownership of mass media facilities and, in the still dominant broadcast medium, insuring that licensees earn their free monopoly over the airwaves by providing program service addressing the needs of the listening public. Newly emerging technologies have the potential to be positive or negative in their societal impact. They can, on the one hand, fragment audiences and subdivide Americans into ever smaller and increasingly contentious interest groups. Or, if we establish regulatory policies which embody those priorities, they can vastly expand opportunities for all Americans to have access to an ever greater range of issues, ideas and entertainment.

The FCC has historically enforced certain limits on the ownership of mass media properties to foster the First Amendment values of diversity of viewpoints and economic competition. Examples include the "one-to-a-market" rule prohibiting common ownership of more than one broadcast facility in the same community, the multiple station rule limiting the total number of broadcast stations that a single entity can own (now thirty-six), and the prohibition on ownership of both a daily newspaper and a broadcast station in the same city.

The Reagan Administration attempted to repeal some of these rules and succeeded, to some extent, in reducing the effectiveness of these ownership rules. In addition, the Administration missed opportunities to increase ownership diversity by freely waiving remaining rules on a case by case basis. For example, despite rules prohibiting ownership of TV stations with overlapping coverage, the FCC permitted Capital Cities Communications to buy ABC's New York City TV station even though it already owned a Philadelphia station which duplicates coverage over most of New Jersey. The FCC also declined to impose ownership limits on new technologies such as cable television systems, low power television, multichannel MDS and direct broadcast satellites.

A new administration should enforce the existing ownership rules and consider whether similar rules should be applied to other media, particularly the cable industry. By many measures, including assets, cable television challenges broadcasting in power and influence, with subscribers in more than 50% of American homes. The cable industry has become increasingly concentrated. The two largest cable operators now serve almost 40% of the nation's subscribers between them, and they are integrating vertically through acquiring program producers and distributors.

Cable's emerging competitors, such as MMDS and SMATV (pay services delivered via microwave and satellite), claim that the cable industry is interfering with their efforts to obtain programming. These problems may be substantially ameliorated simply by enforcing existing antitrust laws, something the Reagan Administration has declined to do. The next administration should also seriously consider the need for rules limiting concentration and vertical integration in the cable industry.

Another means by which the Commission has historically sought to promote diversity is through policies designed to promote ownership of broadcast facilities by minorities and women. Minority and female ownership and employment in telecommunications profoundly broadens the diversity of debate on issues and ideas in American society. There are three basic mechanisms by which this has been accomplished: (1) granting preference for minority or female ownership in the "comparative hearing" proceedings used to select initial licenses from among competing applicants; (2) the granting of tax certificates for stations sold to minorities; and (3) permitting "distress sales" at below market prices to minorities of stations that are facing regulatory problems. Under the Reagan Administration, the Justice Department has attacked these policies, and the Commission attempted to eliminate preferences for minorities and women in the comparative hearing process until forbidden by Congress to do so.

There continues to be severe under-representation of minorities and women in the ownership of broadcast facilities. The new administration should retain and strengthen the preference awarded minorities and women in the comparative hearing process. It should continue to permit tax certificate and distress sales — and consider whether low interest loans or other forms of financial assistance should be made available — to encourage minority ownership.

The affirmative action employment policies of the last generation, while still inadequate, have nonetheless begun to have an increasing impact at middle and upper management levels, and should be reinvigorated. Similarly, the president must insure that the appointment process yields minority and female appointees, and should also encourage FCC and NTIA appointees to strengthen internal affirmative action procedures and efforts within each agency to achieve national workforce parity at upper levels.

Long a major force for non-discrimination in communications policy, a revived U.S. Commission on Civil Rights should update its landmark study of the status of women and minorities in the broadcast industry titled, "Window Dressing on the Set," and make appropriate recommendations. The Civil Rights Commission should also study the employment practices of the non-broadcasting communications and information industries where information products are produced and distributed.

The role of public broadcasting must be clarified and redefined so that it has an unambiguous mandate to develop and distribute programming not provided by the commercial market. This alternative material should be created in an environment which rewards innovation, creativity and diversity. From its inception through to the present, the system of public broadcasting has been hampered by both political constraints and underfunding. A restructuring of the public broadcasting system is required to minimize these barriers. The Corporation for Public Broadcasting should be eliminated, and a new agency — the National Endowment for Public Telecommunication — should be created to fulfill the necessary administrative functions to develop and distribute non-commercial audio and video programs.[9] Such programs should be produced by the independent radio, film and video community. The Endowment should issue grants in sufficient amounts to develop a wide and varied array of programs. Priority should be given to independent producers proposing to develop programs not otherwise provided by the commercial marketplace. This would be a measure of, and a response to, market failure at the local, regional and national levels. Juries of peers should be involved in the grant-making processes. A model for such a scheme is the now existing National Endowment for the Arts.

Funding for public telecommunications and the Endowment should be insulated from the political process. The new president should work with Congress to create a blue-ribbon study group to fully develop the National Endowment and to address other policy options.[10] Over the long term, once commercial broadband service is available as described above, video spectrum users and commercial video users of broadband wire technologies should be taxed a reasonable percentage of the profits they receive from the transmission of their video products.

Certain initiatives should also be taken to promote broadcast program diversity more directly. First, government must restore the Fairness Doctrine. Right now, a radio station owner has been freed to promote personal objectives, say a zoning measure affecting his or her business, without carrying opposing points of view. Broadcasting remains the most powerful tool ever created for shaping public opinion, and those permitted to hold licenses must share these privileges to ensure that the public has access to contrasting points of view on controversial issues of public importance.

Second, the new administration should also take action to ensure that there is programming that serves the special needs of children. Reagan's FCC has been self-contradictory in addressing this fundamental concern: while it concedes that children cannot influence the marketplace, it has nonetheless removed prohibitions against "program-length commercials" (allowing toy companies to produce and broadcasters to air programs primarily designed to sell toys). It has also declined to mandate a reasonable amount of children's television programming specifically designed to educate and inform rather than just entertain, and to impose limits on the amount of commercialization on children's programs. The new administration can overturn these policies right away, thereby ending the exploitation of the nation's children.

Marketplace forces do not always insure news, public affairs and other programming sufficient to meet broader community needs for adults, either. This is especially the case for audiences not demographically attractive to advertisers — the old, the young, the poor and minorities. Under deregulation, broadcasters have received, free of charge, the benefits of monopoly without being expected to provide even a modicum of service in exchange. By making a minimal level of information and local programming the prerequisite for holding a broadcast license, the new administration can quickly respond to the public's unmet need for information about important issues of the day.

A particular victim of deregulation has been the FCC's concern for the character and responsibility of those who are licensed to use the public's airwaves. Initially, the repeal in 1982 of a rule requiring that TV and radio stations be held for at least three years was generally perceived as insignificant. However, fueled by junk bonds, the change has brought in a horde of speculators concerned only with short-term profitability and disinterested in building audiences through community service. The trend was further exacerbated by the FCC's decision to ignore evidence of applicants' bad character; as a result, convicted criminals and stock swindlers are now free to become broadcasters. Accountability should be restored as a standard for licensure.

The last eight years have been a period of evolution for non-broadcast technologies. The Cable Communications Policy Act of 1984, particularly as interpreted by the FCC, deregulated rates and preempted important municipal cable regulation. A consensus for re-institution of some limits is emerging, as cable has raised rates and dropped popular programming. Having succeeded in striking down "must carry" rules, cable operators have deleted local over-the-air channels, especially public stations, in favor of more remunerative pay services and home shopping services. In addition to the horizontal ownership concentration concerns mentioned above, cable has also integrated vertically into programming, while raising rates and fighting to abandon public service commitments such as public access and other channels serving government and service sectors. The elimination of "must-carry" rules requiring cable carriage of local TV stations poses special problems, especially for public broadcasters who may be dropped by cable companies and lose access to their audience. The new administration should explore ways consistent with the First Amendment to ensure that the public has access to public television stations.

As the inevitable convergence of mass media, telephone, data bases, publishing and entertainment accelerates over the next few years, the first steps towards development of ISDN standards of the next century will be taken. The most important short-term manifestation of this evolutionary process is the coming fight over High Definition Television (HDTV) standards. Battle lines are being drawn. Will HDTV be compatible with existing TVs? Will it be delivered initially over-the-air, using additional scarce spectrum space, or by cable and/or home satellite dishes, and thereby subject to less regulation? Will the first-out-of-box Japanese-developed technology be accepted, despite its limitations and adverse trade implications?[11] And, most important of all, will telephone companies be allowed to compete with cable in providing HDTV?

Thus, in dealing with HDTV, the new administration and its FCC will have to confront broad issues with tremendous long-term impact. The needs of American labor and of consumers, especially minorities and women, have received scant attention during the Reagan years. HDTV offers the opportunity for a fresh start, one that helps insure that the fruits of technology are shared by all Americans. By opting for a system allowing use of existing TV sets, and which will pave the way for a regulatory structure separating control of content from ownership of the means of transmission, the new administration and Congress may, quite literally, determine the course of the democratic process in the next generation.

IV. STRATEGIES

Most of the necessary change described here can be accomplished without legislation. Within six months of taking office, the new president will be able to appoint a majority of the FCC by filling three vacancies and appointing a new Chair. However, since at least two of the new commissioners will have to be members of the other party or Independents, a fresh administration will have less opportunity to establish ideological harmony right away. A new commitment to traditional antitrust enforcement policies at the Department of Justice and the Federal Trade Commission will be an important additional ingredient in promoting a more progressive telecommunications policy.

In the first year, the task will be to set straight the policymaking process at the FCC, Justice and Commerce, and articulate a legislative program that comprehends the needs of the coming generation. Beyond implementation of the goals discussed above, the President's major task will be to insure that policymakers retain the flexibility to adapt to technological change in an area that has repeatedly defied easy prediction.

To the extent that the newly composed FCC does not initiate necessary measures, Congress can take up the slack. Especially during its latter months, the 100th Congress manifested an increasing willingness to act on communications policy matters. The new administration can expect a broadcast bill, including the reinstitution of "must carry" rules and the Fairness Doctrine, to be among the first items to reach the floor of both houses of Congress. Thus, there will be the chance to offer leadership and cooperation at a very early point.

One priority needing legislation is the reinstitution of a federal role in research and standard-setting, along the lines of the former Bell Labs. New legislation could amend the Communications Act to promote the goal of "universal service" to a broadband ISDN telecommunication infrastructure that defines "basic service" as including minimum access to "appropriate technologies of communication and information." Under this new definition, appropriate information technology would be regarded as public utility, available to all on a nondiscriminatory basis and at reasonable price. As with public utilities generally, the government would act as the primary guarantor of acceptable performance or fairness to insure that the public interest is served.

In mass media issues, too, there is very little which cannot be accomplished by a well-run FCC. But only Congress can repair the 1984 Cable Act. In view of cable's increasing clout in Congress, this will not be easily accomplished, and can become an important test of presidential leadership.

Although information policy is integrally related to the functioning of democratic government, the participants in the policy debate are largely limited to private sector industrial interests. But the citizenry must also be represented. One mechanism worth consideration is the establishment of a National Endowment for Telecommunication and Information Policy Research, which would enfranchise broader segments of the public. Such an endowment would commission public-oriented study and advocacy and promote public participation, providing relevant, reliable data for use in future public policy debate on information issues.

V. CONCLUSION

The new administration must provide both leadership and imagination in setting priorities. Communication and information policies should take into consideration our core values, the current state of technology, significant trends and anticipated needs. Policy goals should not be limited to short and intermediate terms, but must inevitably look towards the long haul — the 21st century and beyond. Technology does not determine social structure, but widens possibilities. The questions to be confronted require a democratic vision and a practical resolve. What kind of society do we want to be? ˙ What kinds of communications and information initiatives contribute to or obstruct national policy? How can the national interest best be served?

NOTES

[1] For example, the seven regional telephone companies split off from AT&T may not provide "information services" unless Judge Greene grants a waiver.

[2] The concept of "universal" should mean the full and complete participation of the citizenry, regardless of their ability or willingness to pay. For example, we all have universal access to air, but not necessarily *clean* air.

[3] The FCC reports 1986 telephone penetration rates in 1986 of only 80.1% in Mississippi, 86.4% in Arkansas and 92.2% in the District of Columbia. Penetration rates for the lowest-income groups in November 1985 ranged between 65.2% for blacks and 82.2% for whites; nationally, in 1985, there was only a 72.5% penetration among families with even one member of the household.

4 However, this means that some subsidies will be needed. As discussed in the text below, the concept of universal service requires availability to all regardless of the ability to pay.

5 The Doctrine requires coverage of controversial issues of public importance and reasonable opportunity for the presentation of opposing points of view in such coverage.

6 For example, "minimum service" might be defined to include facsimile document transmission capability (*i.e.,* service similar to current "fax" or telecopier machines).

7 For example, businesses typically paid more than residential consumers for similar service, and long-distance customers generally helped support the cost of local service.

8 The "program" was the FBI's systematic effort to enlist librarians to report "suspicious" library use by nationals of countries deemed unfriendly to the U.S.

9 Distribution of radio programs should continue via satellite to local NPR radio stations as well as other commercial radio stations, mail-order cassettes and other recording media. Distribution of video products should include direct broadcast satellite (DBS), regional satellites to non-commercial television stations, integrated broadband networks (coaxial cables and fiber optics systems), video rental stores and direct sales of various media formats. Universal service as applied to IBNs should include not only the provision of video dial tone but also the reception of public telecommunication programs as an "essential information service."

10 This fall, a private study group organized by Professor John Wicklein of Ohio State University is presenting a different proposal for changing, but not eliminating, the CPB function. The Wicklein report will serve as a useful beginning for a more formal project.

11 In the summer of 1988, the FCC made tentative decisions which effectively dictate a slower path which favors U.S.-developed technologies. The rest of the world, however, is following a different path, and the U.S. may have to change course.

ENERGY:
Department of Energy &
Nuclear Regulatory Commission

Richard Munson*

SUMMARY OF RECOMMENDATIONS

The new president has the opportunity to create a comprehensive, long-range energy policy. By stressing efficiency, competition and preparedness, he can ensure a stable and affordable supply of energy for all Americans and enable our businesses to increase their share of world markets.

Ronald Reagan came to Washington pledging to destroy the Department of Energy. But rather than face the legislative headaches of eliminating a cabinet-level department, he instead transformed it — radically. In reality, our Department of Energy has become the Department of Nuclear Weapons. More than 60 percent of the agency's budget is devoted to the design and production of atomic bombs. This emphasis distorts the focus of key personnel and the direction of our national labs. If we want an effective energy policy, we need a real Department of Energy. Weapons and space defense systems should be transferred to civilian management within another agency.

The Nuclear Regulatory Commission also needs to live up to its name, becoming a true regulator rather than largely a promoter of nuclear power. The public has lost confidence in the government's oversight of reactors — not just because of the Three Mile Island and Chernobyl accidents, but also because the NRC has systematically sacrificed public safety in favor of industry interests. The new president should appoint a White House Task Force to reform the NRC's structure in order to create an effective enforcement policy. It also should aggressively demand the safety of reactors and waste disposal operations.

The next president and Congress can supplement these grand administrative actions with a clear set of themes that will guide a national energy policy. That policy must first curtail the nation's

---

* *Richard Munson is Executive Director of the Northeast-Midwest Institute and author of* The Power Makers. *He was formerly director of the Solar Lobby and the Center for Renewable Resources.*

enormous waste of energy. Perhaps one of the most effective initiatives would be to double the fuel economy of cars and light trucks. Researchers estimate that raising the fuel efficiency of the U.S. auto fleet by just one mile per gallon would save 45 percent more oil than the Reagan Administration claims can be pumped from the Arctic National Wildlife Refuge.

Second, a comprehensive energy policy for the 1990s must encourage competition among technologies and industries. Regarding electricity, the next government can help assure reliable supplies and stable prices by promoting a freer market for suppliers and opening access to electricity transmission.

Third, the nation must be prepared for energy emergencies. In contrast to the Reagan Administration's foot dragging, the new president should fill the Strategic Petroleum Reserve and encourage other consuming countries to create similar stockpiles. It also should urge international development agencies to reduce pressures on world oil prices by helping Third World countries use energy more efficiently. Moreover, it must revise NRC regulations to reduce the probability of severe accidents and large releases of radiation.

I. INTRODUCTION

When it comes to an effective energy policy, progressive policymakers should not look longingly back to previous administrations for their models. Former presidents certainly achieved some major accomplishments — including fuel-efficiency standards for new cars that saved more oil than has been pumped from Alaska. Moreover, President Jimmy Carter's Public Utility Regulatory Policies Act opened the monolithic and backward utility industry to competition from new, efficient technologies. On the other hand, price controls proved ineffective, and Carter's $88 billion synfuels program became an embarrassing waste of money.

Progressives also need fresh themes. Energy policy can no longer be couched as a moral contest between nuclear and solar, between the hard and soft paths, between production and conservation. Nor is energy use merely an environmental concern; its availability also clearly affects the nation's economic development, our national security and the social welfare of our citizens. Finally, progressives must acknowledge the power of market forces and the inefficiency of government acting as an energy retailer. Our nation's most effective energy policies have set clear rules that allowed competitive businesses to operate.

During his first year, the new president should adopt two grand administrative actions that demonstrate his commitment to a future-oriented, investment-driven energy policy.

First, he should create a true Department of Energy, transferring the massive weapons and space defense systems to an independent, civilian-controlled agency. DOE's weapons role is not new, but Ronald Reagan made it predominant. Since the Atoms for Peace Program, policymakers have correctly felt that weapons development should be under civilian rather than military control. But rather than continue to endure a national policy distorted toward nuclear power, a full-fledged Department of Energy can help promote a balanced and competitive energy market.

Second, he should restore public confidence in government regulation of nuclear power. Today's so-called regulators, for example, have overruled the objections of governors concerned with the evacuation of civilians during a nuclear emergency. They're also trying to redefine low-level radioactive waste so that it can be unregulated and disposed in neighborhood landfills.

The agency's gross lack of regulatory oversight demands the attention of a White House Task Force on Nuclear Safety, composed of respected men and women clearly not beholden to the industry. The Task Force must be given a broad mandate to develop proposals that reform NRC's structure as well as to craft the critical safety guidelines that the existing agency has either refused or been unable to develop. At the least, the high-level group should remove NRC's office of investigations from oversight by the Director of Operations in order to provide arms-length enforcement. It should establish low-level radioactive waste guidelines for states and encourage the use of dry cask storage for spent fuel. Moreover, it should withdraw policy statements that conclude reactors are currently safe, as well as curtail cost-benefit analyses for backfits.

These two actions, of course, do not constitute a comprehensive energy policy. They would be, however, dramatic and early signals about the federal government's willingness to focus long-term on energy issues.

The new president also should educate the American public about energy's continued importance to our nation's economy and environment. He should outline three principles — efficiency, competition and preparedness — to guide the formation of a long-term energy policy that permits our industries to compete in world markets and our consumers to afford stable and safe supplies of power.

Efficient energy programs would tackle this country's energy wastefulness. Inefficient energy use increases costs for our businesses, reducing their competitiveness. It also adds to severe environmental problems, including greenhouse warming, acid rain and smog. In an age of tight budgets, international economic competition and dirty air, we simply can't afford waste. We must become, as the Marines advocate, lean and mean.

It is true that the nation has become more efficient since the 1973 oil embargo. We use little more energy today than we did 15 years ago, even though we produce almost 40 percent more goods and services. Efficiency improvements, according to some estimates, have cut the nation's annual energy bill by $160 billion. Despite this progress, the U.S. still uses twice as much energy per unit of industrial output as its competitors in Japan and West Germany. A new administration can improve U.S. economic vitality by creating partnerships with industries and universities to advance research and development of energy efficient technologies.

Regarding the second theme, the new president and Congress can together help assure reasonable energy supplies and prices by promoting competition among both companies and technologies. The U.S. energy market is anything but free. Even conservative administrations have adopted a blatant industrial policy toward energy, picking corporations and technologies that it would promote. Throughout this century, Washington spent billions building hydroelectric dams and subsidizing oil wells. Since World War II, it devoted billions more trying to create a nuclear reactor that would be "too cheap to meter." The federal government can certainly help overcome market imperfections, but it must devise a level playing field that allows the most efficient and cost-effective technologies to compete equitably.

Finally, the nation must be prepared for and cushioned from the effects of another energy supply disruption. Over the past year, U.S. demand for oil has risen by a surprising 5 percent, domestic production is down and imports have soared by 17 percent. Recognizing how interdependent the world oil market is, the new administration must fill the Strategic Petroleum Reserve and urge other consumer nations to create or add to similar stockpiles. At the same time, it must move aggressively to reduce the probability of severe nuclear power accidents and large releases of radiation.

II. LESSONS FROM THE PAST

The federal government has long been involved in the energy business. In 1907, President Theodore Roosevelt's Inland Waterways Commission concluded that the "streams of the country are an asset of the people" that should be protected from monopolies and developed to enhance irrigation, navigation, flood control and power production. The Federal Power Act of 1920 promoted hydroelectric dams and created a Federal Power Commission that granted 50-year leases to waterways, with a preference given to municipalities over private power companies. In the early 1930s, Senator George Norris (R-NE) and President Franklin Roosevelt led efforts to create the Tennessee Valley Authority and the Rural Electrification Administration, bringing electric power to millions of poor and rural Americans. Similar regional power authorities were eventually established in the Pacific Northwest, the Southeast and Alaska.

Regarding petroleum, turn-of-the-century policymakers concluded that the free market couldn't determine the proper rate of production for such a critical commodity. To conserve the resource and maintain stable prices, the government developed complex quota systems that tended to provide market control to a few large oil companies. World War II, however, shifted concerns to increasing petroleum production dramatically. Government and industry leaders subsequently developed an array of tax subsidies and incentives to promote domestic drilling and refining. According to the Battelle Memorial Institute, from the beginning of the century through 1978, market tinkering on behalf of the oil industry cost taxpayers almost $200 billion.

In 1946, Congress created the Atomic Energy Commission (AEC) to "conserve and restrict the use of atomic energy for the national defense, to prohibit its private exploitation and preserve the secret and confidential character of information concerning the use and application of atomic energy." Scientists at the AEC initially gave only token attention to nuclear reactor development, preferring to test bigger bombs at the Bikini atoll in the South Pacific's Marshall Islands. In 1951, after the Soviet Union ignited an atomic bomb, Congress amended the original Atomic Energy Act to allow the sharing of certain nuclear information with members of the newly established North Atlantic Treaty Organization (NATO).

President Eisenhower promoted the concept of nuclear commercialism in his famous "Atoms for Peace" speech before the United Nations General Assembly on December 8, 1953. After reviewing the bomb's terrible destructiveness, he pledged the United States would seek ways "by which the miraculous inventiveness of man shall not be dedicated to his death, but consecrated to his life." Moreover, Eisenhower redefined the purpose of atomic energy: "It is not enough to take this weapon out of the hands of the soldiers. It must be put into the hands of those who will know how to strip its military casing and adapt it to the art of peace." The AEC, as a result, became the prime promoter of nuclear power.

Federal energy policy entered a dramatic new phase in response to events that began on October 6, 1973, when Egyptian troops crossed into Israeli-occupied Suez and closed the canal. In response to President Nixon's massive $2.5 billion arms shipment to Israel, angry

Arab ministers agreed to increase oil prices 70 percent, to $5.12 a barrel, and to cut production 5 percent each month "until the Israeli withdrawal is completed...and the legal rights of the Palestinian people restored." Within days, Saudi Arabia slashed production 20 percent and announced a total embargo on oil to the United States and the Netherlands, Israel's key allies.

Although the Arab cutbacks accounted for less than 10 percent of the world's supply, pandemonium ensued. Within a month, the price of oil on the spot market had increased from approximately $3.00 to $17.00 a barrel. In December, OPEC ministers settled on a floor price of $11.65 a barrel, a 400 percent rise in two months. President Richard Nixon subsequently announced Project Independence and created the Energy Research and Development Administration (ERDA) to coordinate federal initiatives promoting energy development. "Let us set as our national goal," said Nixon, "in the spirit of Apollo, with the determination of the Manhattan Project, that by the end of the decade we will have developed the potential to meet our own energy needs without depending on any foreign energy sources." President Gerald Ford pledged to reduce U.S. reliance on OPEC oil by building 250 major coal mines, 200 nuclear reactors, 150 coal-fired power plants, 30 oil refineries and 20 synthetic fuel plants.

By the mid 1970s, America was not significantly closer to energy independence and oil prices had soared above $20 per barrel. Within 100 days of his inauguration, President Jimmy Carter declared the country was "running out of gas and oil" and that "we will live in fear of embargoes" that will threaten "an economic, social and political crisis." He argued successfully for a Cabinet-level Department of Energy. And in perhaps his most memorable phrase, the new president said the campaign to solve the energy crisis must amount to "the moral equivalent of war."

Carter's first volley — the five-part National Energy Act of 1977 — moved slowly through Congress, in part because the Carter administration failed to give clear signals to its Capitol Hill supporters. The White House, for instance, initially declared energy conservation to be the legislation's "cornerstone," but officials later spoke of raising the price of natural gas through deregulation as the plan's "centerpiece." In the early stages, Carter called nuclear power the energy source of "last resort," but as political deals were cut, Energy Secretary James Schlesinger proclaimed that nuclear power was "enshrined in the President's program." In 1979, after the Iranian crisis hiked oil prices further, Carter focused his subsidies on synfuels, proposing a massive $88 billion development program.

From the perspective of the late 1980s, it's clear that some post-embargo energy programs proved enormously effective, while others accumulated only costs and regulations. The successful initiatives, in short, seem to have been those in which the federal government set clear rules and allowed the marketplace to function.

The 1975 Energy Policy and Conservation Act (EPCA), for instance, permitted automobile manufacturers to determine how they would meet the requirement that new cars obtain an average 27.5 miles per gallon by 1985; EPCA, as a result, helped reduce the gasoline required per mile for the average car by almost 30 percent. Moreover, the 1978 Public Utility Regulatory Policies Act (PURPA) opened the electricity market to competition, enabling independent power producers to install some 24,300 megawatts of capacity from unconventional power sources, equal to the output of 24 large nuclear reactors.

The residential energy conservation tax credit, on the other hand, produced little evidence of additional conservation over what consumers would have done anyway. Yet the credit proved to be the single most expensive federal conservation measure. Other failures occurred when the federal government, rather than the private sector, tried to retail new technologies, from solar water heaters to energy audits of buildings.

III. SETBACKS IN THE 1980s

President Reagan has been unusually lucky on the energy front. Policies of his predecessor continued to enhance the economy's energy efficiency, helping to reduce the nation's energy use per dollar of output by an average of 2.7 percent per year between 1976 and 1986. At the same time, inflated oil prices spurred discoveries in the North Sea and the Soviet Union. These two factors led to the collapse of U.S. oil prices from a peak of $33 per barrel in 1981 to almost $10 per barrel in 1987. The price fluctuates around $16 per barrel today.

In some respects, the United States is better positioned to withstand oil supply disruptions than it was 15 years ago. Congress, despite the Reagan Administration's reluctance, developed the beginnings of a strategic petroleum reserve to cushion the economy. Moreover, every sector of the nation's economy responded to higher prices by reducing its energy intensity.

Yet major energy problems persist. Oil imports, for instance, are on the rise for the first time since the mid-1970s, jumping 30 percent since 1985. If present trends continue, the Department of Energy projects that the U.S. will import 60 percent of its oil in 1995, well above the 35 percent level of 1987, and even high compared with the 43 percent dependence in 1979. Petroleum, of course, is one of the world's most unevenly distributed resources. Ninety-five percent of proven reserves are in only 20 countries, and Arab nations and Iran control 56.3 percent of the world's total. Policymakers must remember that the nation's oil supply can be disrupted when the U.S. or its allies rely too heavily on imports from the volatile Middle East.

Some of the positive efficiency gains of the last decade, of course, resulted from disastrous economic setbacks for several industries. Declines in steel and auto manufacturing may have reduced energy demand, but they also slashed employment.

At the same time, the oil price collapse of 1986 provided a mild stimulus to much of the country, but it battered the U.S. oil producing states. U.S. production fell by a record 800,000 barrels per day in 1986, leading to bankruptcies and growing unemployment in hard-hit areas such as Texas and Oklahoma.

Under the Reagan Administration, the nation's energy programs have suffered seven years of neglect and abuse. Avoiding crises such as '73 and '79 should have allowed the U.S. to further prepare for the future by increasing both the diversity of energy sources and the efficiency with which those supplies are used. Instead, the Reagan Administration proposed the virtual elimination of programs to advance energy conservation, renewable resources and coal; it vetoed and only grudgingly accepted legislation to set appliance efficiency standards which both the industry and environmentalists endorsed; and it rolled back automobile fuel efficiency standards and recently proposed to eliminate them entirely.

Rather than promote efficiency, Reagan's Department of Energy advocated increased consumption. Administration officials, for instance, projected that electricity use would continue to grow approximately 3 percent annually. To meet this demand and replace a few oil-fired burners, they argued for the construction of 438 new power plants by the year 2000, or approximately two large stations each month. Such expansion would cost a whopping $1.8 trillion, equal to half a year's gross national product or more than four times the utility industry's existing net assets. The Administration's projected expansion would not even stop at the century's end; the "grow and build" advocates anticipated an ever-accelerating demand for more power plants and more capital.

At the same time, the Department of Interior tried to "open up" and develop America's frontier oil provinces in Alaska and on the Outer Continental Shelf by proclaiming an oil emergency. Under the Administration's proposal, enormous areas of land would be leased for energy development at a time when energy values are severely depressed, thus providing a bonanza to giant petroleum companies.

While the Reagan White House promoted more reactors and oil wells, it advanced no major response to the major energy shock which occurred on April 26, 1986, when one of the Soviet Union's nuclear reactors at Chernobyl exploded and caught fire, spewing radioactive debris more than 1,800 feet into the air and over sizable portions of the Soviet Union and Europe. After the accident, more than 100,000 people had to be evacuated to avoid the substantial amounts of radioactive fallout. Several months later, Soviet scientists announced that 31 people died and 203 remained hospitalized with radiation illness. Following on the heels of the 1979 accident at the Three Mile Island nuclear reactor near Harrisburg, Pennsylvania, the Chernobyl disaster spurred most nuclear nations to re-examine their programs and to place a new emphasis on nuclear safety. In the United States, however, the NRC adopted few new initiatives to regulate reactors.

IV. INVESTING IN OUR ENERGY FUTURE

Energy policy continues to have a critical impact on the nation's economy and environment. Each year, the United States spends almost $440 billion on energy, equalling 11 percent of our gross national product. Rising oil imports account for about one-quarter of our merchandise trade deficit. Government researchers project the oil import bill could reach $100 billion by the end of the 1990s.

Energy use also profoundly affects the environment. It is, for instance, the main factor reducing stratospheric ozone levels and driving climatic change; more than three-quarters of the carbon remaining in the atmosphere each year originates in fossil fuel combustion. Acid rain, caused largely by sulfur emissions for coal-fired power plants, annually costs the U.S. at least $10 billion in materials damage and crop loses.

A short chapter cannot address the myriad of initiatives needed to achieve a comprehensive energy plan. Listed below, however, are several specific policy recommendations based on the themes of efficiency, competition and preparedness.

1. **Efficiency.** The United States wastes an enormous amount of energy. Our businesses consume twice as much power as our major international competitors. We possess the technical ability to double the fuel economy of cars and light trucks, but American automobiles remain some of the world's greatest gas guzzlers.

Energy waste presents clear economic and environmental dangers. Unnecessary fossil fuel burning accelerates greenhouse warming, acid deposition and urban smog formation. Inefficient consumption accounts for much of the nation's $40 billion annual oil import bill, which some government studies project will soar to $100 billion per year by the century's end.

Scientists agree that the least expensive means to obtain new energy is to reduce current energy waste. Environmentalists want the U.S. to set a goal of trimming its energy intensity — the rate of energy used per dollar of economic output — by 2.5 percent per year well into the next century.

Unfortunately, the nation is losing momentum in energy efficiency. The economy's total energy intensity has remained virtually stable over the past two years, compared to 2.7 percent annual reductions over the previous decade. After ten years of improvements, automobile fuel economy has leveled off. Correcting for changes due to structural shifts, industrial energy intensity also became flat in 1983.

The 101st Congress and 41st president can invest in the nation's energy future by reducing energy waste in the nation's vehicles, buildings and factories. To realize this enormous potential, Washington should:

* Double the fuel economy of the nation's cars and light trucks by the year 2000. To achieve this improvement, engineers say the new administration can amend the Energy Policy and Conservation Act to raise new car and new light truck fuel standards to 45 and 35 miles per gallon, respectively, by the end of the century. A substantial tax should be imposed on manufacturers failing to meet the new standards. Automobiles and light trucks account for a third of U.S. petroleum consumption. Although they've increased their efficiency since 1973, technology exists to dramatically increase fuel economy standards and reduce petroleum consumption.

* Aggressively implement the national appliance efficiency standards adopted by Congress in 1987 and supported by equipment manufacturers and environmentalists. These standards are expected to cut peak electricity demand in the year 2000 by 22,000 megawatts.

* Propose legislation to create regional research centers that would investigate more efficient industrial processes, such as chemicals separation or metals casting. These public-private partnerships would help energy-intensive businesses reduce costs and increase productivity.

* Endorse efficiency standards for common lamps and fluorescent lamp ballasts. Lighting consumes one-fifth of U.S. electricity, and engineers project increased efficiency could reduce the nation's power demand by 11,000 megawatts by the century's end.

* Encourage the Federal Energy Regulatory Commission to allow efficiency projects to compete with proposals for additional generating units.

* Set aggressive energy efficiency goals for federal buildings, which now cost $4 billion annually to power. Environmentalists suggest a 20 percent savings per square foot of floor space within ten years. The next government also should restore federal responsibility for setting energy standards in public and subsidized housing, require individual metering in federally-assisted rental housing and set high energy standards for those buildings.

* Increase federal research and development for energy efficiency technologies, fuel conservation, renewable energy sources and alternative fuels. While several federal agencies — Defense, Health and Agriculture — spend up to 12 percent of their budgets for R&D, DOE invests only 0.5 percent of its funds.

* At least double the federal funds (to $315 million) available to weatherize the residences of low-income families. More than 17 million low-income homes need to be weatherized, and particular attention must be given to multi-family buildings which have undergone few efficiency improvements. Families below the poverty line spend an average 19 percent of their income on home energy costs, more than four times that spent by middle-income families. Increasing energy efficiency would make housing more affordable for thousands of Americans.

2. Competition. For industries to be competitive in international markets, the U.S. needs to encourage competition among its industries. In the energy field, however, government subsidies and regulations have long favored selected technologies and industries, discouraging competition and retarding efficiency. Electric utilities, for instance, burn subsidized fuels, pay few taxes and enjoy guaranteed profits.

To free the energy market of distortions working against emerging technologies and innovative enterprises, the federal government faces two options. In late 1984, the Reagan Administration's Treasury Department proposed sweeping reforms to simplify the tax code by eliminating almost all energy credits and deductions. Because representatives of the oil, coal, electric and solar industries protested the proposed loss of their targeted benefits, few of Treasury's provisions were enacted, moving analysts to conclude that a truly free energy market is politically unrealistic. Treasury's approach also was criticized by lawmakers believing that Washington has an important role to play in helping to solve the nation's energy problems.

The government's preferable option is to develop a balanced energy program that curtails market barriers to efficient new enterprises. To enhance competition among both technologies and industries, the next president can:

* Encourage the Federal Energy Regulatory Commission (FERC) to aggressively promote a freer market for electricity suppliers. As mentioned before, the Public Utility Regulatory Policies Act (PURPA) opened the electricity industry to competition. While utility monopolies virtually stopped building large power plants over the past decade, PURPA enabled independent power producers — some big companies, many entrepreneurs — to install more than 24,300 megawatts of capacity from unconventional power sources, equal to the output of 24 large coal plants or nuclear reactors. While not

discouraging state innovation, FERC can set clear and consistent standards for PURPA that promote bidding among the least-cost sources.

* Introduce legislation and propose FERC regulations that open access to electricity transmission lines. Charles Ross, a former federal power commissioner, told the Senate Commerce Committee in 1965 that "it is the parties who control the transmission lines, the arteries of the industry, that control the destiny of millions of ratepayers of this nation." Unfortunately, existing antitrust laws and FERC's limited authority have retarded wheeling, thus decreasing competition and efficiency.

* Remove the barriers that prevent competition in the natural gas industry, and examine whether the nation has adequate interstate pipeline capacity to deliver the gas we will need in the future. Lean-burning and abundant natural gas can significantly improve the quality of our air and water.

* Increase the government's commitment to a diverse energy mix by creating a level playing field of incentives and tax benefits so that all energy technologies — nuclear, fossil fuels, renewables and energy efficiency — can compete in the marketplace on equal footing. So Congress should adjust federal procurement, export promotion and financing provisions to help build innovative renewable energy ventures. It also should curtail the disproportionate subsidies now directed toward nuclear power, in part by enacting legislation that requires the nuclear industry to pay a fair price for federal uranium enrichment, waste disposal and other services.

* Establish programs to translate basic energy R&D results into commercial products. Currently, Japanese and European manufacturers are making the most use of U.S. basic research results to introduce energy-efficient products that capture world markets. Moreover, the next president should create an office within the Department of Energy to monitor and distribute information on foreign energy efforts, particularly those to enhance energy-efficient technologies.

3. **Preparedness.** The United States, the world's largest buyer of imported oil, is spending hundreds of millions of dollars to protect the flow of petroleum through the Persian Gulf's shipping lanes. After the limited 1973 oil embargo, we should have learned that the United States and its allies must be prepared to weather supply interruptions. Unfortunately, the nation is allowing petroleum imports to climb rapidly, risking OPEC's recontrol of the world oil market. A series of oil price increases could further burden the U.S. and other debtor countries with severe economic troubles.

After the Three Mile Island and Chernobyl accidents, we also should have learned to stress nuclear safety and to prepare procedures that will limit damage from future accidents. To help prevent energy emergencies and increase the nation's preparedness, the new president and Congress should agree to:

* Fill the Strategic Reserve. While the Reagan Administration has tried to reduce the SPR's size by 50 percent, energy experts and Congress maintain that the six hallowed-out salt domes along the Texas and Louisiana coasts must be filled with 750 million barrels of crude oil. To assure adequate supplies during an emergency, the new president also should urge other consuming countries to create or add to strategic oil stockpiles.

* Encourage the World Bank and direct AID to help developing countries use energy efficiently. Some developing countries spend as much as 60 percent of their export earnings on imported oil. Increasing energy efficiency can help stimulate economic growth, raise local living standards and reduce pressures on world oil prices. The new administration also should propose exchange programs that help Third World engineers and policymakers learn how to implement energy-efficient technologies and practices.

* Push NRC Commissioners to reduce the probability of severe accidents and large releases of radiation. At the least, they should remove cost-benefit analysis for backfits, establish low-level waste guidelines for states and call for an expert, unbiased reassessment of the nation's high-level nuclear waste program.

SECURITIES REGULATION:
Securities and Exchange Commission

Harvey J. Goldschmid[*]

SUMMARY OF RECOMMENDATIONS

Not since the trauma of the stock market crash of 1929 and the various crises of the early 1930s have our financial markets seemed so fragile and the need for reform so great. During the past decade, our financial markets have both greatly expanded and grown increasingly complex. New financial products (*e.g.*, stock index futures, options of various kinds, so-called "junk" bonds), new trading strategies and technologies (*e.g.*, program trading, stock index arbitrage, portfolio insurance), the internationalization of markets, the blurring of boundaries between previously diverse financial markets, manic merger and acquisition activities, the growing corporate dependence on debt financing and issues related to the shareholder's role have emphasized the critical need for regulatory change.

During this period the Securities and Exchange Commission (SEC) has by and large stuck to its old knitting, properly regulating disclosure and market manipulation, but inexcusably neglecting the regulatory implications of market change. This policy paralysis has been costly. A dramatic illustration of the vulnerability and volatility of our financial markets took place in just four trading days between October 13 and 19, 1987, when publicly held stock values declined 31%, resulting in a loss of approximately $1 trillion. But more is at stake for the nation than unnecessary volatility in its securities markets. Financial markets allocate capital and influence business and consumer conduct in the most basic ways. The 41st President should recognize that the economic health of the nation will be fundamentally affected by the regulatory road that SEC commissioners elect to travel down starting in 1989. The new administration should take the following steps to stem the flight of investors from the nation's

---

[*] *Harvey J. Goldschmid is Dwight Professor of Law at Columbia University. He is a reporter for the American Law Institute's Corporate Governance Project and is chair of the Corporate Takeover Legislation Committee at the Association of the Bar of the City of New York.*

securities markets and to restore the vigor and integrity of these markets:

* Legislation should give the SEC regulatory responsibility for the stock, option and futures markets. Separate monitoring by the SEC and the Commodity Futures Trading Commission (CFTC) has resulted in inconsistent and ineffective regulation. More basically, the nation's financial markets and key players in them (*e.g.*, commercial banks, savings and loan associations, investment banks and insurance companies) are now inextricably linked in economic terms, but are regulated by a host of different federal and state agencies. The predictable result of this "market for financial regulators" is laxity and inconsistency.

* Because the Reagan SEC turned a blind eye towards calls for analysis and evaluation, we do not now have the theoretical or empirical basis for making final judgments on most new financial products and trading strategies, or on other major issues (*e.g.*, involving the internationalization of financial markets and corporation debt). We need the most thorough-going examination of the securities markets since the Kennedy Administration's Special Study (under similar circumstances) in the early 1960s.

* Certain unfair and destabilizing trading practices (*e.g.*, so-called "front running" and short selling of futures in a declining market) should be prohibited. Early in 1989, action should be taken on: (i) insider trading legislation; (ii) legislation providing new budgetary resources and remedial powers for the SEC; (iii) proposals for the imposition of stricter disclosure requirements on local governments issuing municipal bonds; and (iv) proposals for reform of securities industry arbitration.

I. A BRIEF BACKGROUND SKETCH[1]

The federal securities acts of 1933 and 1934 mandated broad disclosure about securities being sold for the first time or publicly traded, provided for the prosecution of misrepresentation and regulated various Wall Street practices. Congress acted in response to public demand. Between September 1, 1929 and July 1, 1932, the value of stocks listed on the New York Stock Exchange shrank from nearly $90 billion to just under $16 billion. "The annals of finance," the Senate Banking Committee wrote, "present no counterpart to this enormous decline in security prices."[2] Approximately half of the $50 billion of new securities that were sold in the United States from 1920-30 proved nearly or totally valueless. In the words of Congress, "The flotation of such a mass of essentially fraudulent securities was made possible because of the complete abandonment by many underwriters and dealers in securities of those standards of fair, honest and prudent dealing that should be basic to the encouragement of investment in any enterprise."[3] Federal intervention had long been advocated because state "blue sky" laws[4] could not provide adequate national protection.

The SEC, created in 1934, is a traditional independent administrative agency. It has five commissioners (no more than three may be appointed from the same political party) and has in general been blessed by high quality leadership and able staff. The first chairman of the SEC was Joseph P. Kennedy. The day President Roosevelt informed his cabinet that he would appoint Kennedy, Interior Secretary Harold Ickes wrote in his diary:

> He has named . . . a former stock market plunger. The President has great confidence in him because he has made his pile, has invested all his money in Government securities and knows all the tricks of the trade. Apparently he is going on the assumption that Kennedy would now like to make a name for himself for the sake of his family, but I have never known many of these cases to work out as expected.[5]

By the time of Kennedy's resignation in September, 1935, however, his achievements in organizing and staffing the SEC and moving the securities markets towards stability were widely applauded. Professor Joel Seligman, who has written the definitive history of the SEC, summarized the Commission's early years as follows:

> [G]one are the days when new securities sales were dominated by private investment banks, such as J.P. Morgan and Company, when references to "bear raids" or stock market "pools" daily appeared in the nation's press, when the New York Stock Exchange fairly could be described as a "private club," when Senate hearings riveted the nation's attention with revelations of fraudulent Peruvian bond sales, "preferred" stockholder lists, bribed journalists who "touted" securities, or stock price manipulation.... The principal actor in this transformation of corporate finance has been the Securities and Exchange Commission.[6]

The SEC's performance after World War II receives mixed reviews. Indeed, in December 1960, President-elect John Kennedy was advised by James Landis, a former SEC chairman and dean of the Harvard Law School, that federal regulatory agencies were in a state of disarray. The SEC suffered from "budget starvation" and Kennedy was advised that the "key to improvement" was the "selection of qualified personnel."[7] For the chairmanship of the SEC, the President nominated my late colleague, William L. Cary of Columbia Law School.

Cary recognized that while the nation's securities markets had changed greatly between the New Deal and the New Frontier, the SEC had not done an in-depth study of these markets in over twenty years. In 1961, a Special Study of securities markets was commissioned. It "undoubtedly was the single most influential document published in the history of the SEC," concluded Professor Seligman.

"It provided a foundation for most of the reforms that occurred in the securities industry during the ensuing fifteen years."[8]

Chairman Cary and his successors at the SEC reinvigorated a tired agency, and the Special Study and other initiatives produced a process of reform that changed securities laws and financial markets enormously for the better.[9] But as a new chairman takes office in January, 1989, he or she will face a situation remarkably similar to the one Cary faced in 1960.

The 1989 financial markets and substantive problems are, of course, very different from those of 1960. The basic needs, however, remain similar: reinvigoration of staff and redefinition of the SEC's jurisdictional boundaries; adequate budget; in-depth study of market change with an eye towards regulatory reform; and, in certain key areas, new legislative initiatives or rulemaking proposals.

On balance, the Reagan SEC has performed adequately — and at times superbly — in enforcement areas involving market manipulation and insider trading. The Reagan Administration as a whole, however, has inexcusably neglected many areas of fundamental importance. A rigid free-market, hands-off approach has characterized much of its thinking. Even when it has been forced to grapple with a financial markets problem, the Reagan answer has usually been myopic, with an emphasis on muddling through.

II. PRINCIPAL CHALLENGES AND REFORMS

NEW FINANCIAL PRODUCTS, STRATEGIES & TECHNOLOGIES

Attacks on new financial products and trading strategies came quickly in the wake of the stock market crash of October, 1987. Futures products, various kinds of options, program trading,[10] portfolio insurance[11] and index arbitrage were all included in the leading critiques.

Valid questions have been raised, for example, whether these new products and strategies increase speculation, increase volatility, work unfairly from the standpoint of the small investor and interfere unduly with long-term corporate governance goals. On the other hand, reducing risk exposure is a legitimate goal for money managers and many "abolition" proposals would produce costly substitutes or be easily avoided.[12]

We do not now have the theoretical or empirical basis for making definitive judgments on most new financial products and trading strategies. This, in substantial part, is because the Reagan SEC spent almost seven years ignoring dramatic changes in financial markets and rejecting calls for analysis and evaluation. After the crash of October, 1987, serious but hurried reports done by the Brady Commission, the CFTC, the SEC, the General Accounting Office, the New

York Stock Exchange and the Chicago Mercantile Exchange, in the words of one commentator, did "not draw the same conclusions, nor . . . [did] they arrive at the same policy solutions, and in some instances, their recommendations . . . [stood] in glaring conflict."[13]

Clearly in this area, as well as in many others, what is called for is the most thorough examination of the securities markets since Cary's Special Study. In addition, there are important lessons to be drawn from the October crash, which can be put into effect right now.

1. Adopt single-source (SEC) regulation of the stock, option and futures markets. The SEC has jurisdictional responsibility for stocks and options. The CFTC regulates stock index futures. According to Stephen Friedman, a former SEC commissioner, there "is no intellectually respectable argument for the existing system of separate regulators for securities and options on securities, and for financial futures and options on financial futures."[14] Similarly, economist Henry Kaufman concluded that the "current system of regulation and surveillance [of financial markets] is really archaic."[15] Single-source regulation would allow for both consistent regulatory requirements and more effective monitoring and prohibition of counterproductive practices.[16]

The Brady Commission properly recognized the need for overall regulation of these financial markets, but recommended that the Federal Reserve "coordinate" the activities of the other regulators. It is now clear that almost everyone in Washington, including the Federal Reserve, rejects this idea. Although the political difficulties are real, Congress should be asked to transfer jurisdiction over "all stock products" — no matter how denominated — to the SEC. The SEC's track record and general expertise (particularly when compared to the CFTC) dictate this organizational solution.

2. Harmonize margin rules and prohibit certain practices. Both the Brady Commission and the SEC have recommended harmonizing the conflicting margin rules applicable to stocks and futures. The Reagan Administration has, however, resisted this proposal. Currently, the margin requirement for stocks is 50%, but is only 15% for most futures traders. Margin rules protect the financial integrity of brokers and the clearing system, restrict leveraged speculation and probably reduce volatility. The margins for stock traders (both public and professional traders) and futures traders should come from a single source and be coordinated in order to avoid conflict.

According to the Brady Commission, aggressive professional traders, aware of the strategies of their major clients, traded "just in front of them" on October 19, 1987. This so-called "front running" intensifies market volatility and is manifestly unfair because it gives market insiders an unearned informational advantage at the expense of their clients and public traders. The same is true of short selling in a declining market, which has been illegal since 1938 for stocks, but for which no current rule exists for futures. Both practices ("front running" is arguably illegal now) should be clearly prohibited. Again, the absence of SEC jurisdiction over the futures market impedes effective rulemaking and enforcement.

THE INTERNATIONALIZATION DILEMMA

By every statistical measure, the internationalization of securities markets has dramatically increased during the past decade. According to a 1987 SEC Staff Report, the total amount of bonds issued internationally in 1980 was approximately $38 billion. Last year, that figure was $254 billion. Of that amount almost $44 billion was raised by U.S. issuers. Last year, U.S. investors' transactions in foreign equity securities reached a record $102 billion, while foreign investors purchased and sold approximately $277 billion in U.S. equity securities.[17]

This development — while both unavoidable and economically desirable in many respects — presents significant regulatory dangers for the SEC. The growing fungibility of the world's financial markets puts pressure on the Commission to dilute existing standards of investor protection in order to hold financial business on U.S. shores. The internationalization of markets also facilitates insider trading.

To meet the challenge of internationalization, Bevis Longstreth, a recent commissioner of the SEC, recommends paring away rules that "impose unnecessary burdens on foreign issuers." He urges, instead, a "careful review of the SEC's role in a global competitive and multi-market setting, looking to balance investor protection interests with the national goal of maintaining our nation's preeminence as a capital market center."[18]

What is clear at this time is that the 1989 SEC should conduct an intense and sophisticated study of internationalization issues. As opposed to the past, this area must receive priority and sufficient resources. Also necessary will be additional mutual assistance agreements (bilateral agreements aimed at insider trading and other violations) and a major diplomatic effort to coordinate the regulation of financial markets.

THE BLURRING OF BOUNDARIES BETWEEN DIVERSE FINANCIAL MARKETS

Many of our principal financial markets and the key players in them (*e.g.,* commercial banks, savings and loan associations, investment banks and insurance companies) are inextricably linked in economic terms but are separately regulated. We have too many different financial regulators at the federal and state levels. Predictably, this has led to duplicative, inconsistent and lax regulation.

It is, for example, unwise today to separately regulate banks and savings and loan associations, different kinds of bond issuers and (as indicated) stocks, options and financial futures. Explanations for this regulatory crazy quilt focus on some combination of history, accident, expertise accumulated over time, political clout and the preservation of executive, legislative or administrative turf.

The SEC in the next administration should play a significant role in helping to consolidate and rationalize our structure for regulating financial markets. Transfers of jurisdiction, deregulatory steps and new regulatory steps will all be necessary.

MANIC MERGER AND ACQUISITION ACTIVITIES

Mergers and acquisitions — both friendly and hostile — may play important roles in furthering basic corporate law and industrial organization goals. They may, for example, prune "deadwood managements," create incentives for efficient operation, provide liquidity for shareholders and move corporate assets to those who can use them best.

Mergers and acquisitions may also have efficiency-retarding effects. They may, for example, be the product of career protection and empire building instincts among managers. Or they result from perverse monetary, career and psychological incentives for investment bankers, lawyers and other professionals; anti-competitive market incentives may also play a role.

The overall economic impact of takeovers remains the subject of legitimate dispute. At this time, however, a new administration should reach two basic policy conclusions.

1. In the antitrust area, the societal costs of the dramatic merger and acquisition wave of the 1980s have overwhelmed all gains. In 1982 and 1984, the Reagan Administration issued merger guidelines that were intellectually defensible, yet too permissive. In practice, however, the Administration's merger policy has been even more permissive than its guidelines. This practical nullification of already permissive guidelines has been accomplished by sharply reducing the Department of Justice and FTC staffs assigned to the merger and acquisition area, by using implausible "multi-factor analyses" to approve mergers that should have been challenged under the guidelines and by winking at gerrymandered market analyses presented by merger proponents.

In terms of antitrust enforcement, the Reagan Administration has jettisoned roughly fifty years of bipartisan support for an effective merger policy. Although data for precise measurement are not yet available, there is widespread recognition that the bottom line on the past eight years is a national economy that has grown increasingly concentrated (*e.g.*, the airline, energy and chemical sectors), and, therefore, increasingly vulnerable to single firm and group manipulations of markets in order to extract monopoly profits.

A basic philosophical underpinning to modern antitrust is the belief that competitive markets will discipline excessive economic power. The Reagan Administration's merger policy has worked against: (i) the preservation of markets with diverse producers; (ii) easy access to markets by new entrants (particularly because of its vertical merger policies)[19]; (iii) the preservation of viable small competitors in concentrated markets; and (iv) broad consumer choice. Worse, all this has occurred during a period when the merger inclinations of senior corporate managers and other key players (*e.g.*, investment bankers, lawyers) have often been driven by motivations that have nothing to do with efficiency.

The appropriate approach is to view horizontal mergers that tend to concentrate markets with concern and suspicion. While efficiency concerns and realistic market analysis[20] should keep us from returning to some of the overly restrictive merger case law of the 1960s, effective antitrust law enforcement requires less permissive merger guidelines than those of 1982 and 1984. The enforcement practices of the Reagan Administration — which substantially disregard the Administration's own merger guidelines — are indefensible.

2. **New federal takeover legislation is required.** The patchwork of federal and state rules now governing the takeover process is inadequate on both legal and economic grounds. New federal legislation should reform the takeover process without basically tilting the playing field in favor of target firms, acquiring firms or various shades of white knight.

In brief, such legislation should: (i) substantially extend the time required for hostile takeovers (buying or selling important, complex industrial or financial businesses in days, as opposed to months, is simply mad in industrial organization terms); (ii) prohibit or sharply curtail counterproductive offensive tactics (*e.g.*, two-tier, front-loaded offers; greenmail) and defensive tactics (*e.g.*, poison pills, lock-ups); and (iii) clean up various technical problems (*e.g.*, closing the "ten-day window" for share acquisitions after a purchaser has accumulated 5%).

THE GROWING CORPORATE DEPENDENCE ON DEBT FINANCING

Although approaches to measuring corporate debt vary, as do levels of concern, there is no doubt that corporate debt has grown greatly during recent years. From 1984 through 1987, for example, roughly $75 billion of stock was retired each year, and, in general, debt was substituted in its place. Corporate restructuring and share repurchase plans (often parts of takeover defenses) and so-called "LBOs" (leveraged buyouts, usually by a management-led group) have played substantial roles in the movement from equity to debt. The negative consequences of this surging debt (which often is short term) may emerge when the business cycle turns down or interest rates substantially increase. At issue will be the economic viability of thinly capitalized corporations.

Our present tax laws favor corporate debt. High on the agenda of a new administration should be an evaluation of the risks of this growing corporate dependence on debt and of the costs and benefits of revisions of tax and regulatory policies.

FINE TUNING THE EXISTING REGULATORY SCHEME

Various proposals have been made during the past eight years that generally deserve to be implemented by legislative action or the promulgation of administrative rules. My candidates for early action in 1989 are: insider trading legislation; legislation providing new budgetary resources and remedial powers for the SEC; proposals for the imposition of stricter disclosure requirements on local governments issuing municipal bonds; and proposals for reform of securities industry arbitration. The explanation for these choices follows.

* The names Boesky, Levine, Siegel, Winans, Milken and Drexel Burnham, among others, have dominated insider trading headlines for nearly two years. In general, those who have admitted guilt in these scandals have committed hardcore, willful offenses and deserve harsh criminal and civil sanctions. They have seriously undermined the honesty and integrity of our securities markets, unfairly accumulated huge, unearned profits and jeopardized the willingness of potential investors to support the nation's capital formation needs.

But a number of important legal questions related to insider trading (*e.g.*, the definition of "insider," standing to sue, the damage and "aiding and abetting" concepts) have not yet been definitively answered or are in dispute in the federal courts. The result has been unnecessary litigation expense and judicial burdens, potential traps for the unwary and a danger that significant issues could be resolved the wrong way. Insider trading law, which has grown out of the very general language of Section 10(b) of the Securities Exchange Act of 1934,[21] now constitutes a "judicial oak which has grown from little more than a legislative acorn."[22] At this time, however, further legislative refinement and elaboration are desirable.

New insider trading legislation should resolve a 4-4 deadlock in the Supreme Court[23] by incorporating a "misappropriation" approach as part of its "insider" definition. Such a step would prevent a crimped, unworkable definition from developing and would broadly strengthen the SEC's enforcement hand. Pending legislative proposals demonstrate that important insider trading questions can be resolved fairly and with enough breadth to preserve judicial flexibility in the future.

    * On September 9, 1988, Chairman Ruder of the SEC acknowledged that the Commission lacked the funds to carry out its responsibilities. "We are a peanut agency" doing a large job, he testified; "we have reached limits of efficiency with current resources [*i.e.*, about $135 million.]"[24]

    There can be no doubt about the reality of the budget squeeze at the SEC. From 1981 to 1986, for example, the SEC's staff grew by only 3%. When inflation is taken into account, its budget has been flat during the 1980s. From 1981 to 1986, however, the volume of trading on the New York Stock Exchange rose 186%, the number of mutual funds went up 86% and the number of corporate filings increased by 35%. This growth combined with the dramatically increasing complexity of securities markets and the demands on the SEC's resources made by the insider trading and market manipulation scandals have precluded the SEC from properly regulating in major areas (*e.g.*, corporate disclosure, municipal bonds, internationalization issues and mutual funds).

    The SEC's efforts are, of course, supplemented by state securities regulators and private plaintiffs, and both have served the nation well during a difficult period.[25] The stakes, however, are too high to continue to drastically underfund the SEC. The Commission must be given a budget commensurate with its critical responsibilities. Similarly, to increase the effectiveness of SEC enforcement, the Commission should be given additional civil money penalty authority and cease-and-desist remedial powers.

    * The bond default by the Washington Public Power Supply System (WPPSS) in 1983 (at $2.25 billion, the largest bond default in securities history) and a 376-page report by the SEC released on September 22, 1988, have again[26] raised the basic question of whether issuers of municipal bonds should be subject to stricter disclosure obligations — *i.e.*, closer to those the SEC administers for corporate issuers. According to the SEC, WPPSS "avoided disclosure of negative developments." WPPSS's financial advisers "did not seek negative information from the Supply System to the degree they might have, and some information was withheld from them. They also tended to avoid causing full disclosure of negative information in their areas of expertise."[27] The SEC concluded that the bond underwriters also might have discovered disclosure inadequacies, if they had conducted a more probing investigation of the offerings.

    Chairman Ruder indicated that the SEC's budget squeeze and the pendency of private litigation affected the Commission's decision to close its WPPSS investigation without bringing an enforcement action.

On September 22, 1988, the SEC released for public comment Proposed Rule 15c2-12, which would: (i) require underwriters of municipal bonds (for offerings of over $10 million) to review statements before bidding for offerings, and to have a reasonable basis for believing the truthfulness and completeness of key representations; (ii) make disclosure statements available to investors; and (iii) establish a central repository of information.

These proposed steps are welcome, but the overall picture remains troubling. More than a decade of experimentation with industry-generated disclosure guidelines puts in doubt their efficacy.[28] SEC mandated disclosure (at least for large issuers of municipal bonds) would create uniform standards of reference for investors, rating agencies and the financial press. At a minimum, this recommendation for SEC mandated disclosure and the SEC's proposed steps should be put into effect by the new administration.

* During the past decade, arbitration has become the almost exclusive means of resolving disputes between investors and the securities industry. In 1980, for example, 800 investors filed securities arbitration claims; the figure was about 4,100 in 1987. For many claimants, arbitration offers a relatively fast, efficient and inexpensive means of resolving disputes.

In order for an arbitration process to be successful, however, it must be procedurally fair and impartial. It should be entered into by investors (who thereby forgo use of the judicial process) on the basis of an informed choice and not as a result of industry coercion.

In early 1987, Sheldon Elsen, chairman of an American Bar Association Task Force on Securities Arbitration, stated that the brokerage "houses basically like the current [arbitration] system because they own the stacked deck."[29] Since that time, through the efforts of the securities industry, Mr. Elsen's Task Force, the SEC and the North American Securities Administrators Association (NASAA), among others, substantial improvements have been made in the arbitration process. But more needs to be done. In June, 1988, James C. Meyer, president of NASAA, testified as follows:

> Individual investors are now skeptical about participating in capital markets they perceive to be dominated by institutions and insiders — and rigged against them. The exodus of individual investors from the capital markets commencing with the events of last October, and the attendant rise in market volatility, illustrate once again that the confidence of the investing public is crucial to stable, sound financial markets. If steps are not taken to make securities arbitration voluntary and fair to both the industry *and* investors, this new crisis in investor confidence could become chronic.[30]

Arbitration reform proposals by NASAA and others, which basically provide for voluntary arbitration and procedural reform, are now before Congress. They should provide the new administration with the basis for action in early 1989.

THE SHAREHOLDER'S ROLE IN THE MODERN PUBLIC CORPORATION

A lively (indeed, heated) debate has developed about the proper role of the shareholder of the modern public corporation. The growing importance of institutional shareholders has raised new issues. The SEC's mandate, which includes the administration of disclosure, proxy (*i.e.*, shareholder voting) and takeover rules, is broad enough to warrant giving shareholder issues an important place in the proposed in-depth study of securities markets.

As is obvious, the reform agenda for the SEC — both in terms of action and study — is large, yet is commensurate with the gravity of the issues facing our financial markets. William L. Cary was fond of quoting two aphorisms. The first counseled patience: "Law reform is not for the short winded," he would say. The second urged both idealism and professional skill: "Technique without ideals is a menace; ideals without technique are a mess."[31] The 41st president should be mindful of both aphorisms as he entrusts a new chairman of the SEC with the task of restoring vigor, decency and fairness to the nation's securities markets. But time is now of the essence. A financial time bomb is ticking. The new administration and Congress must understand that we cannot waste another four years.

NOTES

[1] This discussion is based on Chapters 1-4, 9-11 of Seligman, Joel, *The Transformation of Wall Street* (1982).

[2] *Id.* at 1.

[3] H.R. 85, 73rd Cong., 1st Sess. at 2 (1933).

[4] The first modern "blue sky" law was adopted in Kansas in 1911. The term "blue sky" referred to speculative schemes that, in the words of a judge of the period, had no more substance than "a square foot of Kansas blue sky." *See* North American Securities Administrators Association, *Protecting Individual Investors and the Efficiency of the Capital Markets*, 1, April 1988.

[5] Ickes, Harold, *The Secret Diary of Harold Ickes: The First Thousand Days*, 173 (1953).

[6] Seligman, Joel, *supra* note 1, at X.

[7] *Id*. at 291.

[8] *Id*. at 299.

[9] *See* McGowan, Werner and Goldschmid, "In Memoriam — Professor William L. Cary," 83 *Columbia Law Review*, pp. 765, 767, 769, May 1983.

[10] Program trading may be defined as the buying or selling of a portfolio of stocks by selling stock index futures when the value of the portfolio decreases a specified percentage.

[11] Portfolio insurance is a strategy designed to reduce market risk on a portfolio of stocks by selling stock index futures when the value of the portfolio decreases a specified percentage.

[12] For example, if program trading were prohibited, there is evidence that essentially the same process of trading baskets of securities would occur even if traders did not have access to computers.

[13] Edwards, *Studies of the 1987 Stock Market Crash: Review and Appraisal*, 3, CSFM-Working Paper, March 1988.

[14] *New York Times*, Jan. 14, 1988, at A31.

[15] *New York Times*, Dec. 17, 1987, at A1.

[16] *See e.g.*, discussion in Section IIA 2 *infra*.

[17] SEC, *Staff Report on Internationalization of the Securities Markets*, 1-1, July 1987.

[18] Longstreth, *Global Securities Markets and the SEC*, 8, 20-21, unpublished paper, March 1988.

[19] In the interest of brevity, I have limited my critique of the Reagan Administration's merger policies in the vertical and conglomerate areas. In both areas, the Administration is vulnerable. In the conglomerate area it should be noted, however, that successful hostile takeovers have, in fact, corrected some of the excesses of the 1960s and 1970s. The so-called "bust up" takeover (or corporate re-

structuring done under threat) often reflects a widely shared view that the conglomerate merger wave of the 1960s and 1970s has on balance had efficiency-reducing effects.

[20] It should be noted that concerns about concentration in certain domestic (U.S.) markets have been alleviated by (i) new foreign competition, (ii) the diminished significance of old industrial sectors and the increased importance of generally less concentrated service industries and (iii) a general entrepreneurial spirit in the nation, which at times results in the development of new businesses even in the face of market power.

[21] 48 Stat. 891, 15 U.S.C. Sect. 78j(b). Section 10(b) has been supplemented by other federal securities law provisions and by federal mail and wire fraud statutes.

[22] *Blue Chip Stamps v. Manor Drug Stores*, 421 U.S. 723, 735 (1975).

[23] *See Carpenter v United States*, 108 S. Ct. 316 (1987).

[24] 20 *Securities Regulation & Law Report*, 1394, September 1988.

[25] The North American Securities Administrators Association recently explained:
The dual system of state and federal regulation of the securities markets in the United States began in 1933, when the SEC was created by Congress. The 1980s have been marked by cutbacks in the budget of the SEC and the Commodity Futures Trading Commission (CFTC), in spite of record-breaking expansion of the securities markets. As a result, increasing responsibility for investor protection and the day-to-day policing of the capital markets devolved to state securities officials. Enforcement actions conducted by the state offices rose more than 65 percent between fiscal years 1982 and 1986, with the sharpest increase coming in the initiation of criminal proceedings. Today, state securities agencies carry out more enforcement and disciplinary actions each year than the SEC, the National Association of Securities Dealers and the stock exchanges combined. NASAA member offices are largely responsible for preventing fraud in all but the largest securities offerings...This trend is expected to become even more predominant in the wake of the "Black Monday" stock market crash of October 1987.

NASSA, *Protecting Individual Investors and the Efficiency of the Capital Markets*, 1-2, April 1988.

[26] This same issue was raised prominently, over ten years ago, by an SEC staff report on New York City's near-default in 1974-75. *See* SEC, *Staff Report on Transactions in Securities of the City of New York*, August 1977.

[27] 20 *Securities Regulation & Law Report*, 1435-36, September 1988.

[28] *See* Seligman, Joel, *The SEC and the Future of Finance*, 281-94

[29] *New York Times*, March 29, 1987, sec. 3, at 8, col. 1.

[30] *Statement on Arbitration of James C. Meyer*, Hearing before a Subcommittee on Telecommunications and Finance of the House Committee on Energy and Commerce, 1, June 1988.

[31] The first aphorism is generally attributed to Chief Justice Vanderbilt of the Supreme Court of New Jersey and the second to Professor Karl Llewellyn of Columbia Law School.

EXECUTIVE MANAGEMENT:
Office of Management and Budget

Gary D. Bass & David F. Plocher*

SUMMARY OF RECOMMENDATIONS

Although best known for developing and supervising the federal budget, the White House Office of Management and Budget (OMB) over the past decade has also become recognized for its review of regulations, information collection and dissemination and government management reforms.

The concentration of these powers in one office has transformed OMB from a mere managerial office into one that both develops and implements policy. This has given the president a heightened ability to implement his agenda through the administrative process, independent of Congress. But the cost to the American public has been significant: legislative deadlines and even judicial orders have been ignored or circumvented on the basis of executive orders and internal memoranda; and agency decision-making has been displaced by OMB's behind-the-scenes pressure. The results range from watered down health and safety regulations to management directives that impose substantive duties on agencies, at odds with accepted public policy.

This chapter focuses on five issues that taken together point out the need for a new direction at this very important office.[1] Each demands decisive action by the new president, as well as consideration for legislative action:

* *OMB Leadership and Organization.* The new director should be skilled in budget matters, understand the congressional process and have direct access to the president in order to rebuild morale within the agency and credibility outside OMB. While preparation of the budget remains the highest priority, there should be better coordination between OMB management and budget activities.

---

* *Gary D. Bass is executive director and founder of OMB Watch, a nonprofit research and advocacy organization created in 1983 to monitor the White House Office of Management and Budget (OMB). David F. Plocher is a staff attorney at OMB Watch.*

  * *Regulatory Review.* OMB's micro-management review of agency regulatory decisions should be replaced with a process limited to broad policy review and coordination. OMB should not be involved in substantive agency decision-making. Greater opportunities for public participation must be insured.
  * *Paperwork Reduction and Information Policy.* OMB's bias toward reckless elimination of the "burdens" of federal paperwork and regulations should be replaced with a commitment to objective improvement in the management of federal information resources. OMB must take the lead in guiding agencies into the electronic information age, and in developing a more open national information policy.
  * *Privatization.* The president must stop OMB's short-sighted dismantling of government operations and reaffirm the government's responsibility to ensure the provision of needed public services.
  * *Grant Administration and Intergovernmental Relations.* OMB must establish rules to foster cooperative relations between the federal government and the public and private nonprofit sectors, including a recognition of the importance of the voluntary sector in delivering public services. Nonprofit involvement in public policy debates — particularly those pertaining to program delivery — should be encouraged.

  In general, OMB's reach into agency activities should be significantly restricted and should operate much more in the sunshine. And OMB should better enable the president to fulfill his constitutional duty to "take care that the laws be faithfully executed."

I. HISTORY

  Originally envisioned as a technical budget office, OMB has become a very powerful, politically charged arm of the president. During Ronald Reagan's Administration, particularly, OMB has come to exercise more power than at any other time in its history.

  Established in 1921, as a part of the Department of the Treasury, the office was called the Bureau of the Budget (BoB). BoB's primary task was to coordinate the annual preparation of the federal budget. Prior to that, agencies sent their budgets directly to Congress without any executive branch review.

  Shortly after its creation, BoB's authority was enlarged with management functions, such as the authority to "clear proposed legislation." This process accelerated during the administration of Franklin Delano Roosevelt when, in 1939, BoB was moved to the newly-created Executive Office of the President and given more power, ranging from fiscal policy and planning to administrative research and the review of agency information services. This concentration of powers established a precedent for the modern day OMB as a very powerful office closely identified with the policies of the president.

After World War II, BoB's management responsibilities continued to grow. By 1970, BoB was involved in management reform, agency organization, personnel management, regulatory matters, grants-in-aid programs and policies on intergovernmental relations. The extent of these powers was finally acknowledged when, on July 1, 1970, BoB became the Office of Management and Budget (OMB).

Still, OMB was not expected to do everything. For example, when OMB was created, a White House Domestic Council was also formed, with the idea that the Council, as President Nixon put it, "will be primarily concerned with what we do; the Office of Management and Budget will be primarily concerned with how we do it and how well we do it." The failure of this neat division of labor has been a continuing dilemma for OMB — how to justify deep involvement in both policy and administration, and how to respond to the accompanying charges of over-politicization.

Another functional problem was the balance between OMB's budget and management activities. Although the management side appeared to have nearly equal weight on the organizational chart, it languished in practice. The real power of OMB rested with the budget examiners. Management staff simply lacked the clout to influence agency personnel, let alone the budget examiners.

Although maligned for its management failures, OMB did leap at some opportunities, such as the Paperwork Reduction Act of 1980. This law established the OMB Office of Information and Regulatory Affairs (OIRA) to coordinate the information collection activities of federal agencies, with a thrust toward reducing their cost to government, businesses and individuals. OIRA was also given other information management responsibilities, such as developing information resources management policies, promoting greater information sharing among agencies and overseeing planning for the use of computers and other information technology.

Within two months of the law's enactment, newly inaugurated President Reagan added to OIRA's powers with Executive Order 12291, which called for review of agency regulations according to a test of economic costs and benefits. OIRA combined this process with paperwork clearance to create an integrated review system.

This regulatory and paperwork review process has become one of the most controversial and politically charged activities in OMB's history. It subordinates OMB's management improvement mandate to that of political censor — reviewing substantive agency decisions for consistency with presidential policies and priorities. Not surprisingly, OIRA's emergence as the president's "hitman" in such areas as occupational health and safety, environmental protection and food and drugs has contributed to OMB's image as being overly politicized. Nearly all observers now decry the loss of OMB's "neutral competence."[2]

In other management areas, as well, OMB's accomplishments have been largely overshadowed by charges of politicization. For example, recent efforts to reform federal credit policy, revise program administration regulations and even to better integrate OMB management and budget staff have been identified not with management improvement, but with efforts to assist presidential ideological initiatives such as New Federalism, Reform '88 and privatization. These charges have been fueled by the growing use of political appointees at OMB and the loss of career civil servants who provide "institutional memory," as the National Academy of Public Administration put it.

Most striking is that as OMB has become more visible in executing the president's agenda, the size of its professional staff has decreased (excluding employees from other agencies temporarily "detailed" to OMB). In FY 1981, there were 610 full-time permanent positions; in FY 1988 and FY 1989 there were only 570. The biggest cut was in OMB's management staff. While budget positions were cut five percent over the FY 1981-1989 period (from 385 to 366 positions), management lost 21 percent (from 158 to 125). This trend reinforces the notion that management activities neither command the respect of budget functions nor are pursued in a serious or systematic way.

OMB's powerful gains and political losses are not completely due to institutional changes. Much is due to the personal impact of President Reagan's first OMB director, David A. Stockman. Stockman was only the second OMB director who had served in Congress, and had an uncanny recollection for numbers and process. For example, he gained the national spotlight when he used his understanding of the budget process (especially reconciliation) to win, in a single congressional vote, legislation to significantly reduce federal spending for domestic programs and to transfer responsibility for many programs to states and localities.

With the loss of Stockman, the arrival of James C. Miller III and the accumulated congressional reaction to President Reagan's first term victories, OMB's position as presidential point man became more tenuous. As OMB's political efforts have become more transparent and less effective, Congress has, for example, come to rely less and less on OMB's economic assumptions and spending forecasts when writing the budget or appropriating funds.

II. FIRST STEPS FOR THE NEW PRESIDENT

OMB DIRECTOR AND THE BUDGET

To set a new direction for OMB, the president-elect should select an OMB director within two to four weeks after the election. Selection of a director with an understanding of congressional budget processes, as well as with direct access to the president, will reassure Congress that OMB will be a knowledgeable (and trustworthy) participant in the give-and-take between Congress and the White House.

The new director must also be well-versed in budgetary and economic theory and practice. Although both management and budget should be comparably significant functions of OMB, budget, given the large federal debt, remains the top priority.

A review of the strengths and weaknesses of the Reagan Administration's first two OMB directors — David A. Stockman and James C. Miller III — can assist the new president when selecting a director. While Miller was loyal to the president, his stubborn adherence to the public pronouncements of the White House gained him little respect elsewhere, particularly in Congress. Unable or unwilling to compromise, and lacking Stockman's budget expertise, Miller simply had little to offer Members of Congress.

Stockman's strengths were the reverse and played right into his budget director role. Stockman became the spokesperson for Administration policy; Miller could not. Stockman had access to the president; Miller did not. Stockman was very visible; Miller was not. Stockman commanded respect of career civil servants; Miller did not.

When Stockman was director, the office was abuzz; staff worked long and hard with a firm sense of direction. They knew their work would be understood and used. Under Miller this certainty vanished, particularly as they found themselves, at times, briefing White House staff instead of the OMB director.

Appointing new leadership at OMB will, of course, only be the first step.[3] The new director will have to deal with the consequences of OMB's politicization during the Reagan years. Some critics have simply called for "depoliticizing" the office, but that really begs the issue. The real issue is not the political nature of OMB; it has always been political. In fact, that was why it was moved into the Executive Office of the President almost fifty years ago. It was and is the President's right hand for supervising the executive branch, an inherently political task.

The real issue is OMB's attempt to impose the presidential will on the rest of government regardless of all else, be it statutory mandate or economic reality. Most of these unabashedly partisan attempts have simply resulted in a loss of credibility. When OMB sends the budget to Congress, for example, people smirk and say,

"Dead on arrival." When OMB issues economic assumptions, people roll their eyes at the "rosy assumptions."

The new OMB leadership must recommit the office to producing credible numbers and credible recommendations. While still serving the president, they must not be so partisan as to be more often dismissed than respected.

As a practical matter, the OMB director should immediately request access to OMB computer files and permission to participate in agency budget reviews — even prior to the administration's taking office in January. While the current Administration is not obliged to honor such a request, it has been a frequent transition recommendation. Most likely, the existing Administration would have fewer objections to permitting access to the computer files than to allowing actual participation in agency budget reviews.

Three aspects of the budget process deserve emphasis. First, one of the highest priorities of the incoming administration is the revision of the budget sent to Congress by President Reagan. Although the budget takes about six months to put together, the new president only has about 30 to 45 days to submit changes. This time pressure is intensified by the truncated timetables of the Gramm-Rudman-Hollings balanced budget law. So the new president must quickly appoint an OMB director who can immediately begin work on the budget — even if access to the OMB computer files is denied.

Second, thanks to David Stockman, it is now easier for new administrations to prepare budget revisions. One of Stockman's legacies is the computerized Central Budget Management System operated by the OMB Budget Review Division. This system permits the director to quickly compare proposals, including alternative executive and congressional ones. Thus, the new director will have an advantage if he/she becomes familiar with the system.

Finally, budget submissions for the past few years have been very similar. The same proposals basically have appeared year after year. Thus, the new director — even if denied access to current OMB information — can accomplish a great deal before officially taking office by working from past budgets.

REGULATORY REVIEW

On February 17, 1981, shortly after taking office, President Reagan issued Executive Order 12291, "Federal Regulation." The order vastly changed agency rulemaking by giving enormous power to OMB's Office of Information and Regulatory Affairs (OIRA). The Reagan order built on regulatory review experience gained under Presidents Nixon, Ford and Carter (see chart). But, it went far beyond them to create a centralized OMB regulatory control process.

Under the earlier schemes, while OMB was responsible for regulatory improvement, it did not specifically review all agency regulatory proposals. Further, other bodies played important roles, for example, the White House Council on Wage and Price Stability and President Carter's Interagency Regulatory Analysis Review Group.

The regulatory review programs of Nixon, Ford and Carter are often criticized for their lack of formal enforcement mechanisms. Relying primarily on agency initiative and cooperation to improve regulations, they did not allow OMB to intervene in rulemaking.

This limitation subordinated the interest of presidential control to the principles of delegation and agency discretion — the underlying tenets of the basic rulemaking authority, the Administrative Procedure Act. The result was a system that encouraged regulatory improvement, but did not insure compliance with presidential policies and priorities. This may have suited some presidents, but did not satisfy President Reagan.

Reagan's Executive Order 12291 went far beyond its predecessors by requiring that agencies not only assess the economic costs and benefits of every proposed rule, but also be guided by the results of those assessments as reviewed and interpreted by OMB. This significantly restricted the discretion of the rulemaking agencies, while giving unprecedented power to OMB.

Strictly speaking, E.O. 12291 does not grant OMB control of agency regulations. The order states that its requirements shall not be "construed as displacing the agencies' responsibilities delegated by law." Yet an agency cannot issue a rule until the completion of the OMB review. As a practical matter, this perogative gives OMB veto power over agency regulations.

OMB interference in agency decision-making under E.O. 12291 has ranged from delaying to changing and halting regulations as diverse as consumer product safety requirements, asbestos, grain dust, underground storage of dangerous chemicals and worker exposure to hazardous chemicals. OMB's actions in these cases have been documented and criticized in academic studies, congressional hearings and court decisions.[4]

Each year since 1981, the percentage of regulations reviewed under E.O. 12291 and altered by OMB has increased. In 1981, 16% of agency regulatory proposals underwent some type of change due to OMB review; in 1987, 30% did.

The Reagan Administration, however, was far from satisfied with E.O. 12291. In 1984, Douglas Ginsburg, then-head of OIRA, said: "Agencies have been working on proposed regulations long before they come to notice and comment. Then we get ourselves in a confrontation with the agency over the end product." The solution was found in Executive Order 12498, which established a "Regulatory Planning Process." The order had three significant elements:

* It increased the scope of OMB review of agency rulemaking to include "pre-rulemaking" activities. Pre-rulemaking includes any activity that may lead to regulatory action at some future date.

* Unlike E.O. 12291, which halts rulemaking only until OMB finishes its review, E.O. 12498 prohibits an agency from doing any work unless OMB gives the go-ahead.

* The standard of review is not a single objective, such as cost/benefit analysis, but rather a broader concern about "consistency with Administration policies and priorities" — in essence, a political litmus test.

While a few cases of E.O. 12498 review have received public attention — such as OMB's 1985 disapproval of a study of the relationship between federal budget cuts and infant mortality rates — most have not. Since the entire process is cloaked in secrecy, it is nearly impossible to determine OMB's role. The only product available to the public is a description of what has been approved by OMB — those proposals disapproved never appear.

Over the past year, the President has issued three executive orders that increase OMB's control of agency regulations. These orders — "The Family" (E.O. 12606), "Federalism" (E.O. 12630) and the so-called "Takings" (E.O. 12630) — add substantive criteria to the generic themes of the regulatory review orders.

THE DEVELOPMENT OF PRESIDENTIAL OVERSIGHT
OF AGENCY RULEMAKING

President	Program
Nixon	**Quality of Life Review** — Required interagency review, with OMB supervision, of environmental, consumer protection and health and safety regulations prior to publication as final rules.
Ford	**Economic Impact Statements** — E.O. 11821 expanded Quality of Life Reviews to all federal agencies, and required the preparation of inflationary impact statements (later called Economic Impact Statements) for proposed "major" rules. The EISs were reviewed by the President's Council on Wage and Price Stability; OMB supervised the process and prescribed procedures for economic analyses.

Carter	**Regulatory Improvement Program** — E.O. 12044 required agencies to: (1) publish semi-annual agendas of "significant" regulations; (2) have agency head approve all significant regulatory proposals before initial development and prior to publication as a proposed rule; (3) write regulations in plain English and encourage public participation; (4) prepare a Regulatory Analysis of "major significant" proposed rules; and (5) periodically review existing regulations. The program was supervised by OMB, but carried out in a decentralized manner, with interagency review by the Regulatory Analysis Review Group and the Regulatory Council.
Reagan	**Cost/Benefit Review** — E.O. 12291 went beyond the Carter program to create centralized OMB review with specific substantive and procedural requirements. Not only did agencies have to do cost/benefit analyses, but those assessments had to be reviewed by OMB. The Order required agencies to: (1) publish semi-annual agendas of all rules; (2) conduct cost/benefit analyses of all regulatory proposals, and submit proposed and final rules to OMB; (3) conduct a Regulatory Impact Analysis for "major" rules; (4) refrain from publishing proposed or final rules until completion of OMB review; and (5) periodically review existing regulations.
	The Regulatory Planning Process — In January, 1985, E.O. 12498 added that each agency was to submit a "draft regulatory program" for each year, including an overview of "regulatory policies, goals and objectives" and detailed descriptions of "significant regulatory actions." OMB reviews agency proposals, including pre-rulemaking actions (i.e., anything that "could lead to the commencement of rulemaking" in the future) to determine "consistency with the Administration's policies and priorities" and to "identify such further regulatory or deregulatory actions as may be necessary." Unlike E.O. 12291, which caused delays, under E.O. 12498, OMB can reject an agency activity as "inconsistent," and thereby stop it.

The combination of regulatory review with the clearance process created by the Paperwork Reduction Act of 1980 gave an additional dimension to OMB review of agency decisions. Under the Act (discussed in the following section), OMB reviews information collection activities, many of which lead to or are required by regulations. Consequently, OMB rejection of agency "paperwork" can have a significant impact on agency regulatory activities.

The paperwork process is far more open than the regulatory review process, and provides substantial documentation of OMB interference in agency rulemaking through paperwork review. Examples range from the development of standards for woodburning stoves to pre-rulemaking studies of the health risks of personal cosmetics. The most recent example to gain public attention is OMB's interference with OSHA's worker right-to-know regulation, which was held up and altered, despite repeated court orders.

In these various ways, the Reagan regulatory program is a flagrant misuse of executive power. It has gone beyond the constitutional mandate that the President "take care that the laws be faithfully executed," by subordinating statutory mandates and agency discretion to the political needs of the president.

It has also undercut the Administrative Procedure Act, especially its requirement for public participation in agency decision-making. By the time the public is informed, the most significant decisions have already been made — with OMB's unrecorded pressure. Moreover, OMB decisions are all too often made without proper expertise — OIRA public policy generalists overrule agency professionals and scientists, whose recommendations have often been tested by peer review.

While criticism can be leveled at the President and OMB for grabbing regulatory power and using such power to achieve ideological goals, Congress deserves criticism, as well. It has sat idly by while the administrative government has grown, without providing comprehensive legislation to help cope with the changing conditions. While Congress has been critical of OMB interference in agency activities, it has primarily attacked the problem piecemeal, through oversight of specific programs.

To reorient OMB regulatory review, the new president should take two steps:

1. Rescind the regulatory review executive orders — E.O. 12291 and 12498.[5] This move should be accompanied by the implementation of a significantly revised regulatory review process. It should be designed as an interim process pending congressional consideration of more comprehensive regulatory management legislation.

The interim regulatory review process should be simplified and geared explicitly toward conformity to substantive statutory standards. It should help avoid conflicting requirements and coordinate the development of common standards, such as methods for evaluating regulatory cost-effectiveness. This sort of OMB review can assist the agencies to more effectively manage their activities. But, again, it should be the responsibility of the agency heads, also political appointees confirmed by the Senate, to balance the substantive and political merits of any initiative.

The reviews should be conducted in the sunshine so the public knows what is being reviewed and has an opportunity to participate, consistent with the Administrative Procedure Act. Records of all communications concerning a regulatory proposal, including contacts with other agencies, individuals, or nongovernmental organizations, should be placed in a public record by OMB, as well as the agency. Time limits should be established for OMB review of regulations. And, most important, OMB comments must be explained in writing. Such comments, as well as related OMB communications, should be placed in the agency rulemaking record and considered by agencies in their rulemaking decisions. They should not, however, compel agencies to refrain from or take any specific action.

2. Develop a legislative proposal for a comprehensive regulatory management process. In addition to addressing the appropriate limits of centralized regulatory review, the proposal should include amendments to the Paperwork Reduction Act to distinguish between review of regulatory and non-regulatory information collection activities. This will help minimize OMB review of regulations through the paperwork process and reorient OMB's activities under the Act towards information management.

PAPERWORK REDUCTION AND INFORMATION POLICY

Since 1942, with passage of the Federal Reports Act, OMB (then called the Bureau of the Budget) has had the authority to "determine whether or not the collection of information by a Federal agency is necessary for the proper performance of the functions of the agency or for any other proper purpose." However, according to OMB, by 1979 over 80% of the federal paperwork burden had been exempted by Congress from OMB control.

One of the last acts of President Carter was to sign into law the Paperwork Reduction Act of 1980, which was partly designed to correct the failings of the 1942 Act. Under the 1980 Act, OMB was given renewed power over government paperwork and other information activities.

The Act eliminated the exemptions that had hobbled the 1942 Act, to ensure OMB review of virtually all federal information collection activities (including surveys, questionnaires, record-keeping requirements) that affect ten or more people. It also mandated that OMB generally improve the management of federal agency information activities — through the concept of "Information Resources Management" (IRM).

Reagan's OMB had different priorities. It viewed the Paperwork Reduction Act almost exclusively as a way to assist the Administration's agenda of deregulation and reduction of federal government operations. OMB used the Act's paperwork clearance process as an adjunct to its regulatory review powers, and virtually ignored the rest of the Act. Federal programs suffered accordingly — from delays in releasing the new IRS W-4 tax form to second-guessing the formulation of the decennial census, and from weakening health research on worker exposure to dioxin and video display terminals to curtailing evaluation of housing programs. And programs unpopular with the Reagan administration were hurt more than others — a Harvard University study shows that between 1984 and 1986, OMB was seven times more likely to disapprove environmental or occupational health research than studies focusing on infectious or other conventional diseases.[6]

Despite widespread scholarly and media criticism of OMB's implementation of the Act, Congress reauthorized the Act in the fall of 1986. There was no public debate; the reauthorization slipped through Congress as part of the Continuing Resolution (an omnibus spending bill). In doing so, Congress not only failed to repair the Act's recognized flaws, but also granted OMB even greater power over regulations.

Most significantly, the reauthorization extended the three year maximum period of paperwork approval to regulatory paperwork. This effectively created an unprecedented regulatory "sunset" provision. Now, regulatory paperwork must go through the OMB screen at least every three years. Since enforcement of regulations often depend on paperwork (e.g., reporting or recordkeeping requirements), OMB in effect reviews the substance of the regulation. With paperwork disapproved, regulations can be stymied.

The management of federal information resources has also suffered under OMB's implementation of the Paperwork Reduction Act. OMB has played a significant role in restricting access to government records under the Freedom of Information Act (FOIA). It has rushed headlong into computer matching and other automated uses of information about individuals with little regard for the protection of individual privacy. It has cut budgets and personnel for the eight major statistical agencies, seriously jeopardizing the quality of essential national statistics. And, it has disregarded many of its responsibilities for the management of government information technology, such as automated data processing and telecommunications equipment.

Information dissemination activities, too, have suffered. In 1981, OMB mandated wholesale cutbacks in agency publications. By early 1984, OMB claimed to have eliminated a quarter of all federal publications and reduced the costs of nearly another quarter. While costs were cut, the public also lost. Eliminated publications ranged from educational pamphlets, like *Infant Care* and *Your Housing Rights*, to comprehensive reports, like the annual *Geographic Distribution of Federal Funds*, which lists the distribution of federal program dollars by congresssional district.[7]

When OMB finally issued a directive for the management of information resources in December, 1985, it restricted information dissemination even further. It stated that unless specifically required by law, federal agencies should not disseminate information that "would otherwise be provided by other government or private sector organizations." This criterion is unprecedented in its subordination of public service information planning to the marketing whims of the private sector.

The new president must provide new direction to the management of federal information activities on four fronts:[8]

1. Articulate a national information policy. The new president, through an executive order and in proposed legislation, should affirm that the federal government must:

* Collect and evaluate comprehensive data about national and international conditions, government programs and public policies.

* Disseminate information (to be widely available and equally accessible) about government operations and other public issues and concerns.

* Maintain the free flow of information, in all formats, to ensure unrestricted access for an informed citizenry to speak out on issues of concern, while protecting fundamental privacy interests.

2. Reform legislative direction and oversight. Congress must reassess its current information policy statutes. At a minimum, the legislative agenda should include:

* Revision of the Paperwork Reduction Act to limit OMB's paperwork clearance domination, and to shift the focus from paperwork reduction to information management — perhaps renaming it the Information Management Act to capture its primary focus.

* Revision of the federal printing laws and the Freedom of Information Act to provide practical guidance for the dissemination of and public access to information in electronic format.

* Examination of the roles of the Government Printing Office, the Joint Committee on Printing and the federal depository library system to strengthen federal capabilities to disseminate public information, including through electronic means.

3. Reduce centralized review. As with regulatory review, the issue is not centralization of paperwork review, so much as centralization of control through paperwork review. The excesses of the past eight years demonstrate that it is necessary to reduce the scope of OMB's review powers, replacing the current micro-management and clearance of agency decisions with more general oversight of information practices. At the same time, the paperwork review process must be made more open, to encourage public participation.

An executive order should redirect OIRA's focus from paperwork reduction, with its decision-making bias against "burden" without regard to benefits, toward improved information management. This will require new kinds of staff expertise to guide agencies into the computer age and coordinate the vast information resources of the federal government.

PRIVATIZATION

It has long been the policy of the federal government to look to the private sector to supply commercial products and services to the government. The Reagan Administration, however, has extended the logic of avoiding unnecessary competition with the private sector into an imperative to dismantle all but "inherently Governmental" functions in favor of the private sector.

OMB's dedication to this privatization drive, particularly after James Miller became OMB director in October 1985, is well known. According to OMB:

> [Privatization] merely recognizes that what matters is the service provided, not who provides it. Thus, it is indifferent to whether such services are provided by profit-making enterprises or by public agencies and Government employees.

Since 1986, the Administration has intensified the privatization drive. First, it created a new OMB office, the Office of Privatization, with six staff members to spearhead the effort. Second, a Presidential Commission on Privatization was appointed to make recommendations for furthering the drive — this was the fourth privatization advisory group created during the Reagan Administration. Third, the President issued Executive Order 12615, "Performance of Commercial Activities" to "[ensure that...commercial activities are provided by private industry, except where statute or national security requires government performance or where private industry costs are unreasonable." E.O. 12615 also puts new stock into OMB Circular A-76, which requires cost comparisons of commercial functions to determine whether to contract out services to the private sector. Examples of such functions include: cleaning federal buildings; warehouse operations; motor pools; ADP centers; libraries; weather reporting and management of military bases and radar installations. In 1988, Circular A-76, itself, was revised "to provide more authority for agencies to contract activities without competitive cost comparisons."

Finally, the Reagan privatization efforts have been described and championed repeatedly in annual reports, such as Management of the U.S. Government, which has gone beyond discussions of contracting out commercial activities to include plans for studies, pilot projects and "full privatization." The philosophy behind the effort involves the hope that a one-time infusion of money from the sale of government resources or cessation of government activities will help lower the deficit; it also reflects the desire to reduce the role of the federal government, deferring to the private sector.

As a practical matter, the approach has several obvious drawbacks. First, many of the activities proposed for privatization became government functions because the private sector would not or could not reliably provide the services. Thus, private companies may be unwilling to pay the asking price, if they are even interested — loans and assets already put up for sale have not drawn as much money as projected. And, even if they pay the price, what assurance does the public have of continued service?

Second, several studies have shown that while asset sales may bring in quick revenue, the gains are more than offset by the loss of revenue the asset would have generated over time. Thus, a short-term gain becomes a long-term loss.

Third, shifting government services and assets to the private sector reduces the federal government's ability to independently assess public needs, provide public services and protect resources for future needs.

In the FY 89 U.S. Budget, the Administration maintains that the federal government should defer to the private sector because:

In some cases, the fact that no private provider exists is a reflection of government policy to prohibit competition — as with first class mail service. In other cases, an absence of private providers reflects a government policy of providing large subsidies — as with uranium enrichment

Invariably, the taxpayer ends up paying more for less.

In the case of postal service, there is an accepted public responsibility to provide first class mail service regardless of volume to every home and office in every hamlet, village and town. It is unrealistic to assume that private providers could fulfill that daunting task — the economies of scale are too out of balance. Competition for some routes might interest private companies, but it would increase public costs for supplying mail to the more remote and lower volume areas. Invariably, the taxpayer would pay more for less.

Similar problems are apparent in the case of government subsidies for endeavors such as uranium enrichment. Such subsidies resulted from prohibitively high market risks that kept private companies from investing in and developing the technology and products. Government subsidies were required, if there was to be any progress at all.

While it is reasonable to facilitate private sector use of the government supported technology, products and services, it is another matter to simply transfer the program to the private sector. That only results in increased costs to the public and amounts to an enormous subsidy for private companies for all the research and development they were unwilling to undertake in the first place. Again, the taxpayer would pay more for less.

The new president should halt the divestiture of federal responsibilities on the basis of distorted assessments of short-term economic gains. Specifically:

1. Revise Executive Order 12615 and OMB Circular A-76. The thrust should be shifted from a mandate to contract out all commercial activities to a determination of the best manner, both short- and long-term, in which to perform needed services.

2. Eliminate the OMB Privatization Plan. OMB should not strive "to create an environment conducive to greater privatization successes."[9] Rather, it should work for improved service delivery, which involves a supporting role for the private sector and the public nonprofit sector, as it has historically.

3. Eliminate the OMB Office of Privatization.

GRANTS MANAGEMENT AND INTERGOVERNMENTAL RELATIONS

State and local governments, working hand in hand with the private nonprofit, voluntary sector, have formed an integral partnership with the federal government in the delivery of services to the public. From the delivery of day care to services for the aged; from job training to community development; from community services for low-income people to services for the disabled; from pre-school programs to adult education; from general health care to mental health services — the federal government has traditionally depended on the nonprofit sector and state and local governments to help get the job done.

Despite the important connections and the need for continued partnerships, the relationship between these entities and the federal government has deteriorated, especially for the private nonprofit sector. At the heart of the problem are OMB's policies affecting intergovernmental activities and its grants management policies, which affect every federal agency.

The main elements of OMB's policy regarding grants management and intergovernmental relations can be summed up as follows:

* A shift in the role of the federal government to reduce its size, authority and responsibility in domestic affairs.

* A reduction in federal funding and regulations, and increased reliance on states to carry out federal mandates, while simultaneously increasing OMB control of grants-in-aid programs.

* An ideologically inspired attack to "defund the left," targeted at the private nonprofit voluntary sector.

* Greater reliance on state government and the private sector without added resources to help.

In his second State of the Union address, President Reagan announced a plan to realign the federal system in "a single stroke." The plan called for a "swap" of the major means-tested programs and a "turnback" to states of roughly 45 categorical programs. The "swap" involved a proposal for the federal government to take over funding for Medicaid while states would take responsibility for funding Food Stamps and AFDC. The "turnback" included most major domestic categorical programs that would become state responsibilities to continue if they so chose.

Although Congress formally rejected the plan, OMB found other ways to impose federalism on the entire system. These ranged from budget cuts, to the transfer of specific program responsibilities to state and local governments and proposals to eliminate federal cross-cutting requirements, such as anti-discrimination regulations.

These efforts created an uneven patchwork quilt of service delivery and regulatory enforcement. Some states possessed the resources to provide needed services and administer programs, others did not; some communities were well served by private philanthropy, others suffered as competition for fewer funds forced nonprofits, churches and volunteers to do more with less.

As human services advocates (and other public interest non-profits) became better acquainted with the problems caused by these changes, they began to fight the new federalism initiatives and the OMB cutbacks in funding and regulations. In response, OMB took the battle to new grounds.

As recommended in the 1981 transition report of the Heritage Foundation, in January 1983, OMB proposed to revise Circular A-122, "Cost Principles for Nonprofit Organizations." By revising its grants management cost allocation policy, OMB hoped to greatly restrict the role of nonprofits in public policy debates.

After 15 months of controversy, more than 140,000 public comments and several redrafts of its proposal, OMB issued a final rule that was greatly scaled back from the original. The initial proposal, characterized as a "gag rule," would have: (a) redefined lobbying in such broad terms as to include nearly any type of public policy initiative, including commenting on proposed regulations at any level of government; and (b) disallowed federal payment for any activity covered by the new definition and any activity associated with it. Further, the disallowed activity and associated costs would then be "tainted" so that no portion of the costs, even when not involving the expanded definition of lobbying, could be billed to the federal government. Thus, if a copy machine were used, even after hours, to copy a paper that was used for lobbying, then no portion of the copy machine's cost could be allocated to the federal grant because it was tainted.

It became very clear that this small change in cost principles could have enormous policy and economic impact on a significant portion of the nonprofit sector. Even though the final rule was not nearly as onerous as the original proposal, it had a chilling impact on the nonprofit sector. Even now, many nonprofits continue to fear that commenting on regulatory proposals, attending public hearings or being involved in policy debates may cause them to lose their federal funds or pay heavy penalties.

More recently, OMB again demonstrated its antipathy toward the nonprofit sector with new debarment and suspension rules that establish a national blacklist of people and organizations who are deemed "irresponsible" or "seriously improper" and who are to be barred from federal nonprocurement assistance, such as grants and loans. Ostensibly intended to curb fraud, waste and abuse (for example, to weed out those who have failed to repay government loans or did unsatisfactory work on a government grant) many worried about the vague reasons for being placed on the list, such as "performed poorly" on a grant, and the potential to "shut down groups with views opposing the Administration."[10]

After much controversy, OMB issued final rules that make the nonprocurement rules comparable to those for contractors. This is the heart of the problem: OMB's decision to treat the for-profit and not-for-profit sector, contracts and grants, the same. For example, it may be easy to determine if a contractor has performed poorly — if the paper clips don't work — but it takes different standards to determine whether a nonprofit grantee, running a Headstart program, for example, has performed poorly.

First, you cannot apply procurement contract-type evaluation methods. Second, the sort of performance evaluation methods that might assist in assessing service delivery are exactly the kind of activities that OMB has rejected in a number of ways — budget cuts to evaluation programs, paperwork clearance disapprovals of surveys, questionnaires and reporting requirements and substitution of final audit controls for ongoing performance monitoring.

There is also great irony in OMB's attack on the nonprofit sector. OMB's stated goal is to stop the misuse of federal funds. However, there is neither evidence of significant violations of federal grant rules, nor of significant sums wasted out of the small portion of direct federal grants for nonprofits. Federal procurement, on the other hand, which involves a much larger pool of federal funds, appears to be subject to considerable abuse — witness defense contracts. Nevertheless, OMB has never vigorously pursued procurement reform.

Given the likelihood of continued budget constraints and the important contributions that can be made by the public and private nonprofit sector, OMB should:

1. Sort out the proper role of the federal government. Over the last eight years, federalism has become a euphemism for slashed budgets and abrogation of federal responsibilities. This approach should be replaced by responsible management decisions. When empirical data and policy determinations support shifting federal responsibility, then a carefully phased in plan should be implemented, ensuring continuation of the needed program delivery infrastructure. To this extent, OMB should increase its efforts to involve state and local governments in program planning and evaluation, particularly with regard to payment for federal mandates.

2. Revise grant management rules to facilitate service delivery by private nonprofits. The role of the private nonprofit sector has been critical throughout the life of this country. Grant rules should not be designed to make things difficult for them, but rather to support their essential service. Further, these grant rules should encourage the free expression of nonprofits to discuss and debate problems and gaps in service delivery so that the issues can be dealt with effectively.

3. Revise debarment and suspension rules to reflect the differences between nonprofit and for-profit organizations, and between nonprocurement and procurement activities.

4. Develop guidelines for and actively support agency program evaluation efforts. Guidelines should be provided to grantees and agencies involved in demonstration projects. These evaluations should incorporate the views of individuals and organizations affected by the program being evaluated. It is essential that policy and program decisions depend on much more than accountants and audit controls. They must involve ongoing program-specific assessment of service delivery.

NOTES

[1] Of the issues we do not address in detail, the most notable are those of the budget process and economic policy; they are discussed by others in this volume. Also, we believe the heart of the problem is not the budget *process*, but rather the budget *debate*, which can be characterized as institutional gridlock between Congress and the president.

[2] See, for example, National Academy of Public Administration, *The Executive Presidency: Federal Management for the 1990s*, September 1988; U.S. House of Representatives, *Report of the Task Force on Safety*, Au-

gust 1988; Public Citizen, *Risking Americans' Health and Safety*, October 1988; Congressional Research Service, *Office of Management and Budget: Evolving Roles and Future Issues*, February 1986.

3 The selection of director should be quickly followed by recommendations for key positions, in particular: (1) Deputy Director of Budget; (2) Deputy Director of Management (a new position — to elevate OMB management functions); (3) The four Program Associate Directors (PADs) that monitor agency budgets; (4) The Administrator of the Office of Information and Regulatory Affairs (OIRA); (5) The Administrator of the Office of Federal Policy Procurement.

4 See, for example, Harold Bruff, *Report to the Administrative Conference of the U.S.: Presidential Management of Agency Rulemaking*, 1988; U.S. Senate, Committee on Governmental Affairs, *Oversight of the OMB Regulatory Review and Planning Process*, Senate Hearing 99-839, January 28, 1986; *Environmental Defense Fund v. Thomas*, 627 F. Supp. 566 (D.D.C., 1986); and *Public Citizen Health Research Group v. Tyson*, 796 F.2d (D.C. Cir., 1986).

5 The new president should also rescind three related executive orders that are largely implemented through regulatory review, "The Family" (E.O. 12606), "Federalism" (E.O. 12612) and the so-called "Takings" (E.O. 12630).

6 Barbara Boardman, Ian Greaves, *et al., OMB Review of CDC Research: Impact of the Paperwork Reduction Act*, U.S. House of Representatives, Committee on Energy and Commerce, Committee Print 99-MM, October 1986.

7 When Congress subsequently learned of the demise of this report, it voted to reinstate it. Most other lost publications did not have constituencies with comparable power.

8 We have provided a more detailed description of these issues, as well as recommendations for the new president, in *Federal Information Collection and Dissemination: The Role of OMB*. The report is published by the Benton Foundation, Washington, D.C.

9 *Management of United States Government, Fiscal Year 1989*, Privatization Plan, p.100.

10 "Blacklisting," *National Journal*, p. 2826, November 7, 1988.

CAMPAIGN FINANCE:
Federal Election Commission

SUMMARY OF RECOMMENDATIONS

Money plays far too large a role in today's American politics — especially in our congressional elections. Large campaign gifts can make Congress subservient to special interests rather than to the broad national interest, and shape the kind of legislation Congress passes — or doesn't pass.

Money thwarts the principle of one person/one vote and has made blatant conflicts of interest the order of the day in Congress, although those same conflicts are prohibited in the executive and judicial branches of government.

Too often, money determines who wins — and even who *runs* — in congressional elections.

All of this runs directly counter to what the Founding Fathers had in mind for our Congress and for our democratic process.

The principal remedies lie in:

* public financing of congressional elections, achievable simply by broadening the system already in the law for presidential elections to cover races for the House and Senate;

* an end to all giving by all political action committees (PACs) in federal elections;

* prohibiting contributions in House and Senate elections by nonresident individuals, under a formula, "If you can't vote for a candidate, you can't give";

* free broadcast time given to political parties (which could parcel out the time among candidates as they see fit), plus TV time sold at sharply reduced rates to candidates willing to *talk* to the cameras, without the use of film or other production aids;

* a prohibition of honoraria accompanied by an increase in congressional salaries.

---

[*] *Philip M. Stern, a former Congressional aide and Director of Research for the Democratic National Committee, is the author of six books, most recently* The Best Congress Money Can Buy. *He is also founder and co-chair of* Citizens Against PACs.

I. INTRODUCTION

Of course a president can and should appoint federal election commissioners zealous about maximum disclosure and enforcement — in distinct contrast to the present Commission's majority. (See "Beefing up the Federal Election Commission", below.) But that would not scratch the basic money-in-politics problems, principal among which are these four:

* Conflicts of interest as senators and representatives routinely and shamelessly accept large campaign contributions from industries they regulate. One former House committee chairman, Fernand St Germain, who chaired the banking committee, took in $316,000 from the PACs of banks and other financial institutions (cabinet officers and judges caught in such knowing conflicts are subject to criminal prosecution).

* Soaring (and limitless) campaign costs that make fundraising an ever-present obsession in the minds of lawmakers. U. S. Senators must now, on average, raise $10,000 *every week during their entire six-year term* to win re-election.

* Special-interest campaign contributions financing congressmen's personal retirement funds, under a special law that permits House members elected before 1980 to transfer campaign surpluses to their own personal bank accounts when they retire from Congress. (Rep. Dan Rostenkowski, the chairman of the tax-writing committee and a consistent four-to-one winner in his Chicago district, has a private retirement account of $904,000 waiting for him, financed in considerable part by special-interest PACs.)

* The ability of political action committees to aggregate political money and thereby enable small special-interest groups to impose enormous costs on the rest of the population (e.g., 200,000 dairy farmers forced tens of millions of consumers to pay higher prices for milk and butter, because the dairy PACs contributed to the campaigns of hundreds of lawmakers, including big-city congressmen who haven't a dairy cow in their districts).

In sum, the present system of financing congressional elections distorts representative democracy and undermines the one person/one vote ethic and involves even the best of lawmakers in a system bordering on legalized bribery.

Since the onus for those infirmities lies in the basic election laws themselves, rather than with the FEC, the bulk of this chapter will be devoted largely to proposed changes in those laws.

II. OPTIONS FOR REFORM

To choose among the many legislative remedies available requires clearly defining one's goals. My own are: to reduce the role that money now plays in shaping Congress — who runs, who wins, what kinds of laws they pass once they're in office; to increase competition among candidates as well as their accountability to their constituents; to free them from their never-ending preoccupation with fundraising that the current system imposes; and, finally, to shrink the influence of "interested" money — that is, money contributed by people and groups who hope to benefit financially from their contribution.

PUBLIC FINANCING

Our country needs a system where campaigns are financed as much as possible by "disinterested" money, meaning money that comes from all the taxpayers, through their government. When campaign funds come from all citizens, candidates and officeholders cannot identify any special person or group as the source, and hence cannot be tempted to accord them special favors or undue attention.

Taxpayer financing of American elections is neither radical nor new. In fact, it is the law of the land now for presidential elections. If it works in presidential races, why not in congressional elections? That is, why not have full public funding in House and Senate general elections and public matching grants in primary elections, as in the presidential system?

Public financing is the most urgent reform, for without it even the most honorable of candidates will continue to be obsessed with fundraising and even the best intentioned will be driven, for lack of an alternative, into the arms of special-interest givers.

To end the political arms race, any public-financing plan must include a ceiling on spending for candidates accepting public money. To prevent contestants from gaining an advantage by declining public money and avoiding the spending ceiling, complying candidates should get one dollar for every dollar by which the privately-funded candidate exceeds the spending ceiling. Thus the playing field would be kept level at all times.

PACS

The second crucial reform is to prohibit all PAC contributions to federal candidates. (While an individual cannot give more than $2000 to a candidate per election cycle, a PAC can give $10,000, and PACs that run in packs can give many times $10,000.)

As noted, PACs are the instrument whereby tiny groups like the dairy and sugar lobbies and the auto dealers have been able to prevail in Congress more by money than merit. As lawmakers get an ever-increasing share of their campaign dollars from PACs head-quartered outside their states and districts, they become less and less accountable to their own constituents. More than four-fifths of U.S. Representatives have come to depend on outside PACs for at least a third of their campaign funds. It is not uncommon for lawmakers to get 70% of their money from outside PACs.

Are all PACs equally evil? Is the Sierra Club PAC really equiv-alent to the AMA's? To me, they are, in that all PACs distort the democratic process by placing money-power over people-power. In fact, that is their avowed purpose. Democracy is far better served by *individual* citizens giving to candidates they believe in, rather than delegating that choice to some distant, and largely unaccountable, PAC manager.

The abolition of PAC giving would not impair the legitimate role of interest groups or crimp citizens' rights of association. Without PACs, citizens would still have an undiminished right to form or join groups, and to petition Congress through the group's lobbyists. Orga-nizations would have unimpaired rights to endorse candidates and engage in other political activity. And of course the right of group members to make political contributions as individuals would be unaffected.

The demise of the PAC contributions would deprive groups of only one power: the power to aggregate money and hand it out to candi-dates in amounts that the average citizen cannot equal. That is the power that distorts representative democracy.

CONTRIBUTIONS BY NON-RESIDENTS

Third, contributions to congressional candidates by non-residents of their states or districts should be prohibited under a formula, "If you can't vote for a candidate, you can't contribute to him/her."

If representatives get substantial portions of their campaign funds from outside special-interest PACs or individuals who cannot vote for them (in addition to what they receive from outside special-interest PACs), how can it be said that such legislators are accountable to their own constituents?

To be sure, Congress is a *national* legislature, and lawmakers from, say, South Dakota cast votes affecting the people of Chicago and New York on issues such as aid to the Contras, farm price supports and military budgets. But that doesn't give the people of Chicago and New York the right to *vote* for South Dakota legislators. Why should New Yorkers be allowed to cast proxy ballots with financial contributions larger than all but a handful of South Dakota citizens could afford?

Some fear that prohibiting outside money would doom to perpetual defeat non-incumbents from small, poor states like South Dakota and candidates like Mike Espy, the new black representative from Mississippi. Under current rules, those fears might be well founded. But those rules are not immutable. With a total end to the pro-incumbent PACs, with publicly funded congressional campaigns and a "level-playing-field" guarantee, the picture would be far more equal.

A ban on contributions from non-resident individuals runs counter to the prevailing Supreme Court doctrine that, in politics, money is speech and is therefore protected from regulation by the First Amendment. On the other hand, the Supreme Court did rule that those money-is-speech rights are not absolute but may be subject to limits (e.g., the $2000 per person ceiling in federal elections) where there is a "significant" governmental interest in doing so — in, for example, preventing public corruption or its appearance. In the years since the Court so ruled in the *Buckley v. Valeo* case of 1976, the evidence of public corruption has multiplied, offering hope that a future Court might be induced to broaden the limits it has already approved on individual giving.

Moreover, the Court has enunciated a governmental interest in the principle of one-person/one-vote. Specifically, it has opposed the "dilution of the weight of a citizen's vote" by reapportionment plans that thwart that principle. Could it not be persuasively argued that the vote of, say, a resident of a small and relatively poor state such as South Dakota is significantly diluted by the $2,000 that a wealthy California couple sends a South Dakota candidate?

Moreover, aren't South Dakotans' votes diluted when their senatorial candidates, in mid-campaign, scurry to Chicago, Houston and New York to court wealthy commodity traders, oil men and investment bankers in preference to meeting and hearing the problems of South Dakota citizens?

TV TIME

Few aspects of current American politics are as obscene as the spectacle of candidates going in hock to special interest groups primarily in order to buy TV — now *the* accepted medium for selling political candidates — to swell the already-bulging coffers of broadcasters by their free use of the public airwaves.

There are myriad complexities to any proposal to provide political candidates with free or reduced-rate broadcast time. Here is a first-cut suggestion: radio and TV broadcasters should be required to donate, free, a portion — say, ten percent — of their program and spot-announcement time in each major time category to the political parties during the last sixty days before each congressional general election. The parties would be free to apportion their free time for general party purposes or among their respective congressional candidates as each party saw fit. The time should be allocated among major, minor and new parties according to a past-performance or petition formula similar to that in the present presidential public financing law.

Such a plan would impose minimal burdens on broadcasters, obliging them to devote a mere eight tenths of one percent of the total time now at their disposal, and leaving them free to use (and profit from) the other 99.2 percent of the time granted them by their free use of the *public* airwaves.

In addition to the time granted free to political parties, Congress should require that TV broadcasters sell time at, say, one-eighth the usually-quoted rate to candidates who wish to buy time for advertisements of not less than a minute's duration that would consist solely of the candidate in a studio talking to the camera, with no use of extraneous film footage of baby-kissing, crowd-cheering, "voter" endorsements or other techniques better suited to selling cars than candidates or issues. Just the candidate talking — hopefully about the issues.

BEEFING UP THE FEDERAL ELECTION COMMISSION

In a 1981 study, Common Cause called the Federal Election Commission (FEC), the agency charged with enforcing the post-Watergate reform laws, "an agency born of necessity but truly unloved by its parents" — the Senate and House.

The Administrative Conference of the United States had previously said that if the FEC could be analogized to an automobile, the Commission's behavior led to the conclusion that Congress had "lavished [more attention] on the brakes than on the engine."

Both of those statements were dramatically emphasized by the Commission's conduct during the Reagan years. For example, even while the number of political action committees increased 63 percent and PAC donations nearly tripled, the FEC staff suffered a 17 percent cutback.

Perhaps as a result, the FEC repeatedly levied fines so minuscule that, as campaign finance expert Herbert Alexander put it, campaign operatives consider them "part of [the cost of] campaigning." Similarly, the Republican members of the FEC have blocked probe after probe, including one in which the Commission's action was later castigated by a Federal judge as "contrary to law."

In October, 1987, *The Wall Street Journal* reported that the FEC "got rid of all its trained investigators long ago" and that it "seldom uses its subpoena power and only rarely takes sworn testimony from witnesses." The FEC, continued the *Journal*, "seems more intent on pinching off disclosure of campaign-money abuses than investigating them." For example, in late 1987, the Commission sought to prosecute two private organizations that sought to disseminate data drawn from FEC candidate reports.

The FEC also rejected a staff recommendation to probe so-called "soft money" fund-raising practice of both parties (whereby gifts of unlimited size may be made, *in secret*, to the parties for so-called "party-building activities"). And then, when ordered by a federal judge to take action on the soft-money problem, the commission remained inert for an entire year. Among the reasons for such misfeasance are its appointees. President Reagan reappointed anti-enforcement minded commissioner Lee Ann Elliott (who voted against probing an alleged violation by the American Medical Association, even though she was, at the time, drawing an $18,831 pension from the AMA) while declining to reappoint pro-enforcement commissioners like Democrat Thomas Harris and Republican Frank Reiche.

These incidents reflect more deep-seated structural flaws in the FEC's nature, the most important among which are:

* *Its BI-partisan, as opposed to NON-partisan, nature.* As currently structured, the FEC is made up of three Democratic and three Republican commissioners, and since four votes are required to arrive at a decision or initiate an investigation (e.g. of the AMA), the partisan structure of the FEC is a built-in prescription for stalemate.

* *The fact that its mission is to stand watchdog over its employers.* Exhibit A is the manner in which the FEC lost its initial authority to conduct random audits of the campaign reports filed by Members of Congress. By chance, one of the earliest of the audit targets was the chairman of the House Rules Committee. Not long thereafter, the FEC was stripped of its random audit powers. That could hardly encourage Commission members and staff to act independently and forcefully in enforcing the law.

Exhibit B is the Congress' parsimonious treatment of the FEC's budget, which has an effect not only on enforcement but on disclosure, particularly the failure to affect prompt computerization of candidate reports.

* *Inadequate enforcement powers.* As the FEC interprets the law, it is forbidden to levy even the most minor of fines without undergoing a period of "conciliation." In the opinion of many, that results not only in delay but in a watering down of the fines to the point of inefficacy.

In light of the above, the next president's agenda for strengthening the Federal Election Commission should include at least the following changes in the election laws. First, add a seventh, nonpartisan member to the commission to be chosen by the President from among an array of nonpolitical persons proposed by a prestigious "blue ribbon" panel. Second, the FEC should be freed from congressional control; that could, for example, be achieved by protecting the Commission from legislative budget cuts, as some states have done with local election commissions. Third, Congress should enhance the FEC's enforcement powers by, for example, empowering the Commission to levy meaningful fines without having to go through the conciliation process.

In addition to these statutory changes, the new president could do much to restore the seriousness of purpose that characterized the early days of the Commission by, for example, appointing commissioners of stature and encouraging public use of the tax checkoff to finance presidential elections.

He could do that by personally checking the necessary box on his own tax return, amid Easter-seal-like publicity. (Ironically, Ronald Reagan checked "no" on his personal tax return, even though he had accepted more public money from the checkoff fund than any other presidential candidate.)

OTHER IDEAS

Members of Congress should be prohibited from accepting honoraria (just as employees of the Executive branch are now) to preclude lawmakers "serving two masters." At the same time, to avoid the pressure to seek out such dishonoraria, the salaries of senators and representatives should be raised to, say, the $135,000 recommended in 1986 by the Commission on Executive, Legislative and Judicial salaries (the Quadrennial Commission).

Members of Congress should no longer be permitted to build up large campaign surpluses that discourage challengers. Instead, funds remaining in their campaign coffers after each election should revert to the Treasury or be passed back to the donors to the extent feasible. Also, the "golden parachute" law that now permits many members of Congress to transfer surpluses to their own bank accounts upon retiring from Congress should be repealed.

To strengthen the political parties, as well as to free them from their present dependence on special-interest donors, federal aid should be given the parties by tax credits to match small contributions from individuals. At the same time, we should repeal the so-called "soft money" loopholes in the present law that permit unlimited (and undisclosed) gifts to political parties, including contributions from corporate and union treasuries.

III. THE COST OF CHANGE

A fair appraisal of any menu of reform proposals requires recognizing that no reform is perfect or risk-free. The question is: how do the potential *future* risks of a given reform compare with the *here-and-now* problems in the present system?

To illustrate: many worry that any public funding of elections handled by bureaucrats subject to control by the "ins" in Congress would operate to the disadvantage of congressional challengers. That danger does exist. But it is an "iffy" future danger that should be weighed against the system as it is today. Remember, in the 1986 House elections, the PACs gave 88 percent of their money to incumbents; incumbents outspent challengers nearly 3 to 1; and 98 percent of the sitting representatives who sought re-election won. Incumbents could hardly fare better under the public financing process recommended above.

Critics also argue that public financing will encourage "frivolous" candidates to run for Congress. But which risk poses the greater danger to the Republic — "too many" candidates, or "too few"? The existing system, with its pro-incumbent bias, errs on the side of "too few." It often freezes out challengers, solely for want of money.

America's interests are ill-served by rationing candidacies according to the money a person possesses or can raise, mainly from rich people and PACs. What if there were another Abraham Lincoln among the citizenry who would be prevented or discouraged from running for office merely because of money?

But in sheer dollar terms, can America afford the reform plan outlined here? How much will it cost?

The cost of a public financing program for congressional *general* elections can be precisely calculated, for the number of candidates and the amount of the public grants to each is a known quantity. The cost of companion public finance bills introduced in 1985 was $87 million a year for the House and $49 million for the Senate.

The total for all congressional elections is less than the $150 million the Pentagon spends every year on military bands!

The cost of a partial public financing plan for congressional *primary* elections is much more difficult to calculate. The expense hinges on a large number of unpredictable variables, such as how many candidates will enter the primaries and qualify for federal matching funds.

But again, the important question is: how would the cost of the plan proposed in this chapter compare with the cost of the existing system? Just three legislative measures* on which campaign money

---

*The three measures are the dairy and sugar subsidies and a hospital cost containment measure proposed by President Carter but vigorously (and successfully) opposed by the American Medical Association and its PAC — second largest in America.

appears to have had an impact cost consumers and taxpayers $16 billion every year. Even on the ultra-conservative assumption that only one-tenth of that may be fairly laid at the feet of the current campaign finance system, that still comes out to $1.6 billion a year.

Even if congressional public financing cost $500 million per election — $250 million per year — that would still be only one-fourth the added cost to the taxpayers of the higher dairy subsidy passed by the House after three dairy PACs had showered over a million dollars in campaign contributions. That added taxpayer cost omits the $2 billion surcharge that consumers are paying daily at supermarket check-out counters. And the dairy program is just one expensive subsidy apparently affected by campaign money.

Moreover, the existing campaign finance system carries a hidden price-tag over which the public has little control. That would not be true of a legislated program of publicly-financed congressional elections, which could be pared back any time Congress decided it was too expensive.

But the dollars-and-cents cost is too narrow a measure of the price America pays for the current campaign finance system. More important are the intangible costs — the cost, for example, of insulating lawmakers from effective challenge (by denying their opponents the wherewithal to make that challenge); the cost of rationing candidacies by the amount of money a person possesses or can raise from special interests; the cost of growing cynicism and shrinking participation by average voters who come to feel their voices are drowned out by monied interest groups and therefore no longer count; and, above all, the cost of submerging the national interest in a "me-first" political ethic.

Justice Policy

OVERVIEW:
Department of Justice

Stephen Gillers[*]

As late as 1948, neighboring home owners in the United States could agree to place restrictive covenants in deeds to their homes as a way of assuring that none could sell to a person of a particular race or religion. If a homeowner tried sell a home to an excluded person, neighbors could get a court order preventing the sale. Courts routinely issued such orders.

In 1948, in the case of *Shelley v. Kraemer*, the Supreme Court was asked whether the Fourteenth Amendment's Equal Protection Clause prohibited a state court from enforcing a racially restrictive covenant. The United States was not a party to the case. The Department of Justice had to decide whether to file a friend of the court brief urging the Supreme Court to forbid judicial enforcement of racially restrictive agreements. While the Justice Department had often filed *amicus* briefs in the past, they were in cases involving a federal agency or where the supremacy of federal law was at issue. Neither factor was present in *Shelley*.

Nevertheless, the government asked the Court to allow the United States to file a brief and present argument because the case raised "questions of outstanding importance, not only because of the nature of the constitutional and legal questions involved, but also because of the impact which the decisions will have upon the lives and well-being of millions of Americans." The Department's brief and argument strongly condemned restrictive covenants and asked the Court to prevent their enforcement. When the Court ruled, it agreed with the government.

While the issue in *Shelley* may seem tame today, it was controversial four decades ago. We cannot know exactly how influential the government's intervention may have been. But we can know that it took courage for Attorney General Tom Clark to enter the case and argue for an expansion of the Fourteenth Amendment rights of blacks

---

[*] *Stephen Gillers, professor of law at New York University Law School, teaches legal ethics and other subjects. He is the author of, among other books*, Getting Justice: The Rights of People *and* Regulation of Lawyers: Problems of Law and Ethics.

and other victims of restrictive covenants. This kind of courage from the nation's top law enforcer and his subordinates — to pursue justice even though it may carry political risk — has been all too rare in the decades since. How can we restore it?

Although many administrations, Republican and Democratic, have treated the Justice Department as another facilitator of the president's political agenda, thereby confusing politics for justice, rarely in modern times has the Department been so depleted, so weakened, so suspect and so distrusted as in the final years of the Reagan Presidency.

It would be wrong to lay the blame for this predicament wholly at the feet of former Attorney General Edwin Meese 3rd. Although Mr. Meese obviously undermined the Department's credibility and eroded any claims it wished to make to being the servant of law and not politics, still he had help from his subordinates, some of whose defaults are described in the chapters that follow.

Allowing for all that, it is hard to think of any man or woman in this postwar period who has come to personify as fully as Mr. Meese what the Department of Justice should not be and must be rescued from becoming.

The next president faces a major challenge in restoring the Justice Department to a position where it will enjoy the trust and confidence of the American people. The papers that follow offer specific proposals. Here, I want to discuss two remedies of different magnitude. First, there is the identity of the women and men who will be chosen to lead the Justice Department in the years ahead. Who they are will determine whether the specific proposals that follow, and others, have a chance to succeed. In short, we need a new standard for nomination. Second, one way ethics can play a more prominent role in the future operation of the Justice Department is by creating the position of Special Assistant to the Attorney General for Professional Ethics.

First and foremost, the next president must break with our tradition of choosing Attorneys General based on narrow considerations of political reliability. America is blessed with a strong and independent legal profession and with many lawyers of stature, women and men who enjoy excellent reputations in their communities and areas of practice. The next Attorney General must come from among them. He or she must be a person whose very nomination will invite renewal of our trust in the Department of Justice.

The next Attorney General must also be someone largely uninvolved in the president's political operation. No more campaign managers, political cronies or family lawyers. This is not because lawyers of stature cannot be found in or close to the campaigns of either candidate. They can. It is because the next Attorney General must be and *appear* to be free of the president's dominance. The next Attorney General must be and appear to be a person who would rather pack up and go home than compromise the Justice Department's obligations fairly to enforce the law and assure equal justice.

Unlike any other cabinet officer, the Attorney General has a dual allegiance — to the president but also to enforcement of the law and to our traditions of equal justice and constitutional liberty. Although law may in part be a product of politics, it is not the servant of politics. It has a separate and superior domain. When law and political expediency conflict, the law must prevail. The next Attorney General must appreciate that and be able to say no to a president who instructs otherwise.

The obligation to uphold the law in the face of political expediency requires further clarification. The law commands certain acts and gives officeholders discretion as to others. Legally mandated conduct cannot be refused for any reason, including the Administration's political popularity, no matter how pressing. Consider, for example, the Attorney General's responsibilities under the Voting Rights Act of 1965. If a jurisdiction covered by the act wants to change voting practices or procedures, it must obtain clearance from the Attorney General or a court. The Attorney General must not approve the change unless the jurisdiction proves that the change does not have the purpose and will not have the effect of denying or abridging the right to vote on account of race, color or membership in a language minority group. It would be unthinkable for an Attorney General to approve a change without such proof as a way of increasing the president's popularity in a particular state.

But that's the least of it. The real test comes in the discretionary acts: How shall an issue be argued in the Supreme Court? What priority shall we give civil rights enforcement? What shall be our position on the Freedom of Information Act? What shall be our position on the right way to interpret the Constitution?

Because the discretionary acts are largely unreviewable, the pattern of their resolution will be determined by the way in which the Attorney General thinks about law and justice. We have recently seen an approach to law and justice that is mean-spirited, miserly, narrow and insensitive. Instead, we need an Attorney General who recognizes that the law has a moral dimension and works by example. The Attorney General must understand the great desire of all people, weak and powerful, to be able to look to the law for the fair and compassionate treatment of their claims. The Attorney General must be the legal legatee of America's constitutional tradition, its historical commitment to equal justice, and not merely an advocate for the parochial interests of a particular president of the United States.

It is especially important that the Attorney General of the United States recognize the capacity of the law to correct injustice and, by example, encourage just behavior in others. This is so because the Justice Department is far and away the single most important law enforcement body in the nation. It not only has the resources to do things — sometimes the sole statutory right to do things — but the Justice Department also has the capacity to be a leader in the law that no other entity in our nation enjoys.

The Attorney General who can do this job will not abide an Administration that chooses his or her subordinates. Give the transition team due regard. Consider its candidates. Consult at length. But the Attorney General must, of all Cabinet members, be free to pick the men and women who will join in running the Department and fashioning its policies. No one who will yield this right deserves the office. Prime loyalty of the Attorney General's subordinates must be to the same goals of enlightened law enforcement and constitutional liberty that also command the loyalty of the Attorney General. Departmental independence cannot be limited to its leader; it must run deep within the staff.

Is politics irrelevant in the operation of the Justice Department? Of course not, as any Attorney General would recognize. For example, limited resources must be allocated among the Department's various assignments. The Department cannot do everything. Choosing what it will do, within limits, is a political decision. Similarly, while merit is still indispensable, choosing federal judges is essentially a political decision. No one suggests delegating this function to a non-partisan commission. But the fact that politics has its place does not mean that it can be allowed to dislodge all other considerations, not even for the most discretionary of functions. It is a question of degree and if there is one way to summarize the errors of the past eight years, it is to say that those who have determined the degrees at the Reagan Justice Department have been extreme in their willingness to politicize it.

Judicial selection provides a good example of the need to place a limit on politics even for a task appropriately receptive to political considerations. The full story may not be known for some time, but enough has leaked out about the Reagan Justice Department's inquisitions of potential nominees to the federal bench to sadden any admirer of that institution. It is one thing to seek to learn a nominee's general judicial philosophy and his or (for President Reagan rarely) her approach to constitutional interpretation. It is quite another to require, as there is good reason to believe the Reagan judge-pickers have required, particular answers to focused questions from a menu of current controversial judicial issues, including reproductive freedom, affirmative action and school prayer.

Edwin Meese, though not he alone, has brought the Justice Department to a new low in the regard of Americans. He has shown disregard for our history of constitutional liberty and disdain for the appearance of impropriety in high office. Mr. Meese has made us suspicious of our most important heritage: the rule of law. The most important thing the next president can do is recognize how much damage Mr. Meese has done and set about correcting it with an appointment so inspired that we are persuaded to restore our trust in the Department's integrity.

Once chosen, the next Attorney General must act to underscore the importance of ethical behavior, in fact and appearance, in the operation of the Department. There are many ways to do that. Perhaps the single most important way is to create the position of Special Assistant to the Attorney General on Professional Ethics. The man or woman who occupies that position would be answerable, and have ready access, to the Attorney General. In urging this position, I do not mean to suggest that the ethics apparatus mandated by the Ethics in Government Act be supplanted. The Department's Office of Professional Responsibility (OPR) has day-to-day tasks that must continue to be performed. To the extent it can be done in a way that protects OPR's independence, the new assistant should have a close working relationship with that office.

The job description of the new assistant might read as follows:

"This position requires a man or woman who will search out problem areas and take corrective action before a problem actually arises. He or she will work with all Department lawyers, in Washington and in U.S. Attorney's Offices, and with all agency lawyers who work with the Department. The special assistant will have an 800 number and be available to receive complaints or inquiries from any persons — including judges — who believe that a Department lawyer, or agency lawyer delegated to work with the Department, has acted improperly. The assistant will have authority to investigate and question conduct that is or appears to be improper under traditional rules governing the behavior of government lawyers.

"All lawyers working with or for the Department will be required to respond to the inquiries of the special assistant, who will report directly to the Attorney General. The assistant shall also be available to consult with the Attorney General regarding the propriety of the Attorney General's own conduct and shall be encouraged to raise issues about such conduct with the Attorney General whenever he or she deems it appropriate. Finally, the special assistant shall make it his or her special responsibility to raise ethical standards among government lawyers through innovative educational efforts calculated to make the Department a leader and an example for all."

Character and ethics, then, are two answers to the Justice Department's current sunken state. They are, of course, not separable. Without character, problems over ethics are inevitable, as we have witnessed during the Meese administration at Justice. With character, ethical conduct (and the appearance of such conduct) is not guaranteed — it remains something that must be worked at, actively pursued — but the chance of achieving it is high. Both character and ethics are within our grasp. Reaching them requires only the commitment and will of American presidents in the 1990s and beyond.

CIVIL RIGHTS:
Civil Rights Division, Equal Employment Opportunity Commission & Office of Federal Contract Compliance Programs

Lani Guinier & Barry Goldstein*

SUMMARY OF RECOMMENDATIONS

Under the leadership of the Department of Justice, the Reagan Administration identified race-specific civil rights policies as a spectral presence haunting our democratic political horizon. It called for the repeal of affirmative action, the end of many effective class-based remedies and the abandonment of most racial discrimination cases except those filed on behalf of actual, identifiable victims. Propelled at least in part by the philosophic engine of cost-benefit analysis, the Administration attempted to drive civil rights laws out of our socio-economic system on the ground that they cost more than they have been worth.

Recently, civil rights strategists have been congratulating themselves because so many of these attacks on civil rights over the past eight years were defeated. The Reagan Administration, for example, tried to gut the Voting Rights Act by insisting in 1982 that only intentionally discriminatory election laws should be covered. Congress emphatically rejected that notion by enacting a statutory results test. Subsequently, in 1985, the Department took the position that discriminatory results may not be actionable if blacks enjoy *any* (but concededly unequal) electoral opportunity. A unanimous Supreme Court, supported by a bipartisan consensus of the leadership in both the House and Senate, repudiated this Administration view. (*Thornburg v. Gingles*, 478 U.S. 30 (1986)).

The Administration tried to put Robert Bork on the Supreme Court, but the largest Senate majority in history voted against his

* *Lani Guinier is an associate professor at the University of Pennsylvania Law School and former assistant counsel of the NAACP Legal Defense Fund (1981-1988). Barry Goldstein is director of the NAACP Legal Defense Fund's Washington, DC office.*

confirmation. The President cast the first veto in 121 years on a civil rights bill, but Congress overrode his veto to enact the Grove City bill. Significantly, the Administration failed to enact one major item on its (anti-) civil rights legislative agenda.

Discrimination continues, however, both quietly and overtly. As a result, the new administration and Congress must make civil rights a first-tier priority in both the short- and long-terms. Specific actions in this regard include:

* The new administration must set a new tone immediately by issuing a Statement of Policy that the eradication of racial discrimination requires the full commitment and resources of the federal government to address generations of inequality.

* Congress must use its "advice and consent" in considering presidential nominations to ensure that appointments in *every* department and agency are broadly representative of minorities and women.

* The Equal Employment Opportunities Commission should be clearly directed to take the lead in enforcing equal employment laws, with adequate staff, training and funding.

* The administration should endorse and Congress should approve the Universal Voter Registration Act, setting uniform national standards and allowing election-day registration. Universal Voter Registration is necessary to overcome the pervasive, systematic exclusion of potential voters that the passive registration system now tolerates and indeed encourages.

I. THE REAGAN LEGACY

INTRODUCTION

The Reagan Administration will leave an enduring legacy on civil rights in America. In considering nominees to the federal bench, for example, it pursued an ideological litmus test on civil rights issues such as school desegregation, affirmative action and other race-conscious remedies. Of the 366 Reagan appointees who now represent over half the federal judiciary, only seven were black, proportionately fewer even than were appointed by Richard Nixon from a pool of available minority talent then one-seventh its present size.[1] And Reagan's predominantly white, male, "philosophical" legacy, with life time tenure, will continue into the 21st Century.

The message sent was clear from the first days of the Administration when it abruptly changed sides in several cases, most notoriously the *Bob Jones University* case involving tax breaks for segregated private schools. For the first time in the history of the Civil Rights Division, the Department of Justice filed briefs in employment and voting cases *opposing* women and minority plaintiffs, and generally focussed more public attention upon the so-called white male victims of "reverse discrimination" than even those "actual, identifiable" black victims of state-supported legal segregation. The President fired members of the United States Civil Rights Commission for doing their jobs and vetoed the Civil Rights Restoration Act.

The Reagan legacy endures as well in the framing of civil rights issues in general. The Administration recast civil rights as "special interest" politics. While political appointees admitted that blacks might in fact be worse off than whites, they blamed this on individual failings rather than entrapment by the awful legacy of discrimination. Relying on the extension of formal equality before the law, conservative civil rights theorists/policy-makers took an entrepreneurial approach to civil rights issues.[2] They argued that aggressive, affirmative government efforts to end discrimination were no longer necessary because individual blacks held within themselves the key to their own advancement: hard work and the Protestant work ethic in a robust free market economy.

The Administration sowed conflict between itself and civil rights groups, contributing to an increasing sense of isolation among many black Americans. It gave free rein, for example, to the Radical Right to recast, refocus and polarize a debate that had often previously won bipartisan support. In as emotional an area as race relations, the Assistant Attorney General for Civil Rights proposed in a 1988 memorandum that the Administration should seek "not consensus" but "confrontation."[3] This extraordinary exhortation to polarize the debate exacerbated tensions between people of color and other Americans; it also effectively promoted cynicism about the role of the public sector in advancing the status of historically disadvantaged groups. Moreover, even liberal political, social and economic analysts have recently tended to discount or ignore pervasive vestiges of America's racist heritage. It is in these contexts that we consider specific aspects of the Administration's civil rights programs over the last eight years.[4]

VOTING RIGHTS ENFORCEMENT

The Civil Rights Division of the Department of Justice was never, in the words of a Reagan official, a "hotbed of radicalism or of overreaching in government."[5] Deeply committed to the goals of civil rights enforcement, line attorneys generally adhered to the Division's traditions of "caution, moderation, respect for precedent, patience in the face of protracted litigation, commitment to the system as is and painstaking attention to detail."[6] These career professionals considered themselves apolitical guardians of the middle ground.

During the Reagan Administration, however, all this changed. While the career attorneys attempted to preserve the Division's standards of professionalism, moderation and, above all, "sense of obligation to the law,"[7] the political appointees in the Reagan Administration, under the leadership of Attorneys General Smith and Meese, and Assistant Attorney General William Bradford Reynolds, engaged in a profound assault on Division policies and intended beneficiaries. In the context of voting rights, an experienced litigator summarized the problem when testifying in 1985 in opposition to Mr. Reynolds' promotion to Associate Attorney General:

Despite the fundamental importance of the right to vote, Mr. Reynolds, as Assistant Attorney General for Civil Rights, has adopted policies and taken positions which have failed to protect, and indeed have undermined, the right to vote. He has opposed voting rights legislation designed to strengthen the statutory protections for minority voting rights, he has defaulted in numerous instances in his sworn duty to enforce statutory voting rights protections, and he has placed his imprimatur on racially discriminatory redistricting plans and other discriminatory voting law changes which diluted minority voting strength.[8]

A 1982 report on the Justice Department[9] recited a litany of examples of undue influence by Republican politicians who circumvented the channels normally relied upon for fair decision-making. The report concluded that in several voting cases, partisan politics or neoconservative ideology had been allowed "to corrupt the fair administration of the law."[10]

The Department's lackluster enforcement of routine voting rights matters is also ideologically rooted. Most prominent was the Department's rearguard action on the statutory standard for discerning discriminatory voting results. From the beginning, the Department opposed strengthening statutory protections for minority voting rights. It declined to testify in 1981 about the pre-clearance provisions of the Voting Rights Act or any other aspect of the Voting Rights Act during eighteen days of hearings while the matter was before the House of Representatives. Its explanation: despite being the primary agency charged with promoting the statutory scheme and after enforcing the law for close to seventeen years, the Administration claimed it needed time to "study it."

When finally they did come up with a position, nine months later, both Mr. Reynolds and Attorney General Smith testified in favor of an extension of the pre-clearance provisions, but only on the condition that the Congress also enact a wide-open release provision so that southern jurisdictions could liberally exempt themselves from the requirement of having to comply with administrative monitoring in the first place. The Administration's position on a "liberal bailout" was soundly rejected by both houses of Congress.

The Administration falsely takes credit for the 1982 amendments to the nationwide prohibition on discriminatory election laws, claiming it worked closely with Congress in devising a compromise amendment on Section 2 of the Voting Rights Act.[11] Section 2 raised the question whether plaintiffs in litigation challenging longstanding discriminatory practices would have to prove that the jurisdiction and the legislature intended to discriminate when they originally devised the practice, even if it was a hundred years ago. Mr. Reynolds, contrary to claims made in speeches or briefs, testified *against* any modification to the extremely difficult intent test of Section 2.[12] The Administration reluctantly did sign on to a "results test" in Section 2 only after the House of Representatives, by a 389 to 24 vote, had passed an amendment to Section 2 permitting minority plaintiffs to win based on proof of discriminatory election results alone.

For the next year and a half, despite the Administration's alleged support of the amendment, Mr. Reynolds failed to file any new lawsuits to enforce Section 2. Moreover, having failed to persuade Congress to retain an intent test, the Administration seized the first opportunity to limit the meaning and application of the results test. When black voters, who were 24% of the electorate, went to court in North Carolina challenging a legislative apportionment plan that used large, multi-member conglomerations to submerge minority neighborhoods, the Administration filed a brief in opposition to the black plaintiffs. As a result of the dilution of minority voting strength, only four black members of the North Carolina General Assembly had ever been elected. The Administration asked the United States Supreme Court not to apply the 1982 results test to North Carolina, however, because it felt enough blacks had gotten elected in 1982 — after the lawsuit was pending and as a result of efforts to influence the case — to show that some, though concededly not equal, electoral opportunity existed. It lost.[13]

In an earlier Supreme Court case, the Administration declined to file a brief supporting black voters, even though both the district court and the court of appeals had found evidence of discrimination based on proof of discriminatory intent (*Rogers v. Lodge*, 458 U.S. 613 (1982)). A January 4, 1982 memorandum from Mr. Reynolds to Solicitor General Rex Lee, in fact, revealed that, for Mr. Reynolds, "the preferred course of action," but for a timeliness problem, would have been to formally support the white commissioners.[14]

In addition to filing briefs to promote the incumbency of white politicians, the Division failed to vigorously protect the intended beneficiaries of the Voting Rights Act in its most important mission: administration of the Section 5 pre-clearance provision. This requires those places with a history of discrimination to submit any "standard, practice or procedure affecting voting" for advance federal approval. Between 1981 and 1985, there were at least 30 instances in which Mr. Reynolds overruled his staff, which was urging him to object to a voting law change that they had determined was discriminatory.[15]

In the section 5 pre-clearance process, Mr. Reynolds had the responsibility of acting both as judge and as prosecutor. In *Major v. Treen*,[16] Mr. Reynolds refused to act to stop a race-conscious effort to assure the re-election of a white New Orleans Republican incumbent to the Congress. As a prosecutor he failed to investigate fully the facts. As the judge, he listened only to one side.

Pursuant to its responsibilities under section 5 of the Voting Rights Act, the staff of the Division investigated the 1981 Congressional reapportionment in Louisiana and recommended an objection on the grounds that the plan was racially motivated. During the time that the matter was under submission to the Department of Justice, Mr. Reynolds met at least twice — and spoke by phone nine times — with Republican Governor David Treen, whose role in threatening to veto an earlier plan with a majority black congressional district was pivotal in getting the Louisiana legislature to pass the subsequent "Donald Duck" gerrymander. During this time, Mr. Reynolds had no telephone conversation or meetings with black legislators or black community leaders from the State of Louisiana about the plan.

On June 19, 1982, Reynolds refused to object to Treen's gerrymander. Speaking for the Reagan Administration, he condemned what he claimed were earlier decades of affirmative action and other race conscious remedies which, he said in a speech at Amherst College, created a "racial spoils system" in America. Yet, in neglect of his statutory duty, Reynolds endorsed a racial spoils system in Louisiana when it was necessary to insure the re-election of a white incumbent politician.

The Division's record in the area of voting rights, however, has a bright spot. Because voting rights has not been an area of maximum controversy, the Division has remained relatively active in routine enforcement matters. From January 1981 through September 30, 1986, the Division reviewed more than 82,000 changes pursuant to its administrative pre-clearance responsibilities. Most of the credit for holding the line goes to the 28 career attorneys in the Voting Section of the Division. No other litigating organization, even those specializing in voting matters, has even a fourth of these resources. It is to these special civil servants that the next administration and Congress must look to rescue the Act from its political contamination.

EMPLOYMENT POLICIES AND ENFORCEMENT [17]
Marked by conflict between civil rights groups and the Justice Department over fundamental principles of employment law, the last eight years was largely a period of defending established principles rather than moving forward to deal with current problems. A similar

conflict among the Federal departments — EEOC, Labor and Justice — also paralyzed creative law enforcement.

1. Equal Employment Opportunity Commission.[18] The EEOC is the lead agency in equal employment policies under Executive Order 12067. During the past eight years, however, the EEOC was not able to perform this role because the agency was largely ignored or its advice expressly rejected by the Reagan Justice Department.

In a 1987 speech to the Heritage Foundation, Clarence Thomas, who served as the Chairman of the Commission since 1982, defined the problem in personal terms. After observing that in the Reagan Administration "[t]he emphasis in the area of civil rights and social policies was decidedly negative," he stated that "there was a general refusal to listen to the opinions of black conservatives. In fact, it appeared often that our white counterparts actually hid from our advice. There was a general sense that we were being avoided and circumvented."

Several examples demonstrate the conflict between agencies:

* In 1981 the Justice Department adopted a policy opposing the use of affirmative action goals. The EEOC, however, continued to rely upon and use them.

* After the Justice Department filed a brief opposing the use of affirmative action as a remedy, the EEOC Commissioners wrote to Attorney General William French Smith on January 26, 1983, criticizing as "unacceptable" the Department's attempt "to initiate a major...change in the government's Civil Rights policy, without ever consulting [the EEOC]."

* In *Local 28, Sheet Metal Workers v. EEOC* (478 U.S. 421, n.24 (1986)), the Supreme Court noted that the Justice Department challenged the affirmative action goal provision in the Supreme Court "even though the EEOC has, throughout this litigation, joined the other plaintiffs in asking the courts to order numerical goals, implementing ratios and timetables."

In view of this internal Administration conflict, it is not surprising that the EEOC never presented a clear, consistent policy supporting the use of affirmative action in the enforcement of the fair employment laws. While adhering to the affirmative action guidelines adopted in 1978, the EEOC chairman nevertheless criticized the use of affirmative action goals a "fundamentally flawed approach to enforcement of the anti-discrimination statutes," and stated that he hoped to reverse this approach. Without any opportunity for public comment or any proposed change in its Affirmative Action Guidelines, the Acting General Counsel informed the Commission's attorneys that goals should not be included in settlements. The EEOC staff was informed that goals were "dead."

Prior to 1980, the EEOC played an important role in the development of fair employment law by two principal means: the filing of *amicus curiae* briefs and the promulgation of guidelines. Especially during the Carter Administration, the EEOC used the promulgation of guidelines to advance and define the proper application of the fair employment laws with respect to the use of selection procedures, sexual harassment, sex discrimination, national origin discrimination and affirmative action. While not universally accepted, the Guidelines have influenced significantly the interpretation of the law by the courts.

In the last eight years, however, not only were these important tools rarely used, but the Commission also attempted to undercut important fair employment principles. For the first time, the Justice Department and occasionally the EEOC filed briefs in fair employment cases opposing the positions of minorities and women.[19]

Finally, the policies adopted beginning in 1984 to improve the role of the EEOC as a "law enforcement agency" were criticized as ineffective. For example, the GAO has found that the EEOC process for investigating charges of discrimination is inadequate for determining whether discrimination exists.[20] It is significant that proportionately twice as many charges were resolved favorably for plaintiffs in 1982 (32.3%, 1,970 by cause finding and 19,705 by settlement) than in 1986 (15.5%).[21]

2. Office of Federal Contract Compliance Programs (OFCCP).[22] Affirmative action must be at the center of effective fair employment policies. In particular, the OFCCP in a new administration must be more aggressive in enforcing the affirmative action requirements of Executive Order 11246, which in 1984 applied to some 215,000 federal contractor establishments and more than 30 million workers doing over $167 billion dollars worth of business with the government. As defined in the regulations, affirmative action is "specific and result-oriented procedures designed to achieve prompt and full utilization of minorities and women at all levels and in all segments of the contractor's workforce where deficiencies exist."[23]

The potential advantage of the OFCCP program is that it does not require a finding of discrimination. Unlike the remedy in a fair employment case, the affirmative action requirements apply when there is "underutilization." Several recent studies conclude that the affirmative action requirements of the Executive Order program have removed barriers to fair employment opportunities for minorities and women. In a series of detailed studies, Professor Jonathan Leonard has demonstrated that the Executive Order's affirmative action program has increased the job opportunities for black workers. Professor Leonard compared EEO data over a period of six years (1974-1980) involving more than 16 million employees in more than 68,000 establishments. He concluded that "the claims that affirmative action has been ineffective have been overstated."

Moreover, despite ideological attacks from the Department of Justice, the OFCCP affirmative action program has survived. But while the Labor Department did defend its use of goals and timetables during the Reagan Administration, enforcement of the affirmative action requirements were hindered by the lack of resources — the number of actual staff positions declined from 1304 in 1980 to 840 in 1987.[24]

Also, there were problems with the implementation of the requirements. For example, OFCCP directed its staff not to require goals in excess of current availability, and, in some cases, not to permit such goals. Thus, if blacks comprised only 5% of the skilled workers in a community where blacks comprised 30% of the workforce, contractors were under no obligation to take reasonable, good faith affirmative action efforts to increase the number of black workers above 5%.

Enforcement was stymied by policy conflicts and lack of guidance. The Director of the OFCCP has had no direct authority over the field staff and the budget, and is separated by three levels of authority from the Secretary of Labor. The well-publicized conflict between the Justice Department and the OFCCP over the use of goals undercut the credibility of the program: "there appeared to be a general consensus among the field office staff that the agency no longer has the authority it once had to enforce the antidiscrimination laws within its jurisdiction."[25]

3. Department of Justice. The primary criticism of the Justice Department is its ideological emphasis. The Department took positions against not only affirmative action but also against effective attorneys' fees awards and the definition of illegal discrimination. It was particularly hypocritical in urging an enforcement theory on the basis of *individual* violations, given its positions in the Supreme Court that made it difficult for individuals to obtain lawyers in order to assert their rights.

The zealotry of the Department was exemplified by their attempt to use the Supreme Court's decision in *Memphis Firefighters Local 1784 v. Stotts* to shut down affirmative action altogether. In the case, the Supreme Court ruled as illegal, in 1984, a lower-court order to retain black firefighters against the seniority rule and a last-hired/first-fired provision, without a finding of prior discrimination. The Department took the position, which the Supreme Court subsequently rejected, that *Stotts* forbade all racial or gender affirmative action goals, even if those goals were designed to overcome prior discrimination. The unpopularity of its position was reflected in the almost universal rejection by the state and local governments of the

Department's effort. Indeed, the positions of the Department led to conflict within the Administration. The Department also seriously interfered with the operations of the EEOC and the Department of Labor, as described above.

II. DEMOGRAPHY & POLICY

The next administration and Congress must restructure the civil rights agenda to reflect American reality in the next century. Certain demographic facts can't be ignored:

* 60% of blacks are now concentrated in America's central cities, where infant death rates are nearly double those of whites, unemployment rates among young black males are nearly triple those of their white counterparts, and the disparity between whites and blacks, both in income and wealth, is the same as it was fifteen years ago.[26]

* In 56 of 100 cities with the largest black population, blacks are 30% or more of the populations, but they are "more economically isolated, more socially alienated, than ever before."[27]

* California and 53 major cities will have a nonwhite majority population by the year 2000; at the same time Texas and 11 other states will have a public school population that is majority nonwhite.

* Seven states already have black populations that are over 22%.

* There are no blacks or Hispanics in the United States Senate; no black governors have been elected in this century.

* Only 1.5% of the elected officials nationwide are black (mostly mayors from majority black towns with populations under 1,000).

Blacks and other minorities are increasingly geographically concentrated and demographically isolated. A new administration must begin by immediately seeking out black, Hispanic and Asian and Native American allies, by supporting — not undermining or patronizing — minority leadership, by appointing a diverse group of minority federal officials and by encouraging potential minority candidates for federal, state and local office.

In other words, civil rights issues can be ghettoized from the Left as well as the Right. Speaking before the civil rights organization he founded, the Rev. Jesse Jackson asserted that critics who accuse him of being "out of the mainstream" are correct. "The mainstream is too narrow, too elitist.... What we need here is a broad river. We need a river wide enough for a big boat with a lot of people."

The fair employment laws of 1989, for example, may need to be changed to deal with 21st Century discrimination problems, or with the predicted domination of minorities and women as new entrants into the workforce by the year 2000. If this country is to produce up to its capacity, a concerted effort must be made to include minorities and women fully in both the labor force and the political process.

III. POLICY CHANGES

IMMEDIATE ACTION

The next White House must establish a new tone immediately by announcing a coordinated statement of principles and policies to deal with discrimination both within the federal bureaucracy and between government and affected groups.

This Statement of Policy should govern not just agencies responsible for civil rights enforcement but also agencies responsible for training, education and information policy. It should declare that the eradication of racial discrimination requires the full panoply of existing remedies, including goals and timetables which are needed to address generations of inequality. The administration should acknowledge its commitment, in particular, to use the resources of the federal government to protect the rights of minorities, women and the disabled, to eliminate the effects of past discrimination, and to prevent future discrimination against the intended beneficiaries of the nation's civil rights laws. The statement must also explicitly recognize that substantive equality means not only that the process treat people equally but also that the results reflect the effort to remedy the effects of a century of official discrimination.

Secondly, the administration should send a clear signal that its political appointees, from Cabinet level nominations to the deputy assistant secretary in *every* department and agency, shall be broadly representative of minorities and women. This commitment must be demonstrated from the earliest appointments, and cannot be satisfied simply by making visible, but token, efforts at recruitment. It is critical that administration civil rights policies be enforced and supported by a diverse and representative group of federal officials.

Congress can play an important role in encouraging diversity in the appointment process by withholding its "advice and consent" until enough nominations have been made to establish a pattern of "affirmative recruitment." For example, the Senate Judiciary Committee should begin evaluating federal judicial nominations with reference to specific goals for increasing minority and women nominees. The Committee could decline to consider any nominee until a sufficient number — such as twenty or thirty — were made so as to enable the Committee to consider not only the individual qualifications of each, but also the impact of these twenty or thirty nominations as a totality on the composition of the federal bench.

Third, the administration should announce its intention to use the courts, the Congress and public interest institutions to enlist their power to further the goal of eradicating the effects of racial discrimination from our national landscape, root and branch. The administration must commit itself, with appropriate budgetary support, to enforce effectively anti-discrimination policies within the federal government itself.

SHORT-TERM CHALLENGES

Given the ideological attack led by the Justice Department on affirmative action and race-conscious remedies, as well as conflicts among civil rights agencies, a new administration should make clear that the divisions of the prior administration will be replaced by a coordinated plan. Going further, it should also consider changes in the civil rights laws that address fundamental flaws in our democratic arrangements. For example, the new administration should fight for the Universal Voter Registration Act that no doubt will be re-introduced in the next session of Congress.[28]

There are a number of short-term steps that the administration may consider both to enforce and reform the civil rights laws.

1. There should be a clear public commitment to the EEOC as the lead agency in the enforcement of equal employment laws, with adequate staff, training and budget resources. A Congressional study, for example, found that "there are insufficient travel funds or qualified clerical staff" and that there are "non-existent" or inadequate law libraries in some offices.

The EEOC should be encouraged to assert its leadership by taking aggressive, visible actions, which surely include filing *amicus* briefs on the side of minority and women plaintiffs and improving the process for investigating charges.[29] Of course, it will be necessary for someone on the president's staff to monitor this effort closely. The five EEOC Commissioners serve five-year terms and the General Counsel serves a four-year term. It is crucial that the next president appoint an EEOC staff that is committed to an aggressive and coordinated enforcement approach.

2. The agencies should agree on a joint approach to the development of legal issues, including affirmative action, a standard for the award of attorneys' fees, imposition of sanctions in civil rights cases and the standard for the burden of proof. To the extent possible, the government should follow a law development strategy and not simply react to the cases that are before the courts. The administration must, early on, evaluate and decide how to act on the cases pending before the Supreme Court.

The agencies should consider the coordination of a joint enforcement strategy. For example, the OFCCP and the EEOC may jointly decide to investigate and enforce the fair employment laws against a particular industry or in a particular job category. Moreover, the agencies should consider the coordination of enforcement efforts with other agencies of government; the NLRB, to take one example, has not been actively policing discriminatory practices by unions.

Since targeting of efforts is time-consuming and expensive, the agencies involved should explore the extent to which they may share information and procedures for targeting. To effectively use the contract compliance program, for example, the Department of Labor should have an effective targeting program. The agencies also should seek to develop short-range and long-range plans for insuring the best way to measure the inclusion of minorities and women in the internal workforces of companies, on the one hand, and the availability of those groups in the labor force, on the other hand. Other agencies, such as the Bureau of Labor Statistics and the Census Bureau, must be included.

While some of these issues are not suitable for a quick resolution, it is important that the agencies establish publicly that they are working together on common problems or, if necessary, that the White House is exerting leadership to establish a uniform position.

3. The OFCCP should announce its policy on the appropriate use of affirmative action goals. It is important that the agency proceed in a fashion that clearly indicates that affirmative action will be required in practice as well as in theory. In particular, it is important that companies be required and encouraged to set ultimate goals in excess of availability, to the extent permissible by law.

The OFCCP should also explore the expansion or use of the affirmative action requirements of Executive Order 11246. For example, the agency should determine if there are feasible methods for relating affirmative action requirements to other job training, education or creation programs. And the OFCCP should promulgate a regulation that prohibits contractors from paying for the expenses of employees which are incurred in clubs which discriminate on the basis of race, gender, religion or national origin. Such regulations were proposed at the end of the Carter Administration but were withdrawn under Reagan.

4. The agencies should focus on legislation and longer-term administrative changes:

* Title VII of the 1964 Civil Rights Act, which bars discrimination in the workplace, was developed at a time when the focus was upon prospective relief aimed at breaking down patterns of segregation. The Act contains minimal monetary relief for the victims of discrimination (two years of back pay); yet discrimination often continues in a more subtle and harder-to-prove form. More substantial monetary awards for individuals would provide both an incentive for

persons to challenge discriminatory practices (and lawyers to take the cases on a contingency basis) and an added spur for employers to eliminate discrimination from their workforce. Accordingly, Title VII should be amended to provide for an automatic trebling of back pay awards. If the victims of violations of some business laws may receive treble damages, the victims of employment discrimination should receive such awards.

* The proof of disparate treatment is becoming more difficult. Such treatment has regularly been proved by the use of "testers" (officials posing as prospective tenants) in housing discrimination cases. The agencies should explore the possibility of using testers for the investigation of employment discrimination, which has been done in England.

* The courts have undercut the effectiveness of the fees provisions. We need a new fees act. For example, the standard for the enhancement to hourly fees due to contingency risk must be broadened; prevailing parties should receive interest on fees and back pay awards against the Federal government; the acts should provide for the reimbursement of expert fees and other reasonable expenses.

* Because the OFCCP program is critically important, the administration should consider raising the position of the Director within the Department of Labor to an Assistant Secretary position, as proposed by the House Education and Labor Committee.

* The administration should endorse the Universal Voter Registration Act (the Conyers/Cranston bill). This legislation sets national, uniform standards for voter registration in federal elections, encourages state and local governments to assume the burden of canvassing eligible voters by mail or in government agencies and allows voters to register on election day. Universal Voter Registration — automatic one-step registration and voting — is necessary to overcome the pervasive, systematic exclusion of potential voters that the passive registration system now tolerates and indeed encourages.

LONG-RANGE CHALLENGE
The civil rights laws with which we are entering the 1990s are the product of the 1960s and early 1970s when patterns of segregation were clear. But laws and procedures which were effective in dealing with segregated job opportunities in blue-collar positions may not be suited to deal with subtle discrimination throughout the job structure. It is urgent that the civil rights agenda for the 21st Century be reshaped by the plight of underclass blacks and other people of color. Moreover, the promise of our political system must include a commitment to mainstreaming black issues and black candidates. Eliminating registration and other discriminatory barriers to political participa-

tion,[30] for example, only increases black turn-out where blacks have someone, and something, to vote for.

The White House, consequently, should convene in the Spring of 1989 a White House Summit on Civil Rights in the 21st Century to assess the scope, impact and effectiveness of present laws in light of emerging new realities (where 80% of new job entrants are likely to be nonwhite or women by the year 2000). As an outgrowth of the conference, a task force should be established that includes a majority of nonwhite and female policy analysts, scholars, economists, lawyers, elected officials and public interest leaders. By the fall of 1990, it would submit a proposed plan of action for aggressive federal initiatives and legislative reform.

The president leads not only by his rhetoric but also by his willingness to introduce legislative reforms to remedy continuing and new inequities. After all, it was the Attorney General in 1965 who wrote the Voting Rights Act, an act that is widely hailed as the most successful piece of civil rights legislation and certainly the only civil rights legislation that has kept abreast of demographic and political changes. It may similarly now be the time to consider the development of new rights: to a job, to a decent place to live, to an education, to health care, to be informed about important public policy issues that affect all of us. A partnership with state governments and business firms should also be explored to bring minority youth into the economic mainstream.

In fashioning its immediate, short-range and long-term civil rights agenda, the 41st president and 101st Congress should harness the moral, coercive and consensual power of the law. Vigorous enforcement of the law by the federal government, and a race-consciousness that encourages diversity and representation of both gender and hue, is absolutely critical. No private organization or combination of private organizations can compete with the resources of the federal government to enforce the law. In his commencement address at Howard University, June 4, 1965, after passage of the Civil Rights Act of 1964, and while the Voting Rights Act was being considered by Congress, President Johnson set the tone that the next administration needs to understand: "We seek not just legal equity but human ability, not just equality as a fact, but equality as a result."

NOTES

[1] Of the 366 Reagan appointments to the federal bench since 1981, 7 have been black, 15 Hispanic, 2 Asian and 32 women.

2 K. Crenshaw, "Race, Reform and Retrenchment: Transformation and Legitimation in Antidiscrimination Law," 101 *Harv. L. Rev.* 1331, 1339 (1988).

3 See "Memorandum for Heads of Department Components," February 22, 1988, from Wm. Bradford Reynolds, Assistant Attorney General and Counselor to the Attorney General, p.1.

4 Our focus on voting rights and fair employment law reflects our expertise.

5 Joel Selig, "The Reagan Justice Department and Civil Rights: What Went Wrong," 4 *Univ. of Illinois L.Rev.,* 785, 788 (1985).

6 *Id.*, quoting V. Navasky, *Kennedy Justice*, 194 (1971).

7 *Id.*

8 Frank Parker, Esp., Lawyers Committee for Civil Rights, Director, Voting Rights Project, *Nomination of William Bradford Reynolds to be Associate Attorney General* Hearings, June 5, 1985, at 450.

9 *Justice Department Voting Rights Enforcement: Political Interference and Retreats*, by Frank Parker and Barbara Phillips, Lawyers Committee for Civil Rights Under Law, Washington, D.C.

10 *Without Justice*, A Report on the Conduct of the Justice Department in Civil Rights in 1981-82, The Leadership Conference on Civil Rights, February 1982, at 65.

11 Statement of William Bradford Reynolds, NAACP Legal Defense Fund Civil Rights Institute, May 20, 1983, New York, NY.

12 *Voting Rights Act, Hearings on S.53, S.1761, S.1975, S.1992 and H.R.3112, Before the Subcommittee on the Constitution of the Senate Committee on the Judiciary*, 97th Cong. 2nd Sess., 1655-1850 (1982).

13 *Thornburg v. Gingles*, 478 U.S. 30 (1986).

14 *Hearings before the Committee on the Judiciary, United State Senate*, 99th Cong., 1st Sess., Nomination of William Bradford Reynolds to be Associate Attorney General, June 18, 1985, at 887-888.

15 *Id.*, at 448.

16 574 F. Supp. 325 (ED La. 1983) (three-judge court).

17 There are four principal fair employment laws which bar discrimination on the basis of race, color, sex, national origin, religion, age and handicap which are enforced by three Federal agencies: the Equal Employment Opportunity Commission, the Office of Federal Contract Compliance Programs of the Department of Labor and the Department of Justice. In addition, the OFCCP enforces Executive Order 11246 prohibiting discriminatory practices as well as requiring affirmative action by federal contractors.

18 The EEOC is responsible for the enforcement of two statutes, the ADEA and the EPA, and significant parts of Title VII and Section 501 of the Rehabilitation Act of 1973.

19 See, e.g., *United States v. Paradise*, 107 S.Ct. 1053 (1987); *Local 28 Sheetmetal Workers International Assn. v. EEOC*, 106 S.Ct. 3019 (1986); *Local Number 93, Intern. Assn. of Firefighters, AFL-CIO C.L.C. v. City of Cleveland*, 106 S.Ct. 3063, 478 U.S. 501, 92 L.Ed. 2d 405 (1986); *Firefighters Local Union No. 1784 v. Stotts*, 104 S.Ct. 2576, 467 U.S. 561, 81 L.Ed. 2d 483 (1984). Moreover, the number of *amicus* briefs filed by the commission dropped precipitously since 1980: 89 briefs were filed in 1980, compared with 16 *amicus* briefs in 1985. Of course, the EEOC was limited in the positions which it could take by the positions taken by the Justice Department in the Supreme Court.

20 The proportion of findings of cause to believe that discrimination occurred has remained constant from 1982 to 1986 at approximately 3%, while the proportion of no cause findings has steadily increased from 35% to 59.5%. Moreover, the proportion of settlements of charges has also continued to decline, from 29.4% in 1982 to 12.5% in 1986. Therefore, of the 62,203 closures in 1986, 9,513 or 15.5% were resolved in a manner favorable to the charging party, whereas, 52,580 were closed administratively or as a result of a no cause finding.

21 While focused only upon one office, a GAO study found that the EEOC failed to investigate adequately 29% of the charges.

22 The OFCCP is responsible for the enforcement of the nondiscrimination and affirmative action provisions of Executive Order 11246, Section 503 of the Rehabilitation Act of 1973 and the Vietnam Veterans Readjustment Assistance Act of 1974.

23 It is important that the requirements for affirmative action be carefully analyzed in light of the recent Supreme Court opinions. There has not been a recent court decision on the constitutionality of the affirmative action requirements of the program. To some extent this follows from the lack of aggressive enforcement of the program;

we can expect substantial new litigation challenging the affirmative requirements of the program.

24 The OFCCP is operating under regulations implemented in 1976. Compounding the problem of enforcing the Order under old regulations is the process by which the OFCCP has implemented policy changes. Officials have issued changes in speeches, in information notes to field staff, in directives which are often conflicting with other directives and in briefings given to contractors. Recently, the OFCCP recognized that its policy guidance was in disarray, and stated that it will organize the directives and engage in training efforts to standardize enforcement.

25 See *Staff Report on OFCCP* at 67.

26 See *U.S. Bureau of the Census, Statistical Abstract of the United States,* 72 table 112, 457 table 766 (106th Ed., 1986); *The State of Black America* 51 (J. Williams ed., 1982).

27 Statement of Fred R. Harris, Roger W. Wilkins and David Ginsburg before the Subcommittee on Civil and Constitutional Rights of the House Committee on the Judiciary, May 25, 1988 at 4.

28 There are still too many cumbersome and outdated administrative impediments to registering to vote and to casting a ballot. These barriers have a disproportionate impact on poor people and minorities.

29 Most importantly, the EEOC may move to provide for a hearing *after* the decision of the agency.

30 Structural barriers, such as at-large elections, dilute minority voting strength and make voting a futile gesture where the electorate is racially polarized.

CIVIL ENFORCEMENT & DEFENSE:
Civil Division

David C. Vladeck & William B. Schultz[*]

SUMMARY OF RECOMMENDATIONS

The 500 lawyers assigned to the Civil Division of the Department of Justice represent the federal government in a wide array of court cases, many of which have a direct impact on the lives of every American. The Division's principal mission is to defend the policies set by other agencies in court, which it has done uncritically over the past eight years. Thus the Civil Division has fought to limit access to the courts, to restrict the public's access to government information and has given low priority to enforcing our nation's health and safety laws.

The new administration must take a fresh look at the Civil Division's current "win-at-all-cost" approach to litigation; its ultimate goal should be to advance the administration of justice in this country. In order to set this new tone, it should create a policy planning component within the Civil Division to implement new policies relating to issues such as access to the courts, access to government information and enforcement of federal health and safety laws.

The next administration should implement the following recommendations.

* *Reversal of the Reagan Administration's policy of blocking access to the courts by consumers, environmentalists and members of Congress.* A policy directive should be issued to all Civil Division lawyers directing them to avoid raising standing and other arguments that deny citizens access to the courts unless the argument is required by existing law or serves a compelling policy function.

* *A wholesale revision of the Reagan Administration's policies regarding access to government information.* An Executive Order should be issued reaffirming the principle that all government information should generally be available to the public, and establishing as a matter of Executive Branch policy that no agency shall be permitted to withhold records unless it can demonstrate that a significant, identifiable harm would flow from the record's release.

---

[*] *David C. Vladeck and William B. Schultz are attorneys at Public Citizen Litigation Group, a public interest law firm in Washington, D.C.*

* *The Civil Division should initiate enforcement actions under the health and safety laws and the laws pertaining to government contract fraud.* An important task is to revitalize the role of the government in enforcing laws administered by the Food and Drug Administration, the Consumer Product Safety Commission and other regulatory agencies. Civil Division attorneys should play a lead role in this effort rather than simply wait for referrals. In addition, the resources devoted to bringing fraud cases against government contractors and grantees should be significantly increased.

* *A Policy Planning component should be created within the Civil Division to implement these recommendations.* Because the Civil Division is so segmented and because much of its work is defensive, the creation of a section with oversight over the entire Division will be necessary to implement policies such as those contained in the recommendations made here. After a new policy is implemented, this section would review briefs discussing these policy initiatives to insure that they are properly and consistently presented to the courts.

I. INTRODUCTION

The Civil Division of the Justice Department is unlike any other litigating arm of the federal government because its posture in court is typically defensive. Attorneys who work in the Civil Division represent the federal government in a wide range of cases involving matters such as the personal injury claims of shipyard workers exposed to asbestos; suits for access to documents under the Freedom of Information Act; and cases brought by both industry and public interest groups against regulatory agencies. Because the attorneys who work in the Civil Division touch the lives of so many Americans, their approach to defending cases brought against the government has a significant impact both on whether justice is achieved and on the public's perception of whether we have a just government.

Unfortunately, the attorneys who set policy there have undervalued their importance for many years. Instead, the consistent theme that we heard in interviews with more than 20 attorneys, many of whom have either litigated against the Civil Division or have been employed by it, is that Division attorneys approach litigation in much the way a private practitioner would. They seek to win their cases at all costs, but without any real appreciation that as representatives of the United States government they are obligated to factor the public interest into their decisions.

Attorneys in the Civil Division routinely raise an array of technical and jurisdictional defenses such as standing, mootness, ripeness and failure to exhaust administrative remedies. The practice is so notorious and the division's attorneys can be so aggressive in making their arguments that lawyers who litigate against the Justice Department sometimes joke, only half in jest, that in the Civil Division attorneys believe they have lost a case if the court reaches the merits.

Nevertheless, general rules about when it is appropriate to raise technical defenses are not possible. Rather the controversy is over the frequency with which the Civil Division raises these defenses, not with the fact that they can be raised. To dispel this attitude, the head of the Civil Division should convey the message to the Division's attorneys that defending the government is different from defending a private client in one important respect: the ultimate goal must be justice, not necessarily winning.

Consider the case where the government has an argument that a private party has not exhausted its administrative remedies (because it did not seek relief from the agency first) but it is clear that the agency would have denied the request in any event. In this circumstance, it is unjust for the government to raise an exhaustion defense, although many attorneys in the Civil Division would take precisely that approach.

Having made this point, it should also be said that the attorneys who work in the Civil Division are among the most talented in the government. During the Reagan Administration the Division was managed more professionally and less politically than many other divisions in the Justice Department and agency general counsel's offices. That's why the most important of any of our recommendations will be the choice of the chief of the Civil Division. Only a capable attorney with sound judgment and substantial litigation experience will be able to promote justice in the Civil Division of a progressive administration.

II. OVERVIEW AND HISTORY*

The present day Civil Division can trace its origins back to 1868, when Congress gave the Attorney General responsibility for all government litigation before the Court of Claims. Today, the Civil Division is the largest litigating unit within the Department of Justice, employing about 500 lawyers and nearly 400 support personnel.

The Division was not created by statute; rather, its authority is derived from laws assigning the Attorney General the responsibility for advising heads of executive departments on questions of law and

---

* *Much of the discussion in this part of the report is drawn from a 1987 Department of Justice booklet entitled the "Civil Division."*

handling the federal government's litigation. The role of the Civil Division has been defined by regulations issued by the Attorney General, which spell out in considerable detail the breadth of the Civil Division's responsibilities. (*See* 28 C.F.R. §§ .45 *et seq.* (1986)).

The Civil Division handles the federal government's general civil litigation in both district and appellate courts. The nature of the litigation is as diverse as the activities of the government itself. As a result, many of the Civil Division's cases have significant domestic and foreign policy implications. For example, the Division

* Defends the United States in cases challenging the constitutionality of federal statutes, government programs and presidential action;

* Handles fraud, international trade and bankruptcy cases involving billions of dollars;

* Initiates litigation to enforce a number of federal statutes, including the nation's consumer protection and immigration laws, and defends against challenges to those statutes and associated agency enforcement actions; and

* Handles general tort claims, including those involving toxic substances, aviation, admiralty and so-called *Bivens* actions, where federal officials are sued personally for official actions.

The Civil Division is headed by an Assistant Attorney General and five Deputy Assistants. In the Reagan Administration, most of the Deputies were political appointees, which is a shift from the approach in prior administrations, where the Deputies were principally career government lawyers. The Division has six major litigating units: Federal Programs, Commercial, Torts, Immigration, Consumer Affairs and Appellate.

1. *FEDERAL PROGRAMS*

The Federal Programs Branch, with approximately 90 lawyers, litigates on behalf of approximately 100 federal agencies, the president and cabinet officers, members of Congress and other government officials. Its principal role is to defend against challenges to the constitutionality of federal statutes, and attacks on the legality of federal programs and policies. Among its principal responsibilities are:

* **Regulatory Enforcement.** The Branch is responsible for bringing affirmative litigation to ensure compliance with federal statutes, such as the National Highway Traffic Safety Act or the Employment Retirement Income Security Act.

* **National Security and Foreign Relations.** In the course of its representation of the president, the Defense Department, the State Department and the CIA, the Branch is involved in highly visible national security and foreign relations litigation. This includes litigation stemming from the Reagan Administration embargo of Nicaragua and its non-compliance with the War Powers Resolution.

* **Federal Personnel Policy.** All litigation stemming from federal personnel policies is conducted by the Branch. Thus, it has represented the government in challenges to the Office of Personnel Management's efforts to exclude advocacy organizations from the Combined Federal Campaign and it has defended the Reagan Administration's drug testing programs. It also handles some of the cases charging the federal government with discrimination based on race, age, gender and handicap.

* **Freedom of Information and Privacy.** This unit represents the federal government in litigation under a number of open record and meeting laws, including the Freedom of Information Act, the Privacy Act, the Government in the Sunshine Act and the Federal Advisory Committee Act. Until 1983, the Civil Division also was in charge of formulating and coordinating the government's policies regarding FOIA and the Privacy Act, through the Office of Information and Privacy. However, those functions were transferred to the Office of Legal Policy, which was created in 1981 principally to assist in the selection of judges. We recommend that the Office of Information and Privacy be transferred back to the Civil Division, which conducts all of the government's litigation under the two Acts.

2. TORTS BRANCH

The Torts Branch, with 130 lawyers, represents the interests of the United States, including its employees who are sued individually, in suits where money judgments are sought for damages resulting from negligent or wrongful acts. The Torts Branch's major work falls into three categories:

* **General Tort Claims.** This category includes traditional problems in tort law such as personal injury and medical malpractice. Among the important emerging issues are radiation claims, brought by those alleging injury from the government's testing and production of nuclear weapons and materials, and "Agent Orange" litigation, brought by veterans claiming injury from exposure to the defoliant in Vietnam.

* **Environmental and Occupational Disease Litigation.** Increasingly, the government is involved in litigation involving hazardous substances. The lion's share of these cases involve the use of asbestos in ship construction during World War II, though there are mounting numbers of cases alleging environmental contamination from the use and disposal of toxic substances on and around U.S. facilities — particularly arsenals and military bases.

* **Constitutional Tort Litigation.** Prompted by the Supreme Court's 1971 decision in *Bivens v. Six Unknown Agents of the Federal*

Bureau of Narcotics, federal officials are now often the target of tort cases alleging violations of constitutional, statutory and common-law rights. These cases run the gamut from one alleging a conspiracy among federal law enforcement officials in the Greensboro Ku Klux Klan shooting in 1979 to others involving alleged radiation of sheep, deliberate medical malpractice and issues of national security. These cases can be highly sensitive, often involving top-level federal officials and key federal operations.

3. COMMERCIAL LITIGATION BRANCH

The Commercial Litigation Branch, with over 140 attorneys, is the largest unit within the Civil Division. It prosecutes claims for the recovery of monies fraudulently secured, enforces the government's contract and patent rights and defends the country's international trade policy. Among its major responsibilities are:

* **Civil Fraud.** The Commercial Litigation Branch is responsible for bringing suits to recover losses that result from frauds in federal programs and contracts and the bribery and corruption of federal officials. These cases can involve mischarging, false claims for payment, the substitution of substandard goods, multi-million dollar loan frauds, employee embezzlement and abuses involving federal grant monies. Although this work is important and cost-effective (this litigation more than pays for itself), at present only 35 Branch lawyers are assigned to civil fraud cases.

* **Debt Recovery.** Branch lawyers handle suits for money and property on behalf of the government. Much of this work is to protect the government's interest in bankruptcy proceedings, where the government often has a multi-million dollar stake in the outcome.

* **Customs and International Trade.** Branch lawyers represent the United States in customs and international trade matters before the International Trade Court and the Court of Appeals for the Federal Circuit. These cases often involve significant issues including dumping, countervailing duties and international trade agreements.

4. OFFICE OF CONSUMER LITIGATION

The smallest unit within the Civil Division, with 15 lawyers, is the Office of Consumer Litigation, which is responsible for the enforcement of federal consumer protection statutes through civil and criminal litigation. Among the office's clients are the Food and Drug Administration, the Consumer Product Safety Commission, the Federal Trade Commission and the National Highway Traffic Safety Administration.

5. OFFICE OF IMMIGRATION LITIGATION

This office was created in 1983 to conduct civil trial and appellate litigation under the immigration laws. With 30 attorneys, the office handles litigation arising under the Immigration Reform and Control Act of 1986, including the new employment authorization and sanction provisions. The Office also handles cases brought by individual aliens challenging orders of deportation and exclusion, denials of political asylum, as well as class actions challenging immigration policy and enforcement actions by the Attorney General.

6. APPELLATE STAFF

The Appellate Staff, with 55 lawyers, is responsible for the appellate work of the entire Civil Division. Its caseload includes matters from all of the Division's branches and offices, as well as cases that are brought in the Court of Appeals directly from administrative agencies. By giving the Appellate Staff this broad jurisdiction, the Division retains centralized control over the government's vital litigation in the appellate courts.

The Civil Division's caseload has risen dramatically over the past decade, and can be expected to continue to rise in the foreseeable future. During 1981, Division attorneys were responsible for over 15,000 newly filed cases. By 1987, that number grew to nearly 20,000 cases — an increase of nearly 30 percent. Of course, the 500 Division lawyers in Washington, D.C., cannot handle all of that litigation on their own. Rather, the Division relies heavily on the various United States Attorney's Offices, which are located throughout the nation.

All cases are initially screened by Civil Division lawyers in Washington, who decide whether the case should be handled by the Division, "delegated" or turned over to the U.S. Attorney's office, or "monitored," which means that the U.S. Attorney's office will be responsible for the litigation, but that a Civil Division attorney will be kept informed of the progress of the litigation. Through this process, Civil Division lawyers retain control over all cases that are legally, politically or economically significant.

Apart from the assistance of the U.S. Attorneys' offices, the Civil Division also draws upon the legal resources of the various agencies it defends. Thus, in many instances, the Civil Division delegates the case directly to the affected agency. Or, as often happens, even if the Civil Division decides to handle the case itself, it will rely on agency attorneys to prepare the briefs and other court submissions.

III. POLICY CHANGES THAT WORK

Although the defensive nature of the work done by the Civil Division limits the kinds of policy changes that can realistically be implemented, there are a number of directives that should be issued to advance the public interest and to make the Division work more efficiently. Our recommendations take two forms.

First, as already discussed, one fault is philosophical: Civil Division attorneys, in their quest for victory, sometimes defend cases or make arguments that are contrary to the public interest. More important than any specific recommendation will be the selection of the Assistant Attorney General for the Civil Division, who can set a tone that rewards attorneys not only for winning but also for avoiding technical arguments that lead to unjust results and for persuading clients to settle cases or moderate their positions where appropriate.

Second, there are a number of specific policy measures that will help promote a progressive Civil Division. Among the most important recommendations are that the Civil Division: (1) be more selective about raising jurisdictional defenses; (2) return to the policy adopted by the Carter Administration with respect to defending cases brought under the Freedom of Information Act; and (3) initiate more enforcement actions, particularly in the areas of consumer protection and government contract fraud:

1. The Civil Division Should Not Routinely Raise Standing and Other Technical Defenses Which Deny Citizens Access to the Courts. As mentioned, a lawsuit against the government must often overcome several hurdles before the court can reach the merits. The plaintiff must show that the federal court has jurisdiction over the case. Next the government will typically raise a number of other defenses in an effort to persuade the court that it should dismiss the case rather than reach the merits of the plaintiff's claim. Defenses that the government typically raises are: failure to exhaust administrative remedies; lack of standing (plaintiff does not have a sufficient interest in the case); sovereign immunity (no authority to sue the government); statute of limitations (specific time period for bringing case has expired); mootness (case filed too late); and ripeness (case filed too early).

Two examples will show how these doctrines can delay justice and deny the courts the ability to resolve claims. The first example involves the asbestos cases brought under the Federal Torts Claims Act.

These cases grew out of worker exposure to asbestos while working in shipyards during World War II. After being sued by the workers, the manufacturers then sued the federal government for indemnification under the Federal Torts Claims Act. In the early

1980s, there were hundreds of such claims. The government's policy was to deny the administrative claims and require the asbestos companies to prove their cases in court. Nevertheless, where the asbestos companies sued directly, bypassing the administrative process as futile, the Civil Division argued that the court should dismiss the case on exhaustion grounds. The effect was to delay the resolution of the judicial claim and to drive up the cost of litigation.

Although it may be hard to feel much sympathy for asbestos companies, this same principal has been applied hundreds of times to individual personal injury actions against the government and to public interest groups who have sued regulatory agencies alleging violations of the law. Obviously, the exhaustion requirement serves a legitimate purpose where there is a realistic possibility that the plaintiff can obtain the relief requested from the agency or where consideration by the agency will sharpen the issues to be resolved in court. But where neither of these purposes is served, then the Civil Division should refrain from futilely invoking this doctrine.

A second example involves the issue of standing. The foundation of the doctrine of standing is Article III of the Constitution which limits the jurisdiction of the federal courts to "cases" and "controversies." The courts have held that Article III requires that the dispute between the parties be real rather than theoretical, and that in general the plaintiff must identify some "injury" that the lawsuit could redress. Few people dispute these general propositions, but the Justice Department has often used the standing doctrine to argue that the court should not reach the merits in extremely important cases.

A good example is *Barnes v. Kline*, 759 F.2d 21 (1985). The case was brought by the U.S. Senate, the Speaker of the House, the House's Bipartisan Leadership Group and 33 individual members of the House of Representatives. The issue in *Barnes* concerned the meaning of the pocket veto clause of the Constitution and the requirements for exercising the veto by the President. That particular case concerned a bill that placed certain conditions on continued military assistance to El Salvador. The President thought he had validly exercised the veto because Congress had adjourned before the 10 days for vetoing legislation had expired. The Congress, on the other hand, took the position that the pocket veto had not been validly exercised because it had appointed a clerk to receive any bill vetoed after its adjournment.

Since the law in the D.C. Circuit gives members of Congress standing to bring such challenges, this is a classic case that should be decided by the courts. The Civil Division initially did not challenge standing, and a panel of the Court held that the President's veto was not valid. However, prodded by a dissent by Judge Robert Bork, the

Justice Department appealed the decision to the U.S. Supreme Court. There it argued that Congress never has standing to challenge illegal action by the Executive Branch, a position which would cut the courts out of resolving extremely important disputes between the two other branches of government. (Before the case could be decided, the statute which the President had tried to veto expired, and thus the case was dismissed as moot. The Supreme Court has still not decided the question of congressional standing.)

2. Freedom of Information Act Cases Should Be Litigated Only Where There Is An Identifiable Governmental Interest In Withholding Documents. For the past twenty years, Congress has engaged in a sustained effort to make the concept of an accountable government a reality by enacting a number of statutes granting broad access to government records and opening government meetings to the public. Yet the Reagan Administration has waged a systematic assault on these laws. Indeed, within one year of taking office, it radically transformed the government's information policy by cutting back on access to government records under the Freedom of Information Act (FOIA).

The attack on the FOIA has taken a number of forms. For example, the Reagan Administration rescinded the policy announced by former Attorney General Griffin Bell that the Justice Department would oppose FOIA requests only where there was a showing of "demonstrable harm" to the government. Under this standard, the Justice Department had declined to defend large numbers of FOIA cases where either the government's position was not well-founded or where the agency could not demonstrate that serious harm would flow from disclosure.

However, in early 1981 the Bell memorandum was replaced with a policy requiring the Department to defend all suits challenging an agency's decision to deny a request submitted under the FOIA unless it is determined that: (a) the agency's denial lacks a substantial legal basis; or (b) defense of the agency's denial presents an unwarranted risk of adverse impact on other agencies' ability to protect important records.

As is evident, under this standard, *unless* an agency's position is clearly frivolous, it will be defended by the Justice Department. Compounding the problem, the Reagan Administration, through the Civil Division, has pressed hard in the courts to narrow substantially the types of records that *must* be released.

The Justice Department's policies on fee waivers also impede access under FOIA. In the Act itself, Congress sought to encourage use of FOIA by the press, scholars and public interest organizations by directing that agencies make documents available free of charge when disclosure of the records would serve the public interest. Prior administrations had liberally granted fee waivers. Under the Reagan Administration, however, the Justice Department has drastically cut down on fee waivers by engaging in a cumbersome review of the requester's purpose for seeking the documents and ability to publicize them, as well as the value of the documents. The Administration's new fee-waiver (or non-waiver) policy has made the Act dauntingly expensive to use by many who inform the public. Predictably, it has dissuaded requesters who do not have the stamina to endure the Department's fee-waiver examination from pursuing their requests for records.

The Administration's opposition to the dissemination of any information relating to national security culminated in its withdrawal of Executive Order 12065 governing classification and its replacement by Executive Order 12356. The Executive Order has great significance under FOIA, since under Exemption 1 only information properly classified in accordance with the Executive Order may be withheld. While there are many differences between the Executive Orders, two changes have had profound affects. First, Executive Order 12065 provided for balancing the public interest in disclosure against the injury to national security in determining whether to disclose certain classified materials. Yet the present Order discards this balancing test and categorically forbids disclosure of classified material *regardless* of whether there might be an overriding public interest in the material.

Second, under the prior Executive Order, classification could not be restored to documents once they had been declassified and released to the public. The rescission of this provision in the new Executive Order has led to a number of ugly incidents: books seized off library shelves because they contain newly reclassified information, and scholars threatened for publishing information gleaned from once declassified sources. Executive Order 12356 should be withdrawn. It should be replaced with an Order directing that classification and declassification decisions take into account the public interest in disclosure and prohibiting, or at least restricting, the reclassification of formerly declassified materials.

3. The Civil Division Should Initiate More Enforcement Actions. The Civil Division not only defends (usually), but also prosecutes regulatory cases on behalf of agencies such as the Consumer Product Safety Commission, the National Highway Traffic Safety Administration and the FDA. Historically, these cases have been referred to the Division by the relevant agencies, but the Justice Department has the authority to initiate such actions on its own. Of course, as a practical matter, the relevant agency would have to be consulted prior to initiating any litigation.

With the possible exception of contract procurement cases brought on behalf of the Department of Defense, the entire Reagan Administration has de-emphasized affirmative civil cases. For example, the CPSC has brought only one significant enforcement action (involving All Terrain Vehicles or ATVs), and the Justice Department immediately entered into a settlement agreement that has been severely criticized by public interest groups and the Attorneys General from a number of states. The FDA's enforcement efforts have similarly been curtailed. For instance, although the FDA's scientific panels have concluded that two-thirds of the ingredients on over-the-counter drugs lack the statutorily required evidence of effectiveness, including many big-selling products, it has not initiated any enforcement actions against OTC drug manufacturers for promoting products in violation of the efficacy requirement of the statute. Similar examples can be cited at NHTSA, OSHA and other agencies.

The next Civil Division should study the enforcement policies of the agencies under its jurisdiction and consider new areas for enforcement actions. Of course, such decisions should be made in conjunction with officials at the relevant agencies, but the Division can take the initiative where appropriate.

This may require some re-education for the Division's defense-minded lawyers. For Civil Division attorneys often do not comprehend the important role of affirmative enforcement cases in implementing regulatory statements. In order to restore the role of the United States in enforcing federal health and safety laws, any disagreements between agency counsel and Civil Division attorneys should be reviewed by a Policy Board to be established by the Assistant Attorney General.

Greater emphasis also needs to be placed on the prosecution of civil fraud cases in the government contracts area. At present, the Commercial Branch of the Civil Division has allotted 35 lawyers to handle all of the government's civil fraud litigation — which encompasses all of the defense contracting and procurement cases and fraud in federal grant programs cases. Even though the Civil Division has the support of the U.S. Attorneys around the country, agency lawyers and possibly other attorneys on the Justice Department, the available resources are far too meager to meet the task at hand. Indeed, every one of the dozen or so major corporate law firms that specializes in government contracts work has more lawyers engaged in government contract litigation than the entire Civil Division.

The Civil Division should allocate additional resources to this important work, even if it requires an increase in the Division's budget. It should be stressed that cases brought by the fraud section of the Commercial Branch more than pay for themselves — given the enormous amount of money typically at stake in a government contracts case. In addition, to ensure inter-agency coordination in this area, a high-level task force, headed jointly by the Assistant Attorneys General in charge of the Civil and Criminal Divisions and including representatives of the Defense Department, should be established to formulate new strategies to fight fraud and abuse in government contracts.

4. The Civil Division Should Adopt A Formal Policy Of Working With The State Attorneys General. One positive fallout of the Reagan Administration's policy of not enforcing regulatory laws is that the state Attorneys General have become much more aggressive in bringing consumer protection litigation. Such cases include ones against odometer tampering and opposing the Justice Department's settlement of the ATV case. The Attorney General's office in New York has brought a number of false advertising cases to fill the gap left by the Federal Trade Commission's lack of enforcement activity. And New York and Massachusetts have been active in pesticide litigation; the State of New York, for example, joined a lawsuit against the Environmental Protection Agency that challenged EPA's reversal of its staff's initial decision not to ban the pesticide Alar.

The work of state Attorneys General offices is federalism at its best. The Civil Division should adopt a policy of formally encouraging appropriate enforcement by the state Attorneys General and working with the states where federal and state interests overlap.

5. The Civil Division Should Review The Relationship That Its Attorneys Have With Agency Counsel. One issue which any incoming administration should address is the division of responsibility between counsel at regulatory agencies and the attorneys in the Civil Division. Unless a particular regulatory statute provides otherwise, the Justice Department has the authority to represent the United States in lawsuits brought by or against agencies. However, the Department has occasionally entered into a Memorandum of Understanding that permits the agency to represent itself.

In the typical case, however, an attorney in the Civil Division is the lead attorney having final say on all decisions and has the option of arguing the case in court, even if the briefs are written by agency counsel. Of course, the general counsel of an agency can always ask a Civil Division attorney's superiors to review any decision, but realistically such an option can be used infrequently. The issue is whether such an arrangement is in the best interests of the United States, the two principal considerations being effective representation in court and the desire to attract the most qualified attorneys to work in the Justice Department as well as in the administrative agencies.

In our view, there are strong arguments both for retaining the present allocation of authority and for delegating more decisionmaking authority to the agencies. On balance, given the overriding need for consistency in the federal government's litigating authority, the final authority should be retained by the Justice Department.

However, the current informal rule that frequently bars agency counsel from appearing in court should be significantly relaxed. The Civil Division ought to adopt a policy of generally allowing agency counsel to argue cases in court where the attorney for the agency did the bulk of the work on the briefs; at the very least, agency attorneys should be permitted to participate in trials to an extent that is commensurate with the work they have performed.

6. The Civil Division Should Create A Policy Section to Implement the Significant Policy Changes Recommended in this Chapter. The Civil Division should adopt a policy planning component which would work directly under the Assistant Attorney General. The purpose of this component would be to consider significant policy issues such as those discussed in this chapter. Once adopted, it could then participate actively in implementing such recommendations. For example, if a recommendation urged the Civil Division to be more circumspect about raising the defense of failure to exhaust administrative remedies, then for a period of time the Policy Section could review briefs raising exhaustion to insure that the new directive is being implemented in a consistent manner.

Even where it is decided that there will not be a significant change in Civil Division policy, the Policy Section could be charged with insuring that Division attorneys are consistent in applying doctrines such as preemption and non-acquiescence to appellate court decisions.

7. The Civil Division Should Review The Following Additional Issues:

* *National Security Cases:* The Civil Division handles virtually all of the highly sensitive civil cases involving national security issues. These include cases (a) to enforce secrecy agreements which forbid security agency employees from publishing information acquired during their employment (such as the case against Frank Snepp), (b) brought by former government employees who have been stripped of their security clearances and/or fired because they allegedly present a security risk or (c) filed by journalists, scholars or public interest organizations seeking alleged national security information under the FOIA.

The government has a well-founded need to protect sensitive information. However, in many of the national security cases that have been litigated over the past eight years, the Civil Division has too often uncritically accepted the agency's representations about the potential for harm — no matter how strained those representations may have been. Thus, in one case the Civil Division argued that it was essential for national security that the CIA have absolute discretion — unreviewable by any court — to fire its employees. This claim was flatly rejected by the Supreme Court. In FOIA cases, the CIA routinely makes broad claims that any disclosure of information will impair national security. To ensure that the national security claims the Civil Division raises in court are well-founded, the head of the Civil Division should issue a directive to staff lawyers stating that, in cases implicating national security issues, staff attorneys must make a reasonable inquiry into the basis for the agency's claims of potential harm and must be satisfied that such claims are grounded in fact. In any instance where a staff attorney determines that there is not an adequate factual basis supporting the agency's assertion, the Civil Division should decline to make the assertion urged by the agency.

* *Homosexual Rights Cases:* Over the past eight years, the Civil Division has handled a number of highly controversial cases involving the rights of homosexuals to retain their jobs in the military and national security agencies. These cases are an outgrowth of the Reagan Administration's effort to bar homosexuals from employment both in the military, because they allegedly interfere with morale, and in the national security agencies, because they allegedly present a security risk. The Civil Division has vigorously defended these restrictive, anti-homosexual employment practices. In our view, and in the view of many of the judges that have reviewed these cases, this all-out attack on homosexuals is unwarranted and unlawful. A task force, which would include the Assistant Attorney General in charge of the Civil Division and representatives from the military and the security agencies, should be formed to review and revise existing policies regarding the employment of homosexuals.

* *Tort Actions Against Federal Officials:* Prompted by a number of Supreme Court rulings in the 1970s that federal officials may be sued in tort cases alleging violations of constitutional, statutory and common-law rights, federal officials are increasingly the target of tort cases based on state law. Recent Supreme Court decisions in *Westfall v. Erwin*, 108 S. Ct. 580 (1987), and *Berkovitz v. United States*, 108 S. Ct. 1954 (1988), unanimously held that the government or its employees could be held liable for negligence in performing non-discretionary functions. These decisions will undoubtedly spur even more litigation.

Apart from their sheer volume, these cases pose special litigation difficulties for the Civil Division. Where a federal official is sued in his or her individual capacity, the Division must initially determine whether it will afford representation, which, in general, it does. However, where the federal agency or multiple officials are defendants, the government frequently has to hire private lawyers to represent one or several defendants, to avoid potential conflicts of interest. As a result, these suits are costly to the taxpayers to defend, and create special burdens on the Division. And where the government declines to furnish a federal official an attorney, it places an enormous burden on that official who then must pay for an attorney.

An injured party should not be denied compensation simply because he or she had the misfortune to be injured by a federal official. But there are steps that can be taken by the Department itself and the agencies it represents to alleviate the burden on the Civil Division, without impairing the rights of individuals to sue. One step that warrants careful consideration is whether the government should indemnify officials against tort claims flowing from non-discretionary duties. Adoption of regulations assuring indemnification in appropriate cases would help solve the Division's problems.

DRUG ENFORCEMENT:
Criminal Division

Kenneth R. Feinberg*

SUMMARY OF RECOMMENDATIONS

Not since the presidential elections of the 1960s has the specter of violent crime played such a visible role in a presidential campaign. Charges and countercharges of being "soft on crime" were leveled at both presidential candidates, particularly Governor Michael Dukakis.

Voters of every political stripe agree that the nation's drug abuse problem has reached catastrophic proportions. A June, 1988 Gallup poll showed that a majority of Americans would even support increased taxes to pay for an effective war on drugs. Yet there is an increasing frustration exhibited by voters and elected officials alike that our nation is losing the battle against drug abuse. Many proposals currently being touted by various lawmakers to combat drugs make for splashy headlines but poor policy.

One casualty of the recent crime debate is the political perception, developed over the past decade, that law enforcement and crime control are non-partisan issues that mandate the development of consensus among Republicans, Democrats, Liberals and Conservatives. During the past decade, disparate members of Congress have been able to work together to enact comprehensive crime control legislation. At the forefront of this effort have been four members of the Senate Judiciary Committee — Senators Kennedy, Thurmond, Biden and Hatch — who have worked collegially in enacting a variety of law enforcement measures free from political posturing.

One irony of the recent polarizing debate is the high priority now given to issues of law enforcement and criminal justice. Nowhere is the subject of crime more visible than when it comes to the problem of drug abuse and drug enforcement. The recently enacted comprehensive drug legislation originally had its fair share of so-called litmus test "tough on crime" measures, e.g., the death penalty for drug king-

---

* Kenneth R. Feinberg, a lawyer in Washington, D.C., is a former Assistant U.S. Attorney and was Special Counsel to the U.S. Senate Judiciary Committee. This article was prepared with the assistance of Rima Sirota.

pins, harsh civil penalties, modification of the exclusionary rule. Most of the more draconian provisions were dropped in conference, but a few remain.

What follows is a modest proposal to combat the growing drug problem in America. While these ideas are not comprehensive in scope, they offer some relatively small steps that might be tried on an experimental basis to refocus and strengthen our Nation's war against drugs:

* Regional "drug emergency" areas should be declared and special "drug courts" designated.

* The financial risks of drug involvement must be substantially increased through targeting forfeiture, money laundering, tax and selected benefits programs.

* Local law could require landlords to evict tenants from rental units where police have turned up narcotics.

I. REAGAN ADMINISTRATION BUDGET AND ENFORCEMENT PRIORITIES

As its major strategy in the "war on drugs," the current Administration has overwhelmingly focused on cutting off the supply of illegal drugs. Of its proposed $3.96 billion drug abuse budget for fiscal year 1989, for example, the Administration seeks $2.8 billion for enforcement, $612 million for prevention and $431 million for treatment. Of the $2.8 billion to be spent on enforcement, almost half is targeted for interdiction efforts. $646 million is earmarked for investigating high level drug traffickers while only $230 million is targeted for assisting state and local street-level enforcement efforts.

The Administration's priorities are well-intentioned but ineffective. Interdiction efforts must fail because there are simply too many ways to smuggle drugs into the United States. With thousands of miles of coastline to defend, planes are able to fly into desolate regions of the country to dump their goods. Smugglers continually shift their drop points, always staying a step ahead of the authorities.[1] The results are shocking: according to the General Accounting Office, an estimated 138 tons of cocaine, 11,000 tons of marijuana and 172 tons of heroin and hashish were smuggled into the United States, while only 27 tons of cocaine, 1,106 tons of marijuana and 9 tons of heroin and hashish were actually seized by authorities. Even if drug seizures were doubled, the effect on availability and price would be negligible.[2]

Federal investigations of high-level drug dealers have also proved unsuccessful. The Drug Enforcement Administration (DEA) now devotes almost all of its resources to arresting and incarcerating high-level drug distributors. The costs of such a strategy — including undercover operations, surveillance techniques and trial preparation — are enormous and change only the composition of the "kingpin" population, not the number of dealers or availability of drugs.[3]

So despite an increase in funding from $645 million in 1981 to over $4 billion in 1987, drug use has increased dramatically. This failure is due, in some part, to the current Administration's abandonment of an effective local, street-level enforcement policy.[4] Local drug dealers and users understand that the current risks of engaging in the trade are relatively minimal. A street-level dealer selling marijuana for one year has approximately a 0.1 percent chance of spending time in prison! A cocaine dealer faces about the same risk. One study estimated that only 4.3 percent of all marijuana dealers in California were even so much as arrested.[5]

II. 1988 PROPOSALS

In an election year it is not surprising that lawmakers have rushed to judgment when it comes to drug enforcement. One by one, pieces of legislation are introduced, each more draconian than the next, each touted as one more *ultimate* solution in the war against drugs. Indeed, over 200 bills and resolutions pertaining to the drug issue were introduced this past session.*

Various House Committee bills proposed in the past session include: (1) denying certain federal benefits to convicted drug offenders; (2) creating a "drug czar" position to coordinate all federal anti-drug efforts; (3) requiring drug companies to keep records as to the sale and distribution of compounds that may be used to manufacture illegal drugs; (4) coordinating a joint United States-Latin America anti-narcotics task force; (5) imposing the death penalty for drug-related deaths; and (6) a statutory exception to the exclusionary rule for drug cases.

The Democratic Substance Abuse Working Group, chaired by Senators Moynihan and Nunn, offered a series of proposals that redirect federal priorities toward prevention, treatment and rehabilitation. The plan included (1) a five-year loss of eligibility for federal mortgages and the right to practice before certain federal agencies for those convicted of certain drug crimes; (2) the earmarking of 60% of federal anti-drug dollars for various programs designed to reduce de-

---

* Not surprisingly, no Congressional effort is underway to legalize (or decriminalize) the use of currently prohibited drugs. Politics is the art of the possible. Legalization may be debated in articles and among the experts, but it is not a politically realistic alternative to current drug enforcement policies.

mand; (3) block grants to the states for treatment programs; (4) a computerized passport security program to improve interdiction efforts; (5) funds earmarked for additional federal judges, prosecutors, prisons and state and local law enforcement assistance.

The Senate Republican package emphasized civil sanctioning of drug offenders and a "zero tolerance" policy: (1) the drug testing of all members of Congress and their staffs; (2) increased testing and penalties for drivers in possession or under the influence of drugs; (3) the denial of all federal licenses and other federal benefits to drug offenders; and (4) increased airport interdiction efforts.

The White House Conference For a Drug Free America issued its final report in June, 1988. This document contains over 100 specific recommendations in the areas of prevention, education, criminal justice, treatment, workplace, transportation, sports, public housing, media and entertainment, international drug control, federal reorganization and system-wide problems. The report embraces a zero tolerance policy and includes such measures as stiffened mandatory sentences (including the death penalty) and mandatory drug testing for every public and private employee.

The 1988 anti-drug bill was the last major piece of legislation passed by the 100th Congress. The House and Senate negotiators were unable to agree on a measure that would relax the exclusionary rule in drug-related prosecutions; as a result, the entire provision was cut from the bill. The bill does, however, allow the death penalty for major drug traffickers. It also includes also increased prison terms and fines for drug dealers and users, creates a Cabinet-level "drug czar" position to coordinate national drug policy, provides increased funds for treatment and prevention, creates a special Asset Forfeiture Fund, directs still more resources at drug interdiction efforts and requires improved record-keeping by banks to combat money laundering.

III. "DRUG EMERGENCY" AREAS AND DRUG COURTS

The current Administration's failed efforts at interdiction and "drug kingpin" prosecutions strongly suggest that law enforcement priorities must be aimed not only at the source of supply and initial distribution, but also at the middleman wholesaler, street dealer and consumer of illegal drugs. Such an effort would, of course, require increased prosecutorial, judicial and prison resources. Obviously, the federal government has neither the resources nor the statutory authority to mount a major, all-encompassing offensive against drug distribution and use.

The president does, however, have the power to declare the existence of an emergency or major disaster area. (42 U.S.C.A. Sect.

5121 *et seq.* (1983)). Presidential authority to make such a declaration is predicated upon a gubernatorial request for aid, but is otherwise unlimited. (42 U.S.C.A. Sect. 5141.) Once an emergency is declared, local disaster victims receive public funds in whatever way best responds to the immediate crisis.

A new administration could institute a modest, model program for certifying that a "drug emergency" exists in a given jurisdiction, triggering additional federal financial and technical assistance. While most emergencies have been declared in response to "acts of God," such as flooding and drought, President Carter's declaration of Love Canal as a national disaster area demonstrates that such an approach need not be limited to so-called natural emergencies. A designated certification would trigger the provision of additional federal resources to the area. Such aid would include federal investigative and prosecutorial coordination with state and local officials resulting in, for example, special joint organized drug task forces; a telephone hotline providing a reward (on an anonymous basis) for information leading to the arrest and conviction of drug offenders and drug testing, treatment and counseling as conditions of bail and probation.

A major component of the drug emergency area program would be the creation of temporary federal drug courts providing prompt trials aimed at the small scale drug trafficker and drug abuser. Even at the present level of arrests and indictments, the judicial system in many jurisdictions is close to the breaking point. Prosecutors are inundated with drug cases and courts often experience massive delays. The increased pressure to deal with the drug problem in federally designated emergency areas would, if successful, lead to even greater demands on the judicial system. Enforcement authorities may be reluctant to significantly increase the rate of arrests if they have reason to fear that the additional caseload would hopelessly bog down the system. Increased judicial resources are therefore a necessary component of the program.

Specially designated drug courts would result in other advantages as well. Judges would develop increased expertise in the area, allowing for expedited processing of cases, as has occurred in the Nation's tax and bankruptcy courts. In addition, due in part to judges' differing exposure to felony drug cases, an uncoordinated system results in widely disparate sentences. The establishment of emergency drug courts could increase the likelihood of consistent and even-handed sentencing.[6]

The New York experience illustrates the connection between a high arrest rate, judicial backlogs and the resulting decrease in drug offender convictions. A substantial increase in New York drug felony indictments in 1986 was not met with a corresponding increase in drug case dispositions.[7] Prior to New York's establishment of a special state drug court, 820 of the 975 drug-related felony cases over a six month period were still pending, with 752 defendants free either on money bail or their own recognizance. Because the high arrest rate created an enormous backlog in New York's courts, many strong cases against drug offenders never went to trial.[8] During Operation Pressure Point I, for example, narcotics felony arrests increased by more than 2,000 while narcotics felony convictions rose by only 6![9] In addition, the prosecution of drug cases displaced the prosecution of other criminal cases, including those involving violent crimes.

In response to 1987's significant increase in crack-related arrests, New York created a special "drug court" known as "Part N" (for Narcotics). The drug court concept was aimed at resolving drug felony cases in an average of six days (through plea bargaining); the regular court system averages six months to a year. This innovative program has successfully helped relieve the strain on the rest of New York's judicial system.*

IV. INCREASING THE COSTS OF DRUG DEALING

Attacking illegal drug trade profits is an inherently appealing idea. Current federal proposals include greater use of asset forfeiture, improved money laundering statutes, greater involvement of the IRS and the withholding of certain federal benefit programs. Each of these sanctions, as discussed below, could and should be strengthened. Their principal problem, however, is that they do not and probably can not make participation in the drug industry an unprofitable venture. Illegal drug revenues total approximately $100 *billion* per year and the industry's profit margin is estimated to be *at least* 50%.

The almost inevitable "drop in the bucket" quality of such programs does not, however, negate the need for new and better financially-targeted strategies. It does suggest that these and other similar ideas must be promoted on the basis of results that can realisti-

---

* It is, of course, true that the effectiveness of such a targeted program will result in more drug offenders being imprisoned. Yet, the problem of prison overcrowding has been well-documented; approximately three-quarters of the states are currently under federal court order regarding prison overcrowding. There are simply no shortcuts to the prison space problem. Additional prison facilities are needed. But the modest, targeted program proposed in this chapter should not be challenged on the ground that available prison space is inadequate. Rather, the prison problem must be separately addressed as part of *any* comprehensive law enforcement program.

cally be expected and not as an antidote to the profitable nature of the drug trade. Financial penalties have certain advantages: (1) as compared to lengthy trial procedures, they are relatively speedy mechanisms; (2) a defendant's assets can be frozen prior to trial and thus disrupt his ongoing drug operations; (3) they do serve to punish the individual offender; and (4) perhaps most importantly, they can significantly increase the funds available to maintain and expand the war against drugs.

ASSET SEIZURE AND FORFEITURE

The use of various civil and criminal asset seizure programs has increased markedly in recent years. The categories of forfeitable property have expanded steadily since the 1970s, well beyond mere contraband and the instrumentalities directly used in drug distribution. Current seizure efforts have, however, failed to produce an increase in the retail price of drugs. The value of assets seized simply pales in comparison to the potential profits to be made in the massive drug market.

The current federal Asset Forfeiture Program directs federal authorities to share the proceeds from seized property with local and state law enforcement agencies. The local agencies then use their discretion in allocating the funds. Although the federal government must not trample local priorities and discretion, a greater federal presence can help coordinate local and state efforts to provide more effective prevention and enforcement programs.

The federal government might also legitimately retain more control over the money distributed to states and cities in exchange for increasing the amount shared. (Of the approximately $11.8 million in assets seized by the DEA between 1984 and 1987, about $800,000 was distributed to local authorities with an additional $700,000 pending.) Furthermore, while the program appears to enjoy wide popular support, some serious complaints have been raised about bureaucratic delays encountered by localities waiting to receive the promised revenue. While the Department of Justice has ordered faster distribution, huge delays still exist. One reasonable suggestion is to authorize local United States Attorneys to make the distributions, thus eliminating the current requirement that all state requests be made through the Justice Department in Washington.

MONEY LAUNDERING

The ability of prosecutors to trace accurately the flow of money derived from illegal drugs is important both for establishing the basis of a criminal prosecution and for seizing the offender's drug-related assets. Money laundering, in all its varied forms, is the drug dealer's obvious solution for avoiding detection.

The Bank Secrecy Act (BSA), enacted in 1970, is the federal government's primary anti-money laundering weapon. The BSA and subsequent enactments are meant to generate a paper trail that will facilitate the tracing of criminally based cash flows. A relatively sophisticated drug trafficker, however, has little trouble evading the law. Banks, for example, are only required to report currency transactions in excess of $10,000. A drug dealer can, therefore, simply keep numerous individual deposits below that amount. The BSA also exempts from coverage organizations that do a large cash business, permitting the drug dealer to launder his money through such entities. Banks are not required to report wire transfers with foreign banks or interbank transfers within the United States, thus opening further windows of opportunity for the resourceful drug dealer.

A major problem with closing these apparent "loopholes" in the BSA is that to do so would result in an informational overkill — with the possible result that certain suspicious transactions would get lost in the piles of paperwork. It may well be, therefore, that the most effective solution lies in the coordination of BSA efforts with other enforcement tools, such as RICO, conspiracy and wiretap laws. Within the framework of the BSA itself, however, substantial fines should be imposed on banks that fail to make accurate and timely reports under the existing money laundering laws.

Because the most direct route to BSA avoidance is the depositing of drug profits in foreign accounts, money laundering enforcement cannot be effective without some increased measure of international cooperation. The United States must demand investigative access to financial documents that relate to identified drug enterprises. Such efforts must focus on countries with traditionally strict bank secrecy laws and should make use of such "incentives" as the denial of landing rights and the withholding of U.S. foreign aid.

IRS INVOLVEMENT

The problem with current attempts to involve the IRS in the war against drugs appears to be one of underutilization rather than fundamental defects in existing tax enforcement laws. Prosecution for tax evasion has been successfully implemented against major career criminals and is certainly available for use against drug traffickers. It has been suggested that the primary problem is the IRS's reluctance to act as a criminal law enforcement agency. A new administration must be committed to reorganizing agency priorities. Increased cooperation between the IRS and other relevant agencies should also be encouraged. As a starting point, any conviction for drug-related offenses should automatically trigger an IRS investigation.

FEDERAL BENEFITS

Various schemes denying drug offenders the federal benefits to which they might otherwise be entitled have recently become quite popular. As already discussed, some elected officials have suggested cutting off the rights of convicted drug offenders to benefits such as VA and FHA loans and the right to practice before federal courts or federal agencies. A 1988 presidential task force has suggested that federal student aid funds be denied to offenders and to schools failing to implement appropriate anti-drug programs.

That such programs would serve as a deterrent seems a dubious proposition at best. Their desirability as additional punishment is also questionable. Why keep a drug offender who has served a criminal sentence from getting an education? How does it help society to withhold the opportunity for drug offenders to earn a living outside of the drug industry? Options should instead be developed that would open rather than shut avenues toward rehabilitation. One possibility would be the development of a WPA-style employment program funded by the federal government, perhaps in partnership with the private sector, which would give an individual the opportunity to be relocated far from his or her former drug environment.

There is, however, room for the development of innovative asset seizure and benefit denial programs that do in fact help win battles in the war against drugs. New York has recently implemented a particularly innovative program aimed at "seizing" the leasehold rights of drug users and dealers. Manhattan District Attorney Robert Morgenthau has directed his staff to order landlords to evict tenants from rental units where police have turned up narcotics. If the landlord fails to act within five days of the order, he can be fined $5,000 and the District Attorney's Office will take over the eviction proceeding. These actions are being brought under a 60-year-old law authorizing evictions from apartments that are being used to conduct illegal business. (The statute is popularly known as the "bawdy house law" as it was originally used against houses of prostitution.) The District Attorney's office will set aside a Narcotics Eviction Part to process these cases and a housing or civil court judge will be reassigned to the courtroom.

These are not, of course, ordinary landlord-tenant disputes. The denial of specific housing is not an arbitrary stab in the dark at the drug problem but rather a measure specifically targeted at drug use and dealing. The eviction program is an extraordinary measure taken in response to an extraordinary situation and might well be expanded to encompass federally-supported housing.*

---

* The 1988 anti-drug bill has embraced this concept, terminating the tenancy of public-housing tenants who are convicted of drug-related

V. CONCLUSION — A WORD OF CAUTION

Many of the "solutions" recently put forth by members of both parties are justly criticized as headline-grabbing measures with little likelihood of having a serious impact on the drug problem. Peter Reuter, the Rand Corporation's chief economist, has commented that "the 'war on drugs' imagery is quite dangerous. It leaves the notion that there is such a thing as victory.... [The problem should be] treated...more as a chronic social problem."[10]

A particularly persistent criticism has been that even a large increase in the number of arrests and asset seizures will not begin to make a real dent in drug usage or drug dealing and that our best hope lies with long-term education and prevention. There is, of course, a great deal of merit to this argument, particularly when one candidly assesses the scope of the problems confronting our law enforcement authorities. But emphasizing drug treatment and prevention — the social service priorities in the struggle against drug abuse — does not mean that law enforcement proposals should be shelved. Rather than the false dichotomy of either/or, a comprehensive drug abuse program must seek the dual goals of both law enforcement initiatives and social service programs. Above all else, we must be realistic in our expectations. If, for example, toughening asset forfeiture provisions fails to have an impact on drug use, the funds seized could still be used to promote long-term public awareness and education as to the dangers of drug abuse.

It is essential to acknowledge that these "modest proposals" are not "the answer" to the drug problem; they are, instead, a rational experiment designed to be used on a model, limited basis. The "drug emergency area" proposal, for example, should be instituted on a trial basis in one jurisdiction, such as southern Florida or northern New England. If the program does not prove successful, that failure should be acknowledged, the lesson learned and new approaches tried. The threat on drug abuse demands no less.

NOTES

1 Polich, *et al., Strategies for Controlling Adolescent Drug Use,* Rand Report, February 1984, p.75; Reuter, *et al.,* "Risks and Prices: An Economic Analysis of Drug Enforcement," 338 *Crime and Justice: An Annual Review of Research* 289 (1986).

---

crimes. How effectively this program will be enforced remains to be seen.

[2] Rand Report, p.60. If drug seizures doubled, prices would increase an estimated five percent. In the case of marijuana, that would be the equivalent of nine cents per cigarette.

[3] Reuter, p.326. From an economic standpoint, someone will always want to supply the drug market. To that extent, new market suppliers will spring up as fast as other ones are arrested. See also Dombrink and Meeker, "Beyond 'Buy and Bust': Nontraditional Sanctions in Federal Drug Law Enforcement," *Contemporary Drug Problems* 711, 715 (1986).

[4] "Epidemic," a concept paper by the Democratic Substance Abuse Working Group, June 29, 1988, p.10. The Administration's funding request for street level enforcement, $230 million, represents 5% of the total budget request.

[5] Rand Report, p.59.

[6] See U.S. Department of Justice, Bureau of Statistics, "Felony Outcomes in 18 Felony Courts," 1985 at v. (The use of jail in felony sentencing varied from 1 percent of sentences in Harris County, Texas, to 57 percent of sentences in King County, Washington. There were also substantial differences in average terms and rates of imprisonment. For example, only 2 percent of drug traffickers were sentenced to prison in Hennipen County, Minnesota, whereas 50 percent were sentenced in Dade County, Florida. *Ibid*, p.13.)

[7] Crime and Justice Annual Report, Division of Criminal Justice Services, New York State, 1986, p.165.

[8] John Pekkanen, "Drug Law Enforcement Effects," *The Facts About Drug Abuse*, Drug Abuse Counsel, 1980, pp. 89-90.

[9] Kleiman, "Bringing Back Street-Level Heroin Enforcement," Program in Criminal Justice Policy and Management, JFK School of Government, November 14, 1986, p.28.

[10] "Reluctant Recruit in the War on Drugs," *National Journal*, p.1810, June 18, 1988.

ANTITRUST LAW ENFORCEMENT:
Antitrust Division

Harry First & Eleanor Fox*

SUMMARY OF RECOMMENDATIONS

The 41st president and 101st Congress must resuscitate antitrust.

Minimalist antitrust enforcement, especially in the area of mergers, is the legacy of the Reagan Administration. Not only have there been few actual challenges to mergers, but lax enforcement policy has also emboldened business firms to propose mergers of a size which would not have been entertained seriously a decade ago. These mergers will adversely affect our economy in many areas, from airlines to supermarkets, from the oil industry to computers.

Reagan antitrust enforcers have also refused to enforce the law which prohibits resale price-fixing, thereby increasing the prices that consumers must pay. Although vigorously prosecuting small-scale bid rigging conspiracies, Reagan antitrust enforcers have not looked for illegal cartel behavior in major industries or for foreign cartels seeking to dominate United States markets.

It will not be enough, however, simply to revive antitrust. Antitrust enforcement in the next administration must recognize the impact of foreign competition and trade policy. Antitrust must be coordinated with trade policy to assist strategic industries while still maintaining the spur to innovation that only competition can provide.

Specific proposals recommended to the 41st president and Congress include:

* Immediate revision of the current Department of Justice Merger Guidelines.

* Review of recent mergers to determine whether any have resulted in a substantial lessening of competition, thereby rendering them appropriate for court challenge.

---

* *Harry First is Professor of Law at New York University and co-author of* Free Enterprise and Economic Organization: Antitrust. *Eleanor Fox is Professor of Law at New York University and co-author of* Corporate Acquisitions and Mergers. *She served on the National Commission for the Review of Antitrust Law.*

* Working in coordination with the State Attorneys General, who have been increasingly active in antitrust enforcement throughout the country.
* Immediate withdrawal of the current Department of Justice Vertical Restraint Guidelines and Guidelines for International Transactions.
* Investigation and prosecution of resale price-fixing.
* Investigation and prosecution of international cartels aimed at United States markets.

I. HISTORY AND BACKGROUND

Antitrust law was born from a distrust of power. It embodies a preference for pluralism, concern for consumers and a commitment to business opportunity and market access for firms outside of the circle of power. The overarching concept that has unified these concerns over time is *competition as process* — the idea that competition, not private or government power, should control markets.

The principal antitrust laws are the Sherman Act and the Clayton Act; the Justice Department is charged with enforcement of both of them. Section 1 of the Sherman Act prohibits contracts, combinations and conspiracies in restraint of trade. Section 2 of the Sherman Act prohibits monopolization and attempts to monopolize. The Clayton Act prohibits anticompetitive mergers (Section 7), as well as a variety of restrictive practices such as anticompetitive exclusive dealing and tying (Section 3). The Robinson-Patman Act is an amendment to the Clayton Act and prohibits certain price discrimination.

In recent years, Congress passed the Foreign Trade Antitrust Improvements Act, which limits the reach of the Sherman Act to domestic competition. A companion statute, the Export Trading Company Act of 1982, provides a procedure for obtaining limited immunity from the Sherman Act for export ventures not likely to hurt domestic competition. In 1984 Congress passed the National Cooperative Research Act, which provides limited immunity for research joint ventures filed with the Justice Department and the Federal Trade Commission.

The Assistant Attorney General in Charge of the Antitrust Division normally sets policy, brings appropriate cases and advocates competition policy before administrative agencies and elsewhere. The Division coordinates with the Federal Trade Commission in areas of overlapping jurisdiction, including merger enforcement. The Department of Justice and the FTC review large mergers under the

Hart-Scott-Rodino review procedures.* On request from private parties, the Department issues business review letters, which may express an intent not to challenge a given course of conduct. The Department sometimes issues guidelines stating its own enforcement policy in certain fields, such as mergers and international operations.

While the vigor of antitrust enforcement has been cyclical, prior to the Reagan Administration the Division normally took its law enforcement responsibilities seriously. It has virtually always paid close attention to consumers' interests, and has sought to protect the competition process for the benefit of consumers by challenging power-enhancing mergers, resale price maintenance, anticompetitive combinations and various acts of monopolization. The Division has been a staunch advocate of deregulation of markets. Partially as a result, much deregulation was set into motion by the end of the Carter years, with the understanding that antitrust authorities would then police the newly deregulated markets.

Unfortunately, in the 1980s, antitrust enforcement nearly disappeared. When Ronald Reagan ran for President in 1980, he promised to get government off the back of business. He identified government as the culprit that had destroyed American business supremacy. Since antitrust was a restraint on unbridled business discretion, it therefore became a candidate for near extinction.

Reagan appointed William F. Baxter III as his first Assistant Attorney General in Charge of Antitrust. A self-styled economist, Baxter's number one priority for the nation was "maximizing allocative efficiency," which he believed he could do by the application of theoretical economic models. He, like others associated with the "Chicago School" of economics, posited certain extreme assumptions before applying his models. One was that efficiency is the goal of the law and that businesses virtually always act efficiently — presto, there was little need for antitrust. The one exception (or perhaps a concession to existing law) was clear price-fixing cartels.

The Reagan Administration's pattern of antitrust enforcement has dutifully followed the Chicago School model. Baxter and his successors have spent most of their professional time prosecuting highway contractors for bid-rigging. The Reagan Justice Department does not bring monopoly cases. It will not bring a resale price maintenance case because it believes that resale price maintenance, if used, must be good for consumers. Also, because the Administration regards

---

* The Hart-Scott Rodino Antitrust Improvements Act of 1976 requires parties planning a merger to file and wait if, in general, one party to the transaction has assets or net sales of $100 million or more and the other has assets or net sales of $10 million or more.

mergers as efficient, it seldom brings a merger case. The result of a policy that encourages mega-mergers has not, of course, been a more efficient economy but a dramatically restructured economy of ever-larger corporations. Takeover strategies, not productive strategies, have become the focus of managerial attention.

A brief recitation of facts surrounding the 1980s merger wave illustrates the effects of the sea-change in merger enforcement ushered in by the Reagan Administration: In 1982, the year the Reagan Administration introduced its own Merger Guidelines, the total value of mergers and acquisitions was $53.8 billion; in 1986 it was $176.6 billion. In 1982 there were six deals in excess of $1 billion; in 1986 there were thirty-six. We have seen huge consolidations in the oil industry (for example, GE-RCA for $6.28 billion and Sperry-Burroughs for $4.4 billion); in retailing (the 1988 takeover of Federated Department Stores by Campeau for $6.6 billion, plus $200 million in fees for the investment bankers and lawyers); and in food products (for example, Philip Morris' acquisition of General Foods for $5.75 billion and R.J. Reynolds acquisition of Nabisco for $4.9 billion). And we have witnessed large acquisitions by foreign firms that would prefer to buy U.S. firms than to compete with them (for example, Bridgestone's acquisition of Firestone for $2.6 billion and Sony's acquisition of CBS Records for more than $2 billion).

No opposition to these mega-mergers has come from the Reagan Administration. In fact, out of 2254 mergers notified to the federal government in 1987, the Justice Department filed six cases (the FTC filed only eight more). In other words, the federal government challenged only 0.62% of all 1987 mergers notified. Indeed, this was the *highest* percentage of cases challenged since 1982, when the government challenged 1.4% of all mergers notified.

Perhaps nowhere is the effect of non-enforcement of the law so stark as in the recently deregulated airline industry. As a result of Justice Department policy combined with Transportation Department policy, we have seen a dramatic consolidation of the airline industry, with no successful new entry. Texas Air, owner of Continental and New York Air, acquired Eastern. Then it acquired People Express, competitor of New York Air and Eastern. Delta acquired Western. United acquired Frontier. Northwest acquired Republic and TWA acquired Ozark (with the blessing of the Department of Transportation despite objection from the Department of Justice).

The result: air fares began to move upwards while government officials expressed amazement; how could they have known? On non-enforcement fronts, in contrast, the Antitrust Division has been actively at work. The Antitrust Division had a long, venerable history of filing *amicus* briefs on behalf of antitrust plaintiffs seeking to enforce the law, but Reagan's Antitrust Division filed *amicus* briefs on behalf of *defendants* trying to cut back the law. It filed briefs with the Supreme Court to abolish the "per se" rule against resale price maintenance and to jettison private merger suits. It has issued guidelines to facilitate mergers and vertical (distribution) restraints.

Even while rhetorically decrying "too much government," the Administration has an arrogance and acquisitiveness about federal executive power. Its contempt for private attorneys general — and even state attorneys general enforcing federal law — is a reflection and extension of the Borkian view of the all-powerful Executive: if the people don't like the policies of the Executive they can elect another administration. Administration officials are tying to sabotage private actions (in antitrust and civil rights as well). They argue that a competitor has the incentive to challenge a merger only if the merger is efficient and not if it is price-raising, and therefore competitors should lack standing to sue. While competitor/plaintiffs are "discredited" as seeking private rather than public gain, so too are state attorneys general who enter the breach of federal non-enforcement. State AGs are denigrated as seeking private political ends.

II. NEW PRIORITIES AND INITIATIVES

The priorities and initiatives of a new administration must take account of the Reagan Administration retrenchment — and begin an antitrust resuscitation.

First, we need a visible antitrust policy for the benefit of consumers, businesspeople and the U.S. economy. To do so, we need to reset the terms of antitrust in form and substance, in ways we describe below.

Second, we need carefully chosen industrial strategies to ensure a sound infrastructure, especially in areas of high-technology world competition. The new administration should integrate antitrust and trade policy with an eye on both long-term consumer benefits and strong American business.

In short, initiatives should be taken in connection with mergers, monopolization, agreements among competitors, vertical restraints, transnational restraints and industrial strategies.

MERGERS

The most pressing need is sound merger policy. The following actions should be taken:

1. Merger Guidelines: Virtually the first act of a new administration should be to announce that the Merger Guidelines will be revised. Pending a complete review of the Guidelines, the new administration should announce that it will *at least* enforce the market concentration levels specified in the current Guidelines (it is well known that the Reagan Administration now uses "shadow guidelines" which are even less restrictive than the published version), and that it will not generally include within the definition of a "market" firms that are not currently producing and selling within that market. (The current Guidelines include within markets firms that might enter two years hence.) This announcement should also state that the new administration will no longer indulge a presumption that most mergers "are either competitively beneficial or neutral."

2. **Reviewing past mergers:** Under *United States v. du Pont* (353 U.S. 586 (1957)), the government may challenge a merger if anticompetitive effects can be shown at the time of suit, even if the merger occurred years before. This case gives the government authority to review the legacy of Reagan Administration non-enforcement and to correct the most egregious failures of antitrust policy. A task force should be established to select appropriate cases for litigation. Widespread divestitures would probably be costly, but there may be industries in which competition could efficiently be restored. One obvious target is the airline industry.

3. **Merger doctrine:** A new government must alter several merger doctrines that the current Administration is applying. Some examples are: defining markets realistically; taking account of (rather than assuming away) barriers to entry and effective competition; widening the net of concern from a minimal focus on power over price to a dynamic focus, including the effects of mergers on innovation and consumer choice; developing realistic approaches to analyzing acquisitions by foreign firms, with particular focus on market definitions for international competition; and taking a closer look at the strategic implications of non-horizontal mergers (a type of merger ignored by the current Administration).

4. **State enforcement:** The new administration should announce that it will no longer view the states as adversaries in merger enforcement, but as partners. It should meet with representatives from the National Association of Attorneys General to work out a cooperative program of merger enforcement in which state views can be heard and government resources can be effectively extended.

5. **Hart-Scott-Rodino Antitrust Improvements Act:** Tremendous government and private resources are now devoted to preparing and reviewing merger notifications filed pursuant to the Hart-Scott-Rodino Act. It is time to assess the utility of this allocation of resources. This statute, however well-intentioned, may serve principally to divert resources from enforcement to paperwork.

MONOPOLIZATION

While monopolization cases are not expected to be common, the new administration should examine potential cases with more understanding of the strategic uses and abuses of power. The Baxter-Bork view notwithstanding, monopolization *is* possible and can happen. For example, high technology companies astride two or more markets can manipulate markets and suppress competition. As high technology flourishes and single firm dominance in bottleneck markets becomes more likely (as might predictably occur in data/communications networking of the future), antitrust enforcement must develop and apply principles of fair and reasonable access.

CARTELS AND OTHER HORIZONTAL AGREEMENTS

The new administration should continue and expand the Reagan Administration's strong enforcement policy against bid-rigging and price-fixing — the one bright spot of current enforcement. As with merger enforcement, however, the new Antitrust Division should seek to use the resources of the State Attorneys General. Much of the collusive behavior prosecuted by the federal government has involved rather small-scale conspiracies with local effects. Where possible, these could be prosecuted by the states, leaving more widespread cartel behavior (in the defense contracting industry, for example) to the federal government.

Although the current Administration has been vigorous in prosecuting cartels, it has also been narrow. In this decade of lax antitrust enforcement, major industries have become bolder in engaging in cartel behavior with respect to price and territories. Two target areas are the most promising.

The first is the area of international cartels. When Thurman Arnold headed the Antitrust Division in the late 1930s following a period of antitrust disfavor, he filed 52 suits against international cartels involving 165 firms. The need to pursue international cartels is even more urgent today. Foreign firms should not be able to use collusive behavior to force United States firms from the market. To be certain that this does not occur, an interagency task force should be established to permit the Justice Department to coordinate its investigative efforts with agencies that are involved in trade policy and that are most aware of foreign firm conduct.

The second area is industries that have recently undergone deregulation. For example, over the past several years there have been numerous newspaper accounts of parallel pricing behavior in the airline industry, yet there has apparently been little investigation into whether overt collusive behavior is occurring with more than usual frequency. It would not be surprising to find such behavior where an industry is a newcomer to the rules of appropriate behavior in competitive markets.

Finally, more attention must be paid to the anticompetitive potential of joint ventures. This is particularly the case where the joint

venture involves major industrial firms that have the capital resources to engage in the venture individually. If, for example, AT&T
wishes to work with IBM to advance the state of the art in
data/communications, the red flags should rise.

VERTICAL RESTRAINTS

The Reagan Administration has discontinued antitrust scrutiny of
restraints imposed between levels of the distribution system. This
includes resale price agreements, customer and territorial agreements
and tying and exclusive dealing agreements. The Justice Department's enforcement policy is embodied in its Vertical Restraint
Guidelines (which technically do not apply to resale price-fixing).

The next administration should, first, withdraw the current
Guidelines and, second, announce its intention to pursue cases of resale
price-fixing. The policy should be a return to the law, under which
resale price-fixing is *per se* unlawful, and other vertical restraints are
unlawful if unreasonable.

An aggressive policy of pursuing resale price-fixing would be particularly helpful to consumers. For example, the State Attorneys
Generals were able to secure a $4.5 million refund for approximately
300,000 consumers in nearly 40 states for fixing the resale price of a
popular camera. Surely the federal government could find more such
cases. In addition, based on developments in the past several years,
manufacturers can now terminate discounting retailers with virtual
impunity. Courts have permitted such terminations even after a full-
price retailer pressured a manufacturer to cut off an exemplary discounting competitor. (See *Garment District, Inc. v. Belk Stores Services,
Inc.,* 799 F.2d 905 (1986), *cert. denied,* 108 S. Ct. 1728 (1988).) A new
Justice Department should turn these results around, by litigation if
possible or by legislation if necessary. Thus, the new president and
attorney general should announce their support for the pending
"Retail Price Competition Act," which would make it easier to prevent discounter terminations.

Enforcement in the area of non-price vertical restraints should focus on market access. A dynamic marketplace, with entry open for
new products and products consumers prefer, is critical to our economy.
Indeed, at a time when we are arguing in favor of increased access for
our products in foreign markets, we should be certain that domestic
markets likewise remain open. Thus, exclusive dealing and tying arrangements should come under renewed scrutiny. Antitrust policy
need not assume that every such restraint is illegal; but it need not
assume legality, either.

INTERNATIONAL ANTITRUST

In its waning days the Reagan Administration has issued a new set of Guidelines for International Transactions. These Guidelines are basically a recitation of how it believes antitrust problems in general should be analyzed; the international aspect of transactions is a minor part of the document. A new administration should withdraw these Guidelines upon taking office, because the Guidelines do not reflect appropriate government enforcement policy on a wide range of doctrinal issues.

There is need for a thorough rethinking of antitrust enforcement with regard to international transactions. Of particular importance are: the question of the proper antitrust approach to "Voluntary Restraint Agreements" (VRAs), which have proved costly to the United States economy; the question whether the United States should be less deferential to foreign governments that tolerate restraints that harm United States firms or consumers; and the proper analysis of multinational joint ventures and distribution arrangements that might reduce competition between foreign and domestic firms. These issues could be developed in a new set of guidelines or through the litigation process.

ANTITRUST AND NATIONAL INDUSTRIAL STRATEGIES

The Antitrust Division of the new administration should play an affirmative role in articulating national industrial strategies, providing constructive criticism of other strategies and helping to implement any chosen methodologies. By national industrial strategies, we mean the active use of government to coordinate and assist private business decisions relating to entry, output, investment and innovation.

Strategies should focus on two phases of industrial development: distressed industries and strategic industries. Distressed industries are those industries suffering severe substantial economic losses, often on a long-term basis at the hands of foreign competitors. Strategic industries are those industries where it might be possible, through government intervention, to create economic advantage for a domestic industry that could provide important spillover benefits in the United States economy.

The Antitrust Division has two possible roles to play in this arena. The first is its role in shaping economic policy. The Antitrust Division should not take a reflexive position in favor of "free" markets in all circumstances, but should recognize that government intervention can advance national economic welfare in a way that is consistent with long-run consumer welfare. Simultaneous with shaping a national economic strategy, the Antitrust Division should be actively involved in advocating three antitrust insights:

* Industrial strategy should be government policy. If the government seeks to alter marketplace outcomes, the government should then actively supervise the industry to be certain that public gains are achieved.

* The ultimate goal of national industrial strategy should be the creation of industries that can stand the test of the market.

* Executors of industrial strategy should pay attention to the structure of interfirm relationships. They should be vigilant to prevent cooperation from degenerating into collusion.

The second role for the Antitrust Division is to effectuate an appropriate accommodation of antitrust and industrial strategies, through specific legislative or enforcement activities. With regard to legislation, the Antitrust Division should be guided by the principles expressed above, seeking change that is least likely to alter market structures permanently. For example, the administration should not support legislation exempting mergers in distressed industries (such as the Reagan Administration proposed), which would facilitate permanent structural alteration. In a crisis, tailored legislation creating short-term distressed industry cartels closely supervised by government would entail lower risks. With regard to enforcement, the next Antitrust Division should resist *ad hoc* changes in its approach to antitrust law based on pleas of competitive distress. Legislative solutions are preferable to selective non-enforcement decisions because they can require continuing government supervision under carefully considered circumstances.

III. FUNDING

In 1981 the Antitrust Division had 939 authorized positions. The fiscal year 1989 budget projects 549 positions, a drop of nearly 40% over the course of the Reagan Administration. This reduction in staffing is, of course, consistent with the Reagan Administration's views with regard to antitrust enforcement. At a time when the Administration believed very little in enforcement beyond criminal price-fixing cases, it would have been hard to justify requests for increased expenditures.

Congress must provide a new Division with additional resources if it is to carry out the program outlined above, just as the Antitrust Division's resources were increased in the 1970s to deal with the structural competitive problems of that time. The amount of increase cannot be accurately determined at this point, but two aspects of increased antitrust enforcement should be noted for their lack of budgetary impact. First, if the new Justice Department is able to work in effective partnership with State Attorneys General, those offices can help share the burden of increased antitrust enforcement. Second, the next Justice Department should reverse the current Administration's position of hostility to private actions. As has traditionally been recognized, parties injured by antitrust violations — "private attorneys general" — were intended by Congress to assist in the enforcement of the antitrust laws. By seeking to reestablish enforcement of the law as a priority, the new trust-busters can encourage private litigants to carry out their intended role in antitrust law enforcement.

JUDICIAL SELECTIONS:
Department of Justice

SUMMARY OF RECOMMENDATIONS

Judicial selections represent a major challenge both to a president's political skills and to his statesmanship. In the immediate political environment, judicial nominations that fail to win confirmation are not merely inefficient but are, in fact, damaging to a president's credibility and therefore to his ability to achieve his policy goals. And when they win confirmation, judicial nominations exert a major influence over our national life, for better or for worse, that extends far beyond the term of any administration.

Deciding how to handle judicial selections must consequently be among the first and highest priorities of the next president. He must be clear in his own mind about the role such selections will play in advancing his policy goals, with a due regard both for the politics of the moment and for the long-term national interest.

While Reagan used litmus tests to appoint conservatives to the bench, Presidents Kennedy and Johnson undermined their own policies by appointing anti-civil rights nominees to the bench in the South. The next president must strike a balance between these two extremes. He must develop appropriate, specific criteria for choosing his nominees, and establish a clear-cut chain of responsibility for recommending nominations. He must also decide how and when outside organizations are to be consulted in the course of choosing nominees. And finally, he should pursue an early understanding with the Senate and the Senate Judiciary Committee on how he will seek both the Senate's advice and its consent to his nominations. There should be no ambiguity about any of these considerations, and none of them should be deferred.

I. POLICY GOALS

The role of judicial nominations in the pursuit of legal and social policy has varied widely through past administrations. Some presi-

---

* *Mark Gitenstein is chief counsel of the Senate Judiciary Committee.*

dents — Eisenhower and Ford come to mind — made no discernable effort to advance any particular legal agenda by the selection of judicial nominees. Others, like Kennedy and to a certain extent Johnson, tended to defer almost exclusively to senators in the selection of district judges. As a result, they often nominated judges who frustrated their policy goals, especially as those goals related to civil rights.

Conservatives believe that past Republican administrations made a serious mistake in focusing more on a candidate's reputation and standing rather than their legal and policy views. As Bruce Fein, a former Reagan Justice Department official, put it, "A president who fails to scrutinize the legal philosophy of federal judicial nominees courts frustration of his own policy agenda." The Reagan Administration made no secret of its determination to avoid that mistake. Probably no administration in our history has engaged in as single-minded an effort to use judicial nominations to implement its policy goals as has the Reagan Administration.

At least this Administration has been candid about its agenda with respect to the courts: it has been engaged in a deliberate effort to stack the courts with conservatives who share the Reagan agenda, especially his social agenda. It has been equally candid about its intention to "lock in" its policy goals with its judicial nominations. Former Attorney General Edwin Meese stated frankly that the Reagan Administration aimed to "institutionalize the Reagan revolution so it can't be set aside no matter what happens in future presidential elections."

This Reagan legacy on judicial nominations will present the new president with a dilemma: should he correct the imbalance that has been created in the courts or should he preserve the agenda and the process of his predecessor?

Judicial nominations should neither overemphasize nor ignore the judicial philosophies of the nominees. President Reagan's litmus-test approach, his single-minded emphasis on nominees with a reliably conservative perspective on legal and social policy, however, threatens to interrupt the philosophical evolution of our jurisprudence, and in so doing to deprive our courts of the confidence of the American people on which they ultimately depend. And we don't have to speculate about what happens when the courts send contradictory signals. Presidents Kennedy and Johnson sowed similar confusion and inflicted similar damage on the credibility of the courts by overlooking the policy consequences of choosing anti-civil rights nominees to the federal bench in the South. The next president should aim at some happy medium between these two extremes.

Certainly, a president should pay attention to the philosophical balance of the courts in selecting nominees, with a view to maintaining and, if necessary, redressing that balance. To ignore that consideration would be to risk the credibility that is the courts' greatest single source of strength. But a president who suspects that a nominee has been proposed solely on the basis of judicial philosophy should not proceed with that nomination, or risk undermining his own credibility as well as his ability to pursue his own policy goals.

If there is any clear lesson to be drawn from the bloody nomination fights we have endured over the past six years, it is that any nomination made for purely ideological reasons will provoke a fierce reaction in the Senate. That's what happened with the Daniel Manion nomination, which was confirmed in 1986 by one vote; the Bernard Siegan nomination, which was recently defeated; and, most emphatically of all, with the nomination of Robert Bork.

Consider the background to the Bork nomination. A new national administration arrives in Washington with a bold determination to overturn, in one way or another, a host of constitutional precedents. They turn first to the Supreme Court in an attempt to reverse landmark decisions of recent years, but the Court refuses. They then try to secure Constitutional amendments from Congress, but Congress refuses. All else having failed, the President seeks to achieve through nominations to the Supreme Court what he was unable to obtain by legislation or litigation.

The Court arrives at a precarious balance that pivots around Justice Lewis Powell. Then, to the surprise of everyone, Justice Powell resigns, and the President sees an opportunity to achieve a majority on the Court which will support his political agenda. Leaving no doubt as to his intention, he nominates Robert Bork, who as a legal scholar and judge has for years espoused a radical judicial philosophy directly and openly at odds with the very precedents that Justice Powell has voted to uphold.

The meaning of the Bork nomination was clear; as *The New York Times* observed: "Judge Bork's extensive record as a lawyer, teacher, government official and member of the court of appeals strongly suggests that he would change the court's delicate balance."

Although Robert Bork was clearly nominated precisely because of his controversial judicial philosophy, the White House promptly adopted a vigorous public-relations campaign to paint him as a moderate rather than an extremist. As part of that effort to obscure the sharply featured and well-documented outline of Judge Bork's judicial thought, the White House circulated to Congress and the press a briefing book intended to demonstrate that Judge Bork, in fact, was a moderate on social issues, civil rights and civil liberties.

But both the Congress and the American people knew better, and the Senate had no choice but to consider the consequences, for the Court and for the country, of Robert Bork's judicial philosophy.

Ultimately, after Judiciary Committee hearings which *The New York Times* characterized as "the deepest exploration of fundamental constitutional issues ever to capture the public limelight," the Senate rejected the Bork nomination by an unprecedented margin, 58-42. It was no doubt a painful and frustrating experience for Judge Bork, but the most unfortunate consequence of that nomination was the significant damage it inflicted on the credibility of both the President and his judicial selection process.

II. CRITERIA OF THE SELECTION PROCESS

What, then, are the appropriate criteria for a president to apply in selecting judicial nominees? The first quality to seek in a judge is proper judicial temperament — open-mindedness and a willingness to review each case on its own merits, with due regard for precedent and without any ideological predisposition. Perhaps the most important trait is the capacity for *detachment*. Without it, the other qualities we seek in a judge are meaningless, as Judge Learned Hand reminds us with his customary eloquence: "[A judge] must approach his problems with as little preconception of what should be the outcome as it is given to men to have; in short, the prime condition of his success will be his capacity for detachment."

The next president should also take into account other important criteria the Senate has traditionally — and properly — applied to judicial nominations:

1. Does the nominee have that intellectual capacity, competence and temperament to be a Supreme Court Justice?

2. Is the nominee of good moral character and free of conflict of interest?

3. Is the nominee a person of acknowledged and proven integrity who will interpret the Constitution consistently in the light of a long judicial tradition that has translated its magnificent generalities into practical laws of the land?

These criteria of personal and intellectual integrity — of a standard of judgment that navigates consistently within the broad but well-defined channels in the mainstream of our judicial nominations — are to serve the permanent national interest as well as his own more immediate policy interests. The question of integrity is, moreover, the threshold question for the Senate, and the first to lead to a rejection if the answer is perceived to be wrong.

Who in the administration will discover these demigods? Here again there are as many models as there have been presidents. Any model is a truly personal decision of the president, but it depends in large part on how the president staffs his administration.

President Franklin Roosevelt wanted to be personally involved in judicial selection, and his Justice Department was not very happy about it, as FDR's Solicitor General, Francis Biddle, made clear in a letter to Attorney General Robert Jackson: "[This] should not be [the President's] practice, and I cannot help feeling that he doesn't realize the immense importance to his whole program of these federal judges." President Eisenhower, on the other hand, true to the military tradition in which he rose to supreme command in World War II, delegated the function of selecting nominees completely to his Attorney General, Herbert Brownell.

President Reagan, in his usual style, has been almost totally detached from the selection process. A review of the last eight years makes it clear that the locus of judicial selection has been wherever Ed Meese has been serving. When Meese was White House Counsel, the decisions were made there; when he became Attorney General, the Justice Department assumed the dominant role.

A word of caution is in order here: the more the judicial selection process seems to reside in the White House, and especially in the hands of White House staff, the more political it appears — and the more difficulty the nominee is likely to encounter in a Senate which is increasingly and legitimately concerned about the politicization of the judiciary. Ideally, the initial selection should rest in the Justice Department, with the White House, through the Counsel's office, reviewing selections before a final presidential decision.

Another, more practical warning is also implicit in the demanding criteria judicial nominees must meet: by the time a judicial nomination is sent to the Senate, there should be no surprises lurking ahead for the president, as there was, for example, in the Douglas Ginsberg nomination. The fullest possible inquiries should be made by the Justice Department and the FBI, and their findings, as well as the recommendations of competent outside groups like the American Bar Association (ABA), should be carefully reviewed before any nomination is made — because the Senate Judiciary Committee has made it clear that it will conduct exhaustive inquiries and reviews of its own.

III. CONSULTATION WITH OUTSIDE GROUPS

No matter who identifies and selects judicial nominations within the administration, there will be, and should be, consultation with outside organizations. Such consultations make political sense, if for no other reason than to find out how a particular nominee is likely to fare with certain influential groups, but there are even more fundamental reasons. Local chapters of civil rights organizations, for example, know whether a particular lawyer has some appreciation of civil rights issues. The customs bar can advise a president whether a member of the International Trade Commission has competently administered the trade laws and deserves promotion to a federal judgeship.

Over the last 40 years, the ABA has had the predominant outside consultative role. That role should continue. Indeed, the ABA should be involved as early as the administration feels comfortable with its inclusion. The value of its assessment is, in the first place, that the ABA is the organization most likely to render a disinterested and nonpartisan *professional* judgment. Moreover, the ABA procedure for evaluation avoids stalemate by not insisting on a consensus, and its rating system — ranging from "Exceptionally Well Qualified" through "Well Qualified" to "Not Qualified" — tends to improve the odds for endorsing the president's choice.

But even the ABA's relationship to the judicial selection process has ebbed and flowed. In the Eisenhower Administration, it had unparalleled influence. In the Reagan Administration, the ABA's influence has waned, in part, no doubt, because it has not always conferred its professional blessing on those whose primary credential was their conservative ideology. By the same token, other outside groups which had significant input into Carter Administration selections — women's groups, civil rights groups, *et al.* — have been completely cut out of the process by the current Administration.

As a general proposition, all of these groups — the ABA, the National Bar Association and outside groups on both the Left and Right — ought to have a channel into the selection process, as a matter of common courtesy and common sense. But none of these groups, including the ABA, should hold a veto over nominees. To the extent that any nominee seems to be the candidate of a particular group, the appearance of open-mindedness and detachment is certainly undermined. That will jeopardize not only the nominee's independence but perhaps the nomination itself, in a Senate that is becoming more and more jealous of its prerogatives under the advice-and-consent clause of the Constitution.

IV. ROLE OF THE SENATE

What role should the Senate play in the selection of or consultations about the nomination of federal judges and justices? This is an important question for the next president and Senate.

When the president takes the oath of office next January, he will face something no modern president before Ronald Reagan has had to face: a Senate which takes its "advice and consent" function *very* seriously. With respect to Supreme Court nominations and to district and appeals court nominations as well, the Senate not only intends to exercise its "consent" role aggressively but also expects to be asked its "advice."

Such an advice and consent role is consistent with that contemplated by the Framers. The repeated considerations of the Constitutional Convention concerning the judiciary make it clear that the delegates intended the Senate to play a broad role in the appointment of judges.

The delegates' first conclusion, in fact — when they adopted what was known as the "Virginia Plan" as a working paper at the outset of the Convention — was to lodge exclusive control over the judicial selection process with Congress and to leave no role for the President at all. As the debates proceeded, there were proposals, each rejected after further consideration, to entrust the selection of judges exclusively, first to the president, then to the Senate, then again to the president. Next, a compromise was proposed to provide for appointment by the Executive "by and with the advice and consent" of the Senate, but that proposal failed on a tie vote.

All told, there were four different attempts to include the president in the selection process, and four times he was excluded. In the closing days of the Convention, the draft left the appointment of "judges of the Supreme Court" still in the hands of the Senate, but finally, on September 4, 1787, the Special Committee on Postponed Matters reported the advice-and-consent compromise, which the Convention adopted unanimously.

It is difficult to imagine that after four attempts to exclude the president from the selection process, the Framers intended anything less than the broadest role for the Senate. Even Alexander Hamilton, the great champion of a strong executive, declared in *Federalist* 77 that "If by influencing the President, be meant *restraining* him, this is precisely what must have been intended." In dividing responsibility for the appointment of judges, the Framers intended to prevent the president from encroaching upon the integrity and the independence of the courts. That is why the Framers finally insisted on a broad role for the Senate, and that is why it remains the Senate's constitutional obligation today.

In the 100th Congress, under the leadership of Chairman Joe Biden and Senator Pat Leahy, the Senate Judiciary Committee conducted its own investigations of judicial nominees far more thoroughly than any of its predecessors. That process, which reflected a steadfastly independent state of mind in the Senate itself, will continue.

Moreover, members of that kind of Senate will continue to insist on what they believe to be their prerogative to select nominees to district courts in their states. They will be equally aggressive in sharing in the decision on who will serve on the courts of appeals, and they are not likely to relinquish the consultative role Senator Biden has forged for them on Supreme Court nominations. When Justice Powell resigned in June, 1987, Chairman Biden insisted on consultations with the Administration on the selection of successor. The consultation on the Bork nomination failed to avert controversy, but *only* because the Administration failed to take advantage of the opportunity to do so.

Chairman Biden had sought to head off a confrontation. Invoking a convention that had not been used in decades, he suggested to Chief of Staff Howard Baker that the Senate leadership consult with the President's advisors *before* the nomination. Accompanied by Senate Majority Leader Robert Byrd, he met with Baker and Attorney General Meese. They displayed to Byrd and Biden a list of 15 names under consideration.

Chairman Biden told them that a distinguished nominee who possessed open-minded, conservative views comparable to those of Justice Powell would generate little controversy, in the Senate or in the country. He said that any one of a number of the nominees under consideration could move through the Senate in time to have nine justices sitting on the Court when it convened in October.

Judge Bork's name was on the list. In anticipation, Chairman Biden had studied the judge's many writings and decisions. As a result of the careful and detailed review, he urged that Judge Bork not be the nominee. He made it clear that the judge's controversial record would ensure an immediate confrontation with the Senate, delay the confirmation and divide the country. The Administration rejected his advice. Within 24 hours of the meeting, the President announced Judge Bork's nomination to be an Associate Justice of the Supreme Court and the confrontation began.

A similar process was undertaken with the Ginsberg and Kennedy nominations. The process failed again with the Ginsberg nomination. But the Administration finally heeded the Senate's advice on Anthony Kennedy, and his nomination was approved unanimously.

V. THE BORK NOMINATION

The Senate's action in defeating the Bork nomination was a watershed event that will affect the whole judicial selection process through the next few presidencies. Neither Bork's opponents nor his proponents will soon forget what happened and why it happened. Both are likely to view any future nominee through that lens.

That is why any nominee to the Supreme Court, or indeed to any court, who seems to have been selected for purpose of implementing some political or ideological agenda is going to provoke a serious struggle in the Senate. This is not simply a political fact of life; it is a salutary development. For it was a disastrous mistake when the Administration tried to use judical selection to implement a social agenda in the courts that it had failed to legislate in Congress.

That fundamental error brought the Reagan Administration to its greatest, and most unnecessary, constitutional confrontation with the nomination of Robert Bork. But it was a confrontation that also produced constructive consequences, because it demonstrated beyond all question that not only the United States Senate and its Committee on the Judiciary, but even more importantly the vast majority of the American people are steadfast in their belief that all Americans are born with certain inalienable rights — rights not derived from the majority, the state or the Constitution, but rights that from at least the time of the Magna Carta have been inextricably woven into the fabric of tradition from which the Constitution itself was derived. Americans believe that these rights represent the essence of human dignity.

This is how Justices Brandeis, Frankfurter, Harlan and Powell, among many others, approached the Constitution — and this is the approach on which the majority of Americans insisted in the consideration of the Bork nomination.

To a majority of the Judiciary Committee, Judge Bork's writings showed that he had long been at odds with this tradition and history, and his own testimony demonstrated clearly that he had not altered his positions to any significant degree. He left no doubt in the minds of the Senate or the public that, had his philosophy been the governing one for this country, the Supreme Court would not have served as the last bulwark for the protection of our rights when the government was unduly intruded into the realm of individual liberty. It was his fidelity to his own long-held views and his frankness before the Judiciary Committee — not the winds of controversy that swept through the media — that assured the rejection of his nomination.

The struggle over the Bork nomination came to a head when the context was a Supreme Court which stood gingerly in balance on the critical issues of the social agenda. It was an inevitable and appropriate example of the constitutional principle of separation of powers in action that the Senate should have responded to the President's thrown gauntlet to preserve the balance on the Court. That balance remains delicate and any new nomination will affect it.

The Bork precedent is a palpable and obvious warning to the next administration. Any ideological extreme — left or right — that is permitted to distort the constitutional process of judicial selection will prompt an equally strong and probably successful blocking action in the Senate.

No one in the Senate seeks or enjoys these struggles. Most members would be quite happy if they never had to vote against another judicial nominee. Should the next administration seek to turn the judiciary into its policy arm, however, it will find seasoned adversaries in the Senate. Such "warfare between the branches" is not only self-defeating but undermines the independence and integrity of the third branch over which the struggle occurs — the federal judiciary.

VI. THE PRESIDENT, THE SENATE AND THE COURTS

The appointment of federal judges and Supreme Court justices is a power shared between the president and the Senate, but when vacancies occur on the federal bench, the initiative and the major responsibility lies with the president. It is a great responsibility, but, prudently pursued, it is also a great opportunity.

No other power possessed by the president can be applied both so directly and so broadly. Except for treaties — which also require the advice and consent of the Senate — no other power possessed by the president offers equally enduring influence over the long-term achievement of his policy goals. By the will of the voters and the Constitutional two-term limit, presidents come and go; but federal judges and Supreme Court justices are appointed for life. The wisdom of a president in selecting his judicial nominations and his success in having them confirmed by the Senate clearly play a major role in determining both the success of his administration and his ultimate place in history.

Social Policy

OVERVIEW:
A New Direction For the 1990s

Stuart Eizenstat*

There is an exciting and innovative domestic policy available for the 1990s if only the political leadership is there to articulate it. Substantively sound and politically attractive, it has three components — a new social contract based on mutual responsibility, investments in people to build a more competitive America and a new federalism.

The first leg of this domestic vision should define a new social contract between the government and the people of the United States, a social compact premised on mutual responsibilities and obligations.

For too long, progressive social policy has been perceived by the public as one of "handouts and welfare dependency." Indeed, in the modern era, Democrats have been regarded as the party of government while the Republicans have been the party of the marketplace. But I believe there is a growing bipartisan consensus that our social needs require some government assistance. Government has responsibilities to remove barriers to individual opportunity, to assist the weak, to provide a helping hand to those who need assistance to enter the mainstream of American life. Government can play a constructive role by increasing the number of seats at the banquet table of America for Americans of all races, colors, creeds and religions.

What we must do, however, is stress that government's responsibilities and obligations must be matched by the obligations and responsibilities of citizens and recipients of government benefits.

Therefore, Senator Daniel Patrick Moynihan's efforts to tie Aid to Families with Dependent Children (AFDC) to job training, job search and education is appropriate. While we want to provide aid to poor mothers with young children and no means of support, this is not an end in and of itself. The ultimate goal is self-sufficiency. Welfare is not doing its job if it becomes, as it has in many instances, a way of life not just for one generation but for multiple generations. The recipients of welfare, to the extent that they are physically ca-

---

* Stuart Eizenstat is a partner in the law firm of Powell, Goldstein, Frazer & Murphy and an adjunct lecturer at the John F. Kennedy School of Government at Harvard University. He was formerly assistant to the President for domestic affairs and policy in the Carter White House.

pable of doing so, should be expected to seek work, take reasonable jobs and enter into job training and education programs so that they will not need welfare in the future. It is government's responsibility to help them make the transition, to assist them with child care, job search, education and job training. And as Congressman Tom Downey and Senator Moynihan championed, we must be sure that they are not penalized by immediately losing Medicaid and other benefits when they make the difficult transition from welfare dependency to independence.

So, too, with student aid for college education. We have a right to insist that the recipients fulfill their obligation as citizens by paying back those loans. But we can go further to suggest that they provide a period of public service in return for the assistance the government is providing them.

The same principle can apply to unemployment insurance. Rather than see this as pure income support for the unemployed, America, like West Germany, should tie a training component to unemployment insurance so that those receiving long-term (as opposed to temporary) unemployment insurance benefits are obligated to participate in education and job training programs so they can be prepared for the more complex jobs of the future.

We should also positively consider Senator Sam Nunn's proposal for voluntary service in either the military or in civilian work. There are certain obligations of citizenship. While we should not make the program mandatory, a voluntary service program, particularly one tied to the benefits Senator Nunn would provide — assistance in college or in home ownership — is a positive way of inculcating a sense of citizenship.

This principle of mutual responsibility can be applied not simply to programs involving individuals but to benefits extended to industry as well. For example, corporations seeking trade relief from the federal government should be required to provide positive adjustment plans to indicate the ways in which they will rationalize their capacity, change their management, reduce costs and otherwise become competitive so that they do not need additional import relief in the future. This is a concept which Senator Lloyd Bentsen championed in the trade bill.

The second basis for a new domestic policy involves the concept of investment — not simply investment in plant and equipment, but investment in healthier, more productive human beings. In a time of limited budget resources, our emphasis should be on investments in children. A child born in the United States is two to three times more likely to be poor than one born in most major industrial democracies with lower per-capita incomes. There are currently about 13 million poor children, some 3 million of whom are chronically poor.

Of this number, it is estimated that about half a million live in urban ghettoes. The earlier the intervention and investment, the more the likelihood that the poverty cycle can be broken. Early intervention in investment programs have real paybacks in savings. Thus, for example, it is estimated that $1 invested in prenatal care saves over $3 in the cost of later care for low-birth-weight infants. One dollar invested in pre-school education can save almost $5 in lower costs for special education, public assistance and crime.

Yet, programs such as children's immunization, Medicaid, Women, Infants and Children (WIC), Head Start, Compensatory Education and the Job Corps serve only a fraction of their eligible populations. It would cost roughly $13 billion to serve the entire target population for these programs. We should set a goal that by the year 2000, if not earlier, we will increase spending on these proven effective programs by that amount.

But our investment agenda should not be limited to low-income children.

Perhaps the principle reason for our lack of competitiveness in world markets is the poor quality of our education system, and the equally poor quality of our employment and training system. In an era of global markets where the jobs of the future will require increasingly complex skills, we must view education as a lifetime necessity. The average worker will require retraining several times during his or her career. Industry spends $30 billion on education and training of its employees, much of that to compensate for the absence of basic skills.

According to the National Center for Educational Statistics, we have an effective dropout rate of one in every four high school students — even higher among minorities. Yet, for the workplace of tomorrow fully one in every three jobs will be filled by a minority. The National Assessment of Education Progress estimated that some 13 percent of the nation's 17-year olds are functionally illiterate, or unable to read or write sufficiently to perform everyday tasks, such as reading job notices, filling out job applications, making change correctly or reading a bus schedule.

Early education programs like Head Start and Compensatory Education should receive expanded funding. And a Secretary of Education, with presidential leadership, should encourage longer school hours, emphasize a need for basic skills for all high school graduates and seek to broaden access to higher education by all those qualified for college.

Similarly, our employment and training system is a wreck. The employment service is ill-equipped to do its job; there is an inadequate amount of on-the-job training because the Job Training and Partnership Act has been underfunded by the Reagan Administration. It is time to revamp the employment service and restructure our unemployment insurance system so that it focuses more on retraining the unemployed rather than solely providing income support, including dedicating a portion of the U.S. payroll tax to pay for unemployment insurance to training; and we should adequately fund the private industry councils of the Job Training and Partnership Act.

An innovative investment agenda should also include promoting more research and development, because we can only stay competitive by staying at the cutting edge of change with new products. Since America can never hope to compete on unit labor costs or wages, we must therefore make innovative products. The key is more research and development. Yet, this Administration has starved the research budget of the federal government.

We need a permanent extension of the R&D and university basic research tax credits; increased support for the National Science Foundation in promoting joint federal-corporate research and development; support for programs like SEMITECH and encouragement for the modernization of antiquated R&D facilities and non-profit institutions where much of the basic research of the nation must be done. Investments are necessary not only in education and job training and R&D, but are also required to modernize the infrastructure upon which our economy is based — our bridges, roads and highways, as well as our harbors.

The third leg of the new direction we should take on domestic policy is the development of a new federalism dramatically different from the Reagan model. President Reagan initially proposed devolving AFDC and Food Stamps to the states while federalizing Medicaid. This made no sense from a public policy standpoint since all serve similar low-income populations. In the process, he destroyed whole groups of important federal programs.

A new federalism should attempt to better sort out state and local responsibilities. States should be called upon to assume greater responsibilities for education, infrastructure, social services and a whole range of programs where their knowledge of local conditions is critical. The federal government should assume responsibilities for programs where uniformity is necessary, such as protection of minorities and the environment, since racism and pollution do not respect state boundaries. The federal government should be increasingly seen as a catalyst and stimulant to encourage progressive state action and to provide seed money for local and voluntary initiatives. By trying to do too much, however, the federal government has done too few things well. States are better able to assume more responsibilities. They have been at the forefront of innovation in education, welfare and export promotion. They should be given greater flexibility in how they accomplish national goals. States should no longer be viewed with suspicion but, together with local governments, should be seen as important resources. We need a true federal-state-local partnership.

Perhaps the most unfortunate and lasting legacy of the Reagan era are massive federal deficits. By cutting revenues from their modern average level of about 21-1/2 percent of the gross national product to 18-1/2 to 19 percent, together with massive increases in defense spending, he has left this country with an enormous mismatch between available resources and social needs.

The Congressional Budget Office estimates that the federal deficit, without changes in policy, will decline by only $30 billion to $121 billion between Fiscal Year 1989 and 1993. Even this projection is optimistic — assuming no recession for another 5 years and zero real growth in defense spending. Yet this would mean no recession for a 10-year stretch. And maintaining defense spending at levels no greater than inflation will require the Pentagon to cut $200 billion over 5 years from its projected levels. Indeed, the deficit situation is really much worse. The growing Social Security surplus masks the magnitude of the deficit. In 1994, the surplus in the Social Security Trust Fund will be some $100 billion, meaning that the operating deficit would be about $230 billion, not $121 billion.

The Gramm-Rudman-Hollings Act requires budget balance by 1993, which means that the next President and Congress must slice the deficit by over $120 billion. Deficit reduction, not domestic investments, will be the order of the day. Cutting, not adding, will be the imperative.

There is one easy way to square this circle — to make the needed deficit reductions essential to a sound fiscal policy and at the same time to meet the needs which have grown so acute.

We clearly run the danger of an economic catastrophe if we continue to pile up debt as the Reagan Administration has done. Interest on the debt has tripled since 1980 and is the fastest growing part of the budget. One in seven federal taxpayers' dollars now goes simply to make debt payments — some 14 percent of the budget. This would be bad enough in and of itself. But it is compounded by the fact that roughly half of the debt must be financed from abroad, giving foreign investors a lever over our economic policy, leading the U.S. to become a debtor nation for the first time since World War I and complicating our monetary policy. We cannot expect to maintain Free World economic and political leadership as long as we run mammoth trade and budget deficits.

Yet our domestic social needs cry out for assistance. America's housing situation is but one of many examples. Every night in this most affluent of societies 750,000 are homeless — 2.5 million a year — while our production of public housing has plummeted from 50,000 units annually to 5,000. There is a shortage of 3 million rental units of moderate income housing — with 12 million families chasing 9 million units, yet rent subsidies have been slashed. The rate of home ownership has declined over the past 2 years for the first time in decades, yet no steps have been taken to make home ownership more available.

In order to make any progress in meeting our domestic challenges at a time of pinched resources, we will need to consider the following possibilities:

* Earmarked or dedicated revenues to pay for particular problems, as was done in the catastrophic health bill which the Democratic Congress passed in 1988.

* Finding areas to cut, such as the Economic Development Administration, Amtrak subsidies and farm subsidies, to match additional spending in higher priority areas, such as children's initiatives.

* Private sector mandates, such as Senator Christopher Dodd's child leave proposal, in which corporate America bears some reasonable burden of meeting our social obligations.

* Small pilot programs to test the success of ideas before more expensive programs are created.

* Using limited federal dollars to stimulate state and local government and voluntary action by matching grants.

* Requiring states and localities to bear a greater share of the burden of infrastructure programs from which they benefit.

* Greater use of user fees to pay for some government services.

There is an exciting fresh new domestic agenda — one based on mutual responsibility, investment and a Democratic new federalism. But the fiscal legacy of Ronald Reagan will make its fruition slower and more difficult than the nation deserves.

EDUCATION:
The Department of Education

Norm Fruchter*

SUMMARY OF RECOMMENDATIONS

The new administration and Congress should emphasize two primary goals for federal education policy: expanding the Department of Education's equity agenda; and supporting the comprehensive restructuring of American schooling.

Expanding the equity agenda involves adequately funding existing entitlement programs for disadvantaged students and creating new federal programs to: provide pre-school education for all low-income children; reduce intra-state school funding disparities; provide direct grants to districts for school construction and repair; increase college grant levels; recruit and train an expanded teacher corps; and develop a national literacy campaign.

Comprehensive restructuring involves creating new federal initiatives to: develop new models of school organization, curriculum and assessment responsive to student diversity; transform teaching into a genuine profession by creating more autonomous teacher roles; involve parents and students in effective school governance and support; and create school-to-work linkages which insure decent futures for all non-college bound students.

The cost of these initiatives would significantly increase the Education Department's $20 billion budget. Yet the cost of ignoring the failures of our current factory model school system will be incalculable damage to millions of American students, as well as a a debilitating drain on our national economy. To continue as a flourishing democracy, we must invest more in young minds.

I. HISTORY

Until the advent of the Reagan Administration, the federal government had long championed policies designed to achieve educa-

---

* Norm Fruchter is an educational consultant and activist, an elected school board member in Brooklyn, New York and co-author of Choosing Equality: The Case for Democratic Schooling.

tional equity and improve educational quality. These efforts included the G.I. Bill, which opened access to colleges for World War II veterans; the National Defense Education Act of 1958, which upgraded instruction in mathematics, sciences and foreign languages; and the Elementary and Secondary Education Act of 1965, which funded reading and math improvement for poor students, particularly minorities, in public and non-public schools. During the 1970s, in response to federal court decisions and Congressional mandates, Washington developed programs for bilingual and handicapped students, and helped expand college grant and loan programs, particularly for disadvantaged students.

The Reagan Administration set out to fundamentally change this equity agenda. Funding for Chapter I, the comprehensive effort to improve the skills of poor students, was slashed by almost a third early in the first term. Recent Congressional increases have restored most of these cuts, but the damage to compensatory programs during the past eight years has been considerable. The Reagan Education Department also cut the Follow Through program and resisted other efforts to provide pre-school and early childhood education for poor children, although research increasingly demonstrates that these programs provide significant short- and long-term gains for minority students.

Reagan's Education Department was particularly hostile to efforts to respond to the class, cultural and racial diversity of American students. In a consistent effort to impose "the one best system" on all our schools, Secretary William Bennett advocated a narrow, traditional curriculum as the proper education for all students. Under Bennett's leadership, the Department fought an unceasing war against bilingual and multicultural education and reduced funding, weakened guidelines and even mis-stated research results in an attempt to demonstrate program ineffectiveness. It also attacked women's studies, cut the Women's Equity budget and persistently derided efforts to modify college curricula to reflect the art and thought of non-Western cultures.

As a complement to this attack on diversity, education policy embraced a very traditional right-wing agenda: increasing school discipline, legitimating school prayer and attempting to impose a voucher system. Department leadership stressed the supposed collapse of school order, publishing several reports which misused statistics in efforts to suggest that permissive policies were eroding traditional standards of discipline. In response to this diagnosis of impending anarchy, Secretary Bennett and President Reagan celebrated "get tough" principals whose claim to restoring order involved violating students' rights within school while unlawfully expelling many other students defined as resistant to learning.

Department leadership also supported consistent attempts to find some formula which would permit prayer, vigil or a mandated period of silence in public schools. Though the Constitutional separation of religion and schooling has been consistently upheld by federal courts, federal officials urged the Justice Department to intervene in court actions to support or defend attempts to legitimate some form of school prayer.

President Reagan's Education Department also waged a single-minded battle to establish "choice" as the primary governance principle in education. Through its discretionary grants program for encouraging increased choice in public school systems, and through its conversion of desegregation funding into a national magnet school grants program, the Department emphasized choice at the expense of equity. Its repeated efforts to introduce parental vouchers in the Chapter I program was, in effect, an attempt to dismantle the structure of federally-supported compensatory education. The ultimate goal, explicitly articulated in early reports, was to develop programs of choice which would effectively privatize American public education. That this goal has failed is a tribute to the strength of what remains of the American ideal of a universal public education system, which aims to develop both the academic capacities and the common heritage necessary for effective citizenship.

There was also a strong federal push for educational excellence at the expense of equity. With the publication of *A Nation At Risk* in 1983, Secretary Terrel H. Bell established a rhetoric which linked national productivity and international economic competitiveness to the need to restore academic excellence in American schools. Secretary Bennett subsequently used his bully platform to insist that quantitative reforms — more school days, more class hours, more requirements, more testing — would insure excellence. Though a second wave of reformers such as John Goodlad, Theodore Sizer and Ernest Boyer demonstrated that such reforms would neither improve the quality of education in good school systems nor stem the increasing failure and high dropout rates within poor ones, the Department refused to support efforts to restructure our 19th century factory model schools. It insisted instead that imposing higher standards on an increasingly dysfunctional system would produce excellence for all students.

To support this rigidly quantitative notion of higher standards, the Department also championed standardized testing as a critical accountability measure. Through state-by-state "report cards" which compared student achievement on a range of often inappropriate and misleading indicators, federal policy intensified the use of testing as the critical measure of academic achievement. But when test results become the most important criteria for assessing student achievement, the pressure to teach toward what will be tested is difficult to resist.

Curriculum becomes distorted by the need to develop effective multiple-choice testing skills. Test-oriented drills take precedence over classroom discussion and exploration. Teacher creativity is sacrificed to the need to insure higher scores. Yet even when higher test scores are achieved, they reflect only limited mastery of fragmented and mechanical skills. Such scores do not indicate that students have developed the capacities for the critical thinking and independent analysis necessary to become productive citizens in the complex economy and democracy they will inherit.

II. NEW PRIORITIES AND INITIATIVES

Given the damage wrought during the past eight years, a new administration must emphasize two paramount education goals:

1. To restore and expand the equity agenda so that students do not suffer inadequate schooling because of physical, social, economic or familial disadvantage.

2. To support the restructuring of schooling necessary to define achievement as both sound academic skills and the capacity for critical thought, and to make public education capable of developing such achievement across the diversity of student learning styles.

THE EQUITY AGENDA

* *Restore cuts in traditional equity programs.* Chapter I, at its highest levels of past funding, served only approximately 40% of eligible students; Head Start only 20%; bilingual programs even less. The federal funding envisioned by the Education For All Handicapped Children Act of 1975 has never been provided. These entitlements require funding to effectively improve schooling for disadvantaged children. College grants-in-aid, which the Reagan Administration tried to reduce and convert into loan programs, must reach far more students and provide an increased proportion of yearly college costs without hobbling students' subsequent careers with millstone debts.

* *Integrate entitlements into the mainstream.* Adequately funding current equity programs is only a first step. Many Great Society and subsequent educational entitlements operate through procedures which identify, label and segregate students in order to provide the help they need. Such procedures create varieties of stigma; they also create subsidiary schooling tracks — remediation, special education — which often deliver inferior education. Current entitlement programs must be restructured to provide the help students need within regular classrooms — the educational mainstream — rather than shunt recipients into ancillary settings.

Provide high-quality pre-school programs. Our economy is multiplying social distress for increasing numbers of poor children. Projections indicate that 30% of children now entering school will be latchkey kids, 20% will be in poverty, 40% will experience broken homes, 15% will speak English as a second language, 10-20% will have poorly educated or illiterate parents and 15% will be physically or mentally handicapped. Other estimates indicate that at least 30% of today's schoolchildren are at risk of school failure; by the year 2000, if present trends are not reversed, half of all public schoolchildren may be similarly at risk.

To reduce these odds, a high-quality pre-school program which guarantees universal access through federal support and subsidy is a critical necessity for all low-income three- to five-year-olds. The Perry Preschool Study and other research efforts have demonstrated the enduring strengths that such high quality preschools create. Expanding Head Start should be the focus of this new initiative, but public schools and other non-profit childcare providers should be encouraged to offer similar programs. All new initiatives should stress the equality of access, a high level of parent education and involvement in governance and the high quality of staff training which characterize the best Head Start programs.

Reduce per capita spending disparities within states. Current state funding formulas hurt students from property-poor or tax-burdened districts. In some states, per capita school spending disparities can range from $1500 to $5000. As a recent New Jersey decision in the *Abbott v. Berke* state funding suit indicated, neither equality of opportunity nor equality of results is possible when state policies tolerate such vast disparities. Moreover, in many states, low per capita spending districts often serve predominantly poor and minority students, whose achievement levels reflect the few resources afforded them. A federal campaign based on incentives which encourage states to reduce funding disparities could significantly reduce intrastate disparities. If such incentives proved insufficient encouragement, penalties could be imposed which progressively reduced federal categorical funding (in Chapter I, for example) when inter-district disparities remained substantial.

Rebuild our educational infrastructure. Reducing the inequality of intra-state per capita expenditures will not resolve another critical need in American public education: restoring and rebuilding our decaying school buildings. In thousands of schools, primarily in rural and urban districts, schoolchildren face conditions of overcrowding, decay and hazard caused by district inability to fund improvement of physical plant. Facing limited capacity to tax and the demographic shifts which often result in defeat for school bond issues, many local districts cannot raise the funds required to repair or replace their disintegrating buildings. Nor can states supply the necessary revenues. But a federal school reconstruction fund, offering grants to districts to repair deteriorating school buildings and construct new buildings, could provide the scale of funding necessary to start to restore our schools.

* *Provide new college grant and loan-forgiveness programs.* Federal grants and loans have not kept pace with rising college costs. Worse, the Reagan Administration made repeated attempts to skew federal grant/loan ratios in favor of indebtedness. But accumulating debt is a steep price for a college degree, and one which many poor and working students cannot choose to pay. To attract significantly larger proportions of disadvantaged students to college, and to support them through graduation, federal college-aid grant levels must be raised. Loan-forgiveness programs could exchange specified years of service in critical occupations and needy areas for college tuition and support.

* *Recruit effective teachers.* During the next decade, many districts will face the retirement of more than half their teaching corps. Urban districts, which are currently losing large numbers of experienced teachers to other professions as well as to retirement, will be the hardest hit. Moreover, minority teachers will be increasingly in short supply, because minority graduates are choosing other careers over teaching and minority teachers are leaving the profession at higher rates than whites. Therefore many districts enrolling increasing percentages of minority students will be unable to recruit the minority teachers they need.

Although recent efforts to improve teacher wage rates may reduce the percentage of teacher loss, such increases will not significantly alter the drastic teacher shortages most systems will face. A federal teacher recruitment initiative, offering full scholarships and subsidizing the cost of graduate training in exchange for specified years of service in areas of teacher shortage, could attract and train a high quality teacher corps. Patterned after the Public Health Service Corps, such a program should develop a particular focus on the recruitment and support of minority teachers.

* *Organize a national literacy campaign.* A full commitment to educational equity must include helping illiterate adults victimized by inadequate schooling. Community-based literacy programs funded by federal and state grants have begun to significantly improve adult skills. But these efforts are dwarfed by the extent of adult need. A more effective response would be a federally-funded literacy campaign which enlists community-based and neighborhood agencies, churches, local civic, social and recreational organizations and provides the training necessary to make such institutions centers of effective literacy education. Incentive grants to business and industry

could subsidize both the workplace cost of literacy efforts and the time on-the-job devoted to literacy instruction. Moreover, a concerned Education Department could help recruit local service institutions — hospitals, clinics, social welfare agencies and schools — to develop informal, site-specific literacy programs.

SCHOOL RESTRUCTURING

Our schools are in crisis because they have preserved, unchanged, policies and practices which mirror 19th century industrial organization — a pyramid hierarchy, concentration of resources, economies of scale, bureaucratic discipline. Although successful industry has long since abandoned such practices for smaller scale, more decentralized enterprises, our schooling systems persist as monuments to yesterday. The conservative response to school dysfunction is no solution. Longer school days, higher standards and more testing cannot catapult a 19th century factory model system into the 21st century. What is required is the comprehensive restructuring of our schools to effectively meet current and future challenges.

Such restructuring requires federal resources and support. Although local and state authorities bear primary responsibility for developing schools that meet today's challenges, a progressive Education Department can play a key role.

* *Replace our school factories.* The school structures we've inherited from the 19th century — large schools based on supposed economies of scale, age-grading, grade retention, whole class instruction, student tracking or ability-grouping, competitive classroom practices — don't effectively educate all our children and increasingly don't develop the critical thinking capacities they need.

Federal incentives could provide the support districts need to replace these outmoded structures. Many districts would like to institute smaller schools and develop more comprehensive cross-age grading divisions, such as early childhood units which allow students to move at their own pace without stigma. But often the support, technical assistance and planning time necessary to launch such initiatives are not available from local or state sources. Similarly, federal initiatives could help districts develop alternatives to retaining less successful students by building on the varieties of differentiated classroom, small-group and individual instructional methods which provide effective responses to the diversity of student learning styles.

Many districts would like to replace tracking by ability, the dominant mode of classroom organization, by mixed-ability grouping methods which encourage the academic growth of all students and don't stigmatize those regarded as less able. Again, given the limits of local support, federal programs could supply the necessary incentives to leverage local practice. Finally, federal support for

disseminating teaching methods which encourage classroom collaboration, such as peer tutoring, cooperative learning and project-based
instruction, could make such non-competitive modes of classroom organization far more widely available.

   * *Develop curricula which stress critical thinking and cultural diversity.* To replace current emphases on atomized skills and fragmented
responses, federal policy should support a wide range of new curriculum development. Students deserve programs which stress the primacy of reading for content, the capacity to understand and analyze
what is read and the ability to write clear and articulate responses.
Federal policy should also assist schools in helping all students master a language other than English through the development of language curricula which begin in the early grades. To replace traditional school cultures still rooted in Dick, Jane, Spot and their myth-
ical American home, a progressive Education Department should support the development of curricula which build on the cultural
strengths of our very diverse families and students.

   * *Replace hierarchy with collegiality.* As the key on-line professionals in schooling, teachers need to participate in the decisions which
determine instruction in their schools. Reforms in several districts
are creating more teacher autonomy and shared decision-making and
a wave of expanded teacher experiments is underway. In Toledo, for
example, teachers are involved in peer review of their colleagues,
while in Dade County teachers and parents compose school councils
which share significant discretionary power over budget, hiring and
curriculum. Rochester has differentiated its teacher ladder by creating master teacher positions. And the newly created National Board
for Professional Teaching Standards is developing new career roles
for teachers and more collegial procedures for teacher evaluation.
These efforts would be enormously aided by concerted federal incentives designed to encourage the emergence of teaching as a true profession, relatively autonomous and fully accountable.

   * *Support new forms of student assessment.* Several decades of research have effectively demonstrated the limitations of all forms of
standardized testing, from SATs to multiple-choice reading and math
tests. Moreover, the damage such testing does to curriculum, teaching
and ultimately to student capacity for higher-order thinking is becoming increasingly clear. Yet effective assessment of student learning, both to improve instruction and to ensure accountability, is still a
necessity. Federal support could encourage the research necessary to
develop assessments which help teachers, parents and students
themselves identify and understand what they have learned and
how they can build on what they know to expand their knowledge
and capacities.

* Experiment with new forms of school governance. Though we know that active learners are successful learners, students are still treated as passive receptacles in most of our classrooms. Yet several districts have involved students in new and exemplary forms of instruction, curriculum development and school-community linkages. Other efforts have involved youth in reducing conflict through peer mediation and reducing substance abuse through student-initiated campaigns against drugs. Such innovations deserve federal support and, when successful, effective dissemination to the wider education community.

Current efforts to build community service programs into school curricula, in which student placements are developed in a wide range of civic, social service and helping agencies, should also receive specific federal support, perhaps through a national School-Community Service Program. Traditional definitions of student participation — student councils and other limited, formal modes of representation — should be broadened to challenge and mobilize the energy, caring, commitment and dedication that our youth possess.

* Experiment with new forms of parent participation. Successful schools also depend on strong parent and community involvement. Current experiments in school-based management in California and South Carolina and other forms of district-level collaborative governance, deserve support from a progressive Education Department. Several states, including New York and New Jersey, have recently initiated community school programs which attempt to make neighborhood schools the focus of services — health, recreation, social service, employment, neighborhood revitalization — for students and their families.

* Support successful transitions from education to employment. Finally, effective education policy should address the needs of those students who intend to go to work, rather than college, after graduation. Although such students represent approximately half our high school graduates each year, current policy provides little support for their transition from school to work. Public funds massively support the school-to-college link, directly through federal grants and loans, and indirectly through the allocations, subsidies and research grants provided to state-supported, locally-funded and private colleges. Yet "the forgotten half" who attempt to find work after graduation can tap no comparable support. Federal programs could insure decent futures for non-college bound students by encouraging initial job placements and training options which provide the necessary skills and subsequent opportunities for meaningful careers.

Current vocational programs, too often dumping grounds for less successful students, should be restructured to stress the primacy of academic skills and critical thinking. A national system of internships and apprenticeships, modelled after successful school-to-work programs in western European and Scandinavian countries, should be explored. A National Youth Service Corps should be instituted to engage non-college bound youth, particularly dropouts, in programs of public service, civic improvement, environmental conservation and infrastructure repair.

The cost of all these suggested programs would be considerable. But the cost of continuing to tolerate our increasingly dysfunctional system is even more massive — in escalating expenditures in health care, welfare, other social services and criminal justice. Moreover, there are the incalculable costs in unskilled workers, in our deteriorating quality of life and in the increasing apathy and cynicism of our citizenry. The cost of providing an effective federal role in improving education is modest compared to the damage to our vitality as a nation if we ignore the necessity to restructure our schools.

HOUSING:
Department of Housing and Urban Development

John D. Atlas
Peter Dreier
Derek Shearer*

SUMMARY OF RECOMMENDATIONS

The five housing policy goals of the next president and Congress should be:

1. Expanding the Supply of Affordable Housing. Congress and the President should create a *Housing Opportunity Program (HOP)* to subsidize the construction and repair of affordable rental, cooperative and for-sale housing. The funding should include a mix of *entitlement grants* to states and cities (based on a formula that includes the quality of existing housing, poverty levels, population size and other factors) and *matching grants* to cities and states to encourage their involvement in building affordable housing. At least 25 percent of all HOP funds should be directed toward non-profit community-based housing corporations. If initially funded at $6 billion (evenly divided between entitlement and matching grants), HOP could help build and repair 250,000-400,000 units annually — more than the level reached in the 1970s. HOP should be funded from a mix of sources, including increased appropriations from Congress, dedicated revenues from real estate transactions and by capping the mortgage-interest tax deduction for the very rich and for vacation homes.

2. Assisting First-Time Homebuyers. The federal government should lower and stabilize mortgage interest rates; lower required downpayment and closing costs for first-time buyers; restrict the spec-

---

* *John D. Atlas is President of the National Housing Institute, editor of* Shelter Force *magazine and Chair of New Jersey Citizen Action. Peter Dreier is Director of Housing at the Boston Redevelopment Authority and housing policy advisor to Boston Mayor Raymond Flynn. Derek Shearer is Professor of Public Policy at Occidental College and a former appointee to the National Consumer Cooperative Bank. He is the co-author of* Economic Democracy *and* A New Social Contract.

ulative resale prices on homes subsidized with federal funds or insurance, to help subsequent purchasers and change tax laws to encourage employers to offer housing assistance as an employee benefit (similar to health, education and other benefits).

3. *Assisting the Homeless and Preventing Further Homelessness.* Create a homelessness prevention program which would make short-term loans or grants to households facing eviction or foreclosure — and imminent homelessness. Also, the next administration should extend housing assistance to every household that qualifies for welfare.

4. *Protecting the Existing Inventory of Public and Subsidized Housing.* Establish a moratorium on the "prepayment" of privately owned, federally subsidized low-income housing. (Prepayment would otherwise allow owners to convert over 2 million units of low-income housing to market rate housing, or to tear it down and redevelop the site.) The new government should additionally establish tax incentives and/or regulatory requirements (rent control, condominium conversion limitations) to encourage the owners of federally subsidized low-income housing to sell to non-profit organizations.

5. *Attracting Additional Private Capital for Affordable Housing.* Reform the *Community Reinvestment Act* to eliminate "red-lining," and strengthen the *Home Mortgage Disclosure Act* to include more specific information on banks' lending practices in order to detect red-lining practices. Also, revise the tax-code to encourage long-term private investment in low-income housing and revise pension fund laws to permit investment in affordable housing.

I. HISTORY OF FEDERAL HOUSING POLICY

The clear goal of federal housing policy should be to guarantee that every American has an opportunity to live in decent, safe, affordable housing. To achieve this goal today would require a dramatic overhaul of our federal housing policy. Currently, the U.S. spends less on housing than any other western industrial democracy. We not only have to change national priorities and spend more federal funds, but also spend it in more cost-effective ways that reduce development costs and target assistance to low-income and middle-income consumers. What we propose here is not a dramatic overhaul of federal housing policy, but a number of progressive programs and policies that can be viewed as stepping stones toward more fundamental reform.

For the past 50 years, federal housing policy has been characterized by its "stop and go" nature, its internal inconsistency and its lack of coordination. In fact, housing policies have been designed to serve so many different goals — some at cross purposes — that federal housing policy has had a "crazy quilt," self-defeating quality.

In 1949, Congress adopted a national goal of "a decent home and suitable living environment for every American family," but it has never come up with the money to meet that goal. Over the years, some federal housing efforts have improved the quality of housing and increased the stock of affordable housing for millions of families. But in the 1980s, we have witnessed a dramatic turn-around from the progress made in the postwar period.

A brief historical overview* provides a sense of both the achievements and the incoherence of federal housing efforts.

In the late 19th and early 20th centuries, housing reformers focused their attention on the housing conditions of the urban poor who suffered from overcrowding, poor ventilation, lack of sanitation and shoddy construction. These early reformers sought to eliminate the evils of the slums through various forms of regulation at the local level. They helped enact laws setting minimum standards for light, air, room access and occupancy as well as prescribing electrical, heating, plumbing and materials standards for newly built housing.

By the 1930s, these housing reformers had shifted their focus to eliminating slums through federal intervention — grants and loans for "slum clearance" and public housing. Spurred by the Great Depression, various interested constituencies — home builders, the banking industry, trade unions and the poor — pushed the federal government to act. The result of these political forces was the country's first home financing program and the first public housing program.

In 1932, Congress created the Federal Home Loan Bank, owned and governed by member thrift institutions, to make the flow of mortgage funds more dependable and to create a national market for mortgages. The Housing Act of 1934 created the Federal Savings and Loan Insurance Corporation, which insured individual depositors' accounts from bank failures, and the Federal Housing Administration (FHA), which guaranteed individual mortgages against their default; the latter gave banks the confidence to change their practices from short-term to long-term (i.e., 30 year) mortgages. The Housing Act of 1937 created the public housing system. Local housing authorities were created to build and administer public housing, using the proceeds from the sale of their own tax-free bonds. The federal government would provide additional funds to make up the difference

---

* Even though HUD has become identified with federal housing policy, a comprehensive review of federal housing efforts must broaden its focus beyond HUD.

between what tenants could afford and the cost of operating these apartments.

The original advocates of public housing (like their counterparts in Europe) envisioned it for the middle-class as well as the poor, but lobbying by the private real estate industry (warning about the specter of "socialism") led to limiting public housing to the poor. Both public housing and home mortgage insurance were viewed as jobs programs as well as housing programs.

In the immediate post-war period, the Veterans Administration (VA) created a home loan program providing below-market interest rates and small downpayments. Whereas the FHA program was an insurance program for lenders, the VA program was a government subsidy to housing consumers. The VA and FHA programs stimulated the unprecedented post-war home construction boom and significant growth in homeownership (from 44 percent in 1940, to 62 percent in 1960, to 65 percent in the mid-1970s) during the next three decades. In 1946, housing starts passed the one million mark for the first time, more than tripling the prior year's figure. Housing starts during the 1950s averaged 1.5 million a year. Almost 90 percent of these new units were single-family dwellings. IRS tax policy, which allows homeowners to deduct local property taxes and mortgage interest from their federal income tax, also prompted the construction and home-ownership trends. New highway construction, VA and FHA housing programs and the IRS deductions combined to encourage the post-war exodus from the central cities to the suburbs.

The federal government's home finance policies (involving VA, FHA, FHLB, FISLIC and the IRS) successfully stimulated construction and homeownership for the emerging middle-class. Public housing progress suffered as a result of both World War II and the anti-communist mood of the immediate post-war period, fueled by the real estate industry's opposition. Public housing only made headway when it was joined, in the Housing Act of 1949, with central city re-vitalization. Mayors, builders and business lobbied for a program that would use federal funds to assemble large tracts of land, raze existing buildings, make site improvements and sell them to private developers primarily for commercial use. This was called "urban renewal."

Today, almost 40 years after the 1949 Act, only 1.3 million public housing units have been built. Meanwhile, the urban renewal program, which lasted until 1972, actually tore down more housing units than it replaced.

The cross purposes of federal housing policy in the post-war period are obvious. One set of policies promoted the exodus of business and residents to the suburbs, thus leading to the economic decline of core cities. Another set of policies promoted the revitalization of core cities, but in doing so pushed out the poor at the expense of commercial development and market-rate housing. Another set of policies promoted low-income housing, but local governments, which selected whether and where public housing was built, gave priority to high-rise projects concentrated in low-income neighborhoods.

The civil rights movement of the early 1960s, and the urban riots later that decade, triggered a new round of federal housing initiatives. The major civil rights acts prohibited discrimination in housing and other areas of American life. The War on Poverty, begun in 1965, sought to improve ghetto life by raising the income of those in poverty and, indirectly, provided them with the means to improve their housing. Advocates for bringing housing programs under one administrative roof made progress when HUD was created in 1965. HUD's first effort to coordinate urban-oriented programs was the "Model Cities" program, which lasted a few years until the urban riots, which led to several presidential reports on urban problems. All cited the condition of ghetto housing as an explosive problem and recommended a major new commitment to low-income housing.

Following these recommendations, the Housing Act of 1968 established a housing production goal of 26 million units within 10 years. But public housing was meeting increasing disfavor. A growing number of tenants were minorities displaced by urban renewal; more were the so-called "underclass" (welfare recipients) instead of the "working poor." Operating expenses were going up, creating serious financial problems. As an alternative to public housing, Congress looked for ways of involving the private sector in building low-income housing, as well as market-rate rental housing. Beginning in 1968, several new programs provided developers with low interest mortgages, tax breaks and, later, rental subsidies (Section 236, 221(d) and Section 8). A low-income homeownership program (Section 235) provided low downpayment, low-interest mortgages. Eventually, over 2 million privately owned subsidized housing units were built — almost double the overall number of public housing units.

Each of these programs was eventually criticized as expensive "bribes" to lenders and developers, exceeding the per-unit costs of public housing. But they did succeed in establishing record levels of new housing starts in the 1970s. Although the 26 million goal was not reached, in several years housing starts exceeded 2 million, with a sizable number targeted for the poor.

President Nixon put a moratorium on low-income housing programs in 1972. That lasted a year. The urban renewal program was terminated because of criticism that it destroyed housing, favored downtowns over neighborhoods and displaced the poor.

The Housing and Community Development Act of 1974 folded a number of urban-oriented programs into "block grants" distributed to cities under a "needs formula." It gave control of the dispersal of these funds to local governments, particularly mayors, under the theory that they understood local needs better than Washington. The 1974 act also created the Section 8 program which had three components — new construction, rehabilitation and rent supplements. The latter, which provides tenants with "certificates" in order to find apartments in the private market, would later become the major focus of Reagan's housing policy.

Under President Carter, the federal government continued, and slightly expanded, the urban-oriented housing programs. It added small programs targeted for neighborhood "self-help" efforts and nonprofit development, as well as a competitive Urban Development Action Grant (UDAG) to stimulate private commercial and residential development. With Carter's HUD budget reaching about $30 billion, the federal government added about 200,000 subsidized units a year.

The Reagan Administration became the first since the New Deal to attempt to withdraw the federal government from the business of building or subsidizing low-rent housing. After Reagan's Presidential Commission on Housing issued its report in 1981, calling for a "free and deregulated" housing market, Reagan put an ax to federal programs. HUD's budget dropped from over $30 billion in 1981 to about $8 billion by 1987. In place of production programs for the poor, Reagan substituted a slightly expanded rent supplement program (vouchers); in tight markets with few vacancies, however, many vouchers could not be used. For many of the poor who received vouchers, it was not unlike being provided with food stamps while the grocery shelves are empty.

The Reagan Administration failed to come to grips with a major problem facing privately owned subsidized housing. Unless these subsidies are renewed, up to 2 million low-income units could be lost through conversion to luxury apartments, condominiums or torn down for commercial construction. Reagan also initiated a small "demonstration" program to sell off public housing to tenants, but without providing adequate subsidies to make it feasible. Part of the Reagan plan to "privatize" government functions, it has had few takers among local public housing agencies. Reagan also unsuccessfully sought to penalize cities that had enacted rent control by withholding federal housing funds, but Congress balked at that approach.

As an agency, HUD itself was decimated under Reagan. Housing shouldered the largest cutbacks of any domestic social program. HUD experienced major layoffs of staff. Some of the more innovative programs, such as the "self-help" neighborhood programs, were terminated.

II. THE CURRENT CRISIS

America is now experiencing a severe housing crisis. The disgrace of an estimated 2 million homeless people haunts our cities. During the 1980s, homeownership declined for the first time since World War II, especially for young families. The abrupt slowdown in the normal graduation to homeownership, in turn, has intensified the squeeze on rental housing. Today, only one quarter of low-income households live in subsidized housing. The rest of the poor must compete in the private rental market, where rents are now at a two-decade peak.

A tenant of even moderate means suffers from a shrinking supply of rental housing, the threat of condo conversion and steadily escalating rents. Average rental costs have risen from 23 percent of household income in the mid-1970s to over 30 percent today. The crunch is worst for young people, families and the poor. Between 1972 and 1986, 2 million units that were once occupied by low-income tenants were demolished or converted into high-priced condos or coops. Close to one-half of our country's 14 million low-income renters are now paying more than half of their incomes on rent. More than 800,000 families, some homeless, are on waiting lists for the few (1.3 million) federally subsidized housing units that exist.

III. A FIVE POINT FEDERAL HOUSING AGENDA

Any new comprehensive federal housing policy must address at least the following five key problems:
* Expanding the production of affordable housing.
* Providing assistance to first-time homebuyers.
* Assisting the homeless and preventing further homelessness.
* Protecting the existing inventory of public and subsidized housing.
* Attracting additional capital for affordable housing.

1. EXPANDING THE PRODUCTION OF AFFORDABLE HOUSING

The key to any meaningful solution to the nation's housing crisis is expanding the production of affordable housing. There will continue to be a need for the federal government to fill the gap between what the poor and working families can afford and what it costs to build and maintain housing. The question is, What is the most effective way to spend federal dollars? Congress is unlikely to return to programs that "bribe" for-profit developers to build housing for the poor and working families with expensive tax breaks, mortgage subsidies and short-term (20-year) restrictions on affordable housing use.

A recent report of a task force headed by developer James Rouse and David Maxwell, chairman of Fannie Mae, recommends the creation of a *Housing Opportunity Program*, with funds in the form of entitlement grants to cities and states (based on a formula that includes such criteria as housing stock, poverty, population and other factors), and matching grants to cities and states. The report estimates that a $3 billion HOP fund (matched by $1.5 billion from state and local governments) could build and repair 150,000 to 200,000 housing units annually.*

This approach is an excellent use of federal dollars. It sets federal standards (i.e., targeting funds for low- and moderate-income housing), while allowing maximum local flexibility. It also leverages federal dollars by helping those communities that help themselves. But the panel's modest $3 billion sum is small when measured against the nation's serious housing problems.

The severity of the nation's housing crisis, and the almost decade-long withdrawal of the federal government from housing, calls for a deeper commitment if we are to reach the task force's own goals of decent affordable housing for all by the year 2000. In that light, we would recommend an initial commitment of $6 billion to the HOP program — $3 billion in entitlement funds and another $3 billion in matching grants.

The matching funds would go to communities that are willing to go beyond the entitlement. This provides housing advocates with a tool to demand more local and state dollars for housing. This would provide sufficient funding to produce 250,000 to 400,000 units annually — more than the level reached in the 1970s. Even this level of funding would not meet the need for affordable housing, but it would be an important step in moving the nation forward.

In addition, any matching grant approach must recognize that not all cities and states have equal capacities to generate matching funds. During the 1980s, many cities and states did attempt creative housing programs, and in the process developed considerable sophistication in housing production, rehab, management and regulation.

---

* In September 1987, Senate Housing Subcommittee chairman Senator Alan Cranston, along with Senator Alfonse D'Amato, the Ranking Republican on the subcommittee, asked James Rouse, a prominent developer, and David Maxwell, chairman of the Federal National Mortgage Association, to head a blue-ribbon panel charged with recommending a housing policy for the post-Reagan era. Their report, "The State of the Nation's Housing," was released in March, 1988.

But the playing field is not even. Some cities, states and regions are poorer than others and have less ability to generate revenues, or provide land, or get business or foundations to contribute funds, for housing development. While some localities might be able to afford a 1:1 (federal/local) match, others may only be able to afford a 3:1 match. HUD will need to develop objective criteria for determining the capacity of a city or state to generate matching funds.

The new approach can learn some lessons from past mistakes in federal housing programs. For example, housing built with federal funds should provide long-term affordability, in order to avoid the problems we are now facing with the "vanishing subsidy" dilemma. Speculation restrictions and rent ceilings should be incorporated into all units built with HOP funding. Further, HOP funds should be used, as much as possible, as capital grants to reduce overall housing development costs, rather than more expensive long-term debt financing.

The Rouse/Maxwell task force also recognized the important contribution made by nonprofit housing groups during the 1980s. It calls for a 10 percent set-aside of all HOP funds for nonprofit developers. One successful example is Nehemiah Homes, a nonprofit community-based housing corporation in an East-Brooklyn neighborhood of New York City. A coalition of churches in the neighborhood was able to raise $12 million from their national organizations for a no-interest construction-loan fund. Nehemiah Homes then pressured the city to donate 30 blocks of the desolate city neighborhood and agree to provide each homebuyer a $10,000 interest-free second mortgage. The state of New York provided below market mortgages to the homebuyers through the sale of tax-exempt housing revenue bonds. Nehemiah hired a well-known retired builder to supervise construction, and today, over 700 homes have risen out of the rubble and ruins — each one selling for under $50,000.

Another successful example is the Boston Housing Partnership, an umbrella organization of business leaders, city and state government officials and 10 non-profit community development corporations (CDCs). The BHP has enabled the CDCs to expand their capacity for development of affordable housing. In five years, the CDCs have rehabbed (and now manage) over 1600 low-income apartments. Funding comes from a variety of sources, including city and state governments, private foundations, the United Way and corporate investment through the federal low-income tax credits.

The silver lining in the dark cloud of the Reagan Administration's housing cuts has been the emergence of many community-based nonprofit housing developers in cities across the country. When the federal government turned off the spigot and the private developers went elsewhere, churches, unions, community development corporations (CDCs) and tenant cooperatives filled the vacuum. Overcoming enormous odds, they have been responsible for most of the affordable housing rehabbed and constructed during the decade. They have patched together financial support from local and state governments, private foundations, financial institutions and religious organizations to build low-income housing and rebuild neighborhoods. The current generation of nonprofit builders combine social concern with hard-nosed business skills.

A number of national foundations and intermediaries now support the non-profit sector. These include the Local Initiatives Support Corporation (LISC), created by the Ford Foundation, the Enterprise Foundation, started by developer James Rouse, Habitat for Humanity, a church-based group, the Neighborhood Reinvestment Corporation and the United Way. The key missing link in the burgeoning non-profit community-based sector is the federal government. For all their effort, local and state governments, foundations and church groups cannot — on their own — provide the necessary resources to meet our nation's affordable housing needs. What is needed is a partnership with the federal government.

Toward that end, Rep. Joseph Kennedy introduced the *Community Housing Partnership Act* (HR 3891) in February 1988, based on the success of the Boston Housing Partnership and its counterparts across the country. Through this program, the federal government would provide matching funds to locally based non-profit housing groups. It would provide funds not only for the construction and rehab of affordable housing, but also for technical assistance to help groups develop the expertise to undertake substantial housing development. The legislation has already been endorsed by the U.S. Conference of Mayors, the National League of Cities, the National Low-Income Housing Coalition and other groups.

The Community Housing Partnership program should become the model of reallocating 25 percent of HOP funds instead of 10 percent recommended by the Rouse/Maxwell task force.

Building on the success of state housing trust funds,* the HOP should be funded *not only* by a general increase in taxes, but by a nationwide trust fund. One source of funds would be a 1.5 percent tax on mortgage-backed securities. Another would be to re-use the regressive mortgage-interest and property tax deductions for wealthy homeowners and luxury homes. The savings could be targetted for low- and moderate-income housing. Another approach would be to treat this

---

* Residential security deposits, a surtax on legal documents filed in real estate deals and other self generating funding sources are presently used by states to generate housing funds.

massive tax subsidy as a loan, and require the homeowner to repay it to the treasury out of any eventual capital gain from the sale of the property. This would generate an annual renewable $6 billion fund.*

2. ASSISTING FIRST-TIME HOMEBUYERS

For most families, buying a home is the most important goal of their lives. They dream about, sacrifice and save for it. Federal policies in the postwar period turned this dream into reality for most American families. The FHA and VA provided young families with extremely low mortgages and low downpayment requirements. Tax laws that allow owners to deduct mortgage interest payments and local property taxes added millions of families to the ranks of home-owners. Secondary mortgage market institutions provided lenders with the protections they needed to make long-term loans. Federal law allows state housing agencies to use tax-exempt bonds to provide homebuyers with below-market mortgages.

But the steady rise in homeownership rates after World War II changed direction in the 1980s. A 1986 report by the Harvard-MIT Joint Center for Housing Studies warned that "young households feel thwarted by the high cost of homeownership and alarmed about their prospects of ever being able to buy." Most new homes are purchased by those who already own a home and are "trading up." But the homes they are leaving behind are beyond the financial reach of the majority of young families. The very rich are buying larger homes and often more than one of them.

With some exceptions, homes built by the private homebuilding industry are geared toward the wealthiest one-third of the population. The typical new home in 1988 cost $120,000; in many parts of

---

* The one housing subsidy that has not fallen to the Reagan budget axe is the one that goes to the very rich. The Internal Revenue Service tax code allows homeowners to deduct all property tax and mortgage interest. This cost the federal government $35.1 billion in lost revenue in 1987 alone. This amount is more than four times the HUD budget for low-income housing. Two-thirds of the foregone tax revenue goes to the 10.7 percent of taxpayers who earn over $50,000 annually. Another one-quarter of this subsidy goes to the two percent of taxpayers who earn more than $100,000 annually. One-half of all homeowners do not claim deductions at all. Because low-income subsidies (such as public housing) are more visible than the hidden (tax) subsidies to the wealthy, few Americans worry about getting the rich off welfare. *Tax deductions that help working class and middle class homeowners should remain.* Congress should place a cap on mortgage-interest and property tax deductions for homeowners with very high incomes or who own more than one home.

the country, it was considerably higher. Downpayment requirements of 20 percent means a would-be buyer needs at least $24,000 up front, in addition to several thousand additional dollars for closing fees. This is simply beyond the means of most American families under 40 years of age. Even if these families can find the downpayment, they face monthly costs of $1,500 to $2,000 for mortgage principle and interest, insurance and taxes, in addition to basic maintenance costs that often exceed expectations. Despite fluctuating interest rates, young families can expect to pay 9 to 11 percent , plus points, or else face a variety of alternative mortgage instruments (such as adjustable-rate mortgages) that seem confusing and insecure in terms of planning for the future.

The key components of a program to assist first-time homebuyers would include policies to (a) lower overall housing construction prices; (b) lower and stabilize mortgage interest rates; (c) lower required downpayment and closing costs; (d) restrict the speculative resale prices on homes, to help subsequent purchasers; and (e) change the tax laws to encourage employers to offer housing assistance as an employee benefit.

One contributing factor to the high cost of housing is so-called large-lot "snob zoning" through which communities (primarily suburbs) discourage affordable housing. Several states, notably New Jersey, California and Massachusetts, have enacted "anti-snob zoning" laws, which require developers to set-aside a portion of each development for affordable housing, particularly in communities which have historically excluded affordable housing. Such laws preserve open space, restrict overly dense development and, through innovative planning, reduce land costs and encourage affordable housing. Federal laws (including the matching funds aspect of the proposed HOP system) should look at such zoning provisions as one of the criteria in awarding matching funds.

FHA insurance programs have been a major force behind increased homeownership, by allowing for low downpayment requirements. Unfortunately, in recent years the FHA's mortgage limits have not kept pace with rising home prices. Thus, many potential home buyers are ineligible for FHA programs. By revising its limits, the FHA could expand the potential for homeownership for many young families. The FHA could also reduce its downpayment requirements. The Rouse/Maxwell task force has suggested, for example, that the downpayment requirement be limited to three percent for the first $50,000 of a home's value and five percent in excess of $50,000.

The federal government should continue the mortgage revenue bond program for low- and moderate-income homebuyers. Currently, such programs (run by state housing agencies) typically target homebuyers with incomes below 115 percent of the region's median income, and then provide mortgages at tax-exempt rates (a few points below conventional rates). Federal funds could be used to reduce mortgage interest rates, thereby breaking down a barrier to homeownership for many households. All homes purchased through tax-exempt funding of additional mortgage assistance should incorporate deed restrictions to keep the homes affordable for subsequent buyers.

For moderate-income families, the federal government should create a *downpayment revolving loan fund* — whose loans would be repayable within five years — to help first-time homebuyers overcome downpayment obstacles. In exchange, any appreciation of the home's value would be shared with the federal government, based on a formula that included the size of the loan, the income of the buyer and the amount of appreciation. Those proceeds would be placed in the revolving loan fund to help future first-time homebuyers.

Federal tax laws should be revised to encourage employers to provide housing benefits to employees as part of the personal benefit package, as well as to enable companies to create employee home-ownership plans (modeled on employee stock ownership plans).

HUD should also start a national lease-purchase homeownership program modeled after the successful program in New Jersey where the state housing agency makes attractive loans to for-profit and non-profit builders who allow qualifying households to lease the homes they build with an option to buy. Part of the lease-purchaser's monthly rental payment is set aside as a downpayment. Within 24-36 months, the households have accrued the necessary downpayments to purchase the home.

3. ASSISTING THE HOMELESS AND PREVENTING FURTHER HOMELESSNESS

Imagine a hypothetical disaster befalling our cities — a bomb, a ferocious hurricane or an earthquake — in which two to three million Americans lost their homes. We know that the President and Congress would be swift to act, declaring a national emergency and funnelling whatever funds were necessary to help those who lost their homes.

In fact, a national disaster of this magnitude has occurred already. But our national leaders have taken little action to help repair the damage to the lives of the homeless.

For most of the 1980s, the task of dealing with the burgeoning homeless population was left to local groups — churches, community groups and city halls. During this time, many of these institutions distinguished themselves by stretching their own limited resources to provide basic survival services to the homeless — emergency shelter, meals in makeshift soup kitchens, health care, job training and mental health care. In 1987, advocates for the homeless pressured

Congress into passing legislation providing $355 million to groups providing these services to the homeless.

But the last few years have witnessed a growing dissatisfaction among advocates for the homeless and service providers with these short-term band-aid approaches. It has become increasingly evident to virtually all those dealing with the problem of homelessness that we must address the permanent underlying causes of homelessness and take measures to prevent homelessness from occurring.

There are many causes for the the rising tide of homelessness during the 1980s: Growing poverty; stagnant wages; cuts in the so-called "safety net" (unemployment, disability, welfare and food stamp benefits) that provides a cushion for the poor; the impact of deinstitutionalization, which has dumped about one-half million persons with a history of mental illness onto our streets with little or no facilities and professional help available to them in the community. But most experts agree that the growing shortage of affordable housing is the fundamental cause of the problem.

A federal program to serve the homeless would have (in addition to production programs outlined above) at least the following components: First, an emphasis on homelessness prevention. Prevention keeps families together in their home and is more cost-effective than housing the homeless in either emergency shelters or welfare hotels. Homeless groups in New York and Chicago are organizing to preserve SROs. Massachusetts, New Jersey and New York have enacted tough condominium conversion laws. California, Massachusetts and New Jersey have locally administered flexible rent stabilization laws that prevent rent gouging, and Maryland, New Jersey and Pennsylvania have adopted programs which make timely intervention by way of short-term loans and grants to stave off eviction or mortgage foreclosure, helping people stay in their own homes or apartments.

In 1985, Massachusetts began a Housing Services Program, which funds community-based organizations to mediate landlord-tenant disputes *before* the tenants become homeless. More than 12,000 tenants and 7,600 landlords were served by this program in its first 18 months.

The best protection against arbitrary eviction is found in state laws that prevent eviction except for "just cause" in force in New Jersey, New Hampshire and the District of Columbia. Rather than allowing a landlord to evict a tenant for virtually any reason, such statutes limit the acceptable reasons for eviction to causes within the tenant's control — such as extended nonpayment of rent, property destruction or violation of reasonable lease terms — preventing much unnecessary homelessness.

These states provide excellent models for national legislation. Families facing eviction due to nonpayment of rent through no fault of their own, families who do not have the up-front funds often required by landlords (first and last month's rent, plus security deposit), and other families identified by social service agencies threatened with homelessness due to a medical emergency, rent increase, layoff or other factor beyond the individual's control should be provided with a short-term loan or grant to tide them over.

Second, in light of the obvious relationship between homelessness and poverty, the federal government should at least deal with the two underlying causes of poverty — inadequate welfare payments and the minimum wage. Only 28 percent of America's twelve million low-income households live in subsidized housing. Nearly three of every four poor persons must compete in the private market, which means that most are paying more than they can afford, and are just one small calamity away from losing their ability to pay their rent or mortgage altogether. They should be entitled to housing vouchers, just as they are entitled to food stamps.

Both the "welfare poor" and the "working poor" need and deserve subsidized housing. For the welfare poor, a housing allowance should become part of AFDC benefits. AFDC payment standards should be made uniform nationally (although still requiring state matches) to cover such basic necessities as food, clothing and transportation — all of which are relatively similar from region to region. But because housing costs vary so dramatically from region to region, a housing allowance should be added to all AFDC payments, based on rents in local housing markets. The housing allowance for AFDC recipients would help them pay rent and thus avoid the threat of homelessness.

Current AFDC payments, which are paid for through matching grants with states, are highly uneven across the country, as a recent study by the Urban Institute revealed. Some include allotments for housing, while others have none. Of those that do have housing allotments, some are pegged to actual local rent levels, while most are not. This is a highly inefficient, unfair and costly system, based on both lack of coordination between HUD and HHS and wide variations in state-level AFDC matching funds.

The link between homelessness and low wages has become increasingly obvious. As the U.S. Conference of Mayors survey revealed, about one-quarter of the homeless work. About half of the jobs created in the last decade pay poverty-level wages, according to a Joint Economic Committee report. An increase in the minimum wage — which has not been increased in seven years — is long overdue. This, too, would serve as a major homelessness prevention policy, providing families with adequate incomes to afford basic housing, while engaging in productive work that expands the nation's wealth, rather than drains government resources.

Finally, a national policy to limit condominium conversions would serve to prevent homelessness. Beginning in the 1970s, and accelerating in the 1980s, hundreds of thousands of rental apartments were converted to condominiums. Condominiums are not bad in and of themselves. They often create an entry-level market for first-time homebuyers. Most often, however, affordable apartments are transformed into expensive condominiums, with little or no physical improvement in the unit. In Boston, for example, a study found that the typical monthly housing cost *for the same unit* doubled when an apartment became a condominium. Regulation of condo conversion has typically been done at the city and state level — from advance notice periods, to requirements for relocation expenses, to limits of eviction (especially for the poor and elderly), to outright bans on conversions while vacancy rates remain at emergency levels. In many housing markets, condo conversion is a major cause behind the shortage of affordable rental housing and, thus, a leading contributor to homelessness.

The federal government's role might be to require localities with very low rental vacancy rates to demonstrate that they have put in place some appropriate policy to deal with condominium conversion. A stricter version would be to deny some federal housing funds to localities that do not deal with a condominium conversion trend that exacerbates the rental housing shortage. There are some scenarios where apartment conversion might be encouraged. Whenever possible, federal housing funds can be used to help renters purchase their buildings as limited-equity cooperatives, thus providing tenants with the security and other benefits of homeownership along with the responsibilities of self-management.

4. PROTECTING THE EXISTING INVENTORY OF PUBLIC AND SUBSIDIZED HOUSING

The U.S. has the smallest percentage of subsidized housing of any major industrial nation. In Canada and most of Western Europe, for example, a substantial portion of the housing stock is developed by nonprofit organizations and/or by the government, not only for the poor, but also for the middle-class. In the U.S., however, even the tiny portion of our low-income housing stock subsidized by the federal government — owned by either local housing authorities or private developers — is in jeopardy.

Unfortunately, of the 3,000 public housing authorities across America that manage 1.3 million units, it is the few troubled ones that get most public attention. While the vertical public housing ghettos of Southside Chicago and St. Louis get most of the publicity, however, much "garden apartment" style public housing in smaller cities is decent and well-managed. Still, Abt Associates estimates that to bring the deteriorated big city projects up to sanitary code standards would cost $2 billion a year for 10 years. To ensure their upkeep, those agencies would be required to modernize their management and bring tenants into the decision-making process.

The Reagan Administration's efforts to "privatize" public housing have been so far unsuccessful, but the poor public image of public housing in general lends some popular support to that approach. The plan to sell public housing is a British import. Under Margaret Thatcher, more than half a million units of public "council housing" have been sold to renters. American enthusiasts for the Thatcher program say that the British program proves its feasibility. But there is a vast difference between American and British public housing. In Britain, it represents one-third of the entire housing stock, and its residents represent a broad spectrum of the population. In 40 percent of council housing units there are two or more wage earners; only 29 percent of council housing units — primarily for the elderly — have no wage earner. Local public housing agencies there do not evict families, as they typically do in the U.S. when their incomes rise above the original selection standards.

In the U.S., where public housing represents less than two percent of all housing, occupants are very poor; 62 percent are minorities and 46 percent are elderly. A 1979 survey (the latest figures HUD has) reported an average household income of $5,033; only 30 percent depended primarily on salary and wages for income.

One of the Reagan Administration's major goals has been to get rid of the worst units, which require the deepest subsidies. But the British found, not surprisingly, that the best units sell best, and that the tenants most likely to buy are those with the highest incomes. This leaves the worst units, housing the poorest tenants, in the public housing inventory.

The Reagan "demonstration program' was designed to prove the critics wrong. Like many experiments, it was rigged to get the desired results. For example, 77 percent of the units offered for sale in the demonstration program were single-family homes, which are newer, need fewer repairs and are generally located in attractive residential areas. The tenants there also have higher incomes than their public housing counterparts.

If there is a lesson to be learned from Europe, it is not just to sell off public housing willy-nilly. If some public housing is to be sold, it should be transformed into limited equity cooperatives, which is a midpoint between owning and renting. It gives occupants greater control over their homes, and by restricting the resale price, it keeps them affordable over the long run. But to make it work, government would have to provide residents with substantial subsidies. These would include help to repair long-neglected projects, funds to help residents pay the monthly costs of ownership and maintenance and adequate training to give owner-residents the tools to manage (or sub-contract management of) their housing. Any way you approach it, government support is needed to fill the gap between what it costs to maintain public housing and what low-income residents can afford.

Construction of new public housing has come to a standstill, which is unfortunate since most public housing has been a success. In most cases, public housing is cost-effective, building and maintaining housing for the very poor without all the incentives needed to induce private developers. Successful projects are generally smaller, low-rise, with active tenant involvement in management, close to other residential neighborhoods and commercial shopping districts, and with either on-site or nearby social-service programs to assist public housing residents to lift themselves out of poverty.

The fate of the more than 2 million units of federally-assisted privately-owned housing for the poor, built primarily in the 1960s and 1970s, is even more precarious. They face two problems. First, the 20-year "lock-in" period for low-income occupancy is now at hand. Close to one million units could be eliminated from the low-income supply by the mid-1990s if owners decide to prepay their mortgages when they reach the 20th anniversary. Second, rent subsidies needed to make these apartments affordable to low-income tenants will soon expire if Congress does not renew them. Between 1988 and 1993, about one million subsidy contracts will expire. As with public housing, the country has a large investment in these units, which would re-quire substantially more to replace than to preserve.

At minimum, the federal government should establish a morato-rium on the prepayment of these subsidized mortgages until an ade-quate solution can be worked out.

HUD should renew the rent subsidy controls in all subsidized projects so that low-income families can continue to live there. Rent subsidies average about $3,500 to $4,000 per unit each year; the mortgage subsidies, according to OMB, average another $1,185 per unit annually. Replacement of these units through new construction, however, would be substantially higher at today's construction costs and interest rates.

The long-term solution to this problem is for the government to encourage owners to sell their projects to nonprofit organizations, ten-ant limited-equity cooperatives, or public housing authorities, enti-ties committed to preserving the units for low-income residents. Pro-viding owners with tax breaks on capital gains if sold to non-profits is one approach. Imposing various regulatory requirements (i.e., rent control, condominium conversion limitations) on projects that prepay is an option available to local governments. (Federal projects are ex-empt from such regulations so long as they remain under the federal programs.) Federal funds could be utilized to accomplish these goals, particularly, as an example, where local or state governments contribute matching funds for tenant equity to purchase buildings as co-operatives.

5. ATTRACTING ADDITIONAL PRIVATE CAPITAL FOR AFFORDABLE HOUSING

While public housing is financed with public revenue, raised directly through taxes or indirectly through the issuance of bonds, most of the funds for the other 98 percent of housing construction or rehabilitation in America comes from private lenders, whose market-rate loans add considerably to the cost of housing over the life of a typically 30-year mortgage. Public funds are used to fill in the "gap" between what poor families can afford and what housing costs to build or maintain.

In the long term, creating more housing through direct capital grants, allocated by Congress, is more cost-effective — i.e., less expensive to finance, to build and to maintain — than current approaches. It is cheaper, for example, to build a $100,000 house and pay for it today, out of existing revenues, than to finance $80,000 at a fixed or adjustable interest rate over a 30-year period. It also preserves affordable housing if it cannot be sold at speculative prices ("whatever the market will bear"), but is restricted so that subsequent buyers (and generations) can afford to rent or own it. Such an approach would require, of course, a sizable amount of up-front revenues, which in the initial budget years would appear to be a substantial increase in the national housing budget. Over a 10-, 20- or 30-year period, however, the real cost of the housing would be significantly cheaper. Political realities make it difficult, however, to propose such an approach, when it is easier to "mortgage the future."

Our current housing system requires us to find many sources of private as well as public capital to invest in housing in general and to provide affordable housing in particular. Current arrangements are not favorable toward encouraging private capital to invest in affordable housing. To change this situation, the federal government can create several programs and policies.

First, it can reform the Community Reinvestment Act (CRA). The CRA, enacted in 1977, mandates that the Federal Reserve Bank and other bank regulatory bodies, in evaluating a bank's performance, must assess its performance under the CRA. With the help of other governmental agencies, notably state consumer advocates and lawyers, community groups have challenged banks' .performances. In many cases, to avoid unfavorable publicity, banks have pledged to provide capital for a variety of low-income housing developments, typically through CDCs, or provide home improvement loans in neighborhoods where residents were having difficulty obtaining such loans.

The initial goal of CRA was, in fact, to deal with banks' so-called "red-lining," the systematic withdrawal of investment from certain neighborhoods, leading to a self-fulfilling decline. In many instances, community groups have used the CRA to reverse this process. Complementing CRA is the Home Mortgage Disclosure Act, which requires banks to disclose their mortgage lending activities by census tract. The CRA requires banks to lend in low-income neighborhoods, but it does not say to whom. This means that a bank can be lending all its money to investors who are building solely market-rate housing, thus "gentrifying" a neighborhood, and still fulfill CRA requirements. The CRA needs to be changed so that banks have to invest in *affordable* housing, regardless of the neighborhood.

The current climate of bank deregulation has dramatically increased bank takeovers, mergers and interstate banking. This creates a political opportunity for an effort to reform the CRA to require that banks seeking regulatory relief provide loans for affordable housing. Community groups in Massachusetts, California, Maryland, New Jersey and elsewhere have used the CRA to negotiate such agreements with lenders, but these provisions should be a mandatory part of the federal CRA law.

Second, the federal government can revise the tax code to encourage long-term private investment in low-income housing. As noted above, current tax policy not only favors homeownership, but overwhelmingly benefits the wealthy. Federal tax policy toward rental housing has been uneven, making the investment market less predictable and thus more risky for investors. The 1981 Tax Act provided substantial tax benefits to investors in rental housing; these benefits were virtually eliminated in the 1986 Tax Act and, not surprisingly, rental housing production has witnessed a dramatic decline.

A section of the 1986 act provided tax benefits for low-income rental housing, but the provision was so restrictive that few developers have utilized it. The federal government should expand and improve the low-income tax credit in the 1986 law, restore some of the accelerated depreciation benefits to owners of low-income rental housing and place long-term use restrictions on rental housing that gets favorable tax treatment.

Third, the federal government should continue tax-exempt financing for low-income apartments. Statewide ceilings (or caps) on the use of such bonds should be increased or even eliminated. Tax-exempt financing has built much of this nation's affordable rental housing, including mixed-income housing. So long as it is clearly targeted in terms of the income of residents, and so long as long-term use restrictions are required, they provide a valuable incentive for private developers to enter the rental market. Used in tandem with the proposed HOP funds, tax-exempt bonds could increase the levels of low- and moderate-income housing that is built and rehabilitated in the future.

Fourth, the Rouse/Maxwell task force report has recommended federal support for "benevolent lending" toward affordable housing. Some individuals, corporations, religious groups, foundations and others target part of their portfolios to housing at very low interest rates. Investors receive a more modest return than they would with conventional investments. There is considerable evidence that individuals and institutions would be willing to make such charitable contributions to low-income housing. The federal government can insure these deposits in lending institutions to secure the risk of lending institutions, as well as to insure the mortgages (through FHA) made with funds from such "benevolent" investors. The Rouse/Maxwell task force estimates that several billion dollars could ultimately be generated by such an approach, if only the federal government were willing to become a partner in making it work.

Finally, the federal government should revise the pension fund laws to allow investment of union pension funds in affordable housing. A federal guarantee on pension fund investments in affordable housing would make these untapped resources available at very low risk, with little cost to the federal government. The program would pool affordable housing development projects, and issue federally guaranteed bonds — backed by the revenues from the housing — after it is occupied. Pension funds would purchase the federally guaranteed bonds, which would guarantee a fair rate of return without putting a single retiree's pension at risk. These bonds would be as prudent an investment as Ginnie Mae and Fannie Mae securities that pension funds now hold.

RELIEVING POVERTY:
Welfare & Non-Welfare Approaches

Robert Greenstein*

SUMMARY OF RECOMMENDATIONS

The new administration and Congress will inherit a poverty rate higher than at any point in the 1970s, with especially high levels of poverty among children. If both the president and his Secretary of Health and Human Services accord high priority to new policy initiatives to reduce poverty, significant progress can be made.

* Their central focus should be on initiatives outside the welfare system, with emphasis on a coordinated series of reforms designed to "make work pay." A goal could be established that if a family has a parent working full-time, year-round, the family should not have to live in poverty. To achieve this goal, the administration should seek to restore the minimum wage to its level of the 1960s and 1970s, expand the earned income tax credit (a credit for working families with children) and adjust it for family size and provide working poor families better access to child care and health care coverage.

* Another critical ingredient of a "non-welfare" approach to poverty consists of action to boost child support collections from absent parents. The recently enacted welfare reform legislation took some significant steps in this direction. A further round of promising initiatives is now being tested at the state level and could be ready for national application in several years.

* Targeted expansions of several key programs for poor children that have been found highly effective but reach only a fraction of the eligible children (such as Head Start) would represent a sound investment in the future. An initiative to improve the "basic skills" of children, youth and some poor adults should also be tested.

In a number of these areas, the new administration and Secretary of Health and Human Services will find opportunities to build some measure of bipartisan consensus among liberals and conservatives — and consequently should have a meaningful possibility of translating new proposals into national policy.

---

* *Robert Greenstein is founder and Director of the Center on Budget and Policy Priorities. He was formerly Administrator of the Food and Nutrition Service of the Department of Agriculture and Special Assistant to the Secretary of Agriculture.*

While designing (and securing approval of) new policy initiatives represents the most important anti-poverty activity for a new administration, implementation of the new welfare reform law will also represent a major task for the HHS Secretary.

For example, the Secretary should encourage states to design welfare-to-work programs that seek to upgrade skills and improve the job prospects of those recipients who face significant employment barriers.

I. THE NEED AND OPPORTUNITY FOR ACTION

In 1987, nearly one of every seven Americans lived in poverty. (The poverty line was $9,056 for a family of three in 1987.) Although the nation was in the fifth year of an economic recovery, poverty rates failed to decline.

Poverty rates traditionally have followed economic trends, rising and falling with the unemployment rate. Yet while the unemployment rate in 1987 was about at the same level as in 1978, poverty rates were significantly higher in 1987 — and eight million more Americans were poor.

The poverty figures for 1987 are disturbing:

* The poverty rate stood at 13.5 percent in 1987, higher than the poverty rate in any year in the 1970s, including the major recession years of 1974-75.

* Poverty rates for children have climbed substantially. One in every five children is poor, including two in every five Hispanic children and nearly half of all black children.

* While the number of poor who receive welfare has remained relatively constant over the past decade, the number of poor who work has grown substantially. The number of people who work full-time year-round but remain poor was 43 percent higher than in 1978.

* Perhaps most disturbing, those who are poor have grown considerably poorer, on average. Census data show that the average poor family now falls $4,635 below the poverty line — farther below the poverty line than in any year since 1962.

The higher levels of poverty that have marked the 1980s have been accompanied by rising indicators of need, including the growth of homelessness, and increases in reports of hunger and in requests for emergency food and shelter assistance.

While poverty has risen to higher levels in this decade, the costs of poverty to society also appear to be growing. The increased levels of poverty in the 1980s, especially among children, have come at the same time that the number of children reaching working age each year has fallen in the aftermath of the passage of the "baby boom" generation into adulthood. The combination of these two trends — increased child poverty and a decreased number of youth entering the labor force — means both that employers have fewer prospective employees for entry-level jobs and that the proportion of new entrants into the work force who are from low income backgrounds (and who are minorities) is rising substantially. The result is that the stakes in reducing and ameliorating the effects of child poverty now appear to be unusually high for employers — and for the American economy as a whole.

These developments suggest not only that the next administration must address these problems, but also that the potential exists to include both liberals and conservatives in building a broader base of support for such efforts. Indeed, a rough bipartisan consensus for some changes is emerging. Since 1986, the following events — which few would have predicted a few years earlier — have occurred:

* In 1986, the Southern Governors Association asked the Congress to provide states with a new Medicaid option under which states could extend Medicaid coverage to pregnant women and young children who are not on welfare but who fall below the poverty line. The ensuing legislation featured Senate cosponsors ranging from Edward Kennedy to Strom Thurmond. It passed easily, and within 18 months at least 40 states had elected the new option.

* Legislation was enacted into law in 1988 that will *require* states to extend Medicaid coverage to pregnant women and infants with incomes up to the poverty line and also to children up to their seventh birthdays whose families have incomes below the state's welfare income limit (which is below the poverty line in virtually all states). In the late 1970s, similar legislative proposals proposed by a Democratic president failed to make it through Congress.

* Welfare reform legislation was enacted into law, after periodic attempts had failed in the past.

In addition, in 1987 the Committee for Economic Development, consisting of more than 200 corporate executives and educators, called for increased investment in a series of "preventive" programs for low income children, such as Head Start, compensatory education, immunizations, pre-natal health care and the Special Supplemental Food Program for Women, Infants and Children (WIC). The Committee warned of the consequences for the nation's economy if stronger steps are not taken to address the needs of poor children.

Finally, during the presidential campaign, both candidates called for increased health care coverage for low income families, increased federal spending on Head Start and child care and at least some increase in the minimum wage.

II. OBSTACLES TO CHANGE

While both the need and the opportunity for action are present, major obstacles also exist. Most formidable, of course, is the over-sized federal budget deficit. The deficit crisis effectively precludes new initiatives that carry a price tag running into the tens of billions of dollars. Any new administration will only be able to target a modest number of areas for increased resources of any magnitude.

Reducing poverty rates among children and their families should be one of these priority areas. Yet this will mean reducing less critical areas in both defense and domestic spending to free up resources. Congress started down this road by including a "Children's Initiative" in the Congressional budget resolution passed in 1986. This led to a broadening of Medicaid coverage for poor pregnant women and children and to expanded funding for such programs as Head Start (which provides preschool education to poor children), compensatory education for disadvantaged school children and nutrition supplements for low income pregnant women, infants and young children (provided through the WIC program). The added costs of the Children's Initiative were more than covered by retrenchments in other areas, such as reductions in Urban Development Action Grants and termination of General Revenue Sharing.

In a speech late in 1986, Senator Pete Domenici (then chairman of the Senate Budget Committee) spoke of "national needs that are...compelling and deserve new resources," identified "welfare" as one such need and spoke of a society that is not adequately meeting its responsibility in such areas as "the seamless web of poverty, homelessness, hunger and mental illness." Domenici called for reducing spending in low priority areas to meet these needs. Rep. William Gray, the House Budget Committee chairman, speaking in the same month as Domenici, sounded a similar note. While the budget deficit will constrain what can be done, it need not pose an insurmountable obstacle to progress. The basic question is one of priorities.

THE RISKS OF TOO NARROW A FOCUS

A second potential obstacle is that too narrow a focus will be adopted in approaching the problems of poor children and their families. Currently, two types of policy interventions are growing in popularity: welfare-to-work programs for welfare recipients and "preventive" education or health programs for poor children (Head Start, compensatory education, WIC). Both of these types of interventions should be part of a larger agenda, not the entire agenda itself.

In particular, there is a risk in overselling the benefits of welfare-to-work programs. In evaluating such programs, the Manpower

Demonstration Research Corporation (MDRC), the leading authority in this area, has found that the programs typically increase employment rates for welfare mothers by three to eight percentage points. Such employment gains make these programs worth undertaking, even if they won't have a profound impact on poverty rates. According to Judith Gueron, MDRC's president,

> welfare employment initiatives...can provide meaningful improvements.... [But t]he modest nature of the improvements also indicates that [they] can be only part of a 'solution' to poverty. Other reforms — for example, changes in the tax laws and expansion of the earned income tax credit to increase the rewards for work, educational reforms, training and retraining, increased child support enforcement and job creation programs — are important complements if welfare is not only to be made more politically acceptable but also to succeed in reducing poverty substantially.

Also, welfare-to-work initiatives appear to have much less impact on unemployed young men than on single women with children. Most such men are not on welfare. More than 90 percent of the adults on the Aid to Families with Dependent Children program, the welfare program for families with children, are women. This is true even in the typical state that extends AFDC coverage to two-parent families.

There is a corresponding danger that some policymakers may believe it sufficient to expand a number of health and education programs that have proven effective in aiding poor children but that, due to funding limitations, reach only a modest proportion of eligible poor children. While such expansion is called for, it also needs to be viewed as part of a broader agenda.

For these successful programs are not likely, by themselves, to improve markedly overall employment levels or wage rates in the general economy. As a result, they may largely just "shuffle the deck": that is, some children from poor backgrounds may grow up to earn more because of these programs, but if overall employment and earnings in the economy do not increase, then other low income children may eventually do less well. If this occurs, overall poverty rates are not materially altered. To achieve a larger effect, expansion of these valuable programs needs to be a component of a larger strategy.

Finally, there is a risk of policymakers adopting too narrow a geographic focus. Special efforts aimed at inner city poverty are very much needed. But contrary to popular impression, fewer than one in every 10 Americans who are poor lives in a high poverty area of a central city. (A high poverty area is defined here as an area where at least 40 percent of the residents are poor.) Nine of every 10 Americans in poverty live elsewhere — either in another part of a city, in a suburban area or in a rural area. (For example, the rural poverty rate has risen as fast over the past decade as the central city poverty rate, and it is nearly as high as the central city rate.) Broad-based efforts need to be undertaken that address problems of poverty in a variety of geographical settings.

III. THE BROADER FOCUS

Much attention was focused on the enactment of welfare reform legislation in October 1988. However, to achieve a compromise acceptable to the White House as well as to Members of Congress from both parties and both chambers, the legislation was very limited in scope. As some observers have noted, the new law would more accurately be termed welfare "revision" than welfare "reform." It is not likely to result in large reductions in poverty.

Moreover, most of those who are poor are not on welfare. Of the 13.9 million poor households in 1986 (including the 10.8 million nonelderly poor households), only 3.1 million received benefits under AFDC. Only about half of the children who were poor in 1986 received AFDC in a typical month.

Both politically and substantively, greater progress likely can be achieved during the next several years through approaches to poverty that operate *outside* the welfare system. The Tax Reform Act of 1986 is an illustration. It not only removed six million working poor households from federal income tax rolls, but also gave a further boost to the after-tax incomes of 12 million low income working households through an expansion of the earned income tax credit. And while the Tax Reform Act improved the incomes and purchasing power of poor families, it in addition strengthened work incentives by increasing the remuneration from low paid work and enlarging the gains of work over public assistance. This is a combination that is generally harder to achieve through welfare policy.

Overall, the Tax Reform Act increased the after-tax incomes of low income working families by more than $5 billion a year, the largest gain for low income families from any federal legislation in more than a decade. (It should be noted, however, that this gain only reversed the large increases in federal tax liabilities that had been imposed on low income working families since the late 1970s. Now that the Tax Reform Act has passed, combined federal income and payroll tax burdens on these families are about back to the levels of the late 1970s.)

A KEY REFORM: MAKING WORK PAY

One of the most important elements of a broader "non-welfare" agenda is a coordinated series of reforms designed to "make work pay."* Such an approach can lift many of the working poor out of poverty and raise many others closer to the poverty line. It should also have a strong work incentive effect, bringing more people into the labor market and making work relatively more attractive as compared either to welfare or various illicit endeavors in the underground economy.

The new administration should establish a basic goal: if a parent works full-time, year-round, that parent and his or her children should not have to live in poverty. This goal should be acceptable to both political parties and most Americans, and can be achieved at surprisingly modest cost to the federal government.

To achieve this goal, there are two basic steps: restoring the minimum wage to its traditional level and enlarging the earned income tax credit while adjusting it for family size.

The Minimum Wage. Throughout most of the 1960s and 1970s, full-time year-round work at the minimum wage raised a family of three to the poverty line. From 1960 to 1979, full-time year-round minimum wage earnings averaged 104 percent of the poverty line for a family of three.

The minimum wage was last raised — to $3.35 an hour — in January 1981. But since then, consumer prices have risen 37 percent. Consequently, in 1988, full-time year-round minimum age earnings leave a family of three approximately $2,500 below the estimated poverty line.

Low minimum wage levels have significantly increased the ranks of the working poor. In 1987, nearly three of every five workers who were paid at any hourly rate and whose households fell below the poverty line earned $4.35 an hour or less. Had the minimum wage kept pace with inflation and remained at the average levels of the 1960s and 1970s, it would have been slightly more than $4.35 in 1985. As a result, the incomes of nearly three-fifths of the working poor households in the country where a worker was paid at an hourly rate likely would have been improved, and some would have been lifted out of poverty.

Moreover, from an economic standpoint, now is a good time to raise the minimum wage. Due to tighter labor markets and a reduced number of youths entering the labor market, a minimum wage increase would be likely to have only a small adverse effect on employment opportunities.**

---

* For a fuller discussion of proposals to "make work pay," see David T. Ellwood, *Poor Support: Poverty in the American Family.*

** Important new work on the potential job loss from an increase in the minimum wage, covering labor market data through 1986, finds a

The Earned Income Tax Credit. The second leg of this approach is an expanded earned income tax credit that is adjusted either for family size or for the number of children in a family. Restoring the minimum wage to its traditional level can bring full-time earnings back to the poverty line for a family of three. Reforms in the earned income credit, a tax credit for low income working families with children, can bring most families of more than three people up to (or close to) the poverty line if the families have a full-time worker.

Today, working poor families with several children face a cruel paradox. Family needs increase as family size grows. Recognizing this fact, the poverty line rises with family size. Welfare benefits also increase with family size. But wages do not.

As a result, large working families with several children are more likely to be poor than are smaller families. In addition, those large families that are poor are likely to fall further below the poverty line than smaller families that are poor. Furthermore, as family size increases, low paid work becomes less and less competitive with welfare.

What is needed, then, is a wage supplement for working poor families geared to family size. The earned income tax credit is nearly ideal for this purpose.

The earned income credit is solely available to working poor families in which parents live with and support children. Adults who do not work, as well as fathers who have left their families, do not qualify. Thus, the credit is widely regarded as being strongly "pro-work" and "pro-family."

The credit is also "refundable." This means that if the credit for which a family qualifies is greater than the family's income tax liability, the family receives a check from the Internal Revenue Service for the difference. Thus, if a family has income too low to owe federal income tax but qualifies for a $600 earned income credit, the IRS will send the family a check for $600. The refundable aspect of

---

substantially smaller job loss effect than many other studies which have been cited by opponents of raising the minimum wage. Most of the higher job loss estimates that have been cited rest on studies of labor market data only through 1979. However, labor market conditions, especially for teenagers, are substantially different now than in the 1970s. See Allison J. Wellington, "Effects of the Minimum Wage on the Employment Status of Youth: An Update," presented at the Demography Seminar at the University of Michigan, March 22, 1988; and Isaac Shapiro, "The Minimum Wage and Job Loss," Center on Budget and Policy Priorities, July 1988.

the credit was designed as a way to help offset the high burden of regressive payroll taxes (i.e., Social Security and Medicare taxes withheld from paychecks) that low income working families still must pay regardless of whether they owe any income tax.

In 1988, families with incomes between about $6,000 and $10,000 will qualify for the maximum credit of approximately $875. The credit rises with earnings up to $6,000 and declines as earnings surpass $10,000. It phases out at about $18,500 of income.

In addition to being a well designed element of tax and poverty policy, the earned income credit has support across the political spectrum. One of the first calls to establish an earned income credit came in 1972 from then-Governor of California Ronald Reagan. It was championed in Congress in the mid-1970s by Russell Long, then-chairman of the Senate Finance Committee, and enacted in 1975.

In the past two years, the idea of expanding the earned income credit through family size adjustments has gained a growing and impressive number of both conservative and liberal adherents. Its virtues have been extolled by the White House Task Force on Families (staffed by conservative White House aide Gary Bauer), the House Democratic Task Force on Social Policy, Representative Thomas Petri (R-Minn.), Senators Daniel Patrick Moynihan (D-N.Y.), Bill Bradley (D-N.J.) and Rudy Boschwitz (R-Minn.), leading poverty analysts such as Robert Reischauer and David Ellwood and organizations as disparate as the Children's Defense Fund and the Heritage Foundation.

Expanding the credit and adjusting it by family size would cost in the range of $2 to $4 billion a year, when phased in. If a revenue raising measure considered during a new administration includes some regressive tax increases, such as increased taxes on gasoline, alcohol or tobacco, there would likely be a political imperative to include some offsetting low income tax relief to reduce or eliminate the regressive nature of the legislation. A provision to adjust the earned income credit by family size could perform such a role, helping to make the tax legislation more palatable. The result could be a piece of legislation that would reduce the deficit and make a significant advance in anti-poverty policy at the same time.

The federal government should consider one other step regarding the earned income credit: providing the credit to all eligible working families in their regular paychecks. Currently, the credit is provided to most families in one lump sum as a tax refund at year's end. Yet the credit is likely to be more effective both in helping families meet ongoing living expenses and in increasing the attractiveness of work if it is reflected in workers' regular paychecks. This could be achieved by having an employer add the earned income credit payment due to an employee into the employee's regular paycheck.

Health Care and Child Care Costs. The combination of restoring the minimum wage to its traditional level and adjusting the earned income credit for family size holds the prospect of raising most families with a full-time worker close to the poverty line. Still, these families must have access to affordable health and child care. Otherwise, a substantial amount of their small incomes may be diverted to pay for these services, often leaving their remaining income still well below the poverty threshold.

Some modest steps to address gaps in health care coverage have been taken by Congress in recent years. As noted, recently enacted legislation requires states to extend Medicaid coverage to: 1) pregnant women and infants in families — including low income working families — with incomes up to the poverty line; and 2) children from their first to their seventh birthdays in families with incomes up to the state's income limit for AFDC. States are also allowed, but not required, to extend Medicaid coverage up to the poverty line for children up to the eighth birthdays. Finally, under the new welfare reform law, families that work their way off welfare will receive Medicaid coverage for one year after leaving the welfare rolls.

While important, these steps fall short of what is needed. Medicaid is not provided for most parents in working poor families who are not pregnant women or for most of the children in these families. If their employer does not provide health insurance, some or all family members are likely to be without coverage unless the family spends a substantial portion of its small income for insurance.

Similar problems arise with child care costs. For many working poor families, no government assistance is available. The bulk of federal child care support is provided through the tax system and goes to middle and upper income families, not to poor ones. Unlike the earned income tax credit, the child care tax credit is not refundable. Working mothers too poor to pay income tax receive no child care tax credit, unlike families at higher income levels.

Further expansions of Medicaid coverage to more children in poor families that are not on welfare, along with reforms to make the child care tax credit refundable, should be regarded as integral elements of a strategy to "make work pay." These changes, however, would still leave unmet the bulk of the health and child care problems of low income working families. Further changes are needed and are discussed in a subsequent chapter by Marian Wright Edelman.

Benefits to Urban and Rural Areas. This strategy of "making work pay" would have benefits for inner city and rural areas alike. In rural America, where the poverty rate is higher than in metropolitan areas and not far below the poverty rate for the nation's central cities, one of the principal causes of poverty is low pay for work. More than two of every three poor families living in rural areas include at least one worker and nearly three in 10 have two or more workers. In nearly one in every four poor rural households, the household head works full-time throughout the year. A strategy to make work pay could have a significant impact on rural poverty rates, while boosting rural economies at the same time.

In the inner cities, the proportion of the poor who work is somewhat smaller. Yet the effects could be substantial here, too. A key policy goal in the inner city should be to transform the working poor more into role models, and to make them seem less like "chumps" who work all day at jobs that pay little more than what can be obtained through public assistance or minor hustling. A strategy to make work pay may in the long run do as much or more to affect attitudes in such communities than the exhortations for changes in "values."

ENFORCING FAMILY RESPONSIBILITY THROUGH CHILD SUPPORT COLLECTIONS

A second key non-welfare strategy involves boosting child support collections from absent parents. Some 57 percent of all poor children live in female-headed families. While the fathers of some of these children are unemployed or have little income themselves, the fathers of many others could contribute, or contribute more than they currently do. Greater responsibility for their children needs to be placed on absent parents who have the means to provide support.

The level of child support collections in this country is a scandal. In 1985, only 61 percent of the mothers of children whose fathers were absent were covered by child support awards. Of those who had awards and were supposed to receive payments, 26 percent received no child support at all (and another 26 percent received less than the full amount owed). As a result, more than half of all mothers of children whose fathers were absent either had no child support award or had an award but received no payment.

Collections are even lower for poor children. For example, in 1987, child support payments were received for only 14 percent of the families with children on AFDC.

Major improvements in child support enforcement efforts are both desirable and achievable. There appears to be no other area of anti-poverty policy with so strong a bipartisan consensus.

The new welfare reform legislation reflects this consensus. It places increased emphasis on establishing paternity so that child support awards can more readily be established. It requires states to set guidelines for child support award levels that the courts generally will have to follow, in order to make award levels both more consistent and more adequate. Child support payments ordered in the future will (in most cases) be withheld automatically from wages by the absent parent's employer and then transferred to the custodial parent, in order that awards be more regularly and fully collected. Finally, states will be required to review and update award levels periodically, so that as the absent parent's income rises with job experience or inflation, child support payments rise accordingly.

These changes represent a first phase of needed improvements in child support collections. A second phase of changes should be considered in future years. This second phase would be more far-reaching: it involves the potential replacement of part of the welfare system with a child support payment system, an approach that is currently being tested by the State of Wisconsin (and a variant of which will be tested soon in New York). Until the results of these tests are known, federal action in this area is premature. Enough may be known for a new administration to move in this area before the end of its term, however, if the state tests prove successful.

The approach being tested in Wisconsin involves three key elements. The first two are consistent with the child support provisions of the new federal welfare reform law. The third element — including the partial replacement of the welfare system — goes beyond current federal law.

In Wisconsin, state standards have been set for child support awards, a step all states will now have to take as a result of the new federal law. (In Wisconsin, these standards require that child support awards must equal 17 percent of the absent parent's income if one child is involved, 25 percent of income for two children, 29 percent for three children, etc., unless the court finds a reason to set an alternative award level.) In addition, in a step pioneered in Wisconsin and Texas that will now be mandated nationwide, child support payments are automatically withheld from the absent parent's paycheck and transferred by the state to the custodial parent.

The third element of the Wisconsin system, which will start being tested in 1989, is perhaps the most striking. The state will establish a minimum child support "assurance level." If the child support payment provided by the absent parent falls below this level (because the father's income is too low or the father is unemployed, or for another reason), the state will supplement the absent parent's payment and provide the mother with a combined child support payment that is equal to the "assured level." The state thus will pay the difference between the assured level and the child support payment made by the absent father.

This system is designed to increase the living standards of poor children in single-parent families while at the same time lessening the families' need for (and reliance on) welfare. Fewer mothers and children will qualify for welfare if the child support payments they receive (including the portion of the payment financed by the state) lift them above the welfare income limits.

This approach also should boost incentives to work. Welfare payments are reduced one dollar for each dollar that a mother on welfare earns (after her fourth month on a job). The child support payments in Wisconsin will be reduced by a much smaller amount when low income mothers go to work, however.

The new system will move away from a welfare-type approach in another respect as well. All single parents with children — not just those who are poor — will be eligible for these payments, thereby creating something more like a social insurance program than a welfare program. This may serve both to broaden popular support for the system and to reduce the stigmatizing and at times demeaning aspects of welfare.

The designers of this approach, led by Irwin Garfinkel of the University of Wisconsin, believe that it can have a significant impact in ameliorating child poverty at a relatively modest cost. A significant part of the money for increasing the incomes of these children would come from absent parents rather than the taxpayers. In addition, the government's costs in supplementing low child support payments (and bringing these payments up to the "assured level") would be partially offset by reduced welfare costs.

It should be noted that the various "non-welfare" approaches discussed here go hand-in-hand. For example, in many states, the "Wisconsin approach" to child support would be unlikely to work effectively unless Medicaid were made more broadly available to poor families not on welfare. Otherwise, if child support payments were to lift a family modestly over the welfare income limit and the family lost Medicaid coverage as a result, the family could be worse off than when it was on welfare.*

WELFARE IMPROVEMENT

In the aftermath of the 1988 welfare reform battle, it is unlikely that a new administration or Congress will have great interest in revisiting welfare policy in the near future. This is another reason for concentrating now on initiatives that operate outside the welfare system. Nevertheless, there are several areas of unfinished business in welfare policy that ultimately should be addressed (and some as-

---

* Similarly, a family might not be helped if child support payments lifted it over the welfare income limit, and the family lost the ability to receive education, training or employment services (and child care support during a transition to work) as a result.

pects of the new welfare reform law that eventually need to be reexamined), even if this is not done early in the new administration.

Ending discriminatory treatment of poor two-parent families. One of the major gaps in the American welfare system has long been its treatment of poor two-parent families. Despite the oft-stated goals of strengthening families, our welfare system has long denied to many poor two-parent families the benefits available to poor single-parent families.

Until now, the decision to provide welfare benefits to two-parent families has been left up to the states. Currently, 28 states cover these families, while 23 states do not. In the states failing to cover these families, some or all of the family members are also denied Medicaid coverage.

The new welfare reform law takes a step toward addressing this problem. It requires, effective in fiscal year 1991, that these 23 states provide public assistance for at least six months of the year to two-parent families that meet their state's welfare eligibility criteria. Medicaid coverage will have to be provided throughout the year to these families.

Yet in at least three areas, discriminatory treatment of poor two parent-families remains. First, while single-parent families can qualify for public assistance if their income and assets are sufficiently low, two-parent families must meet an additional criterion: they must have worked in at least six of the past 13 calendar quarters. This is a requirement of federal law; it applies to all states. As a result, a two-parent family in which the parents are young and lack significant work experience — or in which the parents have been out of work for a long period of time before applying for welfare — is ineligible for assistance, regardless of how destitute it may be. If a young woman from a poor background becomes pregnant by a young man without sufficient prior work experience, she may find that she and her child can be eligible for public assistance only if she and the child's father do not marry.

This restriction has an anti-family effect. It also represents a gap in the safety net for two-parent families.

Second, as noted, the 23 states now without public assistance for poor two-parent families will be required by the new welfare reform law to provide aid to these families for only six months out of the year. (The other 28 states will be required to maintain coverage throughout the year.) While this represents an improvement over providing no aid at all in these 23 states, it means that some two-parent families will have assistance ended after six months even if they are still in need and unable to find work. The only way for these families to continue receiving aid for the next six months would be for the father to leave the household. Moreover, there will now be one set of federal requirements applied to these 23 states, while a different set of requirements applies to all other states.

Requiring that these 23 states eventually be brought under the same requirements as the other states — so that two-parent families in all states are protected from arbitrary benefit terminations after six months — should be a federal policy goal. Achieving the goal would further strengthen two-parent families in these states, while mending one of the remaining gaps in the safety net for these families and their children.

Finally, the new welfare reform law imposes a different and more rigid set of work requirements on adults in two-parent families than on adults in single-parent families. States will be required to enroll a much higher percentage of adults from two-parent families in their welfare-to-work programs than of adults from single-parent families. At the same time, states will be given less flexibility concerning the types of education, training, or employment programs that they can provide to the two-parent families.

The new work requirements governing two-parent families are thought to be misguided by many researchers in the field as well as by many state officials. The research findings in this area clearly demonstrate that welfare-to-work programs are more effective for single mothers than for fathers in two-parent families. The welfare-to-work programs generally have little impact on those recipients who are the most employable and have the most prior work experience, since these people usually find jobs on their own with or without a program. The programs typically have a greater impact on those who have greater barriers to employment and are less likely to find jobs on their own. Since the only two-parent families that can qualify for AFDC are those in which an adult has significant prior work experience, these are the very families on which welfare-to-work programs are least likely to have an effect. Yet they are the families that states will now enroll in the greatest proportions.

In states with limited resources for welfare-to-work programs, serving so many of the two-parent families will generally mean providing less service to needy single-parent families. Some resources are likely to be diverted from providing the education and skills a young single mother needs to attain self-sufficiency and avoid years on welfare — and focused instead on temporarily unemployed men in two-parent families who generally will find jobs anyway.

The new law is also unnecessarily rigid in its restrictions on the types of education, training or employment programs that states may use for adults in two-parent families. While states will be allowed to select from a broad range of programs for the single parents, most education or training approaches will be effectively barred for the adults in two-parent families. Most job training programs effectively will be ruled out for them, and educational programs largely will be precluded unless the adult is under age 25 and has not graduated from high school. If a state finds that an adult in a two-parent family who is 25 or older needs remedial education or other skill improvements to make him more employable, the state effectively will be precluded from providing such education or skills upgrading. If the adult in question is a single parent, however, the education can be provided.

These excessively rigid restrictions were contained in neither the welfare reform legislation originally passed by the House of Representatives nor the bill introduced by New York Senator Daniel Patrick Moynihan. The restrictions were added later at the insistence of White House officials who wanted to enroll all fathers in two-parent families receiving public assistance in workfare programs (i.e., in programs where the benefits are "worked off" for no pay) and who did not want to permit education or training programs as an alternative to workfare. Another goal in the welfare area should be to ease these special work rules and restrictions concerning two-parent families.

National Minimum Benefit Level. Another goal is long range but important nonetheless: to establish a federal "floor," or minimum benefit level, that states may not fall below in setting benefit levels for poor families with children. Proposals that the federal government establish such a minimum benefit level for poor families with children — as the federal government has done since 1974 for poor elderly and disabled individuals and couples — are exceedingly difficult to pass. Presidents Nixon and Carter both tried and failed, and another attempt failed in Congress in 1987. Yet the need for a minimum benefit level for poor families with children is, if anything, more acute now than when Nixon and Carter proposed it. In the typical state, AFDC benefits for a family without other income have fallen 33 percent since 1970, after adjusting for inflation. In 19 states, the benefit for families with no other income now falls below 40 percent of the poverty line. The sharp erosion of these benefit levels is one of the factors that has contributed to the increase in child poverty rates in recent years.

IMPROVING THE FOOD STAMP PROGRAM

The food stamp program is the nation's principal defense against hunger. While the basic food stamp structure is sound, several needed changes could help both to reduce hunger and to advance self-sufficiency and family responsibility.

Currently, a drop-out or a high school graduate who does not attend college may be eligible for food stamps if his or her household has sufficiently low income and assets. However, if a poor high school graduate goes on to college, he or she is automatically disqualified from the food stamp program as a result of the college attendance — and his or her family's benefits are lowered as a result — unless the student works at least half-time, cares for young children or is disabled. This harsh treatment toward poor youth who continue their education represents unwise social policy. If a student who is poor lives with his or her parents, the student should not be disqualified from food stamps simply because he or she is in school (especially if the student looks for but cannot find a part-time job). The food stamp program should not be in the position of discouraging students who are poor from continuing their education or of reducing the benefits of the student's family if the student stays in college rather than dropping out.

Change is also needed in the food stamp program's treatment of child support payments so that it conforms to the practice followed in the AFDC program. Under AFDC, a mother is allowed to keep the first $50 a month she receives in child support payments without a reduction in her AFDC benefits (after the first $50, her AFDC benefits are reduced one dollar for each dollar received in child support payments). Allowing the mother to keep the first $50 in support gives her some modest financial stake in identifying the absent father, helping to track him down and collecting child support from him.

This policy is partially undermined, however, by a conflicting policy in the food stamp program where the first $50 in child support payments is counted against benefit levels. The result is that a welfare mother's net gain from child support payments (after both AFDC and food stamp benefit reductions are figured) is as low as $27.50 a month in many cases.

To increase the number of cases in which paternity is established and child support is collected, the food stamp program should also disregard the first $50 in child support payments. This would promote administrative efficiency as well, by eliminating an important source of inconsistency between AFDC and food stamp rules.

Both of these changes — enabling poor students who live with their families to remain eligible for food stamps if they cannot find work and disregarding the first $50 in child support payments — were approved by the House of Representatives on a bipartisan basis in 1987 as part of the House welfare reform bill, but the changes did not make it into law. Another try is warranted when legislation governing the food stamp program comes up for renewal in 1990.

Consideration should also be given to modifying the manner in which the food stamp program treats housing costs when food stamp benefit levels are determined. The food stamp benefit structure is supposed to ensure that poor households have enough resources (including their food stamps) to purchase a minimally adequate diet, after they meet the cost of other necessities such as paying the rent. While the program's benefit structure takes into account all housing costs borne by elderly and disabled households, however, it takes into account only a portion of the housing costs of those non-elderly households (including poor families with children) who bear especially high housing cost burdens. The result is that a number of families with very high housing expenses do not have sufficient resources both to meet the costs of other necessities and to buy enough food. At a time when new Census data shows that 63 percent of all poor renters in the U.S. are paying more than 50 percent of their income for housing, the food stamp policy in this area warrants reexamination.

A BASIC SKILLS INITIATIVE

Consideration could be given to a "basic skills initiative" aimed at high school dropouts and others with skills deficiencies. Recent research by Gordon Berlin and Andrew Sum shows that youths ranking at or near the bottom in basic skills are much more likely than youth with better skills to be poor, jobless, school dropouts, on welfare, unwed parents or arrested for suspected criminal activities. The evidence is mounting for upgrading basic skills, such as reading and basic arithmetic, to combat the emergence of what has been termed an urban underclass.

Of particular interest are positive results from demonstration programs funded by the Ford Foundation. The results suggest that a new administration and Congress should seek to direct a greater proportion of the funds in several existing programs (such as state Job Training Partnership Act programs, the summer youth employment program, the vocational education program and state welfare-to-work programs) to basic skills remediation. The results also suggest that some modest new investments in basic skills training, accompanied by testing and evaluation, are warranted.

IMPLEMENTATION OF WELFARE REFORM

Finally, one of the major tasks for the new Secretary of Health and Human Services will be implementation of the welfare and child support enforcement provisions of the new welfare reform law. The Secretary will need to ensure that states implement the child support provisions in a timely and effective manner and that standards for child support awards are established and energetically enforced by states. If the Secretary permits weak standards or ineffective updating mechanisms, for example, much of the potential for improved child support collections may be lost.

In the welfare-to-work area, the Secretary should encourage states to design programs aimed at upgrading skills and improving the job prospects of recipients who face significant employment barriers. The Secretary should prefer such approaches to state programs that devote so many of their resources to the most employable recipients rather than those more likely to remain on welfare for longer periods of time.

IV. CONCLUSION: THE NET AND THE LADDER

Attacking poverty in America requires two elements: better "ladders" out of poverty so that families can gain self-sufficiency, and a stronger safety net, especially for poor families with children.

In the late 1960s and early 1970s, emphasis was placed on strengthening the safety net through instituting or expanding such programs as Medicaid, food stamps and Supplemental Security Income (SSI). Significant gains were made in health care and nutrition for the poor and in income support for the elderly. However, much less was done to provide "ladders" — that is, to assist and enable the long-term poor to achieve self-sufficiency and work their way out of poverty.

In the late 1970s as inflation severely eroded benefit levels and in the 1980s as a number of programs for the poor were reduced, the safety net was materially weakened. And while increased rhetorical emphasis was placed on attaining self-sufficiency and providing ladders out of poverty, the rhetoric frequently was not matched with federal action. For example, while interest in welfare-to-work programs increased, federal appropriations for these programs were reduced by more than 70 percent (a trend the new welfare law will reverse).

The new administration needs to focus attention on both tasks. Currently, interest seems greatest on measures to foster self-sufficiency and on "preventive" programs for poor children. While this interest is encouraging, attention needs to be paid to the safety net as well. Census data show that in 1979, nearly one of every five families with children that otherwise would have been poor was lifted out of poverty by government benefits; by 1987, however, only about one in every 10 such families was lifted out of poverty by such benefits. To focus exclusively on sturdier ladders — or exclusively on a more adequate safety net, for that matter — would reduce the effectiveness of a new administration's anti-poverty efforts and repeat the mistakes of the past.

Following the course discussed here will require new resources, of course. Yet these resources need not be massive or unrealistic in a time of fiscal belt tightening. As noted, expansion of the earned income tax credit (and making the child care tax credit refundable as well) may be able to be included in a revenue-raising measure that achieves sizeable reductions in the deficit. Similarly, other initiatives outlined here may be able to be linked to freezes or reductions in lower priority spending areas, so that the net effect, once again, is deficit reduction. It should be possible to find the resources to move on a substantial part of this agenda.

AMERICA'S CHILDREN:
Health and Child Care

Marian Wright Edelman*

SUMMARY OF RECOMMENDATIONS

Millions of American children are not getting off to a good start, due to poverty, growing hunger and homelessness, lack of access to health care, inadequate education, declining immunization rates, lack of quality child care while their parents work or adolescent pregnancy. These problems are growing at the same time that we are going to need every American child to be as educated, healthy and productive as he or she can be, since the share of the population that consists of young workers will be declining. Moreover, a growing proportion of those young workers will be from minority groups or disadvantaged backgrounds. If we want to remain competitive internationally and build a stronger America, we will have to rely on and invest in every one of America's children.

We are threatened by a growing chasm between the needs of the society for more skilled and educated workers and a population of children which is under-educated, untrained and poorer. The new president must make preventive investment in children and families the cornerstone of national domestic policy:

* He must act to expand programs that have been proven to be effective and save the society money in the long run, but which reach only a fraction of the eligible children who can benefit from them. Key programs needing substantial growth are the Special Supplemental Food Program for Women, Infants and Children (WIC), Head Start and Chapter 1 educational assistance for disadvantaged children.

* He must act to restore wages that have been battered by economic change and eroded by inflation to such a degree that the median real income of families headed by a person under age 30 and with children fell by 26 percent from 1973 to 1986.

* He must get Congress to pass the Act for Better Child Care (ABC), which will help states improve the accessibility and quality of child care and help lower-income families pay for these services,

---

* *Marian Wright Edelman is President of the Children's Defense Fund, which she founded in 1973.*

while preserving and building on the current variety of available options for care.

* He must get Congress to extend Medicaid coverage to reach all uninsured pregnant women and children in families with incomes less than twice the poverty line. This will address a significant part of the rising tide of "disinsuredness," with one out of five American children currently lacking any public or private health insurance.

I. OVERVIEW

The first high school graduating class of the twenty-first century entered first grade in September 1988. They are the future workers, parents, college students, taxpayers, soldiers and leaders of America in the twenty-first century. Many of these young children are off to a healthy start, but millions of them are not. Today:

* one in four of them is poor;
* one in five is at risk of becoming a teen parent;
* one in five has no health insurance;
* one in seven will drop out of school, if current dropout rates do not decline;
* one in two has a mother in the labor force but only a minority have safe, affordable, quality child care.

Our society is aging and the proportion of Americans who are young is declining. So America will need all of our young to be healthy, educated and productive workers. But if current trends continue, a disproportionate number of them will grow up poor, undereducated and untrained. In a recent report of the Committee for Economic Development, *Children in Need: Investment Strategies for the Economically Disadvantaged*, 225 corporate executive officers and university presidents stated the compelling national self-interest in investing in children:

This nation cannot continue to compete and prosper in the global arena when more than one-fifth of our children live in poverty and a third grow up in ignorance. And if the nation cannot compete, it cannot lead. If we continue to squander the talents of millions of our children America will become a nation of limited human potential. It would be tragic if we allow this to happen. America must become a land of opportunity — for every child.

The new president and Congress must make preventive investment in children and families the cornerstone of national domestic policy. This commitment must go beyond rhetoric and be bolstered by a comprehensive, well-conceived national investment strategy in specific, cost-effective, successful programs for children and families beginning in 1989 and sustained over the next decade. While children cannot vote, lobby for or implement the policies and investment they need to grow up secure, the rest of us must.

Although there are no single fixes for the too-long neglected needs of our children and families, there are solutions within our means that can save millions of children. We know a lot about what works and have a foundation of cost-effective successful public programs to build on that did not exist twenty years ago. What has been missing is the moral and political urgency required to make children a leading national priority. For the facts of their distress are undeniable:

Our children are not physically safe from preventable infant mortality. A black baby born in our nation's capital or in Boston or Indianapolis is more likely to die before his or her first birthday than a baby born in Jamaica. Any American baby is more likely to die in the first year of life than a baby born in Singapore. In 1985 the infant mortality rate for whites alone placed the United States fourteenth worldwide, behind Hong Kong and Japan. The black infant mortality rate alone placed us 28th in the world, behind Bulgaria and equal to Costa Rica and Poland. Many of these deaths are preventable with cost-effective prenatal care. That black babies still die at twice the rate of white babies and at rates worse than babies in some Third World countries cannot but tarnish the appeal of the American Dream and send a signal of racial injustice to a world two-thirds nonwhite and predominantly poor.

American children are not safe from preventable childhood diseases. At a time when UNICEF is mounting a worldwide immunization campaign, American leadership on immunizing our own children has faltered. The incidence of infectious childhood disease among American children is rising while child immunization rates are declining. In 1985 one in three nonwhite inner-city children (1-4) had received no immunization against measles, mumps or rubella.

American children are not safe from hunger and malnutrition. Although child hunger was virtually eliminated in the 1970s with the expansion of federal food programs in the Nixon years, the Physician Task Force on Hunger in America reports it now afflicts an estimated 20 million Americans each month. Nearly half a million children are malnourished. Yet the number of food stamp recipients, one half of whom are children, dropped from sixty-eight to sixty for every 100 poor people between 1980 and 1986.

American children are not safe from growing homelessness. Hundreds of thousands of children literally have no place of their own to lay their heads as family homelessness escalates, as family housing supply shrinks and as wages fall behind inflation and rents soar. When eight-month-old Shamal Jackson died a couple of years ago in New York City, the cause of his death was poverty complicated by low birthweight, poor nutrition, homelessness and viral infection. During his short life he had never slept in an apartment or house. He had been in shelters with strangers, in hospitals, in welfare hotels, in the welfare office and in the subways which he and his mother rode late at night when there was no place else to go. Shamal was only one small victim of our nation's failure to respond to the pervasive child poverty that kills an American child every fifty-three minutes. We lose more children to poverty every five years than we lost in battle casualties during all of the Vietnam War.

American children are not safe from abuse, neglect and violence. There were an estimated 2.2 million reported cases of abuse or neglect in 1986. The violence in too many of our homes is mirrored in the violence in too many of our streets. Homicide is the fifteenth leading cause of infant death. Every year guns take the lives of 3,200 innocent children and auto accidents, many at the hands of drunk drivers, steal 10,500 children's lives, three times more than cancer. Every day parents and children in the Henry Horner Homes in Chicago walk to school through a war zone controlled by lawless gangs. *The New York Times* editorial page described children "exposed daily to stray bullets and to the violent deaths of siblings and schoolmates. Their experience at times sounds like that of the children of Belfast or Beirut."

American children are not safe from too-early sexual activity, pregnancy, abortion and parenthood. A million American girls under the age of twenty get pregnant each year and half of them have their children. Two-thirds of teen parents are white, two-thirds are not poor and two-thirds are not living in inner cities, although poor and minority girls are disproportionately likely to become teen parents.

Our children are not educationally safe. One in seven drops out of school. And millions more who remain in school are not developing the strong basic skills they need to become productive workers. This has disastrous consequences for the young people themselves and for the American economy now and in the future. Youths who by age eighteen have the weakest reading and math skills, when compared with those with above-average basic skills, are eight times more likely to bear children out of wedlock, nine times more likely to drop out of school before graduation, five times more likely to be out of work and four times more likely to be on public assistance.

Our children are not economically safe. Of every 100 children born today, thirteen will be born to teenage mothers, fifteen will be born into households where no parent is employed, fifteen will be born into households with a working parent earning a below-poverty wage and twenty-five will be on welfare at some point prior to adulthood.

In particular trouble are America's youngest families. For the last fifteen years, even during periods of economic expansion, Americans younger than 30 have been suffering from a cycle of plummeting earnings and family incomes, declining marriage rates, rising out-of-wedlock birth rates, increasing numbers of single-parent families and increasing poverty rates. Families headed by persons age 30 and older generally have held their own, but young families (headed by individuals younger than 30) have been sliding backward.

The median income of young families with children fell by 26 percent from 1973 to 1986 — a loss virtually identical to the 27 percent drop in per capita income that occurred during the Depression from 1929 to 1933. As a result, 35 percent of all children in young families were poor in 1986, compared to 21 percent in 1973. Young families also increasingly are likely to hold jobs that don't have health insurance, are unable to get a foothold in the housing market and are in desperate need of child care help as more young mothers enter the workforce to try to prop up the families' income in the face of the young fathers' declining earnings. The rising proportion of young female-headed families also is related directly to the declining earnings of young workers. Young men who earn enough to support a family are three to four times more likely to marry than those without such adequate earnings. As the earnings of young men fell sharply between 1973 and 1986, their marriage rates dropped by one-third and the proportion of births to young women that were out of wedlock nearly doubled, rising from 15 percent in 1973 to 28 percent in 1986.

Given these growing dangers to America's children, Washington must demonstrate throughout the 1990s a commitment to families and children by acting to build on known, successful preventive investments in children and families.

First steps include:

* Assuring that every eligible mother and child receives the nutrition supplements provided by the Special Supplemental Food Program for Women, Infants and Children (WIC). Currently fewer than half of those who are eligible receive WIC services, even though every $1 invested in WIC saves an estimated $3 in reduced health costs.

* Extending Head Start over five years to at least half the poor 3-5 year-old children in America. The Head Start program has demonstrated success in preparing and helping children do better in school. Yet Head Start reaches only 18 percent of the eligible children. To reach half of these poor children eligible, we must increase funding for the program by $400 million in each of the next several

years. The estimated long-term savings are at least $4.75 for every
$1 we invest in quality child care programs for poor preschool chil-
dren.

  * Expanding the federal Chapter 1 program of special educational assistance for disadvantaged children. Chapter 1 has demonstrated success in helping children develop strong basic skills. The
average Chapter 1 investment of $600 per pupil also helps avert the
substantially larger cost of $4,000 incurred when a child must repeat
a grade and the much higher long-term cost if a child drops out of
school. And estimates are that each year's class of dropouts costs the
nation about $228 billion in lost earnings and $68 billion in lost taxes
during their lifetime. Chapter 1 funds must be increased until they
are sufficient to reach all rather than just the half of the eligible
children currently served.

  Finally, the new administration must move immediately to confront, as discussed in the following two sections, the nation's growing
child care crisis and a level of health uninsuredness that erodes maternal and child health.

II. CHILD CARE

  This nation must begin to make an adequate investment in child
care for its youngest and most vulnerable citizens. Certainly every
mother should have the choice to stay at home with her young children, and parents should have the job and income security that they
need to remain home during the critical early months after child-
birth. Yet, although we have undergone a massive demographic
shift as millions of mothers of young children have entered the
workforce, our society currently neither supports parenting at home
nor helps parents when they must go out to work.

  Most mothers of young children have joined the labor force, for
example, making decent child care a necessity for families from every income group. Yet our current patchwork child care system is
strained beyond capacity. Because it cannot meet the growing demand, many families — especially low and moderate-income families
— are forced to leave their children in inadequate and sometimes
dangerous child care. Too many are left alone, with slightly older
siblings or in overcrowded, unsafe or unstimulating care.

  The media have reported a growing list of shocking tragedies
that result from a fragile child care system and inadequate support
to working parents. Four-year-old Maurice and his three-year-old
brother, Anthony, who died when left alone in their Dade County
home after their mother's informal child care arrangements fell
through. She and 22,000 other low-income working parents in Florida
were on a waiting list for publicly subsidized child care — a list

that grew to almost 30,000 in the year after Maurice and Anthony died.

The number of children with working parents will continue its rapid rise. There are 9.5 million pre-school children with mothers in the workforce. By 1995 there will be 15 million. By 1995 two-thirds of all pre-school children and four out of five school-age children will have mothers in the work force. Consequently, child care is essential to helping families be self-sufficient. Parents need child care to enable them to work, pay the bills and be more productive on the job. For many two-parent families today, the second income is all that stands between them and poverty. The House Select Committee on Children, Youth and Families found that the number of two parent families living below the poverty line would increase by more than 50 percent if the women in them were not employed.

For millions of single mothers, moreover, working and putting their children in day care is the only route out of poverty. Yet, more than 200,000 single and married non-working mothers of young children turn down job offers each month because child care cannot be found or afforded. The cost currently averages $3,000 per year per child. Infant care costs even more.

Child care is essential to help parents be productive once they are on the job. Employers are increasingly concerned about the negative effects of a patchwork system on their current and future labor force. A 1986 *Fortune* magazine study of 400 working parents with children younger than twelve concluded that dissatisfaction with child care was the most reliable predictor of workers' absenteeism and unproductive work time.

Young parents with young children and single parents are those least likely to be able to afford child care without public help. The median annual income for a single mother with at least one child younger than six was only $6,400 in 1985, less than the federally established poverty line for a family of two. The cost of child care for one child equals nearly half of that median wage. Young families' falling income — whether they are married couples or single-parent families — makes it increasingly hard for them to pay for care.

As families cannot find or afford care, millions of young children are left to care for themselves. Children spending a great deal of time alone are often consumed by fear. In 1984, children were invited to write to the language arts magazine *Sprint*, published by Scholastic, Incorporated in New York City, in response to the theme: "Think of a situation that is scary to you. How do you handle your fear?" The readership of this magazine includes fourth, fifth and sixth graders from all over the country, and the exercise was designed purely as a way of stimulating children to practice their writing. The editors were stunned to discover that nearly 70 percent of the

7,000 letters that poured in dealt with the fear of being home alone, mostly while parents were working.

A study for the Metropolitan Life Insurance Company quoted a majority of the more than 1,000 teachers interviewed as citing isolation and lack of supervision after school as the major reason children have difficulty in school.

Despite the tremendous growth in demand for decent and affordable child care, federal leadership has been non-existent during the 1980s. The child care crisis can only be met through an active collaboration between the federal government, state and local government, parents and the private sector. While some state governments and employers have made valiant efforts to meet the demand, they are too few and those who have tried still have not come anywhere near fulfilling the need. Only about 3,500 out of six million employers have made any significant investment in child care help for employees, and only a handful of these provide funding assistance.

The federal government currently has no program with the sole purpose of providing direct assistance to help lower-income families pay for child care. The Title XX Social Services Block Grant is the largest source of direct federal funds to states for child care, but it also covers a wide range of other social service needs. Only about 18 percent of Title XX dollars go to child care, and that 18 percent is sliced from a shrinking pie. Title XX suffered a 20 percent reduction in FY 1982 due to budget cuts requested by President Reagan and passed by Congress, and since then has received only two modest increases, not enough to offset the impact of either the 1982 cut or years of inflation. After adjusting for inflation, the federal Title XX appropriation for FY 1988 is less than half that of FY 1977. In 1987, twenty-eight states spent less in real dollars for child care funded through the Title XX Social Services Block Grant than they did in 1981. Only 18 states were serving more children than they did in 1981. At the same time, the number of children younger than six living in poverty rose by more than 40 percent.

Some states have attempted to make up for shrinking federal help by increasing their own commitments for child care. Particularly in the mid-1980s, more governors and state legislatures acknowledged the link between investing in child care and their states' economic vitality. But states' overall spending for child care in real dollars is still stuck at roughly 1981 levels.

The result is that states assist only a fraction of lower-income families which need child care help. For example, half the counties in Kentucky do not offer child care assistance to low-income working families; Seattle and New York City each serve only one of five eligible children.

There is one large federal effort to help families pay for child care: the dependent care tax credit, which allows working families a partial credit on their federal income taxes to offset some day care costs. Spending on the credit has grown substantially in the past decade, but nearly all of this tax break goes to better-off families. Low and lower-moderate income families, particularly after the 1986 tax reform, have no or very small federal income tax liabilities and therefore are not able to use the credit. Also, the credit neither expands the supply of child care nor improves the quality of care.

Even refundable tax breaks would not substitute for direct assistance because the tax relief usually proposed comes nowhere near the cost of care. A family living at the poverty line, even if it were to receive a $1,000 credit from the government, simply cannot afford the additional $2,000 or more that quality child care will cost.

The Alliance for Better Child Care, now composed of more than 130 national organizations, has devised an excellent response: the Act for Better Child Care Services (ABC). ABC, when enacted, will build a stronger state-federal partnership to start creating an adequate child care system in this country. Under ABC each state has the freedom to design its own program, and each parent has the freedom to choose among a variety of safe child care arrangements for the best setting for the child.

ABC reserves most of its $2.5 billion funding to go to states to help poor and low-moderate income families pay for child care. States will design sliding fee scales, giving greater help to the poorer families. Some of the funds would be reserved for additional help to state and local public preschool programs, Head Start and Chapter I programs for preschool children and preschool programs for handicapped children, enabling these programs to extend their hours of service to full day and full year. It makes good sense to build on these programs which typically are excellent but cannot serve the needs of working parents because they only operate part-day.

Recognizing that states use a variety of funding mechanisms, the bill encourages that variety — from contracts with a range of child care providers to the provision of child care certificates to parents. States choosing to use child care certificates would also provide resource and referral programs to help families locate and choose child care that best meets their needs. The use of family day care homes as well as child care centers (both non-profit and profit) is encouraged.

Research consistently shows that children's development is enhanced in programs with adequate numbers of staff trained in early childhood education skills. Only 27 states now require continuing training for teachers while they are employed in child care centers. Forty-two states do not require training for family day care providers. ABC will take a first step toward expanding the number of trained caregivers by requiring that all states offer all caregivers a minimum of 15 hours of training per year, in areas essential to working successfully with young children.

ABC would also establish minimum health and safety protections for children in care. Current child care standards set by individual states vary widely and are often so inadequate that they fail to provide for the most basic safety of children. Thirty-one states, for example, do not establish any maximum group size for preschoolers, and 25 states do not set a maximum for infants, even though a small group is the key to each child's learning, health and safety. Ten states have no specific health training requirements for staff in child care centers. And 29 states have no regulations guaranteeing unlimited parental access to child care centers — another key safeguard of quality and safety.

Because the absence of standards endangers children and families, ABC will establish a bare minimum national safety floor for children in both child care centers and family day care homes. A national Advisory Committee will establish standards in five particular areas that have a great impact on the quality of care: staff-child ratios, group size, parent involvement, caregiver qualifications and health and safety. With regard to ratios and group size, the standards will be set at the current median for all states. For example, the staff-child ratio for infants would be one to four, which would improve care for infants in forty percent of the states. Those states with even better standards will be encouraged to keep their current requirements. ABC will make funds available to enable family day care providers and child care centers to come into compliance with the safety and health protections.

ABC does not create a new federal bureaucracy to monitor day care services or provide them. The entire range of existing day care providers — profit and non-profit, public and private, center-based and family day care — will provide the ABC services. States will assure compliance with health, safety and quality standards. ABC thus builds upon existing efforts and offers states and localities maximum flexibility in tailoring child care to the needs of the families in their communities. The only option that will not be available to states is allowing children to be placed in substandard child care. We need more child care, but it must be child care in which children will not be abused or endangered.

III. HEALTH CARE

Access to medical care for pregnant women and children should not be a privilege reserved for those who can afford it. Our society has a fundamental self-interest, as well as a moral obligation, to make sure that its children are not suffering and grow up as healthy as possible. Every industrialized nation except the United States and South Africa ensures that its citizens, particularly its pregnant women and children, have access to basic care through health insurance or a public health service.

Good health care yields major and long-term benefits to children and to the nation:

* Babies born to mothers who receive early and adequate prenatal care are only one third as likely to die and one-fourth to one-half as likely to be born at low birthweight — a major cause of infant death and long-term disability — as babies whose mothers receive no prenatal care.

* Children who receive routine health exams and preventive medical care for diagnosed conditions, such as vision and hearing problems, emotional illness or physical disabilities, are at lower risk of poor school performance and lifelong poor health than those who do not.

* The benefits to society of good health programs far outweigh the costs. Every dollar spent on prenatal care saves more than $3 in costs to society during infancy alone by reducing the need for expensive neonatal hospital care, and $11 over the child's lifetime by avoiding the medical, social and educational costs associated with preventable lifelong disabilities. Every dollar spent to immunize children has been shown to save more than $10 by reducing the incidence of serious illness and death.

Health services are very expensive in this country, so expensive that access to health insurance paid by an employer or the government has become a crucial determinant of access to health care. Yet, many — especially lower income working families and unemployed families — are covered by neither private nor public insurance. Many others are insured for only a portion of each year.

Among low-income children, those who are uninsured receive only about one-half as much medical care as those with health insurance. Yet the cracks in both our private and public health insurance systems have been widening. Between 1982 and 1986, the number of uninsured Americans grew from 30 million to 37 million.

Private health insurance payments are the largest means by which non-elderly Americans pay for health care, and most private insurance is provided as an employment-related fringe benefit. Seventy-five percent of all privately insured Americans are covered by employer-based plans. But a child's access to this system depends on whether and where his or her parents work. The system not only generally excludes the unemployed and their families, it also does not help members of families — usually at the lower end of the wage scale — which are headed by parents whose employers do not offer their employees subsidized health insurance coverage as a fringe benefit. For example, 30 percent of all employers who pay the minimum wage to most of their workers offer them no health insurance. The system also excludes children when employers either do not offer coverage to employees' dependents or offer only an unsubsidized plan with monthly premium costs that are unaffordable for lower income workers.

Not surprisingly, therefore, low-income adults and children are the groups least likely to be privately insured. In 1985 two out of three uninsured persons and three out of four uninsured children had family incomes less than 200 percent of the federal poverty level.

A high proportion of the uninsured live in families that work. In 1985, 70 percent of the uninsured were either full-time, full-year workers or the spouses or children of such workers. A child living in a poor working family has only one-half the chance of a non-poor child to be insured privately.

The number of privately uninsured families has risen dramatically in the 1980s for three main reasons. First, lower wage service sector jobs (especially part-time jobs) that do not offer insurance account for an increasing proportion of all employment. Second, even among employers that do make health insurance available, a growing number are choosing to subsidize less or none of the cost of coverage, and many employees can not afford the resulting premiums. In a recent survey, one-third of employers reported a reduction in their contributions toward their employees' family coverage. Third, the growing number of children living in single-parent families face a reduced possibility that at least one parent will have employer-based health insurance that covers dependents.

The United States has no uniform public health insurance program for lower income families with children that parallels Medicare's blanket coverage of the elderly and the long-term totally disabled. Instead, we have a patchwork of health programs that do not have sufficient funds to reach even a majority of those in need.

Medicaid is a federal-state program that offers insurance-like benefits to some poor families with children, but the federal Medicaid law has never required states to cover all poor children. Mandatory coverage extended basically only to those receiving Aid to Families with Dependent Children. Yet AFDC rules deny help to most poor two-parent families and set eligibility levels far below the poverty line, thereby effectively excluding millions of indigent children from Medicaid. As AFDC benefits have fallen drastically compared to the cost of living, Medicaid coverage has shrunk further.

Hundreds of thousands of additional children lost their Medicaid insurance due to the Omnibus Budget Reconciliation Act of 1981, which both eliminated certain Medicaid coverage groups and severely curtailed AFDC (and thus Medicaid) benefits for poor working families.

As a result of these limitations and cut-backs, the percentage of poor children covered by Medicaid fell dramatically, from 66 percent in 1976 to 49 percent by 1986.

Recent changes made by Congress have improved Medicaid substantially for pregnant women and children — a hopeful shift in direction after the disastrous reductions in coverage made in the early 1980s. Policymakers at all levels of government saw that these cuts were followed by downturns in key health indicators such as prenatal care delivery. A new consensus gradually is emerging at all levels of government that the traditional rules arbitrarily limiting Medicaid to a fraction of poor children and parents are simply inappropriate in an era when so many millions of low-income persons, from both working and non-working families, are uninsured.

The recent federal reforms have in some cases required states to expand Medicaid eligibility and in other instances given them options to do so. For example, Congress approved progressively broader legislation in 1984, 1986, 1987 and 1988 that requires states to provide Medicaid coverage to any pregnant woman and infant up to age one with a family income below the federal poverty level, and to any child age one to eight who has a family income below state AFDC eligibility standards, regardless of the composition of the family. These new laws also permit states to provide Medicaid to pregnant women and infants with incomes above poverty but below 185 percent of the poverty line, and to children age one to eight with family income above state AFDC financial eligibility levels but below 100 percent of the federal poverty line.

These federal reforms, taken together, are a significant first step — but only a first step — toward the restructuring of Medicaid from what was essentially a companion to welfare into a basic public health payment system for persons without access to private insurance.

Several other federally funded public health programs provide direct grants to states and communities to develop health care systems to serve particular needy populations. The Title V Maternal and Child Health Block Grant program primarily funds state and local public health clinics that provide free or low-cost basic maternity and pediatric care to millions of poor and near-poor women and children each year. Nearly 600 federally funded Community and Migrant Health Centers served more than 5 million persons in 1986, about two-thirds of them children or women of childbearing age. Federal immunization grants are used to purchase and administer life-saving vaccines for millions of American children. In 1986 the federal immunization grants program purchased more than 16 million doses of the vaccines.

These public health programs have been effective and saved money. In 1963, before most of the current programs existed, only 63 percent of pregnant women in America began prenatal care during the first trimester of pregnancy. By 1979 that figure had grown to 76 percent. Between 1964 and 1975 poor children increased their use of physician services by three-fourths, so that by the late 1970s publicly insured low-income children were visiting physicians nearly as frequently as other children.

Predictably, the improved access to health care resulted in improvements in health. The nation's rate of low-birthweight births, which had been rising, declined substantially from 1965 to 1980. While overall infant mortality fell only 15 percent from 1950 to 1965, it fell by 49 percent between 1965 and 1980. The death rate among black infants dropped only 5 percent in the fifteen years before Medicaid, but it plummeted by more than 50 percent in the fifteen years that followed.

The immunization program also has chalked up remarkable successes. Through this effort, smallpox has been eradicated and the incidence of such fatal and crippling diseases as diphtheria, pertussis, congenital rubella, measles, mumps and polio have been reduced drastically. Our nation has achieved up to a 99 percent reduction of these infectious diseases that previously led to suffering, permanent impairments and death. The measles vaccine, for example, has meant that 80,000 children who would have died in the past twenty years are healthy and thriving today because they did not contract measles. Institutions serving children with severe mental retardation have had 80,000 fewer patients in the past two decades because of reductions in the number of children suffering brain damage from measles.

While they have made a crucial difference for public health, these federal public health programs are hampered by inadequate funding and often arbitrary eligibility rules. None of them can take the place of comprehensive insurance coverage.

During the 1970s, when many of these health programs achieved their highest funding levels in real terms, they still reached only a fraction of the women and children in need of them. Since 1980 their effectiveness has been curbed severely by federal budget cuts and freezes. While some of the funding lost early in the 1980s has been restored in more recent years, most of these programs have not received enough funding to keep pace with inflation, much less meet the additional demand for their services caused by increases in poverty and disinsurance. The Title V Maternal and Child Health Block Grant and Migrant Health Center programs are operating at funding levels below the amounts needed to maintain their services at 1981 levels. Community Health Centers are operating at levels that barely match those of 1981. Immunization funding has failed to keep pace with either demand or skyrocketing vaccine price inflation. Each year in the 1981-1986 period, fewer doses were administered in the public sector than in each year from 1978 to 1980. The 1986 total is estimated to be only 80 percent of the doses delivered in 1979.

The Reagan Administration also ceased collection of data through the key statistical system that was capable of showing unmet need for immunizations. Despite the fact that surveillance has been identified as an essential element of immunization efforts, the Administration in 1986 discontinued the U.S. Immunization Survey (USIS), the only report that provided an annual snapshot of childhood immunization levels.

All of these cutbacks and freezes, combined with the growing disinsurance of children and young adults, has led to an erosion in key maternal and child health indicators:

Infant mortality: Improvement in the rate of infant mortality (deaths in the first year in life) is seen as a very sensitive indicator of a nation's health status. 1985 was the first year since 1960 that the national rate of neonatal mortality (deaths within the first twenty-eight days of life) did not improve over the prior year. Moreover, this overall lack of progress masked an even more troubling 3 percent nationwide increase in neonatal mortality among black infants. Not since 1964, prior to the advent of critical public health programs such as Medicaid and community health centers, have neonatal mortality rates among black infants increased.

Low birthweight and prematurity: Between 1970 and 1979, the percentage of infants born at low birthweight (weighing less than 5.5 pounds) decreased 13 percent nationally. However, between 1980 and 1983, the percentage of low-birthweight births failed to decline at all. Following a slight improvement in 1984, the incidence of low birthweight rose in 1985, returning to 1980 levels. A national increase in the incidence of low birthweight had not been seen previously in the United States since 1961. This increase was accompanied by a nationwide rise in prematurity.

Adequacy of prenatal care: Between 1984 and 1985, the percentage of all women who received early prenatal care (beginning in the first trimester) declined, and the percentage of women who received either no care or none until the last three months of pregnancy rose for the fourth time since 1980.

Childhood Immunization Rates: The rate of immunization of our nation's children against polio, measles, mumps, rubella, diphtheria and tetanus generally declined between 1980 and 1985, reversing progress toward national goals in this area and inviting outbreaks of a range of diseases. For example, the proportion of children younger than one not fully immunized for their age against polio was 20.4 percent in 1985. Among nonwhite infants, a staggering 41.5 percent were not adequately immunized, up from 26.8 percent in 1980.

Sexually transmitted diseases: More than half of all teens are sexually active today, putting them at risk of sexually transmitted diseases (including AIDS) and too-early and unintended pregnancies. Sexually active adolescents ages fifteen through nineteen suffer the highest overall rates of sexually transmitted diseases among any age group of Americans. The risk of disease is estimated to be two to three times higher for teens than for individuals age twenty or older.

Teenage pregnancy: Each year one million American teens become pregnant. While American teens are no more likely to be sexually active than teens in Great Britain, France or Canada, their pregnancy rate is twice as high as the rates found in these countries and three times as high as that in Sweden. Although black teen pregnancy rates are higher than white rates in the United States, the pregnancy rate among white U.S. teens alone is higher than the rate among teens of all races in several other industrialized countries.

The nation's lack of progress or, in some cases, outright regression on maternal and infant health measurements and childhood immunization means that the nation will fail to meet many of the health goals set by the Surgeon General of the United States for 1990. These modest goals were established in 1979 and reaffirmed by the Reagan Administration in 1984.

The nation must renew its commitment to making progress in maternal and child health, but it cannot make progress while so many millions of families are excluded from necessary medical care by poverty and lack of health insurance. All Americans need health insurance, either through their employers or through public programs.

As a first step, the federal government must extend Medicaid coverage to reach all uninsured pregnant women and children in families with incomes less than twice the poverty line, which would cost under $2 billion.

Additionally, every eligible mother and child must be assured the nutritional supplements provided by the WIC program. Funding for the Title V Maternal and Child Health Block Grant and the Community Health Centers program should be sufficient to permit the development of health services in all medically underserved areas. And to prevent the rising incidence of infectious childhood diseases and declining immunization rates and to reach the modest immunization goal of the U.S. Surgeon General for 1990, an immediate and substantial increase in the appropriation is required. In FY 1988 the total immunization program cost less than we spend each year just on military musical bands and less than the federal government has spent since 1980 on price supports for honey. Increasing spending on the vital and cost effective immunization program is one of the wisest federal investments that can be made. The U.S. Department of Health and Human Services must also resume immediately surveillance of the immunization status of our nation's children.

A nation that cannot, or even worse, will not shield its defenseless babies from preventable death and sickness in the first year of life when it has the means at hand forfeits its right to be called decent. Saving our babies' lives is not a budget issue. It is not a deficit issue. It is an issue of self-preservation. And it is a moral issue.

CITIZEN PARTICIPATION: ACTION & The Peace Corps

Mimi Mager & Francis A. Luzzatto*

SUMMARY OF RECOMMENDATIONS

Citizen participation and voluntarism have a long and rich history in America. As early as 1830 de Tocqueville noted how volunteer activities were tightly woven into the fabric of society.

In his inaugural address, President Kennedy challenged each of us to do more for our country. Recognizing the role the federal government must play in supporting full-time volunteers, he created the Peace Corps and proposed a National Service Corps. President Johnson, building upon these initiatives, proposed the creation of Volunteers in Service to America (VISTA), a federally supported full-time domestic anti-poverty volunteer program as an integral component of his War on Poverty. They were followed by President Nixon's creation of the ACTION Agency as the federal volunteer umbrella agency.

Over the past eight years, however, President Reagan broke with his predecessors to undermine the notion of public service and voluntarism. Voluntarism was held out as a means of "filling the gap" caused by draconian cuts in social programs and as a convenient way to divest the federal government of its responsibility to address social problems. Self-service and lip-service rather than public service were the Reagan Administration's trademark in the field of voluntarism.

The next president must encourage, promote and reward voluntary service and citizen participation at the national, state and community levels. Contributing to one's community, country and world is a civic opportunity open to the young and citizens of all ages.

Throughout the ACTION Agency portion of this chapter, the VISTA program receives by far the most attention for two reasons:

---

* *Mimi Mager served as Executive Director of Friends of VISTA from 1981-1986 and as Special Assistant to the VISTA Director from 1979-1980. Francis A. Luzzatto worked for the Peace Corps for more than 13 years and is a contributor to* Making a Difference: The Peace Corps at Twenty-Five.

(1) VISTA represents the federal government's *only* full-time domestic anti-poverty volunteer program; and (2) in the Reagan Administration no programs within ACTION, and few within the federal government, were subject to such continued and vitriolic attacks aimed at eliminating the program.

Key recommendations for ACTION and the Peace Corps include these:

* Depoliticize ACTION, and secure broad-based bipartisan support for the Agency and its programs.

* Use the 25th Anniversary of VISTA as the vehicle to revitalize the program and thereby achieve the goal of supporting 5,500 VISTA volunteer service years by the end of the first term.

* Establish ACTION as the point Agency in the federal government for developing and supporting national and community service initiatives.

* Diversify the Peace Corps' approach to assigning and supporting its volunteers overseas so that it will be able to field more volunteers in more countries, thereby achieving its 10,000 volunteer goal.

* Develop specific methods for the Peace Corps to share its Third World perspective with the American people, thereby giving substance to its third goal "to promote a better understanding of people of other countries among the American people."

* Seek ways for the Peace Corps to have a broader impact by disseminating its field-generated methodologies to others working in community-based international development programs.

Both ACTION and the Peace Corps have proven to be wise federal investments, yielding benefits to the people and countries served by each program, as well as to the volunteers themselves, that far outweigh the expenditure of federal resources.

I. ACTION: HISTORICAL PERSPECTIVE

In July 1971, under reorganization Plan No. 1, President Nixon created the ACTION Agency by bringing together all the Federal volunteer programs previously administered throughout the government. Nixon declared that this reorganization plan would achieve greater voluntary citizen service.

Despite widespread opposition by members of the anti-poverty community, the private voluntary sector and key leaders in Congress, Congress approved the Plan and on July 1, 1971 ACTION was established. ACTION's primary purpose is to foster and expand voluntary citizen service in communities around the Nation through activities designed to help the poor, the disadvantaged, the vulnerable and the elderly. Combined under its one roof were Volunteers in Service to America (VISTA), the Retired Senior Volunteer Program (RSVP), the Foster Grandparent Program (FGP) and other domestic programs, and programs of the Small Business Administration, such as SCORE (Senior Corps of Retired Executives) and ACE (Active Corps of Executives), along with the Peace Corps.

This "shotgun marriage" of programs created administrative havoc and was viewed by both Peace Corps and VISTA advocates as a way to reduce the Peace Corps' visibility and to undermine the coordinated anti-poverty efforts of the Office of Economic Opportunity (OEO).

Since its beginning, ACTION has been guided primarily by the prevailing political winds. To ACTION's detriment, each of the four administrations since 1971 has fought over it with the opposition party in Congress. ACTION has survived due in large part to the strength, popularity and successes of a number of its flagship programs, including VISTA, RSVP and FGP — and in part to the tenacity and commitment of its career civil servants. However, unless attempts to politicize the ACTION Agency and its programs cease, it will never be able to achieve its full potential.

ACTION UNDER THE REAGAN ADMINISTRATION

ACTION was more dramatically affected by the 1980 election of Ronald Reagan than perhaps any other federal agency. Thomas Pauken, Reagan's first Director of ACTION, represented the antithesis of the ACTION Director under the Carter Administration, Sam Brown. A Vietnam war veteran and an avowed right-wing conservative ideologue, Pauken was obsessed with changing what he viewed as ACTION's liberal philosophy and agenda. The directorship of ACTION was Pauken's vehicle to pursue the New Right's agenda to "defund the left."

From the outset Pauken's tenure was mired with controversy. One of his first items of business was to attempt to "phase out" the VISTA program. VISTA was viewed as a haven for "leftist agitators" and a remnant of the War on Poverty. Merely changing the program's direction was unacceptable. Rather, VISTA had to be wiped from the books for fear that a future Democratic Administration might revive it.

Political background checks of former and potential ACTION program grantees became the norm under Pauken's leadership. Longtime career employees of the Agency were given notice, transferred or reassigned to do-nothing jobs, and quickly the agency became inundated with political appointees who shared the Director's philosophy and agenda.

Throughout Pauken's four-year tenure, Congress played a particularly strong and effective oversight role. Congressional committees and the General Accounting Office investigated charges of illegal misappropriation of funds, questionable hiring and funding practices and politicization of the ACTION Agency's programs and staff. As a result of Congressional and GAO actions, attempts to misappropriate and divert funds were halted — and the programs survived.

After four years at ACTION's helm, Tom Pauken resigned and was replaced by Donna Alvarado. By then Congress had firmly secured VISTA's future through the remainder of the Administration; and the first significant new program development and expansion was being forced upon the Agency by Congress.

PROPOSALS FOR ACTION

The first priority is to appoint experienced and committed individuals to the Directorship of VISTA, the Older American Volunteer Programs and other political and career positions in Washington, D.C. and the field. Because the Director will face a demoralized agency, it is imperative that he or she make every effort to involve career staff as trusted allies in rebuilding the Agency and setting its future agenda.   Special attention must be given to rebuilding the Agency's infrastructure.

Next, the Agency must reestablish a positive working relationship with Congress, the private voluntary sector, anti-poverty and senior advocates and agency program sponsors and volunteers. Other critical tasks include:

* Serving as the advocate for voluntarism and public service within the federal government;

* Establishing ACTION as the point agency in the federal government for developing and supporting national and community service initiatives;

* Reactivating the National Volunteer Advisory Council;

* Reestablishing ties with the Peace Corps; and

* Mounting a national recruitment and public awareness campaign to support the Agency's programs.

Legislative initiatives are the Agency's next priority. ACTION must immediately prepare an amended FY 90 budget submission and a FY 91 budget, as well as prepare for the FY 90 appropriations hearings and the reauthorization of ACTION's enabling legislation, the Domestic Volunteer Service Act. As a part of the reauthorization process, the new administration should consider amending the statute to make the VISTA and OAVP director positions Presidential appointments and changing ACTION's name to more accurately reflect its purpose, programs and volunteers.

At the first term's conclusion, ACTION should no longer be considered a controversial agency and its goals — to encourage voluntarism, citizen participation and expanded opportunities for service

— should have been depoliticized. The agency should have reestablished a permanent working relationship with the Peace Corps and have explored the feasibility of reuniting the agencies. Finally, ACTION by then should have built a solid program and budgetary base and generated strong bipartisan support.

II. VISTA: HISTORICAL PERSPECTIVE

VISTA (Volunteers in Service to America) was officially created as one of several anti-poverty programs authorized by the Economic Opportunity Act of 1964. The seed was planted, however, during the summer of 1962 when President Kennedy appointed a task force, headed by Attorney General Robert Kennedy, to investigate the need for a National Service Corps and develop an outline for such a program.

In his State of the Union address in January 1963, President Kennedy made his first public reference to what was to become VISTA. Despite broad public support for the concept of a National Service Corps to address poverty in the United States, the National Service Corps proposal barely passed the Senate and effectively died following a fierce attack on the program by House conservatives.

The idea of a national anti-poverty service program was still very much alive when President Johnson on March 6, 1964 delivered a message to Congress, declaring: "The War on Poverty is not a struggle simply to support people, to make them dependent on the generosity of others. It is the struggle to give people a chance." VISTA is the federal government's only full-time domestic anti-poverty volunteer program. Over the past 24 years nearly 100,000 Americans have served as VISTA volunteers. Young and old. Rich and poor. VISTA volunteers commit themselves to work for one year, full-time, without regard for hours. They live within the low-income communities they serve and receive a subsistence level allowance.

Throughout the nearly 25 years of its existence, the VISTA program has evolved to more closely reflect the profile and needs of the low-income communities it serves. In 1965, VISTA volunteers were overwhelmingly white, middle-class college graduates who spent one year in a poor community away from their homes. During the early 1970s, community VISTAs were recruited from the low-income communities served by VISTA. These volunteers worked side-by-side with nationally recruited volunteers with special skills, thus enabling VISTA not only to serve the needs of the poor, but also to nurture local leadership capacity and community self-sufficiency.

VISTA UNDER REAGAN

Despite the extraordinary attempts by many of the six different Reagan VISTA Directors to dismantle the program, VISTA miraculously survived the Reagan reign. As the *New York Times* reported on the occasion of VISTA's 20th anniversary during the height of the assault on the program: "VISTA is the Agency that will not die....Despite the best laid plans for its demise, VISTA hangs on."

Friends of VISTA, a support and advocacy organization, led the battle against the Reagan Administration onslaught. Staffed by an Executive Director who was a former VISTA official in the Carter Administration and supported by a committed board and an active and highly respected Co-Chairman, Sargent Shriver, the group effectively galvanized VISTA's supporters at the grassroots and national levels, as well as in Congress.

Still, the Reagan Administration slashed VISTA's budget from $34 million, supporting approximately 4,500 volunteers in 1980, to $22 million, supporting 2,600 volunteers today. This is up from its low point of $11.8 million in FY 83, the year they slated the program for final phase-out.

Under Pauken, VISTA's anti-poverty mandate was subverted and VISTA'S funds were diverted to new "pet projects" that lacked a poverty focus. The Agency leadership went so far as to remove VISTA's name from the ACTION Agency stationery and ordered the destruction of all VISTA recruitment, public awareness and promotional materials. "Hit lists" of VISTA projects viewed as leftist were drawn up and targeted for elimination.

Young people in particular have suffered the most from ACTION's refusal to conduct national VISTA recruitment and public awareness efforts. As Derek Bok, President of Harvard University, testified before the Congress in 1986: "VISTA recruitment efforts and awareness programs on the nation's campuses have virtually ceased. I hope that VISTA's reauthorization will be a catalyst for increased awareness of VISTA on college campuses and greater recruitment efforts among students." Today a mere 12% of the volunteers are between the ages of 18 and 25, as compared to 74% in 1967 and 33% in 1978.

The popular perception today is that VISTA is either dead — or a credit card. Rather than encouraging and enabling the broadest range of citizens to serve as VISTA volunteers — as mandated under the law — the ACTION Agency has created stumbling blocks that act as disincentives for VISTA service.

Far too many people enrolling in VISTA today are doing so because they perceive it as the "best job" available. They are not necessarily the best qualified for the positions or committed to the notion of anti-poverty service. VISTA was never intended to be a low-income employment, income supplement or job training program. Despite these problems, VISTA's advocates achieved many victories during the Reagan years. Congress not only has continued the program but in 1986 created and funded a new VISTA Literacy Corps program to supplement and build upon VISTA's impressive attack on illiteracy at the community level throughout the United States.

With an FY 88 appropriation of $2.8 million, the Literacy Corps is supporting nearly 700 VISTAs. This is in addition to the nearly 400 literacy VISTAs, which are funded by the core VISTA program. Although the Reagan Administration requested zero funding for the VISTA Literacy Corps in FY 89, Congress approved the continuation of the program at its FY 88 funding level.

Through the eight years of the Reagan Administration, VISTA advocates managed to preserve the "body" and the "spirit" of the VISTA program. It will be up to the next administration and Congress to revive the heart and the soul of the program.

PRIORITIES AND RECOMMENDATIONS FOR VISTA

Key to the revival of VISTA is the appointment of a committed and experienced VISTA Director, coupled with the enthusiastic support of the ACTION Director and the White House. The VISTA national headquarter's staff, which has been reduced to four professionals, must be expanded and revitalized.

The VISTA Director should immediately seize the opportunity of VISTA's 25th anniversary (late 1989) to kick-off a major public awareness, recruitment and recognition campaign in support of VISTA. The Director must determine the quickest and most cost-efficient way to reinstate a VISTA national recruitment structure, with particular emphasis on recruiting young people and people with special skills into the program. Further, the director should establish a goal of 4000 volunteer service years by 1990 mandating that at least one-third of them be nationally recruited volunteers. First term goals must include the support of at least 5500 service years.

Attention needs to be focused on increasing VISTA's budget and preparing for VISTA's reauthorization. ACTION/VISTA must seek significant increases in the VISTA authorization levels and funding floors, as well as a continuation and expansion of the VISTA Literacy Corps.

Further amendments to the law are necessary to a) clarify that the legislative requirement that volunteers live at the economic level of the people they serve means that the VISTA subsistence allowance not be lower than the U.S. government's poverty index for a single individual and b) increase the end of service allowance from the $75 a month level for each month of completed service to $125 a month. (The Peace Corps level is $175.)

Programmatic goals and objectives need to be clearly articulated to the agency staff and the public at large. Specifically, new VISTA guidance papers clearly outlining the program's mission, philosophy and criteria for selection of projects must be developed and issued. A re-emphasis of the essential role of VISTA volunteers as catalysts and mobilizers of financial and volunteer resources, rather than as direct providers of services, is essential. ACTION/VISTA must actively seek grassroots, minority and citizen participation organizations as sponsors.

Agency officials must serve as advocates for VISTA within the federal government, identifying creative ways that VISTA could work with other federal agencies that share the anti-poverty mission of the VISTA program. Further, it is crucial that they promote the student loan deferments currently available to VISTA volunteers, seek expansion of the narrow loan forgiveness provisions currently available only to students with NDSL loans and encourage the efforts of universities and institutions of higher education to provide academic and financial incentives in recognition of full-time VISTA service on the part of students. And finally, VISTA must once again work in partnership with private sector organizations and advocacy groups such as Friends of VISTA that share the mission and support the goals of the VISTA program.

III. ACTION'S OLDER AMERICAN VOLUNTEER PROGRAMS: HISTORICAL PERSPECTIVE[*]

When ACTION was formed in 1971, the Older American Volunteer Programs included the Foster Grandparent Program (FGP) and the newly funded Retired Senior Volunteer Program (RSVP). The Senior Companion Program (SCP) was authorized as a new program in 1973. The Older American Volunteer Programs (OAVP) have been the fastest growing programs in ACTION. There were a total of 4,200 volunteers in 1971. Today, there are nearly 450,000, with a program budget of $163 million.

The Foster Grandparent Program was designed to link low-income seniors 60 years of age or older to children with special needs, whether they be physical, mental, emotional or social disabilities. Foster Grandparents work 20 hours a week and receive a stipend of $2.20 an hour. Currently 17,600 low-income seniors are serving as FGP volunteers in 250 federally supported projects across the nation.

---

[*] Another element of ACTION, not discussed here because of space limitations, is the Service Learning Programs, which promote and support studdent volunteer service on poverty-related issues.

The Retired Senior Volunteer Program (RSVP) is the largest, most flexible and most cost-effective of ACTION's senior volunteer programs. RSVP volunteers need not be low-income, receive no stipend and serve on the average 4 hours a week. If needed they are reimbursed for their meals and mileage. By the end of FY 88, 400,000 RSVP volunteers will be contributing approximately 75,000,000 hours of service at a cost to the federal government of less than fifty cents per volunteer. The 750 community-based RSVP projects in turn assign RSVP volunteers to over 45,000 community agencies nationwide.

The Senior Companion Program (SCP) is the newest and smallest of ACTION's senior volunteer programs. SCP provides service opportunities to low-income seniors 60 years of age or older who serve older adults, particularly the frail and the homebound elderly who are at greatest risk of being institutionalized. SCP volunteers, like FGP volunteers, receive a $2.20 an hour stipend and normally serve 3 to 4 persons for a total of 20 hours a week. Currently, there are nearly 8000 volunteers supported by SCP's $23 million budget. With the high cost of nursing home care, SCP is a model program for reducing the heavy burden of long-term care by providing services to the frail elderly in their homes or familiar surroundings.

PRIORITIES AND RECOMMENDATIONS FOR OAVP'S

The next administration must select a committed and experienced individual as the OAVP Director who has the ability to look beyond the programs' past track record and provide a vision that addresses the changes in demographics, life expectancy, lifestyles, health care needs, attitudes and desires of the growing senior population. Each of the three programs requires its own experienced, committed and visionary director. The OAVP Director must work cooperatively and reestablish ties with the three OAVP Project Directors Associations, national aging organizations, related government agencies and public and private agencies associated with older Americans.

Priorities of the Director should include seeking expanded visibility and recognition for OAVP programs, serving as an advocate for national and community service by older Americans and using the 25th anniversary of FGP and the 20th anniversary of RSVP as the vehicles to highlight the programs and their volunteers.

In conjunction with the reauthorization of the OAVP programs, ACTION should a) examine the stipend level provided to FGP and SCP volunteers and determine if it should be increased and if the income eligibility level for FGP and SCP should be increased from 125% to 150% of the poverty index, and b) amend RSVP's purpose clause to place equal emphasis on providing meaningful volunteer opportunities and serving community identified needs.

The next administration would benefit by identifying new program initiatives for FGP volunteers such as working with homeless children and pregnant teens and engaging RSVP in innovative partnerships with the private sector, such as the recent RSVP literacy initiative. Goals for the next administration should include the development of one new FGP and SCP project in every state.

IV. BUDGET REQUIREMENTS

The first domestic operations budget for the ACTION Agency in FY 72 was approximately $79 million. At the conclusion of the Carter Administration and prior to the FY 81 rescissions, ACTION's domestic budget was approximately $153 million. In constant dollars ACTION's budget in FY 88 would need to be $196.2 million just to keep pace with its level at the end of the Carter Administration; in fact, the FY 88 budget is $163.085 million and the FY 89 budget will be $168.420 million.

The FY 89 VISTA budget is expected to be $21.6 million to support a total of 2600 volunteer service years (VSYS) plus an additional $2.8 million to support the Literacy Corps. (The Reagan Administration requested zero funding for the Literacy Corps.)

If the new administration chooses to request a supplemental appropriation for FY 89, VISTA should be seriously considered for inclusion. A $3.4 million VISTA supplemental would support an additional 400 VSYS and enable an additional 700 VISTAs to address pressing problems such as illiteracy, unemployment, drug abuse, child care and the lack of low-income housing. This would bring VISTA to the 3000 service year mark as it begins its 25th year of operation — which still would be below the 3660 service year level achieved back in FY 67! An additional $1.5 million is critical to enable VISTA to immediately re-establish its national recruitment and public awareness mechanism to provide the program with a more diverse volunteer pool that would include special skill volunteers and recent college graduates. It might also be necessary to request a supplemental appropriation to increase the Agency's administrative budget to enable it to restore necessary functions.

V. THE PEACE CORPS: A HISTORICAL PERSPECTIVE

The Peace Corps' lofty mission was and remains "to promote world peace and friendship." Its three statutory goals are 1) "to assign volunteers to interested countries to help them meet their need for trained personnel"; 2) "to promote a better understanding of Americans among the people served"; and 3) "to promote better un-

derstanding of people of other countries among the American people."
In the vernacular the three goals are sometimes referred to as 1) we
help them, 2) they get to know us and 3) we get to know them.

By articulating three presumably co-equal goals, Sargent Shriver,
the Peace Corps' first director, made it clear that technical assistance (i.e., "we help them") was *not* the Peace Corps' exclusive *raison
d'etre*. He and his collaborators insisted that the Peace Corps would
have to go beyond the more traditional modes of "trickle down" development assistance. They likewise committed the Peace Corps to
reaching beyond the scope of existing international educational and
cultural exchange programs. What they devised was a hybrid — a
technical assistance program based on the the intrinsic value of having people from diverse cultures living and, above all, working together to address local problems.

Thus the Peace Corps was designed as an investment in the future. One of the benefits was creating a cadre of Americans who
would come to understand the beauty and strength of other cultures
while contributing to the development of participating Third World
nations. The founders firmly believed that it was in this country's
long-term interest to learn more about the rest of the world, just as it
was in the interest of other nations to learn more about us. That returning volunteers would share their insights with America and
would ultimately help shape national policy was also an essential
element of the Peace Corps vision.

Over the years, succeeding administrations and a long string of
Peace Corps directors saw themselves as stewards of a precious
legacy. Without exception, each new director tried to keep faith
with the original vision, as they saw it, making only those adjustments that seemed essential to maintaining an effective program.

And yet, possibly because those first few years were characterized by such creativity, the program has gradually, almost imper-
ceptibly, slipped into an orthodoxy that has preempted some of the
very innovations necessary for survival in the long run. Over the
past twenty years or so, the Peace Corps has become overly cautious
and defensive.

This programmatic conservatism has precluded any serious
thought on how the Peace Corps should pursue its three statutory
goals in a changing world. With few exceptions, there are no serious
"program" efforts that can be identified as embodying goals two and
three (we get to know them, and they us). Virtually the entire Peace
Corps budget and staff are devoted to deploying volunteers in Third
World countries. And while goals two and three are not forgotten, it
is commonly assumed that they will take care of themselves — that
they will be attained when volunteers have a positive experience

overseas and share that experience with others upon their return to the United States.

Yet, given our nation's ever-increasing interdependence with the rest of the world, goals two and three have become even more important than the founders of the Peace Corps even imagined. What was a theoretical benefit has become a practical necessity. The next administration and Congress will be in a unique position to see that more Americans learn more about the Third World through the work of the Peace Corps. Indeed, after twenty years the Peace Corps should feel secure enough to be innovative. It will not have to fight a rear-guard action to retain its programmatic independence from ACTION, nor will it be subject to debilitating partisan disagreements.

PERFORMANCE UNDER REAGAN

The appointment of the right-wing Tom Pauken's appointment as director of ACTION had a direct impact on the Peace Corps when his service with a military intelligence unit was revealed. Immediately, Peace Corps' supporters on Capitol Hill and across the country pointed to Pauken's appointment as a violation of the Peace Corps' statutory prohibition against hiring anyone with even the slightest connection with an intelligence-gathering agency. When the President refused to withdraw Pauken's nomination, the Congress voted to separate the Peace Corps from ACTION. After a ten-year association with ACTION, the Peace Corps once again became an independent agency.

Peace Corp Director Loret Miller Ruppe performed admirably. In short order, she succeeded in making the Peace Corps truly bipartisan — at the very time when bipartisanship within the executive branch was virtually nonexistent. Moreover, she managed to obtain the support of President Reagan and his allies in the House and Senate while retaining the enthusiastic support of the Peace Corps' traditional constituency. Ruppe's seven-year tenure as director should be seen as a reaffirmation that government-supported volunteer programs are firmly grounded in fundamental American values and are capable of achieving broad-based political support from all segments of the political spectrum.

The Ruppe years were characterized by administration budget requests designed to keep pace with spiraling overseas costs and appropriations which were significantly higher than in previous years — a remarkable fact given the severe reductions suffered by most other social programs. Many friends of the Peace Corps believe that Loret Ruppe has been the Peace Corps' best advocate since Sargent Shriver, its first and still legendary director.

PRIORITIES AND RECOMMENDATIONS FOR THE PEACE CORPS

The first responsibility of any incoming administration is to make sure that the agency's on-going programs are able to continue without any undue disruption.

There are several program initiatives the Peace Corps should undertake, however, that will make the program even more effective and relevant in the future.

Over the past ten years the Peace Corps has either taken the initiative to leave, or has been asked to leave, a number of countries, such as the Ivory Coast, Brazil, Malaysia and Venezuela. When the Peace Corps left these countries, the point was made, either by the country or by the Peace Corps or both, that the country had "graduated," that it did not *need* the Peace Corps any more. Objectively, the argument may be correct. Such "middle-income" countries often do not require the type of technical assistance the Peace Corps is known to provide. But such a narrow interpretation of the word "need" misses the point. No country, including our own, is ever so developed that there is no work left to be done. Moreover, the world we live in is so interdependent that, almost be definition, we "need" each other. If these assertions are correct, the Peace Corps must begin articulating a rationale that goes beyond "technical assistance" as its primary justification.

The Peace Corps' failure to articulate a different, more inclusive, vision has resulted in having most countries see the program principally, if not exclusively, in "giver-receiver" terms. And while such a relationship is certainly descriptive of the program's basic relationship with many of the lesser developed countries, inevitably fewer and fewer nations will find it acceptable to host a Peace Corps that has come to symbolize their dependence on external assistance. It seems clear that the Peace Corps has failed to involve its host countries in the noble vision of interdependence and understanding which are the underpinnings to goals two and three.

Unless the Peace Corps begins to develop a program rationale based equally on all three goals, we may wake up someday to discover that the Peace Corps has been bypassed by history. In fact, in the Ivory Coast, Brazil, Malaysia, Venezuela and in a number of other countries, the process has already begun.

Consequently, the Peace Corps must develop alternative program models for assigning and supporting volunteers overseas with a) middle-income countries, b) countries with strong national service programs, c) countries more likely to accept volunteers assigned directly to their institutions and d) countries with strong relations with private voluntary agencies (PVOs).

In recent years the Peace Corps assigned a small group of volunteers to a PVO in the Sudan, and it is about to assign a similar group of volunteers to a PVO in Equatorial Guinea. What is noteworthy is that the volunteers are being placed without the usual requirements — a formal Peace Corps country agreement, the appointment of a country director, the assignment of Peace Corps staff members and the establishment of a Peace Corps office. This approach can be replicated in countries that are not willing to accept the symbol of a Peace Corps office but have an established relationship with a reputable PVO.

Numerous Third World countries have developed their own form of national service, and have developed the skills that are required to program and support grass-roots "volunteer" development workers. A case in point is Indonesia, which has many thousands of volunteers throughout the country supported by BUTSI, the Indonesian equivalent of VISTA. Over the years, BUTSI has approached the Peace Corps informally to inquire whether Peace Corps volunteers could be assigned directly to their organization. The Indonesians did not want an official Peace Corps presence other than the volunteers. It was willing, however, to accept one or more Peace Corps staff members to assist it in coordinating the work of the volunteers, provided that they were assigned to its organization. The Peace Corps should be prepared to accept and, moreover, seek out similar relationships where appropriate.

Such alternative approaches would allow the program to gain access to a number of countries willing to host Peace Corps volunteers but not willing to highlight their use of external technical assistance or to accept the trappings of an official Peace Corps presence. Eventually, such alternative relationships would lead to a new perception — a rejuvenated Peace Corps which is no longer seen as a symbol of dependency and which has become symbol of "partnership."

The failure to develop such alternative strategies will limit, over time, the Peace Corps to fewer and fewer LDCs such as Mauritania, Chad, Haiti and Nepal, and will inevitably lead to a much smaller program.

As has been mentioned previously, the Peace Corps' third goal, "getting to know them," has received little institutional attention. Rather, it has been seen as a process that occurs naturally once individual volunteers return to this country. Indeed, until recently, most Peace Corps loyalists felt that it was a process that should be not be influenced by the agency. And while we take it as an article of faith that former volunteers are having some impact on the communities where they live, there is little visible evidence. The only exceptions are in those few institutions where there are large concentrations of former volunteers such as in AID, the Department of

State, numerous PVOs and, to a much lesser degree, the Congress, state and local governments and isolated multinational corporations, banks and schools.

What is missing is one, or more, mechanisms through which former volunteers can more effectively share their understanding of Third World cultures with the public at large. It bears repeating — this is no longer a subject which may have been of interest to a few, it has become a practical necessity for the nation.

If we are to successfully compete for international markets in the future, we will have to better distribute around America our learning about the rest of the world. Indeed, in the long run, the Peace Corps' contribution to this process may be its most significant.

So the Peace Corps should seek legislative approval for: a) a small-grants program aimed at existing and emerging former volunteer groups that are willing to develop returned Peace Corps volunteer (RPCV) speakers bureaus and other local development education activities; b) an operations grants program to stimulate the development of material/papers/articles on Third World concerns for dissemination to the general public through the media; and c) the creation of Peace Corps teaching fellowships in geography, history, language and cross-cultural studies. RPCVs would be assigned to local school systems for a period of one year to teach special classes and to develop additional development education activities in their communities. Such a program could be jointly funded by the U.S. Department of Education, local school systems and/or other institutions in the private sector such as the Carnegie Corporation, or the National Geographic.

In all cases the test must be whether these activities are designed to share the Peace Corps' experience with the public at large, rather than "preaching to the converted," or being satisfied with indulging in personal Third World nostalgia.

Over twelve years ago the Peace Corps instituted the Information Collection and Exchange (ICE). ICE's purpose is to collect and disseminate field-generated technical information derived from the work of the volunteers and their counterparts. Such information runs the gamut of community-based development activities including: small-scale irrigation practices, reforestation in arid areas, oral-rehydration-therapy for infants, rural health education clinics, primary and secondary school science curricula, single-story construction techniques, assistance to small-scale enterprises and intensive vegetable gardening, to name a few.

ICE was founded on the premise that volunteers, through their work, learn some of the most important lessons about development — what works, what doesn't work, why and under what circumstances. As volunteers live and work for extended periods of time at the grassroots level, they begin to see what specific localized inhibitions to development exist, and how these inhibitions affect the people with whom they work. During the course of their assignments, almost by necessity, the volunteers and their counterparts adapt tools, approaches and methodologies to numerous local factors such as culture, the availability of resources and climate. At times volunteers even evolve approaches that have not been tried before. In a sense, ICE has enabled the Peace Corps to become a unique worldwide source of "Appropriate Technologies."

From the very beginning, it was clear that ICE could perform two worthwhile services. First, it could provide technical information to Peace Corps volunteers and staff; second, it could offer Peace Corps-generated technical information to other organizations similarly involved in grassroots development.

Indeed, in the intervening years, ICE has supported volunteers and staff by publishing a series of technical manuals, and by responding to technical questions from the field. And while the Peace Corps has not systematically promoted ICE to PVOs, international development agencies and host country ministries, word has spread. ICE today receives an increasing number of requests for its technical manuals from other organizations.

Unfortunately due to severe funding restrictions, ICE is limited both in the number of technical manuals it can produce and disseminate outside the Peace Corps. As a result it has not had nearly the impact on development that it could have. The Peace Corps has the opportunity to develop a strategy for systematically disseminating this technical information where it can have a much broader impact.

Conceptually and programmatically, the dissemination of such technical information must be seen as co-equal to the assignment of volunteers. Third World countries, whether or not they host Peace Corps volunteers, will come to regard the Peace Corps as a source of technical information as well as as source of volunteers. In fact, the dissemination of such field-generated technical information gives form to the heretofore elusive notion of devising a "multiplier effect" for the work of the volunteers. Moreover, it does so without damaging what the Peace Corps does best — fielding motivated and effective development workers at the community-level — only now what they do may be widely replicated through host country institutions.

THE BUDGET PROCESS

From 1961 on, the amount of money appropriated to the Peace Corps has been seen primarily, if not exclusively, as supporting volunteers abroad. Such costs include all expenses relating to the recruitment, selection, placement, training and living expenses for the volunteers, and all administrative and program expenses related to supporting the volunteer on their assignments.

Thus annual budget requests are calculated by multiplying the number of volunteers projected for a given fiscal year by a series of cost factors. Successive Peace Corps directors have kept a wary eye on the inevitable increased cost of fielding volunteers. The cost per volunteer year has steadily risen from $8,336 in 1962 to $10,931 in 1972, and $23,031 in 1982. It now appears that by 1992 the per volunteer year cost will be $30,000, or more.

Peace Corps' budget request for 1989 is for $150 million. According to Reagan administration calculations, this figure should support 5,200 volunteer-years and allow for 3,600 new trainees. If past form hold true, it is likely that the Congress will appropriate somewhere between $150 and $160 million.

The Congress has established a goal of fielding 10,000 Peace Corps volunteers by 1992. In barely four years the program would have to virtually double in size in order to achieve that goal. There is a real question whether the Peace Corps can responsibly program for so many additional volunteers in such a short time. The impetus to reach the 10,000 volunteer-year figure in part stems from a desire to demonstrate that the Peace Corps is alive and well and show that it has regained some of the ground lost since its "heyday" in the late sixties, when the program fielded close to 15,000 volunteers.

It is appropriate that the Peace Corps be seen as a symbol of what is best in how America relates to the rest of the world. Nevertheless, it is unfortunate that the achievement of a 10,000-volunteer Peace Corps has become a benchmark of effectiveness. While the Peace Corps is certainly smaller than it ought to be, it should be allowed to grow responsibly without the imposition of arbitrary targets.

In its first year the next administration should assess whether the 10,000 goal can be met responsibly by 1992, or whether it may take a few more years. If it chooses to support the movement towards a 10,000 volunteer Peace Corps by 1992, it will have to request annual budget increases of between $45 and $50 million. The variable cost of running a program in over sixty countries and the exact pattern at which the Peace Corps is able to grow responsibly will dictate the precise amounts that will have to be requested, but they should be in the neighborhood of $200 million for 1990, $245 million for 1991 and up to $290 million for 1992.

In addition, if the next administration chooses to support the program ideas proposed in this paper, it should request that these initiatives be separated from the traditional "Volunteer-Sending" budget categories. It is essential that the initiatives described above are not seen as threatening the Peace Corps' more traditional

"Volunteer-Sending" activities. Requesting $10 million specifically for these activities in their own right will go a long way to attentuating any criticism. Future requests might grow, but most likely would not exceed $25 million by the fifth year. Should the Congress decide not to support a 10,000 volunteer Peace Corps, it could allow the program to level off at 8,500 volunteers, or extend the 1992 target.

In any case, the program initiatives proposed here would not require large expenditures of additional money and would give the Peace Corps a visible "bang for the buck." They should be funded regardless of whether the Peace Corps is allowed to grow beyond where it will be on January 21, 1989.

HEALTH CARE:
Department of Health &
Human Services

Ronald F. Pollack & Bruce Fried*

SUMMARY OF RECOMMENDATIONS

Two major gaps in the health care safety net have grown even wider over the last eight years.

First, access to basic health care has seriously eroded. Even as the number of jobs grew, so did the number of Americans with no health coverage. By 1987, the count stood at 37 million people, up more than a million people per year during the Reagan era.

Second, millions of Americans of all ages, because of their chronic conditions, are in need of help with long-term care. Demographic changes assure that the number will grow dramatically, and no existing program can save these Americans and their families from financial exhaustion and destitution.

The Department of Health and Human Services, therefore, should develop major new initiatives to help provide this necessity of life.

* *Health Care for All Working Families.* Following the congressional leadership of Sen. Kennedy and Reps. Waxman and Stark, a proposal should be developed and implemented to require employers to provide health coverage to their workers.

Since such a plan would include some cost-sharing, there should be a corresponding protection, provided by government, for lower-income workers. Care must be taken to avoid harm to new or marginal employers. Strong cost controls must also be built in.

* *Health Care for Those Outside the Work Force.* To cover the twelve million still untouched by an employer-related plan, HHS

---

* *Ronald F. Pollack is the Executive Director of the Villers Foundation, a private, non-profit foundation working to empower elders, especially those with low and moderate incomes. Bruce Fried is the Executive Director of the National Health Care Campaign, which coordinates hundreds of national groups and 35 state campaigns working for a national health care system.*

should propose "Americare." It would be administered through states, with federal standards, and federal and state financing. All those not connected to the labor force would be eligible, with their financial participation (in effect, their premium) related to their income.

   * *Long-term Care for all Ages.* Though the biggest catastrophic expense for older people is for the cost of long-term care, the recent Medicare Catastrophic legislation does virtually nothing to address the problem. Medicaid provides some protection for nursing home care, but requires pauperizing the family seeking help (if it's available at all). Private insurance policies, though growing in number, cover only a half million people — and not at all well. Solutions to encourage individual savings for long-term care needs are aimed only at the better off.

   A social insurance plan, patterned after Social Security or Medicare, would include coverage for all persons who have a specified level of disability; universal, contributory participation; inclusion of all services needed, especially home and community-based services; administration through states using care coordination and management; beneficiary cost-sharing, with low-income protection for those who cannot afford it; and progressive, dedicated financing.

I. THE CRISIS IN ACCESS TO HEALTH CARE

   In the past eight years, we have learned that the crisis in access to health care is largely one of financing (though rural Americans face significant geographic impediments as well). Currently, 37 million Americans, one in six of those under age 65, have no health care insurance, public or private. Data documents the crisis:

   1. The number of uninsured has risen dramatically. Since 1980, over one million people each year have been added to the ranks of the uninsured (see chart). The growing number of uninsured persons results from a decline in relatively high-wage manufacturing and the growth of lower-wage retail and service jobs; federal and state cutbacks in Medicaid eligibility; increases in the number of persons living below the poverty level; large increases in private insurance policy premiums and deductibles; refusal of insurers to cover persons with pre-existing conditions and an increasing number of employers eliminating coverage for dependents.

   2. Most of the uninsured don't get Medicaid. Contrary to the myth, Medicaid — the HHS-run, federal/state program covering the health needs of cash welfare recipients — does not reach the uninsured. In 1975, 63% of the poor benefitted from Medicaid. By 1986, only 37% of families with annual incomes below $15,000 had Medicaid coverage.[1] At least half of America's poor children are not covered by Medicaid.

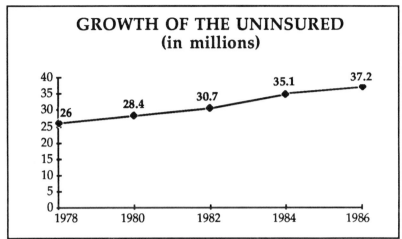

GROWTH OF THE UNINSURED
(in millions)

26   28.4   30.7   35.1   37.2

1978   1980   1982   1984   1986

Source: The Employee Benefit Research Institute, derived from the March 1986 Current Population Survey.

3. A substantial majority of the uninsured are workers and their families.[2] More than half of all uninsured persons are full-time, full-year workers. Working families (workers, their spouses and children) account for more than two-thirds of the uninsured. Less than 14% live in families where no adult is employed.

4. Children account for nearly one-third of the uninsured.[3] Perhaps the most shameful consequence of this growing crisis is measured by our nation's infant mortality rate. After 20 years of steady improvement, our progress in reducing the rate at which infants die in America has stalled. By 1985, the U.S. infant mortality rate, which had been the sixth best among 20 industrialized countries in the early 1950s, had slipped into a tie for the very worst.

While the majority of the twelve million uninsured children live in families where other members lack insurance as well, one out of five live in households where an adult is covered. Employers are excluding dependents from job-based insurance or are raising deductibles or premiums to unaffordable levels.

5. The problem is not limited to persons living below the poverty level. Almost two-thirds of the uninsured (64%) live in households with incomes above the poverty level.[4]

6. Lack of health insurance affects a greater percentage of minorities than whites. While 15% of all whites are uninsured, 25% of blacks and 21% for other minority groups lack coverage.[5]

7. **The lack of insurance, predictably, worsens the accessibility of health care for the uninsured.** A recent Robert Wood Johnson Foundation survey[6] shows that 31.2% of the uninsured have no routine source of care, compared to only 16.4% of the population with some form of insurance. Since 1982, medical visits by poor adults fell 30%.

II. HEALTH CARE FOR ALL

The principal health policy objective for the next administration must be the development of a rational, unified, national health system that is universally accessible, cost-controlled and prevention-oriented. While achieving that objective is crucial, such a program is beyond the country's political reach at this time.

Perhaps the greatest hurdle is the federal budget deficit. Based on current policies and projected economic trends during the first session of the 101st Congress, the federal budget deficit for Fiscal Year 1990 will be $30 billion greater than the deficit target set for that year under the Gramm-Rudman target legislation.

Also, despite the failure of private sector efforts and competition to expand access to the uninsured or control health care costs, powerful political interests — business and insurers — are still not prepared to abandon their ideological romance with marketplace forces as the answer to the health care crisis.

Given the realities of the budget deficit, the political potency of interests opposed to a national health care system and the public's ambivalence — for a national health program on the one hand, and against paying for it on the other — the country must seek achievable solutions to the access and cost crisis.

HEALTH CARE FOR ALL WORKING FAMILIES: THE PRIVATE SECTOR

During the working life of most Americans, health insurance is a benefit of employment. Yet in 1985, 25 million uninsured Americans, 69% of the uninsured, were in families where the family head worked full-time for the full year.[7] Virtually all businesses with more than 100 employees provide health insurance for their workers, although only some 55% of employers with fewer than 100 employees offer coverage.[8]

While the U.S. economy has grown steadily for the past six years and while employment is high, there has been no expansion of employer-provided health benefits. Indeed, it is likely that employer-provided benefits will become less available as employers are faced with continuing inflation of premium costs.

During the 1970s, business interests argued that the private sector could solve the nation's health care problems. Yet, cost containment efforts failed to restrain costs from exceeding, often by large margins, annual increases in the Consumer Price Index. And access to care, far from being broadened, eroded year after year.

There are only two approaches to addressing the access crisis — a national health insurance system (which virtually all other industrialized nations have) or a more complex mix of public and private financing methods. If a national health plan is preferable though politically unobtainable now, a system of private and public insurance that will make health care available to all Americans can be fashioned. Twenty four million Americans, two-thirds of the uninsured, can be insured without affecting the federal budget deficit by relying on the private sector.

Just as employers are required to pay a minimum wage and contribute to Social Security and unemployment protections, so too should employers be required to provide health coverage for workers and their families.

In the past year, policy initiatives obligating employers to provide health care to their employees and their families have been offered in several variations. Sen. Edward Kennedy (D-MA) and Rep. Henry Waxman (D-CA) would require all employers to provide a minimum package of benefits to full-time employees (and their dependents) through the Fair Labor Standards Act. Rep. Pete Stark (D-CA) would obligate employers to provide health coverage to full-time employees (and their dependents) or be taxed. Both plans would 1) prohibit excluding employees or dependents with pre-existing conditions from coverage, 2) preempt the states from requiring health insurance plans to offer benefits greater than those required by the federal minimum and 3) encourage self-employed persons to purchase health insurance by increasing the portion of health insurance costs that are tax-deductible from 25% to 100%.

A third approach, enacted in Massachusetts, imposes a surcharge on unemployment insurance premiums paid by employers for every employee. Employers who provide health coverage can deduct the cost from the surcharge payment. (A similar mandate has been in effect in Hawaii for more than a decade.) The uninsured, including employees who do not receive coverage from their employer, would obtain insurance from a state insurance system.

While employer-mandated benefits are attractive, given their minimal impact on the budget deficit, this approach must recognize the limited ability of low-income workers to participate in the financing of their health coverage. After all, a single mother of two children, working at a minimum wage job 40 hours a week, has below-poverty-level income. To require that mother to spend a portion of her salary on health benefits means that other necessities will be beyond her reach. Some public subsidy is required.

The mandated benefits approach must also be concerned with its impact on new and marginal employers, lest this new benefit obligation cause the closure of these businesses and loss of jobs.[9] Finally, the mandated benefits approach should have a complementary cost control mechanism. The choices would include a Canadian-style unitary budgeting approach, a national all-payer cost containment system, or health care sector wage and price controls. Whatever the approach, substantial opposition, particularly from providers, is certain. Still, without some form of cost containment, health care costs will continue to grow, again jeopardizing access to care.

BEYOND MEDICAID TO AMERICARE: WHAT ABOUT THE UNEMPLOYED?

If our nation's health care strategy is going to require the private sector to provide coverage for people in the workforce, then the public sector must provide for the health care of the twelve million people (including early retirees, some people with disabilities, the unemployed, displaced homemakers and half the poor) who are outside of the work force and not now covered by a public program.

The Department of Health and Human Services should develop a comprehensive public health care system for individuals outside the work force, regardless of age, income or health status. This new public health care system can be called "Americare."

Americare will be built upon a significantly revised, expanded and improved Medicaid program. Americare will be administered at the state level, with financing criteria, minimum benefits and other standards set federally. Americare will be state and federally financed, as was Medicaid, with additional resources coming from other programs and individuals buying into the program.

As described below, long-term care, which currently accounts for one-third of Medicaid expenditures, would be covered by a new program. Some state and federal funds previously spent for Medicaid long-term care would be available to fund Americare's coverage of all unemployed low-income people. Five billion dollars would be a reasonable estimate of funds that could be made available.

In recent years, steps have been taken to uncouple Medicaid eligibility from welfare cash programs. In 1986, Congress permitted states to expand Medicaid coverage to all pregnant women, infants and young children with incomes below the poverty line, and permitted states to pay Medicare cost-sharing for the elderly and disabled with incomes below the poverty line, or to enroll them in Medicaid. In response, most states expanded their coverage for pregnant women and infants and a few expanded coverage for the elderly and people with disabilities. In 1988, Congress obligated all states to provide Medicaid coverage to all pregnant women and young children, and required the states to pay cost-sharing on Medicare benefits for the elderly and disabled with incomes below the poverty level.

A recent study by Dr. Kenneth Thorpe of the Harvard School of Public Health concludes that the current Medicaid program, long-term care excluded, could be expanded to cover the entire uninsured poverty population for $9.6 billion above current spending.[10] If Medicaid eligibility turned only on the question of income, it can be expected that an additional three million people with income below the poverty level, who currently purchase health insurance privately, would drop their existing coverage. In that event the cost of extending eligibility to all persons with below-poverty-level income would require $13 billion in increased public spending.[11]

This cost would be significantly reduced if a mandatory employer-provided health benefits program, such as one of those described above, is enacted. Providing Medicaid coverage to the remaining uninsured poor would require $3.3 billion in new net public spending.[12]

Americare is still only a step toward a universal health care plan. But Americare does provide the framework for such a universal plan. The Department should begin discussions with other federal, state and private entities to explore how best to build a coordinated, rational, efficient system on the foundation of Americare.

Though it would be built on the base of current health care programs for the poor, Americare would not simply be a larger, more coordinated Medicaid program. Instead of focusing on income to determine eligibility, as in Medicaid, the Americare program would make eligible anyone not receiving coverage through his or her employment.

Income would serve only as to determine the level of financial participation in the program. People and families with income below the poverty level would not be required to contribute to their health care coverage. People with incomes between, say, 100% and 200% of the poverty level would be allowed to "buy in" to Americare. Persons with incomes above 200% of poverty could pay an actuarially sound, cost-based premium to obtain coverage.

Following the successful integration of these low-income programs into Americare, a longer-range planning process should examine these prospective steps:

* Integrating Medicare into the new program, along with other public health care programs (CHAMPUS, veterans' health system).

* Offering employers and employees, especially federal employees, the chance to use Americare as their health care.

* Final broadening of the program to cover all Americans.

Although the political difficulties of such a series of steps cannot be underestimated, long-range planning in this direction will be invaluable. The benefits of a unified public insurance program, which would replace a hodgepodge of uncoordinated programs, would be significant. Administrative complexity and cost would be substantially reduced and efficiency would be heightened. Beneficiaries would find a far simpler program to serve them, compared to the bureaucratic nightmare that presently exists.

III. LONG-TERM CARE: A MULTIGENERATIONAL APPROACH

Beginning in January 1989, the 32 million older and disabled Americans enrolled in Medicare will begin receiving the benefits of the Medicare Catastrophic Coverage Act. By the time this bill's provisions are fully phased in, in 1993, most older and disabled Americans will have true protection against financial devastation from the cost of acute health care. That was Medicare's original mission. When Lyndon Johnson signed Medicare into law in 1965, he hailed it as the dawn of a new era: "No longer will illness crush and destroy the savings that [older Americans] have so carefully put away over a lifetime."

Despite the new catastrophic bill, that new era has not yet arrived. The principal reason is that the specter of financial and family devastation still looms over millions of elders: the risk that they will need care for their chronic conditions — *long-term care* — either in the community or in a nursing home.

The basic catastrophic protection under the Medicare bill will limit out-of-pocket spending to about $2,000 a year (with some important gaps, not discussed here). But among elders spending $2,000 or more on health care in a given year, the odds are *four to one* that what caused the expense was not hospital or doctor bills, the most important items covered by Medicare, but long-term care.

There are approximately 1.5 million elders in nursing homes, and about three times that many living in the community and needing some assistance in the activities of daily living to maintain independence. Two-thirds of those at home and in the community rely completely on unpaid care to meet their needs.

Persons over age 85 are much more likely to need long-term care than other elders — 17 or 18 times as likely as someone in the 65-74 age group, for example, to be in a nursing home. And the growth rate for that segment of the population has been dramatic over the last quarter-century:while our population as a whole has increased by about a third, and the number over age 65 has nearly doubled, the population over age 85 has *tripled*. The 85+ population will double *again* in the next 30 years, and double once more by 2050, when "baby boom" survivors will all have reached the age of 85.

But chronic illness and disability know no age limits. Extraordinary and burdensome long-term care costs can befall children and their families, as well as the elderly. And by definition, "long-term" disability in the case of a child is likely to mean substantially longer periods of time than with an elderly person.

Families with ill or disabled children are denied health insurance when they need it most. They face extraordinary out-of-pocket expenses that force them to choose between family bankruptcy and institutionalizing their child.

Nor is this a trivial aspect of the problem. Though the risk of needing long-term care increases greatly with age, projections indicate that, by the year 2000, fully 40% of functionally dependent Americans will be under 65 years of age.[13] The current mix of public and private attempts to respond to long-term care need is inadequate. Medicare and Medicaid, HHS's principal health care programs, offer limited, flawed protection against long-term care needs.

Medicare, the federal acute care insurance program for the elderly and disabled, provides no chronic care coverage, other than the extremely modest respite care benefit added in the recent Catastrophic legislation.[14] Medicaid, on the other hand, does cover nursing home care. In fact, it spent $14 billion for nursing homes for the elderly in 1986. Since Medicaid has been the fastest growing budget item in many state budgets, these costs have received critical attention from governors and state legislators.

Medicaid is a means-tested program. Only persons who are — or *become* — poor are eligible for Medicaid assistance. Indeed, that is how many persons institutionalized in nursing homes become eligible for Medicaid assistance. According to the Department's Health Care Financing Administration, half of all current Medicaid nursing home residents were not initially eligible for Medicaid, but they "spent down" or exhausted their life savings while in the institution.

The recent Medicare catastrophic improvements did allow the spouse left at home to retain more of the couple's income and savings and still not prevent the institutionalized spouse from getting Medicaid help with nursing home costs. But since the levels of protection are still relatively modest,[15] the spouse at home is likely to suffer a substantial drop in her level of living.

Medicaid, therefore, has several inherent flaws as a major mechanism for the funding of long-term care. First, because it offers very little home care coverage, its bias is clearly toward institutional (nursing home) care, though in many states even that benefit is denied to many people unable to pay for care. Second, the program forces most people to spend their entire life savings to qualify for help, and thereafter to pay virtually all of their income toward the cost of care. Third, Medicaid offers mainly medical solutions to persons with chronic disabilities, while most people are also in need of a variety of social services. Finally, Medicaid was designed to provide health care for the poor of all ages. Spending one-third of its funding for long-term care is making it more difficult for the program to fulfill its main purpose.

PRIVATE SECTOR OPTIONS ARE UNSATISFACTORY

During the past several years, as a new appreciation has developed about the seriousness of growing long-term care needs and costs, the Reagan Administration and its ideological allies have taken the lead in searching for private sector solutions to the problem.

Two basic strategies have emerged. The first involves strengthening the ability of individuals to pay for their own long-term care out of their own savings. Tax-advantaged Individual Medical Accounts (IMAs, similar to IRAs) and home equity conversion plans are examples of this approach. They are aimed squarely at better-off parts of the population, and do almost nothing to reduce current public programs' long-term care burden. Indeed, IMAs would create a drain on revenues which would deepen the budget deficit.

The other private sector approach is to bring people together to pool the risk of high long-term care expenditures. Examples are social health maintenance organizations (S/HMOs) and continuing care retirement communities (CCRCs).

Private long-term care insurance is another way to spread the risk of chronic care needs among a broader segment of the population. Since it is non-compulsory, this non-public option may be viewed favorably by those who can afford to pay the premiums.

But the disadvantages of private insurance are many. The most obvious is cost. The Brookings Institution, in its recent landmark study, *Caring for the Disabled Elderly: Who Will Pay?*, sets the cost for an average "high-option" long-term care policy at $684 a year if bought at age 65, and $1,500 a year at age 79-80. In a recent *Consumer Reports* article rating private long-term care policies,[16] premiums for the ten highest ranked policies averaged $781 a year at age 65. Though group coverage could presumably lower that somewhat, costs would still be formidable. Lower and moderate income older people simply could not afford them.[17] And policies may not guarantee that the premium will stay constant over time.

Even if an older person can afford the policy, he or she may not be allowed to buy it. Companies worried about paying too many claims typically turn down applicants whom they believe are likeliest to need care. Turn-down rates of 20-25% are not uncommon. The right to renew the policy is not necessarily guaranteed.

Most policies pay no benefits at all unless there is a prior hospitalization, yet most nursing home residents enter without being in a hospital. As a result, one recent study calculated the average probability of not collecting *any* benefits from private insurance at 61%, if one is actually admitted to a nursing home. For home care, the probability of not collecting is *greater than* 90%.[18] Further, almost all policies are limited to a specified time, a majority three years or less, regardless of the continuing need for care.

Most policies state benefits in terms of money per day — so-called "indemnity" plans. Virtually none adjusts the benefit amount for inflation without increasing the premium. Since the need for long-term care typically occurs a decade or two after the policy is first bought, the daily benefit limit may be almost worthless by the time it is needed. A $50 per day nursing home benefit, after 20 years at expected inflation rates, would be worth only $16 in constant terms.

Nor would private insurance provide much relief for Medicaid budgets at either state or federal level. The Brookings study estimates, using the most generous of assumptions, that the widespread purchase of those policies could reduce Medicaid's nursing home expenditures by just one to five percent.

Then there's the unwillingness of most of us to admit, 30 or 40 years before a long-term care need might arise, that we might actually suffer an incapacity like those for which insurance is offered.

Finally, private insurance is inherently more costly than a public program like Medicare. A public program avoids entirely the expense of marketing and profits — as much as 25-30% of total premiums — and could negotiate better rates from providers because of its market leverage.[19]

THE SOCIAL INSURANCE PROGRAM

There is no disagreement that catastrophic long-term care expense is inherently insurable. Though the individual cost is more than almost anyone can reasonably afford, it occurs sufficiently infrequently (just five percent of the 65+ population is institutionalized) that pooling the risk among a large enough group of people can make it affordable individually. While private insurance does involve the pooling of risk, its market limitations, described above, impose parallel limits on the risk-sharing potential. A social insurance approach, such as that employed in Social Security and Medicare, instead would allow the widest possible risk-sharing across society.

Under a social insurance approach, those receiving benefits will, for the most part, have contributed to the plan, and their earned right to the benefits will be generally recognized. And although access to benefits is universal and uniform, such a program can easily be designed so that contributions and cost-sharing can take into account the ability to pay.

Under a social insurance approach, it is easier to control costs than in a multiple-payer system. This is especially important given projections showing that, if nothing is changed from current policy, Medicaid nursing home expenditures will *triple*, in real dollars, by the year 2020.[20]

In addition, the social insurance approach has the support of the American people[21] and of prominent legislators in both Houses of Congress.[22]

Here are the principles along which HHS should fashion a social insurance plan for long-term care:

1. Anyone who becomes chronically ill or disabled should be covered, regardless of age. Although the elderly run a far greater risk of needing long-term care than younger people, an equivalent number of Americans under 65 also need such care, usually not in institutional settings. Administrative ease may dictate that coverage for those beyond current Medicare beneficiaries be phased in, but universal coverage should be a clear goal from the beginning.

2. The plan should be universal and contributory. The goal is a plan that delivers benefits to everyone who needs them, and is supported by everyone who can contribute.

3. A full range of services should be covered. In-home and supportive services, as well as institutional care, should be included. In order to strengthen informal caregivers, services such as respite and adult day care should be covered as well.

4. States should administer the program. Every state, through Medicaid, is spending a large share of its budget on long-term care. A growing number have moved aggressively to set up home- and community-based service networks for much of their populations. Home care is actually the fastest growing Medicaid service, although only 10% of long-term care under Medicaid is delivered in the community. This experience and expertise cannot be ignored. States should administer the new program, though with far more explicit federal guidance than in Medicaid for such areas as quality control, reimbursement levels and eligibility.

5. Care coordination and management are essential. Both to control costs and ensure quality, states should designate a public or non-profit care coordination agency in each area. That agency would establish eligibility, devise a plan of care for each person, and see to it that providers carry out that plan of care. The mechanism should reinforce the individual's say in choosing both preferred services and qualified providers.

6. Modest cost-sharing should be incorporated. To hold down overall program costs, modest co-insurance should be included. Payments for community services should be substantially lower, thereby encouraging community and home care over undesired and unnecessary institutional care. A short deductible period, no longer than one month, would serve to simplify administration without great hardship, because of the large number of persons with short-term need for those "long-term" care services.

7. Low-income protection is needed. Persons with lower incomes could not afford to pay for a month of care, at home or in a nursing home, nor could they afford even modest co-insurance payments. The program should waive these amounts for all those whose expenses for care bring their net incomes below twice the poverty line.

8. Progressive, dedicated financing should cover the program's cost. Clearly, this plan must be self-financed and, thus, deficit-neutral. Fortunately, it seems clear that Americans are willing to pay more taxes to solve the long-term care crisis.[23] The precise mix of a financing package will depend on a number of factors, but here are possible major elements:

* *Gift and estate tax reform.* There is a clear nexus between insuring against the loss of life savings, and recapturing part of those savings when they are being passed to succeeding generations by those who received the protection. Coincidentally, the estate tax is currently more loophole than tax, largely as a result of 1981 legislative changes. No estate of $600,000 or less pays a cent of federal estate tax. The 1981 legislation alone resulted in an annual loss of estate tax revenues that now exceeds $10 billion.

* *Eliminate cap on payroll deductions for Hospital Insurance.* Currently, there is a $45,000 ceiling on payroll deductions for Social Security and Medicare (Part A - Hospital Insurance). By abolishing the ceiling on the Medicare part of the tax, a substantial amount of money would be raised — about $7 billion a year initially — from people relatively better able to pay it.

* *Charge a premium for elderly persons who did not pay into the trust fund.* This amount could easily be related, at least partly, to the person's ability to pay, as in the case of the supplemental premium that was a feature of the Medicare Catastrophic bill.

* *Establish a residual payroll tax or surtax to be paid into the long-term care trust fund.* It is intended that this portion of the financing would eventually amount to no more than 1 to 1-1/2% of payroll, depending on how much is raised from the other financing sources. The initial amount could be much less, since trust fund balances could be built up gradually to cover future expenditures. At the same time, the earned income tax credit should be adjusted to hold low-wage workers harmless.

BUDGET REQUIREMENTS

1. Health Insurance Through the Work Place. If the Kennedy/Waxman approach is followed, there are no budget requirements save for additional staffing in the Department of Labor to enforce the new provision of the Fair Labor Standards Act and the Employee Retirement Insurance Security Act. If the Stark approach is followed, there would be no budget consequence in terms of expenditures, though income from non-complying employers would be received by the Treasury.

The Massachusetts approach, revised for federal purposes, would have implications for the budget. Expenditures through the Americare program would be required for working people and their families who are not insured through their place of employment. It is impossible to project what the scope of those expenditures might be; however, revenues derived from taxing employers who refuse to provide adequate health care to their employees and their dependents would substantially offset any expenditures.

2. Health Care for People Outside the Work Force. The first phase of Americare's implementation, providing protection for people outside the workforce, could be accomplished with $6.5 billion of new federal spending. If this first phase is implemented with a mandatory employer provided health benefits program, the federal cost for covering all uninsured low-income people would be reduced to approximately $3.3 billion.[24]

Approximately $5 billion of public funds (half federal, half state), previously allocated for Medicaid-funded long-term care, could be made available to fund Americare, as a result of the creation of the new long-term care program discussed above.

Americare, when fully implemented, will be a comprehensive system of financing health care assuring both universal access and effective cost controls. Americare will result in significant savings by eliminating the need for advertising and overly complex bureaucracies, and by allowing the rational allocation of resources. As a result, the growth in the proportion of the Gross National Product expended for health care, (11.2% in 1987, projected by HHS to reach 15% in 2000) will be reduced as Americare becomes the health care financing system for all Americans.

3. Long-term Care. During the first full year of implementation, which would undoubtedly have to be three to four years after enactment, this plan would require $20-25 billion in new public spending (in 1988 dollars). This additional amount could be raised among the various financing options suggested above.

IV. AIDS*

Within a year, more Americans will be lost to AIDS (Acquired Immune Deficiency Syndrome) than died in the Vietnam War — and within four years, AIDS deaths will equal our World War II combat losses. Someone dies from AIDS every half-hour. From one to 1.5 million Americans may already be infected with the human immunodeficiency virus (HIV, the virus responsible for AIDS). One million new cases can be expected in the world within the next five years.

As the death toll of AIDS is rising, so is the financial burden. The direct cost in the United States was $1.64 billion in 1986, and the indirect cost was $7 billion. Projections indicate that in 1991 the total figure will be $66.5 billion, including $10.9 billion in direct medical costs.

Despite these numbers, the Reagan Administration all but ignored the disease until 1987. The first panel Reagan appointed to study the problem failed to overcome its ideological leadership and disbanded. He has since disregarded the recommendations of a highly-respected second panel — the Watkins Commission — and of Surgeon General C. Everett Koop.

The AIDS crisis is unique in two respects. First, it affects the most productive segment of society, young adults, and it has as yet no cure or vaccine. (Only one approved drug, azidothymidine (AZT), has been shown to prolong the lives of patients, but it is so toxic that almost half the patients cannot take it for long periods.) Second, since it developed initially among groups already stigmatized by society — homosexual men and intravenous drug users — the task awaiting the next president is both urgent and difficult.

PREVENTION: THE NO.1 CURE

As long as there is no cure or vaccine for AIDS, the only protection against the virus is prevention. The president must lead a massive effort a) to educate people about the means of transmission in order to induce the needed changes in individual behavior and b) to sharply increase available treatment for drug-users.

The government must target its educational effort about safer sex and clean needles to the various communities most affected by the disease, including gay men, drug users, ethnic minorities, the poor and the homeless. Information must be available both in Spanish and in English, and it must be accurate and explicit. It is also important to provide correct information explaining how people do *not* catch the virus (holding hands, kissing, etc.).

* *The AIDS section was prepared by Olivier Sultan, a research associate at Democracy Project.*

The government must devise creative programs to insure that the information reaches those for whom it is intended. But Administration policy on AIDS education in schools must be reversed to provide explicit, practical information as early as possible. In the words of John Moore, the British Secretary of State for Social Services, "some people may find some of the material disturbing but we cannot afford to pull our punches if we are to reach the young people who are most at risk."

Four further steps could help begin to change people's sexual and drug-related activities:

1. The next administration and Congress must combat drug-use more effectively. This means expanding methadone maintenance facilities and residential drug-free treatment centers. Admiral James Watkins, the chairman of the Presidential Commission on the Human Immunodeficiency Virus Epidemic, estimated that making drug treatments available on demand would cost the federal government $1.5 billion in state block grant programs for FY 1989. The president should take advantage of the favorable anti-drug political climate to obtain the necessary funds from Congress.

2. Because intravenous (IV) drug users represent the greatest threat of HIV infection to the heterosexual community, the government needs to disseminate not only information but also bleach to sterilize needles. In San Francisco, surveys following the distribution of thousands of one-ounce vials of bleach with instructions showed that bleach use among IV users rose from 3 percent to 68 percent.

3. Enough data is available from Europe and Australia to show the crucial role of needle-exchange programs in protecting the IV drug communities. Needle-sharing in the Netherlands declined from 75 to 25 percent between 1985 and 1987 following the institution of such programs. Applications for drug treatment have also increased as a consequence of the programs, as users become incorporated in the health care and drug treatment system for the first time. In a survey conducted at the Montefiore Medical Center in New York City, 84 percent of IV drug users said they would stop sharing needles if they had ready access to a supply of clean needles.

4. Finally, the use of condoms must be encouraged by making them easily available. At the same time, the FDA should conduct studies to determine the safety of various types and brands of condoms.

RESEARCH: RACING FOR A SOLUTION

AIDS research has proceeded very quickly and provided scientists with crucial information. But there is still a great amount that we do not understand about the virus. We know very little, for in-

stance, about the comparative efficiency of various means of transmission — information that could prove crucial in the search for
treatment.

What is most needed is a change in the way the Food and Drug
Administration (FDA) and the National Institutes of Health (NIH)
respond to the AIDS crisis. The key concepts are flexibility, expediency and safety in research and licensing. Already the FDA has
promised to rule on new drug applications (NDA) for AIDS drugs
within 180 days of receipt — as opposed to the usual two to three
years. But that is not enough. In the case of AZT, the FDA showed
that it could do better, going through the NDA process in three and a
half months by working closely with the manufacturer, Burroughs-
Wellcome, during the clinical trials.

The National Academy of Sciences argues that research facilities
and personnel are currently not adequate to address the needs of
AIDS research. So NIH was allocated $43 million this year by the
federal government for improvement of research facilities. Yet given
the magnitude of the compounding costs, this is grossly insufficient.

The discovery of an AIDS vaccine is still elusive, and it is unlikely that researchers can have a vaccine on the market for another
five to ten years, if then. Human-efficiency trials for as-yet-
undeveloped vaccines will pose great logistical difficulties: for example, they need to be large-scale and occur where the virus is
widespread, probably on the African continent. The FDA can save a
considerable amount of time, and numerous lives, by starting to plan
now to implement such a test.

Finally, the president should encourage greater cooperation between American and foreign scientists to increase exchanges of information and to create an international data base, to be coordinated by
the Global Programme on AIDS.

TREATMENT: GREATER ACCESS TO DRUGS

Since there is no known cure for AIDS, the FDA must recognize
that the only hope for many People With AIDS (PWAs) is to enroll
in clinical trials; the alternative is death. The FDA should provide
better information to PWAs and the medical community about the
current status of research drugs for AIDS and the progress of these
drugs toward FDA approval. Registration of all HIV-related clinical trial information and information on approved substances and
investigational new drugs (INDs) must be made available at one central location.

The AZT experience illustrated some of the drawbacks of current
policies, specifically regarding the Orphan Drug Act of 1983. The
purpose of the Act is to give drug companies market-type incentives
to develop drugs with small markets, which are often cost-inefficient

for the company. In effect, the government agrees to provide companies with tax credits and a seven-year monopoly on production to compensate for the costs of research and the low prospects of recovering the initial investment. Unfortunately, in the case of AZT, Burroughs-Wellcome took excessive advantage of a tragic situation: the drug is available for $10,000 a year or more, making it the highest-priced drug on the market. Because AZT is clearly too expensive for many PWAs, Congress passed a bill in 1987 allocating $30 million to finance individual purchases of AZT, a drug the taxpayers have already paid for! Clearly, the next administration should amend the Orphan Drug Act so that companies like Burroughs-Wellcome do not possess absolute pricing power.

INSURANCE COVERAGE: THE MEANS TO HEALTH CARE

The AIDS crisis is also a financial crisis for many PWAs unable to assume the tremendous cost of caring for themselves. No carrier of HIV should be denied access to cost-efficient, quality care because of his or her inability to pay. About forty percent of PWAs are covered by Medicaid and one percent by Medicare. Federal and state Medicaid expenditures for AIDS patients will approach $600 million in 1988, and close to $2 billion in 1991.

However, this represents little more than 25 percent of AIDS-related medical expenditures. Many private insurance companies have been wary of assuming the burden; indeed, 91 percent refuse to insure patients with antibodies to HIV. In states where mandatory HIV testing of applicants is banned, companies have simply refused all coverage.

What is the solution? In the short term, the federal government should expand Medicaid coverage and mandate more uniform regulations from state to state, so that states which offer broad coverage do not get unfairly burdened. At the same time, HHS should significantly reduce the 24-month disability waiting period for Medicare eligibility for PWAs. The National Academy of Sciences estimates that such a measure would cost $2.1-8.3 billion over the next five years.

Eventually, the solution is a national health care plan for HIV infection and AIDS. Such a plan can be operated by private insurance companies, which would be induced to join through tax incentives and which would fund it through increased premiums for *all* insurance holders, perhaps through the previously described Americare program.

Such insurance coverage would have to include the following: purchase of approved drugs (e.g. AZT), cost of trial drugs, cost of HIV test and counseling and whatever hospital or hospice care is needed.

As more persons develop more advanced cases of AIDS, the strains on hospital and long-term residential facilities for intravenous AIDS patients, for children and infants and for patients with dementia and other neurological disorders will increase. It is estimated that by 1991, 8.1 percent of medical and surgical beds in New York and 12.4 percent in San Francisco will be occupied by AIDS patients.

THE POLITICAL DISEASE — AND THE CURE

Even though the AIDS virus is not transmissible through casual contact, many infected people have lost their jobs, their homes, or have been thrown out of school for carrying the virus. While there is no known cure to protect the immune system from the virus, there is one cure for the attack on the civil rights of HIV-infected people: an anti-discrimination bill. This is not only a civil liberties but also a health issue, for the National Academy of Sciences has concluded that "fear of discrimination is a major constraint to the wide acceptance of many potentially effective public-health measures." Such a bill has been warmly endorsed by the Surgeon General, the Institute of Medicine, the National Academy of Sciences, most medical bodies and the Presidential Commission on the Human Immunodeficiency Virus Epidemic.

The president should, as one of his first acts in office, release an executive order banning HIV-related discrimination in the federal government. He has strong support for such a move: according to a 1987 Gallup poll, 75 percent of the population oppose discrimination in housing and 64 percent in the workplace.

At the same time, the government needs to issue strong guidelines to insure confidentiality of test results. The reason is the same as passing an anti-discrimination bill: as long as potential carriers fear their status could be released either to medical authorities, their state's surgeon general, emergency care workers or their local newspapers — and as long as they are not protected against discrimination — many people in high-risk groups will refuse to be tested. When a 1987 South Carolina law was passed requiring that names and addresses of those testing positive be reported to health officials, the number of individuals seeking to be tested declined by 51 percent, and the overall number of those testing positive fell by 43 percent, indicating that fewer high-risk people were getting tested. In contrast, when Oregon enacted an AIDS testing law that provided confidentiality for test results, demand for tests by members of high-risk groups increased by 125 percent for gay men, 56 percent for female prostitutes and 17 percent for intravenous drug users.

Mandatory testing, on the other hand, is a waste of money. Mandatory premarital testing in the state of Illinois, for example, turned up only nine positive results out of 75,000 people tested, at an aggregate cost of more than $400,000. In tests with such low ratios of positives, it is estimated that up to 90 percent might be "false positives," with all the personal pains they create. The only mandatory tests that health policy experts recommend are those for blood, organ and tissue donors.

Instead, the next administration and Congress need to encourage the availability of voluntary, confidential, expedient and cheap testing and counseling. A person's knowledge of his or her HIV test results encourages a more healthful behavior, protecting others and offering counseling and care to the carrier. On such testing, it is important that statistical figures be released to federal health agencies (while respecting the anonymity of individuals, of course) in order to monitor the spread of the virus in the population. Such projections must be done seriously: they are crucial for planning adequate budgets and facilities.

AIDS challenges not only the ingenuity of our medical researchers, but also the ability of our nation to rise above prejudice and bigotry. For all the tragedies brought about by HIV, a strong president can seize the opportunity to combat homophobia and to treat drug-addiction more as a disease than a crime.

NOTES

[1] U.S. Department of Health and Human Services, *Health United States, 1987*, 1987.

[2] Employee Benefit Research Institute, *A Profile of the Nonelderly Population without Health Insurance*, May 1987.

[3] *Health United States, 1987, op. cit.*

[4] Employee Benefit Research Institute, *op. cit.*

[5] G. Dallek, K. Hurwit and M. Golde, *Insuring the Uninsured: Options For State Action*, Americans for Health, Inc. and Citizen Action, 1987.

[6] Robert Woods Johnson Foundation, *Access to Health Care in the United States: Results of a 1986 Survey*, 1987.

[7] Employee Benefit Research Institute, *op. cit.*

[8] U.S. Small Business Administration, *Health Care Coverage and Costs in Small and Large Business*, April 1987.

[9] Actuarial studies of the impact of the Kennedy/Waxman bill show a net loss of zero to 180,000 jobs. The more pessimistic projections generally do not consider the creation of new jobs in the health sector generated by the coverage of the uninsured. In any case, when balanced against 24 million people newly receiving health coverage, most would find even the larger job loss, though painful, to be acceptable.

[10] K. Thorpe, *The Cost and Distributional Impacts of Employer Health Insurance Mandates and Medicaid Expansion*, Harvard School of Public Health, for the Health Policy Agenda for the American People, Chicago, IL, 1988.

[11] Net social spending to increase coverage of the Medicaid program would be $5.6 billion. This figure takes into account current social spending (state and local indigent care programs, cost shifting, etc.) for health care to the uninsured which would no longer be required with expanded Medicaid coverage.

[12] K. Thorpe, *op. cit.*

[13] Linda Aiken, "The Aging of America: Implications for State Policy," in *Building Affordable Long Term Care Alternatives: Integrating State Policy*, National Governors' Association, Center for Policy Research and Analysis, Washington, DC, April 1987.

[14] Beginning in 1990, Medicare will pay for up to *80 hours a year* of care by a home health aide to relieve family members caring for a patient who has met either the Part B catastrophic expense limit or the prescription drug deductible.

[15] The new law allows the spouse at home to keep the first $786 a month of the couple's income, about twice the level allowed in most states today. Instead of about $2,000 in savings, the spouse, at home will be able to keep at least $12,000 of the couple's savings.

[16] In its May 1988 issue, *Consumer Reports* evaluated 53 long-term insurance policies. *None* was check-rated a "best-buy" by the magazine's editors, who concluded, "People whose income and assets are fairly modest should not buy long-term care policies."

[17] The Brookings study estimated that only the wealthiest 25% of the elderly could afford to buy a relatively good policy if they were

willing to spend an additional five percent of their income on the premiums. Brookings, p. 77.

[18] James Firman, "Private Long-Term Care Insurance: How Well Is It Meeting Consumer Needs and Public Policy Concerns?", United Seniors Health Cooperative, Washington, DC, September 1988.

[19] Dr. Mark Schlesinger, at hearing of Subcommittee on Health and Long-Term Care, Select Committee on Aging, U.S. House of Representatives, August 1, 1988, Somerville, MA.

[20] Brookings, p. 11.

[21] See, *e.g.*, RL Associates, Princeton, NJ, "The American Public Views Long Term Care," July 1987; Hamilton, Frederick & Schneiders, Washington, DC, "Attitudes of Americans over 45 years of Age on Long-Term Care," February 1988; Louis Harris & Associates, Inc., untitled survey, February 1988; Peter D. Hart, untitled survey of 18-44 year-olds for *Rolling Stone* magazine, September 1977.

[22] As of this writing, such key players as Reps. Pepper, Stark and Waxman and Sens. Mitchell, Moynihan, Kennedy and Melcher have introduced or are about to introduce major long-term care legislation.

[23] See, *e.g.*, RL Associates poll, *op cit.*, which showed that 68% of voters were willing to pay taxes of 1-2% of their income to pay for long-term care.

[24] Thorpe, K., *op. cit.*

Acknowledgements

The editors want to greatly thank the authors of this volume, who gave extraordinary time and care to their work, as well as our committed Democracy Project staff, Jim Ledbetter, Suzanne McAndrews and Olivier Sultan. Michael Waldman's *pro bono* editorial eye was especially valuable.

In particular, our deepest appreciation goes to a small group of dedicated backers, without whose generosity and confidence *America's Transition* could not have been begun or completed. These special friends include Smith Bagley and The Arca Foundation, Chuck Blitz and The Threshold Foundation, Mark Dayton, Richard Dennis, Ted Field, Gary Goldberg and Diana Meehan, Colin Greer and The New World Foundation, Nadine Hack, Steve Haft and The Bydale Foundation, Sidney Harman, Norman Lear, Joshua Mailman, Art Ortenberg, Richard Parker and The Sunflower Foundation, Jan Pierce and CWA District 1, Bernard Rapoport, Donald Ross and the Rockefeller Family Fund, Stanley Sheinbaum, Phil Stern, Margery Tabankin and The Streisand Foundation, and the Miriam and Ira D. Wallach Foundation.

Others gave important financial support from the inception. Our sincere thanks go to the following *Founding Sponsors*: Ione Morrison Barber, Baird Brown, Campaign California, William F. Chafin, Stanford L. Glass, Dr. Alexander Gralnick, Sol & Bettina Kornbluh, Albert H. Kramer, Libby & John Morse, Colin Offenhartz, Christopher & Mary Ann Petzt, Sydney Pollack, The Charles & Susan Stachelberg Family, and Mary S. Von Euler.

Finally, the editors want to acknowledge the faith and committment of the boards of both the parent organization, Democracy Project, and of *America's Transition*. They, particularly, understood the need for a fresh approach for America's third century: Arthur Ashe, Samuel Berger, Gale A. Brewer, Sandy Chapin, Lawrence Chimerine, Dr. Kenneth Clark, Joan Claybrook, Noreen Connell, Stuart Eizenstat, Jeff Faux, Nadine Hack, Sidney Harman, Jerry Grossman, Barbara Jordan, Frances Moore Lappe, Alice Tepper Marlin, The Rt. Rev. Paul Moore, Jr., Thomas B. Morgan, Aryeh Neier, Richard Ottinger, Esther Peterson, Jan Pierce, Robert Reich, Randall Robinson, Carl Sagan, Derek Shearer, Stanley Sheinbaum, Philip Stern, Ted Sorensen and Margery Tabankin.

About The Editors

Mark Green is President of the Democracy Project, a public policy institute which he founded in 1981. A public interest lawyer and author of several books on government, business and law, he is a frequent commentator on national affairs on CNN and PBS. In 1986 he was the Democratic nominee for the U.S. Senate from New York. .

Mark Pinsky is Executive Director of the Democracy Project.

Also by Mark Green

Ideas That Work: 60 Solutions For America's 3rd Century
(1988, edited with James Ledbetter)

Reagan's Reign of Error: The Instant Nostalgia Edition
(1987, 2nd Edition, with Gail MacColl)

The Challenge of Hidden Profits (1985, with John Berry)

Who Runs Congress? (1984, 4th Edition)

Winning Back America (1982)

The Big Business Reader (1980, edited with Robert Massie, Jr.)

Taming the Giant Corporation
(1976, with Ralph Nader & Joel Seligman)

Verdicts on Lawyers (1976, edited with Ralph Nader)

The Other Government: The Unseen Power of Washington Lawyers
(1975)

Corporate Power in America (1973, edited with Ralph Nader)

The Monopoly Makers (1973, editor)

The Closed Enterprise System
(1972, with Beverly C. Moore, Jr. & Bruce Wasserstein)

With Justice for Some (1971, edited with Bruce Wasserstein)